The London Consensus

Economic Principles for the 21st Century

Edited by

Tim Besley, Irene Bucelli and Andrés Velasco

LSE Press

Published by
LSE Press
10 Portugal Street
London WC2A 2HD
press.lse.ac.uk

First published 2025
Reprinted with minor changes in 2026

Publisher's Note:
This reprinted edition includes the following changes: simplification of the Table of Contents (removal of chapter sub-headings); relocation of the List of Figures and Tables and the 'About the Editors and Contributors' section to the endmatter; and addition of endorsements in the prelim pages. No changes have been made to the book's content. All changes have been made at the request of the book's editors.

Cover design by Glen Wilkins

Print and digital versions typeset by PDQ Media

ISBN (Paperback): 978-1-911712-43-5
ISBN (PDF): 978-1-911712-44-2
ISBN (EPUB): 978-1-911712-45-9
ISBN (Mobi): 978-1-911712-46-6

DOI: https://doi.org/10.31389/lsepress.tlc

This book has been peer-reviewed to ensure high academic standards. For our full publishing ethics policies, see https://press.lse.ac.uk

Suggested citation:
Besley, Tim, Bucelli, Irene and Velasco, Andrés (eds) (2025) *The London Consensus: Economic Principles for the 21st Century*, London: LSE Press, https://doi.org/10.31389/lsepress.tlc Licence: CC-BY-NC 4.0

To read the free, open access version of this book online, visit https://doi.org/10.31389/lsepress.tlc or scan this QR code with your mobile device:

"*The London Consensus* is a landmark effort to rethink economic policy for our times. In it, the world's most thoughtful economists grapple with such pressing challenges as growth, inequality, climate change, and the future of work. What emerges is clear, pragmatic and deeply relevant. It's the roadmap we need to build more inclusive and resilient economies. I highly recommend it."
— **Janet L. Yellen**, Former U.S. Treasury Secretary and Former Chair, United States Federal Reserve.

"History didn't end. This book is about what we can do next."
— **James A. Robinson**, University Professor, Harris School of Public Policy and Department of Political Science, University of Chicago. Recipient of the Nobel Prize in Economic Sciences.

"A rich tapestry of policy ideas from leading economists who argue that one cannot naively aim for economic efficiency without simultaneously addressing allocative fairness and political stability, even if that would be much simpler."
— **Kenneth Rogoff**, Maurits C. Boas Chair Professor of International Economics, Harvard University. Former Chief Economist, International Monetary Fund.

"Global problems abound as do mavericks offering implausible remedies. Yet progress in integrating the economic, social, and political sciences offers a more credible basis for hope. In convening and collating the work of these world-renowned scholars into a coherent whole, *The London Consensus* is a landmark publication."
— **Paul Collier**, Professor of Economics and Public Policy, Blavatnik School of Government, Oxford University.

"Policymakers around the globe are navigating an exceptionally difficult environment. Geopolitics involve escalating wars and a fragmentation of global trade that is a major departure from the post-World War II status quo. The potential benefits from new technologies are yet unclear and unevenly distributed across and within countries. Uncertainty has become a centrepiece of the 'new normal'. The collection of essays in this volume could not be timelier. The volume offers practical and insightful analysis on policy choices and is a must read for those that aspire to tackle some of today's challenges at the national or global level."
— **Carmen M. Reinhart**, Minos A. Zombanakis Professor of the International Financial System, Kennedy School of Government, Harvard University. Former Chief Economist, World Bank.

"The turbulent interwar period yielded a geoeconomic architecture that proved adaptable and largely successful over a period of more than sixty years. Like it or not, that system is fracturing in the face of rapid technology change, social dislocation, new collective action threats, and repeated global shocks. The wealth of insights in this book may amount to less than a consensus, but it offers an essential road map for the kinds of solutions we will need to manage our current crisis."
— **Maurice Obstfeld**, Senior Fellow at the Peterson Institute for International Economics and Professor of Economics Emeritus at the University of California, Berkeley. Former Chief Economist, International Monetary Fund.

"While wisely refraining from calling the Washington Consensus of 1990 'neoliberal economics', this impressive and stimulating book proposes fundamental revisions required 35 years later. It features a powerhouse line-up of authors well-suited to thoughtful consideration of some lessons that are missing from textbook economics."
— **Jeffrey Frankel**, James W. Harpel Professor of Capital Formation and Growth, Kennedy School of Government, Harvard University.

"*The London Consensus* offers a timely and vital rethinking of the principles needed to address some of the most urgent questions facing humanity, including climate change, social inequalities, the AI revolution, and increasing threats to liberal democracy. Tim Besley, Irene Bucelli and Andrés Velasco have brought together some of the top minds in academia to chart new paths forward. The book is essential reading for policymakers, scholars, and anyone concerned with building resilient and equitable societies in an era of global challenges."
— **Silvana Tenreyro**, CBE, FBA. James E. Meade Professor of Economics, London School of Economics.

"This is a fabulously important volume, not just as a distillation of current economic thinking to guide research and policy, but also as an antidote to the dangerous notion that economists are unable to reach consensus on the economic principles that should guide our approach to society's most significant challenges."
— **Charles J. Wheelan**, Tuck School of Business, Dartmouth College

"This ambitious volume presents *The London Consensus*: a pragmatic supply-side progressivism that emphasizes good jobs, strong competition policy, and resilience in the face of AI, inequality, and populism. Essential reading for students and policymakers alike."
— **Ioana Marinescu**, School of Social Policy, University of Pennsylvania. Former Principal Economist, US Department of Justice Antitrust Division.

"The editors of *The London Consensus* have succeeded in assembling a group of the world's most authoritative experts to address a breath-taking smorgasbord of economic problems, puzzles, and controversies. In addition to its impressive scope and scale, *The London Consensus* contains a most welcome feature: each chapter is followed by a critique by yet another distinguished expert, with a rejoinder by the chapter's author. This makes *The London Consensus* a most lively and edifying read."
— **Steve H. Hanke**, Professor of Applied Economics, The Johns Hopkins University.

Contents

Preface **ix**

1. Towards a London Economic Consensus: an introduction
Tim Besley and Andrés Velasco **1**

PART I: INNOVATION AND PRODUCTIVITY **39**

2. Fostering green and inclusive productivity growth
Philippe Aghion and John Van Reenen **41**

Response to Philippe Aghion and John Van Reenen
Diane Coyle **61**

Response to Philippe Aghion and John Van Reenen
Timo Boppart **70**

3. On productivism
Dani Rodrik **77**

Response to Dani Rodrik
Jean Pisani-Ferry **97**

Response to Dani Rodrik
Pierre-Olivier Gourinchas **104**

PART II: TRADE **115**

4. International trade since the Washington Consensus: the gains and the pains
Dave Donaldson **117**

Response to Dave Donaldson
Thomas Sampson **133**

Response to Dave Donaldson
Anthony Venables **138**

5. Export-led growth
Ricardo Hausmann **143**

Response to Ricardo Hausmann
Isabela Manelici **174**

Response to Ricardo Hausmann
Danny Quah **181**

PART III: MACROECONOMIC POLICY **195**

6. Fiscal policy and public debt
Ricardo Reis and Andrés Velasco **197**

Response to Ricardo Reis and Andrés Velasco
Olivier Blanchard **211**

Response to Ricardo Reis and Andrés Velasco
Chryssi Giannitsarou **215**

7. Monetary and financial policies
Hélène Rey **219**

Response to Hélène Rey
Paul Tucker **238**

Response to Hélène Rey
Şebnem Kalemli-Özcan **245**

PART IV: LABOUR MARKET **251**

8. Labour markets and the future of work
Christopher Pissarides **253**

Response to Christopher Pissarides
Kirsten Sehnbruch **270**

9. Labour markets and gender inequality
Oriana Bandiera and Barbara Petrongolo **281**

Response to Oriana Bandiera and Barbara Petrongolo
Ashwini Deshpande **292**

Response to Oriana Bandiera and Barbara Petrongolo
Almudena Sevilla **300**

PART V COHESION, EQUITY AND SOCIAL POLICY **311**

10. Is there a 'new consensus' on inequality?
Francisco H. G. Ferreira **313**

Response to Francisco H. G. Ferreira
Ravi Kanbur **340**

Response to Francisco H. G. Ferreira
Nora Lustig **346**

11. Welfare state
Nicholas Barr **351**

Response to Nicholas Barr
Santiago Levy **379**

Response to Nicholas Barr
Paul Johnson **385**

12. Addressing the learning crisis: an emergent consensus
Lant Pritchett **391**

Response to Lant Pritchett
Pedro Carneiro **421**

Response to Lant Pritchett
Miguel Urquiola **426**

13. Towards resilient and sustainable universal health-care coverage
Alistair McGuire, Joan Costa-i-Font and Ranjeeta Thomas **433**

Response to Alistair McGuire, Joan Costa-i-Font and Ranjeeta Thomas
Carol Propper **464**

Response to Alistair McGuire, Joan Costa-i-Font and Ranjeeta Thomas
Michael Marmot **467**

PART VI: ENVIRONMENT AND CLIMATE CHANGE **473**

14. Climate and environment: what we know and what we need to know
Robin Burgess and Tim Dobermann **475**

15. Tackling climate change in low- and middle-income countries
Elizabeth Robinson and Chukwumerije Okereke **507**

PART VII: POLITICAL ECONOMY AND STATE CAPACITY **533**

16. From liberal economic policies to liberal political institutions? Democracy, development clusters and wellbeing
Tim Besley and Torsten Persson **535**

Response to Tim Besley and Torsten Persson
Margaret Levi **564**

Response to Tim Besley and Torsten Persson
Leonard Wantchekon **568**

17. State capacity
Dan Honig, Adnan Khan and Joana Naritomi **573**

Response to Dan Honig, Adnan Khan and Joana Naritomi
Matthew Andrews **602**

Response to Dan Honig, Adnan Khan and Joana Naritomi
Ernesto Dal Bó **607**

Afterword
Pranab Bardhan **615**

List of figures and tables **621**

About the editors and contributors **624**

Index **643**

Preface

The year 2025 marks three-and-a-half decades since the publication of John Williamson's essay on the Washington Consensus. The ideas contained in that essay have many advocates and also plenty of critics, but there is no denying they have been extremely influential as a list of do's and don'ts in economic policy and development.

Mindful of that anniversary, in May 2023 we convened a conference at the London School of Economics and Political Science (LSE), whose aim was to bring together a group of economists and other social scientists to explore what would constitute a new consensus in their respective areas of expertise. In most topics, we also sought the views of discussants.

We did not provide an overall conceptual framework for the conference or a template for the individual contributions. These were entirely developed by the authors in the spirit of provoking discussion, and the meeting fostered a lively exchange of ideas. Many authors chose to edit their contributions in line with the comments that they received at the conference and afterwards. The book is a record of that exchange, but the events and debates that motivated it continue to evolve. The next phase of the project will be disseminating these ideas and to respond to a fast-moving policy landscape. Only time will tell how well the ideas in this book stand the test of time and whether they prove influential.

The project would not have been possible without the generosity and vision of LSE Emeritus Governor, Benefactor and Alumnus Mario Francescotti. His leadership in establishing the research programme on Renewing the Social Contract at LSE launched this process of academic enquiry. His support has been crucial throughout the project, from the original conference in 2023 to the turning of the papers into the present volume. We acknowledge his support with gratitude.

LSE is a cosmopolitan hub for contrasting policy ideas, but also a place where diverse views co-exist in a collegial way. The School's motto is *rerum cognoscere causas*, Latin for 'to know the causes of things'. This book follows in that tradition. Its success will be judged by the debate that it fosters.

Tim Besley
Irene Bucelli
Andrés Velasco

1. Towards a London Economic Consensus: an introduction

Tim Besley and Andrés Velasco

I. Introduction

John Maynard Keynes' well-known epigram that '(i)t is ideas, not vested interests, which are dangerous for good or evil' has special relevance when reflecting on the role of policy approaches and paradigms in shaping the world we live in. New ideas about economic policy are only partly evidence-based, because they try to shape a world not yet created and therefore rely on a combination of logic, evidence, and imagination. There is no 'grand designer' charting the evolutionary course of the world, where trial and error shape change. So does luck: societies have yet to prevent happenstance from determining their destiny.

Today the new challenges are easy to list: climate change, loss of biodiversity, pandemics, assorted inequalities, the unwanted effects of tech, a fragmenting world economy, populism and polarisation, war on the European continent, waning support for liberal democracy in many countries. Much harder is to identify the set of *new* ideas that will guide us through those challenges.

Any such exercise is inevitably in the shadow of similar efforts in the past. Many intellectual historians identify a post-WWII consensus that stressed a role for state-owned businesses, market regulation, welfare state institutions, and Keynesian demand management.[1] Transferred to the developing world, this consensus meant a heavy role for state support (and sometimes ownership) of infant industries, behind trade barriers and controlled exchanged rates. The approach had its critics, but until the 1970s went largely unchallenged as the development model of choice, promoted by the International Monetary Fund (IMF) and World Bank.[2] It paid dividends in Japan, Singapore, Taiwan, and South Korea, but the record elsewhere was mixed. In Latin America, growth petered out after a period of 'easy' import-substituting industrialisation.[3]

The 1970s were a turbulent decade. The period of stagflation in Western democracies led to critical questions being asked about the prevailing paradigm. The mixed record of the model in the developing world became increasingly clear. Thinkers, such as Anne Krueger, soon to become the Chief Economist of the World Bank, pointed to the rent-seeking opportunities

---

How to cite this book chapter:

Besley, Tim and Velasco, Andrés (2025) 'Towards a London Economic Consensus: an introduction', in: Besley, Tim, Bucelli, Irene and Velasco, Andrés (eds) *The London Consensus: Economic Principles for the 21st Century*, London: LSE Press, pp. 1–38 https://doi.org/10.31389/lsepress.tlc.a

that regulation and protection brought, and the mood started to shift.[4] The election of Thatcher and Reagan led to a different approach (although in the United States some of the shift had begun under Carter). Deregulation and trade liberalisation became mainstream.

A potted intellectual history of the last century would claim that Keynesianism held sway in the industrialised world after the Great Depression, only to be replaced by so-called neoliberalism in the late 1970s or early 1980s. And neoliberal ideas found their pithiest expression in the Ten Commandments that another English economist, John Williamson, published under the label *The Washington Consensus* in 1990.[5]

This simplistic history of shifting economic paradigms is somewhat misleading. On the standard account, Keynesianism was progressive and neoliberalism, conservative – focused on the benefits of markets to the detriment of everything else. But Keynesianism was mostly about macro-management. It coexisted with free markets in the US and highly regulated markets in Europe. Neoliberalism, to the extent that it was a coherent paradigm, was mostly about microeconomic deregulation.[6] It coexisted with expansionary policies and large fiscal deficits in the US under Reagan, and with fiscal austerity in the UK under Thatcher.

Those caveats aside, there is no doubt that Williamson's Washington Consensus was hugely influential. By the early 1990s it constituted the predominant view of effective policy for development. Fuelled by support from the IMF and World Bank, which by then had turned their back on the post-war consensus, fiscal consolidation, tariff reduction and deregulation became the new preconditions for adjustment assistance. The fall of the Berlin Wall brought additional willing participants to the policy experiment.

The Washington Consensus did lay down many important ideas, some of which have stood the test of time. It contributed to the spread of globalisation, creating many opportunities along the way: it is hard to argue against the proposition that the huge drops in global poverty that followed were due, at least in part, to greater economic openness. The fall in world inflation that took hold until recently also owed a great deal to the view – well captured by Williamson – that monetary policy should be used to fine-tune aggregate demand (ideally under the aegis of an independent central bank), not to finance large budget deficits. Those were important achievements, but the Washington Consensus also left us with a plethora of important, unanswered questions about the kind of society that would follow. And those questions have become more urgent with the passage of time.

To explore those questions, in May of 2023 we convened a group of authors and discussants and asked them to give their take on what would constitute a new economic consensus for the 21st century. Because the group met at the London School of Economics (LSE), the working label of our project was the London Consensus. We imposed no pre-determined approach or paradigm on this venture, but we hoped some general principles and lessons would emerge. The papers and comments from that 2023 meeting are contained in this volume.

In the time between the Washington Consensus and the London Consensus meetings, the world has changed in fundamental ways. The collapse of the Soviet Union and its area of influence, the rise of China as an economic power, and the increasing recognition of anthropogenic climate change are just three important examples. Today we have the advantage of being able to judge which prescriptions in the Washington Consensus have stood the test of time and which have proven incomplete or just plain wrong.

The discipline of economics has changed too, most notably in its embrace of political economy, and its engagement with psychology to create richer models of individual behaviour and of collective decision-making. The availability of data and new methods have also allowed for a wealth of innovative empirical studies, both micro and macro, that practitioners can draw upon to understand the consequences of alternative policies. Many of the authors and discussants in this volume have lived through this transformation and have played major roles in reshaping the discipline of economics.

II. Are paradigms useful?

In appraising the lessons from the contributions to this volume, we will steer clear from trying to create a supermarket list of reforms that a country needs to complete before it can improve the lot of its citizens. To democratic leaders with limited terms of office, fragmented parliaments, and limited resources, such lists are not particularly useful. An approach that emphasises everything ends up prioritising nothing and can easily become a recipe for policy paralysis.

Nor are we seeking one-size-fits-all recipes. The binding constraints that hold back economic growth and social progress differ across countries with local history, culture, and politics varying widely. Thus, each nation should develop its own bespoke policy priorities. The very notion of international 'best practice' that can be applied across the board can do more harm than good.

Given these caveats, sceptics might question the idea of trying to build a new consensus at all, whether conceived of in London or anywhere else. And given the mixed record of development models or *paradigms*, which can easily become too rigid or too ideological, perhaps one should stay away from them. Dani Rodrik, in his paper in this volume, rightly counsels policymakers to 'beware of economists bearing paradigms'. Earlier, Albert Hirschman titled his influential essay 'The Search for Paradigms as a Hindrance to Understanding'.[7]

But the fact that local circumstances matter, and that countries ought to have differing policy priorities, does not mean that nations cannot seek common lessons from others' experiences, or from the findings of policy-oriented research. There are at least four reasons why a new consensus can assemble useful knowledge for policymakers to use.

The first is the importance of identifying what does not work. We know from experience there are policy approaches that yield disastrous results pretty much regardless of setting or circumstance. Identifying those failed approaches and placing them on a list of policies *to-be-avoided-at-all-costs* can save a lot of time and trouble.

Second is the difference between principles and policies. Politico-economic analysis can yield general principles – perhaps amounting to a paradigm – that help understand development challenges and organise the search for solutions. Using those principles, each nation can decide which policies are best, given its unique history and circumstances. As Jean Pisani-Ferry argues in his contribution to this volume, 'A great advantage of policy paradigms is that they are directional. Whenever new policy directions are to be explored, governments go through a discovery process where they learn from the successes and failures of other governments'.

Third, and to avoid the one-size-fits-all temptation, useful advice can come in conditional propositions, of the form 'if this is your set of circumstances, do this' and 'if that is your set of circumstances, do something else'. This approach must have a diagnostic technique for identifying the relevant set of circumstances and a prescriptive taxonomy that lists the policies that are appropriate for different circumstances.[8]

Fourth is the importance of narratives in political and economic debates. Psychologists have long argued that human reasoning is predisposed to processing information via narratives.[9] Among social scientists there is increasing interest in the power of narratives to shape policy. And paradigms are a kind of narrative: they help structure thinking about appropriate policies. Plus, in democracies voters must be persuaded of the advantage of this or that policy approach. And those debates take place not over the technical advantages of a given policy, but over the paradigm of which it is part and the values it embodies. Policymakers going into political battle without a paradigm do so with an arm tied behind their backs.

In this introduction we focus on the central elements that, we believe, can form the basis of a new policymaking consensus that could displace the Washington Consensus. We begin with some core principles that shape policy and then, drawing on the contributions in the volume, show how they can be combined to form a coherent intellectual framework for a new approach.

III. Five core principles

1. *It's not just the money: wellbeing is the key*

There is an idea with a long history in economic thinking, going back at least to J. S. Mill: the market should take care of what to produce and how to produce it, while the state addresses market failures and redistribution using taxes and transfers.[10] In modern public economics this view is associated with the seminal work of Diamond and Mirrlees, who laid down the argument for production efficiency in a rigorous way.[11]

Out of this grew the idea of the separation of efficiency and distribution. Optimal taxes and transfers to households can redistribute, while businesses operate in a largely undistorted way as long as their profits can be taxed. The implication is that even economists who care about equity should strive to build an efficient market economy. This conclusion brings together the views of advocates of egalitarianism and of a market-based economy, justifying efforts to make the size of the pie as large as possible before deciding how best to divide it.

This way of thinking is also quite consistent with the thrust of the Washington Consensus, even if the latter was largely silent on matters of distribution. The separation of efficiency and distribution was implicit in the prescription that public expenditure was to focus on infrastructure, security, health, and education, while the use of industrial policy was suspect, regulations were to be lifted, and state-owned enterprises were to be privatised.

This intellectual framework also had a political corollary: if achieving a just distribution could be separated from the pursuit of efficiency, failure to respect the interests of the poor was largely at the door of individual countries rather than an indictment of the Washington Consensus *per se*. The Third Way advocated by politicians, such as Bill Clinton and Tony Blair, could also be justified using this core model, with the implication that there was no fundamental trade-off between the pursuit of efficiency and equity if there existed a fiscal response in the form of redistributive taxation and transfer programmes.

The approach still has much to commend itself. Relying on the market for most allocation decisions is often right when considering private production. But in the years since the Washington Consensus, we have had to relearn an old lesson: *what* you produce, *how* you produce it (e.g., via what kinds of jobs), and *where* you produce it, matters. Not all economic and social ills can or should be corrected by post-production redistribution. Some need to be corrected before or during production, in what some are now calling 'pre-distribution'.[12]

Why does the Mill–Diamond–Mirrlees principle sometimes fail? First, because one of its key premises, that all rents (pure profits) can be taxed, is problematic. There are technical issues around identifying and measuring rents rather than normal returns. The task is especially difficult in a world of creative destruction, where profits motivate innovation. An extra layer of complication arises in a globalised world where transfer pricing is used to shift profits to low tax jurisdictions. Finally, many rents are shifted to labour earnings in ways that make it harder to separate productivity from rents. Taxing labour rents separately from standard labour earnings is almost impossible.

Another difficulty for the separation of equity and efficiency is that modern economies are rife with externalities, which in turn may require intervention directly into the productive process. Of course, externalities were not discovered yesterday, nor was the use of policy to correct them. What is new is the emergence of very large externalities, which span economics, politics, and society. An example is the negative multiplier that affects local communities, destroying social capital and undermining cohesion, when large numbers of well-paying jobs are destroyed. The result is not only unemployment, but increases in drug addiction, crime, broken families, etc.

Those large externalities can also be positive. An example is provided by Ricardo Hausmann in his contribution to this volume: there is substantial evidence suggesting that countries that export more grow faster (and more than proportionately so) because they adopt innovative technology with greater speed and because, in doing so, they learn about additional export opportunities at the extensive margin. These benefits are not all internalised by the exporting firms themselves – the very definition of an externality.

The separation of efficiency and distribution requires that governments be able to extract sufficient revenues through broad-based taxation. But there is an active debate about where the limits to taxation lie, now that many countries in Europe raise 40% or more of national income in taxes. So, while there can be significant expansion of taxation in lower- and middle-income countries, it may well be that the limit is near – or has been reached already – in several high-income nations. If so, as Olivier Blanchard claims in his contribution to the volume, 'it may be that more direct intervention in the market process, rather than the redistribution process, is needed'.

Some economists advocate wealth taxes as a way out of this conundrum. But wealth is hard to measure and often portable across borders. Without a level of global cooperation that is unrealistic today, wealth taxes are unlikely to raise much larger revenues. And while taxes could be levied on fixed assets, such as housing, those higher property taxes would have to be phased in gradually, so as not to punish people who bought their homes recently.

A more subtle but also more fundamental issue with the Washington Consensus (and the Mill–Diamond–Mirrlees principle that underpinned it) is its conception of welfare. In a utilitarian world everything is commensurable, and can be put on a single dimension. Transfers can then be used to compensate losers. Yet, as Francisco H. G. Ferreira stresses in his chapter on inequality in this volume, what matters for human flourishing is not simply the distribution of monetary income (even when that includes compensation). The distribution of self-worth, respect, social status, and public recognition matter a great deal, too.[13] They are intrinsically important and cannot simply be written off by a materialist conception of wellbeing.

We agree with Ravi Kanbur, who in this book stresses that recognising the importance of these multi-dimensional inequalities should not be used as cover for forgetting about what can (and ought to) be done with taxes and transfers. But we also believe that taking a wider perspective on the definition of wellbeing and its distribution does point to issues that matter in concrete situations that policymakers frequently confront. For example, in a town where coal mining has been the mainstay for a generation, a 50-year-old miner will understandably be unhappy if forced to swap his job for that of hotel waiter or telephone operator, even if these new jobs pay better. And the jobless resident of an area suffering from high unemployment will not be eager to hear that there are jobs to be had hundreds of miles away, in places where she has no family, friends or links to the local community.

We conclude there is need for an approach that thinks harder about the kinds of reward structures embedded in an economic system. If the system limits competition and fails to tax rents, that is sure to undermine faith in the market system. When markets function imperfectly, there is a case for labour market interventions via, for instance, minimum wages.[14]

Corporate governance arrangements also determine how different groups are rewarded. Crucially, people care about distribution not just after the state has intervened, but instead look at market rewards as a reflection of opportunities – and often conclude that these are unfairly distorted by the distribution of economic and political power.

It is also relevant whether goods are produced, and jobs generated, *in situ*. Geographical areas are often identified with the production of distinctive varieties of goods. When comparative advantage shifts, the loss of social structures that were associated with those goods can undermine workers' sense of identity. This means paying greater attention to the 'place-based policies', which we elaborate on in the following sections.

2. *Growth matters, but so does place*

Even though Williamson's text is often described as a 'neoliberal' (i.e., conservative) manifesto, it is striking that economic growth does not get star billing as a major goal of policy reforms.[15] The lack of emphasis on growth is not unique to the Washington Consensus, nor to so-called neoliberal approaches. Over the last quarter-century, 'progressive' approaches to development have tended to emphasise other policy goals (for instance, distribution) to the detriment of growth. Even in institutions like the World Bank, growth has not received the priority it enjoyed in the post-WWII consensus. This owes more to shifting intellectual fads in the United States and Europe than to changed circumstances in developing and emerging nations. As Timo Boppart stresses in his contribution to this volume, that 'economic growth as measured by average gross domestic product (GDP) per capita is still a proxy of success of first-order importance and will remain so for the years to come – in particular for developing countries'.

In the Washington Consensus, the focus was on static allocative efficiency: liberalisation, deregulation and privatisation were supposed to ensure that 'prices are right' and private agents can respond to those price signals. The implicit assumption seems to have been that, if the market was allowed to do its work, economic growth would naturally follow.

Thanks to the modern approach to growth, we understand much better than economists did back then that static allocative efficiency is very different from dynamic efficiency, and that getting prices 'right' is neither a necessary nor a sufficient condition to ignite economic growth. In 1989 the endogenous growth academic revolution was just getting under way; the 'creative destruction' growth paradigm that Philippe Aghion and John Van Reenen stress in their contribution to this volume would not be formalised until the following decade.[16]

In this Schumpeterian 'creative destruction' paradigm, innovation rents motivate investments in innovation, so doing away with all rents via liberalisation and competition can, in fact, be bad for growth. But those rents cannot be allowed to get too big, because yesterday's innovators are tempted to use their rents to prevent subsequent innovations, since they do not want to be the victims of creative destruction themselves. This all suggests a subtle and complex interaction among the policies, incentives, and decisions governing innovation, which was very much absent from economic analysis in Williamson's time, as discussed in Aghion and Van Reenen's contribution to this volume.

The factors that create an enabling environment for growth are consequently much richer and more nuanced than in the static-efficiency-only approach. Innovation decisions are rife with externalities and market failures, which can benefit from judicious government policy. For example, knowledge spills over in ways that do not benefit the original owners of that knowledge, frameworks have to be found for safeguarding intellectual property, some innovations are not fully patentable so rents may accrue to imitators who did not invest, coordination failures may prevent needed investments in innovation from taking place, etc.

The case for an activist innovation policy is strong, in advanced and developing economies alike, since the state can both expand the technology frontier and ensure that firms get support to adopt and adapt the most appropriate technologies. Beyond having a strong legal system that protects intellectual property rights, the state can help train the required human capital. Policy can also spur innovation by ensuring that the financial system works effectively to channel capital towards firms with growth potential. This is a particular challenge when lack of collateral or other financial market failures prevents the private sector from doing so.

Growth has positive effects that go far beyond higher incomes, wages, and consumption. One example is that growth enlarges government revenues and relaxes budget constraints, making it possible for governments to spend more on health, education, and pensions. That is one reason why, as Lant Pritchett has stressed, indicators of human development, such as those measured by the United Nations Development Programme (lower poverty, higher life expectancy, lower child mortality, enhanced literacy and numeracy, etc.) are closely correlated with economic growth.[17]

At a time of generalised distrust of politicians and of democratic politics, it is remarkable that growth is a reliable predictor of empirical measures of political trust. Citizens seem to trust their politicians more when politicians are able to deliver a growing economy. Interestingly, growth matters more for trust than other economic outcomes, such as low inflation.[18]

3. *Building resilience: government as insurer of last resort*

Most people prefer their lives to be serene, their jobs to be stable, and their consumption to be smooth. That is why countering volatility and stabilising economic outcomes has long been a goal of policy. Volatility comes in many varieties, but the Washington Consensus focused on only one: macroeconomic volatility resulting from irresponsible monetary and fiscal policies. That emphasis turned out to be insufficient. Policymakers must put countering volatility of all kinds at the centre of their concerns and must design policies explicitly targeted at volatility. There are political and social reasons, in addition to standard economic ones, for this change.

The focus of the Washington Consensus made sense at the time. It was conceived of at a conference on Latin America, a region which in 1989 was coming out of the biggest debt crisis in its history, with deep recessions and high unemployment. In most countries, budget deficits financed via external borrowing accounted for the sizeable debt burden. When borrowing was no longer possible, governments turned to money creation to finance fiscal deficits, which under-fixed exchange rates, caused a loss of reserves, and an eventual balance of payments crisis. The lesson that Williamson extracted was simple: fix monetary and fiscal policies and macroeconomic volatility will go away.

Today economists understand much better than they did in the late 1980s that unsound monetary and fiscal policies are one important cause of volatility, but certainly not the only one. Policymakers do not always heed this lesson, as the Great Financial Crisis of 2007–09 showed. The benign economic circumstances that preceded it allowed for the build-up of imbalances in the financial sector – a phenomenon that illustrates how the financial sector can itself be an important source of shocks, and how proper financial regulation is an essential component of policies to keep the economy stable. (Williamson was aware of this: he excluded free capital mobility from his 10 commandments precisely because it could be destabilising, but he did not make this explicit in the original paper.)[19] Today, economists and central bankers are busy developing micro- and macroeconomic prudential regulation, and institutions like the IMF include capital controls as one more tool in governments' toolkits to fight instability, as Hélène Rey explains in her contribution to this book.

Economists also understand better, as Ricardo Reis and Andrés Velasco stress in this volume, that some financial markets never develop (e.g., markets for certain kinds of insurance) and that other markets disappear at times of financial stress, creating an essential role for government. Part of the job can be taken over by monetary policy (think of Mario Draghi's 'whatever it takes' to prop up the Euro), but monetary policy inevitably must be backed by the taxing and borrowing powers of the state. There is strong justification for an activist fiscal policy that goes far beyond the Keynesian role.

Crucially, volatility is not only macroeconomic, and the Washington Consensus paid almost no attention to other sources of volatility. A case in point is the volatility individuals face due to largely uninsurable idiosyncratic shocks: they might lose their jobs, become sick or disabled, live longer than expected and run out of retirement savings, etc. Not only does this volatility result in people's consumption not being smooth. It is also a source of anxiety and stress, with serious consequences for health and wellbeing.

Furthermore, such volatility can have political consequences: a citizen who is unable to find a job or secure healthcare for a sick child will naturally become angry, disenchanted with mainstream politics, and may be drawn towards extremist or populist alternatives. A properly functioning welfare state should provide insurance against these contingencies, as Nicholas Barr stresses in his contribution to this book.

Last, but certainly not least, recent events have underscored the risks associated with yet other kinds of volatility. As discussed by Alistair McGuire, Joan Costa-i-Font and Ranjeeta Thomas in this volume, the pandemic reminded us how costly it can be to run healthcare systems that are not prepared for a sudden and large surge in the demand for their services. But many healthcare systems, including those of many advanced nations, lacked the spare capacity to deal with sudden surges in demand, with insufficient supplies of essential equipment, such as respirators, to cope with an emergency.

Recent years also revealed how fragile global supply chains are and how vulnerable they are to both economic and geopolitical shocks. The Russian invasion of Ukraine showed that food supply and prices can respond in extreme ways to an adverse shock in one large grain producer. And climate change, of course, will produce ever more volatile weather conditions, with all the attendant (and harmful) economic and social consequences. We agree with Diane Coyle when she underscores in this volume that a 'malfunction of the innovation machine is the economy's lack of resilience or security of supply, demonstrated by the multiple shocks occurring since 2008'. The inescapable conclusion is that the resilience of economic and social arrangements should be a central goal of policy. That objective was completely absent from the Washington Consensus.

Because the environment is likely to become an even more important source of shocks, the world will need to come together to engage in carbon-reducing mitigation efforts. But for many countries, adaptation will be the only option in the near term, building structures that are resilient to shocks. This is a point that both Elizabeth Robinson and Chukwumerije Okereke, and Robin Burgess and Tim Dobermann, make in their respective papers in this book. Many nations, for example, will have to revisit the standards used for flood resilience and make the necessary investments. Governments will have to re-engineer public infrastructure to respond to the heightened risk. The way in which states provide social insurance will also need to be reconsidered, with tricky questions arising along the way on how to relocate certain populations as part of the adaptation process.

4. *There is no good economics without good politics*

In Bill Clinton's campaign, James Carville's well-known dictum was *it's the economy, stupid!* The Washington Consensus shared that premise. There is no single mention of the political economy of reform in Williamson's original manifesto. In the background, politics was far from absent: Ronald Reagan and Margaret Thatcher had obtained the political mandate to reshape their countries' economies, while in countries such as Brazil, Argentina, and Chile autocratic generals were applying Washington Consensus-like policies. But in 1989 the underlying premise seemed simple: fix the economy and politics will get sorted along the way. Three decades of experience have taught us that reforms imposed by either local authoritarian rulers or external lenders, however potentially beneficial, often lack legitimacy and 'local ownership', and get overturned once political or financial circumstances change. Plus, policies that are perceived as temporary and therefore lack credibility can have many undesirable effects, as Guillermo Calvo has long argued.[20]

Economic reformers in the 1980s may have overlooked the importance of politics, but it would be unwise to repeat that mistake today. Look around the world today, and the opposite of Carville's dictum seems to apply: now *it's the politics, stupid!* From the end of the democratic dream in Russia to hardening autocracy in China, from democratic backsliding in Hungary and Turkey to the return of dictatorship in Venezuela and Nicaragua, to the recent succession of coups in Sub-Saharan Africa, from chaotic political gyrations in the United States to growing disenchantment with democracy in many long-established democracies in the West, the catalogue of political ills is long and worrying.

One concern is that, increasingly, shocks to the economy will have their roots in politics or will be exacerbated by politics. Of course, this is nothing new; in history, wars have been an enormous source of economic shocks, something we have been reminded of by recent global events. And many countries have fluctuated between periods of dictatorship and democracy in ways that have been a source of economic instability. These dangers are still with us, but today they are not the only sources of instability. As societies cope with the fallout from globalisation, technological change and climate change, and deal with the reality of populism and polarisation, there is a growing risk that politics will be *the* source of economic shocks.

A case in point is the recent Brexit experience of the UK. Whatever stance one takes on the merits of the decision, it created an enormously volatile political environment in a country famed for stability. How politicians in a range of countries choose to respond to dissatisfaction over immigration will have important spillovers to the economy. In many established democracies, populist parties are gaining popularity on the back of this issue. In other places, such as the United States, this cleavage is, sadly, now mainstream.

Politics obviously influences economic outcomes, but economic policies and outcomes also have political consequences – a causal link that was largely absent from Washington Consensus thinking. As Daron Acemoglu and Jim Robinson have argued, many economists long assumed that 'good economics is good politics', meaning that good economic policies necessarily relax political constraints, making it possible to implement even better policies in the future. But both theory and recent experience suggest this need not be the case.

What may seem myopically like 'desirable' policies today may well shift the distribution of incomes and rents in ways that make politics more challenging in the future.[21] For instance, it is hard not to ponder the recent rise of authoritarian populism across the world without reference to wage stagnation and growing inequality in the US and the UK, the left-behind regions caused by the decline in industrial employment, and the massive human suffering triggered by job losses and family bankruptcies during the Great Financial Crisis of 2007–09.[22]

Economists often mistakenly think of politics as *the great constraint* whereby survival-obsessed and special interest-influenced politicians keep benevolent technocrats from implementing the 'right' economic policies. Even though politics does come with its own structure of incentives, we prefer to flip this approach around and think about politics as *the great enabler*: when the politics goes well, then many other good things follow. Plus, the main alternative to politics is conflict and violence, which are unambiguously worse outcomes.

Politics is about creating an environment for policy choice and implementation that rests on voluntary compliance with laws and regulations, facilitated by citizens' perception that they have a stake in the system and are not simply dependent on the whim of a dictator. Democratic values include consent and respect for the agency of citizens – not only as economic actors in the marketplace, but as political actors with the right to play a role in choosing policies and to use their voice in influencing outcomes.

Moreover, the goals of politics include status, respect and dignity, not just monetary rewards. Political equality is also a core value that can never be attained by systems of government that deny political rights to their citizens. Such rights have intrinsic value, not just instrumental value. They are so important that societies might reasonably tolerate paying a pecuniary price for the sake of having a more engaged and empowered citizenry.

Yet these reflections come with a warning: optimism about the potential of democratic politics is not the same as naivety regarding the risk that politics can take the wrong turn. Put in academic jargon, there is no guarantee that decentralised political interactions among large numbers of people will produce Pareto-efficient outcomes. And even if the outcome is efficient, the associated distribution of economic and non-economic rewards may be hard to square with our preferred notions of justice.

The modern political economy view is that institutions for decision-making are a key building block of an enabling environment for economic policy. As stressed by Leonard Wantchekon in his contribution to this volume, describing the project as finding 'optimal' institutional arrangements is not particularly helpful. Experience from successful polities suggest that transplanting institutions without regard to diversity of history and culture is problematic. At the same time, there are do's and don'ts to be learned from the empirical literature. Polities that invest leaders with power that lacks accountability put both economic and political stability at risk. And a failure to build broad-based political coalitions makes it hard to implement policies that share benefits of economic success widely.

In their contribution to the volume, Tim Besley and Torsten Persson emphasise the importance of a liberal political consensus built around a cohesive society as a basis for political and economic development. But Margaret Levi rightly stresses in her comments that this is a mammoth project for political economists, with lots of details to be filled in. Understanding how that consensus is built will require research in many disciplines, along with a plurality of methods. Political economy is increasingly connecting politics and economics with insights from psychology and sociology, which suggest that the roots of cohesion lie as much in informal norms and values as in formal rules. One important lesson for economic policymakers is to be mindful of whether a given policy helps or hinders the building of social cohesion, a consideration that is absent from a purely economic approach.

Embracing politics is central to our new policy consensus, and this stands in stark contrast to the Washington Consensus. We need to appreciate better how politics can make policy inclusive and sustainable – as well as being sensitive to its own political consequences. This will be crucial to the way in which we discuss specific policies below.

5. *A capable state: the essential complement for everything*

Because the state was supposed to be confined to providing policing, defence, and basic education and health, there was no discussion of state capacity in the original Washington Consensus. By contrast, today we understand that even for these allegedly 'simple' tasks the quality of the state matters tremendously. As Lant Pritchett stresses in his paper for this volume, a number of low-income nations have succeeded in teaching basic reading and writing, while others have failed miserably. There is huge variation in state capabilities, even among nations at similar levels of income. Some of those differences reflect conscious decisions by governments not to invest in state capacity. Investing in the state is a key form of infrastructure investment, which goes far beyond bricks and mortar. The 'right' organisational structures of the state do not emerge spontaneously. They have to be *built*.

State capacities are relevant to almost every area of policy. Even behind the narrow vision of the state that maximises the efficiency of production and redistributes its fruits, lie strong assumptions about what the state can do. Contrary to the mythical libertarian ideal of the small state, creating a functional market economy requires an array of market-supporting institutions, both legal and regulatory. A market does not develop in many countries because the state is too incompetent and weak. Product safety rules, employment contracts that ensure employers fulfil their obligations, or loan contracts that guarantee debtors pay back their debts, are infeasible without state capacity. And just as important, providing adequate public services without broad-based consumption and income taxes often proves impossible.

Nowadays, it is broadly understood that at least three kinds of state capacity are crucial: revenue-raising capacity to pay, without excessive recourse to debt, for the things government does; legal-administrative capacity, to provide a stable framework in which private agents can take decisions – especially investment decisions, which involve parting with resources today in exchange for an uncertain return in the future; and delivery-capacity – not just to design policies, but to implement them effectively.

State capacity is also key for the choice of appropriate policies. Depending on the capacity of a given government to raise revenue, employ able professionals, resist short-term political pressures and avoid corruption, a given policy may be highly appropriate or a complete mistake. During the pandemic, for instance, policies to provide households with emergency income succeeded depending on whether government had the required databases, could make electronic cash transfers, etc.

In contrast to the late 1980s, today scholars can draw on an extensive literature on how and why states invest (or fail to invest) in their own capacity, as Besley and Persson explain in their contribution to this volume. And we also have abundant empirical evidence on which bureaucratic arrangements (i.e., hiring and remuneration schemes), with varying degrees of centralisation or local control, work better to motivate bureaucrats and get the business of government done. The chapter by Dan Honig, Adnan Kahn and Joana Naritomi surveys this evidence and provides preliminary lessons. And as their discussant Matt Andrews notes, the idea that such capacities are just a 'copy-paste' process from elsewhere is dangerous. He makes a convincing plea for an adaptive and iterative process to build such capacities.

Politics again is key. States that operate like the private fiefdoms of narrow ruling elites have little incentive to create broad-based taxation, because those elites can simply expropriate the successful. But this very fact destroys incentives to invest in prosperity. Worse still, the lack of constraints on executive power turns politics into a smash-and-grab game where those who hold power think not about the future, let alone the interests of their citizens, but their own short-term interests alone. Staying in power often is their lexicographic priority. This form of fragility can quickly descend into civil conflict, further compromising the task of building an effective market economy.[23]

Industrial policy (also known in some quarters as productive development policy) and competition policy, we will argue, have a great deal going for them. But without state capacity, the idea of an activist state that can conduct industrial policy and competition policy is pie in the sky. These kinds of policies are state capacity-intensive. In those countries where they have been effective, it is largely because they already had such state capacities or because they were built alongside the implementation of the policies. Moreover, such investments in state capacity can lead to persistence in economic success beyond the life of rotating politicians. To function, the state no longer needs to rely on a specific leader, however competent or benevolent. And this, in turn, creates confidence among those who put private capital at risk, spurring investment.

Another dangerous view is that the state can be substituted for by well-meaning outsiders, either from multilateral or non-governmental organisations (NGOs). This can become quite a conundrum when, as is true in a number of low-income countries, the latter are mostly overseas NGOs. Of course, as a palliative when the state lacks capacity, their role can be vital. But though these NGOs are frequently well-meaning, their accountability to local populations is not guaranteed. There is the risk that, bypassing state actors while performing government-like functions, they will diminish the capacities of the state. There is also the risk that by recruiting talented staff who might otherwise work for the government, NGOs unwittingly perpetuate state weakness. Useful international aid policy means thinking about the dynamic consequences of delivering vitally needed goods and services, not just about the outcomes that are achieved in the short run.

IV. From principles to policy

We now explore the implications of our principles for the conduct of policy. In illustrating them we will draw on the papers in the volume. Rather than proposing a neat compartmentalisation of policies and principles, we view our principles as running through all of the policy approaches that we consider.

1. *Macroeconomic policy*

Not surprisingly given its origins, many of the most memorable policy prescriptions of the Washington Consensus concerned the underpinnings of macroeconomic stability. These included fiscal, monetary, financial and exchange rate policy. Of course, guaranteeing macro stability and getting those crucial policies right is a priority of the London Consensus, too. But we stress new elements that reflect the principles we have outlined.

While the Washington Consensus emphasised fiscal discipline to reduce the need for government borrowing, our new proposed consensus encourages fiscal activism, especially in response to crises. The point Reis and Velasco make in their paper is that fiscal policy has a key role in reducing volatility, and that role goes beyond standard aggregate demand management of the Keynesian variety.

There are at least two new fiscal policies governments have been pursuing in recent years (for instance, during the Great Financial Crisis of 2007–09 and during the COVID-19 pandemic), and which can be justified by solid economic analysis. One is to use targeted transfers to help people offset uninsurable shocks, such as the loss of a job during a recession. Here government plays the role of insurer of last resort, given that private markets cannot provide insurance. The second policy is for government to become a market-maker of last resort, helping to prop up financial markets that freeze at times of macroeconomic stress. During the Great Financial Crisis of 2007–09, public institutions provided emergency credit, subsidies, public guarantees, asset purchases, and capital injections to replace the financial markets that had disappeared or to keep markets operating and secure the flow of credit.

Now, government can perform both functions if and only if it can keep borrowing at times of macroeconomic stress, when the private sector cannot because it is largely shut out from financial markets. This means that to make activism possible in bad times, fiscal policy must be prudent (and reduce net debt) in good times. So, the new activism is far from a call for 'anything goes' when it comes to fiscal policy. On the contrary, it requires substantial fiscal prudence, and the institutions that make that prudence possible: many countries, both rich and middle-income, have found that fiscal rules and the autonomous fiscal councils that administer them can play a crucial role. At the same time, as Chryssi Giannitsarou stresses in her comment in this volume, to be credible those fiscal rules have to be sufficiently flexible. The European experience with overly simple and rigid rules makes this point abundantly clear.

The Washington Consensus stressed the importance of market-determined interest rates, with financial markets determining the allocation of credit. This recommendation was a product of its times, given that many systems of government credit allocation had resulted in cronyism and served neither equity nor efficiency objectives. Market-determined credit allocation remains a goal in the London Consensus. But we place a great deal more emphasis on regulation to prevent lending booms and busts. Creating an institutional environment for micro and macroprudential regulation is now the name of the game, for central bankers and banking supervisors across the world. This means recognising political realities and working with a system that has a judicious mix of technocracy and political accountability.

These financial market policies help reduce volatility and create a system of credit allocation that allows small- and medium-size enterprises to flourish. The past 30 years have also witnessed experimentation with innovative forms of credit supply, sometimes in the form of micro-finance, in order to mitigate incentive problems in financial markets and to widen the scope of borrowing, given that most poor borrowers lack collateral. Providing reliable and secure savings opportunities is also important, particularly as individuals try to manage volatility over the life cycle.

Creating better credit market opportunities has both equity and efficiency objectives. In the absence of financial inclusion, only those with wealth can start new businesses, and those businesses that wish to grow must rely exclusively on retained earnings. This limits who can become an entrepreneur and distorts the firm-size distribution – and it also leads to lower wages by lowering labour demand. So financial inclusion plays a key role in building a more productive and more equitable economy.

Competition in financial markets is important, too. Many countries have concentrated banking sectors, which are a source of rents. These rents can translate into political power. In many countries, such rents are in the hands of foreign banks, so they accrue to foreign shareholders. Moreover, there has been growing suspicion that some financial products have become a means of perpetuating rents rather than mitigating risk. Behavioural economics interpretations of the global financial crisis stress that many market participants were easily misled, which accentuated the misallocation of capital. The resulting government support during the crisis was indispensable, but it created political discontent when it seemed to protect the wealth of rich financiers. The lesson from all of this is a renewed emphasis on both macroprudential and competition policy in finance, both to reduce volatility and to create fairer economic structures.

The Washington Consensus stressed low inflation as a priority, and we of course share that goal. In the years since, and in developed and emerging nations alike, policies to control inflation have converged on a broadly used formula, which can be labelled flexible inflation targeting.[24] It consists of controlling the short-term interest rate to target some agreed-upon measure of inflation, while the exchange rate floats.[25] There are, of course, many operational issues that continue to be discussed: which price index to target, whether the short interest rate should be the only tool used (or, rather, be complemented by 'quantitative policies'), whether the exchange rate float should be clean or dirty, and so on. But those important points aside, the overall approach clearly has been successful. Inflation rates declined worldwide after the adoption of inflation targeting and remained there for more than two decades. And when inflation spiked after the pandemic, in part because of unforeseen supply shocks, central banks managed to bring down headline inflation rates without provoking a recession – although, as Paul Tucker points out in this volume, the combination of large fiscal and monetary stimulus turned out to be excessive in several advanced countries.

We have little to add to this conventional wisdom. But we do want to highlight two additional and important points. One has to do with the global financial cycle (GFC) and its implication for exchange rates and monetary policies, particularly in emerging markets (EMs). The other has to do with the link between exchange rates and exports.

Thanks to the pioneering work of Hélène Rey and co-authors, summarised in her contribution to this volume, today we understand much better than a quarter of a century ago that there is such a thing as a GFC. Asset prices and capital flows to EMs are highly correlated with measures of global risk appetite. And given the important share of the dollar in international funding, US monetary policy is the main driver of the risk cycle. Periods of loose monetary policy in the United States coincide with a weaker dollar, higher risk-taking, larger capital flows, rising asset prices, and increasing leverage in EMs. The opposite happens when the United States tightens monetary policy: investors run for the exits, and capital flows, asset prices, and leverage move in the opposite direction.

In addition, Şebnem Kalemli-Özcan underscores in her contribution to this volume, the GFC often induces a local interest rate disconnect: when the Federal Reserve moves rates in one direction, emerging country market rates tend to move in the same direction even when the local policy rate moves in the other, as the local central bank tries to offset the shock coming from the US.

This has important implications for the conduct of exchange rate policy. Allowing the currency to float does not do away with the dominance of the dollar and the difficulties it brings. As Rey puts it: 'There is no "divine coincidence" that guarantees international financial conditions align with the objectives of domestic monetary authorities.' Central banks in EMs can find themselves facing a boom in capital inflows at a time when they are trying to tighten to reduce inflation, and vice versa.

So, the reality of flexible exchange rates is less rosy than suggested by Milton Friedman, the Mundell–Fleming tradition, and the Washington Consensus. Does that mean that, as a general rule, fixed exchange rates are better? Not at all. Rey persuasively argues, as do other recent papers, that even in the presence of GFCs, flexible rates can play a useful stabilising role.[26]

But it does mean, however, that policymakers should be pragmatic, and not be shy about using occasional exchange market intervention, macroprudential regulation, and even exchange controls, to prevent destabilising short-term capital flows. At the same time, whenever there is an attempt to manage exchange rates, there are institutional challenges as to who will conduct the intervention and with what objective. Having competent management of this aspect of macro policy is a key part of state capacity.

Ricardo Hausmann's contribution to this volume makes a persuasive case for a positive and crucial role of exports in the growth and development process. This means that exchange rate policy cannot be conducted while turning a blind eye to the implications of the real exchange rate for export growth – and for overall economic growth. On the contrary, as Hausmann and co-authors Lant Pritchett and Dani Rodrik show in their earlier paper, growth accelerations are associated with periods of persistently undervalued real exchange rates.[27] The conventional wisdom is that exchange rate policy cannot control the long-run real exchange rate, which is driven by real factors. But the long run can be *very* far into the future. Over shorter horizons, exchange rate and regulatory policy matter. This is an additional reason to be pragmatic and keep a dirty float, prudential regulation, and disincentives to speculative capital inflows, in the policymaker's toolkit.

As well as paying attention to the need to create conditions for stability and to support growth, macroeconomic policy must also recognise that different policies have very different distributional consequences. As Nora

Lustig notes in this volume, the Washington Consensus was frequently blind to the distributional consequences of its prescriptions, especially in countries with weak social safety nets. This had political consequences, for instance when public expenditure cuts were seen as the product of externally driven technocratic interventions by actors such as the World Bank and IMF. Our principle that politics matters stresses that policy ownership by countries is of intrinsic importance and that responsive political systems should be sensitive to the distributional effects of macroeconomic policies.

2. *Structural policies*

Our principles stress the importance of the underlying structure of the economy for both equity and efficiency. We saw earlier that the Washington Consensus focused on static efficiency, with little attention paid to both dynamic efficiency (for generating growth) and to distribution. The London Consensus approaches these issues very differently. We have stressed that *what* you produce, *how* you produce it, and *where* you produce it matter. This gives way to a suite of policies that we will loosely label *supply-side progressivism* (in his comment on Rodrik, Pierre-Olivier Gourinchas also argues that what is central to these policies is the emphasis on the supply side, in contrast to the focus on the demand side typical of more traditional progressive approaches). *Supply side progressivism* assigns a central role to productive development policies – such as industrial, competition and technology policies – to promote inclusive growth.

One of the key debates at the time of the Washington Consensus concerned the role of public ownership in sectors of the economy, i.e., whether it matters which goods are produced by the public or private sectors. Privatisation of state-owned enterprises to increase the efficiency and profitability of businesses and to minimise subsidies to state-owned enterprises was a widely used policy, which received fresh impetus following the fall of the Berlin Wall. There can be no doubt that running state-owned enterprises created large governance challenges. Without the right political incentives, in most countries it has proven extremely hard to manage those challenges and avoid inefficiency.

Although there is close-to-a-consensus on ownership in sectors such as consumer goods and services, which are best located in private hands, debates remain about the case for public ownership of natural monopolies and some kinds of core infrastructure. When it comes to natural monopolies, many countries have embraced independent regulation with mandates that focus on price regulation rather than rate-of-return regulation. But it has proven difficult to incorporate social and environmental goals into such systems. And there are questions of whether investments in green technologies should be paid for by higher prices or funded from general taxation. Plus, some systems have also struggled in managing volatility, such as the price shocks in energy markets after the invasion of Ukraine. Reliability of energy supply is certainly now back on the agenda, with the promise that renewables can play a greater role in many countries in reducing dependence on suppliers based in potentially hostile countries.

The London Consensus is not prescriptive about the way that a country chooses to organise these important sectors. Instead, we give primacy to three of our core principles in approaching this issue. First, access to core infrastructure involves a case for a universal service obligation to limit the domain of inequality, with pricing (including subsidies for low-income users) that respects this mandate. So, equity as well as efficiency objectives matter.

Second, environmental goals are central to these ambitions. Infrastructure investment can be an important driver of clean growth, creating new industries but also allowing other industries to benefit from less volatile access to key inputs.

Third, state capacity is key. Without a joined-up approach that combines technocracy and politics, there is little chance that an inclusive and environmentally sound approach will be achieved that supports growth. Politics affects *how* these key goods are produced and whether these industries are run in the public interest.

The Washington Consensus was famously hostile to state activism in industrial policy – though this preference was often rhetorical, with governments that subscribed to the consensus often continuing to use state-owned enterprises for strategic ends. The success of several East Asian economies, styled a 'miracle', was also attributable to state activism.

Today there is much greater acceptance of activist state policies to solve market failures and to coordinate decisions across sectors of the economy. Indeed, these are now frequently seen as the *sine qua non* of an approach to productive development that can support inclusive and sustainable growth. That said, there are large differences of opinion when it comes to the form such policies should take and what the (measurable) objectives should be.

When it comes to industrial policy, for example, some think that a focus on broad non-selective horizontal policies will suffice, while others see merits in a more vertical approach, even one in which government decides *ex ante* which sectors should be given priority. The climate imperative has somewhat lessened the scope for disagreement, since there is (almost) a consensus that state action that makes both production and consumption greener is needed. Many nations are also having to make judgements on where they stand on advanced technology sectors, and whether they will become so strategically important that some home production capacity should be supported. Globalisation has also reignited debates about cultural industries and whether preservation of the production of unique culturally specific public goods ought to be part of that strategy.

Our core principles do provide some useful guidance in shaping a London Consensus approach to productive development policies (we prefer this label to the conventional 'industrial policy', since many of the activities to be promoted need not be industrial – they could be services, high-value added agriculture, etc.). First, many of the past failures of industrial policy can be avoided by building state capacity that increases the competence of the state in supporting productive development. Legal and regulatory structures are now also thought of as a source of comparative advantage.

Second, politics is key, since there is no obvious way to agree on national priorities and the resources that they require without debate and accountability for success and failure. Even though China lacks conventionally democratic institutions, it created frameworks for learning from success and failure, and decentralisation allowed some kinds of yardstick competition to evolve.[28] The state also supported technological upskilling through education and training.

Third, the objectives of industrial strategy, although debatable, could include important non-efficiency-oriented objectives. These include place-based policies to support a regionally equitable distribution of prosperity (this is connected to the issue of *where* goods and services are produced), or encouraging labour-intensive sectors to expand to reduce unemployment, especially among low-skill workers. If the objectives are clear and state capacity is present, then it is perfectly reasonable to go beyond narrow notions of static efficiency.

Fourth, productive development policy should be used to promote growth, not just static efficiency. It is reasonable for policymakers to be concerned if production is locked into sectors with low growth potential, such as traditional agriculture or old-style manufacturing. A forward-looking strategy that tries to support growth through state activism is perfectly reasonable if the structures are in place to deliver. But alongside state intervention, an enabling environment for both job creation and destruction is important. As we stressed in our principles, designing a transition for workers whose dignity and status comes from their work presents difficult challenges. Good politics can support this process without allowing vested interests to form a blocking coalition.

All of these ideas surface in Dani Rodrik's essay on productivism for this volume. He departs from the thinking that dominated the Washington Consensus by assigning a greater role to government and civil society, along with less of a blind faith in markets. This vision also stresses the need to invest in local communities and create good jobs for all. To do so requires new modes of industrial policy and the capacity to build a political consensus around policy objectives. In their contribution, which has many overlaps with Rodrik's, Philippe Aghion and John Van Reenen frame the challenge in terms of a renewed appreciation of Schumpeterian growth theory. They, too, embrace new forms of state activism to achieve inclusive and sustainable growth, through productive development policy and activist competition policy.

Related to these two is technology policy. Our first principle, that economic structures matter, is of first order importance when considering the consequences of technology. At a country level, there is a strong case for government support to help firms adopt frontier technologies. In his contribution to the volume, Ricardo Hausmann links this to export-led growth, arguing that countries that grow exhibit more than proportional export growth, in a way that changes the composition of exports towards new, more complex products. Hausmann frames the challenge in terms of organising a costly search process for growth opportunities, both at the intensive and extensive margins of production, with government playing an activist role in that process. In addition, Isabela Manelici stresses in this volume, exporting itself may contribute to technology adoption, as exporters learn from sophisticated foreign buyers.

Technological innovation has the potential to dramatically improve productivity and raise living standards. But the fact that many technologies hold great promise does not mean that all of their social and economic consequences will be desirable. A case in point is the advent of social media, which has created new economic opportunities but has also changed the nature of social relations, and not necessarily for the better. The rise of artificial intelligence will be similarly transformative, and along with its huge potential benefits lie distributional and social effects we do not yet fully understand. There are also potential negative externalities that need to be taken into account. One crucial area of concern is the development of technologies that simply replace labour instead of serving as complements for labour productivity.

Democratic societies have been reluctant to regulate technology. Much less reluctance has been evident among dictatorships, which have embraced the potential of tech for citizen surveillance. This contrast has fuelled the perception that free societies should follow a Wild West approach to technology. But the principles we are proposing caution against this stance.

The economy we create, and the inequalities it displays, will depend on the way that technologies are used. Governments will have to develop capacities to do the job of regulating technology better – especially in the case of new technologies whose economic and social consequences are not fully understood.[29]

There is also a respectable case for recognising that the internet is effectively a public utility, where pricing and production decisions require greater state involvement. Here our principle that politics matters re-emerges, but in a different guise, not as a counterpoint but to stress that without adequate contexts for public debate and discussion, states could easily weaken public trust further when they appear to restrict technological opportunities.

Concerns about volatility should also have a more salient role. So far, we have seen only tremors from software glitches and cyber-attacks. But it is plausible to think that the next global crisis will have its origins in cyberspace. State capacity to comprehend the nature of these risks and minimise them *ex-ante* is essential, since mopping up after the event could prove extremely damaging and expensive.

Skills and labour market policies are another important class of structural policies that received scant attention from the Washington Consensus, but are a central part of the London Consensus. Access to 'good jobs, at good wages' is an important policy goal along with growing awareness of the importance of the quality of jobs (formal versus informal, with or without benefits, etc.) and of the need to fight discrimination in the labour market. This issue is central to Christopher Pissarides's contribution to this volume, and it also surfaces in the papers by Dani Rodrik and by Oriana Bandiera and Barbara Petrongolo, and the comment by Kirsten Sehnbruch. It is an issue which, in addition to its crucial economic implications, will also have deep and lasting political repercussions. Without 'good jobs, at good wages' it is hard to imagine how politics will remain peaceful and stable in many countries.

The endogenous growth approach has put human capital at centre stage. And to the extent that educational attainment is broad-based, human capital accumulation can be an important source of inclusivity. Delivering education requires systems of finance that recognise that capital market frictions are important, but also that many of the gains from education accrue to those who receive it, as the contribution by Nicholas Barr to this volume stresses. Thus, easy-to-access and flexible loan schemes allow for more skills acquisition. This requires new kinds of lending, some of which may involve state support.

Externalities are important too, and there are good arguments for subsidising strategically important forms of education. This is often taken as code for STEM subjects, but not only that. Good management plays a key role in business success, and requires understanding of organisational behaviour, economics and human psychology. In addition, cultural industries are the lifeblood of thriving societies and communities.

In accordance with our principles, the approach of the London Consensus stresses a wide interpretation of wellbeing and a central role to values and ethics that promote cohesive polities. Creating a public sphere for establishing common ground is a priority – something that social media have made more difficult by coarsening public discourse. We do not regard seeking such common ground as utopian, and shared experiences like living through a global pandemic ought to create new opportunities.

3. *Openness to trade*

The Washington Consensus was fashioned on the eve of a vast wave of globalisation that saw the widespread integration of the global economy, including two countries of continental scale, China and India. The Washington Consensus was optimistic about the potential of trade to spur development – which made sense given the focus of the initial conference on Latin America, a pretty closed region where one did not have to be an ideologue to think that some trade liberalisation could be beneficial. Consequently, Williamson and his colleagues were suspicious of attempts to protect industries using tariffs and quotas. Protection was seen as a source of political as well as economic distortions, as entrepreneurs were driven to rent-seeking rather than focusing on making their firms more productive.

Three-and-a-half decades later, what have we learned about the benefits and costs of international trade? (We focus on capital mobility and migration later.) Dave Donaldson's paper in this volume tackles the question head on, and provides very clear answers.

A long time ago, David Ricardo started us thinking about the 'gains from trade'. Donaldson's first big conclusion is that modern econometric techniques have revealed that in 'most countries and in most circumstances, the aggregate efficiency gains from being open to foreign trade are substantial'. He adds:

> While it is challenging to quantify the aggregate effects of trade, I believe that we can be more confident than ever in the broad view invoked in the Washington Consensus: that trade openness raises aggregate living standards. In fact, given changes to the global economy since 1989, the size of the aggregate gains available to most countries may also be greater ...

In their comments on Donaldson, both Tony Venables and Thomas Sampson agree that recent evidence shows that gains from trade are large (though Sampson stresses that *how* large depends on country size, with smaller economies benefiting a great deal more from liberalisation).

That is an optimistic conclusion, and one that would seem to chime with the general impression that globalisation and trade are at least partly responsible for pulling tens and even hundreds of millions of people out of poverty in the last decades, most notably in China and India but also in a host of other countries in East and South Asia and Latin America. The conclusion also fits the enormous consumer benefits from globalisation. Products that could barely have been dreamed of 30 years ago, such as smartphones and inexpensive portable computers and tablets, today are widely available. They were not created by globalisation, but the increase in the size of the market has been an important force for innovation and lower costs. The poor, in particular, have been beneficiaries of the increased affordability of basic manufactured goods, such as clothing and footwear.

As part of this trend, the digital world has also been opened up to a wide population. Despite creeping concerns about digital addiction, especially in a world of social media, improved access to digital communications has been largely beneficial. And it has the potential to generate even larger gains in education and also in health, as these technologies are harnessed for treatment and diagnosis. Of course, access to digital technology is by no means universal, and some countries limit the use of global digital brands – as when China chooses to ban content providers, such as Google.

But that is not end of the story. With trade liberalisation occurring at a world scale, the global distribution of production has shifted – most notably with China's entry into the world economy, initially on the back of low-cost manufacturing, and then increasingly by moving up the value chain. This massive shift has produced winners, but also losers. Hence the second main conclusion in Donaldson's paper: 'The uneven effects of globalisation cannot be ignored. Changes in the size and composition of trade flows have markedly unequal effects on earnings across individuals'. Of course, he emphasises, this was never in dispute. Over 80 years ago, the Stolper–Samuelson theorem described how income distribution would shift as the result of trade between rich and poor countries. What is new is the size of the changes involved: 'recent empirical work has shown just how unequal these effects can be – and how they can show up in ways that may have surprised economists from Stolper and Samuelson to those behind the [Washington] Consensus in 1989'.

Now, it is important to be clear about who the losers are and where they live. The Stolper–Samuelson theorem shows that, under plausible conditions, trade between a capital-abundant country and a labour-abundant country will shift the distribution of income in favour of workers in the labour-abundant country and in favour of rentiers in the capital-abundant nation. This proposition largely seems to have been borne out in reality, with the losers being low-skilled workers in rich countries.[30] (That said, in his contribution to this volume Danny Quah does outline a mechanism whereby poor countries, too, can lose from trade.)

This distribution of gains and losses helps explain why one observes growing scepticism towards free trade and rising concern over large-scale manufacturing job losses in the US and, to a lesser extent, in the UK and continental Europe. But for many labour-abundant countries, trade liberalisation has been close to an unmitigated benefit, both in terms of equity and efficiency. Granted, there were reallocation and adjustment costs in poor countries, but those are mostly behind them. And, as both Dave Donaldson and Thomas Sampson emphasise in this book, undoing trade liberalisation there would amount to an additional shock, involving new costs of adjustment. That is why – except for lobbies in remaining monopoly sectors – you will not find many leaders in the so called Global South pushing to raise trade barriers. This crucial distinction in the distributional effect of trade between rich and poor countries is not always captured in international debates, dominated as they are by developments in the advanced world and, particularly, in the Anglosphere.

Another insufficiently appreciated aspect of globalisation is how rents are distributed. Those with intellectual property are able to increase their rents by outsourcing manufacturing. Even though tech giants such as Apple produce little in the US, rents from their products accrue to the Apple Corporation where it chooses to declare them. This has enriched the (successful) entrepreneurial classes whose returns are larger when they can drive down production costs. It also has created new sources of inequality within countries.

Where does the London Consensus stand on all of this? First of all, it is in tune with these developments by emphasising the benefits of exports and an export orientation for growth, especially in developing and emerging nations. Now, an export-orientation is not the same as a laissez-faire attitude, as we stressed in the previous section. On the contrary, a successful export performance may require an activist productive development policy. This is part of a more general theme: growth does not just happen when government steps aside and lets the private sector do its job. Economic growth requires an enabling environment, the lion's share of which is created by deliberate government policy.

In the countries of the North there is a drift towards protectionism – first with the tariffs on Chinese electric auto manufacturers in Canada, Europe and the US and, more recently, with the tariff escalation initiated by Donald Trump. These policies rest in part on the accusation that there is no level playing field. In Europe and North America there is also increasing acceptance of security arguments to restrict trade, especially in high-tech products that go into weapon systems.

Our principles do not rule out all protection measures categorically since, as we have argued, economic structures matter. We also stressed the flaws in the argument that the downside from trade openness can always be dealt with by financial compensation. The political system cannot be relied on to deliver financial compensation, much less compensation for the loss of status and dignity that many have endured. But this certainly does not mean that any old protectionist policy is justified. The risk, or course, is that protectionist vested interests will hide behind security arguments, which are vague and hard to evidence.

One important caveat is that concern over the loss of jobs in certain areas, and the social and political consequences this might have, need not feed straight into protectionist policies – that is, into policies that discriminate between foreign and domestically produced goods, and between national and foreign firms. What we have learned in the years since the Washington Consensus is that the negative multiplier, that goes from the loss of jobs to the weakening of whole communities, operates at the local level (the level of a city or a region) and hence is often best dealt with through local policies – or what is known nowadays as policies of place. Instead of tariffs and quotas, Anthony Venables argues in this volume, those policies should involve 'both [local] labour supply – the training and skill development polices traditionally suggested – and labour demand, through active policy to support lagging areas and attract investment'. The aim is often to start a local 'Big Push' of the kind first described by Rosenstein-Rodan and later by Murphy, Shleifer, and Vishny.[31]

Another way of dealing with the issue of local job losses is to stimulate inward foreign investment, as when European, Japanese, or Korean firms build auto plants in the United States. More generally, the growth of foreign direct investment (FDI) is another dimension of openness that has grown in importance since the years of the Washington Consensus. Williamson stressed its benefits as a source of capital, job creation, and building skills, while exposing domestic firms to greater competition. Back then they were greeted with scepticism in some quarters, but the arguments still stand. FDI can have plenty of beneficial effects, especially for developing nations. The London Consensus puts greater stress than the Washington Consensus on the importance of technology transfer as a benefit from FDI and calls on policymakers to create an environment where such transfers will actually take place.

The London Consensus is sceptical, however, on the benefits (or lack thereof) of a completely open capital account, which can lead to large (and potentially destabilising) short-term capital movements. In line with our discussion in the macro section of this essay, and in the paper by Hélène Rey, there are many circumstances where a clash can arise between the objectives of domestic macroeconomic stability (including export growth and full employment) and the pressures of the global capital market. Policymakers should not be shy about using their entire policy toolkit to deal with such situations. This might include serving as lender of last resort and market-maker of last resort, as stressed by Reis and Velasco in their paper.

Prudence is also in order when it comes to the ever-contentious issue of migration. There is a strong global equality case to be made in favour of international migration, as people flow to countries where jobs are plentiful and pay better. This both pushes up wages in the source country and enables the families of the migrants to receive remittances, which is helpful to reduce poverty and improve income distribution. Even when looked at exclusively from the point of view of rich, capital-abundant countries, and given current demographic trends, it is hard to envision how those countries will keep the tax base growing and be able to provide social services to their ageing populations, without substantial migration flows.

But our emphasis on the political effects of economic policies leads us to counsel care and gradualism. Even if migration does not hold down wages in certain recipient-country sectors, there are political consequences of immigration due to the mixing of cultures and difficulties with integration into local communities. It seems fair to say that such difficulties have been larger and more disruptive than most observers anticipated. This is not a case for doing away with migration – in fact, despite evident political stress, so far, no rich country has moved decisively in that direction, and in many nations migration flows are at all-time highs. Rather, it is an argument for being careful and creative regarding the mechanisms that regulate the movement of people across borders – whether by using a point system that prioritises skills that are high in demand, or by creating mechanisms for temporary migration (some call it rotational labour mobility), which can be less politically disruptive.[32]

4. *Taxation and public spending*

The vision of a state funded by broad-based taxation, and spending on programmes with universal benefits, such as health, education, infrastructure, and the environment, is a point of convergence between the Washington Consensus and the London Consensus. But the underlying principles are quite different, and so are some of the policy implications.

Creating broad-based taxation requires investment in state capacities, which in turn include systems of compliance and measurement. Research in this area has grown fast in the past 30 years, as economists have come to understand that computing the optimal choice of tax rates and tax bases is an empty exercise unless there is scope for implementing and enforcing tax policy. The Panglossian view that delivering quality public programmes is only a matter of political will is not much help – on the contrary, it can be quite destructive. And of course, the ability of states to get their hands on the needed resources varies widely: several advanced economies manage to raise 40% of GDP or more in tax revenue, while many countries in the world struggle to get 20% or even 15%.

Similar considerations apply to public spending. Being able to deliver even the most basic health and education services requires attention to organisational design and the standard of training. The chapter on education by Lant Pritchett, and the very good comments it elicited, all emphasise that there are plenty of examples where spending has increased without concomitant improvements in educational attainment. In his contribution, Pritchett stresses that with near universal access achieved, the priority now is to improve on learning outcomes, which requires realigning educational systems but not necessarily higher spending. We may never have a consensus on the granular details that will drive sustained gains in improving learning outcomes, but points of agreement include commitment to universal foundational learning and supporting and rewarding quality teachers. Pritchett also stresses the need for an adaptive and iterative learning process, rather than a universal blueprint for success.

The study of educational provision is part of a new organisational economics of the provision of key public services. This includes pragmatic debates about the role of private schools, as Pedro Carneiro discusses in his response to Pritchett – although both he and Miguel Urquiola stress that private provision can play a useful role but is no panacea. Urquiola also underscores that system design is key. A running theme is that the provision of education relies on state capacity for designing, evaluating, and implementing whichever system is in place. And without a system of political accountability to drive success, often at the local level, the needed changes may fail to materialise. This aligns with a more general theme in Ernesto Dal Bó's contribution to the volume, stressing the role of accountability and decentralisation in building state capacities.

An important lesson is that taxation and public service access should be designed to distort labour market decisions, and the choice by small firms to be formal or informal, as little as possible. As Santiago Levy's research has long shown – the point also comes up in his comment in this volume – well-meaning but misdesigned welfare systems can push workers and firms into informality, with deleterious effects on productivity and equity. An example is the policy of making certain individual social benefits contingent on employment status, so that informal workers lose access to them if they take a formal job.

In keeping with our theme that policy ought to attempt to reduce the volatility citizens are exposed to, state institutions and expenditure programmes ought to be designed for resilience. This implies that the delivery of public services should not add to volatility, instead being as smooth and reliable as possible over time, even in the face of financial and real shocks. This can be challenging, as the chapter by Alistair McGuire, Joan Costa-i-Font, and Ranjeeta Thomas shows. The COVID-19 pandemic revealed that many healthcare systems, including in advanced nations, lacked spare capacity to deal with sudden surges in demand, and lacked sufficient supplies of essential equipment, such as respirators, to cope with an emergency. Moreover, the global community had not agreed on a cooperative system to allocate scarce vaccines and medicines during a pandemic, with weaker and poorer nations predictably paying the price. Now we understand better than we did a few years ago the risks associated with pandemics. Climate change and the degradation of the natural environment will increase the prevalence of natural emergencies. So, we need to incorporate resilience into public service delivery. This means not just increasing spending, but also building the kind of state capacity needed to identify risks and develop strategies for adaptation and mitigation.

Spending and taxation should be viewed not as separable functions of the state, but instead as part of an integrated component of a social contract based on norms of responsibility – and of reciprocity between the state and citizens. People who believe that the government is serving their interests will feel a stronger obligation to pay their taxes.[33] As Margaret Levi has stressed, governments that are credible and trusted in this sense become less reliant on coercion to get things done and therefore are also more efficient.[34]

The implication is that we should build institutions that create such confidence, including the demonstrable use of public resources for collective ends. But building state capacity is far from a technocratic exercise that can be carried out by external experts and consultants who preach the best global practice. State reforms are unavoidably shaped by domestic politics and by the local political culture. As underscored by political scientists such as Robert Putnam, when civic norms are strong, the state emerges stronger.[35]

Even though state intervention is key in areas such as health and education, inequalities in endowments and circumstances are a constraint on health and educational attainment, something that in this volume Michael Marmot stresses in relation to health. Such inequalities are important for many reasons, not the least of which is that they have a direct impact on the distribution of wellbeing in a way not easily quantified in conventional economic terms.

Hence, reducing the domain of inequalities in health and education is an end in itself. But the goal is likely to be elusive for many reasons, one of which is that inequalities interact in ways that can multiply the resulting harms. For instance, as Carol Propper underscores in her comments, inequality in health outcomes depend not just on differential access to healthcare, but also on inequality of incomes, education, and the places where people work and live.

Pragmatism is also required. We agree with Paul Johnson, who writes in this volume that good economics 'do not support simply minimising state involvement, nor ruling out the private sector. It is much more complicated than that'. That is why recent research has paid a great deal of attention to incentives and organisational design issues. Ideas like school vouchers and competition among providers, once dismissed by some as neoliberal ideology, are now sometimes embraced in pursuit of a system that is both equitable and efficient.

In a modern welfare state, and depending on the public goods and services involved, there should exist a mixture of public and private provision, with varying proportions of redistribution and insurance, and with more or less centralisation in delivery, as Nicholas Barr argues in his chapter for this volume. The devil, as ever, is in the details. The chapters on health and education suggest similar conclusions. In this and other policy domains, the London Consensus is not prescriptive about the balance of public finance and provision, and the methods through which that provision occurs. Instead, the focus is on building the capacity and structures to deliver, based on rigorously evaluating what works.

5. *Empowerment*

The London Consensus stresses the role of policies (and politics) as a source of empowerment. It is also a theme Pranab Bardhan emphasises in his closing comments. Labour market flexibility was part of the mantra of the Washington Consensus era. While the consensus was not openly hostile to trade unions, there was an undercurrent at the time that saw them as part of the problem, not the solution. Yet, labour market flexibility and strong unions are by no means contradictory. For instance, the Scandinavian 'flexicurity system' combines flexibility (in the form of low and predictable hiring and firing costs) with a central role for unions in negotiating features of the workplace that matter for productivity (hours, shifts, worker training, and worker voice among them). Similarly, the London Consensus envisions empowered unions playing a role that goes far beyond the traditional role of bargaining over wages.

There is a related issue of great importance today on which the Washington Consensus was silent: policies to promote gender parity in social and economic life. In their essay in this volume, Oriana Bandiera and Barbara Petrongolo stress that, although economic development often leads to convergence in formal rights, this does not necessarily translate into gender parity in the labour market. Direct policies are needed to achieve equality.

Today, Bandiera and Petrongolo show, the bulk of the labour market differential between men and women is driven by differential experiences upon childbirth – what the literature terms the 'motherhood penalty'. While the state has a role to play in correcting this gap, nowadays there is also growing attention to what firms can do, for instance, by adopting family-friendly policies, such as parental leave, childcare support, and flexible work arrangements. This will require a sharp break from the current prevalence of 'greedy jobs' (jobs where there is little substitution between workers), which pose particular problems for women workers, as Almudena Sevilla stresses in her contribution.[36]

Bandiera and Petrongolo argue persuasively that gender inequality is a waste of talent. Therefore, progress towards gender parity can enhance economic efficiency and growth. But the case for parity should not be based on instrumental efficiency grounds alone, Ashwini Deshpande argues in her contribution. Dignity and social justice are at stake.

Now, the extent to which the voices of female workers will be heard and valued depends on the nature of the workplace. This is an issue of wider concern since, in modern societies, many of our waking hours are spent at work. We hope to have our voices heard on this crucial sphere of our lives, but this is frequently not the case. This reduces economic efficiency, since frontline workers often know better than anyone else how to improve productive practices. But it also matters crucially for people's sense of dignity and self-esteem, and therefore for the politics of a nation, which is more often than not driven by citizens' frustration and desire for change. Political philosopher Elizabeth Anderson, well known for her work on equality in social relations, describes company management as a 'private government', and calls for that government to be more democratic.[37] We sympathise with that call.

Earlier in this introduction we have stressed the importance of political democracy as a source of empowerment. Without delegating authority to citizens as the ultimate stakeholders, it is hard to see how there can be any guarantee to protect the economic, political, and social rights of all citizens. Citizen voice and influence matter because they are directly constitutive of human agency, and not just because they can secure greater access to goods and services.

Crucially, people identify with their local communities, and those identities are a crucial component of who they are as human beings. For most of history we lived in tribal societies and communities that were a key source of identity. Some have seen the advent of a globalised cosmopolitan society as a natural evolution that will allow humans to leave such archaic structures behind. We believe that is a mistaken interpretation. The forms of social organisation and identity might change, but communal identities have a way or reasserting themselves in politics and social life even as they are wished away. A key challenge today is to enlarge this human circle of identity and trust, and to build enlarged communities of fate, as Margaret Levi has long argued.[38] These are communities in which people come to believe 'they are in it together' and are willing to act on the interests of anonymous strangers because of this perceived shared collective interest. Even in a globalised world, there are overlapping communities – like the one that came together to produce this book.

V. Concluding comments

This introductory chapter has attempted to draw lessons from the contributions in this volume. While we have not done full justice to the richness of these, which must be read to be appreciated, we have tried to delineate some common threads and ideas. But they are *our* interpretation and *our* views; we cannot even be sure that our proposals will elicit a consensus among our authors, let alone the global policymaking community. But we do think that now is a good time to try to foster a consensus grounded in sound economic principles.

Each author in this volume was tasked with looking for consensus in a specific policy area. There was no attempt to prescribe any core principles of policymaking that could underpin the task. But, as we have emphasised, principles have emerged, which do allow for a clear departure from the Washington Consensus. Some are clear shifts of direction while others attempt to correct blind spots in the underlying economic model. These principles also reflect fundamental changes in the discipline of economics, towards less monolithic conceptual foundations – a flexibility that has also informed new empirical approaches.

Economics has embraced political economy and has also brought in ideas from other social sciences. Economists' measurement frameworks now try to transcend a narrow focus on the implications of policies for consumption and incomes – without losing sight, of course, that these remain core indicators of economic success and failure. We argue for an approach that has its core in economics, but an economics that also thinks about *who* gets *what* and *why* that matters.

We have also stressed that *what* you produce, *how* you produce it, and *where* you produce it is important. The *what* and *how* allow us to discuss the choice of technology and the role of directed technical innovation, and the consequent impact on the quantity and quality of jobs. The *where* opens the door to a discussion of 'place-based policies' – or 'levelling up', as it has been called in the UK. This approach integrates the local and the global. It is also more attentive to the challenges we now face from climate change and the depletion of nature.

The Washington Consensus did lay down many important ideas, some of which have stood the test of time. The framework it proposed contributed to the spread of globalisation, creating many opportunities along the way: it is hard to argue against the view that the sizeable reductions in global poverty that followed were not in significant part the fruit of embracing greater economic openness. But the Washington Consensus also left us with a plethora of important unanswered questions about the kind of society that would follow.

Some of the failings of the Washington Consensus are understandable. In 1989 economics had yet to re-engage seriously with political economy and with the more nuanced psychological models of human behaviour. And welfare economics as practised then found it easier to argue for efficiency rather than engaging with apparently more difficult issues of distribution. There was also much less appreciation of the importance of state capacities and institutional structures in shaping policy effectiveness. The climate crisis was much less salient, as were some of the social and political downsides of globalisation. These new factors are all prominent in the contributions to this volume and should become central to shaping a new approach.

Because the London Consensus is reflective of where economics, as a discipline, is today, it is best thought of as an *economic* consensus rather than a *policy* consensus. The approach we suggest is not a prescriptive list of policies but a set of principles that assist policymakers when choosing among alternatives. We believe that social science is at its best when used as guidance for seeking solutions, while leaving it up to empowered communities to find the appropriate policies to meet the manifold challenges they face.

Notes

[1] See, for example, Gerstle (2022).

[2] For example, Bauer (1976).

[3] The classic reference is Hirschman (1968).

[4] Krueger (1974).

[5] Williamson (1990).

[6] In the UK, the Conservative-Lib Dem coalition that governed in 2010–15 was never particularly keen on deregulation. Most of that was already done by Margaret Thatcher and largely maintained by Tony Blair.

[7] See Hirschman (1970). Distrust of big ideas and general solutions is also a key theme of Banerjee and Duflo (2011).

[8] Rodrik et al. (2008).

[9] For example, Sarbin (1986), or Schank and Abelson (1977).

[10] This sentiment is neatly encapsulated in the following quote from Mill: 'The laws and conditions of the Production of Wealth partake of the character of physical truths. There is nothing optional or arbitrary in them. It is not so with the Distribution of Wealth. That is a matter of human institution solely. The things once there, mankind, individually or collectively, can do with them as they like. They can place them at the disposal of whomsoever they please, and on whatever terms. The Distribution of Wealth depends on the laws and customs of society. The rules by which it is determined are what the opinions and feelings of the ruling portion of the community make them, and are very different

in different ages and countries; and might be still more different, if mankind so chose.' Mill (1848/2004).

[11] Diamond and Mirrlees (1971).

[12] Hacker (2011).

[13] These are core ideas in moral and political philosophy that go back at least to Aristotle and have modern statements in works such as Rawls (1971), Sen (1999), and Nussbaum (2011).

[14] Manning (2013).

[15] Output growth, as opposed to growth of population or exports, merits only a few passing mentions.

[16] Aghion and Howitt (1992).

[17] Pritchett (2022).

[18] See Besley et al. (2025).

[19] See Williamson (2009).

[20] Calvo (1986a; 1986b).

[21] Acemoglu and Robinson (2013a).

[22] Now, these links should not be interpreted mechanically nor generalised too much. If economic frustration and income inequality were its only sources, then populism would not be affecting egalitarian Sweden or fast-growing India – and the rising populism would be of the left-wing, redistributive variety, not of the right-wing, lower-taxes-on-the-rich kind.

[23] Acemoglu and Robinson (2013b) delineate an important distinction between inclusive and extractive institutions as core drivers of state success and failure.

[24] Svensson (2011).

[25] With regard to the exchange rate, the Washington Consensus was often characterised as favouring market-determined exchange rates. This resulted from the fear that managed exchange rates often became overvalued, and required current and capital account restrictions to be sustained. Floating seemed like a ready fix for this problem, even if it added a new source of volatility. But many others who argued for the Washington Consensus favoured fixed rates. Some for technical reasons (they feared a floating exchange rate was not uniquely determined), others for political economy reasons, since fixed rates would presumably induce fiscal discipline.

[26] Obstfeld and Zhou (2023).

[27] Hausmann et al. (2005).

[28] See Wang and Yang (2021).

[29] For an illuminating discussion of these issues, see Johnson and Acemoglu (2023).

[30] There are caveats. Think of Stolper–Samuelson in the context of two factors of production (skilled and unskilled labour) and many countries. It could be that one country (e.g., Mexico) is relatively abundant in unskilled labour vis à vis one trading partner (the United States) and relatively abundant in skilled labour vis à vis another partner (China). Then, multilateral trade liberalisation could either raise or reduce the wage skill premium in Mexico. In practice it seems to have raised it, increasing wage inequality in Mexico. See Hanson and Harrison (1999).

[31] Rosenstein-Rodan (1943), and Murphy et al. (1989).

[32] On this last point, see Pritchett (2024).

[33] For example, Besley (2020).

[34] See Levi (1997).

[35] Putnam (1994).

[36] The term was coined by Claudia Goldin (2021).

[37] See Anderson (2019).

[38] Levi (2020).

References

Acemoglu, D. and Robinson, J. A. (2013a) 'Economics versus Politics: Pitfalls of Policy Advice', *Journal of Economic Perspectives,* 27(2): 173–192. https://doi.org/10.1257/jep.27.2.173

Acemoglu, D. and Robinson, J. A. (2013b) *Why Nations Fail: The Origins of Power, Prosperity, and Poverty*, London: Crown Currency. https://doi.org/10.1111/dpr.12048

Aghion, P. and Howitt, P. (1992) 'A Model of Growth Through Creative Destruction' *Econometrica*, 60(2): 323–351. https://doi.org/10.2307/2951599

Anderson, E. (2019) *Private Government: How Employers Rule Our Lives (and Why We Don't Talk about It)*, Princeton, NJ: Princeton University Press.

Banerjee, A. and Duflo E. (2011) *Poor Economics: A Radical Rethinking of the Way to Fight Global Poverty*, New York: Public Affairs.

Bauer, P. (1976) *Dissent on Development*, Cambridge, MA: Harvard University Press.

Besley, T. (2020) 'State Capacity, Reciprocity, and the Social Contract'. *Econometrica*, 88(4): 1307–1335. https://doi.org/10.3982/ECTA16863

Besley, T., Dann, C. and Dray, S. (2025) 'Growth Experiences and Trust in Government', unpublished working paper.

Calvo, G. A. (1986a) 'Temporary Stabilization: Predetermined Exchange Rates', *Journal of Political Economy*, 94: 1319–1329. https://doi.org/10.1086/261435

Calvo, G. A. (1986b) 'On the Costs of Temporary Liberalization/Stabilization Experiments', in M. Connolly and C. Gonzalez (eds) *Economic Reform and Stabilization in Latin America*, New York: Praeger Publishers.

Diamond, P. A. and Mirrlees, J. A. (1971) 'Optimal Taxation and Public Production I: Production Efficiency', *The American Economic Review*, 61(1): 8–27.

Gerstle, G. (2022) *The Rise and Fall of the Neoliberal Order: America and the World in the Free Market Era*, Oxford: Oxford University Press. https://doi.org/10.1093/oso/9780197519646.001.0001

Goldin, C. (2021) *Career and Family: Women's Century-Long Journey Toward Equity*, Princeton, NJ: Princeton University Press. https://doi.org/10.1515/9780691226736

Hacker, J. (2011) 'The Institutional Foundations of Middle-Class Democracy', *Policy Network*, 6(5): 33–37.

Hanson, G. and Harrison, A. (1999) 'Trade Liberalization and Wage Inequality in Mexico', *Industrial and Labor Relations Review*, 52(2): 271–288. https://doi.org/10.1177/001979399905200207

Hausmann, R., Pritchett L. and Rodrik, D. (2005) 'Growth Accelerations', *Journal of Economic Growth*, 10(4): 303–329. https://doi.org/10.1007/s10887-005-4712-0

Hirschman, A. O. (1968) 'The Political Economy of Import-Substituting Industrialization in Latin America', *The Quarterly Journal of Economics*, 82(1): 1–32. https://doi.org/10.2307/1882243

Hirschman, A. O. (1970) 'The Search for Paradigms as a Hindrance to Understanding', *World Politics*, 22(3): 329–343. https://doi.org/10.2307/2009600

Johnson, S. and Acemoglu, D. (2023) *Power and Progress: Our Thousand-Year Struggle Over Technology and Prosperity*, London: Hachette UK.

Krueger, A. O. (1974) 'The Political Economy of the Rent-Seeking Society', *American Economic Review*, 64(3): 291–303.

Levi, M. (1997) *Consent, Dissent, and Patriotism*, Cambridge: Cambridge University Press. https://doi.org/10.1017/CBO9780511609336

Levi, M. (2020) 'An Expanded Community of Fate', *Noēma* [7 July]. https://www.noemamag.com/an-expanded-community-of-fate/

Manning, A. (2013) *Monopsony in Motion: Imperfect Competition in Labor Markets*, Princeton, NJ: Princeton University Press. https://doi.org/10.1515/9781400850679

Mill, J. S. (1848/2004) *Principles of Political Economy*, Book II, Chapter 1, London: Great Minds Series (1848).

Murphy, R., Shleifer, A. and Vishny, R. (1989) 'Industrialization and the Big Push', *Journal of Political Economy*, 97(5): 1003–1026. https://doi.org/10.1086/261641

Nussbaum, M. C. (2011) *Creating Capabilities: The Human Development Approach*. Cambridge, MA: Harvard University Press. https://doi.org/10.4159/harvard.9780674061200

Obstfeld, M. and Zhou, H. (2023) 'The Global Dollar Cycle', *Brookings Papers on Economic Activity*, Washington, DC: Brookings Institution. https://doi.org/10.3386/w31004

Pritchett, L. (2022) 'National Development Delivers. And How! And How?' *Economic Modelling*, 107: 105717. https://doi.org/10.1016/j.econmod.2021.105717

Pritchett, L. (2024) 'Rotational Labour Mobility Is the Biggest Global Economic Opportunity', Working paper, Labor Mobility Partnerships (LaMP) and LSE School of Public Policy.

Putnam, R. D. (1994) *Making Democracy Work: Civic Traditions in Modern Italy*, Cambridge, MA: Harvard University Press. https://doi.org/10.1515/9781400820740

Rawls, J. (1971) *A Theory of Justice*, Cambridge, MA : Harvard University Press. https://doi.org/10.4159/9780674042605

Rodrik, D., Hausmann, R. and Velasco, A. (2008) 'Growth Diagnostics', in Serra, N. and Stiglitz, J. (eds) *The Washington Consensus Reconsidered: Towards a New Global Governance*, Oxford: Oxford University Press. https://doi.org/10.1093/acprof:oso/9780199534081.003.0015

Rosenstein-Rodan, P. (1943) 'Problems of Industrialisation of Eastern and South-Eastern Europe', *Economic Journal*, 53: 202–211. https://doi.org/10.2307/2226317

Sarbin, T. R. (1986) 'The Narrative as a Root Metaphor for Psychology', in Sarbin, T. R. (ed) *Narrative Psychology: The Storied Nature of Human Conduct*, New York: Praeger Special Studies 1–27.

Schank, R. C. and Abelson, R. P. (1977) *Scripts, Plans, Goals and Understanding: An Inquiry into Human Knowledge Structure*, New York: Psychology Press.

Sen, A. (1999) *Commodities and Capabilities*, Oxford: Oxford University Press.

Svensson, L. O. (2011) 'Inflation Targeting', in Friedman, B. and Woodford, M. (eds) *Handbook of Monetary Economics*, Volumes 3a and 3b. North-Holland Publishing Company and American Elsevier Publishing Company.

Wang, S. and Yang, D. Y. (2021) 'Policy Experimentation in China: The Political Economy of Policy Learning', No. w29402. National Bureau of Economic Research. https://doi.org/10.3386/w29402

Williamson, J. (1990) 'What Washington Means by Policy Reform', Chapter 2 from Williamson, J. (ed) *Latin American Adjustment: How Much Has Happened?* Institute for International Economics.

Williamson, J. (2009) 'A Short History of the Washington Consensus', *Law and Business Review of the Americas,* 15(7): 7–26.

PART I

INNOVATION AND PRODUCTIVITY

2. Fostering green and inclusive productivity growth

Philippe Aghion and John Van Reenen

This chapter explains the main ideas underpinning the Schumpeterian growth paradigm and how it provides a new lens to look at the determinants and effects of the growth process. Schumpeter was pessimistic about the future of capitalism. Indeed, his belief was that capitalism was doomed because in his view it was impossible to prevent incumbent firms from barring new innovations, either directly or by exploiting political connections with government authorities. The chapter uses the lenses of the Schumpeterian paradigm to revisit growth policy debates and also to rethink capitalism and its ability to reconcile the promise of sustained prosperity with the quest for greener and more inclusive growth. We argue that the proper functioning of an economy of innovation and creative destruction rests on the triangle between firms that innovate, the state, which is meant to regulate and invest, and civil society, which serves as a watchdog to induce firms and the state to do the right things.

I. Introduction

One can assess paradigms by their ability to shed new light on major economic trends and enigmas, and also to provide a new lens to look at policy design. Ironically, the Washington Consensus, which was perceived to be based on modern economic theory, was rather untethered from any formal paradigm.[1] It has shown its major limitations and as we seek to go beyond it, we have to consider what alternative growth paradigm should be used.

Up until the early 1990s, the dominant theory of economic growth was the neoclassical growth model first developed by Robert Solow.[2] This model predicts that investing in the accumulation of physical capital equipment

How to cite this book chapter:

Aghion, Philippe and Van Reenen, John (2025) 'Fostering green and inclusive productivity growth', in: Besley, Tim, Bucelli, Irene and Velasco, Andrés (eds) *The London Consensus: Economic Principles for the 21st Century*, London: LSE Press, pp. 41–76 https://doi.org/10.31389/lsepress.tlc.b

stimulates growth of per capita gross domestic product (GDP) – but only up to a certain point, because of diminishing returns on capital. As Solow explained, generating sustained growth requires technical progress to keep improving the quality of machines, i.e., their productivity. But Solow, and the neoclassical paradigm more generally, did not describe the factors that determine technical progress, and in particular the factors that stimulate or inhibit innovation.

The Schumpeterian growth paradigm, also referred to as the 'creative destruction paradigm', was meant to fill this gap. First, by developing micro-founded models of innovation-led growth that give centre stage to market structure, cross-firm heterogeneity and firm dynamics. And second, by confronting these models with new and rich microdata.

In this chapter, we use the lenses of the Schumpeterian growth paradigm to revisit growth policy debates and also to rethink capitalism and its ability to reconcile the promise of sustained prosperity with the quest for greener and more inclusive growth.

The chapter is organised as follows. First, we summarise the main ideas underlying the Schumpeterian growth paradigm, and then provide several examples illustrating how the paradigm allows us to identify faulty reasoning and to question flawed policy recommendations. The subsequent sections use the lenses of the Schumpeterian paradigm to revisit growth policy debates. First, we discuss the issue of how to reconcile industrial policy with competition policy. Then we focus on green innovation and the energy transition, before looking at whether, and, if so, how, one can make capitalism both more innovative and more inclusive. The final section concludes by arguing that the triangle among firms, the state, and civil society is key to achieving the objective of sustained, green, and equitable prosperity.

II. The Schumpeterian paradigm

The paradigm revolves around three main ideas.[3] The first is that long-term growth results from cumulative innovation, where each new innovator builds upon previous innovations. In particular, institutions that favour the diffusion and codification of knowledge contribute to making innovation cumulative, i.e., they make it unnecessary to climb the same mountain over and over again, like Sisyphus. The second idea is that innovation is motivated by the prospect of innovation rents. Institutions that secure those rents, in particular by protecting intellectual property rights, encourage entrepreneurs to invest more in innovation. And the third idea is creative destruction: that is, new innovations render previous innovations obsolete. In other words, there is a permanent conflict between the old and the new.

One could add that policies that foster productivity growth at the technological frontier are not quite the same as those that foster productivity growth far below it: in particular, product market competition fosters innovation-led growth by frontier firms as they innovate to escape competition with their rivals; but competition does not necessarily foster imitation-led growth by non-frontier firms.

At the heart of this new growth paradigm lies a contradiction. On the one hand, innovation rents are needed to motivate innovation investments. On the other hand, yesterday's innovators are tempted to use their innovation rents to prevent subsequent innovations as they do not want to suffer from creative destruction themselves.

Regulating capitalism is in part about how to manage this contradiction. Interestingly, even as he saw creative destruction as a potential driving force of growth, Schumpeter himself was quite pessimistic about the future of capitalism, as he anticipated that previous innovators would turn into entrenched conglomerates that would impede new innovations. Even though to some extent recent economic history seems to support Schumpeter's worries, we believe that it is possible to manage this fundamental tension so as to 'save capitalism from the capitalists'.[4]

The Schumpeterian paradigm provides a new lens to look at the determinants and effects of the growth process: it gives centre stage both to firm dynamics and to cross-firm heterogeneity – between incumbents and entrants, between leaders and followers in the various sectors of the economy, and between small and large firms. And, most importantly, it lends itself to a renewed dialogue between theory and empirics, using new firm-level microdata. It is this creative interaction between micro-founded growth theory and empirical analyses based on microdata that provides the best ground for policy analysis and in particular for questioning common wisdoms and identifying potentially erroneous policy prescriptions.

A first such common wisdom is that de-growth is the only way to effectively fight climate change. At a glance, the relationship between growth and CO2 emissions or temperature over the past centuries seems to support that view: namely, temperature and aggregate CO2 emissions worldwide started to increase precisely at the time of the growth take off in the 19th century. And in China and India CO2 emissions began to rise just when those countries embarked on high growth paths. However, we now know what negative growth looks like thanks to pandemic lockdowns. In France, during the first lockdown between March and May 2020, domestic GDP went down by 35%, while CO2 emissions were reduced by only 8%. Fighting climate change through negative growth could be like imposing such a lockdown indefinitely.[5]

A more promising route to reconcile climate conservation with sustained growth and prosperity, is green innovation: looking for cleaner sources of energy, cleaner products, and cleaner production technologies. We discuss how to induce green innovation later in the article.

A second common wisdom we can question with the Schumpeterian paradigm is that automation is bound to increase aggregate unemployment by substituting capital for labour. Hence, to limit the negative effects of automation on aggregate employment, governments should tax robots.

The fear that machines would lead to mass unemployment goes at least back to 1589, when William Lee introduced his knitting machine, but the most famous manifestation came with the Luddite movement in 1811–12, which resisted manufacturers' use of machines for producing textiles. Then, in the 1930s, economists starting with J. M. Keynes expressed concern about the danger of mass 'technological unemployment'.

More recently, the information technology (IT) and artificial intelligence (AI) revolutions have revived the fear that technological progress will make labour increasingly redundant, with the result that economic scholars and policymakers have proposed robots be taxed in order to protect aggregate employment. The dominant view indeed sees robotisation and other forms of automation as primarily destroying jobs, even if this may ultimately result in new job creation taking advantage of the lower equilibrium wage induced by the job destruction. Hence the policy recommendation that robots should be taxed in order to protect aggregate employment and also wages.

However, there is an alternative view: namely, that firms that automate become more productive, which enables them to lower their quality-adjusted prices and therefore to increase the market for their products, perhaps in part by taking business from other firms – domestic or foreign – that did not automate. This productivity effect may more than offset the direct substitution effect of automation (i.e., the replacement of workers by machines), in which case, automation will result in higher labour demand by the automating firms.

In previous work we have considered various measures of industrial capital, including Daron Acemoglu and Pascual Restrepo's 'industrial automation' measure, showing that an increase in any of these measures results in higher firm-level employment.[6] This confirms an older line of research showing the benefits of firm-level technological innovation for jobs.[7] Taxing robots would reduce firms' incentives to become more productive through automation, and therefore increase their market worldwide and their labour demand. That means the end result of taxing robots may in fact be to reduce aggregate domestic employment – not protect it.

A third common wisdom to be questioned is the idea that subsidising incumbent firms, or relaxing the credit constraints they face, should always be growth-enhancing. By contrast, Schumpeterian models have shown that subsidising incumbent firms research and development (R&D) investments may be detrimental to aggregate innovation and growth if it discourages entry by potentially more innovative firms.[8] Similarly, relaxing the credit constraints faced by incumbent firms may discourage entry by more efficient innovators.[9] Indeed, the Additional Credit Claims programme introduced by the European Central Bank in 2011 to prevent a post-crisis recession by relaxing credit constraints on a subgroup of European incumbent firms resulted in reduced exit by the least efficient firms, thereby discouraging entry by new innovating firms.[10] Getting the balance right between encouraging the new and safeguarding overall economic stability is often hard, but the emphasis is all too often on powerful incumbent interests rather than smaller new entrants.

III. Competition and industrial policy

Empirical studies from the 1990s that used panel data of firms in the United Kingdom pointed to a positive correlation between product market competition and innovation.[11] Subsequent work has shown that more intense competition enhances innovation in 'frontier' firms, which innovate to escape competition with their rivals, but may discourage it in 'non-frontier' firms.[12] One important implication is that competition should be more growth-enhancing in countries that are closer to the world technology frontier, as more firms in these countries are close to the leading edge of technology in their sectors. The idea that growth-enhancing policies are not the same for advanced countries and for less developed countries is in fact more general, and we return to it later in the chapter.

That impediments to competition should be detrimental to innovation and productivity growth is well illustrated by the recent growth history of the United States. Why, after a boost between 1995 and 2005, has US productivity growth fallen since 2005? Why has it fallen despite the IT and AI revolutions? And why have firms' markups increased over the same period? Different explanations for the growth decline have been explored, for example, the view that new ideas may be harder to come by, or the fact that growth may be mismeasured – and there is good evidence supporting both claims.[13] Another complementary explanation is that during the past decades the US economy has experienced a rising hegemony of so-called 'superstar' firms. Studies have shown a sharp rise in market concentration in all sectors of the US economy since the early 1980s.[14]

The ascent of superstar firms has been facilitated by the IT revolution, which allowed them to perform a broader range of activities, but also by loopholes in competition policy that allowed them to expand almost without bound through mergers and acquisitions.[15]

To the extent that superstar firms were more productive – having accumulated social capital and know how, or developed networks that other firms could not emulate – their rising influence contributed to the surge in productivity growth between 1995 and 2005. It also explains the surge in rents as superstar firms tend to have higher markups than other firms. The flip side is that, as they became hegemonic, superstar firms ended up discouraging innovation and entry by other firms, hence the observed decline in growth and entry since the early 2000s.[16]

That competition is key to sustained productivity growth had been acknowledged by policymakers on both sides of the Atlantic long before the aforementioned studies came out. What's more, it was in the name of competition that industrial policy came under strong criticism in the 1980s.

Until then, and particularly in the years following World War II, national champions were at the forefront of industrial policy in many developed countries. In France, this pro-champion policy was a pillar of the reconstruction of the economy, and of the 30 years of post-war growth.

In the United States, it played a decisive role in particular for the defence, aeronautics, and aerospace industries in the pursuit of supremacy over the Soviet Union. At the same time, the World Bank, under the direction of Robert McNamara, supported trade protection and import substitution in developing countries to allow them to nurture their infant industries. In the UK, the 1970s were the era of champions, such as British Leyland, the ill-fated car maker.

However, over time, industrial policy fell out of favour. Economists had been long aware of the problems it creates in practice. First, it favours existing large domestic firms – the national champions – thus limiting or distorting competition. This is the entrenched incumbent we discussed in the last section, who can hold back entrants. Second, governments are not great at picking winners – that is, choosing which firms they should support with subsidies or tariffs – as they do not have access to all of the relevant information. Furthermore, they may be unduly receptive to lobbying by large incumbent firms. The greater these firms' resources, the more they are in a position to influence public policy.[17]

This challenge led to a preference for what are known as 'horizontal' policies for stimulating innovation and growth, meaning policies that apply to all sectors of the economy. Among the main types of horizontal policy are (1) investing in the knowledge economy (especially higher education and research), (2) reforming labour and product markets to make them more dynamic, through appropriate policies for competition, unemployment insurance, and professional training, and (3) developing venture capital and private equity to provide funding for innovation.

Do these horizontal actions suffice? Or does the state still have a role to play in industry, and, if so, what is that role? Objections to industrial policy from the 1950s and through the 1980s are difficult to counter, not least because later work identified several sources of inefficiency in state intervention, due to asymmetric information or the potential for collusion between private actors and the state.[18]

Still, this alone does not suffice to disqualify state intervention, which remains legitimate for several reasons. One is the existence of positive knowledge externalities, or the fact that the benefits others receive from innovative efforts far exceed those appropriated by the agent who exerted the effort. An individual deciding whether to invest in education or in R&D does not take into account the positive externalities on their coworkers or on the economy as a whole. As a consequence, individuals tend to underinvest in education and in R&D. Moreover, credit constraints exacerbate this tendency. However, this alone does not justify state intervention that is not purely horizontal.

A first argument in support of a vertical industrial policy is that, left entirely to their own choices, firms may not spontaneously innovate in the right direction. For example, car manufacturers that innovated in combustion engine technology in the past will tend to innovate in that same technology in the future – despite it being a 'dirty' technology.[19]

Another argument has to do with problems of coordination. Several studies have suggested that government action can help resolve coordination problems, thereby enabling or accelerating entry into strategic sectors where the initial fixed costs of entry are high.[20] Consider a new potential market where entry is costly and where future profits are uncertain and depend on information (such as the level of consumer demand) that cannot be known until the market is active. No single firm wants to be the first to pay the fixed costs of entry. Every firm prefers to let other firms bear the fixed costs first and then to benefit from the information they generate, without bearing the risk and cost of acquiring this information themselves. In other words, the absence of state intervention leads to the 'free rider' phenomenon, which results in delay or even an impasse in creating the market. To solve this problem, the state can subsidise the first entrant, which encourages other firms to follow its example.[21]

This argument explains the success of state intervention in the aeronautics industry (for example, with Boeing and Airbus), where fixed costs are high and demand is uncertain. It also explains the success of the Defense Advanced Research Projects Agency programme established in the United States in 1958 to facilitate the transition from basic to applied research, and also marketing for breakthrough innovations where this transition entails substantial fixed costs and requires coordinated efforts by various economic actors.[22]

But once we recognise that industrial policy can be useful, how can we determine in which sectors the state should intervene? Policymakers should first address economic and social priorities, such as fighting climate change and developing renewable energies, health, and defence. After that, they should focus on sectors using highly skilled labour or having a high degree of competition. A study analysing international microeconomic data showed that public investments targeting skill-intensive sectors are more effective in stimulating productivity growth.[23] Similarly, a study based on Chinese data showed that targeting more competitive sectors helps stimulate productivity growth.[24]

The question then arises of the governance of sectoral state aids. Sectoral aids stimulate productivity growth more when they are not concentrated on a single firm or a small number of firms – in other words, if the aid operates to maintain or increase competition in the sector. Furthermore, such aids should be regularly reassessed in order to avoid the perpetuation of programmes that prove to be ineffective. Co-financing by state and private investors, such as development banks, can facilitate the establishment of adequate exit mechanisms. Finally, as we will explain in greater detail, subsidising established firms can hinder the entrance of new, more innovative firms as a result of a reallocation effect: incumbent firms increase the cost of skilled labour and other factors of production. The state should thus implement sectoral aid that does not impede new entrants and that reconciles, as much as possible, industrial policy and competition policy.

Our work has shown how industrial policy could be effective in stimulating growth, by looking at the effects of the changing European Union state aid rules that effectively randomised certain geographical areas in and out of eligibility for investment subsidies.[25] Importantly, these subsidies were not effective for large incumbents, but very effective when targeted at smaller businesses. Similarly, fiscal incentives for R&D tend to have larger impacts on smaller firms, as shown by one study that exploited the British expansion of the R&D tax credit system to small- and medium-sized enterprises in a discontinuity design.[26]

Overall, industrial policy is not a 'yes-or-no' issue. Rather, the challenge is to redesign the governance of industrial policy to make it compatible with competition, and more generally with innovation-led growth.

IV. The middle-income trap

In 1890, Argentina enjoyed a GDP per capita approximately 40% that of the United States, making it a middle-income country. This level was three times the GDP per capita of Brazil and Colombia, and equivalent to that of Japan at the time. Argentina sustained this GDP per capita relative to the US through most of the 1930s – until 1938, since Argentina's productivity consistently and substantially declined relative to American levels. What explains this drop-off?

Schumpeterian growth theory offers an explanation. Countries like Argentina either had institutions or policies (in particular import-substitution) that fostered growth by accumulation of capital and economic catch-up. They did not, however, adapt their institutions to enable them to become innovating economies. As argued in the joint work of Daron Acemoglu and Fabrizio Zilibotti, the greater the level of development in a country – i.e., the closer it gets to the technology frontier – the greater the role of cutting-edge innovation as the engine of growth, replacing accumulation and technological catch-up.[27]

Japan, where the state has always tightly controlled competition, is another example. Japan's Ministry of Economy, Trade and Industry caps the number of import permits, and the state subsidises investment by the industrial-financial consortia known as *keiretsu*. It is thus not surprising that Japan's growth has fallen from an extremely high level between 1945 and 1985 – the envy of other developed countries – to a very low level thereafter.

In our previous discussion we mentioned some recent evidence for the prediction that competition and free-entry should be more growth-enhancing in frontier firms, which implies that they should be more growth-enhancing in countries that are more economically advanced, since those have a larger proportion of frontier firms. Indeed, one study that used a cross-country panel of more than 100 countries over the 1960–2000 period showed both that average growth should decrease more rapidly as a country approaches the world frontier when openness is low, and that high entry barriers become increasingly detrimental to growth as the country approaches the frontier.[28]

Such empirical exercises point to the importance of testing for interactions between institutions or policies with technological variables in growth regressions, because openness is particularly growth-enhancing in countries that are closer to the technological frontier, and entry is more growth-enhancing in countries or sectors that are closer to the technological frontier.

Similarly, to the extent that frontier innovation makes greater use of research education than imitation, the prediction is that the more frontier an economy is, the more growth in this economy relies on research education. And indeed, we have shown that tertiary education is more growth-enhancing in more advanced countries.[29]

Some developing countries have policies and institutions that foster technological catch-up and imitation, while others fail to take off. Among those that catch up, however, some get stuck midstream. This is the case in particular for countries that are too slow – or fail altogether – to adapt their institutions to transform their economies from catch-up economies to frontier innovation economies. The reason for this is that vested interests and incumbent firms block not only the entry of new competitors but also any reform that would increase competition and more generally help the country move from imitation-led growth to growth driven by frontier innovation. The occurrence of a crisis, as well as international economic competition, can help nations to escape the middle-income trap by compelling the government to undertake the appropriate structural reforms. Thus, by weakening incumbent firms, the financial crisis of 1997–98 opened Korean firms to competition and helped South Korea to enter the club of innovative countries.

V. Green innovation

Why can't we rely on firms alone to generate green innovation? The reason is that those incumbent firms that innovated in dirty technologies in the past tend to continue to innovate in dirty technologies in the future. This phenomenon has been referred to as 'path-dependence'.[30]

We provided the first evidence of such path-dependence by studying data for patents filed by automobile companies from 80 countries between 1978 and 2005.[31] The analysis distinguished between 'green' innovations, which support the development of electric vehicles, and polluting innovations, which support the development of combustion engines. Using these data, we identified which factors determine a firm's propensity to make green innovations rather than polluting innovations.

One might think that a firm that has innovated in combustion engines in the past but is now faced with decreasing returns on this type of innovation would decide to turn to electric vehicles. But we found that this is not the case. The more a firm has innovated in combustion engines in the past, the more it continues to innovate in combustion engines today. In other words, firms persevere in the fields where they have already acquired a comparative advantage. This path-dependence implies that, left to their own choices, firms that have acquired experience in combustion engines will not spontaneously choose to focus on electric vehicles. Therefore, state intervention is necessary to incentivise these firms to redirect their innovative activity from polluting technologies to green technologies.

To determine whether a patent, and thus an innovation, is green or polluting, we used the International Patent Classification, focusing on patents representing a significant advance in knowledge. For this purpose, we examined triadic patents, i.e., those registered in the United States Patent Office, the European Patent Office, and the Japanese Patent Office.

For each innovator, whether a firm or an individual, and for each year from 1978 until 2005, we know not only the number of green and polluting patents obtained by the innovator that year, but also the history of patents that have been granted to the same innovator. This information enables us to analyse the extent to which a firm's propensity to innovate in green or in polluting technologies depends on the green and/or polluting patents it has accumulated in the past.

We found that the probability that a firm would produce a green patent increased by 5% if more than 10% of its past patents were green. In a symmetrical fashion, a firm that has registered more polluting patents in the past has a higher probability to produce a polluting patent today. Firms thus exhibit path-dependence when choosing what innovation to pursue, and we cannot rely solely on the private sector to redirect innovation towards green technologies without the intervention of the state.

The good news is that public policy can be effective in redirecting innovation towards green technologies. We showed that a 10% increase in the fuel price that a firm faces increases by 10% its likelihood of innovating in green technologies.

A first implication of path-dependence is that creative destruction should help: by definition, new entrants are not subject to path-dependence, since they were not around in the past. In other words, in an economy where incumbent firms innovated mainly in dirty technologies in the past, by its very nature creative destruction favours greener innovation.

A second implication is that outside intervention is needed to redirect incumbent firm's innovation towards clean technologies. There are multiple channels and instruments that can be activated for that purpose. Some channels rely primarily on state intervention: carbon taxes and tariffs; subsidies to green innovation; and industrial policy. But other channels also involve civil society: social norms and how much citizens value the environment; consumers' information about the CO2 content of firms' production and inputs; and shareholders' concern for corporate social responsibility. In countries with higher concern for civil society and the environment, more intense competition policy implemented by the state will induce firms to innovate in green technologies in order to escape competition from potential rivals.[32]

In the end, the key to successfully fighting climate change lies both with creative destruction, since new entrants are not subject to the path-dependence, and with the triangle among innovative firms that innovate, the state, which is meant to regulate and invest, and civil society, which serves as a watchdog to induce firms and the state to do the right things.

VI. Rethinking capitalism

The COVID-19 crisis revealed different weaknesses of capitalism on both sides of the Atlantic. In the United States it shed light on the deficiencies of a social system that cannot adequately protect the most vulnerable against the consequences of a big aggregate shock, and/or against the consequences of becoming unemployed.[33] Meanwhile in Europe it revealed the limits of an innovation system that was unable to mass produce messenger RNA vaccines even though the underlying basic research had been conducted in Europe.

This contrast illustrates the extent to which the Western world is currently divided between 'cut-throat capitalism' and 'cuddly capitalism'.[34] The United States is an incarnation of the former, being more innovative but less protective and inclusive, while the Scandinavian countries, and to a lesser extent Germany, are the representatives of the latter, more protective and inclusive but less innovative.

One view is the 'either/or': namely one cannot be both highly innovative and highly protective and inclusive. The argument runs that, insofar as innovation at the technological frontier relies on strong monetary incentives and requires high sunk investments and high risk-taking, the countries that aim for frontier innovation should forego the goals of insurance and equality: in other words, they should renounce cuddly capitalism in favour of cut-throat capitalism. On the other hand, those countries that choose cuddly capitalism have no alternative but growth through imitation of technologies invented by the frontier countries. These countries provide their citizens with greater equality and insurance, but their growth ultimately depends on the growth of the cut-throat countries, which, one might say, work for the benefit of the rest of the world.[35]

We depart from this either/or view for two reasons. First, the strong belief that capitalism cannot be fully dynamic unless it is inclusive, and that it cannot be fully innovative if vested interests prevent the emergence of new talents. And second, the existence of policies that can help move capitalism both towards greater innovation *and* towards more protection or inclusiveness. Here we shall focus policies in three areas: labour market, education, and competition.[36]

Start with labour market policy. Not long ago, Anne Case and Angus Deaton pointed to a worrisome phenomenon: after a long period of decline, mortality within the middle-aged, non-Hispanic white population in the United States began to rise in the early 2000s, with a distinct acceleration since 2011–12.[37] The other striking fact emphasised by Case and Deaton was the increase in so-called 'deaths of despair' in this cohort, meaning deaths resulting from suicide or substance abuse compared to the average mortality rate for the same age range in other developed countries.

The authors' explanation for this trend reversal in the mortality of non-Hispanic whites is heightened job insecurity, one consequence of which is increased family instability. Creative destruction in the United States threatened in particular the so-called 'working class aristocracy' of the 1970s[38] with an increased risk of unemployment and loss of status accompanied by earnings loss. The resulting anxiety led to increased consumption of anti-anxiety medication, opioids, and alcohol, thereby increasing the risk of overdose, alcohol-induced coma, and liver disease, as well as of suicide, which accounts for the observed increase in mortality.

Nothing of the sort happened in Denmark: one study that analysed the effects of job displacement on health in Denmark showed that, in a country with safety nets to protect people in the event of job loss, being laid off has no negative effect on health.[39] Indeed, a noticeable difference between Denmark and the United States is that in 1993 Denmark introduced a system called 'flexicurity' to regulate its labour market. This system has two pillars. First, the labour market was made more flexible by simplifying dismissal procedures for firms. This means, for example, that severance pay is limited, and litigation is rare. To offset this flexibility, there are two forms of security: unemployment benefits equal to 90% of salary – subject to a ceiling – for a maximum of three years, and massive government investment in professional training to give workers the skills they need to re-enter the labour market quickly.

The study in Denmark compared the health of workers whose place of employment closed between 2001 and 2006 with workers otherwise identical but whose employing firms did not close. Firm closure did not seem to impact the various indicators of health status, such as consumption of antidepressants or anti-pain medication, or consulting a general practitioner. Similarly, the study found firm closure had no significant effect on mortality of workers in the firm.

This finding is all the more important because the introduction of the flexicurity system made Denmark not only more protective but also more innovative, by making it easier for Danish workers to move from one job to another, which in turn encouraged more, and more efficient, creative destruction.

Regarding competition policy, in the previous discussion, we argued that by increasing the number of product lines controlled by superstar firms, the IT revolution ended up reducing innovation and growth in the overall economy in the long run. What is more, inadequate competition policy in the US favoured this evolution: in the absence of regulations on mergers and acquisitions, the superstar firms could grow and expand without limit, thereby discouraging entry and innovation by other firms in the economy. Competition policy should be reformed so as to better account for the effects of mergers and acquisitions on future innovation and entry, thereby fostering innovation-led growth and making that growth more inclusive by allowing innovative entrepreneurs to enter the market.[40]

Finally, regarding innovation policy, recent studies have pointed to the fact that parental income and education influences an individual's probability of becoming an innovator. This in turn leads to a so-called 'lost Einsteins', or 'Marie Curie', phenomenon: namely, that highly talented children, who could have become innovators if born to wealthy or well-educated parents, fail to innovate if born to poor or low-educated families.[41] The reason cited was that parents with greater education transmit knowledge and aspirations to their children, both of which are needed to become an innovator. An interesting example can be found in Finland, which in 1970 reformed its education system to make it more inclusive. As it turns out, parental income or education does not affect the probability of becoming an inventor for those individuals that started school after the reform – but it did for those that experienced the pre-reform schooling system.[42] This suggests that investing in a more inclusive and high-quality education system should both stimulate innovation-led growth *and* make growth more inclusive, simply by allowing more talented individuals to become innovators. In other words, by reducing the number of lost Einsteins.

Overall, we are not condemned to choose between innovation and inclusion. Rather, we can activate forces that will make our economies both more innovative and more inclusive, by constantly favouring the entry of new innovative firms and the emergence of new talents.

VII. The triangle among firms, the state and civil society

As previously discussed, Schumpeter was pessimistic about the future of capitalism. Indeed, his belief was that capitalism was doomed because in his view it was impossible to prevent incumbent firms from barring new innovations, either directly or by exploiting political connections with government authorities.

One can argue that Schumpeter was underplaying the role of state intervention. For example, our discussion on stagnant productivity growth in the United States suggested that more appropriate competition policies would limit the power of superstar firms to expand and control most sectors of the economy, thereby encouraging innovation by other firms and thus fostering aggregate productivity growth.

However, nothing guarantees that the government will do what it is supposed to do, nor that it will resist lobbying pressures from incumbent firms. The United States, where lobbying activities have successfully delayed action on competition policy to curb the power of superstar firms, is an illustrative example.[43] Hence the role for civil society and democracy to limit the scope of collusion between public officials and incumbent firms seeking to maintain their rents.

Overall, the proper functioning of an economy of innovation and creative destruction rests on the triangle among firms, the state, and civil society. The market provides incentives to innovate and constitutes the framework within which innovative firms compete. The state is there to protect property rights on innovations, to enforce contracts, and to act as an investor and insurer. Finally, civil society – the media, labour unions, voters – generates or calls for the enforcement of constitutional provisions intended to check executive power and ensure greater efficiency, ethics, and justice in the operation of the market. Indeed, history shows that a mobilised civil society has contributed greatly to the evolution of capitalism towards a system that is better regulated, more inclusive, and more protective of citizens. And, as we have argued, the triangle between firms, the state, and civil society is also key to reconciling prosperity with the environment and the necessary ecological transition.

Acknowledgements

We thank Tim Besley and Andrés Velasco for very helpful comments and suggestions.

Notes

1 For example, see Hausmann et al. (2008). The Washington Consensus refers to the view – shared by the IMF, the World Bank, and the US Treasury in the early 1990s – that anywhere in the world growth relies primarily on the combination of macroeconomic stabilisation, market liberalisation, and broad-based firm privatisation.

2 Solow (1956).

3 Aghion and Howitt (1992); Aghion et al. (2014).

4 Rajan and Zingales (2004).

5 Major et al. (2021).

6 Aghion et al. (2023a); Acemoglu and Restrepo (2022).

7 For example, Van Reenen (1997).

8 Klette and Kortum (2004); Acemoglu et al. (2018).

9 Aghion et al. (2019a).

10 Aghion et al. (2019a).

11 Blundell et al. (1995); Blundell et al. (1999); Nickell (1996).

12 Aghion et al. (2005); Aghion et al. (2009).

13 Bloom et al. (2020); Aghion et al. (2019b).

14 Autor et al. (2020); Autor et al. (2023).

[15] Aghion et al. (2023b); Ridder (2021).

[16] In emerging market economies, large firms can also prevent the necessary move from imitation-enhancing institutions to more innovation-enhancing institutions, as we argue later in this chapter.

[17] Krueger (1993).

[18] Laffont and Tirole (1993).

[19] Aghion et al. (2016).

[20] Bolton and Farrell (1990); Rob (1991).

[21] There is close parallel here with what in development economics is known as the self-discovery problem. See Hausmann and Rodrik (2003).

[22] Azoulay et al. (2019); Moretti et al. (2023); Howell et al. (2022).

[23] Nunn and Trefler (2010).

[24] Aghion et al. (2015).

[25] Criscuolo et al. (2019).

[26] Dechezlepretre et al. (2023).

[27] Acemoglu et al. (2006).

[28] Acemoglu et al. (2006).

[29] Aghion et al. (2006).

[30] Acemoglu et al. (2012).

[31] Aghion et al. (2016).

[32] Aghion et al. (2023c).

[33] Aghion et al. (2021).

[34] Acemoglu et al. (2017).

[35] Acemoglu et al. (2017).

[36] Finance could be mentioned as a fourth policy. Indeed, higher financial development both offers better insurance to individuals against risks, starting with the risk of losing one's job, while also making it easier for firms to borrow against future returns in order to finance innovation. The lack of finance is more likely to be a problem in emerging market economies, where capital markets are more imperfect, making the case for 'cuddlier' institutions even stronger in these economies.

[37] Case and Deaton (2017).

[38] By which we mean particularly the white non-Hispanic working class (and parts of the lower middle class).

[39] Roulet (2017).

[40] Such reform is advocated by Gilbert in his recent book (2021). That entrant innovation should foster social mobility is shown in Aghion et al. (2019c). For a discussion of reforms see Tirole (2022) and De Loecker et al. (2022).

[41] Bell et al. (2019).

[42] Aghion et al. (2023b).

[43] Lancieri et al. (2023).

References

Acemoglu, A. Aghion, P. and Zilibotti, F. (2006) 'Distance to Frontier, Selection, and Economic Growth', *Journal of the European Economic Association*, 4(1): 37–74. https://doi.org/10.1162/jeea.2006.4.1.37

Acemoglu, D., Aghion, P., Bursztyn, L. and Hemous, D. (2012) 'The Environment and Directed Technical Change', *American Economic Review*, 102(1): 131–66. https://doi.org/10.1257/aer.102.1.131

Acemoglu, D., Robinson, J.A. and Verdier, T. (2017) 'Asymmetric Growth and Institutions in an Interdependent World', *Journal of Political Economy*, 125(5): 1245–1305. https://doi.org/10.1086/693038

Acemoglu, D., Akcigit, U., Alp, H., Bloom, N. and Kerr, W. (2018) 'Innovation, Reallocation, and Growth', *American Economic Review*, 108(11): 3450–91. https://doi.org/10.1257/aer.20130470

Acemoglu, D. and Restrepo, P. (2022) 'Demographics and Automation', *The Review of Economic Studies*, 89(1): 1–44. https://doi.org/10.1093/restud/rdab031

Aghion, P. and Howitt, P. (1992) 'A Model of Growth through Creative Destruction', *Econometrica*, 60 (2): 323–351. https://doi.org/10.2307/2951599

Aghion, P., Bloom, N., Blundell, R., Griffith, R. and Howitt, P. (2005) 'Competition and Innovation: An Inverted-U Relationship', *The Quarterly Journal of Economics*, 120(2): 701–28. https://doi.org/10.1093/qje/120.701

Aghion, P., Meghir, C. and Vandenbussche, J. (2006) 'Growth, Distance to Frontier, and Composition of Human Capital', *Journal of Economic Growth*, 11: 97–127. https://doi.org/10.1007/s10887-006-9002-y

Aghion, P., Blundell, R., Griffith, R., Howitt, P. and Prantl, S. (2009) 'The Effects of Entry on Incumbent Innovation and Productivity', *The Review of Economics and Statistics*, 91(1): 20–32. https://doi.org/10.1162/rest.91.1.20

Aghion, P., Akcigit, U. and Howitt, P. (2014) 'What Do We Learn from Schumpeterian Growth Theory?' in: Aghion, P. and Durlauf, S. (eds) *Handbook of Economic Growth*, Elsevier. https://doi.org/10.3386/w18824

Aghion, P., Cai, J., Dewatripont, M., Du, L., Harrison A. and Legros, P. (2015) 'Industrial Policy and Competition', *American Economic Journal: Macroeconomics*, 7(4): 1–32. https://doi.org/10.1257/mac.20120103

Aghion, P., Dechezleprêtre, A., Hemous, D., Martin, R. and Van Reenen, J. (2016) 'Carbon Taxes, Path Dependency, and Directed Technical Change: Evidence from the Auto Industry', *Journal of Political Economy*, 124(1): 1–51. https://doi.org/10.1086/684581

Aghion, P., Bergeaud, A., Cette, G., Lecat, R. and Maghin, H. (2019a) 'The Inverted-U Relationship between Credit Access and Productivity Growth', *Economica*, 86: 1–31. https://doi.org/10.1111/ecca.12297

Aghion, P., Bergeaud, A., Boppart, T., Klenow, P. J. and Li, H. (2019b) 'A Theory of Falling Growth and Rising Rents', *The Review of Economic Studies*, 90(6): 2675–2702. https://doi.org/10.1093/restud/rdad016

Aghion, P., Akcigit, U., Bergeaud, A., Blundell, R. and Hemous, D. (2019c) 'Innovation and Top Income Inequality', *The Review of Economic Studies*, 86(1): 1–45. https://doi.org/10.1093/restud/rdy027

Aghion, P., Antonin, C. and Bunel, S. (2021) *The Power of Creative Destruction: Economic Upheaval and the Wealth of Nations*, Cambridge, MA: Harvard University Press. https://doi.org/10.4159/9780674258686

Aghion, P., Antonin, C. Bunel, S. and Jaravel, X. (2023a) 'What Are the Labour and Product Market Effects of Automation? New Evidence from France', CEPR Discussion Paper No. DP14443.

Aghion, P., Akcigit, U., Hyytinen, A. and Toivanen, O. (2023b) 'Parental Education and Invention: The Finnish Enigma', *International Economic Review*, 64(2): 453–90. https://doi.org/10.1111/iere.12632

Aghion, P., Bénabou, R., Martin, R. and Roulet, A. (2023c) 'Environmental Preferences and Technological Choices: Is Market Competition Clean or Dirty?' *American Economic Review: Insights*, 5(1): 1–20. https://doi.org/10.1257/aeri.20210014

Autor, D., Dorn, D., Katz, L., Patterson, C. and Van Reenen, J. (2020) 'The Fall of the Labour Share and the Rise of Superstar Firms', *The Quarterly Journal of Economics*, 135(2): 645–709. https://doi.org/10.1093/qje/qjaa004

Autor, D., Dorn, D., Katz, L., Patterson, C. and Van Reenen, J. (2023) 'Local and National Concentration Trends in Jobs and Sales: The Role of Structural Transformation', NBER Working Paper 31130. https://doi.org/10.3386/w31130

Azoulay, P., Fuchs, E., Golstein, A. and Kearney, M. (2019) 'Funding Breakthrough Research: Promises and Challenges of the ARPA Model', *Innovation Policy and the Economy*, 19: 69–96. https://doi.org/10.1086/699933

Bell, A., Chetty, R., Jaravel, X., Petkova, N. and Van Reenen, J. (2019) 'Who Becomes an Inventor in America? The Importance of Exposure to Innovation', *The Quarterly Journal of Economics*, 134(2): 647–713. https://doi.org/10.1093/qje/qjy028

Bloom, N., Jones, C., Van Reenen, J. and Webb, M. (2020) 'Are Ideas Getting Harder to Get', *American Economic Review*, 110(4): 1104–44. https://doi.org/10.1257/aer.20180338

Blundell, R., Griffith, R. and Van Reenen, J. (1995) 'Dynamic Count Data Models of Technological Innovation', *The Economic Journal*, 105(429): 333–44. https://doi.org/10.2307/2235494

Blundell, R., Griffith, R. and Van Reenen, J. (1999) 'Market Share, Market Value and Innovation in a Panel of British Manufacturing Firms', *The Review of Economic Studies*, 66(3): 529–54. https://doi.org/10.1111/1467-937X.00097

Bolton, P. and Farrell, J. (1990) 'Decentralization, Duplication, and Delay', *Journal of Political Economy*, 98(4): 803–26. https://doi.org/10.1086/261707

Case, A. and Deaton, A. (2017) 'Mortality and Morbidity in the 21st Century', *Brookings Papers on Economic Activity*, 1: 397–476. https://doi.org/10.1353/eca.2017.0005

Criscuolo, C., Martin, R., Overman H. and Van Reenen, J. (2019) 'Some Causal Effects of an Industrial Policy', *American Economic Review*, 109(1) 48–85 https://doi.org/10.1257/aer.20160034

Dechezlepretre, A., Einio, E., Martin, R., Nguyen, K. and Van Reenen, J. (2023) 'Do Tax Incentives Increase Innovation? An RD Design for R&D', *American Economic Journal: Economic Policy*, 15(4): 486–521. https://doi.org/10.1257/pol.20200739

De Loecker, J., Van Reenen, J. and Obermeier, T. (2022) 'Firms and Inequality', Deaton Inequality Review, POID Working Paper 27. https://ifs.org.uk/inequality/wp-content/uploads/2022/02/Firms-and-inequalities-IFS-Deaton-Review-Inequalities.pdf

Gilbert, R. (2021) *Innovation Matters: Competition Policy for the High-Technology Economy*. Cambridge, MA: MIT Press. https://doi.org/10.7551/mitpress/12686.001.0001

Hausmann, R. and Rodrik, D. (2003) 'Economic Development as Self-Discovery', *Journal of Development Economics*, 72: 603–33. https://doi.org/10.1016/S0304-3878(03)00124-X

Hausmann, R., Rodrik, D. and Velasco, A. (2008) 'Growth Diagnostics,' *The Washington Consensus Reconsidered: Towards a New Global Governance*, in Serra, N. and Stiglitz, E. (eds) Oxford: Oxford University Press. https://doi.org/10.1093/acprof:oso/9780199534081.003.0015

Howell, S., Rathje, J., Wong, J. and Van Reenen, J. (2022) 'Opening Up Military Innovation: An Evaluation of Reforms to the U.S. Air Force SBIR Program', POID Discussion Paper. https://www.nber.org/system/files/working_papers/w28700/w28700.pdf

Klette, T. J. and Kortum, S. (2004) 'Innovating Firms and Aggregate Innovation', *Journal of Political Economy,* 112(5): 986–1018. https://doi.org/10.1086/422563

Krueger, A. (1993) *Political Economy of Policy Reform in Developing Countries*, Cambridge, MA: MIT Press.

Laffont, J. J. and Tirole, J. (1993) *A Theory of Incentives in Procurement and Regulation*, Cambridge, MA: MIT Press.

Lancieri, F., Posner, E. and Zingales, L. (2023) 'The Political Economy of the Decline of Antitrust Enforcement in the United States', Working Paper, University of Chicago. https://doi.org/10.3386/w30326

Major, L. E., Eyles, A. and Machin, S. (2021) 'Learning Loss since Lockdown'. *Centre for Economic Performance Covid Analysis 19.* https://cep.lse.ac.uk/_new/publications/abstract.asp?index=8228

Moretti, E., Steinwender, C. and Van Reenen, J. (2023) 'The Intellectual Spoils of War: Defense R&D, Productivity and Spillovers,' *Review of Economic and Statistics,* 1–46. https://doi.org/10.1162/rest_a_01293

Nickell, S. (1996) 'Competition and Corporate Performance', *Journal of Political Economy*', 104(4): 724–46.

Nunn, N. and Trefler, D. (2010) 'The Structure of Tariffs and Long-Term Growth', *American Economic Journal: Macroeconomics*, 2(4): 69–96. https://doi.org/10.1257/mac.2.4.158

Rajan, R. and Zingales, L. (2004) *Saving Capitalism from the Capitalists: Unleashing the Power of Financial Markets to Create Wealth and Spread Opportunity*, Princeton, NJ: Princeton University Press.

Ridder, M. D. (2021) 'Market Power and Innovation in the Intangible Economy'. Working Paper, University of Cambridge. https://www.maartenderidder.com/uploads/6/2/2/3/6223410/maarten_de_ridder_jmp.pdf

Rob, R. (1991) 'Learning and Capacity Expansion under Demand Uncertainty', *Review of Economic Studies*, 58(4): 655–675. https://doi.org/10.2307/2297826

Roulet, A. (2017) 'The Causal Effect of Job Loss on Health: The Danish Miracle', in *Essays in Labour Economics*. Doctoral dissertation, Harvard University.

Solow, R. (1956) 'A Contribution to the Theory of Economic Growth', *The Quarterly Journal of Economics*, 70(1): 65–94. https://doi.org/10.2307/1884513

Tirole, J. (2022) 'Competition and the Industrial Challenge for the Digital Age?' IFS Deaton Review on Inequalities. https://ifs.org.uk/inequality/wp-content/uploads/2022/03/Competition-and-the-industrial-challenge-IFS-Deaton-Review.pdf

Van Reenen, J. (1997) 'Employment and Technological Innovation: Evidence from U.K. Manufacturing Firms', *Journal of Labour Economics*, 15(2): 255–84. https://doi.org/10.1086/209833

Response to Philippe Aghion and John Van Reenen by Diane Coyle

Innovation is the dynamo of productivity, or in other words getting more valuable economic output from the same or fewer resources; and productivity matters because it is a necessary condition for improvements in living standards over the long run. Both economic history and growth theory underline the importance of innovation for progress.[1] New ideas and techniques have increased the quantity of economic output but more importantly have transformed the quality of life, including the fundamentals of health and longevity.

In their chapter, Philippe Aghion and John Van Reenen describe the role of ideas and innovation as a cumulative process involving 'Schumpeterian' creative destruction.[2] The process is societal, involving not only individual entrepreneurs and firms but also the state, as well as consumers and civil society organisations. These various economic actors have different motivations, incentives, and knowledge.

Yet what Will Baumol vividly characterised as the 'free market innovation machine' has broken down in the 21st century.[3] There is certainly still massive innovation in technologies, including digital, energy, materials, biomedicine and parts of high-value manufacturing, despite some prominent claims that its pace or impact have slowed.[4] For example, even before taking account of advances in generative AI, the cost of computing has continued to fall dramatically, even if the pace has slowed.[5] However, technological advance is not translating into productivity growth or improving living standards. In many advanced economies productivity growth has slowed to a crawl. In most, median earners have experienced little real income growth for a decade. As people live in specific places and tend not to be all that mobile, income inequality has a geography; spatial inequalities are high and some places have entered a spiral of decline.

The innovation machine is manifesting other faults, alongside these macro failures. It has become apparent that the growth the world economy experienced during the 20th century was unsustainable – thanks in part to improved measurement of natural capital.[6] The economy uses many or most of nature's resources without paying for them, and while their marginal cost was apparently low in the mid-20th century, it is clearly high now in terms of both climate damage and biodiversity loss.[7] Nature is the binding constraint on future growth.

Secondly, for the first time in some countries, improvements in life expectancy have halted or even reversed for some groups. This is in part due to the COVID-19 pandemic, but beyond that extreme health inequalities and 'deaths of despair' – which are also spatially concentrated.[8] This is all the more startling when medical innovation has been so dramatic, in areas ranging from gene therapy to personalised cancer treatment.

A third malfunction of the innovation machine is the economy's lack of resilience or security of supply, demonstrated by the multiple shocks occurring since 2008. Surprising shortages have emerged as extended global supply chains involve multiple bottlenecks – a phenomenon being explored in the growing literature on production networks.[9] Although global production networks have enabled ever greater division of labour, the gains from specialisation may be reaching their limit as there is less and less competition at each link of the chain.[10]

Taken together, it is not surprising that many citizens are expressing discontent with the state of the economy in populist votes.[11] There is a dual transition under way as a result of the continuing evolution of two general purpose technologies: non-carbon energy and digital. Although people value digital technologies highly as consumers, as in prior episodes, the diffusion of use and therefore productivity gains from major new technologies is highly uneven.[12] Digital technologies exaggerate the unevenness. Not only are there very high returns to scale at the fundamental levels of the technology stack (such as data centres, undersea cables and generative AI models), but there are also significant network effects amplifying the increasing returns. Digital software and data are also non-rival, hence potentially under-produced, and enabling high monopoly rents to those 'superstar' firms able to exclude other users.[13]

The giant leaps forward in productivity through the 19th and 20th century owed much to process (rather than product) innovation – the factory system, the standardisation of the American System of Manufactures, the assembly line, Just-In-Time production, and most recently extended supply chains and the platform business model. However, by their nature, process innovations require firms to reorganise their production, which is never easy and probably harder than ever when intangible capital, such as software (rather than, say, machine tools), is involved.[14] Now there is mounting evidence in the literature that the highest productivity firms are those using digital tools, and that they are pulling ever further away from the rest of the pack.[15] The organisational capabilities are concentrated in the same firms that benefit from huge scale economies, superstar-type network effects, strong intellectual property protection, monopoly rents, and the consequent ability to shape regulation in their own favour.

While their own employees are well paid – with earning dispersion increasing within rather than between sectors – the market power of such firms means their interests and those of their customers are no longer well aligned. This extends beyond the tech sector: the food industry profits from making people obese and despoiling the environment, the pharma industry requires illness and has scant incentive to promote health, the finance sector largely undertakes zero-sum transactions, and much of the tech sector itself provides its valued services as a by-product of the misinformation and surveillance or privacy loss that generate advertising profits.[16] This description of a malfunctioning economic system is exaggerated – but recognisable.

What shape might a new policy consensus concerning innovation and productivity take? In their chapter, Aghion and Van Reenen cover education policy, labour market policy, and competition policy, all clearly vital in addressing the uneven dispersion of benefits – and costs – involved in the dual transformation in energy and communications technologies currently reshaping the structure of the economy. In this comment I will focus on the competition and innovation policies.

The Schumpeterian process, with a better technology or product creatively disrupting its predecessors, combined with winner-takes-all or superstar markets, implies that competition is now not so much 'in' the market as 'for' the market. Following reassessments of competition policy in digital markets in the European Union, United States and United Kingdom, authorities are updating their practices and guidance to take better account of the business models and dynamics in these markets.[17] For example, the incentive for a digital platform to 'envelop' additional markets in order to exploit their capabilities and capture more spillovers (think Uber extending to Uber Eats, for example), calls for a rethink of the market definition process in a merger inquiry.[18] Platforms will set prices on one or some sides at below marginal cost even in a competitive environment.[19] When markets 'tip' to dominant players, platforms will lose money in their early stages so profitability analysis needs to take account of planned early losses.

Two other points have been less often noted in discussions of the evolution of competition policy.

One is that with market dynamics that tip to a dominant player, any decision by the competition authority – to permit or prevent a merger – will determine the identity of that player. This means other criteria need to be brought to the decision making. Competition policy is in this sense unavoidably more 'political', or market-shaping.[20]

The second is that there are levels of the technology stack where regulators should seek to set common standards to enable interoperability or easy switching. This is similarly not a technical but a normative decision with welfare implications. For example, in the 1980s there was competition between two technical videotape standards, VHS and Betamax. There were presumed gains from the better model winning, but also losses as some consumers bought a soon-to-be defunct technology. A contrast is provided by the industry-devised, EU-mandated Global System for Mobile Communications standard in mobile telephony, which enabled rapid expansion of the market on a global standard, with large gains from learning-by-doing and scale. Mandated common or open standards and interoperability may be desirable in some of the currently concentrated technology markets, but will require case-by-case analysis.

Two other areas of policy require consensus building. One concerns data policy. Data fuels the digital economy, and there is an extensive, lively debate under way, reflecting a general dissatisfaction with current policy frameworks. By and large, datasets are treated as 'owned' intellectual property (IP); there are already legal cases being brought against new AI models alleging breach of copyright through the use of training data.

As with other forms of IP, the societal optimum will likely require a balance of exclusion (to create incentives to invest in a public good) and access (to enable gains from wider use of a non-rival good). Given that useful data is generally relational – linking an exchange or interaction between more than one agent – new data rules will need to set out access rights, permissions, and responsibilities.[21] While much of the public debate concerns privacy and surveillance, another important social welfare consideration is the distribution of benefits generated by the use of data to the public providing it. For example, I will want my health data to remain private (between me and authorised health professionals), but I might be happy for it to also be used in research to develop new medicines – as long as those can benefit me as well as making profits for the data purchaser.

This leads to the final area of a new consensus on innovation: the direction it takes. For innovation needs to generate benefits widely through society. The direction it takes is endogenous to the structure of markets, and relations between the state and individuals in civil society; innovation is a socio-technical process that can take many directions.[22] Some items in the innovation policy toolkit are particularly well-suited to directing innovation in directions that increase social welfare.[23] These include advance purchase guarantees, procurement policy in general, or innovation prizes; standard setting to de-risk future markets; and regulations decreeing a switchover (for example, to electric vehicles).[24] In the context of the renewed interest in industrial policy, governments might also want to encourage innovation in areas of the nation's specific economic strengths – although identifying these requires policymakers to be robust to lobbying efforts – or of specific supply chain vulnerabilities.

Conclusion: policy for a world of increasing returns

The dynamics shaping the nature of Schumpeterian competition 'for the market' in a world of superstar firms and increasing returns to scale require the approach to policymaking to adapt. It needs to recognise that there are multiple possible equilibrium outcomes, that there are likely to be critical tipping points in market dynamics, and that a key task for policymakers is coordination. There are large potential productivity gains from ongoing process innovations including digital platform business models, and large consumer welfare gains possible from improved matching, choice and time saving. But these have been massively unevenly shared thanks to rent-seeking and competition and innovation policies that have been ineffective in the context of these now-dominant market dynamics.

Policymakers need to take a strategic approach to market shaping, including shaping the direction of innovation. This can include advance market guarantees, standard setting, direct regulation, public investment in national competitive strengths and complementary infrastructure, and mitigation of supply chain vulnerabilities. It must also include effective competition enforcement. The bottom line is that the out-of-control innovation machine needs steering if the promise of continuing technological advances is to be realised.

Notes

[1] DeLong (2022); McCloskey (2016); Aghion and Howitt (1992).

[2] Aghion et al. (2023).

[3] Baumol (2004).

[4] Gordon (2016).

[5] Coyle and Hampton (2023).

[6] United Nations (2014); World Bank (2021).

[7] Dasgupta (2021).

[8] Marmot et al. (2020); Case and Deaton (2020).

[9] Carvalho and Tahbaz-Salehi (2019).

[10] Coyle (2023).

[11] Rodríguez-Pose (2020).

[12] David (1990); Perez (2003).

[13] Autor et al. (2020); Manyika et al. (2018).

[14] Bessen and Wang (2024).

[15] Tambe et al. (2020); Cathles et al. (2020); Coyle et al. (2022); Andrews et al. (2015); Loecker et al. (2022).

[16] Dimbleby and Lewis (2023).

[17] Crémer et al. (2019); Stigler Center for the Study of the Economy and the State (2019); Furman (2019).

[18] Coyle (2019).

[19] Rochet and Tirole (2003).

[20] Coyle and Dahmen (2024).

[21] Viljoen (2021).

[22] Acemoglu et al. (2012); Johnson and Acemoglu (2023).

[23] Bloom et al. (2019).

[24] Kremer et al. (2022).

References

Acemoglu, D., Aghion, P., Bursztyn, L. and Hemous, D. (2012) 'The Environment and Directed Technical Change', *American Economic Review*, 102(1): 131–66. https://doi.org/10.1257/aer.102.1.131

Aghion, P. and Howitt, P. (1992) 'A Model of Growth Through Creative Destruction', *Econometrica*, 60(2): 323–51. https://doi.org/10.2307/2951599

Aghion, P., Bergeaud, A. and Van Reenen, J. (2023) 'The Impact of Regulation on Innovation ', *Banque de France Working Paper No. 804*, forthcoming. https://doi.org/10.2139/ssrn.4325116

Andrews, D., Criscuolo, C. and Gal, P. N. (2015) 'Frontier Firms, Technology Diffusion and Public Policy: Micro Evidence from OECD Countries' [Internet]. Paris: OECD. https://www.oecd-ilibrary.org/economics/frontier-firms-technology-diffusion-and-public-policy_5jrql2q2jj7b-en

Autor, D., Dorn, D., Katz, L. F., Patterson, C., Van Reenen, J. (2020) 'The Fall of the Labor Share and the Rise of Superstar Firms', *The Quarterly Journal of Economics*, 135(2): 645–709. https://doi.org/10.1093/qje/qjaa004

Baumol, W. J. (2004) *The Free-Market Innovation Machine: Analyzing the Growth Miracle of Capitalism*, Revised edition, Princeton, NJ: Princeton University Press.

Bessen, J. E. and Wang, X. (2024) 'The Intangible Divide: Why Do So Few Firms Invest in Innovation?', Boston University, School of Law Research Paper No. 24–36. https://doi.org/10.2139/ssrn.4988419

Bloom, N., Van Reenen, J. and Williams, H. (2019) 'A Toolkit of Policies to Promote Innovation', *Journal of Economic Perspectives*, 33(3): 163–84. https://doi.org/10.1257/jep.33.3.163

Carvalho, V. M. and Tahbaz-Salehi, A. (2019) 'Production Networks: A Primer', *Annual Review of Economics*, 11(1): 635–63. https://doi.org/10.1146/annurev-economics-080218-030212

Case, A. and Deaton, A. (2020) *Deaths of Despair and the Future of Capitalism, Illustrated Edition*, Princeton, NJ: Princeton University Press. https://doi.org/10.1515/9780691199955

Cathles, A., Nayyar, G. and Rückert, D. (2020) 'Digital Technologies and Firm Performance: Evidence from Europe' [Internet]. European Investment Bank (EIB) (EIB Working Papers). https://ideas.repec.org//p/zbw/eibwps/202006.html

Coyle, D. (2019) 'Practical Competition Policy Tools for Digital Platforms', *Antitrust Law Journal*, 82(3): 835–60.

Coyle, D. (2023) 'Economic Progress and Adam Smith's Dilemma', *National Institute Economic Review*, 265: 5–11. https://doi.org/10.1017/nie.2023.21

Coyle, D. and Dahmen, H. (2024) 'The Political Economy of Competition Policy', in: Deutscher, E., Lindeboom, J., Makris, S. (eds) *Cambridge Handbook on the Theoretical Foundations of Antitrust and Competition Law*, Cambridge: Cambridge University Press.

Coyle, D. and Hampton, L. (2023) '21st Century Progress in Computing', *Telecommunications Policy*, 102649. ISSN 0308-5961. https://doi.org/10.1016/j.telpol.2023.102649

Coyle, D., Lind, K., Nguyen, D. and Tong, M. (2022) 'Are Digital-Using UK Firms More Productive?' in Economic Statistics Centre of Excellence (ESCoE) Discussion Papers [Internet]. Economic Statistics Centre of Excellence https://www.escoe.ac.uk/are-digital-using-uk-firms-more-productive/

Crémer, J., Montjoye, Y. A. and Schweitzer, H. (2019) 'Competition Policy for the Digital Era' [Internet]. Luxembourg: European Commission. https://data.europa.eu/doi/10.2763/407537

Dasgupta, P. (2021) 'The Economics of Biodiversity: the Dasgupta Review', London: HM Treasury. https://www.gov.uk/government/publications/final-report-the-economics-of-biodiversity-the-dasgupta-review

David, P. A. (1990) 'The Dynamo and the Computer: An Historical Perspective on the Modern Productivity Paradox', *American Economic Review*, 80(2): 355–61.

DeLong, B. (2022) *Slouching Towards Utopia: An Economic History of the Twentieth Century*, London: Basic Books.

Dimbleby, H. and Lewis, J. (2023) *Ravenous: How to Get Ourselves and Our Planet into Shape*, Main edition, London: Profile Books.

Furman, J. (2019) 'Unlocking Digital Competition' [Internet]. HM Treasury Digital Competition Expert Panel. https://assets.publishing.service.gov.uk/government/uploads/system/uploads/attachment_data/file/785547/unlocking_digital_competition_furman_review_web.pdf

Gordon, R. J. (2016) *The Rise and Fall of American Growth: The U.S. Standard of Living since the Civil War, The Princeton Economic History of the Western World 60*, Illustrated edition, Princeton, NJ: Princeton University Press. https://doi.org/10.1515/9781400873302

Johnson, S. and Acemoglu, D. (2023) *Power and Progress: Our Thousand-Year Struggle Over Technology and Prosperity*, London: Basic Books.

Kremer, M., Levin, J. and Snyder, C. M. (2022) 'Designing Advance Market Commitments for New Vaccines', *Management Science*, 68(7): 4786–814. https://doi.org/10.1287/mnsc.2021.4163

Loecker, J. D., Obermeier, T. and Van Reenen, J. (2022) 'Firms and Inequality'. CEP Discussion Paper. https://ideas.repec.org//p/cep/cepdps/dp1838.html

Manyika, J., Ramaswamy, S., Woetzel, J., Birshan, M. and Nagpal, Z. (2018) 'Superstars: The dynamics of firms, sectors, and cities leading the global economy', [Internet]. McKinsey Global Institute. https://www.mckinsey.com/~/media/mckinsey/featured%20insights/innovation/superstars%20the%20dynamics%20of%20firms%20sectors%20and%20cities%20leading%20the%20global%20economy/mgi_superstars_discussion%20paper_oct%202018-v2.pdf

Marmot, M., Allen, J., Goldblatt, P., Herd, E. and Morrison, J. (2020) *Build Back Fairer: The Covid-19 Marmot Review. The Pandemic, Socioeconomic and Health Inequalities in England*, London: Institute of Health Equity.

McCloskey, D. N. (2016) *Bourgeois Equality: How Ideas, Not Capital or Institutions, Enriched the World,* Reprint edition, The University of Chicago Press. https://doi.org/10.7208/chicago/9780226334042.001.0001

Perez, C. (2003) *Technological Revolutions and Financial Capital: The Dynamics of Bubbles and Golden Ages*, Reprint. Cheltenham: Elgar. https://doi.org/10.4337/9781781005323

Rochet, J. C. and Tirole, J. (2003) 'Platform Competition in Two-sided Markets', *Journal of European Economic Association*, 1(4): 990–1029. https://doi.org/10.1162/154247603322493212

Rodríguez-Pose, A. (2020) 'The Rise of Populism and the Revenge of the Places That Don't Matter', *LSE Public Policy Review*, 1(1): 4. https://doi.org/10.31389/lseppr.4

Stigler Center for the Study of the Economy and the State (2019) Stigler Committee on Digital Platforms: Final Report. https://www.chicagobooth.edu/research/stigler/news-and-media/committee-on-digital-platforms-final-report

United Nations (2014) 'System of Environmental-Economic Accounting 2012: Central Framework', New York, NY: United Nations. https://unstats.un.org/unsd/envaccounting/seearev/seea_cf_final_en.pdf

Tambe, P., Hitt, L., Rock, D. and Brynjolfsson, E. (2020) 'Digital Capital and Superstar Firms' [Internet]. National Bureau of Economic Research Working Paper Series. https://doi.org/10.3386/w28285

Viljoen, S. (2021) 'A Relational Theory of Data Governance', *Yale Law Journal*, 131(2): 573–654.

World Bank (2021) The Changing Wealth of Nations [Internet]. Washington, DC: World Bank https://www.worldbank.org/en/publication/changing-wealth-of-nations

Response to Philippe Aghion and John Van Reenen by Timo Boppart

I. The significance of economic growth

Let me start my response with a quote from the late Robert E. Lucas, Jr, in which he asks:

> Is there some action a government of India could take that would lead the Indian economy to grow like Indonesia's or Egypt's? If so, what, exactly? If not, what is it about the 'nature of India' that makes it so? The consequences for human welfare involved in questions like these are simply staggering: Once one starts to think about them, it is hard to think about anything else.[1]

The quote fits well here since the statement was made around the time of the Washington Consensus and precisely concerns the questions of whether and how policy can foster economic growth. And the final sentence underscores the importance of said growth. What also catches the eye is Lucas's selection of countries. Why did Lucas pick India, and why is it compared to Egypt? It is easy to forget from today's perspective that India was indeed once a prime example of a slow growing country. Figure 2.1 shows the GDP per capita of India, Indonesia and Egypt over time on a logarithmic scale such that the slopes of the lines can be interpreted as growth rates. India was consistently growing at a lower rate and falling behind relative to Indonesia and Egypt up until the late 1980s. Remarkably, around the time of Lucas's quote, the growth rate of the Indian economy starts to accelerate and India catches up with the other two countries. There is little doubt that this change in growth trajectory is related to policy reforms in India at the time.[2] Hence, the answer to Lucas's first question has proven to be a clear yes: there definitely are policy actions that affect the long-run growth rate of an economy![3]

When thinking about how many people in India have been lifted out of poverty over the past 30 years the welfare consequences behind Figure 2.1 are indeed simply staggering. Unfortunately, Figure 2.1 also shows a change in the opposite direction: Egypt's growth slowed down around the mid-1980s.

Even though it is easy (and probably right) to criticise the Washington Consensus for neglecting the distributional and environmental consequences of policy actions, economic growth as measured by average GDP per capita is

Figure 2.1: Real GDP (in US$) per capita of India, Indonesia and Egypt on a logarithmic scale, 1950–2020

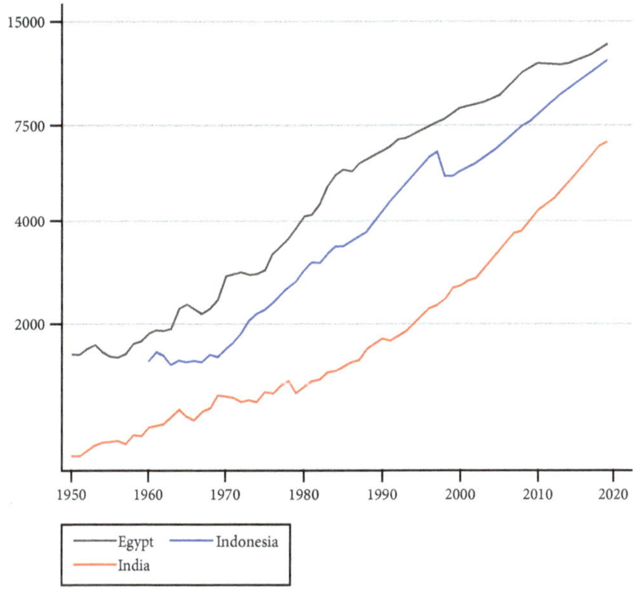

Source: Penn World Table (PWT) 10.01 (variable rgdpna for GDP).

still a proxy of success that is of first-order importance and will remain so for the years to come – in particular for developing countries.

II. What we have learned

Fortunately, over the past decades, the literature has deepened our understanding of economic growth and cross-country income level differences. Back in the 1950s, Robert Solow postulated that all growth is ultimately driven by technological change, and that the lion's share of growth is not accounted for by the primary factors of production (labour and capital).[4] However, Solow's neoclassical growth framework, which assumes that long-run growth happens at an exogenous rate, is simply not designed to study the role of policy in economic growth. It was the modern innovation-led growth literature that set out to change this and to micro-found the process of technical change.[5] The approach of Philippe Aghion and Peter Howitt, which focuses on the disruptive nature of technical change, has proven to be empirically persuasive and sufficiently rich and amenable to speak to the important policy questions.[6] The piece by Aghion and John Van Reenen nicely summarises and celebrates the achievements that came out of this literature.

Another major moment in the literature was the negative result from the development accounting literature, i.e., the finding that human and physical capital differences cannot – at least not from a purely neoclassical perspective

– account for observed income differences across countries.[7] This observation shifted the focus of the literature on cross-country income difference from studying differences in physical and human capital to studying technological differences and differences in the allocative efficiency of production factors across plants and firms.[8] As developing countries are typically not thought of as driving the technological frontier but rather adopting technologies invented elsewhere, the literature on innovation-led growth may appear to have less relevance for the developing world. However, the process of technology adoption is often also characterised by vested interests.[9] Hence, the 'Schumpeterian' mechanism by which incumbent firms have an incentive to block entry and growth – often even with the help of government intervention – is highly relevant for developing countries, too. As a consequence, the literature on misallocation of production factors and differences in life cycle firm growth nicely complements the Schumpeterian perspective.[10]

Figure 2.2: Growth rates, in GDP, GDP per hour worked, and TFP for OECD countries, 1960–2020

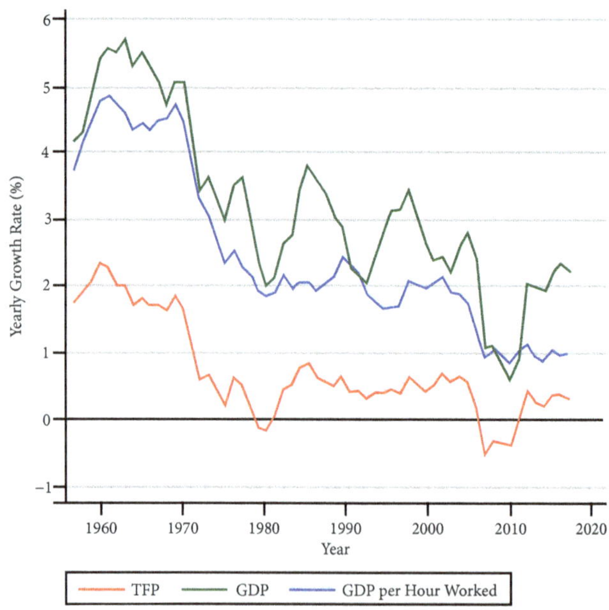

Source: This is an updated version of the figure in Boppart and Li (2023). Data: PWT 10.01 using the following variables: GDP = 'rgdpna', TFP = 'rtfpna', hours = 'avh' times 'emp', GDP per hours = 'rgdpna' divided by hours. 5 year centred moving averages. Averages across countries are weighted by real GDP.

III. Do not take growth for granted

Recently, the relationship between policy and growth has become topical in advanced economies, too. After a period of remarkably stable growth rates, there has been a significant productivity slowdown since the early 2000s (Figure 2.2 illustrates for the OECD countries). The slowdown is visible in labour productivity as well as in total factor productivity (TFP), and it does not seem to be a statistical artefact of output getting harder to measure.[11]

Figure 2.3: US establishment entry and exit rates (%), 1980–2020

Source: Business Dynamics Statistics. Establishment entry/exit rates are defined as the count of entering/exiting establishments in year t divided by the average count of employment active establishments in year t and t – 1.

What is behind this productivity slowdown? And is there a policy mix that can undo it? I think the jury is still out. But a very active recent literature has emerged that builds on the pioneering work of Aghion and Howitt to study these important questions. In line with the Schumpeterian paradigm, the productivity slowdown was accompanied by falling establishment entry and exit rates (Figure 2.3 shows the US entry and exit rates). A major insight of the Schumpeterian perspective is that excessively dominant incumbent firms can actually hamper growth.[12] Generally, an important take-away message is that there is no iron law of steady growth in advanced economies either and economic growth should not be taken for granted.

IV. Complementary aspects and concluding remarks

Despite the achievements of the literature, it is fair to say that we have not yet solved the mystery of economic growth. The Schumpeterian growth paradigm that features centre stage in the piece by Aghion and Van Reenen is empirically persuasive but does not explain all the variations observed in long-run growth rates.

Demographics is another aspect that has been emphasised in the debate about the recent productivity slowdown.[13] To the extent that smaller birth cohorts decrease start-up rates and dynamism of the economy, demographics could indeed become a major drag on future growth. Another potentially fundamental challenge is the extent to which the growth potential has been exhausted or ideas are getting harder to find.[14] As mentioned above, from a purely neoclassical perspective schooling can be rejected as a major driver of growth. However, as schooling might generate important spillovers – which are not captured in a neoclassical framework – it feels premature to completely dismiss the role of human capital. In particular, how an economy's pool of talent is 'used,' i.e., allocated to different firms and tasks, may have a significant effect on output. As a consequence, there is also no conflict between inclusion and economic growth; rather, they should go hand in hand.

At the global level, over the past three decades, output growth was heavily influenced by the catch-up process of the populous countries of China and India. As these countries are now slowing down, a big question is whether a similar transformation will next take place in Africa.

Notes

1 Lucas (1988).

2 See, e.g., Aghion et al. (2008).

3 Whether or not the reforms in India were in line with the Washington Consensus is a different question – Rodrik (2006) argues that this is not the case.

4 Solow (1956; 1957).

5 Romer (1990).

6 Aghion and Howitt (1992).

7 See Klenow and Rodriguez-Clare (1997) and the large literature that followed them.

8 See, for example, Hsieh and Klenow (2009; 2014).

9 Parente and Prescott (2002).

[10] A powerful example of this is when production factors that drive the innovation process (e.g., R&D labour) are misallocated across firms (see, for example, Aghion et al. (2022)).

[11] Aghion et al. (2023).

[12] See, for example, Aghion et al. (2023) and Akcigit and Ates (2023).

[13] See Hopenhayn et al. (2022) and Peters and Walsh (2022).

[14] Gordon (2017); Bloom et al. (2020).

References

Aghion, P., Bergeaud, A., Boppart, T., Klenow, P. J. and Li, H. (2023) 'A Theory of Falling Growth and Rising Rents', *The Review of Economic Studies*, 90(6): 2675–2702. https://doi.org/10.1093/restud/rdad016

Aghion, P., Bergeaud, A., Boppart, T., Klenow, P. J. and Li, H. (2022) 'Good Rents versus Bad Rents: R&D Misallocation and Growth', Technical report, Working Paper.

Aghion, P., Burgess, R., Redding, S. J. and Zilibotti, F. (2008) 'The Unequal Effects of Liberalization: Evidence from Dismantling the License Raj in India', *American Economic Review*, 98(4): 1397–1412.

Aghion, P. and Howitt, P. (1992) 'A Model of Growth through Creative Destruction', *Econometrica*, 60(2): 323–351. https://doi.org/10.2307/2951599

Akcigit, U. and Ates, S. (2023) 'What Happened to US Business Dynamism?', *Journal of Political Economy*, 131(8): 2059–2124. https://doi.org/10.1086/724289

Bloom, N., Jones, C. I., Van Reenen, J. and Webb, M. (2020) 'Are Ideas Getting Harder to Find?', *American Economic Review*, 110(4): 1104–1144. https://doi.org/10.1257/aer.20180338

Boppart, T. and Li, H. (2023) 'Productivity Slowdown: Reducing the Measure of Our Ignorance', In Akcigit, U. and Van Reenen, J. (eds.) *The Economics of Creative Destruction: New Research on Themes from Aghion and Howitt*, Cambridge, MA: Harvard University Press; 283–305. https://doi.org/10.2307/jj.4820341.14

Gordon, R. (2017) *The Rise and Fall of American Growth: The US Standard of Living Since the Civil War*, Princeton, NJ: Princeton University Press. https://doi.org/10.1515/9781400888955

Hopenhayn, H., Neira, J. and Singhania, R. (2022) 'From Population Growth to Firm Demographics: Implications for Concentration, Entrepreneurship and the Labor Share', *Econometrica*, 90(4), 1879–1914.

Hsieh, C. T. and Klenow, P. J. (2009) 'Misallocation and Manufacturing TFP in China and India', *The Quarterly Journal of Economics*, 124(4): 1403–1448. https://doi.org/10.2139/ssrn.1442871

Hsieh, C. T. and Klenow, P. J. (2014) 'The Life Cycle of Plants in India and Mexico', *The Quarterly Journal of Economics*, 129(3): 1035–1084.

Klenow, P. J. and Rodriguez-Clare, A. (1997) 'The Neoclassical Revival in Growth Economics: Has It Gone Too Far?', NBER *Macroeconomics Annual*, 12: 73–103.

Lucas Jr, R. E. (1988) 'On the Mechanics of Economic Development', *Journal of Monetary Economics*, 22(1): 3–42. https://doi.org/10.1016/0304-3932(88)90168-7

Parente, S. L. and Prescott, E. C. (2002) *Barriers to Riches*, Cambridge, MA: MIT Press.

Peters, M. and Walsh, C. (2022) 'Population growth and firm-product dynamics', NBER Working Paper 29424. https://doi.org/10.3386/w29424

Rodrik, D. (2006) 'Goodbye Washington Consensus, Hello Washington Confusion? A Review of the World Bank's Economic Growth in the 1990s: Learning from a Decade of Reform', *Journal of Economic Literature*, 44(4): 973–987.

Romer, P. M. (1990) 'Endogenous Technological Change', *Journal of Political Economy*, 98(5/2): S71–S102. https://doi.org/10.3386/w3210

Solow, R. M. (1956) 'A Contribution to the Theory of Economic Growth', *The Quarterly Journal of Economics*, 70(1): 65–94. https://doi.org/10.2307/1884513

Solow, R. M. (1957) 'Technical Change and the Aggregate Production Function', *The Review of Economics and Statistics*, 39(3): 312–320. https://doi.org/10.2307/1926047

3. On productivism

Dani Rodrik

'Productivism' refers to an approach that prioritises the dissemination of productive economic opportunities throughout the entire economy and segments of the labour force. It differs from what has come to be called 'neoliberalism' by assigning governments and civil society significant roles in achieving this goal. Productivism puts less faith in markets and is suspicious of large corporations. It emphasises production and investment over finance and the revitalisation of local communities over globalisation. It also departs from the Keynesian welfare state by focusing less on redistribution, social transfers, and macroeconomic management, and more on creating economic opportunity by working on the supply side of the economy to create good, productive jobs for everyone. This chapter relates the contemporary labour market problems of advanced economies to the dualism literature in economic development, which focuses on the divergence between 'modern' and 'traditional' segments within poor economies. It then highlights the nature of the new challenges and why established models of economic growth and Keynesian social welfare need to be updated. It describes new modes of industrial policy required to deal with these challenges and questions whether our governments are up to it. It also discusses how the elements of this new strategy are drawing support from both sides of the political spectrum.

I. Introduction: an old problem in a new setting

How to overcome 'productive dualism' is our central economic challenge. Dualism is an old idea that lies at the core of development economics and has become increasingly relevant to advanced economies as well. The economists who founded the field of development economics, such as the Nobel Prize-winning W. Arthur Lewis, noted that the economies of poor nations are split

---

How to cite this book chapter:

Rodrik, Dani (2025) 'On productivism', in: Besley, Tim, Bucelli, Irene and Velasco, Andrés (eds) *The London Consensus: Economic Principles for the 21st Century*, London: LSE Press, pp. 77–113 https://doi.org/10.31389/lsepress.tlc.c

between a narrow 'modern' sector that uses advanced technologies and a much larger 'traditional' sector characterised by extremely low productivity. For a long time, scholars considered dualism as the defining feature of developing countries, in contrast to advanced nations where they assumed that frontier technologies and high productivity prevailed across the entire economy. This marked development economics as a distinct sub-branch of economics, separate from conventional neoclassical economics. Correspondingly, the task of development policy became the establishment of new institutional arrangements to overcome the disparities in incomes, education, health, and life chances more broadly created by productive dualism. While the developed–developing country distinction may have made some sense in the 1950s and 1960s, in the 2020s it no longer appears to be relevant.

Industrialisation has been the traditional vehicle for overcoming dualism; as workers get absorbed into more productive manufacturing activities, wages rise, and the economy's overall productivity increases. But this old and powerful remedy no longer works. As a result of automation and other innovations that have been labour-saving, manufacturing has lost its ability to create plentiful jobs in both developing and advanced economies.[1] Globalisation has accelerated the process as a small number of countries with strong comparative advantages in manufacturing have squeezed production in middle- and high-income economies.

Employment de-industrialisation has been a common feature of all advanced economies. Manufacturing employment has declined (as a share of total employment), even in countries like South Korea or Germany that have maintained strong industrial sectors. Increasingly, developing countries have also struggled to create significant employment in formal manufacturing firms. Changes in manufacturing technologies have made it difficult for low-income countries to successfully compete in manufacturing without using skill- and capital-intensive technologies that absorb limited labour and are inappropriate in light of these countries' underlying factor endowments, since they are abundant in low-skilled labour and scarce in capital.

Hence, productive dualism is becoming an entrenched feature of developing and advanced economies alike, requiring remedies that come straight out of the development policy toolbox. In a 2017 book called *The Vanishing Middle Class*, the MIT economic historian Peter Temin pointed out that the Lewis model of a dual economy had become increasingly relevant to the US.[2] De-industrialisation, globalisation, new technologies that favour professionals and capitalists, and declining protections for labour have widened the gap between the winners from these developments and those who are left behind. Convergence between poor and rich parts of the economy has been arrested, labour markets became increasingly polarised between high- and low-educated workers, and regional disparities widened. In Europe, the increase in inequality has not been as marked thanks to stronger welfare states, but the same forces have operated there too. The gaps between the most productive firms and regions, and those lagging behind, grew while the middle class shrank.[3]

Consequently, policymakers in advanced economies are now grappling with the same questions that have preoccupied development policymakers for a long time: how to attract investment, create jobs, increase skills, spur entrepreneurship, enhance access to credit and technology – in short, how to close the gap with the more advanced, productive parts of the national economy. The starting points may be different, but the problems of a region where good jobs have disappeared, productive employment has become scarce, social problems (such as crime and addiction) have mushroomed, and there is low trust between government officials and various social groups, and the business community looks distressingly familiar to a development economist. The obstacles that racial or ethnic minorities, recent immigrants, or low-educated workers must surmount in such settings are the bread-and-butter of development economics.

Localities that are left behind in advanced economies may have access to greater amounts of financial resources. In the United States, state and local governments spend tens of billions of dollars, not very effectively, on tax incentives and other subsidies to attract large firms.[4] But their officials typically operate under structural and bureaucratic constraints that would be familiar to their counterparts in poor nations. They lack the requisite information on where the most important opportunities and bottlenecks are, they are subject to political pressure and lobbying from parochial private interests, and the capabilities they need to mobilise, even when they exist, are spread across a wide range of public and private organisations that they do not directly control. The new realities of labour markets require updates to established models of growth and the Keynesian social welfare state.

In this chapter, I describe the 'productivism' approach, which is a remedy that targets productive dualism at its source. I first outline this approach and then compare it to other policy frameworks with the help of a taxonomy of public policies. I discuss the relationship between productivist policies and what are commonly called industrial policies, providing an example of how they can be deployed in service sectors. Since economists and many others tend to be sceptical of the capacity of governments to undertake transformational policies, I will address some of the traditional objections to government interference in the productive sphere. I also suggest that productivism carries appeal for many elements of both the right and left side of the political spectrum. I end the chapter with some cautions about the dangers of taking economic paradigms too seriously.

II. A new approach

Productivism is an approach that prioritises the dissemination of productive economic opportunities throughout all parts of the economy and segments of the labour force. Our core economic and social problems – poverty, inequality, exclusion, and insecurity – have many roots. But they are reproduced and reinforced on a daily basis as immediate by-products of firms' employment, investment, and innovation decisions. In the language of economists, these decisions are rife with externalities for society, i.e., they have consequences that spill over to many people, firms, and other parts of the economy. Some of these externalities are well recognised in economics. Learning and innovation spillovers from research and development (R&D) form the rationale for tax credits and other public subsidies. Environmental externalities and the effects of greenhouse gas emissions on climate change form the basis for environmental regulation.

But today, these externalities are broader and include what we can call 'good jobs' externalities. Good jobs are a pathway to the middle class. They pay well enough to allow for a reasonable living standard with some security and savings, are relatively stable, have safe working conditions, and offer some career progression. Firms that generate good jobs contribute to the vitality of their communities. Conversely, a shortage of good jobs comes at social, political, and economic costs. Social consequences can take the form of exclusion, broken families, drug abuse, addiction, and crime. Political ills can follow, such as polarisation, the rise of populism, backlashes against globalisation and immigration, decline in trust in government, experts, and institutions. The prevalence of 'bad jobs' is also symptomatic of economic dualism, which creates its own inefficiency: productive technologies remain bottled up in a few firms and do not disseminate throughout the rest of the economy and the labour force.

Firms' decisions on how many workers to employ, how much to pay, what kind of technologies to deploy and how to organise work affect not just the bottom line, but the life opportunities of prospective employees and their communities. When a company decides to automate its production line or outsource part of its production to another country, society may suffer long-term damage that is not internalised by its managers or shareholders. Framing the problem as an 'externality' – or as a 'coordination failure' that prevents firms and governments from undertaking complementary actions (in training, technology adoption, investment decisions) for broad-based prosperity – clarifies that productivism is about productivity, and not about redistribution or social/labour standards. But it does not presume productivity trickles down. It aims to enhance wellbeing across all sectors of society by directly broadening access to productive employment opportunities.

Productivism differs from what has come to be called 'neoliberalism' in that it gives governments and civil society significant roles in achieving productive employment goals. It puts less faith in markets and is suspicious of large corporations. It emphasises production and investment over finance, and the revitalisation of local communities over globalisation. It also departs from the Keynesian welfare state – the paradigm that neoliberalism replaced – in that it focuses less on redistribution, social transfers, and macroeconomic management, and more on creating economic opportunity by working on the supply side of the economy to create good, productive jobs for everyone. And productivism diverges from both of its antecedents by exhibiting greater scepticism towards technocrats and being less instinctively hostile to populism in the economic sphere.[5]

III. Where conventional models fall short

To see how productivism differs from alternative approaches, it is useful to consider our policy options through a matrix that categorises different approaches to prosperity and inequality (Figure 3.1). First, I divide policies into pre-production, production, and post-production stage interventions. To understand fully the range of options for creating inclusive prosperity, this is a better categorisation of policies than the conventional pre-distribution/redistribution distinction. Within the pre-distribution category, my framework makes a further distinction between policies that affect endowments people bring to markets (such as education) and policies that directly influence production, employment, and investment decisions (such as industrial policies or labour market regulations). Second, I divide interventions into those that intend to redress inequities at the bottom, middle, or top of the income distribution. Minimum wages, for example, target the incomes of the working poor while wealth taxes target incomes at the very top.

The traditional welfare state model operates largely within the first and third columns: it targets the educational and other endowments of workers before they join labour markets and *ex-post* redistribution through taxes and social insurance policies (see Figure 3.2). The government's role is to finance education, engage in progressive taxation, and provide social insurance against idiosyncratic risks, such as unemployment, illness, and disability. The presumption is that good/middle-class jobs will be available to everyone with adequate education and skills.

Figure 3.1: Remedies for prosperity and inequality

		At what stage of the economy does policy intervene?		
		pre-production	production	post-production
Which segment of the economy do we care about?	low productivity			
	middle productivity			
	high productivity			

Traditional growth strategies, on the other hand, focus on the most productive segments of the economy and encompass interventions within the bottom row (see Figure 3.3). These may include innovation systems,

Figure 3.2: Traditional welfare state model

		At what stage of the economy does policy intervene?		
		pre-production	production	post-production
Which segment of the economy do we care about?	low productivity	investments in eduction and training		transfers; full-employment macro policies
	middle productivity			social insurance, pensions, safety nets
	high productivity			

Figure 3.3: Traditional growth model

		At what stage of the economy does policy intervene?		
		pre-production	production	post-production
Which segment of the economy do we care about?	low productivity			
	middle productivity			
	high productivity	innovation systems, IPR rules, trade agreements	market-friendly regulations, R&D and export incentives	corporate tax incentives

intellectual property rules, appropriate regulatory structures, and export and innovation incentives. The presumption is that high growth eventually pulls everyone up and leaves few regions or pockets of the labour market behind.

When the inadequacy of good/middle-class jobs is driven by secular trends, such as technology and globalisation, neither of these strategies work well. Economic insecurity, inequality, and poor productivity (except for those at the very top) are important structural problems today. Secular trends in technology and globalisation are hollowing out the middle of the employment distribution. These trends exhibit themselves in the form of bad jobs that do not offer stability, sufficient pay, and career progression, and in permanently depressed labour markets outside major metropolitan centres. These problems need a different strategy that tackles the creation of good jobs directly. The focus necessarily turns to firms; to help them internalise the economic and social spillovers that they generate. Hence, the productive sector must be at the heart of such a strategy. This calls for targeting the middle cell of the matrix, focusing on direct interventions in the productive sphere with the goal of expanding the supply of middle-skill jobs (Figure 3.4). Altogether, we must change what we produce, how we produce it and who gets a say in production decisions. This requires not just new policies, but also a reconfiguration of existing ones.

Advanced and developing nations alike will need a new breed of coordinated policies aimed at the supply and demand sides of labour markets, combining skill training programmes with support for firms.[6] Good jobs require good firms and vice versa. Active labour market policies designed to increase skills and employability should broaden into partnerships with firms explicitly targeting the creation of good jobs.[7] Industrial and regional policies that currently centre on tax incentives and investment subsidies should be replaced by customised business services and amenities to facilitate maximum employment creation.[8] National innovation systems should be redesigned to orient investments in new technologies in a more employment-friendly direction.[9] Policies that tackle climate change, such as the European Green Deal, should be explicitly linked to programmes of job creation in lagging communities.[10] Recognising that in the future prosperity will have to rely much more on services and smaller and medium-sized enterprises, the focus of industrial policy should be reoriented away from manufacturers and 'national champions', large private corporations that receive priority in government policies.

Figure 3.4: The productivist 'good-jobs' model

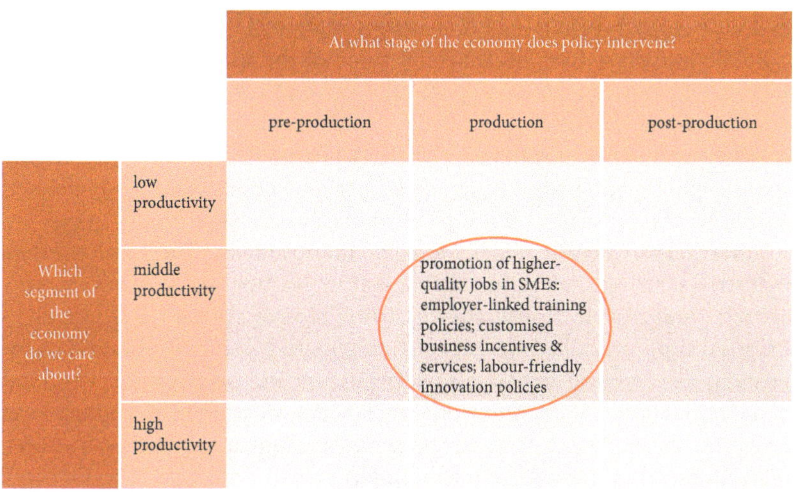

A new economic order requires an explicit quid pro quo between private firms and public authorities. To prosper, firms need a reliable and skilled workforce, good infrastructure, an ecosystem of suppliers and collaborators, easy access to technology, and a sound regime of contracts and property rights. Most of these are provided through public and collective action, which is the government's side of the bargain. Governments, in turn, need firms to internalise the various externalities they produce for their communities and societies when they make their labour, investment and innovation decisions. So, firms must live up to their side of the bargain too, not as corporate social responsibility, but as part of an explicit regulatory and governance framework.

Looking at our policy challenge in these terms makes it clear that the conventional separation between growth policies and social policies no longer makes sense. Faster economic growth requires that new technologies and productive opportunities are disseminated among smaller firms and wider segments of the labour force, and that their use is not confined to narrow segments of the elite. Reducing inequality and economic insecurity is more effective when it happens through better employment prospects than through fiscal redistribution only. The economic growth and the social agenda are increasingly one and the same.

IV. New types of industrial policies

If productivism is to be successful it will have to internalise the lessons learned from the failures of past policies and adapt to fundamentally new challenges. State interventions aimed at reshaping the structure of an economy – so-called 'industrial policies' – have been traditionally faulted for being ineffective and getting captured by special interests. 'Governments cannot pick winners', as the old adage goes. In reality, much of this criticism is overdone. While there have been notable failures,[11] systematic studies in the 2010s and early 2020s find that industrial policies incentivising investment and job creation in disadvantaged regions have done surprisingly well.[12]

Public initiatives have been behind some of the most startling high-tech successes of our time, including the internet and GPS. For every Solyndra, a solar cell manufacturer that failed spectacularly after half a billion dollars in government loan guarantees,[13] there is often a Tesla, the phenomenally successful electric battery and vehicle manufactures that also received government support at a critical phase of its development.[14]

Nevertheless, there is much room for improvement. The most effective industrial policies entail close, collaborative interactions between government agencies and private firms, whereby firms receive critical public inputs – financial support, skilled workers or technological assistance – in return for meeting soft and evolving targets on investment and employment. This kind of industrial policy is likely to work much better, whether in promoting local economic development or in directing major national technological efforts, than open-ended subsidies or tax incentives.

Productivism focuses on enhancing the productive capabilities of all segments and regions of a society. While traditional forms of social assistance and especially better access to education and healthcare can help in this regard, connecting people with productive employment opportunities requires further intervention. It requires improvements both on the demand and the supply side of the labour market.[15] Policies must encourage an increase in the quantity and quality of jobs that are available for the less educated and less skilled members of the workforce, where they choose (or can afford to) live.

In the future, the bulk of these jobs will not come from manufacturing, but from services, such as health and long-term care and retail. In the United States, less than one in ten workers are currently employed in manufacturing. Virtually all new net job creation in the private sector since the late 1970s has taken place in services. Even if policy succeeds in reshoring manufacturing and supply chains, the impact on employment is likely to remain limited. The experiences of East Asian manufacturing superstars, such as South Korea and Taiwan, provide sobering examples. These two countries have managed to rapidly increase the share of manufacturing value added in gross domestic product (GDP) (at constant prices), yet, they have experienced steady declines in manufacturing employment ratios.

This is important since so much of the policy effort in the United States is focused on promoting high-tech manufacturing. The most recent example is the CHIPS and Science Act that the US Congress has passed, providing $52 billion in funding for semiconductors and related manufacturing.[16] The initiative aims at enhancing national security vis-à-vis China and creating good jobs. Unfortunately, even if the first objective is met, the second objective is likely to remain elusive. A strategy fixated on geopolitical competition with China will not be effective on the jobs front. A similar point can be made about the subsidies to green technologies that are a core component of the so-called Inflation Reduction Act that US President Joe Biden signed in 2022. The green transition is undoubtedly an urgent priority that the new paradigm needs to tackle. But here, governments also cannot achieve multiple objectives with a single instrument. Policies that target climate change are not a substitute for good-job policies and vice versa. Shoring up the middle class and disseminating the benefits of technology broadly through society requires an explicit good-jobs strategy.

V. A good-jobs strategy for services

But is an industrial policy for services possible? I have discussed elsewhere what such a strategy might look like in the contexts of the US, French, and British economies. Here, I will briefly summarise the US proposals.[17;18;19]

My proposed programme has both local and national components. The local approach would build on existing development and business assistance programmes that are already loosely structured along the lines advocated here. These are collaborative partnerships between local development agencies, firms, and other partners aiming to revitalise local communities and create good jobs. They are organised around an implicit (and evolving) quid pro quo: the provision of public services (such as business extension services, infrastructure, or customised training) in return for soft commitments by firms on investment and employment creation. Such partnerships align with a new, more flexible, and contextual model of industrial policy that is better suited to the challenge of creating good jobs.

The federal initiative would be the establishment of an Advanced Research Projects Agency (ARPA) focused on the promotion of employment-friendly technologies: ARPA-W(orkers). Starting from the premise that innovations that *complement* rather than *displace* workers are feasible, yet, currently undersupplied, ARPA-W would promote early-stage investments in digital and other technologies that enhance prevailing worker skills and create good jobs.

Consider what is perhaps the toughest test case for these ideas: long-term care. Employment in this sector will increase rapidly in future years as the population continues to age and, consequently, demand for in-home or assisted living arrangements increases. Much of long-term care work is done in homes (through agencies that provide the caregivers or through self-employed caregivers) or in assisted living or retirement communities where, unlike hospitals or nursing homes, regulations are weak. In such settings, remuneration and work conditions have traditionally been very poor – characteristics that epitomise bad jobs. Employees are mostly women and disproportionately are people of colour. Long-term care workers are typically regarded as performing low-skill jobs and are often not viewed as real professionals.

As Paul Osterman has noted, there are three ways in which jobs in long-term care can be improved.[20] First, the government can regulate and impose standards (such as high minimum wages). Second, the government can increase reimbursement rates from Medicaid and Medicare in the hope that higher rates translate into increased wages. Third, the productivity of direct-care workers can be raised, allowing the long-term care system to serve patients' needs better and to reduce costs, generating room for better compensation. While the first two strategies might be useful, greater productivity is ultimately the most reliable source of better jobs.

Osterman suggests that it could be useful to increase productivity in long-term care through a strategy that is analogous to the deployment of innovations in manufacturing pioneered by Japanese car producers. This entails a combination of investing in worker skills, providing workers with greater voice, discretion and autonomy, and giving them more responsibility for the quality of the service. Care workers that are empowered with greater autonomy and decision-making can use their knowledge of residents and patients to customise their services and provide more flexibility (e.g., in schedules, food, and treatment). An important component of the strategy could be the introduction of new technologies that complement caregivers' skills, such as digital tools that enable caregivers to collect real-time information and to respond quickly and efficiently to the needs of individual residents.

These changes would require a willingness to experiment with novel work practices and a continuum of efforts, from R&D and the introduction of new technologies for long-term care, on the one hand, and to their local adoption, adaptation, and contextualisation in specific communities, on the other. If long-term care is managed better in these ways, productivity benefits would show up in lower turnover among care workers, reduced hospitalisation rates, better management of chronic conditions, and quicker and smoother transitions out of acute care facilities. None of this is easy. Enhancing productivity in services is notoriously difficult and often impeded by a myriad of well-meaning licensing, safety, and other regulations. But if we cannot find ways of increasing productivity in jobs that our workers are destined for, we will end up with economies that are both worse performing and less inclusive.

VI. Are governments up to it?

Scepticism about the ability of governments to lead and achieve positive change is near universal. To many, 'effective government action' is an oxymoron. Given the state of our contemporary politics, such doubts may be well-placed. Authoritarian populism and polarisation – which interact with and reinforce each other – have infested our public sphere to the detriment of our capacity to mount collective action against common problems.

But there is a longer-standing concern about government action that relates to administrative capabilities. Governments do not have the information and capabilities, the argument goes, needed to achieve positive structural change in the economy. Give governments too much power and they will direct resources towards the wrong places and turn into captive tools of special interests. That was the argument at the heart of neoliberalism and a key source of its appeal. It is the argument that must be overcome by any successor narrative on economic policy, and productivism especially, if it is to become successful.

In reality, government capabilities are not inherited or static. They are built over time, once appropriate priorities are set and as a result of experience, learning and building trust with private entities. For public officials, the relevant questions should not be 'do we have the capacity?' but rather, 'do we have in place the right priorities and the correct mode of governance?'

The sceptic might say this all sounds good in theory, but it is not achievable in practice. Look around and public governance seems to be failing throughout, from the local and national to the global level. In fact, as Charles Sabel and David Victor point out in their book, effective models of governance already exist and have made a big difference.[21] The practice is there, but so far, theory has been lacking. Sabel and Victor focus on climate change, which is the greatest policy challenge of our time, and it is also an area where governance is doubly difficult: regulations have to be not only effective at the national level, but they also have to be negotiated globally among states with different interests and circumstances. They build their argument on the example of the Montreal Protocol on ozone.[22] First negotiated in 1987, the protocol has been successful at curbing ozone depleting substances (ODS), to the point where the ozone layer is now on course to full recovery.

The ozone layer and climate change challenges looked similar at the outset, with significant scientific and technological uncertainty and considerable differences among the positions of advanced and developing nations. The United Nations Framework Convention on Climate Change of 1992, the first global climate agreement, in fact took the Montreal Protocol as its model. Both global regimes started out as 'thin' regimes, with broad commitments to cut emissions – ozone depleting substances in the first case and greenhouse gases in the second – by a certain date, but otherwise it had little operational content.

But the agreements evolved very differently. The Montreal Protocol made steady progress by bringing firms and governments into collaboration in solving concrete technological problems, while climate change agreements got stalled in global negotiations. Sabel and Victor show that a key difference was the creation of sectoral committees under Montreal, in which ODS-emitting firms joined national regulators and scientists in search for technological alternatives. The groups started small and were few in number, but expanded as knowledge accumulated, actors acquired new capabilities, and parties built trust between each other. The virtue of the sectoral committees was that actual problem solving was devolved to local actors, the firms with the requisite technological know-how. When innovation stalled, targets were reset.

The result was a virtuous loop of on-the-ground innovation and top-level goal setting. In the climate regime, by contrast, firms were kept at arms' length from regulators, for fear that they would control the process. Instead, these entrenched conflicts of interest and resulted in inadequate innovation.

The Montreal Protocol is not the only successful case of what the authors call 'experimental governance'. They discuss in detail a wide range of national and sub-national programmes, ranging from the Advanced Research Projects Agency – Energy (ARPA-E) in the United States to the control of agricultural pollution in Ireland. In each of these cases, governance revolves around ground-level experimentation married to higher-level goal setting. Successful practices that emerge from these collaborations are routinised subsequently through dissemination and standard setting.

These examples are not limited to environmental policy. The operation of ARPA-E is modelled after the Defense Advanced Research Projects Agency (DARPA), a US agency that is responsible for some of the landmark innovations of our time, such as the internet and GPS. At the local level, the most successful initiatives to revitalise communities and create jobs take the form of private–public collaborations that bring training programmes, businesses, non-profit groups, and public officials together to create new pathways to economic opportunity.[23] Effective national industrial policies take a similar collaborative, cross-sectoral approach.[24] The important point is that there are enough concrete, real-world examples of these collaborative approaches to give us hope that these ideas are not utopian.

As Sabel and Victor explain, the general strategy in all these domains is to start out with ambitious, somewhat ill-defined goals. Programme leaders must acknowledge the deep uncertainty and, hence, the likelihood of mistakes and false starts. There must be incentives for the actors with the most detailed and accurate information – typically firms – to look for solutions, which means public agencies must contribute some combination of sticks (the threat of regulation) and incentives (public inputs). Milestones and monitoring are key to permit reassessment and revision. Solutions are generalised, as they emerge, in the form of standards or regulations for all. Innovation is key, since higher standards (cleaner environment, better jobs) are possible only through productivity-enhancing innovations.

This kind of policymaking differs significantly from the conventional approaches that dominate today's thinking. From my perspective, the state versus market dichotomy no longer makes sense. States and markets are complements, not substitutes. Economists' standard top-down, principal–agent model of regulation (with it top-down, principal–agent framing) becomes unhelpful.

VII. A paradigm beyond right and left?

If productivism is to be successful, it will have to transcend the stale ideologies of the past. A new economic paradigm becomes truly established when even its purported opponents start to see the world through its lens. At its height, the Keynesian welfare state received as much support from conservative politicians as it did from left-wing liberals. In the United States, for example, Republican presidents Dwight Eisenhower and Richard Nixon bought fully into its essential tenets – regulated markets, redistribution, social insurance, and counter-cyclical macroeconomic policies – and worked to expand social welfare programmes and strengthen workplace and environmental regulation.[25]

It was similar with the neoliberal approach. The impetus for it came from economists and politicians – such as Milton Friedman, Ronald Reagan, and Margaret Thatcher who were all market enthusiasts. But if the paradigm eventually became dominant, it was in no small part thanks to centre-left leaders, such as Bill Clinton and Tony Blair, who had internalised much of its pro-market agenda.[26] These leaders pushed for deregulation, financialisation, and hyper-globalisation, while paying lip service to ameliorate the consequent rise in inequality and economic insecurity.

As with previous paradigms, productivism will have to find support eventually from both ends of the political spectrum. The polarisation that prevails in our political life makes such an outcome seem outlandish. Yet, there are in fact signs of convergence.

We saw many of these elements in the Biden administration's narrative and in at least some of its policies. The wholesale embrace of industrial policies to facilitate the green transition, rebuild domestic supply chains, and stimulate good jobs, the finger-pointing at corporate profits as a partial culprit behind inflation and the refusal to revoke Trump's tariffs against China are some examples. When the administration's most senior economist, Secretary of Treasury Janet Yellen, extols the virtues of 'friend-shoring' – sourcing supplies from US allies – over the World Trade Organization (WTO), we know we are in a different world.[27]

But similar strands exist on the political right as well. Alarmed by China's rise, Republicans have made common cause with Democrats in pushing for active investment and innovation policies to bolster US manufacturing.[28] Past (and likely future) Republican presidential candidate Senator Marco Rubio has made impassioned pleas for industrial policy – promoting financial, marketing, and technological assistance to small businesses as well as manufacturing and high-tech sectors.[29;30] 'In those instances in which the market's most efficient outcome is one that's bad for our people,' says Rubio, 'what we need is targeted industrial policy to further the common good'. Progressives on the left could not agree more. The architect of Trump's China trade policy, Robert Lighthizer, similarly has won many fans on the left for his hard-ball tactics vis-à-vis the WTO. Robert Kuttner, a leading voice among the progressives, has argued that Lighthizer's views on trade, industrial policy, and economic nationalism 'were more those of a progressive Democrat'.[31]

The Niskanen Center, named after the libertarian economist William Niskanen who was a principal advisor to Reagan, has made 'state capacity', the ability of governments to provide public goods, one of its main planks, emphasising its importance for a healthy economy.[32] Oren Cass, advisor to 2008 Republican presidential candidate Mitt Romney and a former senior fellow at market-promoting Manhattan Institute, is a critic of financialised capitalism and supports reshoring supply chains and investment in local communities. Patrick Deneen, one of the leading intellectuals of the 'populist right' talks about the importance of 'pro-worker policies' and 'the encouragement, through government policy, of domestic production'. Listening recently to Deneen discussing these and other economic policies, the *New York Times* writer Ezra Klein was moved to say: 'What's funny about that to me is that they seem to me to resemble what the current Democratic Party is'.[33]

Pragmatism can override political partisanship when it comes to the real work of fostering local businesses and job creation and the public–private partnerships necessary to achieve that end. That was the revelation of the husband-and-wife team of James and Deborah Fallows when they travelled around America on their single-engine plane to study experiences with local economic development.[34] Confronted by the challenges of economic decline and joblessness, local politicians were engaged along with community groups, entrepreneurs, and other stakeholders in extensive policy experimentation – and in many of those cases whether they were Democrats, Republicans, or Independents made little difference to what they did.

However, deep divides between the two parties on social and cultural issues, such as abortion rights, race and gender, remain. Many in the Republican Party, including key figures such as Marco Rubio, have yet to give up their allegiance to Donald Trump, who continues to be a threat to US democracy. And there is always the danger that the 'new' industrial policies that conservatives and progressives alike favour will fizzle out or turn into the policies of the past.

Whether it goes astray or not, there are signs of a major reorientation in economic policy – one that is rooted in production, work and localism instead of finance, consumerism and globalism. And it might turn into a new paradigm that captures the imagination of both sides of the political spectrum.

VIII. Beware economists bearing paradigms

At present, we are in the midst of a transition away from neoliberalism, with much uncertainty about what will replace it. We might approach the absence of a solidified new paradigm with mixed feelings. On the one hand, we certainly do not need yet another orthodoxy offering cookie-cutter solutions and ready-made blueprints for nations and regions with very different circumstances and needs.[35] On the other hand, economic policy needs to be guided by an overall animating vision. If history is a guide, the vacuum left by the waning of neoliberal ideas will soon be filled by a new paradigm – and the more appropriate and adaptable that paradigm, the better.

All our previous policy paradigms – whether mercantilist, classical liberal, Keynesian, social-democratic, ordo-liberal or neoliberal – had important blind spots because they were conceived of as universal programmes to be applied at all times and everywhere. Inevitably, the innovations they brought to how we think about economic governance were overshadowed by those blind spots. The result was over-reach and a back-and-forth swing in the pendulum between excessive optimism and pessimism about the role of the government in the economy.

The answer to any policy question in economics is 'it depends'. It may seem this would render economics useless and irrelevant. But in fact, the opposite is true. We need economic analysis and evidence to fill out the details of *what it depends upon*. The keywords of a truly useful economics paradigm are contingency, contextuality, and non-universality. Economics teaches us that there is a time for fiscal profligacy and a time for fiscal conservatism. A time when government should intervene in supply chains and a time when it should leave markets to their own devices. Taxes should be sometimes high, sometimes low. Trade should be freer in some areas and regulated in others. Mapping the links between varying real-world circumstances and the desirability of different types of interventions is what good economics is about.

Our societies are confronted today with vital challenges that require new economic approaches and significant policy experimentation. But those who are looking for a new economic paradigm – or actively trying to develop one – should be careful what they are wishing for. Our goal should be not to create tomorrow's ossified vision, but to learn how to adapt our policies and institutions to changing exigencies. Ultimately, what our economy demands is sound ideas, and not necessarily a new paradigm.[36]

By the time any set of ideas becomes conventional wisdom, it is riddled with one-size-fits-all generalisations and truisms that are bound to be unhelpful and misleading as a general orientation to policy. As such, what I have described here as productivism must be understood as a contingent set of policies – a set of policies that at best meets the demand of our time. The more successful it is, the less relevant it will become to future challenges.

Notes

1. Diao et al. (2021).
2. Temin (2017).
3. Vacas-Soriano and Fernandez-Macias (2017).
4. Slattery and Zidar (2020).
5. Rodrik (2018).
6. Rodrik and Stantcheva (2021a).
7. Rodrik and Sabel (2019).
8. Bartik (2019).
9. Acemoglu and Restrepo (2019).
10. European Commission (2019).
11. Lincicome (2021).
12. Criscuolo et al. (2019).
13. Stephens and Leonnig (2011).
14. Overly (2017).
15. Rodrik (2021b).
16. Moore (2022).
17. Rodrik (2022).
18. Rodrik and Stantcheva (2021b).

[19] Doshi et al. (2023).

[20] Osterman (2020).

[21] Sabel and Victor (2022).

[22] UN Environment Programme (2018).

[23] Fallows and Fallows (2019).

[24] Ghezzi (2017).

[25] Gerstle (2022).

[26] Rodrik (2016).

[27] US Department of the Treasury (2022).

[28] Franck (2021).

[29] Rubio (2021).

[30] Rubio (2019).

[31] Kuttner (2022).

[32] Lindsey (2021).

[33] Klein (2022).

[34] Fallows and Fallows (2019).

[35] Rodrik (2021a).

[36] Rodrik (2021b).

References

Acemoglu, D. and Restrepo, P. (2019) 'The Wrong Kind of AI? Artificial Intelligence and the Future of Labor Demand', IZA Discussion Paper 12292. Bonn: Institute of Labor Economics (IZA). https://www.iza.org/publications/dp/12292/the-wrong-kind-of-ai-artificial-intelligence-and-the-future-of-labor-demand

Bartik, T. J. (2019) 'Making Sense of Incentives: Taming Business Incentives to Promote Prosperity', WEfocus Series, W. E. Upjohn Institute for Employment Research; https://doi.org/10.17848/9780880996693

Criscuolo, C., Martin, R., Overman, H. G. and Van Reenen, J. (2019) 'Some Causal Effects of an Industrial Policy', *American Economic Review*. 109(1): 48–85. https://doi.org/10.1257/aer.20160034

Diao, X., Ellis, M., McMillan, M. and Rodrik, D. (2021) 'Africa's Manufacturing Puzzle: Evidence from Tanzanian and Ethiopian Firms', Working Paper 28344, *National Bureau of Economic Research*. https://www.nber.org/system/files/working_papers/w28344/w28344.pdf

Doshi, V., Spencer, H.and Rodrik, D. (2023) '*Creating a Good-Jobs Economy in the UK*', The Economy Inquiry 2030, Resolution Foundation. https://economy2030.resolutionfoundation.org/wp-content/uploads/2023/07/Creating-a-good-jobs-economy-1.pdf

European Commission (2019) 'The European Green Deal'. https://ec.europa.eu/info/strategy/priorities-2019-2024/european-green-deal_en

Fallows, J. and Fallows, D. (2019) *Our Towns: A 100,000-mile Journey into the Heart of America.* New York: Penguin Random House, Pantheon Books.

Franck, T. (2021) 'The Senate Is Set to Pass a Massive Bipartisan Tech and Manufacturing Bill that Takes on China'. CNBC. [8 June]. https://www.cnbc.com/2021/06/08/senate-takes-on-china-with-bipartisan-manufacturing-bill.html

Gerstle, G. (2022) *The Rise and Fall of the Neoliberal Order: America and the World in the Free Market Era*, Oxford: Oxford University Press.

Ghezzi, P. (2017) 'Mesas Ejecutivas in Peru: Lessons for Productive Development Policies', *Global Policy*, (3): 369–80. https://doi.org/10.1111/1758-5899.12457

Klein, E. (2022) 'Transcript: Ezra Klein Interviews Patrick Deneen'. *The New York Times*. [13 May]. https://www.nytimes.com/2022/05/13/podcasts/transcript-ezra-klein-interviews-patrick-deneen.html

Kuttner, R. (2022) 'After Hyper-Globalization'. *The American Prospect*. [31 May]. https://prospect.org/economy/after-hyper-globalization/

Lincicome, S. (2021) 'Industrial Policy: A Bad Idea Is Back', *CATO Institute*. https://www.cato.org/policy-report/july/august-2021/industrial-policy-bad-idea-back

Lindsey, B. (2021) 'State Capacity: What Is It, How We Lost It, and How to Get It Back', *Niskanen Center*. https://www.niskanencenter.org/state-capacity-what-is-it-how-we-lost-it-and-how-to-get-it-back/

Moore, S. K. (2022) 'U.S. Passes Landmark Act to Fund Semiconductor Manufacturing', *IEEE Spectrum*. [19 July]. https://spectrum.ieee.org/chips-act-of-2022

Osterman, P. (2020) *Creating Good Jobs*, Cambridge, MA: MIT Press.

Overly, S. (2017) 'This Government Loan Program Helped Tesla at a Critical Time. Trump Wants to Cut It', *The Washington Post*. [16 Mar]. https://www.washingtonpost.com/news/innovations/wp/2017/03/16/this-government-loan-program-helped-tesla-at-a-critical-time-trump-wants-to-cut-it/

Rodrik, D. (2016) 'The Abdication of the Left', *Project Syndicate* [11 July]. https://www.project-syndicate.org/commentary/anti-globalization-backlash-from-right-by-dani-rodrik-2016-07

Rodrik, D. (2018) 'Is Populism Necessarily Bad Economics?', *AEA Papers and Proceedings*. 2018 May 1(108): 196–9. https://doi.org/10.1257/pandp.20181122

Rodrik, D. (2021a) 'A Better Deal for the World's Workers', *Project Syndicate*. [20 December]. https://www.project-syndicate.org/commentary/new-deal-for-workers-bargaining-power-good-jobs-by-dani-rodrik-2021-12?barrier=accesspaylog

Rodrik, D. (2021b) 'Beware Economists Bearing Policy Paradigms', *Project Syndicate* [11 May]. https://www.project-syndicate.org/commentary/economic-policy-must-abandon-universal-paradigms-by-dani-rodrik-2021-05

Rodrik, D. (2022) 'An Industrial Policy for Good Jobs', *The Hamilton Project Brookings Institution* https://drodrik.scholar.harvard.edu/files/dani-rodrik/files/rodrik_-_an_industrial_policy_for_good_jobs.pdf

Rodrik, D. and Sabel, C. (2019) 'Building a Good Jobs Economy', Working Paper. https://drodrik.scholar.harvard.edu/publications/building-good-jobs-economy

Rodrik, D. and Stantcheva, S. (2021a) 'Fixing Capitalism's Good Jobs Problem', *Oxford Review of Economic Policy*, 37(4): 824–37. https://doi.org/10.1093/oxrep/grab024

Rodrik, D. and Stantcheva, S. (2021b) *Economic Inequality and Insecurity: Policies for an Inclusive Economy*. Report Prepared for Commission Chaired by Olivier Blanchard and Jean Tirole on Major Future Economic Challenges, Republic of France: https://drodrik.scholar.harvard.edu/publications/economic-inequality-and-insecurity-policies-inclusive-economy

Rubio, M. (2019) 'Rubio Releases Chairman's Mark to Reauthorize the Small Business Act', Marco Rubio, U.S. Senator for Florida. SBC Senate [18 July] https://www.sbc.senate.gov/public/index.cfm/2019/7/rubio-releases-chairman-s-mark-to-reauthorize-the-small-business-act

Rubio, M. (2021) 'Exclusive: American Industrial Policy and the Rise of China', Marco Rubio, U.S. Senator for Florida. [21 May] The American Mind. A publication of the Claremont Institute. https://americanmind.org/memo/american-industrial-policy-and-the-rise-of-china/

Sabel, C. F. and Victor, D. G. (2022) *Fixing the Climate: Strategies for an Uncertain World*, Princeton, NJ: Princeton University Press.

Slattery, C. and Zidar, O. (2020) 'Evaluating State and Local Business Incentives', *Journal of Economic Perspectives*, 34(2): 90–118. https://doi.org/10.1257/jep.34.2.90

Stephens, J. and Leonnig, C. D. (2011) 'Solyndra Solar Company Fails after Getting Federal Loan Guarantees', *The Washington Post*. [31 Aug]. https://www.washingtonpost.com/politics/solyndra-solar-company-fails-after-getting-controversial-federal-loan-guarantees/2011/08/31/gIQAB8IRsJ_story.html

Temin, P. (2017) *The Vanishing Middle Class: Prejudice and Power in a Dual Economy*, Cambridge, MA: MIT Press.

UN Environment Programme (2018) *About Montreal Protocol*. http://www.unep.org/ozonaction/who-we-are/about-montreal-protocol

US Department of the Treasury (2022) 'Remarks by Secretary of the Treasury Janet L. Yellen on Way Forward for the Global Economy', U.S. Department of the Treasury [13 April]. https://home.treasury.gov/news/press-releases/jy0714

Vacas-Soriano, C. and Fernandez-Macias, E. (2017) 'Europe's Shrinking Middle Class', *Eurofound*. https://www.eurofound.europa.eu/de/publications/blog/europes-shrinking-middle-class

Response to Dani Rodrik by Jean Pisani-Ferry

Dani Rodrik makes five key points in his ambitious and wide-ranging chapter. The first three are insightful. The fourth is problematic. The fifth is disputable.

1. There is a need for a new paradigm to help define the post-neoliberal economy.
2. Economies nowadays are rife with externalities. A major issue for policymakers is how to tackle such externalities.
3. How to overcome 'productive dualism' between frontier firms and laggards is the central economic challenge we face, yet the traditional growth strategies that focus on manufacturing and the most productive segments of the economy are unlikely to be successful. The new industrial policy should focus on services.
4. The new industrial strategy should rest on an implicit quid pro quo between firms and public authorities, by which the former would commit to internalising externalities while the latter would provide worker-centred services.
5. Governments have the capacity to design and implement this new approach.

In this discussion, I will address these points one by one, before concluding with some broader remarks.

I. The case for a new policy paradigm

Policy is made of actions, but action programmes build on broad paradigms that define economic and societal aims and match instruments to objectives. Since World War II, two successive paradigms have dominated the policy agenda in advanced economies: the neo-Keynesian/welfare state paradigm of the first post-war decades and the neoliberal paradigm that became dominant in the 1980s. According to Rodrik, time has come to outline a new policy paradigm.

One could question whether a new paradigm is really necessary and useful: a policy agenda is best defined by a series of priority problems and a corresponding series of responses, and these can be selected without an overarching paradigm. Worse, broad concepts are easily misleading. Policy innovation often builds on the hybridisation of existing ideas and the notion of a coherent policy paradigm can be regarded as an obstacle to necessary recombination.[1]

However, a great advantage of policy paradigms is that they are directional. Whenever new policy directions are to be explored, governments go through a discovery process where they learn from the successes and failures of other governments. Policy innovation is often decentralised and experimental, especially when cross-country dimensions are considered. In this context, success depends on complementarities between measures implemented in different fields, for example, labour and product markets. This is why the case for outlining a new paradigm and defining its main components is a cogent one.

A common paradigm serves as a coordinating device to ensure policy coherence within countries. It also helps foster experimentation and cross-fertilisation between countries. The economic policies of Margaret Thatcher and Ronald Reagan were far from identical, but they were based on the same rejection of the neo-Keynesian policy paradigm and they were aiming at the same type of transformations. What became known as the neoliberal paradigm was simultaneously experimented in the United Kingdom and the United States.

II. The new political economy of externalities

A second reason to search for a new paradigm is that in modern economies, the nature of the problems policies need to address has changed. Externalities have been known for at least a century, but they were generally regarded as respectable curiosities, not as key challenges for policymaking. The neoliberal paradigm of the 1980s made no room for responding to them in its policy agenda.

Things have drastically changed for reasons that have to do with policy priorities (a much stronger emphasis on preserving financial stability, or the environmental commons, such as a stable climate or biodiversity), but also with the nature of the policy reasoning. Economists nowadays are much more conscious of the limits of simplified models and contemporary economic analysis no longer takes the optimality of unfettered markets as its default hypothesis. The burden of proof has shifted.

Externalities are central in Rodrik's approach. By promoting the notion of a 'good jobs externality' or by arguing that 'firms' decisions on how many workers to employ, how much to pay, what kind of technologies to deploy and how to organise work' affect 'the life opportunities of prospective employees and their communities', he broadens the scope of externalities in a major way. He makes each individual employer accountable for the wellbeing of the middle class and the fate of local communities.

Rodrik's broad concept of externalities goes beyond pure economic perspectives. As he notes, good jobs are also a matter of status, working conditions, and career progression and their shortage comes at 'social, political, and economic costs'. In pure money terms, in some countries today's low-wage employees may be better off than middle-class employees of the 1990s, but their social status and career outlook are much worse. Indeed, numerous surveys indicate that perceptions of a downhill evolution are nowadays much more widespread than they were a few decades ago.[2]

'Good jobs', however, are hard to define economically. If it were only a matter of preventing declines in real wages, the middle-class malaise would not affect countries like France and Belgium where wages, especially at the bottom, are protected by legally binding price indexation provisions. Yet the perception of a broken social contract is as widespread in these countries as it is in the United States, where the minimum wage has lost ground for decades. In earnest, a good jobs economy is as much a sociological notion as an economic one.

III. Overcoming productive dualism, without cultivating the illusion of a manufacturing revival

Productive dualism – meaning the coexistence within the same economy of modern, high-productivity firms and of a low-productivity laggard firms – was traditionally a distinctive feature of developing economies. India, for example, displays such characteristics, and so does China (albeit less so), while homogeneity of firm performance used to be much more pronounced in the United States.[3]

In recent decades, however, the dispersion of productivity performance across sectors, firms, and geographies has increased in the United States and other advanced economies, making them increasingly akin to developing economies. Rodrik regards this evolution as indicative of a perverse convergence between advanced and developing economies. Whereas development traditionally resulted in convergence to the top, whereby the least-efficient firms and sectors were gradually giving way to the more efficient ones, what we have witnessed in recent decades is rather a growing divergence. As documented by Andrews et al., large swathes of advanced economies are increasingly characterised by low productivity, low wages, and low profits.[4]

The resurgence of dualism between firms belonging to the same sector has major economic and social consequences. Inequality, for example, is increasingly attributable to the high heterogeneity of firm performance.[5] It also implies that the mere observation of the dispersion of individual firm performances or of divergences across sectors does not suffice anymore to distinguish advanced from developing economies.

The question is how to cure productive dualism. Rodrik is correct in observing that the traditional remedy to this disease – industrialisation – is not available anymore. As forcefully argued by Posen, among others, re-industrialisation is an illusory therapy to the scarcity of good jobs.[6] The economic strategies of President Biden and President Trump may prove successful and end up countering China's competitive pressure. But whatever the level of success of these or similar policy initiatives, they are unlikely to result in a significant rebound of manufacturing employment.

The basic reason why manufacturing employment has been shrinking is that productivity gains in manufacturing are much higher than in services. Artificial intelligence (AI) may have some impact on the relative productivity gains of educational or healthcare services in comparison to the manufacturing sector, but it is doubtful that its effects will be large enough to change the overall landscape. The future of employment is services employment, and the relevant policy question is whether newly created services jobs will have the same frustrating characteristics as those of the past or, rather, if they will emulate some of the characteristics of yesterday's manufacturing jobs.

IV. The contours of a new industrial strategy

Whereas there is much to agree with in Rodrik's diagnosis and broad policy agenda, his prescription, at least as it is presented in the chapter, is not compelling enough to command support. His view is that good services jobs will be created within the framework of an 'implicit quid pro quo' between the government and private employers. The former would commit to deliver public services in return for 'soft commitments by firms on investment and employment creation'.

Rodrik, however, is short on details about this possible quid pro quo strategy. He gives examples from the successes of the DARPA, yet the DARPA template does not include any soft commitment by firms to create jobs. Rather, it involves an explicit contract whereby the federal government provides funding to risky but promising projects and the private firms deliver concrete innovations. The 'soft' component of the bargain is that because the programme aims at promoting breakthrough innovations, the precise features of these innovations cannot be defined *ex ante*. But the aims are clear and the success criteria reasonably well defined.

The way these problems are solved is well established: the counterpart to the uncertainty on what projects are expected to deliver is a close monitoring of their development by programme officers entrusted with the ability to discontinue funding to unsuccessful projects. Because the combination of high research costs and uncertain outcomes acts as a deterrent to the launching of audacious moonshot projects, government funding helps to overcome *ex ante* risk aversion. As firms engaged in unsuccessful projects have a natural tendency to call for additional support, thorough monitoring of project development facilitates the recalibration or discontinuation of subsidies once the project has taken off.

Applying this template to the creation of good jobs in sectors such as healthcare or other social services would raise several challenges. First, as already observed, whether or not jobs that are being created are in fact 'good' is hard to determine. Second, it is not clear how success and failure should be measured for the project monitoring to be based on objective criteria and to avoid capture. Third, the calibration of subsidies is made difficult by pervasive uncertainty and the unobservability of the characteristics of the jobs that are being created. As observed by Rodrik himself, in a dynamic environment with multidimensional uncertainty, 'subsidies will generally fall short and be dominated by different policy tools'.[7] It may even happen that 'neither the policymaker nor employers have reliable information on the possibilities and costs of creating good jobs'.

The implication is that rather than operating through across-the-board policy schemes with clear eligibility criteria and performance indicators, industrial policy would need to rely on a much more tailor-made approach. This could be attainable for individual projects, assuming government officials in charge of implementing them are specifically trained. But to make a difference, Rodrik's ARPA-W would need to be operated at scale.

V. Do governments have the capacity to foster the creation of good jobs?

Governments in Europe intervene in labour markets much more than in the United States. In continental Europe, they set minimum wages, define health and safety standards, regulate collective bargaining, mandate the employer's workforce training obligations – just to mention their main channels of intervention. The French labour code that defines the mutual obligations of employers and employees is more than 3,000 pages long, not counting collective agreements at industry level. Many of these provisions aim at defining what good jobs are, and yet, dissatisfaction with labour relations and employment conditions are almost as widespread as in North America.

In order to create good jobs, Rodrik's prescription is to let national and local governments bargain with employers, with the aim of entering into agreements with them. The risk, however, is that these agreements will be either ineffective, or incoherent and inefficient. Bureaucrats are not trained to negotiate contractual agreements with firms.

Rather than trust that government officials will be able to perform such tasks, an alternative would be to reform corporate governance with the aim of giving employees and local governments a voice in companies' strategic decisions. Provisions of this sort exist in many European countries, especially in Germany where *Mitbestimmung* (co-determination) is part of the legally mandated corporate governance structure, usually through forming a supervisory body where elected representatives of workers and other stakeholders have a say. Stakeholder capitalism would balance shareholder capitalism, and this type of structure would potentially be more amenable to companies' broader responsibilities.

Stakeholder capitalism is no panacea. There is no guarantee that it would help strengthen the quality of jobs. Employees, for example, could collude with the shareholders to divide up rents at the expense of the local community to which the company is accountable. But a more balanced governance structure, where stakeholders are represented alongside shareholders, would help define the proper responsibilities of a company vis-à-vis its employees and the local communities. This would at least be a step in the right direction.

Notes

[1] Weitzman (1998).

[2] Fourquet et al. (2023).

[3] Hsieh and Klenow (2009).

[4] Andrews et al. (2016).

[5] Furman and Orszag (2018).

[6] Posen (2021).

[7] Rodrik (2022).

References

Andrews, D., Criscuolo, C. and Gal, P. (2016) 'The Global Productivity Slowdown, Technology Divergence and Public Policy: A Firm-Level Perspective', Hutchins Center Working Paper, Brookings Institution. https://www.brookings.edu/wp-content/uploads/2016/08/andrews-et-al.pdf

Fourquet, J., Gariazzo, M. and Jéquier, S. (2023) 'Classes moyennes en tension, entre vie au rabais et aides publiques insuffisantes', IFOP/Fondation Jean-Jaurès. https://www.jean-jaures.org/publication/classes-moyennes-en-tension-entre-vie-au-rabais-et-aides-publiques-insuffisantes/

Furman, J. and Orszag, P. (2018) 'Slower Productivity and Higher Inequality: Are They Related?', PIIE Working Paper 2018-4. https://papers.ssrn.com/sol3/papers.cfm?abstract_id=3191984

Hsieh, C. and Klenow, P. (2009) 'Misallocation and Manufacturing TFP in China and India', *The Quarterly Journal of Economics*, 124(4): 1403–1448. https://doi.org/10.1162/qjec.2009.124.4.1403

Posen, A. (2021) 'The Price of Nostalgia: America's Self-Defeating Economic Retreat', *Foreign Affairs*. [20 April]. https://www.foreignaffairs.com/articles/united-states/2021-04-20/america-price-nostalgia

Rodrik, D. (2022) 'An Industrial Policy for Good Jobs', *The Hamilton Project, Brookings Institution*. https://drodrik.scholar.harvard.edu/files/dani-rodrik/files/rodrik_-_an_industrial_policy_for_good_jobs.pdf

Weitzman, M. (1998) 'Recombinant Growth', *The Quarterly Journal of Economics*, 113(2): 331–360. https://doi.org/10.1162/003355398555595

Response to Dani Rodrik by Pierre-Olivier Gourinchas

Productivism, the economic and political paradigm proposed by Dani Rodrik, embodies an ambitious vision of both the fundamental objectives of our economic system and of how the pursuit of these goals shapes the role of government. By redefining these two elements, productivism also redefines the interactions of government with other economic agents – workers and firms – and lays the foundation for a different economic model. While radical, this vision stems from some of the evident failures of the current paradigm, which Rodrik labels as 'neoliberalism', and the acute social tensions it has generated.

I. Recapping the productivist paradigm

The social challenges that afflict many countries, particularly advanced economies (AEs), makes the need to rethink our economic paradigm evident. The secular slowdown in productivity growth has brought about a scarcity of 'good jobs'. Our economies grapple with 'dualism', whereby the most productive technologies remain corralled within a few firms, hindering innovation from trickling down and spurring aggregate growth. These factors lead to inequality across workers and regions, fuelling discontent, social tensions, and political polarisation.

How did we get here? Rodrik argues that both neoliberal supply-side and Keynesian demand-side policies are responsible. The former spurred investment and growth, but by leaving the private sector actions unchecked, it failed to address the externalities inherent in firms' profit-maximising behaviour. The latter excessively focused on *ex-post* redistribution and social transfers without fostering steady productivity growth and the broad-based economic opportunities that come with it.

Rodrik's solution is productivism. The goal of this paradigm is to achieve broad-based growth and enhance access to economic opportunities across all regions and segments of the labour force. This objective relies on governments playing an active role in supporting the supply side, enabling firms to create good jobs, equipping workers with the right skills to fill them, pre-emptively addressing market failures, and fostering the diffusion of innovation from 'superstar' firms to the rest of the economy.

II. Questioning the premises

It is unquestionable that economic growth over the past two decades has lagged behind the rapid expansion in the second half of the 20th century, with much of it driven by a few countries, notably China. However, the combination of sluggish growth, dualism and rising inequality seems to be more characteristic of the United States than a reflection of the global status quo. Many other AEs have been able to strike a better balance between promoting growth and mitigating inequality through a combination of 'pre-production' policies, such as an equitable education system, and 'post-production' redistribution.[1] In fairness, many of them also grapple with similar political challenges, including rising discontent, polarisation, and the rise of populism.

These challenges are relatively recent. Taking a longer-term view, the post-World War II era witnessed unprecedented global growth with declining poverty rates and a rising middle class driven by both neoliberal and Keynesian policy agendas. For many countries, especially emerging markets and developing economies (EMDEs), this trend has persisted over the past 20 years. Yet, we should avoid idealising the past: many of the so-called good jobs created in the 1950s and 1960s in the US were reserved for white males. Other demographic groups were too often left out.

My second reservation regarding the evidence is whether productive dualism is the true problem at hand. While it is true that new technologies can lead to winners and losers, policies aimed primarily at redistributing resources across firms may have the unintended adverse effect of hindering innovation. The implicit assumption appears to be that latent productivity gains are just waiting to happen in small and medium-sized enterprises (SMEs). Yet, it remains unclear whether small firms are inherently too small and large firms too large. Considering the abundant evidence on the higher productivity of large firms, allowing firms at the technological frontier to expand in size is not necessarily a bad recipe for spurring growth.[2] Instead, the real issue could lie in the lack of competition, as large incumbent firms have progressively gained market power over the years, resulting in monopolies and barriers to entry that impede innovation and hinder the growth of productive firms.[3;4;5]

III. How can governments steer the economy?

In Rodrik's vision, governments are trusted 'to lead and achieve positive change' by playing a very active role in the economy. But extensive interventionist policies are costly. This is a problem when fiscal space is limited from the outset. Does productivism, therefore, risk re-creating dualism, but this time between the countries that have fiscal space and those that do not?

There is also the danger that, under the guise of 'modern-supply side' and 'big government' policies, many special interests will fester, potentially creating a soft budget constraint for workers and firms with access to various forms of protection. I am somewhat apprehensive about the notion that externalities are everywhere. If so, what are the limits on state intervention? How big is too big?

Governments, like markets, can have short horizons. Interventions can be misguided, such as the excessive focus on manufacturing jobs in economies primarily dominated by services, or can be targeting narrow political gains, like relocating a factory from foreign country X to swing county Y, which might seem politically appealing but could prove largely wasteful from a global perspective. This short-termism may be exacerbated in democratic systems, raising an important question: is productivism compatible with democracy?

That being said, there is clearly an important role for the government to steer the economy, albeit perhaps not as widespread as envisaged in Rodrik's productivism. The solution may be more evolutionary than revolutionary. Recalibrating existing policies to address current and future challenges may prove more effective than a new paradigm centred on pervasive domestic-oriented industrial policy.

To start with, policies should be accompanied by a forward-looking vision. It is essential for governments to anticipate upcoming challenges and address market failures, while avoiding overly prescriptive measures on firms. Active policies should provide incentives that encourage firms to navigate these challenges without acting as a rigid framework that hampers innovation and growth. Adopting such an approach would be crucial in three key areas. First, guiding the 'green transition', aiming to combine carbon emissions reduction with promoting inclusive growth.[6;7;8;9] Second, supporting technological change while mitigating potential disruptions from fast-spreading innovations like AI. Third, fostering competition in new sectors like digital markets to counteract the emergence of monopolies in growth-driving sectors.[10]

In the productivist paradigm, an active government role involves connecting supply-side policies with worker-centric outcomes. To start, this requires a precise definition of 'good jobs'. As Rodrik suggests, this definition encompasses various facets beyond a living wage, such as prospects for career advancement, a sense of purpose, and the ability to maintain a dignified standard of living.[11] In the context of rapidly changing production methods and labour markets, it is crucial to translate this vision into a clear working definition to guide policy decisions. This will require addressing practical issues, such as ensuring essential working conditions (e.g., employment security, regular working schedules, and avoiding excessive surveillance of workers' performance). It will also require answering more existential questions about the meaning people find in machine-dominated work or the treatment of workers belonging to categories often perceived to hold differing social statuses, labelled as 'gig economy workers' or 'knowledge economy workers'.

Governments are also responsible for equipping workers with skills necessary for the good jobs of the future, ranging from 'green jobs' to those that will prominently feature AI integration. To achieve this, the education system must prepare individuals before entering the labour force and establish retraining programmes for displaced workers. Additionally, incentivising firms to provide continuous training to their employees to be competitive in a fast-changing economy is essential. Lastly, I fully agree with Rodrik that ensuring geographic inclusion is paramount.[12] Many communities have been left behind during previous waves of structural transformation, whether due to routine-biased technological change or globalisation. We are acutely aware of the long-lasting trauma and social tensions that these community-level shocks can cause. Hence, we must embed inclusivity at the core of structural transformation rather than acting *ex-post* through reparatory place-based policies.

Governments should also take a more active role in structural transformation. The role of government is not simply to regulate privately developed technologies, but can also entail participating in their development to create widely accessible tools and promote applications aimed at public-interest goals. The involvement of public entities in R&D is essential to ensure that innovation is aligned with social outcomes. To give an example, AI research is increasingly dominated by the private sector relative to academia. A recent study finds that in 2021, the US government and the European Commission allocated US$1.5 billion and US$1.2 billion, respectively, on non-defence AI development. Meanwhile, private companies globally spent more than US$340 billion in the same year.[13] With such significant investment gaps, AI applications are more likely to serve firms' profit-maximising objectives, leaving scant public-interest alternatives for key AI tools. A comprehensive understanding of these complex new technologies is essential for positioning governments to regulate their development and uses effectively.

IV. Other factors to consider

Three other factors seem relevant:

Giving workers a voice. Increasing productivity is a necessary but not sufficient condition for creating good jobs. How the benefits of productivity growth are distributed is also crucial. In AEs, there has been a steady erosion of workers' bargaining power over the past decades, resulting in average wages stagnating well below labour productivity growth and widening income inequality. This decline in bargaining power can be attributed to various factors, including a significant reduction in trade union membership since 1980, and an increasing employer concentration in the labour market – known as monopsony – accompanied by the emergence of other non-competitive practices adopted by many firms.[14;15;16;17] It is crucial to restore the voice of workers and rebalance the power dynamics between capital and labour. This would not only help increase wages today, but also ensure the creation of good jobs in the future. When workers have a say in how firms adopt new technologies, the risk of labour displacement decreases, thus fostering innovation that is more inclusive and beneficial for all stakeholders.[18;19]

Firms' incentives, decision-making and accountability. Promoting inclusive growth requires aligning firms' objectives with broader societal goals. To do so, policymakers can provide fiscal incentives to encourage firms to create well-paid jobs for underprivileged groups or in economically disadvantaged areas. However, this endeavour would require fewer interventions by policymakers – and consequently fewer distortionary policy measures – if the fundamental objectives of firms and the core values that guide their operations were inherently aligned with social values and goals. In recent decades, the increasing 'financialisation' of the economy, with firms increasingly relying on financial markets and private equity funding, has led to profit-driven shareholders dominating companies' decision-making processes and more opacity in their internal processes.[20;21;22;23] The emergence of the environmental, social, and governance (ESG) movement has partially countered this trend by promoting corporate transparency, accountability, and encouraging firms to publicly align their actions with social values. Nonetheless, there is a need for further improvements in ESG codes and transparency to ensure that this trend is not merely an act of 'greenwashing' or 'social-washing'.[24]

Competition policy. The rise of 'superstar' firms over the past decades, particularly in the US, can be attributed to a mix of forces, including the roll-back of anti-trust regulation, globalisation, and new technologies consolidating productivity advantages and market dominance. To counter monopolistic tendencies, government should not only collaborate with firms, but also set the 'rules of the game' to ensure fair competition across all markets. The fast-growing digital sector deserves particular attention, as competition dynamics in digital marketplaces, the trading of data, and social media platforms are very different from those of brick-and-mortar sectors. In many countries, competition regulations and anti-trust frameworks are adapting, but there is still a large gap to close.[25]

V. Productivism in emerging markets and developing economies

Before concluding, let me share a few concerns about the implications of productivism for EMDEs.

This group of countries stands to lose heavily from the domestic-oriented industrial policies that many AEs recently enacted.[26;27] While, in the current conjuncture, protectionist agendas are mostly motivated by concerns over supply chain security and geopolitical fractures, they also align with the types of policies envisioned by productivism. This does not bode well for EMDEs, as they would bear the costs of the spillovers from larger economies adopting this new paradigm.

Governments in EMDEs also face greater challenges in applying the productivism paradigm themselves. Firstly, they have lower institutional capacity than AEs: weaker regulatory framework, reduced efficiency in public spending, inadequate revenue collection capacity and higher economic informality. Governments in EMDEs also face higher borrowing costs and a high risk of sovereign debt distress, which reduces their capacity to raise finances to support supply-side fiscal policy. Lastly, high poverty rates, posing immediate threats to the survival of large fractions of the population, make it hard to justify diverting resources away from demand-side social spending in the short term. Overall, governments in EMDEs have a more limited ability to play the active role in long-term growth envisioned by Rodrik.

In this context, the International Monetary Fund (IMF) and International Financial Institutions (IFIs) can play an important role. These organisations have longstanding experiences assisting EMDEs in enhancing the capacity of their governmental institutions through technical assistance. Moreover, the IFIs themselves are adapting to better support countries in facing the long-term challenges ahead. The IMF, for instance, is rapidly integrating climate change considerations into its country surveillance, advising countries on policies for climate change adaptation, and mitigation. This shift is paired with the creation of long-term financing tools for the specific purpose to tackle these challenges, such as the Resilience and Sustainability Trust, established in 2022 with the support of several AEs. Such examples of multilateral efforts to assist EMDEs are all the more crucial when considering the dangers of the recent drift towards a more geopolitically fragmented global economy.

VI. Final remarks

Where does this leave us? I think the first-order solution identified by Rodrik is the right one: bring back growth. Fostering aggregate economic growth is crucial for increasing the supply of good jobs and expanding access to economic opportunities in a politically effective manner. Without economic growth, redistributing the surplus of the few already existing good jobs – despite addressing essential equity concerns – inevitably pits certain societal groups against others. There is a risk that excessive emphasis on *ex-post* redistribution of the socio-economic pie devolves into a zero-sum game, potentially exacerbating current social tensions. Rebalancing governmental actions towards well-designed supply-side policies – with careful consideration of their distributional effects – is necessary to empower firms and workers to expand the pie itself and widen access to economic opportunities.

However, I find that under productivism the pendulum is swinging too far. Yes, we need to acknowledge the failures of the neoliberal system and find solutions to the challenges it has caused. But this can be done through a careful recalibration of policies that is achievable under our current paradigm of what governments can do and how they should interact with other agents. For instance, governments can start by focusing on broadening access to high-quality education and improving the functioning of markets.

The large move towards an interventionist government and more ubiquitous domestic-focused industrial policy envisioned by productivism may result in unintended consequences. For instance, increasing productivity is always advantageous, and efforts to enhance the total factor productivity of smaller firms are commendable. However, we should carefully consider the appropriate policy measures to achieve this. Subsidising smaller and less efficient firms while restraining the expansion of the most productive companies may not necessarily foster growth.

Overall, this ambitious proposal effectively recentres the discussion on the central issue of how government policies must proactively guide productive efforts in the right direction to address current and future challenges, rather than merely rectifying the problems caused by externalities and distorted incentives *ex-post*. This is an important insight.

Acknowledgements

With help and input from Carlo Pizzinelli, Giovanni Melina, and Florence Jaumotte.

Notes

1 Blanchet (2022).

2 Autor et al. (2020).

3 Diez et al. (2018).

4 De Loecker et al. (2020).

5 Eeckhout (2022).

6 International Monetary Fund (2022).

7 International Monetary Fund (2020).

8 Bergant et al. (2022).

9 Bluedorn et al. (2023).

10 Akcigit et al. (2021).

11 Rodrik and Stantcheva (2021).

12 International Monetary Fund (2019).

13 Ahmed et al. (2023).

14 Jaumotte and Osorio Buitron (2015).

15 Azar et al. (2022).

16 Boeri et al. (2022).

[17] Bassanini et al. (2023).

[18] Acemoglu and Restrepo (2019).

[19] Belloc et al. (2023).

[20] Epstein and Jayadev (2019).

[21] Duenhaupt (2012).

[22] Herren Lee (2021).

[23] Morgenson and Rosner (2023).

[24] Elmalt et al. (2021).

[25] OECD (2022).

[26] International Monetary Fund (2023).

[27] Aiyar et al. (2023).

References

Acemoglu, D. and Restrepo, P. (2019) 'The Wrong Kind of AI? Artificial Intelligence and the Future of Labor Demand', IZA Discussion Papers. 12292. https://www.iza.org/publications/dp/12292/the-wrong-kind-of-ai-artificial-intelligence-and-the-future-of-labor-demand

Ahmed, N., Wahed, M. and Thompson, N.C. (2023) 'The Growing Influence of Industry in AI Research', *Science*, 379: 884–886. https://doi.org/10.1126/science.ade2420

Akcigit, U., Chen, W., Diez, F. J., Duval, R. A., Engler, P., Fan, J., Maggi, C., Mendes Tavares, M., Schwarz, D. A., Shibata, I. and Villegas-Sánchez, C. (2021) *Rising Corporate Market Power: Emerging Policy Issues*. Staff Discussion Note 2021/001. https://www.imf.org/en/Publications/Staff-Discussion-Notes/Issues/2021/03/10/Rising-Corporate-Market-Power-Emerging-Policy-Issues-48619

Aiyar, S., Chen, J., Ebeke, C. H., Garcia-Saltos, R., Gudmundsson, T., Ilyina, A., Kangur, A., Kunaratskul, T., Rodriguez, S. L., Ruta, M., Schulze, T., Soderberg, G. and Trevino, J. P. (2023) *Geoeconomic Fragmentation and the Future of Multilateralism*. Staff Discussion Note 23/001. https://www.imf.org/en/Publications/Staff-Discussion-Notes/Issues/2023/01/11/Geo-Economic-Fragmentation-and-the-Future-of-Multilateralism-527266

Autor, D., Dorn, D., Katz, L. F., Patterson, C. and Van Reenen, J. (2020) 'The Fall of the Labor Share and the Rise of Superstar Firms', *The Quarterly Journal of Economics*, 135(2): 645–709. https://doi.org/10.1093/qje/qjaa004

Azar, J., Marinescu, I. and Steinbaum, M. (2022)‘ Labor Market Concentration’, *Journal of Human* Resources, 57: 167-199. https://doi.org/10.3368/jhr.monopsony.1218-9914R1

Bassanini, A., Bovini, G., Caroli, E., Casanova Ferrando, J., Cingano, F., Falco, P., Felgueroso, F., Jansen, M., Martin, P. S., Melo, A., Oberfichter, M. and Popp, M. (2023) ‘Labour Market Concentration, Wages and Job Security in Europe’, NOVA Business School Working Paper 654. http://dx.doi.org/10.2139/ssrn.4321138

Belloc, F., Burdin, G. and Landini, F. (2023) ‘Advanced Technologies and Worker Voice’, *Economica*, 90: 1–38. https://doi.org/10.1111/ecca.12446

Bergant, K., Mano, R. and Shibata, I. (2022) ‘From Polluting to Green Jobs: A Seamless Transition in the U.S.?’, IMF Working Paper 2022/129. https://www.imf.org/en/Publications/WP/Issues/2022/07/01/From-Polluting-to-Green-Jobs-A-Seamless-Transition-in-the-U-S-520244

Blanchet, T., Chancel, L. and Gethin, A. (2022) ‘Why Is Europe More Equal than the United States?’, *American Economic Journal: Applied Economics*, 14(4): 480–518
https://doi.org/10.1257/app.20200703

Bluedorn, J., Hansen, N. J., Noureldin, D., Shibata, I. and Tavares, M. M. (2023) ‘Transitioning to a Greener Labor Market: Cross-Country Evidence from Microdata’, *Energy Economics*, 37, 106836. https://doi.org/10.1016/j.eneco.2023.106836

Boeri, T., Garnero, A. and Luisetto, L. G. (2022) ‘The Use of Non-Compete Agreements in the Italian Labour Market’, Fondazione Ing. Rodolfo Benedetti Working Paper. https://www.frdb.org/wp-content/uploads/2022/05/Boeri-Garnero-Luisetto-Non-compete-agreements-Italy_FINAL.pdf

De Loecker, J., Eeckhout, J. and Unger, G. (2020) ‘The Rise of Market Power and the Macroeconomic Implications’ *The Quarterly Journal of Economics*, 135(2): 561–644. https://doi.org/10.1093/qje/qjz041

Diez, F. J., Leigh, D. and Tambunlertchai, S. (2018) ‘Global Market Power and its Macroeconomic Implications’, IMF Working Paper 2018/137. https://www.imf.org/en/Publications/WP/Issues/2018/06/15/Global-Market-Power-and-its-Macroeconomic-Implications-45975

Duenhaupt, P. (2012) ‘Financialization and the Rentier Income Share–Evidence from the USA and Germany’, *International Review of Applied Economics* 26(4): 465–487. https://doi.org/10.1080/02692171.2011.595705

Eeckhout, J. (2022) *The Profit Paradox: How Thriving Firms Threaten the Future of Work*, Princeton, NJ: Princeton University Press.

Elmalt, D., Kirti, D. and Igan, D. (2021) 'Limits to Private Climate Change Mitigation', IMF Working Paper 21/112. https://www.imf.org/en/Publications/WP/Issues/2021/04/29/Limits-to-Private-Climate-Change-Mitigation-50297

Epstein, G. and Jayadev, A. (2019) 'The Rise of Rentier Incomes in OECD Countries: Financialization, Central Bank Policy and Labor Solidarity', in Epstein, G. (ed) *The Political Economy of Central Banking*, Cheltenham, UK: Edward Elgar: 350–378.

Herren Lee, A. (2021) *Going Dark: The Growth of Private Markets and the Impact on Investors and the Economy.* Remarks at The SEC Speaks in 2021. US Security and Exchange Commission. Speech [12 October]. https://www.sec.gov/news/speech/lee-sec-speaks-2021-10-12

International Monetary Fund (2019) "Chapter 2, Closer Together or Further Apart? Within-Country Regional Disparities and Adjustment in Advanced Economies', in *World Economic Output.* https://www.imf.org/en/Publications/WEO/Issues/2019/10/01/world-economic-outlook-october-2019?intcid=OBanner-WEO1019

International Monetary Fund (2020) 'Chapter 3, 'Mitigating Climate Change', in *World Economic Output.* https://www.imf.org/en/Publications/WEO/Issues/2020/09/30/world-economic-outlook-october-2020

International Monetary Fund (2022) 'Chapter 3, A Greener Labor Market: Employment, Policies, and Economic Transformation', in *World Economic Output.* https://doi.org/10.5089/9781616359423.081

International Monetary Fund (2023) 'Chapter 4, Geoeconomic Fragmentation and Foreign Direct Investment' in *World Economic Output 2023: A Rocky Recovery.* https://www.elibrary.imf.org/display/book/9798400224119/CH004.xml

Jaumotte, F. and Osorio Buitron, C. (2015) 'Inequality and Labor Market Institutions', Staff Discussion Note. 2015/014. https://www.imf.org/en/Publications/Staff-Discussion-Notes/Issues/2016/12/31/Inequality-and-Labor-Market-Institutions-42987

Morgenson, R. and Rosner, J. (2023) *These Are the Plunderers: How Private Equity Runs — and Wrecks — America,* New York: Simon & Schuster.

Organisation for Economic Cooperation and Development (2022) *OECD Handbook on Competition Policy in the Digital Age*, Paris: OECD Publishing. https://www.oecd.org/en/publications/oecd-handbook-on-competition-policy-in-the-digital-age_c8c1841b-en.html

Rodrik, D. and Stantcheva, S. (2021) 'Fixing Capitalism's Good Jobs Problem', *Oxford Review of Economic Policy,* 37(4): 824–837. https://doi.org/10.1093/oxrep/grab024

PART II

TRADE

4. International trade since the Washington Consensus: the gains and the pains

Dave Donaldson

Controversy has always swirled around 'trade liberalisation' – and perhaps more so than for any other policy on Williamson's original Washington Consensus list. Anti-globalisation protests in the 1990s and early 2000s sharpened scepticism of the idea that developing countries could reliably grow if they opened their markets to foreign imports. And two decades later, globalisation remains as divisive as ever. This chapter discusses accumulating evidence that liberalising a nation's international trade gives rise to substantial aggregate gains and yet also substantial costs of adjustment and displacement. However, the trade-off involved is no different from any other policy change that strives to raise aggregate efficiency. While there are no easy options for policymakers who must balance the gains and pains from trade, lessons from recent research offer tentative recommendations for policymakers who are evaluating the prospects of trade liberalisation and seeking to resolve the tension between aggregate gains and concentrated losses.

I. Introduction

When John Williamson coined the term 'Washington Consensus' over 30 years ago, one imagines that policy prescriptions related to 'trade liberalisation' may have flown particularly freely from his pen. But controversy has always swirled around this particular policy – perhaps more so than any other on Williamson's list. Anti-globalisation protests in the 1990s and early 2000s sharpened scepticism of the idea that developing countries could reliably grow if they opened their markets to foreign imports. And two decades later, globalisation remains as divisive as ever.

How to cite this book chapter:

Donaldson, Dave (2025) 'International trade since the Washington Consensus: the gains and the pains', in: Besley, Tim, Bucelli, Irene and Velasco, Andrés (eds) *The London Consensus: Economic Principles for the 21st Century*, London: LSE Press, pp. 117–142 https://doi.org/10.31389/lsepress.tlc.d

Yet, this time there's a vital difference. While many developing countries now embrace trade openness with unprecedented enthusiasm, the centre of gravity for resistance to globalisation has moved to some of the world's richest countries – and to the very heart of their politics. What are we to make of these evolving debates?

Taking the research on globalisation and its consequences since the Washington Consensus was laid out in 1989, two main themes emerge.

First, recent studies have shown that, for most countries and in most circumstances, the aggregate efficiency gains from being open to foreign trade are substantial. The 'aggregate' concept to which this research refers can be thought of as the total amount of consumption a nation can enjoy, without considering the distribution of these goods and services. While it is challenging to quantify the aggregate effects of trade, I believe that we can be more confident than ever in the broad view invoked in the Washington Consensus: that trade openness raises aggregate living standards. In fact, given changes to the global economy since 1989, the size of the aggregate gains available to most countries may also be greater than ever. And so – setting aside the potentially uneven distribution of the costs and benefits of globalisation – both evolving evidence and evolving fundamentals suggest that good policy should, most of the time, favour liberal trade.

But the second key lesson from recent research highlights the naïveté of the previous paragraph: the uneven effects of globalisation cannot be ignored. Changes in the size and composition of trade flows have markedly unequal effects on earnings across individuals. This was never in dispute: for example, 80 years ago the Stolper–Samuelson theorem described how income inequality in industrialised countries would rise as a result of trade with developing ones, and even as the Washington Consensus took root some researchers drew important attention to the potentially unequal outcomes of globalisation.[1] But recent empirical work has shown just how unequal these effects can be – and how they can show up in ways that may have surprised economists from Stolper and Samuelson to those behind the Consensus in 1989.

Take the expectation that any unequal effects would be dissipated by, for example, workers changing firms, regions or occupations: research now routinely documents just how slow, costly, and incomplete this adjustment process can be. Or the belief that unequal effects on earnings would not pass through to consumption, thanks to the taxes and transfers that hold up an effective social safety net: in the few places where researchers have been able to look, the effects of trade shocks on earnings before and after redistribution look similar, implying that the social safety net is far from perfect. What's more, the social consequences of these unequal effects may be even larger than thought in 1989. Recent evidence suggests the presence of a 'social multiplier' of economic distress: that when harm is concentrated in one community, it can have even more destructive consequences.

The upshot of these two themes – aggregate gains and concentrated pains – is that countries considering a more liberal approach to trade will have to evaluate how the consequences will be distributed across society, both in terms of the transition to a more open economy, and the possibility that the volatility of underlying labour demand shocks will be worse once the economy is more open. But I discuss a set of guidelines below.

One key point about unequal effects of globalisation, however, must be emphasised. Recent evidence tells us that the costs and benefits of economic change are borne unequally – especially when it occurs quickly and is clustered within communities. But the same is true of all economic change. It is hard to imagine any element of the Washington Consensus, which was focused on aggregate efficiency rather than inequality, that is immune to the updated caveats described here.

My discussion proceeds as follows. The first section describes our understanding of the magnitude of the aggregate gains from trade, as well as how trade can be facilitated by policy levers beyond mere liberal tariff policy. The next section outlines how trade transitions, such as the sorts of expansions in openness that we expect to produce aggregate gains, come with large transition costs of adjustment. And the final section provides tentative recommendations for policymakers who are evaluating the prospects of trade liberalisation, and seeking to resolve the tension between aggregate gains and concentrated losses.

II. The aggregate gains from international trade

Three strands of evidence from recent research have bolstered the belief that aggregate benefits from trade are likely to be large.

The first involves studies of natural experiments resulting from external shocks that temporarily reshaped countries' openness to trade.

The closing of the Suez Canal between 1967 and 1975 created one such experiment.[2] Suddenly, the shortest distance of sea-based travel between some pairs of countries rose considerably, whereas that between others was not affected at all. This means that, due to their position on the globe, countries were differentially exposed to the Suez closure, with some countries, like India, suffering from a lengthening of many of their important trading routes and others, like Japan, escaping relatively unscathed. The more affected a country was, the greater the reduction in its trade – but this effect reverted once the canal reopened. Similarly, gross domestic product (GDP) per capita in those countries also fell substantially – and reverted to trend upon the canal's reopening. Putting these two findings together, with the plausible assumption that the Suez closure had no other direct effects on GDP per capita beyond changes in trade flows, one study found the sensitivity of real GDP per capita to changes in trade openness to be very large, with an elasticity of per-capita income to trade flows of at least 0.25. This means that every 10% increase in trade openness corresponds to a 2.5% change in per capita income.

Other research has pursued a similar line of inquiry based on the growth of air shipping throughout the second half of the 20th century, which affected countries differently due to their positions on the globe.[3] In this case, the implied effect of trade on aggregate efficiency was many times larger than was found in the Suez study – though this may reflect the effect of air exposure on economic mechanisms beyond those working through trade, such as foreign investment.

The second strand of evidence that has emerged is the accumulation of theoretical and econometric understanding of the 'standard' model of international trade.[4] The basic idea is quite simple. It involves a model economy with broad sectors of production across which there is little ability for consumers to substitute. Within each sector the inputs, beyond primary factors like labour and capital, involve goods made in other sectors, often with little ability for producers to substitute across such inputs, both primary and produced. Finally, when it comes to sourcing the different versions of products produced within each sector, whether for final consumption or for intermediate production use, buyers in the model can only substitute imperfectly across the versions produced domestically relative to those available from abroad. This imperfect domestic–foreign substitutability gives rise to aggregate gains from trade.

Such product differentiation can arise for many reasons. One could argue that it derives from comparative productivity differences, adjusted for wages, among supplying locations around the world. Or it could be that firms, both at home and abroad, make investments in product differentiation, and as a result produce different goods. Either way, at an aggregate level, the result is that when a country buys goods, the domestic versions usually appear to be imperfect substitutes for foreign versions – and empirical estimates do suggest that the implied rate of this substitutability is relatively low. This means that the aggregate gains from trade openness can be large, particularly for small countries that have fewer domestic substitutes for the large set of input suppliers that exist abroad. According to one estimate, a moderately open country, such as Canada, would experience a drop in per capita income of 30–40% if it were to prohibit international trade, whereas for a more closed country like Australia this number is in the 7–16% range.[5] On the other hand, if Australia were as open as Canada – a fanciful thought, perhaps, but also not beyond the realm of possibility with the growth of nearby Asian partners and the rise of services trade – it is possible that it would enjoy substantial gains from the rise in openness.

The third strand of evidence one could point to is more circumstantial, but it still deserves to be taken seriously. It is simply the case – just as it was at the time of the Washington Consensus – that it is hard to find examples of countries that have grown dramatically without being open to foreign trade. Just as an earlier generation would point to the East Asian 'miracle' countries of Hong Kong, Japan, Malaysia, Singapore, South Korea, and Taiwan, an updated list of countries where surges in living standards seem plausibly related to international trade could include Bangladesh, Botswana, Chile, the Dominican Republic, Panama, Peru, Thailand, and Vietnam – and perhaps China and India as well.

Beyond the preceding discussion of evidence, it seems likely that the fundamentals of the global economy have evolved in a way that has only increased the potential gains from trade. For example, improvements in communication technologies have expanded the scope for international outsourcing, trade in services and goods, and the modern web of international supply chains that we now take for granted. Equally, expansions of foreign direct investment have girded the set of arrangements under which goods can be produced far from where they are consumed.

For all of these reasons, I believe that the empirical and theoretical argument supporting large aggregate gains from international trade is in fact stronger today than it was at the time of the Washington Consensus.

1. *How to promote trade*

The Washington Consensus focused on reducing impediments to imports via the reduction of import tariffs and the removal of quantitative restrictions. But recent research has established how tariffs and quotas may comprise only a small subset of the reasons that trade is inhibited. In this sense, a modern prescription for liberal trade can appeal to a wider vision of open trade policy than was emphasised in the Washington Consensus.

On the importing side, red tape, slow processing, insufficient port capacity, slow highways and railroads, and even blatant corruption at border crossings and ports, can all be severe impediments to the free flow of trade, much like explicit taxes and quotas. And many of these same features apply symmetrically to the export side. More export-specific policies, on the other hand, include export processing zones, special economic zones, export banks, trade fairs, and economic diplomacy. The science of evaluating such policies – comparing the trade efficiency bang to the administrative buck – is still in its infancy, but in many settings the net social gains from overcoming obstacles to the movement of goods appear to be positive.

Another broad lesson concerns the nature of such impediments. While tariffs are usually an explicitly variable tax, per-unit quantity or value, increasing evidence points towards a fixed cost of exporting or importing that inherently derives from non-tariff considerations. Around the world there is a striking tendency for large firms to do much more international trading than small firms, which indicates the presence of economies of scale in exporting activities.

Other recent evidence clarifies just how much international trade takes place within the borders of multinational firms.[6] This suggests the presence of synergies between a nation's trade policy and its openness to foreign direct investment. It stands to reason that multinationals may be unwilling to locate in countries where their access to foreign goods and services is costly – especially when those are sourced from within the firm itself. The country that wants to attract foreign investment may find that it must allow free trade in the types of goods and services that are complements for those investments.

2. *Managed trade*

Many of the examples of export-led growth referred to above – such as Japan, Taiwan, or Korea – invoke images of countries that adroitly 'manage' their trade by selectively promoting sectors. By contrast, the Washington Consensus on trade policy explicitly advocated for both low and uniform tariffs. If the goal of trade policy is only to enhance aggregate efficiency, then arguments for strategically managed trade must rest on the presence of market failures. Important examples include environmental externalities, knowledge spillovers in production and innovation, and market power. In the absence of such market failures, aggregate efficiency – and hence per-capita income – will only fall if policies attempt to enlarge favoured sectors at the expense of others.

While domestic market failures surely exist, it is important to recognise that, in principle, the best way to address such problems is domestic policy, not trade policy. In most cases, it would be surprising if the best way to grow an industry were anything other than industrial policy targeted at that industry. While it is possible that pragmatic constraints on policy choices could mean trade policy is after all the best way to correct a domestic market failure, it is hard to imagine that this would generally be the case. Strategies for measuring market failures and designing policies to correct them, ideally in ways that can resist capture by special interest groups, are discussed in other chapters of this volume.

III. The concentrated losses – and painful adjustments – of international trade

It was once held plausible that most workers in a modern economy were endowed with relatively general and malleable skills, capable of retraining in a matter of years. Likewise, that these same workers would be willing and able to uproot themselves and move elsewhere in search of work. Put together, it seemed that 'exposure' to any economic change, such as the liberalisation of a country's international trade policy, would differ in accordance with broad skill groups, but not a worker's occupation, firm of employment, or location of residence.

Recent research has highlighted just how simplistic this 'broad skill groups' view appears to have been. There is by now a great deal of evidence showing that many factors of production, and especially workers, provide services that are extremely specific to their current economic activities, taken to mean the mixture of occupation, industry, region, or even firm at which they are employed.

Such findings can still be interpreted in a skills-based framework, since one can always define a worker's skills as those that are tailored to their current occupation-industry-region-firm match. But the result is a 'hyper-specific' factors model with a plethora of workers possessing different types of skills, each to be affected by trade in myriad directions. That said, it may still be useful to imagine a long-run version of such a model in which workers of the same broad skill group are able to transition from one sector, occupation, firm, and/or region to another. But then the crucial question becomes an empirical one: how costly and long-lived is this adjustment process?

To summarise the answers to this question, it helps to start with the 'job displacement' literature in labour economics. Studies of this sort isolate cases in which a worker-firm match ends, for reasons plausibly unrelated to the productivity of the worker in question. Mass lay-off events are a classic example. Numerous scholars have documented the recurring pattern that, on average, when a worker loses their job in such a manner, the resulting reduction in earnings is extremely large – not just in the immediate sense, but for years to come.[7] Earnings are not only lost while unemployed or out of the labour force, but also upon re-employment, which suggests that the typical job found by a displaced worker is one that is less suited to their skills or circumstances.

The mass lay-off events that drive estimates in the job displacement literature need not have anything to do with international trade. But a recent body of differential exposure studies does estimate effects of import competition on worker earnings that appear consistent with the wider displacement literature.[8] For example, one prominent study followed all US workers employed in manufacturing in 1992 and ranked them according to the extent to which their 1992 industry of employment would go on to see an increase in imports from China over the coming decades. According to such a ranking, researchers can follow the earnings trajectory of two workers: one at a high amount (say, the 75th percentile) of such exposure to import competition and one at a comparatively low amount (say, the 25th percentile). Even though these two workers saw a similar path of earnings prior to 1992, their fortunes subsequently diverged. By 2007 the total accumulated earnings of the highly exposed worker were, on average, lower than that of the less exposed worker by about half of one year's salary.

Findings like these are striking. But they need to be interpreted with care. For one, these studies use theoretical reasoning to differentiate types of workers according to their exposure to trade events, and such reasoning often considers only a subset of mechanisms through which trade events can affect people. This is a necessary and deliberate aspect of the study's research design, since exposure is itself a concept that is guided by the researcher's theory and prior beliefs, but it inevitably shapes what we learn from the evidence.

One way to see this is to consider four simple mechanisms by which a tariff reduction affects individuals in any economy. The first and the focus of the aforementioned studies involves import competition: that a worker in a given sector is likely to suffer reduced earnings or employment when their country imports more goods in that sector. However, an equally important second mechanism involves exports. Most countries find that their trade balance – the difference between its total imports and total exports – does not respond to a change in its tariffs, especially over relatively long-run time horizons, such as a few years. So, there can be no such thing as an event that permanently raises imports without raising exports too. Whenever we find workers who are competing with newly imported goods, there must be other workers who are enjoying a commensurate export boom of approximately equal size, and even countries that do see growing trade imbalances must be experiencing capital inflows that create an investment boom that may have similar effects. A third mechanism returns to the importing side of the ledger but observes that many firms themselves use imported goods as productive inputs via global supply chains. In this case the effect on workers is ambiguous, depending on whether the worker is a complement or a substitute for the imported goods. Finally, a fourth way that trade affects workers looks beyond their role in production and to their role as consumers. We expect that greater availability of foreign goods will reduce prices, giving purchasing power benefits to all workers, regardless of whether their nominal earnings are helped or harmed by trade.

Quantifying, combining, and disentangling these four mechanisms is challenging, not just because of the data required, but also because not all researchers will agree on the right way to define a given individual's exposure to any given channel. Adding to the challenge is the fact that our discussion of these mechanisms has so far only covered so-called direct versions of these phenomena. Indirect versions can also percolate through the domestic economy and easily affect workers in seemingly immune sectors, including those in non-traded activities.[9] To illustrate this, consider three law firms that each exclusively work for three types of domestic clients: import-competing firms, export-oriented firms, and input-importing firms. These law firms do not directly trade anything, but the lawyers who work in them could be just as exposed, indirectly, to the mechanisms of trade as are the workers of their clients. Such indirect effects are dauntingly complex in a modern economy – and even if we could penetrate that complexity, the resulting differences in worker exposure may be so slight that we would struggle to pick them up with differential exposure designs. Nonetheless, many small indirect effects of this kind are very likely to add up to something larger.

Another reason to interpret such findings from differential exposure studies with caution is that these studies are deliberately designed around the goal of providing convincing estimates of relative effects, not aggregate effects. This means that any mechanism that affects all workers equally will go unmeasured. For example, suppose that all workers consume goods according to similar budget shares. In such a case it would be impossible to use differential exposure designs to estimate the consumer price benefits of trade since there is no way to find a non-exposed worker to use as a reference point of 'zero' around which the effects on others can be benchmarked. Indeed, it is typically found that workers who are relatively exposed to greater import competition experienced a reduction in their earnings relative to the earnings of other workers. But this cannot be interpreted as evidence of import penetration actually harming the former group of workers. It is entirely possible that imports caused the earnings (especially the real earnings, incorporating consumption price effects) of both types of workers to rise, implying that no one experienced any actual harm in an absolute sense.

Given these reasons for caution, it is not at all clear how one could use such differential exposure studies to quantify the aggregate effects of trade. But that concern need not trouble us here. The previous section summarised the case for the aggregate effects of trade, appealing to a different sort of evidence that was aggregate in nature, by design. Instead, what studies of differential exposure do illuminate is a sense of just how costly it may be to adapt to shocks, such as an increase in international trade.

Why is this the case? Suppose that two workers have similar skills and live in the same location, but we initially observe them working in different sectors. The economy then opens up to international trade, with imports flooding into one of the two sectors, resulting in a contraction in this import-competing sector. If it were costless for workers to move across the two sectors then we would never see a differential effect on the two workers' earnings – their differential exposure based on initial sectors would be irrelevant because no mobility costs tie them down to such initial conditions. By contrast, if adjustment is costly then we would see differential effects. Going further, if adjustment were costly for two years and free thereafter then we would see differential earnings that follow this same pattern: large for two years and zero thereafter. Seen in this light, the fact that differential exposure studies find such large relative effects, and often for several decades, implies that adjustment costs must be large, even on multi-decadal time horizons.

One point that often gets lost in discussions of this theme is that adjustment costs are, clearly, all about change. That is, whatever weight one attaches to the importance of such costs, that weight should be applied symmetrically to views about both liberalising and hindering trade. The broad push towards greater openness ensconced in the Washington Consensus will have costs of adjustment that are unequally borne, but the same would be true if one considered any other change in the tariff code, such as a move to enhanced protectionism. Adjustment costs speak in favour of maintaining the status quo, not against any particular direction of change.

In the presence of adjustment costs, any changes in a nation's trade policy are likely to produce both winners and losers, especially in relative terms. This is not a surprising statement for those who are used to thinking about international trade. But it is important to remember that the identities of the relatively helped and harmed are unlikely to map neatly onto standard notions of inequality. For example, in a model with exposure based on broad skill groups, we know that if low-human capital workers are those relatively harmed by a shock then income inequality will go up. But when the unequal effects of trade instead play out along dimensions such as workers' firms, occupations, regions or sectors, we lose the ability to make easy connections to income inequality. On the other hand, if social evaluations of inequality are based on changes rather than levels, then concentrated losses caused by trade reforms may be considered harmful regardless of what they do to the shape of the income distribution.

IV. Does policy help with the costs of adjustment? Does it need to do?

The above discussion described earnings effects that are measured at the 'factory gate'. But one might imagine the idyllic extreme in which social policies serve to ensure that workers' earnings are decoupled from the vagaries of their pre-tax and transfer earnings.

There is surely no country that comes close to this level of protection against negative shocks and, equally, in which unexpectedly positive earnings are completely taxed away. Obvious factors, grounded in asymmetric information, place severe limits on the feasibility of such social insurance schemes. But it remains an important empirical question to ask just how far the average worker is from the full insurance limit when it comes to the consequences of trade liberalisation.

This has been studied in the context of the US response to the expansion of imported goods from China.[10] Despite the existence of the Trade Adjustment Assistance programme, which aims to help workers displaced by shocks from international trade, and other forms of redistributive assistance, such as tax policy and unemployment insurance, research has found that the estimated effects of the import shock on post-redistribution earnings are very similar to those on pre-redistribution earnings. At least in this particular context, there is clearly not much trade-adjustment redistribution happening in practice.

In the absence of social insurance, perhaps individuals' self-insurance – whether due to formal insurance schemes, the ability to borrow and save, or the help of friends and family – would mean that shocks to even post-redistribution incomes have little bearing on consumption. Data limitations make it especially challenging to quantify the pass-through of trade shocks to consumption. But it stands to reason that we would not see the sort of social harm from job loss described below in a world of complete formal and/or informal insurance.

A final consideration about private insurance mechanisms concerns the speed of adjustment being asked of households and their social networks in response to a given policy change. With real-world constraints on access to insurance and credit markets, households would be able to cope with a stream of small shocks better than a sudden and large one. Following this logic, researchers have derived the optimal rate of gradualism for a given policy reform as a function of the extent to which borrowing limits depend on borrowers' collateral and how unevenly wealth is distributed throughout the economy.[11] What is unclear, however, is the extent to which smooth policy changes actually translate into smooth household-level shocks. Even if at the macro level sectoral shrinkage driven by trade liberalisation happens slowly, if this change evolves one lay-off or factory closure at a time then at the micro level, the insult to any individual household may be sudden and large.

1. *Aggregate features of adjustment to shocks*

Another strand of research evaluates the extent to which a given worker's experience in response to a job loss is altered when others around them are also subject to the same, or related, economic turmoil. In the job displacement literature, researchers have found the total earnings lost after one's own job loss is considerably worse in a recession than in a boom – especially in the first few years after the separation, and especially for older workers.[12] This may reflect the fact that other, similar workers are also searching for re-employment, as well as a period of diminished investment by firms. Similar findings have emerged from research into Finland's experience with the collapse of its Soviet-era trading arrangements in the early 1990s.[13] Workers who were employed at plants that sold a large share of their output to the Soviet Union in 1989 suffered, on average, a substantial reduction in their relative earnings throughout the 1990s. But this effect was both considerably worse in locations where a large share of other plants were affected and also borne, albeit to a lesser degree, by workers in such locations who did not even work at one of the plants. In other words, the estimated earnings damage done, per worker, appeared to increase with the number of affected workers.

2. *Social externalities*

A final area of evidence about adjustments to trade shocks documents a set of consequences beyond earnings losses. These include the effects of relatively greater Chinese import competition on mortality rates – notably, from drug overdoses – in US localities, as well as impacts on marriage rates, fertility, and children's living circumstances.[14] In the case of Brazil's trade liberalisation, crime rates were found to rise in places more exposed to import competition.[15] Such findings highlight the social externalities that are likely to be associated with job displacement and diminished labour market prospects caused by the import competition side of trade liberalisation. However, it is possible that the export-expansion side of trade liberalisation is accompanied by analogous positive externalities – such as falling crime rates in booming regions.

V. Policy recommendations

The discussion so far can be summarised in two simple statements: first, that permitting liberal international trade is likely to engender substantial aggregate efficiency gains; and second, that changing openness to trade is likely to cause substantial adjustment costs for some workers.

Before examining the policy implications of these statements, it is important to recognise that they could be applied just as accurately to a wide range of economic policy areas, especially those covered by the Washington Consensus. This means that, in most settings, it would be incoherent to cite adverse distributional consequences of adjustment, such as the large costs of job displacement, as a reason to forego or even slow trade liberalisation while simultaneously failing to apply the same prudence to other areas such as monetary, fiscal, competition, or environmental policy.

Nonetheless, recent research suggests the following approach as a guide for policymakers:

1. Embrace the broad principle of openness to trade, because the aggregate efficiency gains from doing so are likely to be large, especially when beginning from a point of high trade barriers. Trade openness can be enhanced, on both the import and export sides, via the traditional means of reducing import tariffs and quantitative restrictions. But technical barriers, customs bureaucracy and corruption, inadequate ports and domestic transport facilities, should also be evaluated.
2. Given a proposed set of policies to boost trade, assess the relative winners and losers that are likely to result. This involves the four mechanisms previously described: (i) import competition, which displaces factor demand; (ii) export engagement, which augments it; (iii) imported inputs into production, which can either displace or augment factor demand to the extent that the inputs are substitutes or complements for the factors in question; and (iv) cheaper prices for imported consumer goods, which should broadly benefit all factors. Further, such an assessment must incorporate the indirect versions of these mechanisms. For example, the workers of firms whose clients are in an import-competing sector may be just as exposed as workers in the import-competing sector itself, even if this exposure is less apparent.[16]
3. Assess the pre-redistribution earnings consequences of a typical job displacement event in the country of interest. If the consequences of factor demand displacement are expected to be borne most heavily by those who lose their jobs and have to transition to new ones, a crucial consideration concerns how long this transition will typically take, as well as the size of any long-run drop in earnings upon re-employment. This may depend on features such as labour market policies and the costs of geographic mobility.[17]
4. Assess the extent to which these pre-redistribution earnings effects pass through into post-redistribution earnings and consumption in the setting of interest. The degree of such pass-through depends on the social safety net, and in particular those policies relevant to the types of relatively long-lived and secular displacement shocks that come with expanding trade. In low-income settings, informal safety nets may be important to assess as well.
5. Assess the extent to which job displacement shocks are likely to involve large 'multipliers' in the setting of interest. This occurs when shocks

that are particularly concentrated – in space, sectors, occupations or firms – have worse effects than those that are spread out.

6. Assess the risk that job displacement, especially when it causes costly consumption losses and is particularly concentrated, creates deleterious social costs such as crime or political unrest.
7. When the costs identified in the previous three points are particularly high, trade liberalisation is likely to come with severe disruption, borne unevenly by the population. In such a case, search for ways to reduce the costs of transition. One strategy is to enhance social safety nets, retraining programmes, and the like, particularly in the places where job displacement is likely to be felt. A second strategy would be to modify the trade liberalisation plan to limit such losses by design – that is, by tailoring it *ex ante* to avoid introducing a constellation of shocks that, for example, due to the presence of multipliers may be particularly harmful.

VI. Concluding remarks

Like so many efficiency-enhancing policies, liberalising a nation's international trade gives rise to substantial aggregate gains and yet also substantial costs of adjustment and displacement. Such choices often prove controversial. While there are no easy options for policymakers who confront this trade-off, lessons from recent research, as described in this chapter, have highlighted the types of events and settings that may be particularly costly. This should empower policymakers to evaluate and implement the types of aggregate efficiency-improving reforms at the heart of the Washington Consensus better than they were able to in 1989.

In this regard, trade liberalisation displays many similarities to the other items on John Williamson's list. However, a distinct feature of trade legislation is that it can be targeted in unusually detailed respects. For example, most countries can, and typically do, set different tariffs and non-tariff measures on thousands of unique products, and then further tailor these tariffs to specific trading partners through the use of trade agreements, as well as anti-dumping and countervailing duties. In contrast, other policy areas are inherently difficult to target, such as monetary policy, or are typically applied with broad brushstrokes in practice, such as those in fiscal or environmental domains. In principle, the freedom to engage in the hyper-targeting permitted by trade policy is no bad thing. But in reality, one does not have to look far to find examples of the abuse of such discretion in the favour of special interest groups who lobby most successfully for policy advantages that harm society as a whole. Policymakers need courage to resist such pressures and the Washington Consensus serves as a reminder that the aggregate dividends afforded by trade openness are worth fighting for.

Notes

[1] Rodrik (1997); Wood (1995).

[2] Feyrer (2021).

[3] Feyrer (2019).

[4] For a summary of the state of this art see, for example, the survey by Costinot and Rodríguez-Clare (2014).

[5] Costinot and Rodríguez-Clare (2014).

[6] Antras et al. (2024).

[7] Jacobson et al. (1993).

[8] Examples include Topalova (2010) on India; Autor et al. (2013), Autor et al. (2014), and Pierce and Schott (2016) on the United States; and Dix-Carneiro and Kovak (2017) on Brazil.

[9] Adao et al. (2022).

[10] Autor et al. (2013).

[11] Beraja and Zorzi (2023).

[12] Davis and von Wachter (2011).

[13] Costinot et al. (2022).

[14] Autor et al. (2019); Pierce and Schott (2020).

[15] Dix-Carneiro et al. (2018).

[16] The methods in Adao et al. (2022) can be used to conduct such an assessment.

[17] The methods in Bertheau et al. (2023) provide guidance on how such an assessment can be done, and this study's specific findings may potentially inform other contexts.

References

Adao, R., Carrillo, P., Costinot, A., Donaldson, D. and Pomeranz, D. (2022) 'Imports, Exports, and Earnings Inequality: Measures of Exposure and Estimates of Incidence', *The Quarterly Journal of Economics*, 137(3): 1553–1614. https://doi.org/10.1093/qje/qjac012

Antras, P., Fadeev, E., Fort, T. and Tintelnot, F. (2024) 'Exporting, Global Sourcing, and Multinational Activity: Theory and Evidence from the United States', *The Review of Economics and Statistics*, 1–48. https://doi.org/10.1162/rest_a_01450

Autor, D., Dorn, D. and Hanson, G. H. (2013) 'The China Syndrome: Local Labor Market Effects of Import Competition in the United States', *American Economic Review*, 103(6): 2121–2168. https://doi.org/10.1257/aer.103.6.2121

Autor, D., Dorn, D., Hanson, G. H. and Song, J. (2014) 'Trade Adjustment: Worker-Level Evidence', *The Quarterly Journal of Economics*, 129(4): 1799–1860. https://doi.org/10.1093/qje/qju026

Autor, D., Dorn, D. and Hanson, G. (2019) 'When Work Disappears: Manufacturing Decline and the Falling Marriage Market Value of Young Men', *American Economic Review: Insights*, 1(2): 161–78. https://doi.org/10.1257/aeri.20180010

Beraja, M. and Zorzi, N. (2023) 'Inefficient Automation', Working Paper 30154, National Bureau of Economic Research. https://economics.mit.edu/sites/default/files/inline-files/Inefficient%20Automation_Revised.pdf

Bertheau, A., Acabbi, E. A., Barceló, C., Gulyas, A., Lombardi, S. and Saggio, R. (2023) 'The Unequal Consequences of Job Loss across Countries', *American Economic Review: Insights*, 5(3): 393–408. https://doi.org/10.1257/aeri.20220006

Costinot, A. and Rodríguez-Clare, A. (2014) 'Trade Theory with Numbers: Quantifying the Consequences of Globalization', in Gopinath, G., Helpman, E. and Rogoff, K. (eds) *Handbook of International Economics*, Vol. 4., Elsevier; 197–261.

Costinot, A., Sarvimaki, M. and Vogel, J. (2022) 'Exposure(s) to Trade and Earnings Dynamics: Evidence from the Collapse of Finnish-Soviet Trade', MIT working paper. https://economics.mit.edu/sites/default/files/publications/Scarring_LATEST.pdf

Davis, S. J. and von Wachter, T. (2011) 'Recessions and the Costs of Job Loss', Brookings Papers on Economic Activity, Fall, 1–72. https://www.brookings.edu/articles/recessions-and-the-costs-of-job-loss/

Dix-Carneiro, R. and Kovak, B. K. (2017) 'Trade Liberalization and Regional Dynamics', *American Economic Review*, 107.10: 2908–2946. https://doi.org/10.1257/aer.20161214

Dix-Carneiro, R., Soares, R. R. and Ulyssea, G. (2018) 'Economic Shocks and Crime: Evidence from the Brazilian Trade Liberalization', *American Economic Journal: Applied Economics*, 10(4): 158–195. https://doi.org/10.1257/app.20170080

Feyrer, J. (2019) 'Trade and Income—Exploiting Time Series in Geography', *American Economic Journal: Applied Economics*, 11(4): 1–35. https://doi.org/10.1257/app.20170616

Feyrer, J. (2021) 'Distance, Trade, and Income – The 1967 to 1975 Closing of the Suez Canal as a Natural Experiment', *Journal of Development Economics*, 153: 102708. https://doi.org/10.1016/j.jdeveco.2021.102708

Jacobson, L. S., LaLonde, R. J. and Sullivan, D. G. (1993) 'Earnings Losses of Displaced Workers', *American Economic Review*, 83(4): 685-709.

Pierce, J. R. and Schott, P. K. (2016) 'The Surprisingly Swift Decline of US Manufacturing Employment', *American Economic Review*, 106(7): 1632–62. https://doi.org/10.1257/aer.20131578

Pierce, J. R. and Schott, P. K. (2020) 'Trade Liberalization and Mortality: Evidence from US Counties', *American Economic Review: Insights*, 2(1): 47–64. https://doi.org/10.1257/aeri.20180396

Rodrik, D. (1997) *Has Globalization Gone Too Far?* Washington, DC: Institute for International Economics.

Topalova, P. (2010) 'Factor Immobility and Regional Impacts of Trade Liberalization: Evidence on Poverty from India', *American Economic Journal: Applied Economics*, 2(4): 1–41. https://doi.org/10.1257/app.2.4.1

Wood, A. (1995) *North-South Trade, Employment and Inequality Changing Fortunes in a Skill-Driven World*, Oxford: Oxford University Press.

Response to Dave Donaldson by Thomas Sampson

The three decades since John Williamson proposed the Washington Consensus have seen an explosion of empirical research on international trade. Aided by more disaggregated datasets and increased computational power, researchers have shed new light on the causes and consequences of cross-border trade. Dave Donaldson elegantly synthesises the findings of this literature and the ways in which the new evidence does – or does not – require us to re-evaluate the role of trade liberalisation in the Washington Consensus.

Donaldson highlights two main themes. First, under most circumstances there are likely to be substantial aggregate gains from openness to foreign trade. This conclusion is consistent with Williamson's arguments for trade liberalisation, but there is now more evidence to support his position than was available 30 years ago. While the evidence establishes a presumption in favour of openness, it also suggests that the gains from trade are likely to differ across countries. In particular, smaller countries have more to gain because they are more reliant on overseas production and demand. To give one example, Arnaud Costinot and Andrés Rodríguez-Clare estimate that the gains from trade are two to three times greater for the United Kingdom than for the United States.[1] Such differences imply that the stakes at play in trade policy debates vary dramatically across countries.

While Donaldson's first theme reinforces Williamson's position, his second strikes a note absent from the original Washington Consensus. Trade policy not only affects aggregate efficiency, but also has important distributional consequences. That trade can, in theory, affect the distributions of income and consumption has long been known. What has changed since Williamson made his proposal is the steady accretion of evidence documenting distributional effects and establishing that they are often both large and long lasting. Adjustment to trade liberalisation is frequently slow and costly with the costs primarily borne by those – be they workers, firms, industries, or regions – that find themselves unable to compete with foreign production. In principle, the state could compensate these losers and support them in transitioning to new activities. In practice, any support provided is generally insufficient to meet their needs.

Thus, Donaldson concludes that while policymakers should continue to seek ways to promote trade openness, they should also pay greater attention to the distributional consequences of proposed reforms and attempt to ensure losses are sectorally and spatially dispersed. How policies can best be designed to reap the benefits of trade openness while minimising adjustment and distributional costs is a question that researchers are only now starting to grapple with, particularly when it comes to addressing social consequences at the level of communities and regions. But, as a starting point, it is worth exploring how policies can be tailored to allow for gradual adjustment, avoid concentrated losses, and provide meaningful support to people, firms, and communities facing the biggest shocks.

However, it is important to remember that the new evidence on the distributional impacts of trade does not provide any rationale for reversing trade liberalisation or for rejecting international cooperation in trade policy formation. For seven decades after World War II governments and international institutions gradually reduced barriers to trade, often through international agreements. The General Agreement on Tariffs and Trade (GATT) proved an effective forum for reducing import tariffs on a multilateral basis, while many countries pursued deeper integration with their most important trading partners through preferential trade agreements such as the European Union (EU) and the North American Free Trade Agreement. The fall of the Soviet bloc also increased integration as former communist states joined the world trading system.

But in the past decade this trend has been interrupted by a return to nationalism in trade policy, most prominently manifested by Brexit, the collapse of the World Trade Organization's (WTO) dispute settlement system, and the US–China trade war. These developments stem, at least in part, from concerns over the distributional consequences of trade. However, we should not expect them to succeed in addressing such concerns.

One reason they will not succeed is that the costs of adjusting to trade liberalisation arise primarily not from liberalisation itself, but from the necessity of adjustment. Any technology or policy shock that shifts production across occupations, firms, industries, or regions will generate adjustment costs, including shocks that result from increased barriers to trade. As Donaldson nicely puts it: 'Adjustment costs speak in favour of maintaining the status quo, not against any particular direction of change'. Provided we accept that change is inevitable, policy should seek not to prevent change but to dampen and share any costs that change brings. Reversing trade liberalisation simply introduces a new shock for agents to grapple with.

But a more fundamental problem with the protectionist turn in trade policy is that it overlooks Donaldson's first theme: the existence of aggregate gains from trade. Acknowledging these potential gains, the key challenge for policymakers is not to prevent trade shocks, but to identify ways to reduce barriers to trade while minimising adjustment costs. Donaldson's discussion focuses on policies that can be implemented unilaterally – customs capacity, transport infrastructure, export support – all of which are undoubtedly valuable. I would add to this list the importance of participating in and supporting international institutions that promote openness by facilitating trade policy cooperation.

Why is international cooperation important? Trade policy generates cross-border externalities that national policymakers do not internalise. When acting unilaterally countries have incentives to adopt policies that are more protectionist than is globally efficient in order to improve their terms of trade or shift profits across countries. And the protectionist impulse may be further magnified by producers lobbying for import protection. International negotiations provide a forum for countries to reduce inefficient protectionism and make all countries better off by trading market access commitments.[2] Trade policy institutions such as GATT/WTO and regional trade agreements facilitate these negotiations and help avoid mutually destructive trade wars. The recent turn to economic nationalism undermines this system of international cooperation by instead prioritising national control over trade policy.

The economic costs of rejecting internationalism are readily apparent from research on current President Donald Trump's trade policy. Increased tariffs on US imports raised prices paid by US consumers and users of imported intermediate inputs without improving US terms of trade, leaving the US as a whole worse-off.[3] Moreover, retaliatory tariffs imposed by countries including China and the EU reduced US exports and increased prices in these countries. Overall, the evidence shows that the trade war harmed all participants, offering a reminder of why international trade policy institutions were established following the trade wars of the 1930s.

Brexit offers a more nuanced, but no less instructive, case study of the risks of unilateral trade policy. Whereas President Trump's rationale for raising tariffs was avowedly protectionist, many proponents of Brexit argued that it would enhance free trade by allowing the UK to reduce trade barriers with the rest of the world.[4] And since the UK voted to leave the EU in 2016, successive UK governments have framed their trade policy in terms of a 'Global Britain' strategy to promote openness. However, actual policy choices have not delivered on these aspirations. Although the UK has signed new free trade agreements with Australia and New Zealand, it has not secured deals with larger markets, such as the US. More importantly, the government has – despite its stated intentions – repeatedly backed away from unilateral liberalisation.

The debate over the UK's most-favoured nation (MFN) tariffs provides one example of why unilateral liberalisation has proved elusive for Brexit Britain. Upon leaving the EU's customs union, the UK regained control over the MFN tariffs it charges on imports from other WTO members. Initially, the UK proposed a substantial liberalisation that would have increased the share of its MFN imports facing zero tariffs from 52% under the EU's tariff schedule to 96%.[5]

But this proposal ran into two difficulties. First, domestic producers objected to greater import competition and lobbied to maintain existing protection. Second, the proposed tariff schedule reduced the incentive for other countries to strike trade deals with the UK. Canada paused negotiations on rolling over its existing trade agreement with the EU to cover the UK post-Brexit and linked the pause to the prospect of obtaining tariff-free access to the UK market without needing a trade deal.[6] In the face of these difficulties the UK backtracked and adopted a new schedule much closer to the EU's MFN tariffs. Under the new UK tariff schedule, only 70% of MFN imports face zero tariffs.[7] After the UK announced its less liberal tariff schedule, negotiations with Canada resumed and a rollover deal was eventually reached.

The other weakness of the Global Britain argument for Brexit was that it ignored the costs of raising trade barriers with the EU. And these costs have proved to be substantial. The Brexit vote caused an immediate fall in the value of the pound, which raised import prices and reduced real wages. Uncertainty and the expectation of future increases in trade costs then led to lower investment and slower output growth, leaving the UK economy around 2–3% smaller by the end of 2019 than it otherwise would have been.[8] These costs materialised even before the UK left the EU. And the implementation of the new UK–EU trade relationship at the start of 2021 resulted in further disruption, causing UK imports from the EU to fall by around 20%.[9]

The UK's struggles illustrate that the route to greater openness lies not in unilateralism but through international negotiation and cooperation. A renewed commitment to working together – and to building, or re-building, institutions that facilitate trade liberalisation, while also affording countries the freedom to address any distributional conflicts that further openness may generate – would leave countries better placed to capture the benefits that international trade can bring, and to face future trade policy challenges.

Notes

1 Costinot and Rodríguez-Clare (2014).

2 Bagwell and Staiger (1999).

3 Fajgelbaum and Khandelwal (2022).

4 Sampson (2017).

5 Garrett et al. (2020).

6 Government of Canada (2022).

7 Garrett et al. (2020).

8 Dhingra and Sampson (2022).

9 Freeman et al. (2022).

References

Bagwell, K. and Staiger, R. W. (1999) 'An Economic Theory of GATT', *American Economic Review,* 89(1): 215–248. https://doi.org/10.1257/aer.89.1.215

Costinot, A. and Rodríguez-Clare, A. (2014) 'Trade Theory with Numbers: Quantifying the Consequences of Globalization', in Gopinath, G., Helpman, E. and Rogoff, K. (eds) *Handbook of International Economics*, Vol. 4., Elsevier: 197–261. https://doi.org/10.1016/B978-0-444-54314-1.00004-5

Dhingra, S. and Sampson, T. (2022) 'Expecting Brexit', *Annual Review of Economics,* 14: 495–519. https://doi.org/10.1146/annurev-economics-051420-104231

Fajgelbaum, P. D. and Khandelwal, A. K. (2022) 'The Economic Impacts of the US–China Trade War', *Annual Review of Economics*, 14: 205–228. https://doi.org/10.1146/annurev-economics-051420-110410

Freeman, R., Manova, K., Prayer, T. and Sampson, T. (2022) 'UK Trade in the Wake of Brexit', Centre for Economic Performance Discussion Paper 1847. https://cep.lse.ac.uk/pubs/download/dp1847.pdf

Garrett, J., Gasiorek, M. and Winters, A. L. (2020) 'New Tariff on the Block: What Is in the UK's Global Tariff?' UK Trade Policy Observatory [20 May 2020]. https://blogs.sussex.ac.uk/uktpo/2020/05/20/new-tariff-on-the-block-what-is-in-the-uks-global-tariff/

Government of Canada (2022) Canada–United Kingdom Trade Continuity Agreement Timeline [18 May 2022]. https://www.international.gc.ca/trade-commerce/trade-agreements-accords-commerciaux/agr-acc/cuktca-acccru/trade-agreement-timeline.aspx?lang=eng

Sampson, T. (2017) 'Brexit: The Economics of International Disintegration', *Journal of Economic Perspectives,* 31(4): 163–184. https://doi.org/10.1257/jep.31.4.163

Response to Dave Donaldson by Anthony Venables

The real value of world trade has grown by a factor of three since the presentation of the Washington Consensus in 1989, and trade has – until recently – grown faster than income. Openness to international trade is now the norm, with trade an important factor in the extraordinary success in lifting more than a billion people out of extreme poverty since 1989.

Trade liberalisation is one of the recommendations of the Washington Consensus. The intellectual case for trade liberalisation rests on the potential for trade to raise aggregate income – in all participating economies – as production becomes located in line with comparative advantage. The case is subject to three well-known provisos. First, while a country as a whole gains, changes in the distribution of income within a country will create both winners and losers. Second, world efficiency is lost if countries restrict trade to exploit their monopoly or monopsony power in particular goods. Third, trade should not interact adversely with distortions in each country, e.g., leading to expansion of activities with negative externalities. Standard responses to these provisos are, in turn: domestic redistribution and compensation policies can be used to sort out distributional issues; rules of the international trading system can prevent beggar-thy-neighbour tariffs or subsidies; and non-trade distortions are not a trade issue, and so are the business of other policy areas.

Intellectual developments in the years since the Washington Consensus have done much to enrich our understanding of the drivers and effects of international trade. The role played by firms has attracted research, thus giving better understanding of intra-industry trade, increasing returns to scale, and market power. International interactions through trade in global value chains, foreign direct investment in services, and intellectual property have been studied. And there is better understanding of the complex set of factors that shape firms' decisions on where to locate production and how to supply markets. On balance, these developments increase the gains from trade predicted by traditional theory. But none of them suggests that trade will lead to a 'first best' outcome. Each comes with trade-offs (e.g., between economies of scale and monopoly power), and the realisation that achieving gains may require complementary policies, beyond the range (and at variance with the spirit) of the Washington Consensus.

This note focuses on two issues, drawn from what could be a much longer list. The first is the problem of the 'left behind' – those people, and those places, that have not shared in the overall gains from trade, or that have suffered from trade-related shocks. The second is the issue of global externalities, in particular those created by carbon emissions (negative) and by the creation and transmission of knowledge (positive).

I. The left behind

Openness to trade has been used successfully by some of the fastest growing developing economies and has been an important part of growth accelerations. But other countries have been left behind, not using trade opportunities to develop new and fast growing sectors. Meanwhile, some high-income countries have experienced a different 'left behind' problem as changing patterns of comparative advantage have destroyed jobs in sectors and regions; traditional comparative advantages have been lost, while expanding sectors are based in other regions. Growing regional inequalities are apparent in many countries, creating acute problems in areas of the United Kingdom and the United States. Some of the places hit by negative trade shocks in the 1970s became deprived areas, and remain so 50 years later, stuck in a low-level trap.

Fundamentally, the gains from trade derive from places being able to expand some sectors – those in which they have a comparative advantage – while other sectors contract. The problem is that growing a new sector is harder than the textbook models of comparative advantage suggest. While every place has a comparative advantage in something, by definition, what that something is depends on policy. The simple idea that markets will lead to an efficient outcome is often incorrect. We see this where negative trade shocks have left places in a low-level trap, persistent across multiple generations, and in those countries that have failed to establish new industries that are internationally competitive. These issues are well known, and have been studied under labels such as the infant industry argument, self-discovery, and coordination failure. They are particularly acute for relatively complex sectors that require institutional, technical and knowledge support from the rest of the economy. These are the high value sectors (with relatively high value added per worker), and failure to grow them results in specialisation in relatively low-value service or resource-based activities.

Which policy responses can address this problem? Some are uncontroversial. Developing countries need the institutions, skills, and infrastructure to create a good business environment that makes them attractive for firms – including those in export sectors – to invest in. Government support for these 'general purpose' investments is widely accepted, but has often proved hard to deliver.

In high-income countries the response to job losses has often relied on workers acquiring – possibly with government support – new skills to ready them for jobs in new sectors. This too is uncontroversial, but encounters two problems. One is that the support has often not been delivered effectively or at sufficient scale, and the other is that skills alone are not sufficient to attract new sectors. 'Social multiplier' effects occur, as negative shocks trigger a vicious cycle with out-migration (principally of the young and more skilled), declining land values, shrinking local business ecosystems, and less ambitious youth aspirations. To escape – or better, to pre-empt – this low-level equilibrium a comprehensive package of 'place-based' policies may be needed. These need to involve both labour supply – the training and skill development polices traditionally suggested – and labour demand, through active policy to support lagging areas and attract investment.

In each of these cases – a developing country making the most of trade openness, or a lagging region redefining its comparative advantage – active industrial policy has a role to play. The difficulties of successfully implementing such policies are well understood, but recent work re-evaluates the possibilities and means of successful intervention.[1] Essentially, the structural changes required to make the most of trade opportunities, and to adjust to trade shocks, often require systematic policy intervention using a wider range of instruments than was envisaged in the Washington Consensus.

II. Global externalities: climate and technology

Climate change is a market failure on a global scale, of an importance that means it should top any list of policy priorities. Carbon emissions are shaped by the structure of production, and the technologies that are used, in countries around the world. These are inherently trade issues. What is an efficient pattern of production and consequent trade in goods and services, taking into account impacts on climate? How should climate imperatives change our thinking about trade-related policy? There are two broad issues here. One is to do with the pricing of carbon (and other greenhouse gases) to secure a pattern of trade that is consistent with comparative advantage but inclusive of carbon emissions in production. The second – and more important – is to do with the development and diffusion of new and greener technologies.

The first of these is conceptually straightforward, although practically difficult. For efficiency, the carbon price needs to be the same in all countries; failing this, the second best policy is a carbon border adjustment mechanism (CBAM), i.e., an import tariff that corrects the differential at the border, such that local producers are not undercut (in their domestic market, at least) by more carbon-intense foreign competition. The practical difficulty is that implementation of this policy requires knowledge of the carbon intensity of imports. Supplying this information places a considerable burden on foreign exporters and will therefore have a 'trade-chilling' effect, reducing trade beyond what is intended. Experience gained as the EU's CBAM comes into operation will be instructive.

The second issue is to ensure that the trading system supports the rapid development of green technologies, and their widespread application. Development of these technologies involves the classic market failures of increasing returns to scale and learning-by-doing, as well as coordination failure (where one element of a new technology becomes viable only when other complementary elements are in place). As such, the market will undersupply innovation, meaning efficiency requires policy support, e.g., to accelerate movement down the learning curve, as we have seen most spectacularly in the development of solar panels. Securing rapid adoption means open trade, competitive (marginal) cost pricing, and widespread diffusion of intellectual property.

These features are desirable from the standpoints of both climate and economic efficiency. However, a corollary of steep learning curves and government support is the likelihood that one country comes to dominate supply, while other countries (or firms) that are slower to secure cost reductions are outcompeted by imports. The prices of these imports may be greater than marginal cost, but are likely to be well below some (ill-defined) measure of long-run average cost. The tensions here are between the urgency of promoting technical change; the role of government support in achieving this; and the market dominance and ensuing trade patterns associated with increasing returns and learning-by-doing. These features do not fit well with current trade rules, with the political economy of importing countries, or with the need for resilience against supply shocks.

The issues pose numerous questions. How are safeguards and other elements of contingent protection to be handled? Is an import surge of cheap green products to be welcomed or restricted? Should there be rules on state aids and subsidies? Is a policy that accelerates the development and adoption of green technologies, but needs protectionist elements to make it politically feasible, to be welcomed or restricted by trade rules?

III. Concluding remarks

The principles of free trade in goods and services promoted in the Washington Consensus have delivered prosperity to many and remain sound guidance. The intellectual case for free trade remains strong, but subject to provisos that have become more important – due to experience and changing circumstances – and that need to be addressed in a new consensus.

Comparative advantage is highly conditional on policy, as demonstrated by the failure of some countries to benefit from trade liberalisation, and by the persistence of the adverse effects of negative trade shocks. Recognition of these facts needs to be a core part of a new consensus designed to enable countries to get the most from trade.

There are now externalities that are fundamentally international. Climate change is a global problem, and addressing it requires the speedy development of new technologies and their rapid dissemination. A new trade consensus must recognise the priority of policies, at the national and international level, that support growth and dissemination of these innovations.

Note

[1] See Juhász et al. (2023), and also chapters on exports and on industrial policy in this volume.

Reference

Juhász, R., Lane, N. and Rodrik, D. (2023) 'The New Economics of Industrial Policy', NBER Working Paper 31538, National Bureau of Economic Research. https://www.nber.org/system/files/working_papers/w31538/w31538.pdf

5. Export-led growth

Ricardo Hausmann

The Washington Consensus dismissed exports as an important focus of economic growth strategies. According to its principles, if countries unified exchange rates, reduced barriers to trade, and brought inflation under control, exports would adjust to their efficient level. Today, many countries have followed these precepts, and yet, the median country has not narrowed its income gap with the United States. Export performance matters for growth, with countries that grow exhibiting more than proportional export growth. In many developing and emerging economies, growth is highly correlated with exogenous movements in their export prices and on fluctuations in international capital flows. Moreover, sustained fast-growing economies change the composition of their export basket substantially towards new, more complex products. This chapter argues that a focus on exports, both at the intensive margin, but especially at the extensive margin, can help countries figure out what policies to adopt in order to achieve sustained growth. It highlights the critical role that technology adoption plays for long-term growth, but also the market failures that make the proverbial invisible hand of the market inefficient. The implication of this analysis is not a new list of fixed policies that all countries should adopt, as the way Washington Consensus intended. Instead, it is an organised and costly search process for growth opportunities, both at the intensive and extensive margins of production.

I. Introduction: exports and the Washington Consensus

Should exports be an important focus of economic growth strategies? The Washington Consensus, summarised by John Williamson some 35 years ago, would have answered in the negative. In the 1980s, when the consensus was

---

How to cite this book chapter:

Hausmann, Ricardo (2025) 'Export-led growth', in: Besley, Tim, Bucelli, Irene and Velasco, Andrés (eds) *The London Consensus: Economic Principles for the 21st Century*, London: LSE Press, pp. 143–193 https://doi.org/10.31389/lsepress.tlc.e

forged, many countries had highly protective trade regimes, multiple exchange rates with large black-market premia, interest rate controls, and high inflation. The consensus was that if countries unified exchange rates, reduced barriers to trade and brought inflation under control, exports would follow naturally. According to the Lerner symmetry theorem, import tariffs are equivalent to a tax on exports. Exchange controls act as an additional tax by forcing exporters to sell their earnings at an artificially appreciated exchange rate. If such policy-induced distortions were eliminated, the Washington Consensus suggested, exports would naturally reach their efficient level.

Today, many countries have unified their exchange rates, eliminated exchange controls, brought inflation to single digits, reduced trade barriers, and signed free trade agreements with many of their main trade partners, and yet, the median country has not narrowed its income gap with the US. Export performance matters for growth, with countries that grow exhibiting more than proportional export growth. In many developing and emerging economies, growth is highly correlated with exogenous movements in their export prices and on fluctuations in international capital flows. Moreover, sustained fast-growing economies change the composition of their export basket substantially towards new, more complex products.

Regional differences in growth and export trajectories confirm these observations. Countries in East Asia – including China – have managed rapid changes to their export baskets, increased their global export shares in new industries, and achieved fast growth. In Latin America, by contrast, even good performers like Chile, Colombia, and Peru stabilised inflation, opened their economies to international trade (tariffs are negligible and they have signed numerous free trade agreements), and capital flows. Yet, they have been unable to diversify their export baskets and achieve sustained growth. The experiences of many nations in Africa and the Middle East resemble those of Latin America.

Export-led growth has been a topic of discussion at least since the 1980s when East Asian economies were undergoing growth miracles that contrasted with the dire performance of debt-stricken Latin America. A central question was whether the growth miracles in the East were associated with their so-called export-led industrialisation (ELI), which was different from the import-substitution industrialisation strategy adopted in Latin America since the 1950s. Clearly, something was amiss in Latin America, but what exactly had worked well in East Asia was less clear. For some, like Balassa,[1] Krueger,[2] Bhagwati,[3] and Talvi et al.,[4] the invisible hand of the market and its discipline had done most of the miracle in the East. For others, like Amsden,[5] the visible hand of activist industrial policies did the trick.

More recently, Dani Rodrik has argued that the success of ELI may no longer be replicable. In the past, manufacturing was low-skill labour intensive, which allowed it to absorb large numbers of workers who were leaving agriculture. Today, manufacturing is much less labour intensive, leading to premature de-industrialisation (measured as declining employment shares) and, hence, will not have the aggregate reallocation benefits of the past.

Acemoglu et al.[6] and Rodrik et al.[7] also ask us to look deeper than the so-called proximate causes of growth – like exports and technology – towards more fundamental determinants of growth such as the quality of institutions. They argue countries do not adopt technology because their institutions do not generate the right incentives. For other scholars like Galor[8] and Weil,[9] the demographic transition, as countries shift from high birth and death rates to low birth and death rates, comes along with improvements in life expectancy, reductions in fertility rates, improvements in education, declines in dependency ratios (the average number of children and elderly per 100 working-age population), and increases in female labour force participation and urbanisation, which all facilitate human capital accumulation, the adoption of technology, and economic growth. The implicit message of this literature is that growth policies should focus on either institutions, demography, or education.

In this chapter, I argue that a focus on exports, both at the intensive margin (where existing products increase their volume), but especially at the extensive margin (where new products start being exported), can help countries figure out what policies to adopt in order to achieve sustained growth. I present six stylised facts about growth and its trends in the decades that followed the Washington Consensus. The first stylised fact relates to convergence. Since 1990, there has been massive convergence in all the factors associated with the demographic transition: life expectancy, fertility, employment per capita, and female labour force participation. There has even been massive convergence in workers per capita, capital per worker, education, and urbanisation. According to the Solow framework, these trends should have generated convergence in income if technological gaps had remained constant, while according to Galor and Weil, these trends should have generated technological convergence. Both logics should have delivered massive income convergence.

But that has not happened. The median country has not narrowed its income gap. The only way to make sense of this result is that there has been widespread technological divergence, despite the demographic transition, urbanisation, and impressive narrowing of education gaps. This calls into question the idea that technology adoption will just naturally follow if we address certain deeper underlying causes. Instead, countries seem to have institutions that can sustain all the dimensions of the demographic transition, including a massive improvement in education, health, and female labour force participation, but apparently cannot sustain technology adoption. What is missing?

The second stylised fact is that poor countries are cheap, meaning that a dollar buys more in poor countries than in rich ones. I show that this is not only true across countries, but also within countries: as countries get richer, they become more expensive. This is known as the Balassa–Samuelson effect and can be explained not only by the fact that poor countries are less productive – that is why they are poor – but that this productivity gap is much more pronounced in tradable industries (e.g., agriculture, manufacturing, mining, and tourism) than in non-tradable industries (e.g., construction, retail trade, and social services). Countries that grow consistently see faster improvements in productivity in tradables than in non-tradables, which is why they become more expensive. This implies that whatever is difficult about technology adoption seems to matter more for tradables; and countries that grow consistently also improve the relative productivity of tradables.

The third fact is that the elasticity of exports to gross domestic product (GDP) per capita is greater than 1, both between and within countries, meaning sustained growth is associated with a more than proportional growth of exports, at least since World War II.

The fourth fact is that countries differ radically in the basket of tradable goods they can produce. Poor countries can usually only produce a few ubiquitous products, while rich countries are able to make those same products, but also make many additional products that are less ubiquitous.

The fifth fact is that, at least in the 1980s, only about 20% of the countries that grew substantially also changed significantly their export basket in the direction of more complex, less ubiquitous products.

I interpret these last two facts considering the theory of technology that underpins the economic complexity approach. According to this theory, technology is really about productive knowledge, but the implementation of this knowledge requires not just the codification of knowledge into shareable codes, recipes, formulas, algorithms, and how-to-do manuals, or the embodiment of that knowledge into tools and materials, it requires tacit knowledge or know-how in brains. However, the know-how that is missing does not reside in a single brain that, if brought into the country, could ensure technology adoption. Individual brains have a limited capacity to acquire know-how, so we put different bits of knowledge in different heads. The required know-how resides in teams of brains spread out between the employees of every firm and that of its suppliers, including institutions that provide public goods.

This makes technology adoption concrete, and not just an abstract parameter that changes the productivity of general factors of production. Technology adoption is rife with market failures arising, like coordination failures, knowledge spillovers, and externalities associated with public goods. These issues are more severe and impactful for tradables than for non-tradables, and more serious at the extensive margin than at the intensive margin. Complementarities among technologies mean that problems in the adoption of one technology, say electricity, will make it more difficult to adopt other technologies that rely on the availability of electricity. This can help explain widening technological gaps in most countries.

I then explore the policy implications of this theory. The Washington Consensus prescribed that market failures were the exception rather than the rule. The bulk of the attention was put on policy-induced distortions that could be addressed through liberalisation of trade, labour markets, investment, and finance. Our alternative approach starts from the presumption that market failures are rife, they come in many different types, they are highly interactive, and are hard to predict or address without contextual information, which must be revealed to policymakers by engaging with the real world.

Since productivity problems are more important for tradables than for non-tradables and more difficult to address at the extensive than at the intensive margin, a focus on the competitiveness of exports with a special attention to its extensive margin is appropriate.

Economic growth requires a search process into the opportunities and obstacles faced by existing industries and into the 'adjacent possible': i.e., industries that do not yet exist and that are promising in terms of their feasibility and attractiveness but remain undeveloped.[10] The policy question becomes how to organise these two search processes at the intensive and extensive margins, given the institutional and corporate structures with which history has bequeathed each country. Policy tools, such as industrial zones, special economic zones, research and development (R&D) subsidies, training subsidies, development banks, investment promotion agencies, and business associations, are no panacea but can usefully be adapted to solve the challenges that the search process faces.

This chapter will proceed as follows. Section II presents the six stylised facts. Section III provides an interpretation of these facts. Section IV discusses what this means for policy. Section V concludes.

II. Six stylised facts

1. *Convergence in fundamentals, but not in income*

The literature has emphasised several channels through which growth and development happens. Richer societies possess more physical capital: installations and machines that make human effort more productive. They also have better health outcomes in terms of life expectancy and have fewer children on whose education they can afford to invest more, leading the next generation to have more human capital. Fewer children also imply lower dependency ratios, hence, more working age population per capita capable of providing potential labour effort. With fewer children and more education, women can participate more fully in employment, giving the economy more human resources to expand production. Finally, a more educated labour force should make it easier to adopt technology. Developed societies are more urbanised, enabling them to sustain a deeper division of labour, greater human interaction, and more accessible markets. So, investment, health, demographic change, education, and urbanisation are key to development because they increase the availability of physical and human factors of production, and because they facilitate technology adoption.

If we focus on fundamental aspects of development, paraphrasing the Washington Consensus, exports will naturally rise to their efficient level. By contrast, without progress in these more fundamental areas, exports alone cannot make a difference.

To show what happened in the world since the advent of the Washington Consensus, I borrow the idea of measuring gaps with respect to the US from Hall and Jones.[11] I ask myself whether countries have widened or narrowed the gap vis-à-vis the US in all these aspects of development. Table 5.1 shows the degree to which countries that started below the US in 1990 narrowed their gaps with the US in the subsequent three decades. It also measures the degree and speed of absolute convergence in each selected development indicator, showing how much of the change in the gap is explained by the initial size of the gap.

The results are puzzling, reporting massive convergence in many aspects of development seen as fundamental. The capital to output ratio has narrowed in 83% of the 83 countries that started below the US in 1990 and the speed of convergence has been massive. Regarding life expectancy, the gap narrowed in 93% of the countries that started below the US, with the convergence term alone explaining 68% of the variance. The gap in fertility rates declined in 91% of the 120 countries that started above the US. With lower fertility gaps, female labour force participation gaps narrowed in 74% of the 117 countries that started below the US. Employment per capita gaps narrowed in 80% of the cases. The gap in urbanisation narrowed in 59% of the cases.

Regarding education, the convergence has been even more impressive. Whether you look at years of schooling of the labour force, tertiary enrolment or the Penn World Table's measure of human capital (see Table 5.1), the gap narrowed between 1990 and 2020 in 97%, 92%, and 95% of the 132 cases considered, with a high convergence speed and a significant correlation between the initial gap and subsequent progress.

With so much progress in all these dimensions of development, it makes sense to expect massive convergence in incomes. Yet, we do not observe this. Instead, barely 55% of the countries narrowed the income gap post 1990. The estimated absolute convergence term is almost zero and not statistically significant.

To make sense of this, standard growth accounting requires a divergent total factor productivity (TFP) gap, with 56% of countries diverging, rather than converging. Economists usually refer to TFP as 'technology': a shift parameter that makes other factors more productive.

So, what does this mean? Countries have been massively converging in all the dimensions we associate with development – except income. This can only be explained by a widening technological gap, which is unrelated to standard measures of human capital, such as education and health, on which there has been massive convergence.

One popular explanation for income differences between countries is the institutional approach associated with Douglass North, Daron Acemoglu, and James Robinson.[12] This approach accepts that income differences are mainly due to differences in technology but argues that institutions create the incentive structure that determines whether technologies get adopted. But this begs the question of how can it be that institutions are good enough to

Table 5.1: The evolution of development gaps vis-à-vis the United States since 1990

	N	N(¡US)	Sh_conv (¡US)	Beta_conv	R2	75pctl/25pctl
K/GDP_(kd	146	83	.83	-.38	.34	1.75
Life_Expectancy	155	135	.93	-.45	.68	1.19
Fertility_Rate	155	120	.91	-.2	.2	2.29
Fem_Laborforce_Part	155	117	.741	-.18	.15	1.46
Urbanization_Rate	121	108	.59	-.18	.22	2.29
Employment/cap	146	123	.8	-.27	.16	1.37
Yrs_of_Schooling_BL	132	132	.97	-.39	.76	1.67
Tert_Enrollment_BL	132	132	.92	-.26	.27	4.19
Human_Capital_(PW)	133	132	.95	-.19	.25	1.59
GDP/cap_(kd)	134	130	.55	-.05	.02	9.51
TFP	95	86	.44	-.23	.06	1.83

Sources: World Development Indicators, Barro-Lee, Penn World Tables.

achieve convergence in demography, health, education, female participation and urbanisation, but not in income and technology? Moreover, there are huge technological and income differences between regions of a country. How can we account for this within-country variance, given that many institutional aspects are national? Another popular explanation emphasises issues of education quality. But what do we need to assume about divergent education quality to overwhelm the fact that education quantities, including in higher education, have been converging so strongly?

2. *Poor countries are cheap*

It is commonly known that a dollar tends to buy more in poor countries than in rich ones (see Figure 5.1). The graph shows the relationship between income per capita relative to the US for 2021 measured at purchasing power parity (PPP), and the PPP adjustment factor. Low-income countries have a PPP of 3, and middle-income regions are at around 2, meaning that a dollar buys, respectively, 3 and 2 times more in those countries than in the US.

Intuitively speaking, poor countries are less productive, hence, they should face higher costs. But because poor countries are less productive, they pay lower wages, hence, they should be cheaper. Combine the first and second intuition and you may think that poor countries should be just as expensive as rich ones with their lower productivity compensated by lower wages. So why are low-income countries three times cheaper?

Balassa[13] and Samuelson[14] ask us to consider splitting the economy into two types of products, according to their international tradability. Tradable goods, like scissors, are those that are relatively easy to ship. Non-tradable services, like haircuts, tend to be sold domestically only. Tradable goods tend to be subject to the 'Law of One Price', meaning that international consumers will not be willing to pay more for a pair of scissors if they can get a similar one from somewhere else, thus, disciplining the price. Non-tradable goods are not subject to this arbitrage, so their prices vary much more.

To square the puzzle, we need to accept that poor countries are *absolutely* less productive than rich countries – that is why they are poor – but *relatively* much less productive in tradable goods than in non-tradable activities. Whatever explains the difference in productivity between rich and poor countries is particularly concentrated in the productivity of tradable (hence, exportable) products.

The negative relationship between the PPP adjustment factor and GDP per capita is not just a characteristic of the cross-country variation: countries that grow become more expensive.[15] This means that when countries grow, they tend to improve their relative productivity of the tradable sector more than the non-tradable sector.

Figure 5.1: Purchasing power parity adjustment factor and GDP per capita at PPP, 2021

Source: author's calculations based on World Development Indicators (https://databank.worldbank.org/source/world-development-indicators).

3. *The elasticity of exports to GDP is higher than 1 both between and within countries*

Rich countries tend to export proportionally more than poor countries. To show this, we first look at the cross section, plotting the log exports per capita to the log of GDP per capita for a sample of 171 countries in 2019 (Figure 5.2). The slope of this curve implies an elasticity of 1.53 with a standard error of 0.09. This means that the gap in export per capita grows more than proportionally with income per capita.

This high export elasticity is not just a feature of the comparison between countries. Within countries, a dynamic estimation of this slope over time delivers an elasticity of 1.37 with a standard error of 0.06,[16] meaning that as countries grow, their exports tend to grow faster than GDP. Empirically, growth is 'export-led' in the sense that exports grow more rapidly than GDP.

4. *Growth in many developing countries is strongly dependent on external conditions, such as terms of trade and access to finance*

In a paper on growth accelerations with Lant Pritchett and Dani Rodrik, we found that improvements in the terms of trade of countries tend to generate growth accelerations that eventually peter out.[17] By contrast, sustained growth accelerations require more substantial changes. Extending this work, Gruss, Nabar, and Poplawski Ribeiro show the great sensitivity of country-specific external demand, terms of trade, and particularly external financial conditions in triggering growth accelerations and preventing reversals.[18]

Why is growth so sensitive to external conditions? External conditions determine how many imports countries can afford, whether they pay for them with exports or with borrowed money. Imports embody technology that make firms more productive. This suggests that the availability of foreign exchange is a binding constraint in many settings and that exogenous relaxations of that constraint – whether due to terms of trade movements or the availability of capital – are associated with temporary growth accelerations.

5. *Richer countries have the capacity to make a greater variety of complex products*

The presence of a product in the export basket of a country indicates that the country has adopted whatever technologies are necessary for making that product. How much of that product it decides to make will depend on the country's comparative advantage, demand, and other factors. Here, I will explore the basic capacity to make the product.

To do this, I build on Hidalgo and Hausmann[19] and look at world trade. Consider a matrix of countries and their exports, classified into about 1,200 different products. The matrix has about 200 rows and 1,200 columns. We fill the matrix with 1s and 0s depending on whether the country exports more than an epsilon of that product, where I consider epsilon to be just 1%

Figure 5.2: Exports of goods and services per capita, and GDP per capita 2019, logs

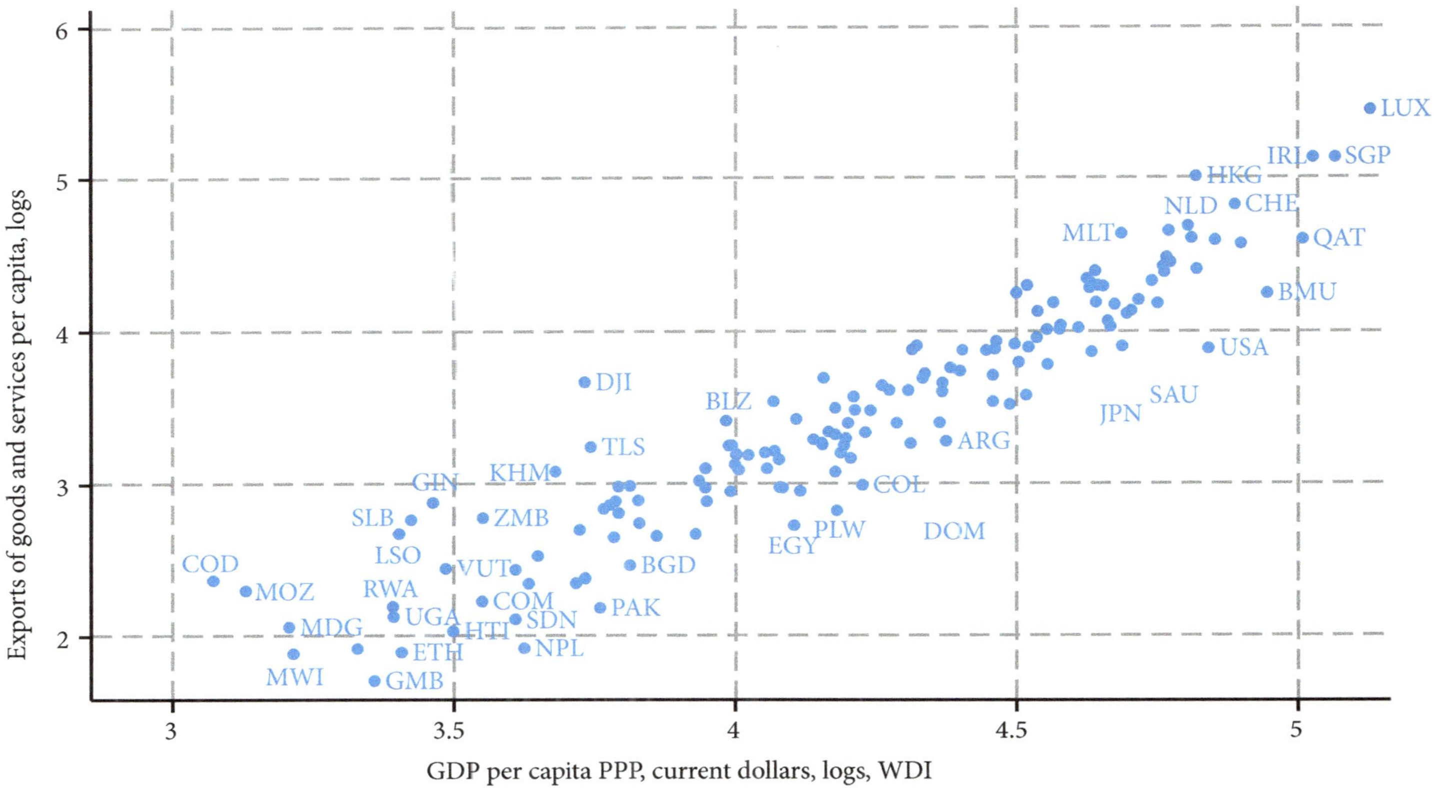

Source: author's calculations based on World Development Indicators (https://databank.worldbank.org/scurce/world-development-indicators).

of what it would have exported if it exported with the same intensity as the global average. I order the countries by how many 1s they have (i.e., I sum the rows and reorder them according to this measure). I order columns by how ubiquitous products are (i.e., we sum the columns and reorder them according to this measure).[20] We order the countries by how many 1s they have (i.e., we sum the rows and reorder them according to this measure). We order columns by how ubiquitous products are (i.e., we sum the columns and reorder them according to this measure).

Figure 5.3 shows the results for the year 2019. Countries at the top make at least an epsilon of almost everything. Countries at the bottom make few things. Products at the left are made in many places (they are ubiquitous, which suggests they are easy to make). Products at the right are made in fewer places. What emerges is a triangular shape where lower rows tend to be subsets of upper rows.[21] This happens because the poorly diversified countries make ubiquitous products, and more diversified countries make more unique products.[22] Countries at the top include Austria, Czech Republic, Denmark, and Sweden. Countries at the bottom include Bangladesh, Ethiopia, Guinea-Bissau, Nigeria, and Sudan.

Figure 5.3: Presence and absence of products in the export basket of countries (2019)

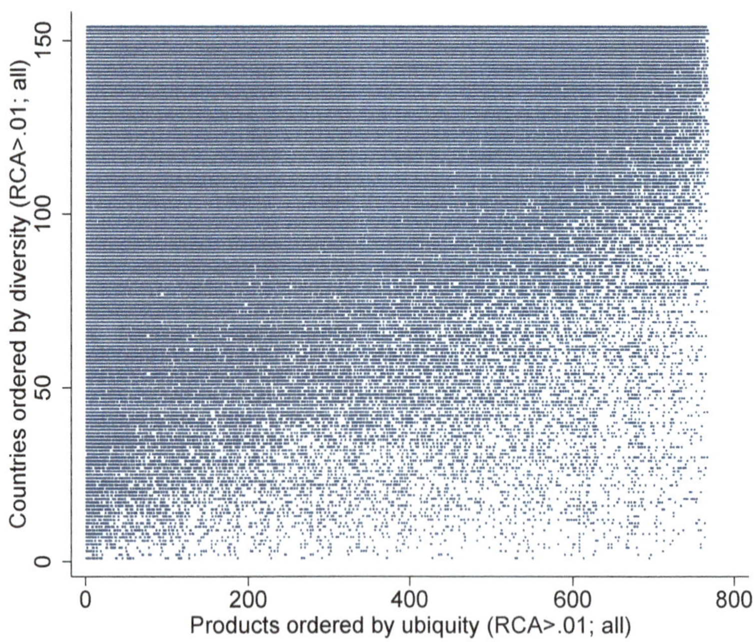

Source: authors' calculations based on the UN-COMTRADE dataset, available at https://comtradeplus.un.org/.

6. *Fast growers significantly upgraded the composition of their export basket*

Hausmann et al. show a strong association between growth and the economic complexity index.[23] Hidalgo and Hausmann developed a method to measure of a country's effective use of technology from matrixes, such as Figure 5.3, which they called the Economic Complexity Index (ECI).[24] Hausmann et al. show a strong association between growth improvements in the ECI.[25] To illustrate this, I focus on the period of the Washington Consensus and look at the developing world, defined as the bottom 75% of countries in 1990 in terms of income per capita. I calculate the cumulative percentage growth of these countries between 1990 and 2019 and split the countries into quintiles according to their 1990–2019 growth rate.

Figure 5.4 (a) shows the evolution of an index of GDP per capita relative to the US, normalised to 1 in 1990, for each of the quintiles. The figure shows that only the top quintile significantly narrowed the gap with the US. The second quintile had modest gains, the third quintile made essentially no progress, and the bottom two quintiles fell further behind.

Figure 5.4 (a): Average income per capita by quintile of growth

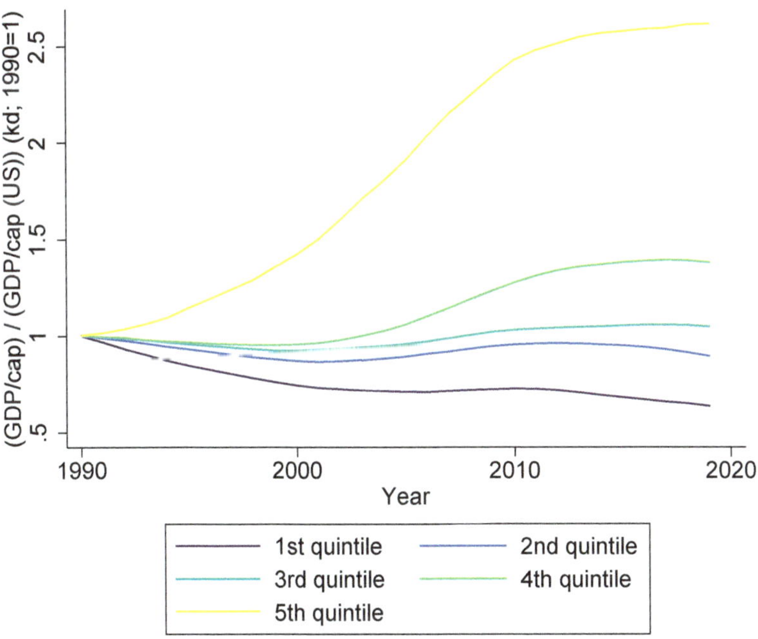

Source: author's calculations based on ECI data.

Figure 5.4 (b) shows the evolution of the economic complexity index for those same quintiles of countries. The graph tells a very similar story: only the top quintile significantly improved its economic complexity. The second quintile shows modest gains and the others fell behind.

Figure 5.4 (b): Change in the rankings of the Economic Complexity Index by quintile of growth

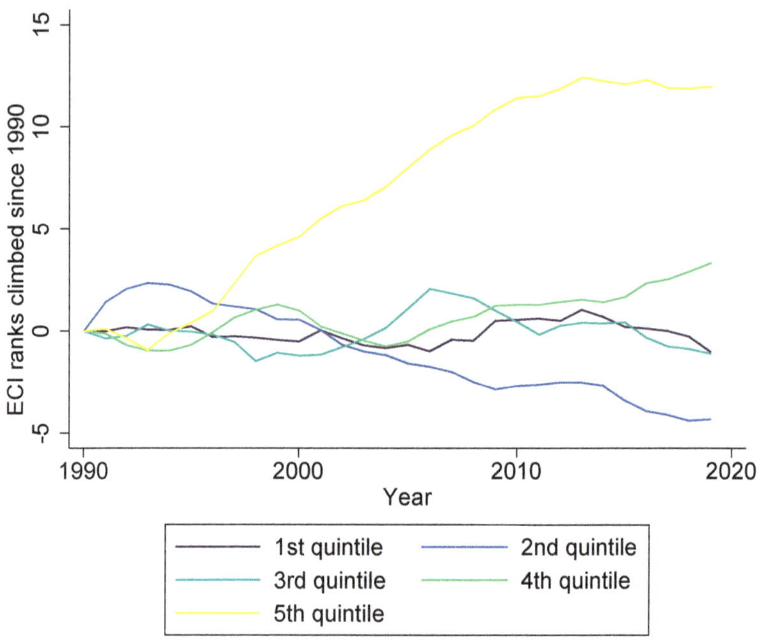

Source: author's calculations based on ECI data.

This means that the countries that narrowed their income gap with the US also acquired the necessary capabilities to expand the extensive margin of their exports towards more complex goods.

III. Making sense of the stylised facts

There has been no unconditional convergence in incomes despite massive unconditional convergence in many broad-based fundamentals, such as demography, health, education, investment, urbanisation, and female labour force participation. This suggests that the typical country exhibits divergence in technology adoption, despite convergence in broad-based fundamentals.

The fact that poor countries are cheap indicates that the productivity gap in tradables is larger than in non-tradables. When countries grow, they tend to become more expensive, suggesting that sustained growth requires technology adoption that is biased towards tradables. Whatever limits technology adoption hurts tradable industries more, and sustained progress requires the ability to revert this technological challenge.

The fact that the elasticity of exports to GDP per capita is greater than 1, both in the cross-section and in the time-series, also suggests that sustained growth is associated with more than proportional growth of exports: it is de facto 'export-led'.

Facts 5 and 6 suggest that technology is adopted in chunks: it is embedded in the capability to implement specific productive processes that go into subsets of products. According to neo-classical growth models, rich and poor countries have the capacity to make everything, but rich countries have a comparative advantage in some products and poor countries in others. That is not what we observe: rich countries do have the capacity to make nearly everything, but may choose not to use that capacity intensely. Poor countries have capacity to make fewer and more ubiquitous products. Figure 5.4 (b) suggests that sustained growth requires an expansion of the capacity to make more products and products that are more complex.

1. *An alternative interpretation of technology*

In some versions of economics, technology is defined by its outcomes: it causes factors of production to become more productive.[26] In other versions, such as in Paul Romer's view,[27] technology is defined as ideas or recipes. The first definition does not help us understand how to act on technology. The second assumes that the hard part is coming up with the idea or the recipe. It is relatively easier to adopt the idea or implement an existing recipe. So why not just adopt the ideas that others have already developed, for free?

In our alternative interpretation, technology is the productive knowledge we use to transform the physical and social world to our liking. This knowledge has grown exponentially for many centuries. However, our individual capacity to absorb knowledge has not. The number of books, scientific publications, and patents shows impressive exponential growth. Our ability to read is no greater than that of Adam Smith or Isaac Newton. To be able to use more knowledge at the societal level, given our limited individual capabilities, the world has used three complementary mechanisms. First, the division of knowledge; we put different bits of knowledge in different heads. By doing so, the whole can know much more than its parts.

Second, modularisation splits the production processes into stages. Each stage requires the coordination of a diverse group of workers that span the productive knowledge to execute that stage. However, each stage relies on inputs that were performed by other organisations in previous stages. The recipe to make a brownie cookie does not include the instructions to make sugar, chocolate, nuts, eggs, pans, ovens, or energy. These are other modules that use and embed different knowledge.

Third, codification converts tacit knowledge in brains into other forms that can more easily be shared through documentation, standardisation, classification, and a deeper scientific understanding of the mechanisms involved. Codification tries to extract the cook's knowledge into a set of recipes. A lot is lost in translation, but something remains that enhances the ability of others.

Tools and codes can easily be moved around. Tacit knowledge moves much more slowly into brains: according to Malcolm Gladwell,[28] it takes 10,000 hours of practice to become good at something.

So, implementing technology means being able to put together the human team – with their differentiated know-how – that spans the knowledge necessary to perform that stage in the production process and secure all the relevant inputs and codified knowledge.

For the human inputs, there is an important distinction between the intensive and the extensive margin of know-how. A violinist can train another violinist, and a baker can train another baker. But what do you do if you do not have a violinist to begin with? This creates a chicken-and-egg problem in the process of diversification, to which we will return.

Two important distinctions must be made about other inputs to the production process; first, some inputs are tradable and others not. To use a modern machine, a firm in a poor country does not need to know how to make the machine. It can simply buy it abroad, provided the country has access to foreign exchange, ports, roads, logistical services, and a legal framework that underpins international trade and finance. To be able to operate the machine, the electricity and repair services need to be provided locally. Hence, operating an imported machine still requires local availability of non-tradable goods and services, which must be provided locally. An entrepreneur in a poor country can take the idea of Amazon and decide to make a similar company in her country. However, the Amazon business model presumes that potential customers have access to the internet, that they have credit cards and that some delivery firms exist. Hence, the Amazon business model requires the prior diffusion of other industries on which it depends.

The second important distinction is between private and public goods. Private goods can be acquired in markets. Public goods have no markets: either some non-market organisation, like a government, provides them or society will have to operate without them. There is a market for cars, but there are no markets for roads, traffic lights, traffic signs, traffic rules, or traffic cops.

Hence, industries can exist if they can secure the necessary capabilities, including workers that span the know-how required, non-tradable market inputs, and public goods. The process of technology adoption implies growth in the availability of these non-tradable capabilities.

2. *Problems with capability accumulation at the extensive margin*

It is not easy for economies to provide the capabilities that their existing industries demand. Workers could have better skills, providers of non-tradable inputs could be more efficient, and the relevant public goods could be better. But these capabilities have been enough for incumbent industries to survive and even for some of them to thrive. More importantly, as time passes, these industries have the potential to improve through learning-by-doing, and through lobbying they might secure a better supply of public goods.

But industries that do not yet exist face a different problem. It is hard to operate a new plant without workers that have industry experience. But how can there be workers with experience in industries that do not yet exist? You cannot make watches without watchmakers, but how do you become an experienced watchmaker in a place that does not make watches? Without this experience, how can new industries get started?

It is much easier if the pioneer industry can bring workers with industry experience from a place where the industry already exists. Interestingly, a growing literature has shown the importance of human mobility,[29] migration,[30] and return migration for growth industries in general[31] and for pioneer firms[32] in particular.

Unfortunately, many developing countries have restrictive immigration policies that are typically biased against high-skill workers. In most countries, the number of foreign workers that a firm can have is limited. Professional accreditation often restricts work to those that have obtained a local diploma, thereby excluding foreigners.

The required non-tradable inputs of a new industry are the output of industries that may not yet exist, partly because the industries that would use their output as an input are also absent. This is the proverbial chicken-and-egg problem: you need car parts to run an original equipment manufacturer (OEM), but how do you set up an OEM if there are no car part producers? This may be why countries with car manufacturing capabilities obtained OEMs through explicit industrial policy that provide assurances to address these issues.

Regarding public goods, governments have enough trouble providing for the needs of existing industries. They have other priorities than worry about the needs of industries that do not yet exist. But without these public goods, those industries may never get started.

These are all examples of coordination failures. They are the norm rather than the exception at the extensive margin, and can be addressed by coordinating activities in non-market ways. Solving these problems may even generate positive externalities that markets fail to consider, and hence, do not fully exploit. If a country acquires a capability because it is demanded by a particular industry, that capability is now available to other industries. Developing the capabilities needed by one industry may cause positive spillovers to other potential industries.

Learning-by-doing can also generate positive spillovers. A pioneer may train workers that are then hired by new entrants, meaning the discovery process creates positive externalities, hence, the market underprovides them.[33] The newly trained workers may even be hired by other new industries that have similar know-how requirements.

Such distortions differentially impact the tradable vis-à-vis the non-tradable sector. Workers and firms improve as they produce, something known in the literature as Wright's Law.[34] They experience cost reductions as they acquire experience. Contrast a pioneer firm in a non-tradable industry with one in a tradable industry. The first one, being a pioneer, is by definition a monopolist in its industry. It will be able to appropriate monopoly rents that may be enough to finance the learning process. The local pioneer in a tradable industry is not a global pioneer. It enters a market with foreign suppliers that have already gone through a learning process, improved their productivity, and lowered costs. The local pioneer cannot expect to earn equivalent monopoly profits to finance the learning because it faces competition from abroad from the beginning. This may make innovation harder in tradable industries, explaining why poor countries are relatively less productive in these industries.

Lucas argues that growth depends on learning-by-doing,[35] but this process peters out within existing industries. To sustain growth, countries need to move to new industries where they can then benefit from new rounds of learning-by-doing. But entering new industries is difficult because of market failures.

IV. What does this all mean for policy?

Clearly, the policy-induced distortions that were the focus of the Washington Consensus – misaligned exchange rates, financial repression, protectionism, and unsustainable fiscal policies – remain a relevant concern, although in a dwindling number of countries. These issues affect stability and short-term efficiency. But long-term growth requires sustained adoption of technology, which is rife with market failures. This explains why the Washington Consensus has been ineffective on this front.

So, what should policies be like in a world rife with market failures? The standard economics answer, going back to Pigou,[36] is that you need to specify the market failure and figure out if externalities are positive or negative. Activities that generate positive externalities should be subsidised, while negative externalities should be taxed.

But this is a simplification that takes poor account of what markets do and what their failure implies. Instead, it is useful to recall what a well-functioning market does – to better understand what happens when it fails. First, **the market is an information system** that reveals highly decentralised and dispersed information. Every good or service has a price that conveys information about willingness to pay, relative costs, and much more. Externalities and other distortions imply that prices may not fully convey the right information.

Second, **the market is an incentive system**. Firms try to make profits by maximising the gap between the value of the output they produce and the value of the inputs used to produce it. Those values embed the information contained in prices. Third, **the market is a resource mobilisation system**: decentralised financial markets try to make money by funding activities that are expected to be profitable because they correctly respond to information contained in prices.

A few market failures have to do exclusively with distorted price signals that can be addressed through taxes and subsidies or through competition policy. But this presumes that the government can figure out what prices are distorted and how.

A couple of examples of such distortions come to mind. R&D create positive externalities that imply that markets tend to underprovide them in general. This justifies some form of subsidy. This is the argument that has made R&D tax credits ubiquitous in developed countries.[37] Out of the 38 OECD countries, 34 countries offered R&D subsidies in 2021, up from 20 in 2000. It is not obvious what should count as R&D spending across industries as different as software, steel, and medicines, or whether they generate the same positive spillovers. It is also not obvious what should count as R&D at different levels of development: setting up a new venture in a developing country involves initial setup and self-discovery costs that generate economies of scale and potential positive externalities for followers. Yet, to solve this, a relatively simple rule[38] could be included in the tax code, as many OECD countries do with R&D expenditures.

Industrial zones can also serve as a generic solution to a class of problems. At the highest level, industrial zones address the fact that manufacturing needs to take place in urban settings, which are highly regulated. Manufacturing requires access to roads, ports, and airports so materials and products can be brought in and out, and it requires urban transport to allow workers to commute. It requires power, water, water treatment plants, security, and other services. Markets cannot ensure that all inputs will be provided simultaneously and continuously everywhere, but governments can make sure that they are provided at a particular spot.

Special economic zones (SEZs) include some exceptions to the general legislation of a country, especially to avoid distortions for export-oriented activities. Their free zone status can reduce transaction costs associated with getting imported inputs through customs for products that are expected to be re-exported. The SEZs avoid value-added taxes and tariffs on imports, avoiding the need to request their reimbursement when exporting. Sometimes they include lower corporate income tax rates that are justified by the fact that optimal tax rates should be sensitive to the elasticity of tax bases to tax rates, and that tradable activities are more mobile than non-tradable activities. In other instances, like Panama, SEZs are exempted from the general immigration law.[39] On the downside, SEZs create a border with the rest of the country and can limit the integration of domestic value chains.

Agglomeration economies can be created in backward regions through a combination of tax incentives, the location of government activities, government procurement preferences, and infrastructure investments. The state of Colorado grew through the relocation of important federal government agencies, the development of the airport, and the highway system. The states of Arizona, New Mexico, Nevada, and California have had similar developments. Yet, there is still no consensus on place-based policies.

R&D subsidies, industrial zones, and SEZs exemplify a common class of problems. Other market failures are more **systemic** as they involve disruptions in all three functions of the market. Public goods are a good example as they have no price; they are not supplied with a profit motive; and they are expressed in millions of pages of legislation, thousands of government agencies, and highly localised and diverse infrastructure. Where is the government supposed to get information about what specific public goods are needed? What is the incentive to respond to the information? And how will resources be mobilised for that purpose?

Missing markets pose a similar systemic challenge: they have no price, there are no profit motivated firms, and there is nothing for capital markets to fund.

Consequently, to overcome systemic market failures policies need to address the information, incentives, and resource mobilisation functions that markets provide. We need to clarify how to handle highly decentralised information, how to implement incentives to respond to that information and how to respond and allocate resources.

Defining such policies is highly context- and industry-specific. First, we must distinguish between existing industries and potential new industries. Second, we distinguish between mature technologies and emerging technologies. Third, we distinguish between technologies and processes in terms of the degree of local adaptation they require. Fourth, we need to consider that industries emerge with different minimum-scale requirements. Fifth, we consider differences among the agents of change that can initiate or participate in an industry: established large organisations versus start-ups, and global corporations versus small- and medium-sized enterprises. Finally, different industries need different types of public goods.

These distinctions mean that horizontal policies, i.e., policies that are industry agnostic, such as the ones emphasised in the World Bank's Doing Business indicators,[40] are woefully inadequate and impractical. Governments should deal with challenges and opportunities at the most appropriate level. Electrical vehicles, mining, and pharmaceuticals need very different public goods and face different coordination challenges and externalities. Policies to address industry needs should be as horizontal as possible but as vertical as necessary.

Governments must help reveal the information that is required to identify opportunities and obstacles for expanding into new industries amid a context of systemic market failures. This critical information revelation process depends on how governments can embed themselves in information flows that are needed to act effectively. Existing industries tend to form chambers of commerce and other associations that lobby for the provision of the public goods they need. The United States has over 20,000 registered lobby groups that speak to 224 committees and sub-committees of the United States Congress. The existence of these associations indicates that there are private gains from influencing policy. A large literature, starting with George Stigler,[41] looks at these activities as rent-seeking and unproductive. However, since many public goods are complements of privately owned productive assets, improving their provision could create value. Rent-seeking can be contained through competition between lobby groups, procedural transparency, and mechanisms of accountability.

It is easier for incumbent industries to coordinate and form lobby groups than for industries that do not yet exist. If a government wants to promote diversification, it must develop mechanisms to learn about agents that explore the adjacent possible, the opportunities they encounter, and the obstacles and market failures they face. A network of public and semi-public entities has evolved to play this role. For example, investment promotion agencies talk to potential investors in firms that do not yet exist. Managers of industrial zones talk to potential tenants that uncover possibilities and obstacles. Development banks offer funding to pioneer firms and get access to their business plans. Agencies that authorise R&D-related tax expenditures get information regarding firms' innovation efforts. Vocational training entities, often organised with the participation of firms and worker representatives, try to align training programmes with business needs. Major investors, as in aerospace in Mexico, medical devices in Costa Rica, or green hydrogen in Namibia, demand university programmes that align with their needs. State-owned enterprises expose the government to information about new markets, technologies, and opportunities. Some governments perform technological surveillance to keep them abreast of challenges and opportunities. The media informs of problems, initiatives, and opportunities that different members of society are facing or considering.

But without incentives to respond, information can go to waste, just like the tragedy of September 11 is said to have occurred because intelligence agencies failed to connect the dots. Connecting the dots between the myriad of information flows that governments possess could do wonders.

The Washington Consensus policies prescribed 10 simplified commandments for government action. A new consensus should recognise that while governments may have clear goals, they often do not know what opportunities can take them there, and what obstacles they will face. Government strategy must consider how to find out about such new opportunities and obstacles.

This is similar to climate change policy, where the goal is clear, trade-offs are difficult, and the instruments to deploy are up for grabs (e.g., carbon taxes, science, technology and R&D subsidies, regulations, government-run labs, and government procurement). Policies require the capacity to do real-time assessments of trends and impacts of adopted policies, so they can be adjusted in light of the learning process. In contrast with monetary policy, where one institution has the bulk of the responsibility, climate change policy involves a network of institutions that must coordinate and align.

Most governments aspire to shared and sustainable prosperity as an ultimate goal of growth policy. But they need smart intermediate policy goals to help them achieve these aspirations. The goal of expanding exports both at the intensive and the extensive margin could be an appropriate intermediate goal that forces governments to figure out how to increase productivity in tradable activities, which is where the gaps are largest. It will force society to explore the extensive margin where externalities, chicken-and-egg problems, and missing public goods are more severe.

To achieve this intermediate goal, governments need to reveal information about opportunities and obstacles, and connect the dots between the information that reaches growth-promoting entities – like development banks, investment promotion entities, export promotion agencies, SEZs, business associations, universities, research centres, vocational training institutions, science and technology policy entities, and diaspora organisations, to promote problem identification and capability building.

I propose a guide to the search process for action with the below set of questions.

Question 1: On current trends, are existing exports poised to grow at a significant pace, compatible with the growth aspirations of the country? If yes, an export focus may not be the right frame for this country's growth strategy. If the answer is no, the country is unlikely to sustain a decent growth rate unless it addresses the export question. One reason for a negative answer may be that the current export basket does not have the capacity to move the country forward. For many countries, such as Saudi Arabia, the United Arab Emirates, Kazakhstan, Colombia, and Venezuela, oil has been a large share of exports, but oil production (measured in barrels per capita) has been falling for decades. For a while, declining production was compensated by high oil prices, but since 2014 that is no longer the case. Given global decarbonisation ambitions, oil exports are unlikely to grow much, if at all. Copper, fruits, forestry, and salmon will not be sufficient to power the Chilean economy forward and the soybean revolution cannot bring many more gains to Argentina's economy.

Question 2: What constrains the export potential of existing industries? Are existing industries constrained by insufficient supply of skills, infrastructure, energy, or other public goods? Or does the country need better access to foreign markets? A diagnostic approach could help identify the binding constraint.[42] For example, South Africa's export performance has been disappointing. The most obvious reason is a recent collapse in the country's electricity, transport, and port capacity due to mismanagement of state-owned enterprises.[43] The concern starts with exports, but the solution may point to other policy areas.

An important aspect of existing activities is that they exist. Incumbent firms understand what matters to them and will complain and lobby for solutions. Many governments engage the private sector constructively at the industry or cluster level to identify and resolve issues, such as deliberation councils in Japan and Korea, Black-Belt teams in Albania,[44] or *Mesas Ejecutivas* in Peru and Argentina,[45] and cluster initiatives in Colombia.[46] Other governments engage through export promotion and investment retention institutions. In other cases, a strong private sector lobby can de facto coordinate the government, as is the case with the Dominican Association of Free Zones (ADOZONAS).[47]

Question 3: What new ideas in tradable goods and services are in the adjacent possible, given existing capabilities? Which ideas are currently being explored by pioneering investors? What obstacles are investors bumping against? Is there a clear pipeline of potential new industries in gestation or is the scene relatively barren? Policymakers may face a costly information revelation problem. The industries that policymakers want to promote may not yet exist for reasons that are hard to pin down. Is it a chicken-and-egg problem among feasible private sector investments that just needs to be coordinated? Or does the new industry require capabilities the country does not yet have and is unlikely to acquire? Are there missing public goods and can they be identified and provided? Can you attract foreign investors to explore the industry's feasibility? Will you be able to negotiate a reasonable deal with investors? Is it worthwhile to risk public resources in the attempt?

These questions can only be answered by organisations that are dedicated to addressing them. Such organisations take several forms: investment promotion agencies, such as Ireland's IDA and Costa Rica's CINDE, engage with new and incumbent investors to figure out which industries they want to attract, what instruments seem most effective, what it takes for the investment to happen, and whether it would be valuable for the country to make the effort. Another approach is the use of investment development corporations, such as South Africa's Industrial Development Corporation (IDC) or the Corporación de Fomento de la Producción de Chile. While IDC has been used for other purposes, it has the mandate to look at new opportunities and consider providing debt or equity. As part of the government, IDC can influence public policy to secure needed public goods. The government does not need an *ex ante* view on what investments it wants to attract in order for these approaches to work. Instead, it has an open window for actors to contribute relevant information, so the government can figure out what opportunities are attractive. This is the idea behind 'Smart Development Banks'.[48]

ADOZONAS is another organisational form with similar effects. The business association of privately-owned free zones stand to benefit from attracting new investors that will rent out their industrial real estate. To do so, it engages closely with investors, connects them with capabilities in the private sector, and lobbies the government for changes in the provision of public goods.

The fundamental problem is that this information is costly to reveal and acquire. It is not obvious what opportunities are feasible, attractive or strategic, and finding out involves significant costs. Hopefully, incurring these costs is an investment that creates valuable information. While these investments are risky, not doing them is potentially extremely costly in terms of forgone feasible growth opportunities.

Question 4: Who are the potential agents of change that can lead structural change? Economists tend to assume that things happen if the incentives are right. Many have even defined economics as the science of incentives. According to this view, people avoid actions because of a lack of incentives. Seldom in this approach is the possibility that things do not happen, not just because people may not have the incentives: they may just not have the capabilities.

Countries differ in the types of capabilities they possess and in the organisations that possess them. Most places do not have an ecosystem of start-ups, venture capital firms, incubators, accelerators, private equity firms, and stock markets. For the few places that do, exploring new business ventures can be done from the proverbial home garage. Most other places require firms that can internalise those functions. In the United States, before the emergence of Silicon Valley, innovation mostly happened inside large corporations, such as AT&T that was a private, regulated monopoly.

Structural breakthroughs often happen within large conglomerates that have the balance sheet to make large investments – meaning they possess an internal capital market. They also have experienced managerial capital that can be reallocated to new ventures. They have the reputational capital to reach complex deals with other organisations and with the government. Toyota, Samsung, Turkey's Koç group, and Colombia's Grupo Empresarial Antioqueño are examples of this.

State-owned enterprises can play a similar role. Companies such as OCP Group in Morocco, Sasol in South Africa, Empresas Públicas de Medellín in Colombia, ARAMCO in Saudi Arabia and many examples in China (e.g., CNPC, China Mobile, ICBC, CNOOC, and Chem China) are organisations that have the capacity to execute strategic diversification bets. In other contexts, the attraction of a multinational corporation can have transformative effects, such as INTEL in Costa Rica, De Beers in Botswana and Namibia, and Volkswagen in Slovakia.

Very often, growth strategies do not spell out who are the agents of change that will execute the strategy. These agents are often bequests of the past and differ markedly across countries and over time. They constitute the organisational endowment that countries have to mobilise in order to catalyse the growth process.

V. Concluding remarks

Technology adoption is critical for long-term growth, but it cannot be delegated to the proverbial invisible hand of the market. Technology adoption is rife with market failures that only concerted actions can address. Technology adoption seems to be more challenging and impactful in tradable activities. The fact that poor countries are cheap reflects that the productivity gaps are larger in tradables than in non-tradables. The fact that when countries grow sustainably their exports grow more than proportionally and they expand the basket of feasible products towards more complex goods, suggesting that it is good to focus technology adoption on tradable activities.

The resulting policy implication is not a new list of concrete policies that all countries can adopt in the way the Washington Consensus was formulated. Instead, it is an organised and costly search process for growth opportunities, both at the intensive and extensive margins of production. This does not require a list of policies, but rather a set of processes that can endogenously generate such policies by actively exploring opportunities and obstacles. A country cannot walk away from the institutional and organisational structure that has been bequeathed by history. Instead, societies need to incur the risks of exploration in a responsible way. This process might be difficult, but its absence is bound to make growth impossible.

Notes

1 Balassa (1964).

2 Krueger (1998).

3 Bhagwati (2004).

4 Talvi et al. (1997).

5 Amsden (2001).

6 Acemoglu et al. (2005).

7 Rodrik et al. (2004).

8 Galor (2005; 2022).

9 Galor and Weil (1999); Weil and Galor (2000).

10 The 'adjacent possible' is a term introduced by Stuart Kauffman to describe the possible evolutionary paths that a complex system can take at any point in time. See Kauffmann (2014).

11 Hall and Jones (1999).

12 North (1990); Acemoglu et al. (2005).

13 Balassa (1964).

[14] Samuelson (1964).

[15] An estimation of the impact of GDP growth on the PPP adjustment factor, controlling for fixed country characteristics and year effects, delivers an elasticity that is slightly smaller than that implied by the cross-section.

[16] These are the results of an estimation of the impact of the log of exports on the log GDP, controlling for fixed country characteristics and year effects.

[17] Hausmann et al. (2005).

[18] Gruss et al. (2018).

[19] Hidalgo and Hausmann (2009).

[20] More precisely, I use Balassa's measure of revealed comparative advantage, which is the ratio of the share of the product in the country's export basket to the share of the product in world exports. A ratio of 1 would mean that the country exports what would be expected given the size of the country's total exports and the size of the product's world market. Our epsilon implies a ratio of just 0.01. I am indebted to Ulrich Schetter for the idea of looking at this extreme of RCA>0.01 rather than 1, as Hildago and Hausmann (2019) did. The latter is plausibly influenced by comparative advantage, while 0.01 just indicates an ability to make the product.

[21] In mathematical terms, this means that the matrix is nested. The literature on ecology has found that ecological networks tend to be nested in the sense that rare species tend to live in highly diversified places while ubiquitous species inhabit both (Hultén, 1937). Bustos et al. (2012) show that the nestedness is stable in international trade data such as that in Figure 5.3.

[22] This observation was first demonstrated in Hidalgo and Hausmann (2009), where they used a revealed comparative advantage of 1 rather than 0.01 to binarise the matrix. We focus on a lower cut-off to emphasise that we are focusing on the extensive margin.

[23] Hausmann et al. (2014).

[24] Hidalgo and Hausmann (2009).

[25] Hausmann et al. (2014).

[26] Solow (1957).

[27] Romer (1994).

[28] Gladwell (2008).

[29] For example, Coscia et al. (2020) study the impact of business travel on the evolution of productivity, employment, and exports at the country–product level.

[30] For example, Bahar and Rapoport (2018) study the impact of migration on the evolution of comparative advantage in receiving countries.

[31] For example, return migration as a source of industry dynamism has been studied by Hausmann and Nedelkoska (2018) for Albania, Bahar et al. (2019) for the former Yugoslavia, and by Diodato et al. (2023) for Mexico.

[32] For example, Mostafa and Klepper (2018) show how the garment industry was seeded into Bangladesh by one Korean company that trained 126 workers who went on to start 56 new high-performing companies. Hausmann and Neffke (2019) study regional pioneer firms in Germany. They found that pioneer firms intensively hired workers with industry experience from other regions. This was particularly important for the re-industrialisation of Eastern Germany post-reunification.

[33] See Hausmann and Rodrik (2003).

[34] Wright (1936).

[35] Lucas (1993).

[36] Pigou (1912).

[37] OECD (2023).

[38] The rule typically involves allowing accepted R&D investments to be deducted from taxable income at a rate greater than 100%.

[39] In the case of Panama, SEZs have exemptions from the rule that firms cannot have more than 10% foreign workers and the SEZs benefit from several special visa regimes (Hausmann et al. 2016).

[40] World Bank (2021).

[41] Stigler (1971).

[42] Hausmann et al. (2008).

[43] Hausmann et al. (2023).

[44] Andrews and Harrington (2023).

[45] Ghezzi (2017).

[46] Llinás (2021).

[47] Jiménez et al. (2012).

[48] Fernández-Arias et al. (2020).

References

Acemoglu, D., Johnson, S. and Robinson, J. A. (2005) 'Institutions as a Fundamental Cause of Long-Run Growth', in Aghion, P. and Durlauf, N. (eds) *Handbook of Economic Growth, Volume 1 Part A*, Elsevier: 385–472. https://doi.org/10.1016/S1574-0684(05)01006-3

Amsden, A. H. (2001) *The Rise of 'the Rest': Challenges to the West from Late-Industrializing Economies,* Oxford: Oxford University Press. https://doi.org/10.1093/0195139690.003.0001

Andrews, M. and Harrington, P. (2023) *Facilitating Learning and Discovery-Oriented Industrial Policy in Albania* (No. 431). Center for International Development at Harvard University.

Bahar, D. and Rapoport, H. (2018) 'Migration, Knowledge Diffusion and the Comparative Advantage of Nations', *The Economic Journal* 128(612): 273–305. https://doi.org/10.1111/ecoj.12450

Bahar, D., Hauptmann, A., Özguzel, C. and Rapoport, H. (2019) 'Migration and Post-conflict Reconstruction: The Effect of Returning Refugees on Export Performance in the Former Yugoslavia', Center for International Development at Harvard University. https://doi.org/10.2139/ssrn.3408310

Balassa, B. (1964) 'The Purchasing-Power Parity Doctrine: A Reappraisal', *Journal of Political Economy*, 72(6): 584–596. https://doi.org/10.1086/258965

Bhagwati, J. (2004) *In Defense of Globalization: With a New Afterword*, Oxford: Oxford University Press.

Bustos, S., Gomez, C., Hausmann, R. and Hidalgo, C. A. (2012) 'The Dynamics of Nestedness Predicts the Evolution of Industrial Ecosystems', PLOS One, 7(11): e49393 https://doi.org/10.1371/journal.pone.0049393

Coscia, M., Neffke, F. and Hausmann, R. (2020) 'Knowledge Diffusion in the Network of International Business Travel', *Nature Human Behaviour,* 4(10): 1011–1020. https://doi.org/10.1038/s41562-020-0922-x

Diodato, D., Hausmann, R. and Neffke, F. (2023) 'The Impact of Return Migration on Employment and Wages in Mexican Cities', *Journal of Urban Economics*, 135. https://doi.org/10.1016/j.jue.2023.103557

Fernández-Arias, E., Hausmann, R. and Panizza, U. (2020) 'Smart Development Banks', *Journal of Industry, Competition and Trade*, 20(2): 395–420. https://doi.org/10.1007/s10842-019-00328-x

Galor, O. (2005) 'From Stagnation to Growth: Unified Growth Theory', in Aghion, P. and Durlauf, N. (eds) *Handbook of Economic Growth, Volume 1 Part A*, Elsevier: 171–293. https://doi.org/10.2139/ssrn.651526

Galor, O. (2022) *The Journey of Humanity: The Origins of Wealth and Inequality*, New York: Vintage Penguin Random House.

Galor, O. and Weil, D. N. (1999) 'From Malthusian Stagnation to Modern Growth', *American Economic Review*, 89(2): 150–154. https://doi.org/10.1257/aer.89.2.150

Ghezzi, P. (2017) 'Mesas Ejecutivas in Peru: Lessons for Productive Development Policies', *Global Policy*, 8(3): 369–380. https://doi.org/10.1111/1758-5899.12457

Gladwell, M. (2008) *Outliers: The Story of Success*, New York: Little, Brown and Company.

Gruss, B., Nabar, M. S. and Poplawski Ribeiro, M. (2018) 'Growth Accelerations and Reversals in Emerging Market and Developing Economies: The Role of External Conditions', IMF Working Papers 2018/052, International Monetary Fund. https://www.imf.org/en/Publications/WP/Issues/2018/03/12/Growth-Accelerations-and-Reversals-in-Emerging-Market-and-Developing-Economies-The-Role-of-45698

Hall, R. E. and Jones, C. I. (1999) 'Why Do Some Countries Produce So Much More Output Per Worker than Others?', *The Quarterly Journal of Economics*, 114(1): 83–116. https://doi.org/10.1162/003355399555954

Hausmann, R. and Nedelkoska, L. (2018) 'Welcome Home in a Crisis: Effects of Return Migration on the Non-Migrants' Wages and Employment', *European Economic Review*, 101: 101–132. https://doi.org/10.1016/j.euroecorev.2017.10.003

Hausmann, R. and Neffke, F. (2019) 'The Workforce of Pioneer Plants: The Role of Worker Mobility in the Diffusion of Industries', *Research Policy*, 48(3): 628–648. https://doi.org/10.1016/j.respol.2018.10.017

Hausmann, R. and Rodrik, D. (2003) 'Economic Development as Self-Discovery', *Journal of Development Economics*, 72(2): 603–633. https://doi.org/10.1016/S0304-3878(03)00124-X

Hausmann, R., Pritchett, L. and Rodrik, D. (2005) 'Growth Accelerations', *Journal of Economic Growth*, 10(4): 303–329. https://doi.org/10.1007/s10887-005-4712-0

Hausmann, R., Klinger, B. and Wagner, R. (2008) *Doing Growth Diagnostics in Practice: A 'Mindbook'*, Center for International Development at Harvard University. https://doi.org/10.18235/0011325

Hausmann, R., Hidalgo, C. A., Bustos, S., Coscia, M. and Simoes, A. (2014) *The Atlas of Economic Complexity: Mapping Paths to Prosperity*, Cambridge: MIT Press. https://doi.org/10.7551/mitpress/9647.001.0001

Hausmann, R., Obach, J. and Santos, M. A. (2016) *Special Economic Zones in Panama: Technology Spillovers from a Labor Market Perspective* (No. 326). Center for International Development at Harvard University.

Hausmann, R., O'Brien, T., Fortunato, A., Lochmann, A., Shah, K., Venturi, L., Enciso-Valdivia, S., Vashkinskaya, E., Ahuja, K., Klinger, B., Sturzenegger, F. and Tokman, M. (2023) 'Growth Through Inclusion in South Africa', CID Faculty Working Paper No. 434 November.

Hidalgo, C. A. and Hausmann, R. (2009) 'The Building Blocks of Economic Complexity', *Proceedings of the National Academy of Sciences,* 106(26): 10570–10575. https://doi.org/10.1073/pnas.0900943106

Hultén, E. (1937) *Outline of the History of Arctic and Boreal Biota During the Quarternary Period,* New York: Lehre J. Cramer.

Jiménez, J. A., Hidalgo, C. A., Jiménez, J., Lawrence, R., Levy-Yeyati, R., Sabel, C., Schydlowsky, C. (2012) Reporte Harvard: Construyendo un mejor futuro para la República Dominicana: Herramientas para el desarrollo. *Ministerio de Economía, Planificación y Desarrollo. República Dominicana.*

Kauffman, S. A. (2014) 'Prolegomenon to Patterns in Evolution', *Biosystems,* 123, 3–8. https://doi.org/10.1016/j.biosystems.2014.03.004

Krueger, A. (1998) 'Why Trade Liberalisation Is Good for Growth', *The Economic Journal*, 108(450): 1513–1522. https://doi.org/10.1111/1468-0297.00358

Llinás, M. (2021) 'Iniciativas cluster una forma concreta y efectiva de «mover la aguja» de la productividad', *Bogotá DC.* https://confecamaras.org.co/wp-content/uploads/2024/03/iniciativas-cluster-marco-llinas.pdf

Lucas Jr, R. E. (1993) 'Making a Miracle', *Econometrica: Journal of the Econometric Society*, 61(2): 251–272. https://doi.org/10.2307/2951551

Mostafa, R. and Klepper, S. (2018) 'Industrial Development Through Tacit Knowledge Seeding: Evidence from the Bangladesh Garment Industry', *Management Science*, 64(2), 613–632. https://doi.org/10.1287/mnsc.2016.2619

North, D. C. (1990) *Institutions, Institutional Change, and Economic Performance*, New York: Cambridge University Press. https://doi.org/10.1017/CBO9780511808678

OECD (2023) 'Mapping Business Innovation Support (MABIS)', OECD R&D Tax Incentives Database. https://one.oecd.org/document/DSTI/STP/NESTI(2023)2/FINAL/en/pdf

Pigou, A. C. (1912) *Wealth and Welfare,* London: Macmillan and Company.

Rodrik, D., Subramanian, A. and Trebbi, F. (2004) 'Institutions Rule: The Primacy of Institutions Over Geography and Integration in Economic Development', *Journal of Economic Growth*, 9(2): 131–165. https://doi.org/10.1023/B:JOEG.0000031425.72248.85

Romer, P. M. (1994) 'The Origins of Endogenous Growth', *Journal of Economic Perspectives*, 8(1): 3–22. https://doi.org/10.1257/jep.8.1.3

Samuelson, P. A. (1964) 'Theoretical Notes on Trade Problems', *Review of Economics and Statistics*, 46(2): 145–54. https://doi.org/10.2307/1928178

Solow, R. M. (1957) 'Technical Change and the Aggregate Production Function', *The Review of Economics and Statistics*, 39(3): 312–320. https://doi.org/10.2307/1926047

Stigler, G. J. (1971) 'The Theory of Economic Regulation', *The Bell Journal of Economics and Management Science*, 2(1): 3–21. https://doi.org/10.2307/3003160

Talvi, E., Serra, P., Birdsall, N., Pack, H., Solimono, A., Stallings, B., Gavin, M., Sabot, R., Lustig, N., Petrei, H., Edwards, S., Hausmann, R., Jaspersen, F., Cunha, P. V., Thomas, V., Shirley, M. M., Page, J., Howard, E., Pfeffermann, G., Ross, D., Shilling, J., Boeker, P., Lee, J. and Bitran Colodro, E. (1997) *Pathways to Growth: Comparing East Asia and Latin America*. Inter-American Development Bank. https://doi.org/10.18235/0012386

Weil, D. N. and Galor, O. (2000) 'Population, Technology, and Growth: From Malthusian Stagnation to the Demographic Transition and Beyond', *American Economic Review*, 90(4): 806–828. https://doi.org/10.1257/aer.90.4.806

World Bank (2021) 'Doing Business', The World Bank Group [Dataset, updated 18 August] https://databank.worldbank.org/source/doing-business

Wright, T. P. (1936) 'Factors Affecting the Costs of Airplanes', *Journal of Aeronautical Sciences*, 10: 302–328. https://doi.org/10.2514/8.155

Response to Ricardo Hausmann by Isabela Manelici

The fundamental cure for poverty is not money but knowledge.

Sir Arthur Lewis, Nobel Laureate in Economics

I. Exports as a bedrock for growth strategies

Hausmann posits that low- and middle-income countries (LMICs) can achieve long-term economic growth through strategies that explicitly promote exports. How much such strategies improve long-term aggregate welfare, whether deviations from policy neutrality favouring exports increase welfare more than alternative policies, and the distributional implications of such strategies are core concerns in academic and policy debates.

Hausmann argues that narrowing the distance to the technology frontier is essential for closing income gaps between countries. LMICs have converged in development goals, such as life expectancy and school attainment – but not in income. Hausmann interprets these patterns as evidence that while local institutions in LMICs can achieve the former development goals, the latter goal cannot be achieved solely 'from within'. Market failures and distortions in LMICs can disincentivise technology upgrading. Hausmann's conjecture is that export-promoting policies would alleviate market failures and distortions that otherwise stymie technology upgrading.

Hausmann advocates for policies that support the exploration of 'productive opportunities' (particularly in tradable goods and services). He portrays the export market as one where firms from LMICs can achieve scale and amortise the large investments that are often necessary for technology adoption. He also highlights the important role of the export basket complexity, arguing that LMICs should prioritise exploration of complex goods that provide greater learning-by-doing prospects. Why is policy needed to facilitate such exploration (i.e., what stands in the way of profit-maximising entrepreneurs undertaking such exploration without government intervention)? And why can exports best facilitate the exploration process? These questions are at the heart of Hausmann's policy recommendation.

Where could the technology necessary to export more complex goods and services come from? Hausmann sees technology as 'productive knowledge' that takes three forms: (1) embedded in tools and materials; (2) codified in recipes, manuals, etc.; and (3) embedded in people as tacit knowledge. Local producers may be able to invest in acquiring the first type of knowledge whenever they have access to capital, and when rents from such investments are protected. In such cases, the role of export-specific policies is more speculative, e.g., will these policies alleviate credit constraints or reduce crime and corruption? The second and third types of knowledge likely require direct exposure to superior technologies and opportunities to gauge whether they will be appropriate for local use. In such cases, we can draw a more direct link to exposure through exports, assuming foreign workers and firms possess more advanced knowledge than local workers and firms, and that they share such knowledge with their suppliers from LMICs.

II. Globalisation-led growth?

According to Nobel Laureate Michael Spence, a major weakness of the Washington Consensus as a guide to development policy formation is its underemphasis on knowledge transfers, as well as on the domestic conditions and investments that facilitate absorption and diffusion of knowledge and technology.[1]

LMICs that encourage trade and the entry of multinational enterprises (MNEs) can expand their productive knowledge by exposing their workers and firms to the more advanced knowledge of workers and firms from abroad. Such exposure could happen through international firm-to-firm trade (where the domestic firm is an exporter or an importer) or intranational firm-to-firm trade (when the domestic firm supplies or buys from an MNE subsidiary in the country). Such exposure could also happen through domestic workers employed by globally engaged firms (domestic importers/exporters or MNE subsidiaries), who then transition to entrepreneurship or employers yet to be globally engaged.

Which pursuit of those favouring exports, imports, or MNE entry will be most effective and the potential complementarities among them requires further research. Estimating the separate causal effects of trade or foreign direct investment (FDI) exposure on workers, firms, and aggregate growth (let alone their interactions) is notoriously difficult. Moreover, the data requirements to pin down these mechanisms are rarely met economy-wide, particularly not in LMICs, where data coverage and quality tend to be lower. The fact that most economic activity and employment in LMICs occur in the informal sector further hinders the ability to provide complete answers on the aggregate effects of trade or FDI-seeking policies. These caveats notwithstanding, importers, exporters, and MNEs (often the same firms) are among the leading firms in each country.[2] Therefore, it is helpful to take stock of what we currently know and do not know about the effects of their trading and MNE status on knowledge accumulation, diffusion, and aggregate growth.

III. Evidence supporting export promotion

The Washington Consensus recommended supporting trade through unified exchange rates and reduced trade barriers. Hausmann goes a step further in recommending explicit support for firms and industries to boost their export performance. His first argument in favour of such explicit support is that it helps countries achieve market scale, which matters in settings with internal returns to scale or fixed investment costs.[3] Whether or not improved market access is accompanied by investment hinges on whether capital access improves alongside market access.

Hausmann's second pro-exports argument relates to the complexity of the export basket. It is yet to be fully settled whether the relationship between a country's development and the complexity of its export basket is one-way or two-way. Atkin, Costinot, and Fukui explore this relationship theoretically and empirically.[4] The classical Ricardian perspective is that development may give countries comparative advantage in more complex goods. According to this perspective, laissez-faire policies are optimal. Alternatively, industrial policies fostering specialisation in more complex goods may lead to faster growth, which could justify export-targeting policies. Atkin, Costinot, and Fukui find evidence of positive dynamic economies of scale in more complex sectors (similar to Young, and Hausmann et al.).[5;6;7] However, this finding does not imply pervasive dynamic gains from trade because such a result would require that more complex sectors face less foreign competition. However, more complex sectors tend to face *more* – not less – foreign competition, which makes them shrink relative to other sectors. Since complex sectors are the source of dynamic spillovers, opening up to international trade can hurt the development of LMICs. Atkin, Costinot, and Fukui conclude by inviting more research into the unexpected correlation between economic complexity and competition.[8]

Another potential benefit of exporting (less explored in Hausmann's chapter) is that exporting may provide opportunities to learn from sophisticated foreign buyers. To probe this channel's existence and quantitative importance, Atkin, Khandelwal, and Osman randomly allocated export orders for high-quality rugs to handmade rug manufacturers from Egypt.[9] The authors provide compelling evidence of knowledge transfers from foreign buyers to the rug manufacturers that were mediated by export intermediaries. A caveat noted by the authors is that finding sophisticated foreign buyers of complex goods is onerous. The chapter did not conduct a cost–benefit analysis of export facilitation programmes, nor did it isolate market failures preventing firms from exporting without assistance. The finding that learning-from-exporting benefits exist is not sufficient to justify policy intervention, and a thorough cost–benefit analysis is necessary before concluding that an export-led growth strategy is net positive for an economy.

IV. Evidence supporting import promotion

Policymakers have long been focused on the risk of labour dislocation from import penetration. However, even when holding production technology constant, imports used as inputs in production can lead to lower production costs and consumer prices (as shown by Blaum, Lelarge, and Peters).[10] A caveat worth mentioning is that it is hard to measure the resources spent on finding trading partners abroad (like in the case of export promotion), meaning that we are yet to have a complete welfare estimate of access to cheaper imports.

When technology adapts in reaction to imports, reductions in import tariffs can increase access to imported input varieties and product scope.[11] R&D as well as technology upgrading can also exhibit complementarities with imported inputs. According to Bøler, Moxnes, and Ulltveit-Moe, cheaper R&D stimulates not only R&D investments but also imports of intermediates, magnifying the productivity gains from R&D.[12] Conversely, trade liberalisation can affect firms' technologies through changed incentives to undertake R&D or quality upgrading.[13] To activate this complementarity between R&D and imports requires well-functioning capital markets. Lastly, Buera and Oberfield argue that imports can lead to dynamic gains from trade as domestic firms may draw insights when importing from the most productive foreign firms.[14] However, the ability to draw insights is likely to depend on the absorptive capacity of domestic importers. If firms have lower absorptive capacity in LMICs, these gains from importing are stifled.

V. Evidence supporting multinational enterprises attraction

Most foreign direct investment is made via the entry of subsidiaries of MNEs. MNE subsidiaries account for most of the exports of countries across the development spectrum (e.g., 45% in Uganda, 84% in Costa Rica, 61% in Belgium) and most complex goods exports (e.g., 90% for medical devices in Costa Rica and a similar percentage for cars in Romania). Therefore, MNEs deserve a centre seat at any discussion over export-led growth and a separate discussion about their benefits for the domestic economy. The need to discuss the gains from MNEs is also motivated by the fact that the abolition of barriers to FDI is a central tenet in the Washington Consensus.

Regarding the benefits of MNEs, there is an emerging consensus that suppliers to MNEs experience substantial improvements in their productivity.[15;16;17] Domestic firms may also benefit from purchasing inputs developed by domestic suppliers for the MNEs or from imitating MNE products.[18;19;20] MNEs can also benefit the domestic economy through former MNE workers joining domestic employers and sharing the knowledge acquired during their MNE tenure or through entrepreneurship after their MNE employment.[21;22] MNEs can further improve welfare through channels that do not hinge on knowledge transfers (such as MNE-driven changes in labour standards within their supply chain).[23]

Whether policies such as SEZs, suggested by Professor Hausmann in his chapter, that warrant a preferential tax treatment to MNEs are welfare-enhancing or not depends on the magnitude of the (knowledge) benefits from MNEs, whether MNEs internalise them or not, the extent to which MNEs interact with the domestic economy, and how distortionary SEZ benefits are. More evidence along these lines is welcome. The merits of other policy instruments, such as investment promotion agencies that aim to reduce information frictions, depend on the market failures plaguing an economy and whether those instruments can address the relevant failures.

VI. Conclusion

Hausmann's chapter on export-led growth is a thought-provoking reflection on the limited role played by exports in the Washington Consensus and the more prominent role exports could play following the London Consensus. In reaction, I welcome the proposal of Hausmann and read it as a broad invitation to scholars to address the remaining open questions on the contributions of globalisation (in its many forms) to development and growth.

Notes

[1] Spence (2012).

[2] Sutton and Kellow (2010).

[3] Bustos (2011).

[4] Atkin et al. (2024).

[5] Atkin et al. (2024).

[6] Young (1991).

[7] Hausmann et al. (2007).

[8] Atkin et al. (2024).

[9] Atkin et al. (2017).

[10] Blaum et al. (2018).

[11] Goldberg et al. (2010).

[12] Bøler et al. (2015).

[13] Eslava et al. (2018).

[14] Buera and Oberfield (2020).

[15] Javorcik (2004).

[16] Alfaro-Ureña et al. (2022a).

[17] Amiti et al. (2023).

[18] Rodríguez-Clare (1996).

[19] Kee (2015).

[20] Brambilla et al. (2009).

[21] Poole (2013).

[22] Liu et al. (2014).

[23] Alfaro-Ureña et al. (2022b).

References

Alfaro-Ureña, A., Manelici, I. and Vasquez, J. (2022a) 'The Effects of Joining Multinational Supply Chains: New Evidence from Firm-to-Firm Linkages', *The Quarterly Journal of Economics*, 137(3):1495–1552. https://doi.org/10.1093/qje/qjac006

Alfaro-Ureña, A., Faber, B., Gaubert, C., Manelici, I. and Vasquez, J. P. (2022b) 'Responsible Sourcing? Theory and Evidence from Costa Rica', Working Paper 30683, National Bureau of Economic Research. https://jpvasquez-econ.github.io/files/Responsible_Sourcing_CR.pdf

Amiti, M., Duprez, C., Konings, J. and Van Reenen, J. (2023) 'FDI and Superstar Spillovers: Evidence from Firm-to-Firm Transactions', Working paper 31128, National Bureau of Economic Research. https://www.nber.org/system/files/working_papers/w31128/w31128.pdf

Atkin, D., Costinot, A. and Fukui, M. (2024) 'Globalization and the Ladder of Development: Pushed to the Top or Held at the Bottom?', MIT Working paper. https://economics.mit.edu/sites/default/files/2024-03/mutvc_LATEST.pdf

Atkin, D., Khandelwal, A. and Osman, A. (2017) 'Exporting and Firm Performance: Evidence from a Randomized Experiment', *The Quarterly Journal of Economics*, 132(2): 551–615. https://doi.org/10.1093/qje/qjx002

Blaum, J., Lelarge, C. and Peters, A. (2018) 'The Gains from Input Trade with Heterogeneous Importers', *American Economic Journal: Macroeconomics*, 10(4): 77–127. https://doi.org/10.1257/mac.20160426

Bøler, E. A., Moxnes, A. and Ulltveit-Moe, K. H. (2015) 'R&D, International Sourcing, and the Joint Impact on Firm Performance', *American Economic Review*, 105(12): 3704–39. https://doi.org/10.1257/aer.20121530

Brambilla, I., Hale, G. and Long, C. (2009) 'Foreign Direct Investment and the Incentives to Innovate and Imitate', *The Scandinavian Journal of Economics*, 111(4): 835–61. https://doi.org/10.1111/j.1467-9442.2009.01589.x

Buera, F. J. and Oberfield, E. (2020) 'The Global Diffusion of Ideas', *Econometrica*, 88(1): 83–114. https://doi.org/10.3982/ECTA14044

Bustos, P. (2011) 'Trade Liberalization, Exports, and Technology Upgrading: Evidence on the Impact of MERCOSUR on Argentinian Firms', *American Economic Review*, 101(1): 304–40. https://doi.org/10.1257/aer.101.1.304

Eslava, M., Fieler, A. C. and Xu, D. Y. (2018) 'Trade, Quality Upgrading, and Input Linkages: Theory and Evidence from Colombia', *American Economic Review*, 108(1): 109–46. https://doi.org/10.1257/aer.20150796

Goldberg, P. K., Khandelwal, A. K., Pavcnik, N. and Topalova, P. (2010) 'Imported Intermediate Inputs and Domestic Product Growth: Evidence from India', *The Quarterly Journal of Economics*, 125(4): 1727–67. https://doi.org/10.1162/qjec.2010.125.4.1727

Hausmann, R., Hwang, J. and Rodrik, D. (2007) 'What You Export Matters', *Journal of Economic Growth*, 12: 1–25. https://doi.org/10.1007/s10887-006-9009-4

Javorcik, B. S. (2004) 'Does Foreign Direct Investment Increase the Productivity of Domestic Firms? In Search of Spillovers Through Backward Linkages', *American Economic Review*, 94(3): 605–627. https://doi.org/10.1257/0002828041464605

Kee, H. L. (2015) 'Local Intermediate Inputs and the Shared Supplier Spillovers of Foreign Direct Investment', *Journal of Development Economics*, 112: 56–71. https://doi.org/10.1016/j.jdeveco.2014.09.007

Liu, Q., Lu, R. and Zhang, C. (2014) 'Entrepreneurship and Spillovers from Multinationals: Evidence from Chinese Private Firms', *China Economic Review*, 29: 95–106. https://doi.org/10.1016/j.chieco.2014.03.005

Poole, J. P. (2013) 'Knowledge Transfers from Multinational to Domestic Firms: Evidence from Worker Mobility', *Review of Economics and Statistics*, 95(2): 393–406. https://doi.org/10.1162/REST_a_00258

Rodríguez-Clare, A. (1996) 'Multinationals, Linkages, and Economic Development', *American Economic Review*, 86(4): 852–873. http://www.jstor.org/stable/2118308

Spence, M. (2012) 'Some Thoughts on the Washington Consensus and Subsequent Global Development Experience', *Journal of Economic Perspectives*, 35(3): 67–82. https://doi.org/10.1257/jep.35.3.67

Sutton, J. and Kellow, N. (2010) *An Enterprise Map of Ethiopia*, International Growth Centre. https://www.theigc.org/sites/default/files/2010/09/An-Enterprise-Map-of-Ethiopia-English.pdf

Young, A. (1991) 'Learning by Doing and the Dynamic Effects of International Trade', *The Quarterly Journal of Economics*, 106(2): 369–405. https://doi.org/10.2307/2937942

Response to Ricardo Hausmann by Danny Quah

I. The trade-technology relation in small and poor economies

In 'Export-led growth', Ricardo Hausmann concludes that what determines aggregate economic performance is (a) not just trade but exports and (b) not just technological progress but economic complexity.[1] This chapter challenges those conclusions on analytical and empirical grounds. I argue that because poor countries are cheap a wage-price mechanism underpins the growth impact of trade and technology. It is that mechanism, rather than exports and economic complexity, that more fundamentally determines aggregate economic performance.

In this commentary I build on Hausmann's framework, but depart from it in two significant ways. First, I show empirically that small economies are surprisingly successful. Their per capita incomes are unexpectedly high relative to larger economies. This finding contradicts theoretical models that feature as key growth drivers the advantages of diversity, scale economies, and economic complexity and experimentation. This is not to say that all small countries are rich, indeed, many are poor. Instead, it is to say the converse: almost all rich countries happen to be small. Smallness is not sufficient for economic success but is (close to) necessary. Good aggregate economic performance is not just the preserve of one or two small countries; rather, success characterises a broad range of small states, each with very different circumstances.

Singapore is a tiny country with a population of only 5.6 million and a land area of just 734 sq km (smaller than New York City or urban London). Yet, Singapore is the world's sixth-richest nation by per capita income (averaged from 2013 to 2023). Does that make Singapore unusual? There is only one large country among the nine richest countries in the world: the United States (ranked eighth). The average population among the nine richest nations, excluding the US, is only 4.2 million, i.e., less than Singapore's. The largest nation in this high-performing group (excluding the US) is Switzerland with a population of only 8.5 million. Among the rich, small states are the norm, not the exception. Second, I argue that in a world where poor countries are cheap, the effects of technological improvements and trade openness are not monotone, but vary with sectoral wage-price characteristics across the economy. On average, economic complexity in advanced technology matters for growth, but less so in countries that are extremely successful.

Why might this be? Conventional wisdom is that both trade and technological advance are good for everyone. In economic analysis this is, typically, unambiguous at the level of the aggregate economy. Following this thinking, moreover, if shifts in trade and technology disadvantage anyone in the economy, government can more than fully compensate those affected individuals while still keeping overall gains positive on net.

However, that poor countries are cheap indicates that those standard mechanisms are failing to function as expected in both rich and poor nations. Instead, in the model of this commentary, a wage-price mechanism with particular features ends up sequencing different dynamic adjustment across different sectors: international price convergence in tradable sectors then implies unconventional and counter-intuitive price response in non-tradables. The result is political resistance to trade and technology advance in specific sectors in the economy as those shifts wind up privileging certain workers and business and disadvantaging others.[2] This divergence between aggregate economic effect and domestic consensus also carries implications for geopolitical relations between nations.[3]

II. Poor cheap countries in the global economy

For four decades, the Washington Consensus has been an important if controversial reference for development policy in the global economy.[4;5;6;7] It provided guiding principles on three broad topics: first, property rights, privatisation, and liberalisation; second, monetary and fiscal policy; and third, trade, and foreign investment.

When Spence surveyed post-1970s growth experiences worldwide, he concluded that two features, not emphasised in the Washington Consensus, have been key for developmental success in the world and, in particular, in Asia: one, knowledge transfer and two, engagement with the global economy.[8] High incomes result from high productivity and advanced technology, and the fastest, most efficient way to improve technology levels in an economy is through knowledge transfer with the rest of the world. But it is not just in technical advancement, driven by knowledge transfer, where gains are obtained from engagement with the global economy. Benefits are obtained from just having access to large markets. Trade and investment opportunities in any country, especially a low-income emerging economy, are dwarfed in comparison with those available in the global economy.

Along the same lines is a third key observation: despite an impression of universalism, the Washington Consensus relates more obviously to the Latin American growth experience than generally elsewhere around the world. Hausmann builds on these three observations. His growth analysis emphasises exports where Asia succeeded while Latin America did not – and technology – to increase productivity rather than just stabilise the macroeconomy. In his approach, Hausmann raises two challenges. First, the Washington Consensus does not work: Latin American countries that followed the Washington Consensus recommendations were not as successful as Asian ones that ignored them. Second, traditional growth models too do not work: across nations, per capita incomes remain widely dispersed whereas convergence (again across nations) has already occurred in the values of neoclassical explanatory variables – number of workers per capita, capital per worker, education, and urbanisation; and in indicators of demographic transition, such as life expectancy, fertility, and female labour force participation rates.

The final ingredient in Hausmann's analysis is that poor countries are cheap, a relation discussed both in Hausmann's chapter and in subsection II.1. This hypothesised empirical regularity does not mean those countries' currencies are undervalued. Instead, the cheapness of poor countries signals that those countries' production structures bear particular features. Hausmann uses this maintained hypothesis to motivate his emphasis on technological progress in products of ever greater economic complexity. I will use this same fact to argue, instead, that certain kinds of economic openness and technical progress can harm economic wellbeing. Thus, in my analysis, a world where poor countries are cheap is a world of potential political resistance to trade openness and technological improvement.

To understand this, we need to begin with an explanation for the cheapness of poor countries. Informal intuition for this is that countries are poor when their technology is less advanced, thus lowering worker productivity. But it is incorrect to say that this implies low prices. If, for instance, wages are pre-determined or less than fully flexible downwards, then reduced productivity results in higher prices, not lower. This is no mere hypothetical possibility. In the early 2000s, many poor countries did not yet have widely available high-speed broadband Wi-Fi internet service at home or at work. Instead, to get online, users visited costly, slow, wired internet cafes. Less advanced technology did not make things cheap. Quite the opposite: poor countries worked with less advanced technology that was both costlier and less convenient.

Farming provides a second example. While traditional, low-tech agricultural methods are appropriate when low-wage labour is plentiful, continuing with that less advanced technology implies ever higher output prices as wages rise. Only by upgrading agricultural technology and raising labour productivity would it be possible to reduce food prices as wages rise. Again, less advanced technology does not make things cheap.

Therefore, a more robust analysis is needed to understand why poor countries are cheap: It is this that will motivate both Hausmann's emphasis on economic complexity and the current commentary's hypotheses on domestic resistance to trade and technical progress.

Suppose the economy produces different kinds of outputs, some of which are not (yet) traded internationally. For sectors producing traded output, prices on their outputs are equalised to world prices, after normalising by market exchange rates. These sectors' outputs are neither cheaper nor costlier than in the rest of the world. In traded-output sectors technology levels together with world prices determine wages. Assuming labour can move freely in the economy, the wage rate across all sectors – both traded and non-traded – is equalised, and is thus exogenously determined relative to technology in non-traded sectors. Therefore, poor countries with low technology levels in their traded sectors will have low wages. Those low wages propagate through the entire economy and result in low prices in non-traded sectors. Thus, poor countries are cheap.[9]

At this point, Hausmann's analysis draws on a key asymmetry between the non-traded and traded sectors. The equalisation of traded-sector prices with the rest of the world means that technical advances in that sector translate into a corresponding rise in wages. That increase in wages, in turn, means that prices rise in the non-traded sector. On the other hand, technical advances in non-traded sectors does not raise wages – those are fixed by technology and price in the traded sector – but instead lowers output price in the sector concerned. It is thus only technical advances in the traded sectors that improve the economy; technical advance overall has ambiguous effects. Because Hausmann associates economic complexity with exports, and thus with trade more generally, he deduces economic complexity to be the key driving variable for exports and thus for growth. The empirical analysis in Hausmann's chapter examines that relation.

An alternative rendering is possible for this Balassa-Samuelson mechanism resulting in a substantively different emphasis: begin by noting that, in general, technical advance in traded sectors is welcomed by all segments of the polity. However, in a world where poor countries are cheap, technical advance in non-traded sectors will be opposed by segments of the population, for its lowering output prices, and thus its being perceived to cause job destruction and to put at risk both employment and business sustainability. In this reasoning, moreover, it is trade that matters, not just exports (or imports). As long as trade causes a rise in output prices, i.e., as long as domestic prices converge upwards to world levels with trade, then wages too rise everywhere in the economy. Non-traded sector output prices are more likely low when technology in that sector is relatively advanced. In these circumstances economic openness attracts popular support. However, a low-tech, non-trading sector will, other things equal, have relatively high output price. Trade for that sector will then drive down output price, and be perceived to cause job destruction, unemployment, and failing businesses. Such economic openness attracts political opposition.[10]

This description highlights yet another difference between my reasoning and the analysis in Hausmann's chapter. On the trade openness side, Hausmann's focus is exports, a quantity variable. Mine is not quantities but instead prices and wages, changes in which emerge from trade. My analysis does not suggest separating out exports and imports: either one of these matters as much as the other.

In summary, understanding why poor economies are cheap can, as in Hausmann's chapter, motivate scrutiny of the economic complexity of exports and can potentially help explain the positive impact on growth of economic complexity. Further extending the reasoning, as I do here, helps shed light on why trade and technical advancements are not always unambiguously accepted by the population in a given economy.

Policymakers have a range of options for trade and technology that can increase growth and lift economic performance. Not all options, however, are politically acceptable. What does not work is to simply boost technology or open up the economy, without first working through their impact on wages and prices.

Section III will present empirical evidence on cross-country aggregate economic performance relative to the large forces of trade openness and economic complexity just discussed. For completeness, however, the following subsection II.1 now discusses the empirics of relating poor countries to cheapness.

1. *Empirics for how poor countries are cheap*

How empirically accurate is the hypothesis that poor countries are cheap – if, as I have argued, poor countries' use of less advanced technology does not lower prices? While that informal intuition is incorrect, the empirical evidence will, indeed, show poor countries are cheap. (Also, I highlight the key features of the data using a format that I will deploy again repeatedly for efficiency in the following section III.)

Hausmann analyses the relation between incomes and prices using PPP adjustment factors. But unless one knows what convention is being used for numerator and denominator in the definition of a PPP adjustment factor, it will be unclear how exactly a downward-sloping line in Hausmann's Figure 5.1 shows what it intends. Does a high adjustment factor mean the country is cheap? Or expensive? What is the direction of adjustment?

Instead then, define R the real price of the economy as the number of local currency units (LCUs) needed to purchase what one international dollar can buy, divided by the market exchange rate (in LCUs per international dollar). This price is low – the economy is cheap – when fewer LCUs are needed to make a purchase than the market exchange suggests.[11] In all the empirical analyses here and in section III, I present snapshots of different variables at the beginning and the end of the available time sample, where beginning means taking the timeseries average over the decade 1980–1989 and end means the timeseries average over the decade since 2013.

Figure 5.5 graphs R the real price of the economy on the vertical axis, and per capita GDP on the horizontal axis. Each panel shows the ordinary least squares line and a nonparametrically-fitted trend line, as well as its 95% confidence interval.[12]

We can conclude that poor countries are indeed cheap on average: both panels of Figure 5.5 have the best-fitting lines slope upwards. However, there is considerable variation in the distribution of data points around the positively-sloped lines. Where the bulk of the cross- section distribution rests, the locally estimated scatterplot smoothed (loess) line is firmly positive with tight confidence interval around the estimate. It is striking, however, that even in that midrange there are significant outliers both upwards and downwards. Singapore, for one, is consistently cheap relative to what its high GDP per capita would predict. In the cross-section Singapore is balanced by other more expensive countries: Switzerland, Norway, Iceland, and Denmark.

While cheapness is the focus of explanation in this discussion, subsequent empirical analysis in this commentary will use measurements at market exchange rates, rather than corrected for cheapness or using PPP. This is because in section III the focus of interest becomes the economy's position in the world. While correcting for purchasing power, i.e., using PPP, is appropriate for understanding the wellbeing of a country's people, it is inappropriate for assessing that country's role in the global economy: jet fighters and Apple iPhones are purchased not with PPP-corrected dollars but with dollars bought at market exchange rates.

Figure 5.5: Relationship between real price of the economy and GDP (per capita)

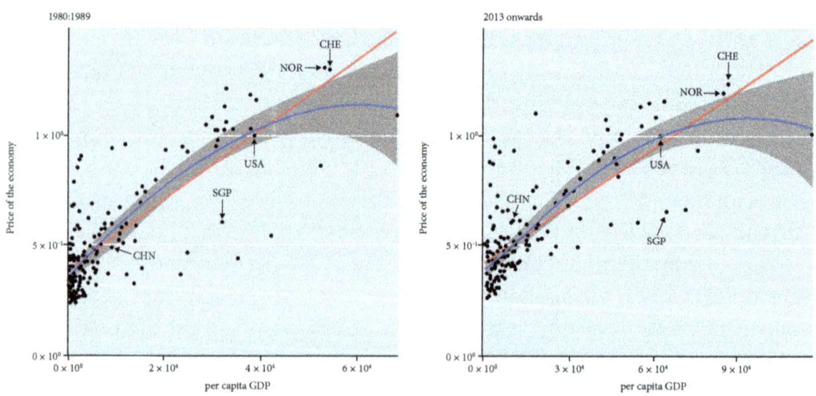

Source: author's own calculations based on World Development Indicators.
Notes: Poor countries are cheap. The left panel shows the situation for the 1980s; the right, that since 2013. The vertical axis is the real price of the economy, R in the text; it is the reciprocal of cheapness. The horizontal axis is GDP per capita. The data points are all the national economies in the World Bank's World Development Indicators database. Each graph displays OLS and nonparametric loess lines, the latter together with its 95% confidence interval. The panels also explicitly indicate Switzerland, Norway, Singapore, the United States, and China – to help calibrate the reader's intuition on what the figures show, and to which the analysis will return subsequently.

III. The global distribution of economic success

This section quantifies the significance of trade and technology in the cross-section distribution of aggregate economic performance across countries. This is to help assess the export and complexity channels for economic growth proposed by Hausmann.

The key finding, however, will be that small countries are surprisingly successful economically. This casts doubt on the idea that complexity and scale are the critical drivers for aggregate economic performance. More directly, this section will also document how the effects of technological improvements are not monotone: economic complexity is good for raising per capita GDP for ordinary economies; however, the richest, most successful economies escape this correlation and are extraordinarily rich without having to be unusually complex.

First, consider the distinction between exports and trade, the sum total of exports and imports. Do exports need to be highlighted as the engine of growth and prosperity? Or will trade suffice?

Figure 5.6 shows how, once business cycle variations have been removed, exports and trade in the cross section of countries are tightly related to the point of being indistinguishable. Over the longer term, total trade just equals twice exports. The slope of the ordinary least squares line equals exactly that ratio, with the exception of one or two instances, deviations from the line too small to be visible to the human eye.

Consequently, it will not be possible to tell if it is exports that drive growth, as suggested by Hausmann, or whether it is more generally trade that does so.

Figure 5.6: Relationship between trade and exports

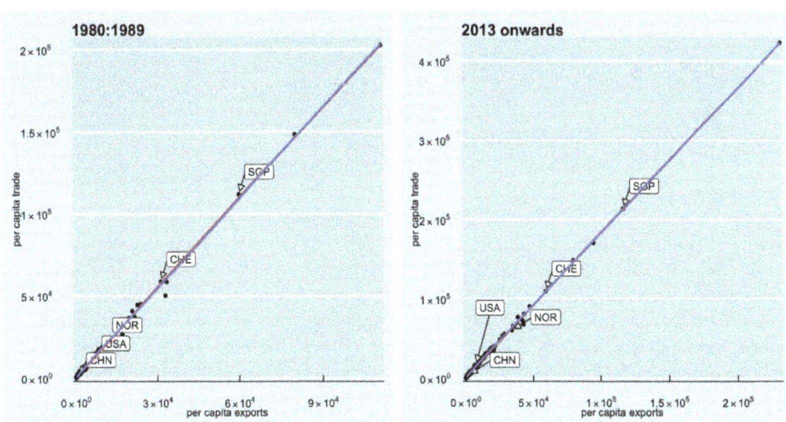

Source: author's own calculations based on World Development Indicators.
Notes: Modulo, a proportionality constant, when smoothed over a decade, exports and trade are indistinguishable in the cross section.

Next, consider the hypothesis that engagement with the global economy encourages technological advance and thus increases growth and raises economic performance more generally.

Figure 5.7 shows that for both beginning and end of the data sample, income and trade are strongly positively related. Economies are richer, the greater their openness. This positive relationship has a relatively narrow confidence interval around it. At the same time, however, the data show significant outliers, e.g., Singapore. Conditional on its trade, Singapore's GDP per capita is unexpectedly low. Two other outliers, but in the opposite direction, are Norway and the United States: these two countries are unexpectedly rich, given the relatively little that they trade.

One of the most interesting features of Figure 5.7 is how China is strikingly unremarkable. For all the attention China attracts in its being nearly every other nation's lead trading partner, the reality is China does relatively little trade per person. Many other countries do much more. Singapore, for one, does 50 times more trade than China per capita. China's trade is notable primarily because its population is so large. In trade per capita, China is unremarkable.

Figure 5.7: Relationship between income (GDP per capita) and trade (per capita)

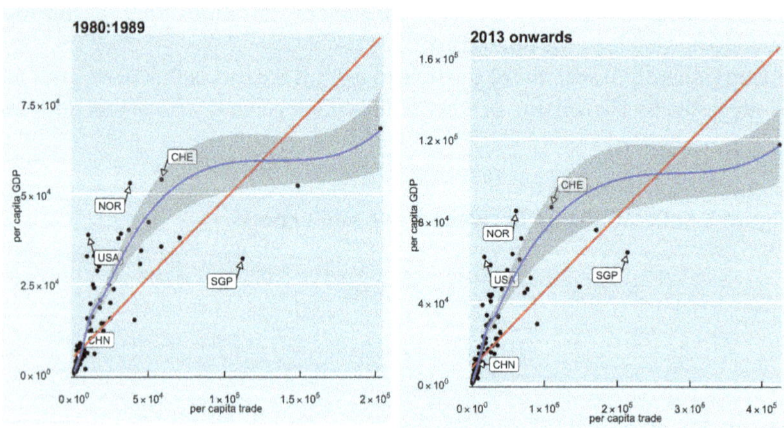

Source: author's own calculations based on World Development Indicators.
Notes: Incomes and trade are positively related. The vertical axis is GDP per capita; the horizontal axis, total trade per capita. The positive relationship has a relatively narrow 95% confidence interval, but with significant outliers. Singapore, conditional on how much it trades, has relatively low per capita income. Norway and the US, on the other hand, deviate in the opposite direction. Relative to how little they trade, those two nations are unexpectedly rich. Finally, given its very large population, China's pattern of trade and income is unremarkable.

Figure 5.8: Relationship between trade (per capita) and population size

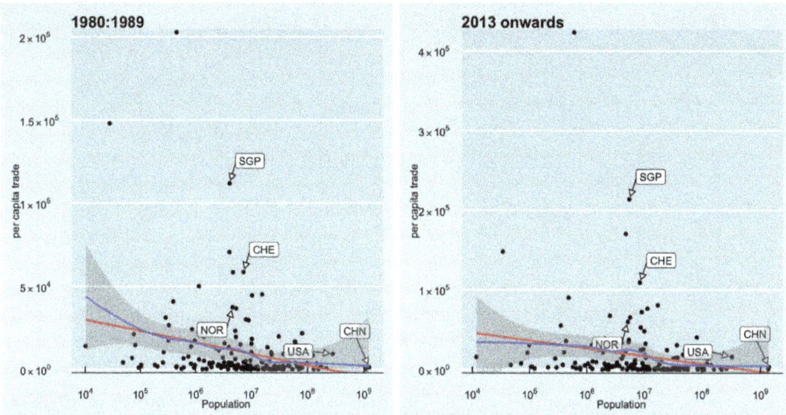

Source: author's own calculations based on World Development Indicators.
Notes: On average, per capita, small states do not trade significantly more than large economies. The vertical axis is trade per capita; the horizontal axis is population, measured on a log (base 10) scale. The most striking feature is how nations like Singapore and Switzerland consistently trade orders of magnitude more than world average.

This empirical regularity on trade and country size is sometimes dismissed with the suggestion that arithmetic alone, mechanically and misleadingly makes small states appear to trade more. However, Figure 5.8 shows that this is not the reality. Many small countries trade as little per capita as large countries. Some large economies trade hardly at all; others considerably more. Countries exercise significant agency in how much they choose to trade. On average the relationship between trade and size is negative, but only slightly so. Instead, the most outstanding empirical feature in Figure 5.8 is how successful countries like Singapore and Switzerland consistently trade orders of magnitude more than the world average. It is not that small countries trade a lot. Instead, it is that successful countries who trade a lot happen to be small.

To expand on this, Figure 5.9 shows the relationship between income per capita and population. The figure shows the sense in which small countries succeed at economics. During 2013–22, of the nine richest nations on Earth, only the United States had a population greater than 10 million. With its over 300 million people, the United States was obviously an outlier. Singapore's population, by contrast, was only 5.6 million. Even more remarkably, the average population of the nine richest states, excluding the United States outlier, only came to 4.2 million. The largest of these eight, Switzerland, had a population of only 8.5 million. To be clear, Figure 5.9 is not a statement that small states always succeed: it shows many small nations are poor. Instead, the lesson in Figure 5.9 is that successful nations are small, not that small states succeed.

Figure 5.9: Relationship between GDP (per capita) and population size

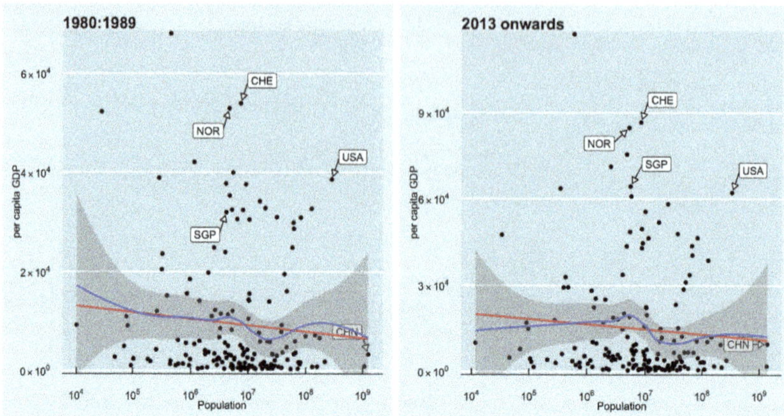

Source: author.
Notes: The richest nations on the planet are almost all small states. Since 2013, of the nine richest nations only the US has a large population. Singapore in this time has only 5.6 million. But, more striking, the average population of the nine richest states, excluding the US, is only 4.2 million, with the largest, Switzerland, having a population of just 8.5 million. Obviously, many small nations are poor. Not all small states succeed but almost all successful nations happen to be small.

Figure 5.10: Relationship between GDP (per capita) and economic complexity

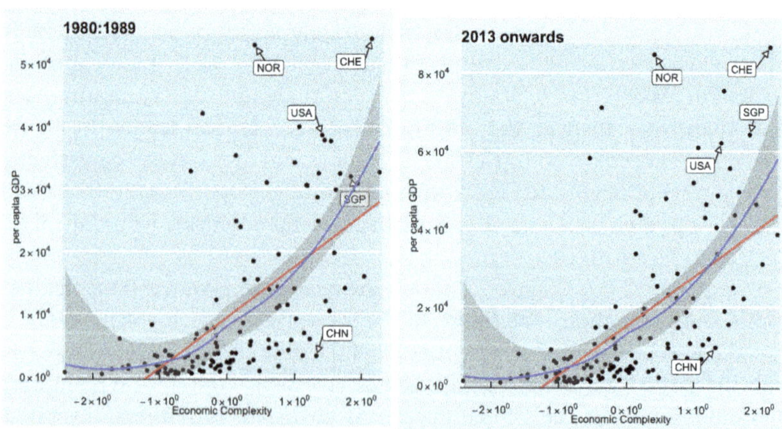

Source: author.
Notes: Incomes and high-complexity production are strongly positively related. At the same time, however, complexity cannot account for the performance of the small-state, successful economies. The figure shows GDP per capita on the vertical axis and the Hausmann–Hidalgo index of production complexity on the horizontal axis.

Finally, and most critical for the analysis in Hausmann's chapter, we turn to economic complexity and economic performance. Does complexity account for the greatest economic successes? Is economic complexity the best, fastest way to improve the level of technology in the tradables sector and to maintain it at a high level? Is economic complexity the best way to raise the price of tradables, thereby allowing incomes, wages, and all prices to rise without mass opposition?

Figure 5.10 shows that the relationship between income and economic complexity is strongly positive. However, the most successful economies are distinct upwards outliers relative to that relationship. By contrast, nations that do not outperform the positive relationship are many and hew close to the ordinary least squares and loess lines. Economic complexity accounts well for average economic performance, but not for successes.

This pattern of outliers is predicted from the earlier finding that small states are surprisingly successful. By logic, small states do not have the size to encompass the wide diversity of skills and insights that create complex products. When they succeed, therefore, they escape in an upwards direction from the predicted average relation between incomes and economic complexity. This reasoning helps explain Figure 5.10. It leaves open, however, the reasons underlying the economic performance of those small countries that do succeed.

Small states will, naturally, tend to make too much of what its people can do, and too little of what its people want. It is trade – both exports and imports together – that overcomes these bottlenecks.

IV. Conclusion

This response has developed a simple analysis of the effects of trade and technology on aggregate economic performance. The core mechanism I draw on is wage–price dynamics in a global economy where poor nations are cheap.

The commentary departed from Hausmann's work in two important conclusions: (1) what matters is trade generally, not exports in particular; (2) what matters is technological progress generally, not economic complexity in particular. It is important, however, that those sectors where technological advancements occur and where trade impacts significantly have particular wage–price patterns. Empirically, for average nations, technological advancement through complexity matters; for extreme successes, it is trade that matters.

This response's key empirical findings, however, concern the economic performance of small states. A small economy, all else equal, tends to produce too much of what its people can do and too little of what its people want. Small states cannot match the scale, variety, or complexity that bigger economies can leverage. They face significant obstacles for growth and economic success. Yet, small states are the most successful economies on the planet.

Small nations, provided they remain open to the global economy, can draw on different channels of knowledge transfer. Advanced technology levels are indeed critical for prosperity and aggregate economic performance – but they can come through multiple pathways, not only home-grown research and complexity of the domestic economy. Trade helps small states overcome their natural bottlenecks.

Trade with the global economy is essential for small states, whereas larger nations can afford autarky. Thus, although a more elaborate analysis is not given in the current commentary, a simple conjecture is natural on the role small states can play in the global economy. All else equal, small states have the most to gain from an open global trading system. Consequently, it is they who will show greatest commitment to such an international order.[13]

Notes

1 The analysis in the current chapter of aggregate economic performance rests on the understanding that that is actually what many observers have in mind when they speak of economic growth. For policymakers, growth rates – the first-differences of log incomes, typically analysed in regressions – are meaningful not for their measured values but for the endpoint to which they draw the economy.

2 While my reasoning might appear unconventional, the differential effect in my argument is, in essence, the same as that in analyses of inequality and growth. Indeed, my use of the specific wage-price mechanism – essentially a Balassa–Samuelson effect – can be viewed as yet another driver for inequality in growing economies.

3 Quah (2024a).

4 Its author notably reported that 'there are people who cannot utter the term without foaming at the mouth' (Williamson, 2002).

5 Rodrik (2006).

6 Spence (2021).

7 Quah (2024b).

8 Spence (2021).

9 This reasoning is basically that of the so-called Balassa–Samuelson effect, named after the economists who first proposed an explanation for this pattern of prices across countries.

10 In the language of Great Power rivalry this is what happened with 'The China Shock' (Quah, 2024a). While the economy in such a situation can always choose to block trade, or otherwise retreat into autarky, the better way to combat this negative impact, according to the analysis in the text, is to improve technology in the traded sector.

[11] Variable R is available as PA.NUS.PPPC.RF from the World Bank's World Development Indicators database.

[12] Being cheap or costly is always relative. The World Bank constructs R in World Bank international dollars, a measure akin to the US dollar. In Figure 5.5, being vertically lower than 1 means roughly that the economy is cheaper than the US; being higher, costlier. To help the reader mentally calibrate the graph, observe that the World Bank's international dollar turns out to be close to but not identical with the US dollar, so the United States appears near but not exactly at the value 1 on the vertical axis.

[13] Quah (2024a).

References

Quah, D. (2024a) 'Economic Principles for a New World Order of Multipolarity and Multilateralism', Working paper, LKYSPP. https://dannyquah.github.io/Storage/2024.03-Danny.Quah-New-World-Order-Multipolarity-Multilateralism.pdf

Quah, D. (2024b) 'Why Small Nations Surprisingly Succeed: Trade, Technology, and the Washington Consensus', Working paper, LKYSPP, Singapore. https://dannyquah.github.io/Storage/2024.02-Danny.Quah-Small-Nations-Success.pdf

Rodrik, D. (2006) 'Goodbye Washington Consensus, Hello Washington Confusion? A Review of the World Bank's Economic Growth in the 1990s: Learning from a Decade of Reform', *Journal of Economic Literature*, 44: 973–987. https://doi.org/10.1257/jel.44.4.973

Spence, A. M. (2021) 'Some Thoughts on the Washington Consensus and Subsequent Global Development Experience', *Journal of Economic Perspectives*, 35(3): 67–82. https://doi.org/10.1257/jep.35.3.67

Williamson, J. (2002) 'Did the Washington Consensus Fail?', *Peterson Institute for International Economics* [6 November 2002]. https://www.piie.com/commentary/speeches-papers/did-washington-consensus-fail

PART III

MACROECONOMIC POLICY

6. Fiscal policy and public debt

Ricardo Reis and Andrés Velasco

The original Washington Consensus fiscal policy principles involved fiscal discipline, public spending on physical and human capital, and broad tax bases with low tax rates. While these principles remain sound, in this paper we add two new principles supported by theory, evidence, and experience. The first new principle involves using targeted transfers to offset shocks that economic agents cannot insure against, and using transfers and public credit to preserve markets when a market-maker of last resort is needed. This policy will involve fluctuating public balances and infrequent but large public deficits during crises, which in turn requires a second principle to ensure the necessary fiscal space. That second principle is to preserve the special nature of public debt, keeping government bonds safe and liquid, via rigorous fiscal rules and credible fiscal and monetary institutions. For most countries, the existence of a global financial safety net is also essential to the successful implementation of this second principle.

I. Introduction

The original formulation of the Washington Consensus included three priorities for fiscal policy:

- Pursue fiscal discipline to avoid the macroeconomic instability associated with excessive debt issuance or money creation.
- Keep public expenditures focused on basic health, education, welfare, and infrastructure, and away from sectoral subsidies of dubious social and economic value.
- Raise tax revenues from a broad tax base, holding marginal tax rates at moderate levels.[1]

How to cite this book chapter:

Reis, Ricardo and Velasco, Andrés (2025) 'Fiscal policy and public debt', in: Besley, Tim, Bucelli, Irene and Velasco, Andrés (eds) *The London Consensus: Economic Principles for the 21st Century*, London: LSE Press, pp. 197–217 https://doi.org/10.31389/lsepress.tlc.f

A generation later, most economists are still in broad agreement with these three principles. But academic views and actual practice have since shifted – at times in ways that complement them, but also in some ways that contradict them. After all, in many advanced economies public debt has risen since the Great Financial Crisis of 2007–09 more than ever during peacetime. The governments of both advanced and emerging nations today often react to crises with aggressive countercyclical fiscal policies, as they did both during the Great Financial Crisis of 2007–09 and during the COVID-19 crisis. And the International Monetary Fund (IMF) routinely recommends progressive tax systems and the use of taxes and transfers to redistribute from the rich to the poor as part of the job of stabilising business cycles. In short: there is a great deal more fiscal activism than the Washington Consensus recommended.

Now, it is one thing to try to fulfil both the old and the new role for fiscal policy; it is something else to be able to do it. The new fiscal activism requires that governments be able to borrow in times of crisis, when private sector agents often cannot. History shows that not all governments retain unfettered market access at reasonable interest rates (or any rates at all) during periods of financial strain. Only those with manageable debt levels and strong fiscal institutions do. These are the prerequisites for safeguarding the privileged role of public debt and being able to undertake an activist fiscal policy.

This chapter develops these points and proposes a new and broader perspective on fiscal policy and debt management, adding two principles to Williamson's original formulation of the Washington Consensus: a rationale for the new activism on both spending and taxation, and a revamped perspective on fiscal discipline and public debt.

II. Fiscal activism

At the time of the Washington Consensus, it was widely accepted that countries should run fiscal deficits during economic contractions and surpluses during expansions. This was either because of neoclassical tax smoothing, which dictates that tax rates and their distortions should be constant over time (so that revenues fluctuate with the cycle), or because of Keynesian output stabilisation, in which the government spends or saves in a countercyclical fashion. Those ideas remain valid and widely accepted today. But there are three additional reasons for fiscal activism, which we analyse in what follows.

1. *Fiscal policy as insurance, completing markets after the event*

People face many risks they cannot insure against, that not only cause large drops in wellbeing when they materialise, but also cause prospective anxiety beforehand. Some of these risks are aggregate, so they cannot be pooled and diversified away by traditional insurance. A recession or a large drop in housing prices affects almost everyone, with no winners around to compensate the losers. In an ideal world, these risks could be traded and efficiently shared in financial markets, but in the real world they cannot. On the contrary, financial markets often end up amplifying these shocks and concentrating them in the most vulnerable segments of the population.

One common macroeconomic risk involves losing one's job during a recession. Finding a new job can take a long time, even after the recession is over. Another macro risk is a sudden and large aggregate income loss – for instance, during a health crisis like the pandemic – that limits sales for a small business owner. Yet a third one is a large spike in unavoidable spending for households whose rigid consumer basket depends heavily on energy. There is no macro market where the millions of people who find themselves in such situations can insure against these contingencies before the fact.

In principle, government can help households smooth consumption across these different possible events. Before a shock happens, it can set up automatic stabilisers, such as unemployment insurance. Afterwards, it can transfer resources to those affected by uninsurable bad outcomes. In addition to the welfare benefits that follow from standard consumption smoothing, there is an important macroeconomic benefit – with a logic dating back to Keynes – that the literature has emphasised in the past two decades. During a recession, the fear of being hit by uninsured shocks leads people to save more, which in turn lowers aggregate demand and deepens the slump, in what is sometimes referred to as a paradox of thrift.[2] Public provision of social insurance can sever this amplification mechanism, since the government internalises the effects that prices do not reflect when insurance markets are missing.

The standard objection to public insurance provision is moral hazard: people would lose the incentive to guard themselves against risk. But the shocks in question are macroeconomic, and depend less (or not at all) on individual actions. This reduces the scope for moral hazard. In the standard story, people who have insured their bicycles are then more likely to leave them unlocked or in unsafe locations, with the result that the 'shock' of having the bike stolen happens more often. That is not the case with aggregate shocks, because no single person can make them more frequent.[3] Moreover, the government can observe, however imperfectly, the realisation of these shocks, so that people cannot misreport them to boost their insurance payout. All these reasons amount to a case for government to intervene.

Examples of these principles in action are easy to come by. Take unemployment insurance: many governments have chosen not just to have such a system, but to raise its coverage and generosity once a recession begins. Other more recent cases include temporary programmes designed to allow businesses to survive the pandemic downturn, such as the United Kingdom's furlough scheme, and the novel transfer programmes that targeted support to the most affected households during the 2022 energy crisis.[4]

These new policies have often been large – in some cases, very large. Germany, for instance, spent €200 billion, or over 5% of gross domestic product (GDP), to subsidise consumers during the 2022 spike in energy prices.[5] The new activism mostly involves transfers to households and businesses. It is very different from the Keynesian activism, consisting of government purchases of goods and services that the old Washington Consensus focused on.

However, the new case for activism has its limits. Such policies ought to provide transfers only to those especially affected by shocks. Looking back at the measures taken during the pandemic or the energy crisis, that was often not the case. This raised the fiscal costs of these programmes while lowering their effectiveness. Moreover, targeting those affected is not the same as targeting those who are poor on average. Insurance is not the same as redistribution. If rich households were affected by the shocks, they could also be recipients of transfers. In practice, this is seldom the case because higher savings and wealth allow the rich to self-insure, but it is still an important principle to keep in mind.

More broadly, the new emphasis on insurance provision need not imply a larger state. The argument is not about the size of the government across the business cycle, but about activism during recessions. The average size of the state could remain unchanged if, during the upswing, government lowered spending and accumulated assets (or repaid debts) to make activism easier to finance during turbulent times. We return to this topic shortly.

The need for and the desirability of these policies varies from country to country. Different societies have different social insurance arrangements to deal with the 'missing markets' problem. In some countries, family and kinship ties can be more effective than government in providing insurance. In others, government may get a bigger 'bang for its buck' by subsidising private agents or providing public guarantees that spur the emergence of private insurance markets, instead of insuring households directly via transfers. And, of course, the extent to which public insurance crowds out or complements private insurance depends both on context and on policy design.

2. *Fiscal policy as market-maker of last resort*

Related to the need to create missing markets is the need to sustain existing markets when they are near collapse. Whereas the first new role for fiscal policy focuses on households and businesses unable to purchase insurance, this second role focuses on the markets and institutions that provide the limited insurance that does exist. Under this logic, a fiscal intervention is triggered by the infrequent (but potentially very costly) collapse of certain markets, especially financial markets. Access to insurance disappears precisely when it is most needed – during crises.[6]

The Great Financial Crisis of 2007–09 provides a prime example. Government, broadly defined to include both treasuries and central banks, stepped in to provide emergency credit, subsidies, public guarantees, asset purchases, and capital injections, either to replace the financial markets that had disappeared or to keep markets operating.

This kind of market failure results from financial imperfections that the academic literature has long explored. To take just one example, imagine that lenders will not allow firm or household debt to rise beyond a certain multiple of collateralisable assets such as real estate or physical capital. If a recession then lowers the value of these assets, firms and households can no longer borrow as much as they did before. Households are forced to cut consumption and firms to reduce investment. This in turn deepens both the recession and its associated welfare losses.[7]

Even worse, the literature shows that crises can also become self-fulfilling. Continuing with the same example, if the borrowing constraint depends on the price of the collateral, and that price falls in response to the expectation that households will not consume and firms will not invest, then the tightening of borrowing constraints causes that expectation to be confirmed.[8]

The role for government here is related to, but also different from, the previous role we discussed. An activist fiscal policy can eliminate the bad equilibrium by committing to use government resources to provide public credit or to buy assets, preventing the downward spiral of prices. This can stop the amplification that arises from the fire sale of assets and can avoid the self-fulfilling pessimism that results from the endogenous tightening of borrowing constraints.

But why should government be in the business of providing such support? What can it do that the private sector is not able to do?

For one, government (at least in advanced economies, and sometimes in emerging markets (EMs)) can borrow when others cannot. This means government can become a lender of last resort or a market-maker of last resort, responding to aggregate shocks, when others are illiquid. In the best-case scenario, and if it is credibly and readily available, the fiscal bazooka may not need to be used. The mere expectation that government would intervene to rule out the bad equilibrium keeps the economy locked into the good equilibrium.

Notice how different from the conventional rules this new role for fiscal policy is. The focus here is not on aggregate demand management or on helping firms directly through bailouts. Rather, it is on supporting the normal functioning of financial markets.

Again, this new activist role for the government is subject to caveats. When it comes to financial institutions, moral hazard is at the forefront. Banks may overborrow if they expect the government to step in, and this places a constraint on how much the government can and should do. But this does not mean it should do nothing. Intervention brings benefits; moral hazard can bring costs. Standard economic calculus suggests that the optimal policy should be somewhere in the middle: large enough to make a difference and rule out the bad equilibrium, but not as large as it could be.[9]

A second caveat is that, for political reasons, policies that are meant to be temporary could end up being permanent. For instance, long-run credit subsidies could allow inefficient firms to survive and reduce aggregate productivity.[10] Again, this is not an argument for doing nothing, but rather for designing policies in a way that ensures they will be as temporary as needed. One way to do that is to introduce state-contingent sunset clauses in the legislation that authorise the initial fiscal intervention. An alternative is to enhance the quality and autonomy of fiscal and monetary institutions, as we discuss shortly.

There is one last constraint on fiscal policy that is central. Government can only step in as a lender of last resort and market-maker of last resort if it retains the ability to borrow during a crisis, when no one else can. The new interventionism implies greater borrowing during turbulent times, a point to which we now turn.

3. *The amplitude of the fiscal balance*

In principle, providing transfers to those most affected by a recession is consistent with raising taxes on the least affected and conducting a zero-deficit fiscal policy. But completing markets after the fact will often yield larger public deficits. One reason is that insurance should be inter-temporal, across groups that live at different times as well as across groups alive today. The 'less affected' groups are not just a (possibly small) subset of those alive today, but also those who will live through better times (with an expansion in economic activity) after the crisis. Accomplishing this inter-temporal risk-shifting is another dimension in which government can complement private markets.

Being a market-maker or lender of last resort could be accomplished without public deficits: the government could accumulate savings that it then disburses during crises. But that is unlikely to be the first-best policy, because holding those assets in a liquid reserve is typically expensive. Yet for some countries, especially open emerging economies, this may be the only available option. For these countries, an increase in the public deficit (in response to a fire sale after an asset price drop) is likely to be accompanied by a rise in the current account deficit. Being able to borrow abroad to finance that larger deficit is far from guaranteed, especially if the asset price that collapses is the (nominal and real) exchange rate, since this lowers the present value of the government's future revenues when measured in foreign currency.

When public borrowing in times of crises is possible, this need not mean more frequent and larger deficits. On the contrary, it can mean larger surpluses in good times to pay for the larger deficits in bad times. As in our earlier argument, here the case is for a larger amplitude of the public deficit, not for a larger deficit on average.

In addition to the 'risk-sharing-across-time' argument, there is another independent case for running larger deficits during turbulent times. Over the last 20 years, advanced economies have experienced an excess of savings relative to the ability of those economies to channel savings to productive investment projects. This has caused low equilibrium real interest rates, and therefore nominal interest rates have hit the zero lower bound more often. At this point the economy is in a liquidity trap, where the central bank cannot cut interest rates further if needed to stimulate the economy. It is widely accepted that under the zero lower bound, fiscal policy can and should take over from monetary policy as the main tool to stabilise the economy across the business cycle.[11]

Moreover, nearly two decades of research on the liquidity trap have yielded novel and varied arguments on why the multipliers of fiscal policy can be enhanced by targeting transfers to groups with different marginal propensities to consume. As a result, the composition of spending and other interventions are key – not just their size, as was the case in older Keynesian analysis.[12] Finally, the last 20 years also saw a widening wedge between the returns to private investment and the interest rate on government bonds. Fiscal and monetary policies may be able to crowd in private investment if they manage to affect this wedge.[13]

An important caveat is that savings and investment move around, and so do real interest rates. When the zero lower bound does not bind, monetary policy – conventional or unconventional – should still play a central role in stabilisation. Moreover, in the years since the Washington Consensus, more nations, especially in EMs, have moved towards flexible exchange rates and reasonably deregulated capital accounts. In those circumstances, monetary policy is more effective than fiscal policy in stabilising output and employment.

III. Preserving fiscal space through prudent debt management

More fiscal activism and a greater amplitude of fiscal deficits and surpluses requires that governments retain their ability to borrow during crises. But this is not something that happens automatically. Rather, fiscal space needs to be built and preserved.

1. *Build and respect strong fiscal and monetary institutions*

The fact that fiscal policy could be conducted in an optimal way does not mean that it always or often is. Far from it: the political economy of fiscal policy is challenging and intricate.[14] Scholars have documented the tendency of many countries to run a deficit over the whole business cycle, implying a 'deficit bias' and a persistent trend of debt accumulation. Also well documented is the common procyclicality of deficits (the opposite of what both old and new arguments prescribe), prompted by the fact that borrowing constraints often become looser in good times and tighter in bad times, especially in EMs.[15] If fiscal policy suffers from both a deficit bias and from procyclicality, then the fiscal space the government requires to play the role of market-maker will be absent.[16]

Creating fiscal space is not easy, but both academics and policymakers have learned a great deal since the Washington Consensus on how to create strong and credible institutions to deliver it. On the side of monetary policy, the expression of these lessons is central bank independence, designed to preserve price stability, prevent fiscal dominance, and keep the public debt reasonably free from inflation risk. On the fiscal side, the debate is much less settled and there exists no one-size-fits-all policy recommendation. Yet there is growing agreement that medium-term fiscal frameworks and fiscal rules (with escape clauses for recessions) can help in this regard.[17]

Over the last two decades many countries have adopted fiscal rules of one kind or another, so there are plenty of cases to learn from. There have been both successful and unsuccessful experiences with fiscal rules, in developed and EMs alike. Among advanced nations, the debate within the Eurozone has been particularly rich, with the principles that guide fiscal rules in Europe having been recently updated.[18] Among emerging nations, arguably the most successful experience with fiscal rules is that of Chile, a country that since 2000 has managed to keep public debt low, not lose market access during the Great Financial Crisis of 2007–09 and the COVID-19 crisis, and pursue countercyclical fiscal policies (including some lending and market-making of last resort) during both crises.[19]

Research and practice have highlighted one trade-off that is increasingly clear: rules must be sufficiently simple so that they can be understood by citizens and, especially, by market participants. However, at the same time, they must be sufficiently adaptable and flexible to deal with large unforeseen shocks – perhaps via escape clauses. The principle guiding this and other trade-offs is that credible budget institutions and sound public finance management during good times preserve market access during recessions and crises.

2. *Transparency and communication to prevent self-fulfilling debt runs*

The seminal work of Guillermo Calvo emphasised the potential for multiple equilibria and self-fulfilling sovereign debt crises.[20] If debtholders, who are concerned about a higher risk of default (whether via inflation or outright non-payment), demand higher risk premia and therefore higher interest rates, they make it more expensive for governments to service the debt. This increases the risk of default and can make the initial worries self-fulfilling.[21]

Because indebtedness does not have to be very high to place a country in the multiple equilibria region, few nations are immune to these risks. Multiplicity can occur even at low levels of debt, since a very high interest rate can make such debts unsustainable. But multiple equilibria are more likely when debt is high; then, even a small increase in the interest rate investors demand can make default fears self-fulfilling. The maturity of the debt also plays a crucial role. If average maturity is short and therefore a large share of the debt needs to be rolled over every period, then it is more likely that small shifts in expectations can cause the government to become illiquid.[22] Self-fulfilling debt panics are also more likely when public debt is denominated in foreign currency, as is often the case in EMs, since in that case the local central bank cannot serve as a lender of last resort.[23]

One implication is that the sustainability of public debt should be understood as probabilistic and potentially subject to sharp and sudden changes. Another implication is that public debt management requires communication and steering of beliefs, to select the best possible equilibrium and prevent others from happening. Institutional design can help: constitutions and laws that rule out some policy actions also prevent policy traps driven by self-fulfilling expectations.

3. *Protecting the special (and potentially fragile) nature of the public debt*

Until recently, the global decline in real interest rates increased fiscal space, since governments could issue more bonds to satisfy the excess supply of private savings. But the demand for publicly issued paper does not depend only on global savings and investment. The government can borrow at lower rates than private agents because of the special features of government debt that give rise to a 'debt revenue'.[24] Preserving these special features requires special care and management.

Government debt is the most liquid security in most countries' domestic financial market. Households and businesses facing the uninsured risks we emphasised earlier rely on this liquidity when they save for a rainy day that can arrive when least expected. In turn, the collapse of financial markets, which we also discussed earlier, is often associated with private assets becoming hard to sell and the premium on the liquidity of public debt rising. In fact, the classic expression of the market-maker of last resort involves not the fiscal authorities directly, but rather the central bank intervening to preserve the liquidity of public debt. This kind of liquidity-preserving intervention is very different from monetary financing, which was the chief concern of the Washington Consensus (although drawing the line between the two of them in practice and in real time can be challenging).

Another special feature of government debt comes from its safety, or at least the perception of safety. In crises, if public debt is perceived as safe (as is usually the case in advanced economies) then the government gains fiscal space even as private entities lose it. The upshot is that governments borrow at rates lower than private agents, and also have that borrowing capacity preserved during crises – but only as long as they can keep the liquidity and safety of the public debt.

The 'debt revenue' resulting from the special liquidity properties of public debt has limits; it cannot finance a fiscal deficit of any size, indefinitely. Moreover, the gap between the private real rate of interest and the rate the government has to pay is in itself a function of the size of outstanding public debt. As governments issue more debt to take advantage of that gap, it can shrink, and even disappear altogether – in which case the public debt is no longer 'special'.

Across the world, the degree to which market participants view government debt as safe and liquid is dramatically different. Not even the United States may be able to take the safety of its Treasuries as a given, and surely nor can the other richest economies of the world, as the 2022 mini-budget crisis in the United Kingdom revealed. Emerging and developing economies face a fickle demand for government bonds. The privileged borrowing position of the public sector can quickly vanish, since the special role of public debt as provider of liquidity can be (and often is) displaced by foreign currency or foreign bonds. Flight to safety at the time of crises manifests itself also as a flight away from the public debt of certain countries and towards that of others. Minimising these problems requires an effective international architecture, a subject to which we now turn.

4. *The importance of the international financial architecture*

For all countries but the United States, national fiscal and monetary institutions must be complemented with international institutions that help preserve fiscal space and permit fiscal activism. These include the IMF at the forefront, and more recently regional financing arrangements, such as the European Stability Mechanism, the Chiang Mai Initiative in East Asia, and the Latin American Reserve Fund. Rather than discuss what each should do, we focus on what they should strive to accomplish as a whole.

First, and as a global by-product of the need to complete markets, the global financial safety net should provide targeted emergency fiscal support. Not only do some of the arguments that we made about aggregate shocks at the national level translate to the global level, but so do the limitations on what government can accomplish. Globally, this support can help compensate for the fickle nature of fiscal capacity as discussed, by preserving it and helping keep the public debt of the affected country safe.

Second, and as a manifestation of the need for market-making of last resort, the global financial safety net should stand ready to anchor governments to the 'good equilibrium'. It should help prevent the self-fulfilling pessimism that can cause runs on government debt, a spike in interest rates, and a collapse in a government's borrowing capacity. This does not mean, of course, financing each and every fiscal deficit, regardless of circumstances. Instead, it requires a strong commitment to support institutions that are solvent.

Third, and closely related, the Washington Consensus view that the international financial architecture should provide emergency financing during balance of payments crises deserves to be reinforced. These crises need not occur because of excessively expansionary or imprudent fiscal or monetary policies but can occur because of 'sudden stops': bouts of self-fulfilling pessimism that cause capital to flow out and asset prices to drop, impairing international creditworthiness.[25]

The overall message is that the new fiscal activism, if it is to be feasible and successful beyond the United States and a handful of advanced economies, requires a global financial safety net that is both vastly larger and more agile than what is in place today.

IV. Conclusion

A new London Consensus should supplement the three fiscal policy principles of the Washington Consensus with two new ones:

- Pursue fiscal activism focused on first offsetting uninsured shocks to income via targeted transfers, and second on preserving markets and the flow of credit during crises, above and beyond the standard government purchases meant to regulate aggregate demand.
- Ensure that these larger cyclical budget deficits are sustained by strong institutions, national and international, which keep debt sustainable and preserve the safety and liquidity of government bonds.

Notes

1 Williamson (1990).

2 Keynes (1933); McKay and Reis (2016); Guerrieri and Lorenzoni (2017).

3 Nor can people insure before the fact because the relevant insurance markets do not exist. The only option open to them is to engage in self-insurance: for instance, a small business owner could accumulate large cash reserves or establish access to a sizeable credit line. But that is expensive, inefficient, and creates the aggregate demand effect that deepens slumps. In extreme cases, it is unlikely that a small business owner, for instance, even if very prudent, could have enough cash in hand to keep paying all employees for six months or a year while receiving zero income, as happened during the pandemic.

4 Pope and Shearer (2021).

5 Bachmann et al. (2022); Lindner (2023).

6 Brunnermeier and Reis (2023).

7 Kiyotaki and Moore (1997).

8 Woodford (1986); Liu and Wang (2014); Céspedes et al. (2022).

9 Of course, ruling out bad equilibria can require doing 'whatever it takes', as the world learned from Mario Draghi during the Euro Area debt crisis of 2010–14.

10 Buera et al. (2013).

11 Blanchard (2023).

12 Eggertsson (2010).

13 Reis (2022b).

14 Alesina and Perotti (1995).

[15] Alesina et al. (2008); Ilzetzki and Vegh (2008).

[16] Moreover, a well-formulated fiscal policy can lower the frequency with which a market-maker of last resort will be needed.

[17] Blanchard et al. (2010).

[18] Ilzetzki (2021); Blanchard et al. (2022); European Commission (2024).

[19] Céspedes et al. (2014).

[20] Calvo (1988b).

[21] Lorenzoni and Werning (2019).

[22] Rodrik and Velasco (2000).

[23] Chang and Velasco (2001).

[24] Reis (2022a).

[25] Calvo (1988a).

References

Alesina, A. and Perotti, R. (1995) 'The Political Economy of Budget Deficits', *IMF Staff Papers*, 42(1): 1–31. https://www.elibrary.imf.org/view/journals/024/1995/001/article-A001-en.xml

Alesina, A, Tabellini, G. and Campante, F. (2008) 'Why Is Fiscal Policy Often Procyclical?', *Journal of the European Economic Association*, 6(5): 1006–1026. https://doi.org/10.1162/JEEA.2008.6.5.1006

Bachmann, R., Baqaee, D., Bayer, C., Löschel, A., Moll, B., Kuhn, M., Peichl, A., Pittel, K. and Schularick, M. (2022) 'What If? The Economic Effects for Germany of a Stop of Energy Imports from Russia', ECONtribute Policy Brief No. 028, University of Bonn.

Blanchard, O. (2023) *Fiscal Policy Under Low Interest Rates*, Cambridge: MIT Press. https://doi.org/10.7551/mitpress/14858.001.0001

Blanchard, O., Dell'Ariccia, G. and Mauro, P. (2010) 'Rethinking Macroeconomic Policy', *Journal of Money, Credit, and Banking*, 42 (Supplement): 199–215. https://doi.org/10.1111/j.1538-4616.2010.00334.x

Blanchard, O., Sapir, A. and Zettelmeyer, J. (2022) 'The European Commission's Fiscal Rules Proposal: A Bold Plan with Flaws that Can Be Fixed', Blog Post, *Bruegel*, 30 November 2022. https://www.bruegel.org/blog-post/european-commissions-fiscal-rules-proposal-bold-plan-flaws-can-be-fixed

Brunnermeier, M. and Reis, R. (2023) *A Crash Course on Crises: Macroeconomics Concepts for Run-Ups, Collapses, and Recoveries*, Princeton, NJ: Princeton University Press. https://doi.org/10.1515/9780691221113

Buera, F. J., Moll, B. and Shin, Y. (2013) 'Well-Intended Policies', *Review of Economic Dynamics, Special Issue on Misallocation,* 16(1): 216–230. https://doi.org/10.1016/j.red.2012.10.008

Calvo, G. A. (1998a) 'Capital Flows and Capital Market Crises: The Simple Economics of Sudden Stops', *Journal of Applied Economics*, 1(1): 35–54. https://doi.org/10.1080/15140326.1998.12040516

Calvo, G. A. (1998b) 'Servicing the Public Debt: The Role of Expectations', *The American Economic Review,* 78(4): 647–661.

Céspedes, L. F., Parrado, E. and Velasco, A. (2014) 'Fiscal Rules and the Management of Natural Resource Revenues: The Case of Chile', *Annual Review of Resource Economics*, 6(25): 105–132. https://doi.org/10.1146/annurev-resource-100913-012856

Céspedes, L. F., Chang, R. and Velasco, A. (2022) 'The Macroeconomics of a Pandemic: A Minimalist Framework', *Journal of International Money and Finance,* 127, 102674. https://doi.org/10.1016/j.jimonfin.2022.102674

Chang, R. and Velasco, A. (2001) 'A Model of Financial Crises in Emerging Markets', *The Quarterly Journal of Economics*, 116(2): 489–517. https://doi.org/10.1162/00335530151144087

Eggertsson, G. (2010) 'What Fiscal Policy Is Effective at Zero Interest Rates?', in D. Acemoglu and M. Woodford (eds) NBER *Macroeconomics Annual*, University of Chicago Press. https://doi.org/10.1086/657529

European Commission (2024) 'New Economic Governance Framework'. Luxembourg: Publications Office of the European Union. https://economy-finance.ec.europa.eu/economic-and-fiscal-governance/eu-assessment-and-monitoring-national-economic-policies/evolution-eu-economic-governance/new-economic-governance-framework_en

Guerrieri, V. and Lorenzoni, G. (2017) 'Credit Crises, Precautionary Savings, and the Liquidity Trap', *The Quarterly Journal of Economics*, 132(3): 1427–67. https://doi.org/10.1093/qje/qjx005

Ilzetzki, E. (2021) *Fiscal Rules in the European Monetary Union*. Vox EU, 10 June 2021. https://cepr.org/voxeu/columns/fiscal-rules-european-monetary-union

Ilzetzki, E. and Vegh, C. (2008) 'Procyclical Fiscal Policy in Developing Countries: Truth or Fiction?', NBER Working Paper 14191, National Bureau of Economic Research. https://doi.org/10.3386/w14191

Keynes, J. M. (1933) 'An Open Letter to President Roosevelt', *New York Times*, Vol. 16.

Kiyotaki, N. and Moore, J. (1997) 'Credit Cycles', *Journal of Political Economy*, 105(2): 211–48. https://doi.org/10.1086/262072

Lindner, C. (2023) 'A Resilient Germany Is Weathering the Energy Crunch', *Financial Times*, 2 January 2023. https://www.ft.com/content/52a8df8d-6a61-4b42-8b36-35d7e95eb70a

Liu, Z. and Wang, P. (2014) 'Credit Constraints and Self-Fulfilling Business Cycles', *American Economic Journal: Macroeconomics*, 6(1): 32–69. https://doi.org/10.1257/mac.6.1.32

Lorenzoni, G. and Werning, I. (2019) 'Slow Moving Debt Crises', *American Economic Review*, 109(9): 3229–63. https://doi.org/10.1257/aer.20141766

McKay, A. and Reis, R. (2016) 'The Role of Automatic Stabilizers in the U.S. Business Cycle', *Econometrica*, 84(1): 141–194. https://doi.org/10.3982/ECTA11574

Pope, T. and Shearer, E. (2021) 'The Coronavirus Job Retention Scheme: How Successful Has the Furlough Scheme Been and What Should Happen Next?' London: The Institute for Government. https://www.instituteforgovernment.org.uk/publication/coronavirus-job-retention-success

Reis, R. (2022a) 'Debt Revenue and the Sustainability of Public Debt', *Journal of Economic Perspectives*, 36(4): 103–124. https://doi.org/10.1257/jep.36.4.103

Reis, R. (2022b) 'Which R-star: Public Bonds or Private Investment? Measurement and Policy Implications', Manuscript, LSE.

Rodrik, D. and Velasco, A. (2000) 'Short-Term Capital Flows', *Annual World Bank Conference on Development Economics*. https://www.nber.org/system/files/working_papers/w7364/w7364.pdf

Williamson, J. (1990) 'What Washington Means by Policy Reform', in *Latin American Adjustment: How Much Has Happened?*, Washington, DC: Institute for International Economics.

Woodford, M. (1986) 'Stationary Sunspot Equilibria in a Finance Constrained Economy', *Journal of Economic Theory*, 40(1): 128–137. https://doi.org/10.1016/0022-0531(86)90011-6

Response to Ricardo Reis and Andrés Velasco by Olivier Blanchard

I fully agree with the general theme of the chapter: namely, a more active role for fiscal policy – but also, by implication, a crucial role for governance to maintain fiscal discipline and debt sustainability.

When thinking about fiscal policy, I like to start with the three public functions identified by Richard Musgrave: allocation, distribution, and stabilisation. I will talk briefly about the first two, and then focus on the third, which is the subject of the chapter by Ricardo Reis and Andrés Velasco.

I. Allocation

New technologies appear more subject to both increasing returns and externalities than those in the past. Increasing returns are clear in the case of networks. Positive externalities are clear in the form of the many intangibles that, once created, can be shared at little cost with others. Negative externalities are clear in the case of, for example, global warming.

Today, industrial policies are increasingly popular. Some of them are justified; others are not. Economists are, rightly, sceptical of industrial policy, emphasising the difficulty of identifying market failures and avoiding heavy lobbying. But a simplistic 'no industrial policy' position is untenable. Redefining the role of the state, and with it the contours, limits, and fiscal implications of the right industrial policy, is very much needed.

II. Distribution

Market inequality has increased, and there are reasons to think it will continue to grow. The traditional advice has been for the state to provide education and training, accept the market outcome, and then rely on redistribution rather than on trying to modify market distribution. For example, economists have typically argued, rightly in my view, that a negative income tax is a better way to help low-income workers than a minimum wage.

However, it may be that we have come to the limit of how much redistribution the state can afford. In European countries in particular, average and marginal tax rates are high, and we may have reached the political limit of redistribution. If so, it may be that more direct intervention in the market process, rather than the redistribution process, is needed. In the context of trade, the idea that it may be better to protect certain jobs, rather than to try to help those who lose their jobs, is clearly gaining political support. Economists are again rightly sceptical. But a simplistic 'trade is good' position is again untenable. Research on what the state can do to affect market distribution – be it through caps on chief executive officer salaries, subsidies for 'good' jobs, or incentives for firms to create job ladders rather than dead-end jobs – is very much needed.

III. Stabilisation

I believe that the dominant view among economists today is that the main stabilisation tool should be monetary rather than fiscal policy. (This was not always the case. Early Keynesians were much more sceptical about monetary policy and more enthusiastic about fiscal policy.) The currently dominant view must be revisited.

In the simplest version of the now-standard macro model – the New Keynesian model – there is one major distortion, namely nominal price rigidity, which leads to undesirable fluctuations in output in response to shifts in aggregate demand. In such a world, the right policy tool is the interest rate. By moving the interest rate appropriately, the central bank can keep output at potential, and avoid undesirable fluctuations in output. There is no need for fiscal policy to intervene. Obviously, the model is too simple, but the message is a clear and influential one: monetary policy is the right tool, and the onus is on central banks to stabilise output.

In reality, there are many other distortions that monetary policy cannot handle and that fiscal policy can, at least in principle. Take, for example, a decrease in aggregate demand in an economy in which many consumers are liquidity constrained, and thus insensitive to the interest rate. In that economy, monetary policy may work rather poorly, but fiscal transfers to liquidity-constrained households will work well. Or, to take a relevant recent example, think of a large increase in energy prices that decreases the purchasing power of households and leads to a large contraction in demand and output. In this case, fiscal transfers aimed at poor households – or, even better, at poor households who spend a larger fraction of their income on energy – can both boost demand and limit adverse distribution effects. This is something that monetary policy cannot do.

More fundamentally, monetary policy has one basic tool, the short interest rate – or perhaps two if we include quantitative easing, though it is not clear that this, thought of as debt maturity management, should be done by the central bank rather than the Treasury. Fiscal policy, by contrast, has a near infinite range of tools, taxes, or subsidies that can be aimed at specific sectors, or at specific groups of households or firms. It can use tools that work primarily through income effects, such as a cut in taxes, or others that work primarily through substitution effects, such as an explicitly temporary decrease in value-added tax rates. It can do targeted intragenerational transfers, or it can do intergenerational transfers through deficit finance.

While there is uncertainty about the values of multipliers associated with various fiscal tools, the evidence shows that the effects of government spending on output are quick and strong, as is the effect of transfers to poorer households. By contrast, and as we are observing today, both the size and the timing of the effects of monetary policy on economic activity are highly uncertain.

The case for fiscal policy becomes even stronger when interest rates are low, for two reasons. First, the fiscal and the welfare costs of debt become smaller. Debt sustainability is consistent with lower primary balances; indeed, if the interest rate is less than the growth rate, it is consistent with some primary deficits. Meanwhile the welfare cost of debt, due to the crowding out of investment and lower capital accumulation, is also lower when rates are low. Second, if interest rates are at or close to the zero lower bound, the scope for monetary policy to increase demand is sharply reduced. These considerations were highly relevant pre-pandemic, before the fight against inflation sent rates higher. They may well become relevant again in the future.

So, should we rely primarily on fiscal policy for stabilisation purposes? One can think right away of strong counter arguments. First, fiscal measures may work quickly, but they often take a long time to pass through the political process. By the time they arrive, they may well be too late. As a result, fiscal policy is often pro- rather than countercyclical. Second, the larger the set of potential measures, the stronger the role of lobbies, and the more likely fiscal policy will be misused. We saw a striking example of this in the American Rescue Plan Act of 2021, which, because of the addition of measures to satisfy many constituencies, was much too large from a macroeconomic stabilisation viewpoint. Finally, fiscal measures have a legacy: higher deficits lead to higher debt, and governments typically suffer from a deficit bias, leaving adjustment through higher taxes or lower spending to subsequent governments.

Is there a way to design fiscal stabilisation so that it solves this Gordian knot, preserving the ability to use many instruments, while making sure fiscal policy remains responsible? I think there is – and it has to rely on two pillars.

First, greater use of automatic stabilisers. The arguments are again well known. Automatic stabilisers eliminate political lags. Whether they act through unemployment benefits or tax revenues, they make fiscal policy by nature countercyclical. The issue is that they are, almost in their entirety, the accidental result of the progressivity of income tax, of the degree of indexation of the tax system, and of the generosity of unemployment benefits. Their size and their macro relevance vary across countries for reasons which have nothing to do with stabilisation. An economy with more progressive income taxes will have stronger stabilisers. We must thus explore and develop quasi-automatic stabilisers – measures that are triggered by the crossing of some threshold, such as an unemployment rate, or an estimate of the output gap. This in turn raises challenges.

One is that cyclical fluctuations in output have different causes, such as weakness in consumption, investment, or exports. Should we try to design different stabilisers depending on the apparent source of the fluctuations, or should we be less ambitious and settle for simpler stabilisers, based on, say, the unemployment rate, no matter what the source?

Another challenge is that it is essential to make sure that these stabilisers work symmetrically and have a neutral effect on debt ratios in the long run. This is harder to design than it sounds. If the threshold is a certain value of the unemployment rate, the stabiliser will respond in the same way whether this is an increase in unemployment above the natural rate, or an increase in the natural rate itself – in which case it should not respond. How can the stabiliser be designed as such that a move that reveals itself to have been incorrect automatically repairs itself over time?

It is clear that quasi-automatic stabilisers cannot be the sole fiscal response, and that eventually they must be completed by discretionary policies. This raises yet another issue. Should we think of stabilisers as first aid until the right policies can be designed, or as the main fiscal policy tool? This has implications for their design, too.

To the extent that discretionary measures remain essential, the second pillar must be strong fiscal governance. In addition to the well-documented deficit bias, the larger the set of potential tools, the larger the scope for misuse. For example, to avoid the addition of ever more fiscal measures – as was seen in the American Rescue Plan – the size of the primary balance must be decided from the top down, rather than from the bottom up. And there must be rules that enforce debt sustainability. In this context, the current discussion of revised fiscal rules for the European Union is extremely interesting. We now know what the new rules will be. The work by the European Commission and the subsequent academic and political discussion has led to a shifting consensus. It has shown that, in a constantly changing environment, rules based on simple and invariant numbers, such as those set in the Maastricht Treaty, are either counterproductive or simply do not work and are violated. It has shown that any assessment must be tailored to the specific country and take the form of a debt sustainability analysis.

In essence, and overlapping very much with the analysis by Reis and Velasco, my belief is that fiscal policy should play a more important role in macroeconomic stabilisation. And in particular, improved quasi-automatic stabilisers and fiscal rules to maintain debt sustainability are two promising directions of research.

Response to Ricardo Reis and Andrés Velasco by Chryssi Giannitsarou

Modern fiscal policy is and should be quite different from what it was 35 years ago. The original Washington Consensus stipulated three main priorities in relation to fiscal policy and public debt: (a) fiscal discipline; (b) public spending for health, education, welfare, and infrastructure; and (c) a broad tax base and moderate marginal tax rates. All of these are largely uncontroversial, and I would imagine very few, if any, economists would disagree with the basic principles behind these three priorities. After all, this is what a good parent would advise their children as they move into adulthood: (a) spend wisely; (b) spend as to keep healthy and happy; and (c) have a good source of income to support your spending. Nevertheless, these principles aimed to promote economic liberalisation and market-oriented reforms, and while the Washington Consensus has often been praised for fostering economic growth, it also faced criticism for exacerbating inequality and neglecting social safety nets. The proposed amendments by Ricardo Reis and Andrés Velasco succinctly summarise the recent efforts of the profession to show that it is possible to combine economic growth with fiscal policies that give a bigger role to governments as entities that efficiently offer such safety nets.

The three priorities of the Washington Consensus can also be thought of as a sensible guide for fiscal policy in normal times and in the long run. But as recent experience has shown, we often face large and asymmetric deviations from normal times, in the form of crises and disaster episodes that we can no longer call 'rare'. Such events generate extreme asymmetries in how their effects are felt by various parts of the population, and the difficulty or non-suitability of applying a 'one-size-fits-all' fiscal policy to address them lies at the heart of the two proposed amendments of these priorities by Reis and Velasco. The first, *fiscal activism* – in the forms of insurance, market-maker of last resort and intertemporal reallocation – describes how fiscal authorities have the ability to respond in times of severe crisis, such as the COVID-19 pandemic. The second, *fiscal space via sound debt management*, prescribes ways in which countries can prepare to face such events, by building solid institutions, managing the expectations of the public, and dealing with the aftermath of crises and disasters.

It is easy to agree with these amendments and accept these as equally important priorities for fiscal policy; here, I would like to both highlight but also expand on some important elements implicit in the chapter by Reis and Velasco.

By nature, activist fiscal policy needs to be adaptable, flexible and creative – especially in times of crisis. The experience with rigid fiscal rules, such as the EU's Stability and Growth Pact, have taught us, if anything, that fiscal authorities and governments need to be prepared to change their minds when the facts change. Also, the much talked about sustainability of debt can be quite an open-ended and vague concept in the absence of a plan to create the fiscal space needed to ensure that governments can give intertemporal transfers in times of disasters.

To the extent that governments can act to prevent and mitigate crises, the amended priorities of the London Consensus can be used as guides to address the mother of all crises: that of climate change. The climate crisis, marked by rising global temperatures, shifting weather patterns, and heightened frequency of extreme weather events, represents a call to action that transcends borders. The ethos of fiscal activism as proposed by Reis and Velasco resonates deeply in this context and should prompt governments to assume the role of fiscal insurers against environmental disasters. Just as fiscal activism served as a lifeline during economic crises such as the COVID-19 pandemic, it can provide a framework for addressing future environmental disruptions. In light of the Paris Agreement of 2015, fiscal activism can become the toolkit through which nations translate pledges into tangible action. Governments, in their capacity as insurers and intertemporal risk sharers, should extend support to vulnerable countries, ensuring they possess the resources to fortify their defences against environmental threats. Such a commitment would underpin the ethos of equity, enabling those who bear the brunt of climate impacts to build resilience.

With the spotlight on climate change, the critical issue of biodiversity loss is one that receives less attention due to its slow evolution and less violent manifestation in our everyday lives. At the time of writing this chapter, there are disappointingly few biodiversity-relevant taxes and subsidies. According to the *Dasgupta Review*, in 2021 there were only 206 biodiversity-relevant taxes in 59 countries, raising just 1% of the total revenue from environmentally relevant taxes, and only 146 biodiversity-friendly subsidies in 24 countries.[1] In line with the aforementioned priorities of fiscal policy, governments must broaden their approach to encompass taxes and subsidies – that is, fiscal transfers that target biodiversity preservation and restoration.

A final point relates to the importance of *international* collaboration and cooperation of fiscal policies. This is especially important when it comes to policies focused on environmental or global health crises. While fiscal policies have traditionally been perceived as a sovereign matter, the complexity of environmental crises demands international collaboration. As such, the London Consensus should amplify the importance of leveraging global institutions and mechanisms to align fiscal policies for environmental preservation. The IMF, World Bank, and initiatives like the EU's Emissions Trading System (EU ETS) serve as potential platforms to harmonise fiscal efforts. The role of the IMF extends beyond traditional economic stabilisation to include addressing climate-related risks and promoting environmentally sustainable economic growth. Direct collaboration with the World Bank facilitates the flow of funds to developing nations, aiding in their transition to sustainable environmental practices. The EU ETS underscores the potential for regional cooperation in decarbonisation.

With international coordination, environmental fiscal policies can enhance the ability of governments to share risk not only across time but also across space. The Paris Agreement stands as a testament to the potential of international collaboration in shaping environmental policy. Nations come together, each contributing according to their capacity, to address the climate crisis. The agreement recognises the differentiated responsibilities of developed and developing nations, encouraging an atmosphere of equity and cooperation. This spirit must extend to all facets of environmental fiscal policies, enabling the mobilisation of resources to aid vulnerable countries, support mitigation and adaptation efforts, and fund green projects that benefit the global community.

The fiscal activism envisioned by Reis and Velasco should extend beyond individual country borders because the urgency of environmental crises requires a new kind of fiscal policymaking – one that embraces international cooperation and goes beyond geopolitical divides. In an ideal world, governments would work in tandem with existing and new global institutions to lay the groundwork for a sustainable future supported by ample fiscal space and sound fiscal policies.

Note

[1] Dasgupta (2021).

Reference

Dasgupta, P. (2021) 'The Economics of Biodiversity: The Dasgupta Review', Technical Report, HM Treasury. https://assets.publishing.service.gov.uk/media/602e92b2e90e07660f807b47/The_Economics_of_Biodiversity_The_Dasgupta_Review_Full_Report.pdf

7. Monetary and financial policies

Hélène Rey

The Washington Consensus helped forge a world view in which opening borders to capital flows was seen as an important way to increase economic efficiency. In the past decades, evidence accumulated of the shortcomings of a largely unmanaged financial system in which the volatility of capital flows was still seen as an exogenous feature of the world economy. This chapter sets the stage by discussing the characteristics of the global financial cycle (GFC) and the role of the United States Federal Reserve, to then discuss the influence of this cycle on the pass-through of domestic monetary policy to market rates for emerging markets (EMs) and advanced economies. It then sets out the implications of limited monetary policy pass-through for the validity of the trilemma in international finance. The chapter calls for the systematic use of macroprudential policy tools in advanced and EMs alike to complement credible monetary policy frameworks. It also emphasises the importance of the development of local currency bond markets. In some cases, capital controls may also be useful.

I. Introduction

The Washington Consensus helped forge a world view in which opening borders to capital flows was seen as an important way to increase economic efficiency. A parallel was drawn between the efficiency benefits of trade in goods and those of trade in assets – supported by certain economic theories that neglected to model frictions in capital markets. That parallel went relatively unchallenged in the 1980s and the 1990s. The International Monetary Fund (IMF) even considered changing its articles of agreements to push for deregulation of the financial account in 1997 – but then capital suddenly began to flow out of Thailand and other Asian economies. The events that followed, culminating in what would be called the 'Asian financial

---

How to cite this book chapter:

Rey, Hélène (2025) 'Monetary and financial policies', in: Besley, Tim, Bucelli, Irene and Velasco, Andrés (eds) *The London Consensus: Economic Principles for the 21st Century*, London: LSE Press, pp. 219–249 https://doi.org/10.31389/lsepress.tlc.g

crisis of 1997', cut short the planned overhaul of the international financial system towards more liberalisation.

Nonetheless, the lingering wisdom held that free capital flows remained desirable, and insuring against their volatility was mainly the responsibility of debtor countries. As a result, some EMs, especially in Asia, went on to accumulate large stocks of foreign exchange reserves to help insulate their domestic monetary and financial conditions from hot money flows. In parallel, important progress was made in terms of macroeconomic frameworks, with more countries adopting inflation targeting, letting their exchange rate float, and enhancing the credibility of their central banks. This was a step in the right direction and improved resilience. Little by little, however, researchers began to analyse the shortcomings of a largely unmanaged financial system in which the volatility of capital flows was still seen as an exogenous feature of the world economy.

Evidence accumulated that the system was not sustainable. We went from a long stretch with no financial crises after 1944, under Bretton Woods, where financial flows and exchange rates were heavily managed and banks in the financial centre tightly regulated, to a rapid succession of major financial disasters following liberalisation and deregulation[1]: the Latin American debt crisis of the 1980s; the Mexican peso crisis of 1994–95; the Asian financial crisis of 1997; the Russian crisis and Long-Term Capital Management bankruptcy of 1998; the Turkish and the Argentinian crises of 2001; the Great Financial Crisis of 2007–09; the Euro Area debt crisis of 2010–14.

This sequence of crises made it urgent to revisit the conventional wisdom and draw lessons to help manage monetary and financial stability going forward. So, what, exactly did we learn?

This chapter sets the stage by discussing the characteristics of the GFC and the role of the US Federal Reserve in section I. It then turns to the influence of this cycle on the pass-through of domestic monetary policy to market rates for EMs and advanced economies in section II. Section III sets out the implications of limited monetary policy pass-through for the validity of the trilemma in international finance. The GFC makes flexible exchange rates less effective, and with full capital mobility, monetary independence is hard to achieve. This does not mean however that exchange rate flexibility and a credible inflation targeting framework are not advisable; they help to absorb large shocks. Finally, section IV reviews the different policy tools and concludes the argument. The chapter calls for the systematic use of macroprudential policy tools in advanced and EMs alike to complement credible monetary policy frameworks. It also emphasises the importance of the development of local currency bond markets. In some cases, capital controls may also be useful.

II. The global financial cycle

Financial globalisation has risen over the last 50 years. The collapse of Bretton Woods and the subsequent financial deregulation greatly encouraged the development of global banking and capital markets. This induced a high degree of co-movement in risky asset prices, capital flows, leverage, and financial aggregates around the world, a phenomenon called the global financial cycle (GFC) in Rey (2013).[2] Risky asset prices and capital flows are highly correlated with measures of global risk appetite, such as the Chicago Board Options Exchange's Volatility Index (VIX). Figure 7.1 shows that the common components of risky asset prices and gross capital flows are highly positively correlated with one another and co-move negatively with the VIX, a 'gauge of fear' in international markets.[3] In financial markets – unlike in other realms of the economy – volumes and prices go hand in hand, and both increase sizably during periods of high-risk appetite. Such periods tend to be ones in which risk taking, proxied by leverage, goes up, and flows into EMs increase. The balance sheet of certain financial intermediaries become larger and more vulnerable to sudden changes in asset valuations.

Countries' exposure to global financial conditions has an important effect on their ability to conduct effective independent monetary policy. There is no 'divine coincidence' which guarantees that international financial conditions align with the objectives of domestic monetary authorities. As a result, central banks in EMs and advanced economies alike may face exuberant international investors at a time where they are trying to tighten monetary policy at home. Vice versa, they may be unable to find liquidity when they are attempting to

Figure 7.1: The global financial cycle

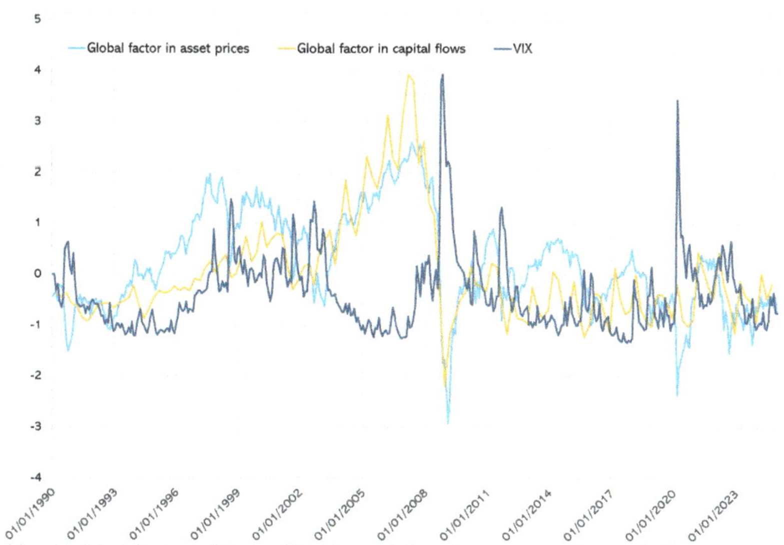

Source: author's calculations, data from Miranda-Agrippino and Rey (2022).

expand demand domestically. The extent to which they can use policy tools to tame the GFC and gain some independence will be discussed in the next sections. But what drives the GFC?

US monetary policy has an important effect on the GFC, in particular through a 'risk-taking channel'.[4] Various papers describe how loose monetary policy and extensive liquidity provision induce financial players to take on more risk.[5] This can happen by relaxing financial constraints and shifting the 'sentiment' of market participants.[6] Given the importance of the dollar as a funding currency, as well as the prevalence of dollars on the asset side of international balance sheets, it is perhaps not surprising that the monetary policy of the US Federal Reserve has a sizeable effect on gauges of 'market fear' such as the VIX or indeed on any index of risk aversion and volatility; there are large positive correlations between the VIX, the VSTOXX, the VFTSE, the MOVE etc... as well as with the excess bond premium.[7] US monetary policy impacts 'risk on' and 'risk off' attitudes in international markets. Figure 7.2[8] shows the effect of a 100 bp monetary policy tightening by the US Federal Reserve on the VIX (left panel) and on a measure of aggregate risk aversion. In both cases one sees large contemporaneous increases, which fade after six to eight months.

Risk taking in turn shapes credit creation, leverage, and the movement of flows to or from EMs,[9] as well as asset valuations around the world. Variation in the leverage of global banks has a large impact in driving current account imbalances.[10] The global dollar cycle is particularly important when it comes to influencing economic conditions in EMs and low-income economies.[11]

Figure 7.2: Federal reserve and risk on, risk off

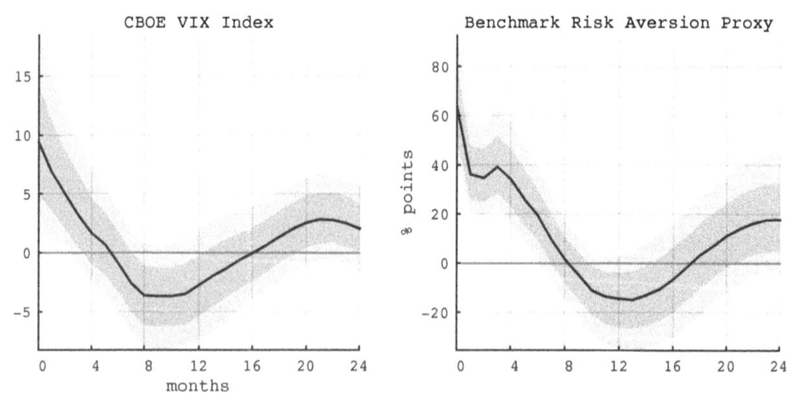

Source: Figure E.3 (parts vi and i), p. 31, in 'Online Appendix' for Miranda-Agrippino and Rey (2020). CC BY licence.
Notes: Impulse response function of US monetary policy on risk aversion: VIX and aggregate effective risk aversion proxy . Effect of a 100 bp Federal Reserve tightening. Months on the x axis.

In sum, we have learned that i) there is a powerful GFC; ii) the risk-taking channel is important for monetary policy transmission, hence theoretical modelling of spreads and premia is of first order importance in monetary models; and iii) the US Federal Reserve's monetary policy has important spillover effects on risk taking well beyond US borders.

III. Monetary policy pass-through and the global financial cycle

What are the implications of the GFC for the managing of monetary and financial conditions in emerging and advanced economies?

Using a large set of emerging and advanced economies at a quarterly frequency from mid-1990s to 2019, one study[12] showed that central banks in emerging economies, just like their peers in advanced economies, tend to follow a Taylor rule, meaning lowering their policy rates in response to deteriorating local economic activity or lower inflation. Yet the pass-through of their policy rate to short-term market rates appears compromised by their exposure to the GFC. The same study found that, in emerging economies, three-month market rates tend to increase when economic activity contracts. In advanced economies, by contrast, they found that policy rates and short-term market rates both decline when economic activity decelerates.

Figure 7.3 contains case A for emerging markets and case B for advanced economies. The first panel in each case shows the correlation between the future interest rate (at horizon t+h) and current gross domestic product (GDP) growth (at horizon t). The policy rate is in blue and the three-month treasury rate is in red. The second panel in each case panel reports the correlation between the future treasury-policy differential (at horizon t+h) and current GDP growth (at horizon t).[13] Thus, monetary policy seems to be counter-cyclical in both emerging and advanced economies over the last three decades. However, emerging economies' market rates, *even short-term ones*, exhibit a striking disconnect from local policy rates, and the wedge between the two appears to increase in times of stress. This disconnect between short-term market rates and policy rates in EMs often reflects their exposure to global financial markets and the ebb and flows of capital as funding costs in emerging economies depend in part on international liquidity. This is strikingly true, for example, in Turkey.[14] Though not the only factor behind the GFC, US monetary policy is a prominent driver of international funding conditions. Many researchers have shown that an exogenous increase in US rates causes a decrease in credit creation, tighter financial conditions, and a decrease of both *gross* capital flows for all economies and of *net* capital flows for EMs.[15]

For EMs, macroeconomic stabilisation can be complicated further by the existence of the 'original sin', a situation in which domestic currency cannot be used to borrow abroad.[16] As a result, if a country's firms borrow in dollars to finance a project that generates returns in domestic currency, an appreciation of the dollar could lead to a financial crisis. Moreover, foreign and domestic borrower panic can interact.[17] Recent research has shown that, historically, the vulnerability of EMs to US monetary policy was stronger both when the original sin was present, in the form of currency mismatch on balance sheet, and when the monetary policy frameworks were less credible.[18] The improvement of monetary policy frameworks, through inflation targeting and floating exchange rates, together with the development of domestic currency debt markets, which eliminate the original sin, helped increase the resilience of EMs to the 2022 US Federal Reserve hikes – even if other factors, such as strong commodity markets, early hikes in EMs, and macroprudential policies, all likely played their roles.

Figure 7.3: Pass-through of monetary policy
Panel A: emerging economies

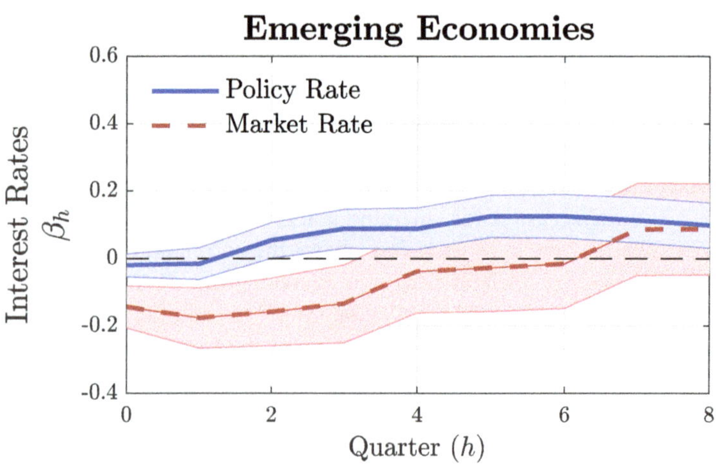

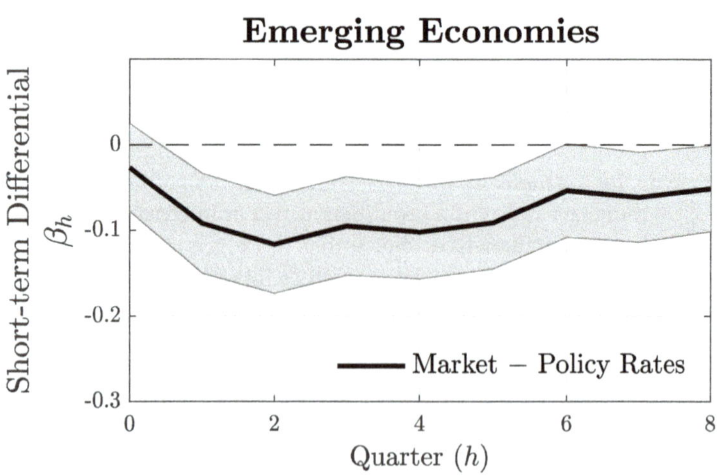

Panel B: advanced economies

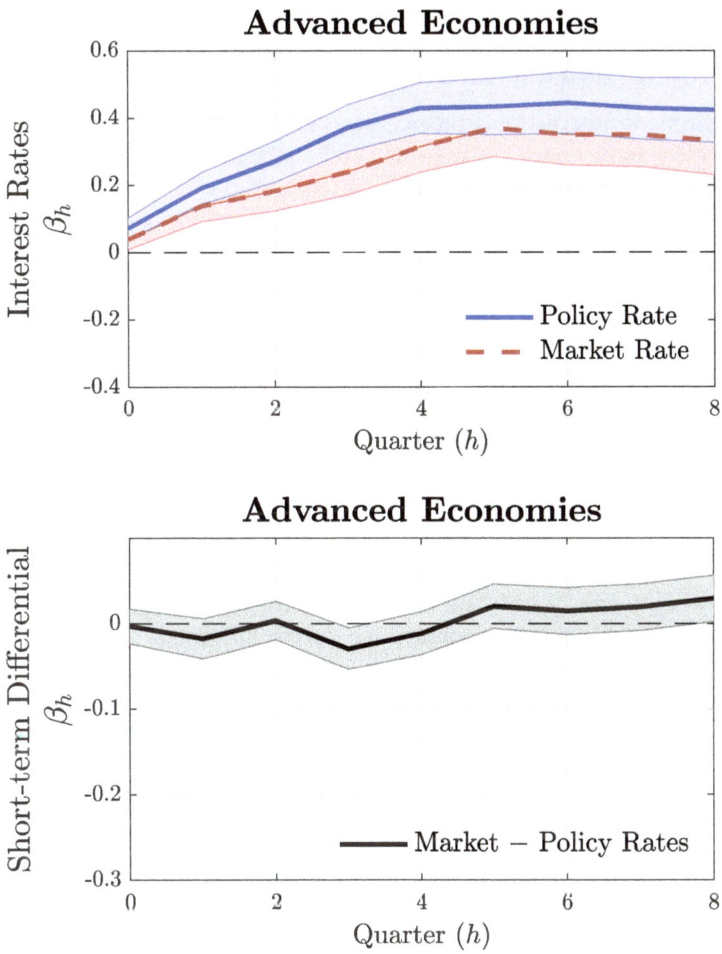

Source: De Leo et al. (2022), Figure 2, p. 10; reproduced with permission by authors.

In fact, the tightening of financial conditions caused by the US Federal Reserve extends to advanced economies, with corporate and mortgage spreads widening even for large economies with floating exchange rates such as the United Kingdom or Germany.[19] Therefore, while the pass-through of monetary policy to short-term market rates is higher for advanced economies than it is for EMs, the monetary and financial conditions of advanced economies are nevertheless affected by the GFC.

In sum, we have learned that (i) monetary policy pass-through for EMs is not straightforward, even for short-term market rates; (ii) monetary policy pass-through is also not straightforward for advanced economies, as far as mortgage rate and corporate lending rates are concerned; (iii) the pass-through of policy is influenced by global financial conditions – and these conditions are, in turn, influenced by the US Federal Reserve's monetary policy.

IV. Trilemmas and dilemmas

The trilemma in international finance states that, at any one moment, it is not feasible to have a fixed exchange rate, full capital mobility, and monetary policy independence. Only two of the three may coexist. The trilemma argument builds on an arbitrage condition in international markets – the uncovered interest parity (UIP) condition – which equates returns across bond markets in a world of perfect capital mobility and risk neutrality. For example: it is evident that under a fixed exchange rate regime and full capital mobility, policymakers cannot set the interest rate at the level they believe appropriate for monetary conditions in their economy. Should they try to free their policy rate from foreign influences, they would quickly be flooded by large capital flows reversing their measures. Meanwhile the 'fear of floating', so well documented by Guillermo Calvo and Carmen Reinhart, is an important illustration of the constraint that full capital mobility puts on the monetary policy of countries resisting exchange rate volatility, whatever the reason.[20]

On the other hand, a floating exchange rate in principle gives a central bank an additional degree of freedom. According to the Mundell-Fleming logic, once the exchange rate has accounted for foreign influences, the domestic interest rate is all that is needed to achieve the internal policy target of macroeconomic stabilisation. This is why the literature testing the empirical validity of the trilemma has focused on measuring the co-movement of interest rates in peripheral and centre countries across exchange-rate regimes. If the domestic policy rate does not closely follow that of the centre country, this is taken as evidence of monetary policy autonomy vis-à-vis the centre. Policy rates will of course be less correlated under a floating exchange-rate than under a fixed exchange-rate regime when there is free capital mobility.[21]

However, in section II we saw that the ability to set the policy rate independently, which is only available under floating exchange rates, far from guarantees the potency of monetary policy – because in emerging economies the pass-through of monetary policy is affected by global financial conditions, even for short-term market rates. This also applies to advanced economies with floating currencies when it comes to longer rates.

This means the trade-off faced by central bankers is much more complex than had been historically acknowledged, partly because many monetary policy models failed to model risk and term premia, or even spreads. However, this does not mean that exchange rate flexibility and a credible inflation-targeting framework are not advisable; they help to absorb large shocks.[22] Indeed, countries with fixed exchange rate regimes are more susceptible to financial fragilities – such as unsustainable credit and house price growth, as well as excessive bank leverage – than those with more flexible regimes.[23]

To summarise this section, we have learned that even if floating exchange rates do provide a degree of insulation for economies when compared to fixed exchange rate regimes, effective monetary policy independence requires additional tools to help 'tame' global financial conditions.[24] In that sense, the traditional trilemma has morphed into a dilemma: to guarantee some pass-through of monetary policy, capital flows and credit should be managed either directly, through capital controls, or indirectly, through macroprudential policies.[25]

V. Expanded set of policy tools

Gross capital inflows, leverage, credit growth, and asset prices all dance to the same tune, co-moving with risk appetite. This is the GFC – and it may not always be beneficial for individual countries. Symptoms can veer from benign to sudden stops or large asset price bubbles and excess credit creation. In the latter case, such conditions have been identified as among the best predictors of financial crises.

To deal with the GFC and the 'dilemma', there are many policy options that can be used to reinforce the pass-through of domestic monetary policy and to help maintain financial stability, while implementing the mandate of price stability (and high employment, where relevant). Different tools will be more or less suitable depending on the country, its institutional structure and legislative arsenal, and the development of its financial markets and preferences. A non-exhaustive list of these tools follows: (a) capital controls; (b) monetary policy framework of EMs (credibility, independence of the Central Bank); (c) monetary policy of the US Federal Reserve and other main Central Banks; (d) national countercyclical macroprudential policies; (e) stricter prudential regulations on, i.e., foreign debt exposure, leverage, concentration exposures, maturity transformation of banks and non-banks; (f) development of local financial markets to ensure that in case of sudden stops there are enough contrarian investors and to limit dependence on foreign currency financing (ending the original sin).[26]

1. *Capital controls*

Capital controls are one measure that can insulate economies from the GFC. These could be either cyclical or permanent, and applied to inflows or outflows – or both.

Permanent capital controls might be applied to a subset of assets on either the inflow or the outflow side. But it is difficult to make a rigorous assessment of the effects of such a policy because, in recent times, permanent controls have been implemented exclusively in a subset of low-income countries, which share very specific characteristics.[27] Overcoming this selection issue is a major challenge.

In contrast, temporary controls, especially on credit and portfolio inflows when the cycle is in a boom phase, can and have been used in various contexts, such as the Chilean 'encaje', the capital controls on firms' production, investment, and exporting decisions imposed by Chile between 1991 and 1998, and the 2010 and 2011 Brazilian taxes on equity inflows. Such controls have often been used with the primary aim of preventing 'excessive' appreciation of the exchange rate when capital flows in, potentially hurting the export sector. In these situations, central bankers sometimes intervene in the foreign exchange market to keep their currency down, accumulating reserves. They face the trade-off of higher inflation or increased sterilisation costs with the likely side effect of a higher interest rate leading to further inflows – something also reinforced by expectations of further appreciation of the exchange rate. Taxing inflows – if effectively implemented – can act as a circuit breaker in such a situation. But there is lively debate on the effectiveness and side effects of temporary capital controls in this context.[28]

When it is excessive credit growth that is the main issue of concern, capital controls should be viewed more as partial substitutes to macroprudential tools. The latter tend to be more targeted.[29] It is important to note that macroprudential policies can weaken the link between domestic monetary policy and capital inflows, without the imposition of capital controls. For instance, the central bank can reduce the incentive for banks to borrow externally when domestic monetary policy tightens by imposing additional capital or foreign exchange reserves requirements. Macroprudential policies have thus been found to be able to 'carve some space' for monetary policy. Indeed, 'pre-emptive' measures to manage capital flow can reduce developing countries' external finance premia during risk-off shocks, especially for the most vulnerable countries.[30]

Capital outflow controls have also proved to be useful in certain circumstances. In the case of Iceland and the 2008 crisis, capital outflow controls that locked in large amounts of carry-trade funds were successfully used as a bargaining tool between the Icelandic government and international investors to help resolve the banks' illiquidity.[31]

2. *Monetary policy frameworks of emerging markets*

In EMs, both the extent of domestic monetary policy pass-through to short-term rates and the ability to insulate from foreign financial spillovers – in particular the US Federal Reserve's monetary policy – depend in great part on the credibility of their monetary policy frameworks.[32] Adopting a floating rate and a credible inflation target can help; floating rates also to some extent help absorb large economic shocks.[33] Meanwhile, the development of bond markets in local currencies also helps make EMs more resilient.

3. *Internalising the global spillovers of the centre's monetary policy*

One might also consider acting on one of the sources of the GFC itself: monetary policy in the main financial centres, and in particular the US. Monetary conditions in large financial centres shape the GFC via the endogenous response of leverage and the procyclicality of cross-border credit flows. Central bankers in systemically important countries have yet to fully internalise the spillover effects of their policies on the rest of the world; they should pay more attention to their collective policy stance.

One practical way of implementing this would be, as Eichengreen et al. propose, for 'a small group of systemically significant central banks to meet regularly under the auspices of the Committee on the Global Financial System of the BIS', and for this group to 'discuss and assess the implications of their policies for global liquidity, leverage, and exposures, and the appropriateness of their joint money and credit policies from the point of view of global price, output, and financial stability'.[34] It could then issue a short report discussing policy trade-offs and international inconsistencies. With time, this should at least help us understand these complex issues, by stimulating more research in these areas – and might encourage central bankers to internalise some of the external spillovers of their policies – and to quantify spillbacks.

But the challenges of such a system are obvious: international cooperation on monetary spillovers may conflict with the domestic mandates of central banks. For example, in the short-to-medium run, domestic activity and inflation targets could very well be at odds with international financial stability. Furthermore, the management of aggregate demand in systemically important economies also has important consequences for economic activity in the rest of the world. The trade-offs are clearly extraordinarily complex.

4. *Muting the transmission of the global financial cycle with macroprudential measures*

Historically, the most dangerous outcome of loose global financial conditions is excessive credit growth, which means monitoring credit growth and leverage in each market is a sensible policy. Some countries have gone to great efforts to set up macroprudential authorities with this mandate.

In response to the Great Financial Crisis of 2007–09, Basel III introduced a countercyclical capital buffer. In the case of real estate, for example, which has historically been associated with severe financial meltdowns, lending can be restricted through loan-to-value ratios and debt service-to-income ratios, limits on exposure or additional sectoral capital buffers.

There is now a wealth of experience on the implementation of such tools. For example, the financial stability reports of national macroprudential authorities in the Euro area set out how they have used their countercyclical buffers in recent years. The 2013 Bank of Korea Report discussed how that institution leveraged caps on a foreign exchange derivatives position and a macroprudential stability levy on non-core foreign exchange liabilities of banks. And the French Haut Conseil de Stabilité Financière discusses in its reports how it has tightened the lending standards in the residential real estate market. Country-specific institutional details and political economy considerations are of course important, but nonetheless a centralised repository of the knowledge and experience gathered so far by supervisors and central bankers would be highly valuable.[35]

Beyond the specific tools to be used, an important practical issue is the timing of an intervention. If a bubble is growing it is important not to wait too long; if a recession is looming one must raise the countercyclical buffer in time to release capital before the credit crunch.

Assembling a set of reliable early warning indicators for such scenarios can help prompt appropriate action. A complementary option would be to stress-test the balance sheet of the financial sector – both banks and non-banks – and identify the scenarios that could jeopardise financial stability. However, stress testing is a difficult exercise in general, and estimating second-round effects is particularly challenging. Furthermore, this is not a popular undertaking with market participants, as it requires regular inputs on top of mandatory reports. It also requires careful thinking about communication policy – and perhaps absolute confidentiality, as the case may be. Moreover, fiscal backstop strategies are needed to guarantee the credibility of the stress testing. None of this is easy. But doing stress tests regularly and often, even if the process is imperfect, is a necessary monitoring tool. It improves the knowledge of supervisors and insures they are up to date with recent market developments. It may also provide constructive challenges to the internal risk monitoring of institutions, or reveal failures in corporate governance in organisations where incentives are not necessarily aligned to keep risk in check, or where information is not adequately available. It may even reveal blind spots of risk-taking activities occurring below the radar screen of the Chief Risk Officer (CRO).

Finally, but importantly, it is worth remembering that excessive borrowing by a country means that *someone else is lending excessively*: macroprudential policies apply to lenders just as much as they apply to borrowers.

5. *Muting the amplification capacity of the financial sector*

At the heart of the transmission mechanism described in this chapter is the ability of financial intermediaries, whether banks or shadow banks, to leverage up to high levels quickly when financing conditions are favourable. Credit seems excessively sensitive to financing costs. Policies should aim to prevent risk taking being excessively procyclical. By putting tougher controls on leverage, limiting the extent of exposures to specific actors, monitoring maturity transformation and demanding liquidity buffers, one can reduce the propensity of the financial system to engage in destabilising feedback loops.

With such a set of tools, one can also help make the macroprudential policies described above more robust. Errors of judgements by supervisors, CROs, chief executive officers, and boards are possible and even likely in our excessively complex financial environment. Tougher limits on leverage ratios, for example, are a sensible way to decrease the (verifiably huge) cost of these errors, without imposing large costs on the real economy.[36] However, greater attention must be paid to non-bank financial intermediaries, which may have fallen outside the regulatory perimeter but have the ability to leverage, if we are to limit the 'leakages' of macroprudential policies.[37] Indeed, although strong prudential policies aimed at global banks do reduce the likelihood of funding stress during times of turmoil, this can cause risk to migrate towards non-banks, warranting an expansion of the regulatory perimeter.[38]

6. *Developing the depth of local financial markets*

Having deeper local financial markets will ensure that, if capital is abruptly withdrawn from a country, there are enough contrarian investors who can absorb the increase in net supply.

One concern for EMs has been the increase in non-bank financial intermediation, particularly open-end mutual funds and exchange-trade funds, which now account for nearly half of the external financing flows into such markets – even exceeding cross-border lending by global banks.[39] Investment funds are inherently more vulnerable to liquidity and redemption risks during periods of global financial market stress, increasing the volatility of capital flows to EMs. Benchmark-driven investments, namely passive funds, appear very sensitive to global risk shocks, such as tightening US dollar funding conditions, and some of these investors hold a large share of the investable assets of a given country. Hence, if they withdraw abruptly, a collapse in valuations may induce highly problematic second-round effects.

Such effects are likely to be less destabilising if there are local contrarian investors with deep pockets, such as pension funds. As discussed previously, developing local currency bond markets also has the advantage of decreasing the prevalence of the original sin.

VI. Conclusions

Of these six options, if history is a guide, establishing effective international cooperation among the main central banks to internalise the spillovers of their monetary policies on the rest of the world seems most difficult. There are many reasons for this, not least that such cooperation may conflict with the domestic mandates of central banks. Furthermore, the management of aggregate demand in systemically important economies has important consequences for economic activity in the rest of the world; other countries cannot simultaneously complain of excessive capital inflows due to loose monetary policy in the centre countries *and* wish for a higher level of economic activity and demand stimulus in the same countries. All of this underlines that fact that the trade-offs are extraordinarily complex, and policy action will most likely remain biased towards national priorities. Still, a transparent forum in which the collective monetary policy stance of the systemically important central banks is actively discussed would be highly beneficial.

The most appropriate policies to support monetary and financial stability seem therefore to require both adopting a credible inflation targeting framework with a floating exchange rate, together with a well thought-out set of macroprudential policies applying both to host and investment countries. This policy needs to be supplemented with an active prudential supervision deploying the tools mentioned earlier, which can boost the development of local markets and help deepen local markets, to reduce the destabilising effect of capital flight. Depending on the source of financial instability and institutional settings, the use of capital controls on inflows and outflows, as a partial substitute for macroprudential measures, should not be discarded.

Such a set of policies should help increase the pass-through and effectiveness of monetary policy in EMs and advanced economies alike, as well as guaranteeing financial stability as much as possible. They constitute a reasonable basis for a London Consensus.

Notes

1 For a summary of the data and a theoretical analysis of trade and financial globalisation and their interconnections, see Martin and Rey (2006).

2 Rey (2013).

3 Miranda-Agrippino and Rey (2022).

4 Bruno and Shin (2015); Kalemli-Özcan (2019); Miranda-Agrippino and Rey (2020); Degasperi et al. (2023).

5 Borio and Zhu (2012); Bauer et al. (2023); Coimbra and Rey (2023); Kim et al. (2022).

6 Boehm and Kroner (2023) emphasise the importance of US news in driving economic sentiments; Aldasoro et al. (2023) present a rich comparison of domestic and global financial cycles.

7 Gilchrist and Zakrajšek (2012).

8 Miranda-Agrippino and Rey (2020). US monetary policy is identified using high frequency instruments (Fed Funds Future; 30-minute windows around monetary policy announcements – see Gertler and Karadi (2015)). Shaded areas are 90% and 95% confidence intervals.

9 Kaminsky et al. (2005).

[10] Acalin (2023).

[11] Obstfeld and Zhou (2023).

[12] De Leo et al. (2022).

[13] Correlations control for t-1 interest rate. The shaded areas are 90% confidence intervals.

[14] di Giovanni et al. (2021).

[15] Degasperi et al. (2023); Kalemli-Özcan (2019).

[16] Eichengreen and Hausmann (1999).

[17] Chang and Velasco (2001).

[18] Kalemli-Özcan and Unsal (2023).

[19] Rey (2016); Miranda-Agrippino and Rey (2020).

[20] Calvo and Reinhart (2002).

[21] It is reassuring that a series of papers has consistently found that short rates are less correlated to the base country rate for flexible exchange rate countries than for fixed exchange rate countries (Obstfeld et al. 2005).

[22] In the case of some small open economies (Singapore, for example), where transaction costs and exchange rate risks are detrimental for trade, a fixed exchange rate vis-à-vis a currency basket may well be preferred to a flexible rate. Characteristics of countries, such as openness and development of financial markets, as well as the traditional optimum currency areas factors matter for the choice of the optimal exchange rate regime. See Mundell (1961).

[23] Obstfeld et al. (2019); Obstfeld (2015). From a theoretical point of view, Cespedes et al. (2004), for example, analyse the effect of devaluation of the domestic currency on the economy when liabilities are in dollars and show that even in that case, floating exchange rate regimes tend to dominate.

[24] For an interesting discussion on the case of Indonesia see Basri and Sumartono (2023).

[25] Rey (2013).

[26] There are of course other relevant policy considerations linked on the one hand to fiscal policy and on the other hand to the IMF, the global safety net, and the use of Central Bank swap lines. They will not be discussed here due to the lack of space; they would warrant another chapter on their own.

[27] Klein (2012).

[28] Forbes (2021).

[29] But capital controls may be appropriate if there is a great deal of direct cross-border lending and the banking system can be circumvented. For a theoretical model showing the optimality of capital controls in a neo-Keynesian framework even with flexible exchange rates, see Farhi and Werning (2014).

[30] Das et al. (2022).

[31] Baldursson et al. (2023).

[32] Kalemli-Özcan and Unsal (2023).

[33] Obstfeld et al. (2019).

[34] Eichengreen et al. (2011).

[35] Tucker (2018).

[36] Admati and Hellwig (2013).

[37] Forbes (2021).

[38] Goldberg (2023).

[39] Chari (2023).

References

Acalin, J. (2023) The Global Financial Cycle Meets Global Imbalances, *mimeo IMF.* https://julienacalin.com/files/JMP_AcalinJ.pdf

Admati, A. and Hellwig, M. (2013) *The Bankers' New Clothes: What's Wrong with Banking and What to Do About It,* Princeton, NJ: Princeton University Press. https://doi.org/10.1515/9780691251714

Aldasoro, I., Avdjiev, S., Borio, C. and Disyatat, P. (2023) 'Global and Domestic Financial Cycles: Variations on a Theme', *International Journal of Central Banking*, 19(5): 49–98.

Baldursson, F. M., Portes, R. and Thorlaksson, E. E. (2023) 'Capital Controls as a Bargaining Device: The Case of Iceland', *Review of International Economics*, 31(4): 1308–1324. https://doi.org/10.1111/roie.12668

Basri, C. and Sumartono, L. (2023) 'The Impossibility of the Impossible Trinity: The Case of Indonesia', *Oxford Review of Economic Policy,* 39(2): 341–355. https://doi.org/10.1093/oxrep/grad010

Bauer, M. D., Bernanke, B. S. and Milstein, E. (2023) 'Risk Appetite and the Risk-Taking Channel of Monetary Policy', *Journal of Economic Perspectives*, 37(1): 77–100. https://doi.org/10.1257/jep.37.1.77

Boehm, C. and Kroner, N. (2023) 'The US, Economic News and the Global Financial Cycle', *Mimeo Austin. National Bureau of Economic Research (NBER).* https://doi.org/10.3386/w30994

Borio, C. and Zhu, H. (2012) 'Capital Regulation, Risk-Taking and Monetary Policy: A missing link in the transmission ?', *Journal of Financial Stability*, 8(4): 236–251. https://doi.org/10.1016/j.jfs.2011.12.003

Bruno, V. and Shin, H. S. (2015) 'Capital Flows and the Risk-Taking Channel of Monetary Policy', *Journal of Monetary Economics*, 71: 119–132. https://doi.org/10.1016/j.jmoneco.2014.11.011

Calvo, G. A. and Reinhart, C. M. (2002) 'Fear of Floating', *The Quarterly Journal of Economics*, 117(2): 379–408. https://doi.org/10.1162/003355302753650274

Céspedes, L. F., Chang, R. and Velasco, A. (2004) 'Balance Sheets and Exchange Rate Policy', *American Economic Review*, 94(4): 1183–1193. https://doi.org/10.1257/0002828042002589

Chang, R. and Velasco, A. (2001) 'A Model of Financial Crises in Emerging Markets', *The Quarterly Journal of Economics*, 116(2): 489–517. https://doi.org/10.1162/00335530151144087

Chari, A. (2023) 'Global Risk, Non-Bank Financial Intermediation and Emerging Market Vulnerabilities', *Annual Review of Economics*, 15: 549–572. https://doi.org/10.3386/w31143

Coimbra, N. and Rey, H. (2023) 'Financial Cycle with Heterogeneous Intermediaries', *The Review of Economic Studies*, 91(2): 817–857. https://doi.org/10.1093/restud/rdad039

Das, M., Gopinath, G. and Kalemli-Özcan, S. (2022) 'Preemptive Policies and Risk-off Shocks in Emerging Markets', NBER Working Paper No. w29615. https://doi.org/10.2139/ssrn.3998788

Degasperi, R., Hong, S. S. and Ricco, G. (2023) 'The Global Transmission of US Monetary Policy', Centre for Economic Policy Research (CEPR) Discussion Paper 14533.

De Leo, P., Gopinath, G. and Kalemli-Özcan, S. (2022) 'Monetary Policy and the Short-Rate Disconnect in Emerging Economies', NBER Working Paper No. w30458. https://doi.org/10.2139/ssrn.4222661

di Giovanni, J., Kalemli-Özcan, S., Ulu, M. and Baskaya, S. (2021) 'International Spillovers and Local Credit Cycles', *The Review of Economic Studies*, 89(2): 733–773. https://doi.org/10.1093/restud/rdab044

Eichengreen B. and Hausmann, R. (1999) 'Exchange Rates and Financial Fragility', *Proceedings – Economic Policy Symposium – Jackson Hole*, Federal Reserve Bank of Kansas City: 329–368. https://doi.org/10.3386/w7418

Eichengreen, B., El-Erian, M., Fraga, A., Ito, T., Pisani-Ferry, J., Prasad, E., Rajan, R., Ramos, M., Reinhart, C. M., Rey, H., Rodrik, D., Rogoff, K. S., Shin, H. S., Velasco, A., di Mauro, B. Weder and Yu, Y. (2011) *Rethinking Central Banking: Committee on International Economic Policy and Reform,* Washington, DC: Brookings Institution.

Farhi, E. and Werning, I. (2014) 'Dilemma Not Trilemma? Capital Controls and Exchange Rates with Volatile Capital Flows', *IMF Economic Review,* 62 (4): 569–605. https://doi.org/10.1057/imfer.2014.25

Forbes, K. (2021) 'The International Aspects of Macroprudential Policy', *Annual Review of Economics,* 13: 203–228. https://doi.org/10.1146/annurev-economics-081020-051248

Gertler, M. and Karadi, P. (2015) 'Monetary Policy Surprises, Credit Costs, and Economic Activity', *American Economic Journal: Macroeconomics,* 7(1): 44–76. https://doi.org/10.1257/mac.20130329

Gilchrist, S. and Zakrajšek, E. (2012) 'Credit Spreads and Business Cycle Fluctuations', *American Economic Review,* 102(4): 1692–1720. https://doi.org/10.1257/aer.102.4.1692

Goldberg, L. (2023) 'Global Liquidity: Drivers, Volatility and Toolkits', Mundell Fleming Lecture, National Bureau of Economic Research (NBER) Working Paper 31355. https://doi.org/10.3386/w31355

Kalemli-Özcan, S. (2019) 'U.S. Monetary Policy and International Risk Spillovers', *Proceedings – Economic Policy Symposium – Jackson Hole,* NBER Working Paper 26297. https://doi.org/10.3386/w26297

Kalemli-Özcan, S. and Unsal, F. (2023) 'Global Transmission of FED Hikes: The Role of Policy Credibility and Balance Sheets', *mimeo University of Maryland.* NBER Working Paper 32329. https://doi.org/10.3386/w32329

Kaminsky, G. L., Reinhart, C. M. and Vegh, C. A. (2005) 'When It Rains, It Pours: Procyclical Capital Flows and Macroeconomic Policies', in *NBER Macroeconomics Annual,* 19: 11–82. https://doi.org/10.1086/ma.19.3585327

Kim, D., Coimbra, N. and Rey, H. (2022) 'Central Bank Policy and the Concentration of Risk: Empirical estimates', *Journal of Monetary Economics,* 125: 182–198. https://doi.org/10.1016/j.jmoneco.2021.08.002

Klein, M. (2012) 'Capital Controls: Gates versus Walls', *Brookings Papers on Economic Activity.* 317–367. https://doi.org/10.1353/eca.2012.0015

Martin, P. and Rey, H. (2006) 'Globalization and Emerging Markets: With or without crash?', *The American Economic Review,* 96.5: 1631–1651. https://doi.org/10.1257/aer.96.5.1631

Miranda-Agrippino, S. and Rey, H. (2020) 'U.S. Monetary Policy and the Global Financial Cycle', *The Review of Economic Studies*, 87(6): 2754–2776. https://doi.org/10.1093/restud/rdaa019

Miranda-Agrippino, S. and Rey, H. (2022) 'The Global Financial Cycle', *Handbook of International Economics,* Chapter 1: 1–43. https://doi.org/10.1016/bs.hesint.2022.02.008

Mundell, R. (1961) 'A Theory of Optimum Currency Areas', *The American Economic Review*, 51(4): 657–665.

Obstfeld, M. (2015) 'Trilemmas and Trade-offs: Living with Financial Globalization', BIS Working Paper 480.

Obstfeld, M., Shambaugh, J. and Taylor, A. (2005) 'The Trilemma in History: Tradeoffs among Exchange Rates, Monetary Policies, and Capital Mobility', *The Review of Economic and Statistics*, 87(3): 423–438. https://doi.org/10.1162/0034653054638300

Obstfeld, M., Ostry, J. D. and Qureshi, M. S. (2019) 'A Tie that Binds: Revisiting the Trilemma in Emerging Market Economies', *The Review of Economics and Statistics,* 101(2): 279–293. https://doi.org/10.1162/rest_a_00740

Obstfeld, M. and Zhou, H. (2023) 'The Global Dollar Cycle', National Bureau of Economic Research (NBER) Working Paper 31004. https://doi.org/10.3386/w31004

Rey, H. (2013) 'Dilemma Not Trilemma: The Global Cycle and Monetary Policy Independence', *Proceedings – Economic Policy Symposium – Jackson Hole*. https://www.kansascityfed.org/Jackson%20Hole/documents/4575/2013Rey.pdf

Rey, H. (2016) 'International Channels of Transmission of Monetary Policy and the Mundellian Trilemma', *IMF Economic Review*, Palgrave Macmillan; International Monetary Fund, 64(1): 6–35. https://doi.org/10.3386/w21852

Tucker, P. (2018) *Unelected Power: The Quest for Legitimacy in Central Banking and the Regulatory State*, Princeton, NJ: Princeton University Press. https://doi.org/10.23943/9781400889518

Response to Hélène Rey by Paul Tucker

> Constitutional liberty will be best worked out by those who aspire to freedom by their own efforts. You will only overload it by your help, by your principle of interference.
>
> Former prime minister Robert Peel, House of Commons, 1850[1]

I. Introduction

Hélène Rey's chapter on the monetary system joins the project of offering to the developing world a map for how to achieve growing prosperity. I am doubtful about any such project, except in the most modest terms. This is for both broad and more subject-specific reasons.

The highest-level reason is approximately summed up in the quote from former prime minister Peel when trying to persuade the Westminster parliament not to force liberty onto other states. The terms on which political communities manage to establish basic order, and make that order acceptable to their people, creating conditions for cooperation, is highly context-dependent. What has worked for advanced-economy states might cut across another political community's way of life – meaning, most significantly, the deep political values embedded in their collective institutions.

Nor, today, is it in our interests to lecture or prescribe. Less than a decade or so into what might easily be a century-long geopolitical and ideological contest, the rich liberal democracies need friends. That means exercising self-restraint in proselytising our way of life, instead letting it speak for itself.

The point is underlined by the harsh fact that our core institutions have not been working well. Monetary-financial policy falls into that ignoble category. In the past 15 years, we have caused the biggest global financial crisis since the 1930s, then opted for a mix of macroeconomic stimulus that fuelled another bout of speculative excess, and recently have struggled to maintain low and stable inflation. What *we* should learn from that takes up the bulk of my remarks.

Prescription, which I am counselling against, is profoundly different from another kind of endeavour. That involves trying to explain what seems to have worked for us, what definitely has not worked, and which successful measures seem to depend on local conditions and, by contrast, which might possibly be transferable to other circumstances. That is what, incompletely and rather crudely, I want to attempt concerning 2022 and 2023's monetary-financial problems. In a nutshell, the problem is that we still have not found institutions that are reliably committed to pre-emptive actions to maintain monetary-system stability.

II. Moral hazard runs through delegated regimes for monetary system stability

The two core functions of central banking are easily stated: price stability and banking stability. Because nearly all the money held and used by nearly all of us is the deposit money issued by commercial banks, the two are umbilically linked.[2] Both functions are increasingly delegated by legislators to independent central banks because each depends upon pre-emptive actions in the face of, respectively, inflationary shocks and banking system vulnerabilities. Over the past decade, however, few such independent power holders have acted pre-emptively.

That is a problem of moral hazard, as it involves deviating from mandates. We need, somehow, to make it harder for policymakers to depart from stability-oriented policies.

III. Price stability

The harder case is price stability, for the simple reason that, writing in mid-2023, we do not yet know, for sure, whether monetary policymakers have let inflation out of the bag. Plainly, the energy cost shocks rooted in Russia's war on Ukraine (and the oil-producing states' geopolitical choice not to offset them) raised the price level, and hence for a while headline inflation. It would have been unnecessary and crazy to seek to offset those shocks entirely. Some accommodation made sense. But, at the time of writing, it remains unclear whether inflation will come back to target or settle some way above it, requiring a policy-engineered slowdown.

Just in case that is the outcome, it is not too early to ask why we find ourselves in this predicament. Some possible proximate causes are already clear enough: relying too heavily on monetary policy to revive underlying growth after the Great Financial Crisis of 2007–09; continuing to add to the monetary stimulus even when, during the COVID-19 pandemic, there was extraordinary fiscal support that could have been funded in the capital markets; not heeding contractions in labour supply after the pandemic, which left some economies with excess demand even though they were not growing rapidly; and nearly a decade of forward guidance leaving policymakers on autopilot rather than responsive to shocks.

Behind those various technicalities, deeper forces might have played a part, including a wish to promote 'inclusive growth' (as the Federal Reserve framed it in what looked like an appeal to progressive politicians);

a desire to steer credit to useful places and away from unworthy ones; and an apparent assumption among the political classes that inflation was an earlier generation's problem, making possible a shift to 'monetary activism' (as a British government stipulated in the Bank of England's 2013 Remit).[3] Putting that together, it was as if central bankers could focus on more pressing problems because medium-term inflation explanations were surely anchored to target. But that was always risky because the true anchor was always central bankers' *own* willingness to act pre-emptively, even when that would be unpopular.

1. *Remedies*

While there is no obvious remedy, several measures could be taken to reduce the chances of revisiting the problem anytime soon. One is to strengthen automatic fiscal stabilisers, overcoming politicians' self-interest in sitting on their fiscal hands when monetary policy is constrained (most obviously by the 'zero' lower bound on nominal interest rates).

A second measure, getting closer to the bone, is to make it clearer that central banks should stick to actions that directly serve their core stability mission. The point is hardly to marginalise other public policy objectives. It is, rather, to retighten the harness binding central bank leaders' desire for professional esteem and public prestige – on which the utility of independence depends – to their success in delivering the mission that warranted their extraordinary powers in the first place. Milton Friedman was half onto something, but not what he thought, when in the early-1960s he claimed in a letter to Stanley Fischer: 'the two most important variables in [central bankers'] loss function are avoiding accountability on the one hand and achieving prestige on the other'.[4] What he missed is that, in some circumstances, exposing oneself to accountability can help sharpen incentives, and so offers a route to prestige.

Third, therefore, a lexicographic objective, under which business cycle stabilisation is subordinated to price stability, remains best as it removes ambiguity about the need, at all times, to maintain *securely* anchored medium-term expectations.

IV. Banking system stability

Similar sentiments can be brought to the banking stability mission, where moral hazard problems were at the root of 2023's banking failures – the collapse of Silicon Valley Bank and other large United States regional banks, and the unravelling of Credit Suisse. In the US, the authorities ignored international norms when they formally decided to cease planning for the failure of large regional banks, and did so even though they must have known they did not have a good plan.[5] In Switzerland, meanwhile, the authorities not only set aside a resolution plan discussed for years with international peers, but they also did not refinance an ostensibly well-capitalised bank, which might have avoided a fire sale of the core business. If there were insufficient unencumbered assets any of them would accept as collateral, the central banks were in a bind (as lending unsecured is for elected fiscal officials).

1. *Complete liquidity insurance for 'safe assets'*

Among remedies, the biggest is to accept that, for a solvent bank, the central bank will act to enable *all* short-term liabilities to be paid out. That implies those with access to central bank liquidity insurance should be required to cover 100% of their short-term liabilities with assets eligible at their central bank, and should pre-position those assets with the central bank (acting, effectively, as a sub-custodian) so that they cannot be used for other purposes.[6]

Access to such insurance cannot credibly be limited to de jure banks unless the state uses a hard-to-amend law to prevent any other kind of intermediary from conducting a systemically dangerous maturity transformation. Except where that condition is met, the insurance should be available to any issuer of 'safe assets', defined as those instruments that users (investors, traders, intermediaries) feel no need to analyse. Like money, they are, as economists put it, information insensitive. And like money, they enjoy network economies, and so are liquid – until some revelation shatters an illusion, there is a run for the exits, and supposedly safe assets become, in a flash, illiquid, or worse.[7]

Under that regime, the amount of capital an issuer of money-like safe assets had to carry against its core banking business would be determined by the excess collateral (known as 'haircuts') required by the central bank. Since central banks suffer political costs when they suffer losses from financial system support operations, they have incentives to be cautious in setting and monitoring haircuts. In other words, in the Western political culture, mitigating moral hazard in the application of banking policy is more incentive compatible for a central bank as lender of last resort (LOLR) than it is for a standard prudential supervisor.

2. *The LOLR and resolution policy for fundamentally bust firms*

Normatively, however, in constitutional democracies such liquidity insurance must be subject to the proviso that the unelected central bankers should not lend to anyone that is fundamentally insolvent. That is a matter of *our* values – specifically, those associated with the separation of powers between executive government and an elected legislature. Lending to fundamentally bust firms distributes resources from longer-term creditors to short-term creditors. In consequence, solvency bailouts and lending to firms that, even after receiving liquidity assistance, will not be able to discharge all their obligations must be reserved to elected politicians, because only they can decently discriminate between different creditors.[8]

When a prospective borrower *is* fundamentally broken but the state wishes to avoid a taxpayer bailout, the distressed intermediary must go into a bankruptcy or special resolution process that is designed to avoid systemic chaos. This is already agreed policy in all major banking centres, but needs to be applied, as it was not in the US, to all significant banks.

Separately, central banks need to make it clear that they stand ready to lend to a resolved bank in case it (initially) suffers liquidity strains. Some have still not done so, leaving the financial system weaker than it needs to be. Being clear about lending into effective resolutions would give the central banks leverage, via their collateral valuations and haircuts, over the size of recapitalisation a resolution must deliver. Even though it might not be widely grasped, central bankers are vital to making resolution policy credible.

V. Summing up

There might seem to be an awkward tension in this comment. On the one hand, I urge rich states to refrain from preaching and proselytising to poorer and weaker states, who need to find their own way. On the other hand, I seem to advocate certain policies for monetary system stability. Where do I stand?

The former consideration dominates. While IMF programme conditions obviously bite, and are framed for specific circumstances, I think states should take the IMF's routine general recommendations as interesting ideas rather than authoritative (in the sense of having content-independent authority). That is partly because real crises focus the mind, as illustrated by a sad example in the banking field. For half a decade or so from the late-1990s, the IMF started proselytising moving banking supervision away from central banks, favouring integrated all-purpose financial regulators instead. This was after the United Kingdom took that course in 1997. At the time, I thought it was a bad idea for Britain as London's culture would not incentivise information sharing between the regulator and the LOLR. Sadly, that is how it turned out, and we reaped the consequences in 2007. The IMF, dare I say, was barely equipped to judge whether it was a good idea in the UK, let alone whether it was a sensible policy to float for the rest of the world.

A happier but still instructive example is inflation targeting. It started in New Zealand. A few years later it was adopted by Sweden, and then Britain. At the time, there was almost no academic literature on the subject, and international organisations were not proselytising it. That is not a bad model: scan the world for good ideas, and ask whether any might work at home.

So, the reform ideas I float here are just that: my take on some serious local difficulties in the rich world, which might or might not be of use to those bearing responsibility elsewhere. This leaves an awkward but important question hanging in the air: what notice developing countries should take of the plethora of standards and codes pushed their way by the IMF and other international bodies and groups. Members of the G20, including some large

EM economies, overtly sign up to them and are in the room when they are being drawn up. This is as close to consent as it gets in international affairs.

Which other states are in a broadly equivalent position depends on the subject matter and, therefore, which international body draws up a standard. Except where a state has been properly involved (entailing something like consent), I suggest they ask themselves whether it would be useful for them, all things considered, to tie themselves to the mast of a particular standard.

The calculus would be different if IMF programme conditions were overtly (and credibly) linked to compliance with codes and standards. But they are not. And if they were, agreeing the standards and codes might well end up involving more demanding processes: what some would misleadingly term global democracy. Given geopolitics, that is not on offer.[9]

Years ago, perhaps a decade before I left office in late-2013, I was visited by a very senior Indian official who asked whether they should bow to international pressure to liberalise capital flows. My suggestion was that they listen very carefully to the substantive arguments of everyone who tried to persuade them one way or another, but without paying much notice of where the advice came from, as few concerned would be around to take responsibility if the choice backfired. Indian officials had to make up their own minds. I did not know at the time that, in a tiny way, I was echoing Peel.

Notes

1. Hurd and Young (2010).
2. Tucker (2018).
3. Smialek (2021); HM Treasury (2013).
4. Fischer (1990).
5. Systematic Risk Council (2019).
6. King (2016); Tucker (2019).
7. Holmstrom (2015).
8. Tucker (2020).
9. Tucker (2022).

References

Fischer, S. (1990) 'Rules versus Discretion in Monetary Policy', in: B. M. Friedman and F. H. Hahn (eds) *Handbook of Monetary Economics Volume II*, Amsterdam: Elsevier Science Publishers. https://doi.org/10.1016/S1573-4498(05)80028-1

HM Treasury (2013) 'Remit for the Monetary Policy Committee'. https://assets.publishing.service.gov.uk/government/uploads/system/uploads/attachment_data/file/221566/chx_letter_to_boe_monetary_policy_framework_200313.pdf

Holmstrom, B. (2015) 'Understanding the Role of Debt in the Financial System', *BIS Working Paper No.* 479. https://www.bis.org/publ/work479.pdf

Hurd, D. and Young, E. (2010) *Choose Your Weapons: The British Foreign Secretary, 200 Years of Argument, Success and Failure*, London: Weidenfeld and Nicolson.

King, M. (2016) *The End of Alchemy: Money, Banking and the Future of the Global Economy*. London: Little, Brown and Company.

Smialek, J. (2021) 'The Federal Reserve Chair Says the United States Needs "More Inclusive Prosperity"', *The New York Times* [22 June]. https://www.nytimes.com/2021/06/22/business/economy/jerome-powell-house-testimony.html

Systematic Risk Council (2019) 'Systemic Risk Council Urges Federal Reserve and FDIC Not to Relax Resolution-Planning Requirements for Large US Regional Banks'. https://www.systemicriskcouncil.org/2019/07/systemic-risk-council-urges-federal-reserve-and-fdic-not-to-relax-resolution-planning-requirements-for-large-us-regional-banks/

Tucker, P. (2018) *Unelected Power: The Quest for Legitimacy in Central Banking and the Regulatory State*, Princeton, NJ: Princeton University Press. https://doi.org/10.23943/9781400889518

Tucker, P. (2019) 'Is the Financial System Sufficiently Resilient?', *BIS Working Papers* No. 792. https://www.bis.org/publ/work792.pdf

Tucker, P. (2020) 'Solvency as a Fundamental Constraint on LOLR Policy for Independent Central Banks: Principles, History, Law', *Journal of Financial Crises*, 2(2): 1–33.

Tucker, P. (2022) *Global Discord: Values and Power in a Fractured World Order*, Princeton, NJ: Princeton University Press. https://doi.org/10.23943/princeton/9780691229317.001.0001

Response to Hélène Rey by Şebnem Kalemli-Özcan

This paper is a clear description of what we have learnt since the Washington Consensus. The main lesson is the importance of the GFC, thanks to Hélène Rey's great work on this topic. The paper describes in great detail alternative policies to deal with the GFC.

I agree with the paper overall. In this discussion I will add some newly available evidence, with a focus on EMs. This evidence is based on the new integrated policy framework developed by the IMF, a Washington institution that seems to be moving away from the Washington Consensus.

I start by highlighting an important theme in Rey's paper, namely the heterogeneity of both borrowers and lenders. This is very important as we move away from the Washington Consensus, because no two countries are the same in terms of capital flows, risk sentiment of investors, size of foreign currency debt, credibility of monetary policy, or institutional environment. Such heterogeneity on the borrower side also affects the lending side, as lenders price loans to reflect the heterogeneity of borrowers. To think about regulation and other related policies, we need to think about differences in the risk-taking behaviour of the lender. Hence, we may need different regulation for global and domestic lenders. These important themes are all in Rey's paper but they are worth stressing.

The first panel of Figure 7.4 shows that debt accounts for 70% of EM external liabilities, and that three kinds of borrowers – sovereigns, banks, and corporates – have roughly equal shares in this stock of debt. The middle panel focuses on portfolio debt and shows that most of the portfolio investment into emerging markets is directed to sovereigns (almost 70%). The last panel shows loans, where corporates and banks, but not sovereigns, have the lion's share.

Figure 7.5 demonstrates the effect of the GFC on emerging markets. It focuses on a typical EM, Turkey, using my work on the subject. The figure plots a period where Turkey is a representative EM, in the sense of having current account deficits, high growth and low inflation, starting in 2003. The period includes the year 2013, when the Turkish central bank was deemed the best across EMs.[1]

The black line in Figure 7.5 is a measure of global risk appetite, VIX. We can see strong co-movement between VIX and the average domestic lending rate in the top left panel. The top right panel shows the capital flow side of this process. Capital flows correlate negatively with VIX: when VIX falls, capital flows to the domestic financial intermediary sector (i.e., banks), rise.[2]

Figure 7.4: Debt in emerging markets

(d) Share of Sectors in Total External Debt Liabiliies - Emerging

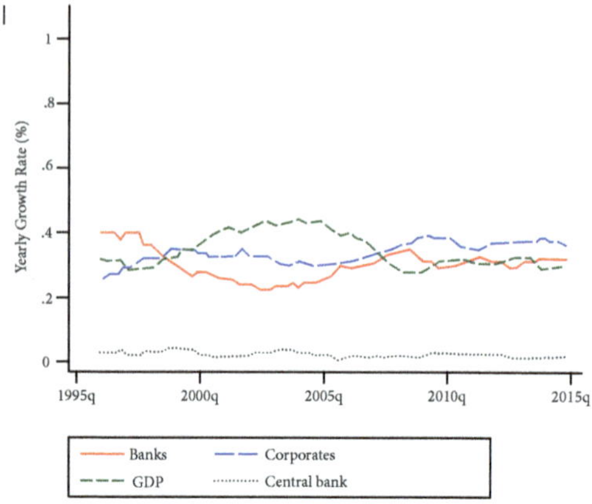

(e) Share of Sectors in Other Investment Debt Liabilities - Emerging

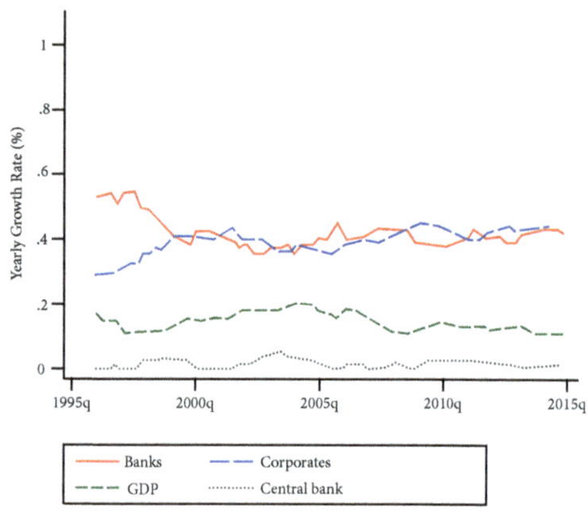

(f) Share of Sectors in Portfolio Debt Liabilities - Emerging

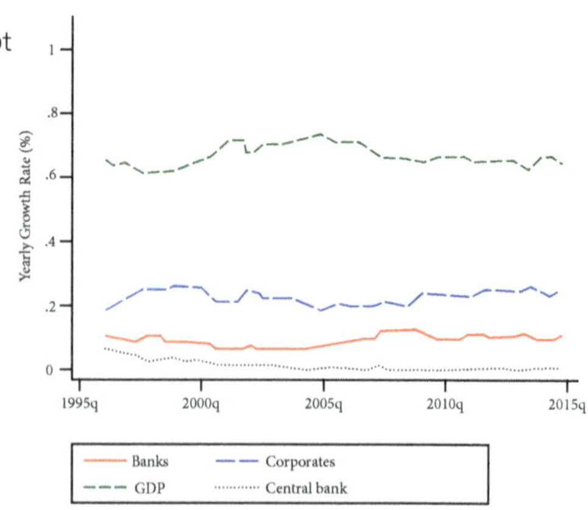

Source: Figure 3 [d, e, and f] in Avdjiev et al. (2022),[3] reproduced with permission from the *Journal of the European Economic Association*/Oxford University Press.

Figure 7.5: Macro facts

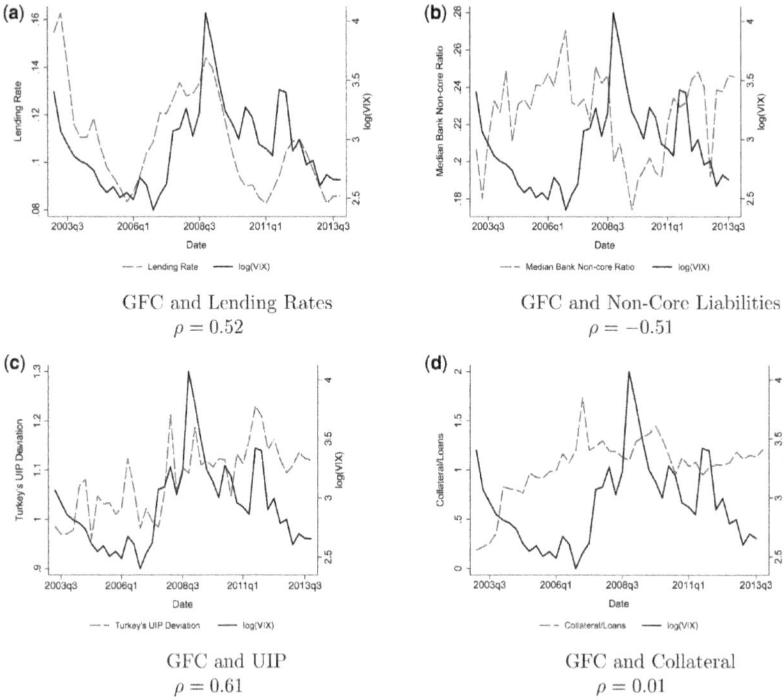

Source: Figure 1 in di Giovanni et al. (2022),[4] reproduced with permission from *The Review of Economic Studies*/Oxford University Press.

The banks with external liabilities have high non-core liabilities, since core liabilities are composed of domestic household deposits only. These so-called high non-core banks tend to cut rates and lend more during the boom phase of the GFC compared to low non-core banks, and vice versa during the GFC downturn.

The bottom panels show other factors that are also important for the transmission of the GFC. The bottom left panel looks at the deviation of UIP. This matters because it reflects the funding cost in local currency versus dollars – and, as Rey explains, one of the issues we need to consider is how to develop local currency bond markets. UIP deviations are reflections of investors' demand for local currency versus foreign currency bonds. The figure shows that UIP never holds in EMs and the gap is always positive, meaning excess returns for EM currencies.

The figure also shows the correlation between UIP and VIX, reflecting the fact that when risk is high it is harder to borrow in local currency and easier to borrow in dollars. If a country is unable to borrow in dollars for other reasons – say, sovereign default risk – then it is in a tough spot, because all sources of funding begin to close off.

The final panel highlights one difference between an emerging market and an advanced economy like the United States. In emerging markets, there is zero correlation between collateral values and the GFC. This is because capital flows not just into the stock market, amplifying asset values used as collateral, but (as shown in Figure 7.4) also into domestic banks and global banks operating locally.

In my work with Gita Gopinath and Pierre De Leo, we showed the disconnect between policy rates and market rates in emerging economies.[5] Market rates go in an opposite direction in emerging markets than they do in advanced economies in response to US monetary policy shocks. Given that disconnect, monetary policy is unlikely to be very effective in EMs, so let me end by discussing what other policies could be used to greater effect.

Using a newly available data set from the IMF, we are also able to document what policies each country uses, according to what they report to the IMF.[6] We can see that most countries use macroprudential (domestic) or macroprudential/capital flow management policies. In fact, up to 80–90% of countries used these policies between 1996 and 2020.

An example of a pre-emptive capital flow management used by Brazil but not by Mexico before the 2013 surge in US Treasury yields known as the 'taper tantrum'.[7] UIP deviation increases more in Mexico than in Brazil, because Brazil deployed a pre-emptive prudential policy and Mexico did not. Our paper proposes and implements an econometric identification strategy to prove this statement causally.

The policy implications of all this accumulated evidence are potentially huge. By reducing the impact of risk-off shocks (financial shocks) on countries' external funding costs and exchange volatility, pre-emptive policies permit countries to enjoy continued access to international capital markets during troubled times. This is an important policy lesson for the London Consensus. Turbulent times are precisely when countries most need access to international capital markets, and also when policies typically used in response to a shock, such as monetary policy, may be least effective, as originally argued by Hélène Rey and confirmed by the data in my own work summarised previously. There is an importance nuance here that shows the power of Hélène's findings. Even if you have an autonomous policy – that is, you set your monetary policy differently than, say, the Federal Reserve or the European Central Bank – the existence of the GFC means that policy is less effective in stabilising your own economy.[8]

Notes

1 Adjiev et al. (2022).

2 The blue line plots the banks' external funding from foreigners called non-core liabilities.

3 di Giovanni et al. (2022).

[4] Things have changed drastically in Turkey after 2017, but this latter period is not covered in this figure.

[5] De Leo et al. (2022).

[6] Das et al. (2022).

[7] Das et al. (2022).

[8] Kalemli-Özcan (2019).

References

Avdjiev, S., Hardy, B., Kalemli-Özcan, S. and Servén, L. (2022) 'Gross Capital Flows by Banks, Corporates, and Sovereigns', *Journal of the European Economic Association*, 20(5): 2098–2135. https://doi.org/10.1093/jeea/jvac038

Das, M., Gopinath, G. and Kalemli-Özcan, S. (2022) 'Preemptive Policies and Risk-Off Shocks in Emerging Markets', IMF Working Papers 2022/003, International Monetary Fund. https://doi.org/10.5089/9781616358341.001

De Leo, P., Gopinath, G. and Kalemli-Özcan, S. (2022) 'Monetary Policy and the Short-Rate Disconnect in Emerging Economies', NBER Working Paper No. w30458. https://doi.org/10.2139/ssrn.4222661

di Giovanni, J., Kalemli-Özcan, S., Ulu, M. F. and Baskaya, Y. S. (2022) 'International Spillovers and Local Credit Cycles', *The Review of Economic Studies*, 89(2): 733–773. https://doi.org/10.1093/restud/rdab044

Kalemli-Özcan, S. (2019) 'US Monetary Policy and International Risk Spillovers', *Jackson Hole Symposium Proceedings*. https://www.kansascityfed.org/documents/6951/Ozcan_JH2019.pdf

PART IV

LABOUR MARKET

8. Labour markets and the future of work

Christopher Pissarides

New technologies are causing a restructuring of labour markets in many countries. While much has been written on how these technologies may destroy jobs, this chapter argues that they do not threaten the end of work but they will require extensive worker transitions. While some of the new job tasks that will be created in the digital economy will require skills at an advanced level with a strong scientific base, it is a basic knowledge of these technologies that will be required practically everywhere in the labour market. The chapter discusses the way in which both companies and governments have a role to play in meeting the challenge of achieving these transitions, in face of increasing demand for 'good work'.

I. Introduction

Modern labour markets are in a continuous state of flux. The reasons for change are many, and include new technologies, demographics, supply conditions, and policy. A good labour market accommodates these changes speedily and with minimum disruption. It also gives companies opportunities to adapt to the latest technologies and improve their performance. But very often the institutional structure of a country or its politics inhibit adaptation to new conditions and the country fails to keep up with its competitors.

The future of work is too big a topic to talk about in general terms. Although most economists would agree that certain features of the labour market make change easier to accommodate, in other cases different shocks might require different institutional structures and different responses. This chapter will focus on technology as the cause of change – though the lessons learned will be relevant to accommodate other changes in labour markets.

How to cite this book chapter:

Pissarides, Christopher (2025) 'Labour markets and the future of work', in: Besley, Tim, Bucelli, Irene and Velasco, Andrés (eds) *The London Consensus: Economic Principles for the 21st Century*, London: LSE Press, pp. 253–279 https://doi.org/10.31389/lsepress.tlc.h

Ever since industrialisation we have had ongoing technological change, sometimes great enough to rise to the status of a revolution. Occasionally, an economy might be hit by a one-off shock that will require special measures, such as the transformation of the former planned economies of Eastern Europe, or COVID-19. But in advanced industrial countries, the main reason for change over the longer term is new technology. Technology drives productivity, which is linked to income from work. It also gives opportunities for the creation of better jobs, which can improve human wellbeing independently of income. But to achieve this goal, the labour market needs to be well-regulated and functional, and its participants need to be aware of the challenges.

All of this begs several questions. What makes a labour market 'good' in the face of frequent shocks? How can the labour market best take on the latest technologies and develop new ones? What determines how workers will be affected – and what is the role of policy in influencing this process for the better? Overall, how can we make sure that new technology helps create good jobs?

Typically, when new technology arrives, some labour needs become obsolete. The most common manifestation of this will be 'role turnover': although workers retain their jobs, the things they do with the new technologies change over time. Bank tellers become 'relationship managers', because dealing with simple transactions has been taken over by automated teller machines. Retail shop floor assistants move to back-room selling over the internet, because people no longer buy from stores but shop online.

Yet, some changes in technology are great enough to demand a change of job, or even the closure of companies – even as they create new jobs and new start-ups. Worker transitions take place continually. Most are within the same sector of employment, doing similar things in the new jobs as in the old. But some technologies are more disruptive and require new capital investment and upskilling of the labour force.

Inevitably, the challenges encountered in a forced job change are much bigger than those encountered because of internal role changes. But unless workers are actively engaged in the evolution of new technologies and make the transitions with minimal disruption to their wellbeing, internal role changes can also be disruptive.

Companies can do certain things to achieve smooth transitions and adapt to new technologies. They can, for example, retain and retrain their employees, engaging them in the evolution of the company, motivating them, and all the while attracting more business through improvements in productivity. I shall argue that the best way for companies to achieve this is through the provision of 'good' jobs, which I will define and elaborate on in the course of this chapter.

The state also has an important role to play in the transition to new technologies. This might mean removing obstacles to change, which, although often well-intentioned, can be deleterious. Or it might mean well-designed social and retraining support to help workers, especially those that have lost their jobs, deal with the transition. Over the long term, governments must maintain a well-functioning infrastructure and provide up-to-date education, training assistance, and incentives for research and development (R&D). A consensus is emerging amongst economists about the best role the state can play in this arena, informed to a large extent by the various international rankings on competitiveness, innovation capabilities, and public sector efficiency.

In this chapter, I start by reviewing the industrial penetration of new technologies, before discussing the implications of that penetration for skills and jobs, and finally examining the role of government in facilitating the adjustment to the new world of work. I will pay particular attention to the impact on jobs and the wellbeing of workers, both in the transition and in the new normal of automation technologies.

II. The background: leading technologies and their industrial penetration

The leading technologies today are based on robotics and artificial intelligence (AI), and their main impact on work is automation. Automation mainly affects tasks traditionally done by workers lower down the skills distribution, which means that, if by introducing the new technologies a company increases profitability, the main beneficiaries are those doing more skilled and managerial work. That said, more recently AI technologies have improved their capabilities and have begun to penetrate activities traditionally associated with more skilled workers.[1]

Much has been written about the ability of robots to replace human labour in many occupations, mostly in manufacturing. This literature has converged on a figure for jobs that are at a high risk of obsolescence in the vicinity of 10–15%, although the pandemic may have raised this figure a little.[2] These jobs are mostly manual and low skilled, such as assembly line jobs, warehouse jobs, certain delivery jobs, and the like. More recently, however, robots capable of service sector tasks have been emerging too.[3]

Rather than view this as a negative development, I see it as positive, in the sense that the jobs that are lost are routine manual jobs, with low productivity and presumably not very fulfilling for the workers either. It is very difficult to turn these jobs into ones that are more productive and better for the workers. Their removal provides an opportunity for workers to acquire more training and progress to jobs that can be more productive, give more satisfaction, and provide more income. This process fits well with Joseph Schumpeter's claim that societies need to undergo a process of creative destruction of old and established work methods, to be replaced by new job creation.[4] According to Schumpeter, this is 'the essential fact about capitalism. It is what capitalism consists in and what every capitalist concern has got to live in'. When the jobs that are being replaced are poor jobs, as in the case of manual labour, creative destruction can have social benefits too. The role of government is to facilitate this transition, by providing a flexible environment for the company sector to replace the obsolete jobs, and by supporting the workers who lose their jobs to retrain and find better jobs, without falling into poverty.

A caveat is that the job creation that follows Schumpeterian job destruction does not benefit all sectors of the economy, or all workers, equally. Societies need to undergo a structural transformation and, for more inclusive growth, workers need to be prepared for the transitions. The main transformations required fall on low-skilled workers, who lose their jobs and need to learn new skills before they find new jobs. The ease with which the transitions can be made depends on the closeness between the declining and expanding sectors. For example, do manual manufacturing workers need to learn how to work as nurses or as hotel staff, or do they transition to being delivery drivers? Policy support is needed here, both to make the economic transitions easier, but also to support families during the transitions.

Robotics have been disrupting employment since the 1990s, when robots were first introduced on a large scale into manufacturing. This happened once robots became commercially viable as self-controlled mobile devices, sometime in the late 1980s. AI penetration remains low but is growing fast. AI learns from historical data, which means it cannot yet be trusted to produce unbiased results in all situations.[5] But the widespread use of the internet on mobile devices has been critical in the proliferation of big data sets that have commercial applications – such as training AI.

The current industrial penetration of robots worldwide is available from the database collected by the International Federation of Robotics, which is sourced from suppliers of robots to industrial companies. They define robots as fully autonomous machines that can be programmed to perform several manual tasks without human intervention. These tasks include handling, welding, dispensing, processing, assembling, and dismantling. They are found almost exclusively in the manufacturing industry, but the use of robots with AI is spreading to the service sector as well. Although in terms of growth rates of robot use China stands out, the countries whose industries are most highly robotised are Germany, Japan, and South Korea.[6] These are also the biggest producers of transport equipment and electronics, in which robot use is at its highest, and among the world's biggest exporters. Robot use improves productivity and competitiveness for its adopter, and so those countries that were first to automate today enjoy exceptionally large markets for their manufacturing goods.[7]

An aspect of robot use that is often ignored in the literature on robot-labour substitutions is that robots are used mainly in the production of tradable goods. Ignoring international trade when evaluating their impact on jobs leads to misleading results.[8] Across industrial countries, the biggest users of robots are also the ones that lost relatively fewer jobs in manufacturing, because robots made them more competitive, and therefore they exported more. This experience contrasts with that of countries like Britain and France, which have been much slower to adopt robots and have fallen behind both in export markets and in job creation in manufacturing.

It is much more difficult to collect data on the use of AI in production, but the general view is that it remains very limited. For example, in the financial sector, despite the hype about fintech and its disruptive potential, only a small fraction of activities has been taken over by AI.[9] AI is based on software that solve problems, so it cannot be counted in the way that self-standing robots can.

However, we can say something about the readiness of countries to adopt AI, based on the 'enablers' that they possess. The main enablers for AI are digital infrastructure, innovation capabilities, well-trained human capital, the country's openness to interaction with other similar countries, and the quality of its labour force institutions, including good social support.[10] The United States and China are the top performers in this respect because of their large internal market and their large digital companies, although they fail on the provision of social support during the transition. Northern European countries, including the United Kingdom, perform well across most criteria, with some differences between them.

The European Union has been compiling statistics on the use of AI in Europe, including comparisons with the US, China, and the UK.[11] The US is the leading country in most dimensions, with China close behind. Although the US has more successful start-ups in the AI sector than any other country, the UK has by far the highest 'AI density', defined as companies that use AI, relative to country size. This contrasts with robotics, in which the UK has low density. So, in the future of work, although robotics has not been a major disruptor in British manufacturing, and British productivity has suffered because of it, the expectation is that AI will make a bigger difference to jobs.

III. Implications for skills and jobs

The jobs at risk of obsolescence as robotics and AI develop are those involving tasks that can be programmed, given the available data. When a task done by humans is taken over by machines, workers could learn new skills and move on to another task within their organisation. Sometimes entire companies may shut down or contract, in which case jobs are lost and the workers must move on. Those companies that innovate successfully create jobs complementary to the new technology and grow large, but they drive out of the market others that do not innovate. Although companies like Amazon, Google, and Netflix are new digital companies and have grown large very quickly, they employ fewer people relative to their turnover than the companies that populated their sectors in the past, such as high street retail outlets, newspapers, or cinemas. The big losers when new technologies come to disrupt a sector are the companies that fail to innovate and either shrink or are driven out of the market altogether, bringing down with them the total number of jobs in the sector.

One thing is certain, however: in a free market economy, there will never be a shortage of jobs. Economists as prominent as John Maynard Keynes and Wassili Leontief predicted that eventually there might be a shortage, but they failed to see the potential of the service sector to create jobs without limits.[12] In Keynes's time, service sectors that employed large numbers of workers, such as hospitality, were practically unknown. Later, when Leontief was writing, the gig economy, which is now growing in response to the digitalisation of production and distribution, did not exist. New jobs are created all the time: any person who invents a way of spending their time that is useful to someone else is effectively creating a service sector job. And human ingenuity will always invent new ways of spending time. As society advances and living standards rise, the hours people spend at work will fall, because leisure is a commodity the demand for which increases with income. Currently, the countries with the highest productivity in Europe, such as Germany and the Netherlands, also have the lowest average hours of work, in contrast to countries with low productivity, such as Greece, that have the highest. In several advanced countries, including the UK, Germany, and the US, there is currently a shortage of labour, not a shortage of jobs. Eventually, the four-day week will become the norm, too, but the point to note is that these reductions in work are not driven by obsolescence due to the takeover of work by machinery, but by voluntary additions to leisure activities – which are themselves creating jobs in services.[13]

New technologies will cause a restructuring of employment. An argument may be made, with some justification, that the destruction can be quick, while the creation that follows it is slower. There is an interim period, during which the workers must learn new skills and transition to their new jobs, that is longer than it used to be in the past. It is essential, in these circumstances, that governments provide social support and training assistance to workers, to avoid them falling into long-term unemployment and disenfranchisement. Good social support is one of the enablers used by organisations that calculate the AI readiness of countries, and it is one of the few where the leading countries, the US and China, fall short compared to Europe.

Most of the transitions that will be necessitated by AI are role transitions within a company. Many fewer will demand job change. The roles that will become more in demand in the future are of two types: those that are complementary to the machines and perform tasks that advance the technologies and their use, and those that serve the people when the machines fail to serve them.

In terms of the latter, it is clear by now that most of the new job creation in response to the coming of the robots and AI will be in the service sectors that cannot be automated. These sectors are mainly ones in which there is direct contact with the people who receive the services. Since they are sectors that rely on human interaction, they are characterised by low productivity growth. They mostly supply services that become more in demand as societies become wealthier, so the services they supply are 'luxuries', in the way that economists use the term, meaning that they consist of goods or services on which expenditure increases faster than income.

Prominent among the sectors that will experience this type of jobs growth are health and care, because of our ageing societies and the 'luxury' element in high-quality, specialised care. As incomes rise, people expect better care for the sick, for their children, and for older people. In societies where incomes are low, care services are often provided by the family. But as incomes and education standards rise, specialist services from outside the home take over. The change from home provision of certain types of services to market provision is known as the 'marketisation' of consumption and it is a major source of job creation as societies grow. This is partly because market demand for services such as care rises, and partly because the family members who used to provide the services at home are now better educated and available to enter the market and seek jobs more suitable to their skills.[14] These factors are behind the observation that, over time, spending on health and care increases by about 1–2% faster than gross domestic product (GDP).

Another sector that can create jobs that cannot be automated is the hospitality and leisure sector, including the creative industries. As living standards rise, people demand better quality services in their leisure activities, such as travel, hotel accommodation, restaurants, and entertainment. In addition, as hours of work fall, especially as full-time workers get more annual leave, the demand for leisure services will increase. Spending on travel to foreign countries has grown much more rapidly than GDP, because of the luxury element of this pursuit and the improvement in safety standards, comfort, and value for money of air travel. It is this kind of job creation that was missed by Keynes – albeit understandably given the structure of employment in his time – when he claimed that there would be a job shortage a hundred years from the date that he was writing. In contrast, William Baumol as early as 1967[15] wrote about the importance of the Arts as employment destinations as technology takes over industrial jobs, because computers will never be able to exhibit the creativity of the human mind in the Arts, even if they can match many aspects of it in simple situations.

The skills required for such jobs are neither new nor different from the ones currently required. The challenge for these jobs is to make them attractive for workers, especially new entrants to the labour market, given that a large number of them will be in the public sector, and many others will be in labour-intensive industries with low productivity growth. The public sector will have to find resources for the funding of health and care services that grow as a fraction of GDP. However, the disparities in spending show clearly in a cross-section of countries.[16] In the US spending on health is as much as 18% of GDP, while in Germany and the UK it is 12.5%, and in China, where care is still largely in the hands of the family, it is a mere 5.1%.

The jobs that are created because of new technologies, which are aimed at developing those technologies and making them commercially useful, are of a different kind and will require new skills. The key to these jobs is technical training to understand the way that robotics and AI work, and data processing skills to gain information about the market and community. They could be highly specialised jobs in research establishments or jobs in companies or government dealing with the development and implementation of the technologies in practical situations. The greatest number of jobs in this class will be in companies that create 'digital jobs', whose remit will be to use the data generated by new technologies to enhance the company's market performance. By their nature, such jobs will be exclusively in the 'knowledge economy'.

In recent surveys of talent shortage by the Manpower Group, IT skills and data processing feature prominently. For the UK in particular, other technical skills in need are operations and logistics, and engineering.[17] The same is found in surveys of skill shortages by the McKinsey Global Institute, in which digital skills for ICT work is the competence most in demand. 'Soft skills' are also frequently listed as skills in short supply. These include reliability and self-discipline, creativity, critical thinking, leadership, and managing others, as well as advanced communication and negotiation skills. These are all skills with very low automation potential, and they will be a critical component of the work of the future.

An important point to bear in mind when talking about skills is that, although the ones that attract attention are the new skills of data analytics, interacting with computers, and generally skills associated with digital technologies, most of the jobs and roles of the future will involve people interaction. The skills needed in people interaction are different from the skills needed to interact with computers – and even the jobs that primarily involve interaction with computers will also involve some degree of people interaction, because any company will have a management structure and collaborative ways of working. This comes out clearly in a recent study of skills for the economy of 2035, which found that, although the new in-demand skills would be those related to information technology (IT) and data, the six most essential skills would be those needed to communicate with people. Namely, communicating with supervisors, peers, or subordinates; organising, planning, and prioritising work; establishing and maintaining interpersonal relationships; making decisions and solving problems; and customer and personal service.[18]

In work done at the Institute for the Future of Work with job vacancies and the skills that they require, we also found that IT and analysis, the two key competencies for the knowledge economy, were the two most rapidly growing skill demands. But the core skills required by most advertised jobs involve competencies like communication, language, and logical thinking.[19]

IV. The role of government

Government will inevitably have a greater role to play in the future labour market. This role will involve both broad control and regulation of new technologies, and, more narrowly, preparing the workforce for the needs of the future.

1. *Choosing AI trajectories*

A feature of AI is that it can do many things and not all are good for humanity. Of course, this is a feature of most of the important discoveries in the history of industrialisation, which are general purpose technologies that relate to our capacity to do things faster and in larger volumes. A key discovery in the first industrial revolution was steam power, which could run factories and move ships and trains more efficiently than in the past. Next came electricity, which was a stronger source of power with many more applications than steam. Digital technologies and AI fall into the same category. They can do more data processing, and solve problems faster, than anything that we had before them.

One difference is that with steam and electricity it was clear what we had to do: replace the current sources of energy with new ones, and transform homes and workplaces to accommodate them. With AI we have much more choice regarding the direction of research and applications. We can, for example, use it for medical research, diagnosis, and treatment – or we can use it for warfare. We can use it to make rich people even richer, by developing it in the way that works best for them – or we can use it to fight poverty and ill health around the world. It is a matter of social choice, and given the way that our societies are organised, along the Smithian principle that pursuing your own objectives will give the best outcomes for society, we are not likely to make the best choices without government intervention.

Because of this feature of AI, governments need to set standards and direct research to causes that are beneficial for humanity. Of course, defining what is and is not beneficial can be controversial. This is a question that has occupied the minds of philosophers and scientists for thousands of years. We need, as a society, to find ways of choosing – and deciding – in which definition and metrics of societal wellbeing to ground that choice. Government needs to take the initiative. And with respect to the theme of the future of work, an obvious starting point is the creation of good jobs. So: what constitutes a good job?[20]

2. *Good jobs*

Good jobs are ones that promote worker wellbeing while remaining productive and beneficial to the employer. This may not be easy to achieve, because in practice it is much easier to create jobs that are beneficial to the employer, but which bring unhappiness and frustrations to workers. It is inevitable that subjective happiness measures of people at work cannot be as high as similar measures taken during leisure hours, otherwise people would not need money to work. But for most people, when given a long list of activities to rank, being at work scores very low and is sometimes preferable only to being sick in bed. There is obviously room for improvement in the provision of good jobs. We spend a large part of our lifetime at work, and so if government can incentivise companies to create good jobs then the improvement in social welfare will be large.[21]

Research from diverse organisations, including some by the Institute for the Future of Work, identify several features of good jobs. The most important of these is the engagement of workers by management in the day-to-day operations of the company, giving them more autonomy and allowing them to take initiative in the performance of their duties. For this to succeed workers need to be treated as stakeholders by their employers, engage in a frequent exchange of ideas with both line managers and subordinates, and take the initiative in restructuring their jobs and learning new roles. This is understood by employers, but it is difficult to put into practice, given the history of clearly defined tasks that has characterised, and continues to characterise, most jobs in the pre-digital era.[22] It is, however, interesting that the ability to communicate well with line managers and subordinates is considered one of the key skills of the future, as previously mentioned.

Another important feature of good jobs that is frequently mentioned in surveys is time flexibility.[23] An employer that is more open to work interruptions because of family or other personal needs is always preferred to one who is not. The ability to have some choice over the way that the working week is organised is also a sought-after feature. An attraction of this and other related features that enable a more targeted work–life balance is that it benefits demographic groups that currently have lower participation in the labour market, such as women, people with disabilities, and minorities.

Other features of good jobs that improve wellbeing in the workplace are a fair pay structure, diversity of employment, and good public health. Though these features are still not common in British labour markets, they are achievable. For example, human resources departments can be given more incentives to hire a diverse labour force, to enable work from home with the technologies developed during the COVID-19 lockdowns, and to provide an office of Occupational Health at work.

The question of how to improve the autonomy of the workforce and the relations between line managers and subordinates is one that needs to be studied more carefully by both employers and government. Information about best practice is useful. Progress needs collaborative solutions, rather than each company developing its own approach. But it is not certain that progress can be made by relying only on company initiatives. More autonomy at work and good quality jobs contribute to worker wellbeing, better health outcomes, and better mental health. Governments need to take a more active role to promote them. One approach would be to include good work as a company purpose and devise legally enforced standards of company performance towards job quality, along the lines of the ones that protect the shareholders of a company.[24]

3. *Health and care*

The education and health sectors, which are largely in the hands of governments, will become more important job destinations than at present. Although they are often treated together, their needs are diverse. Health is the easier one to monitor, although in practice it is the more difficult one to provide for because of its increasing financing needs. AI has enormous potential in the health sector, mainly in diagnostics, for example, matching patients to donors and suggesting treatments. For this to succeed, government needs to devote greater resources to both R&D and organisational adjustments to increase efficiency. It also needs to decide whether R&D will be focused on elite university hospitals or more dispersed throughout the country. R&D designed for pure research might be more fruitful if it is directed at the main research hospitals, but it is important that the whole country benefits from their discoveries. Applying those new discoveries and technologies across the country would require extensive new capital investment, as well as human capital trained in how to use the new AI-driven equipment.

Care has different needs. As pointed out, the challenge for care will be how to meet the increased demand from an ageing population and a wealthier and better-educated society that will expect more and better-quality service. Training for these skills will not be difficult – the difficulty is how to attract enough highly motivated individuals. Ultimately, the main constraint in state-provided health is the macro one of resources, because of the need to increase the resources devoted to health and care as a fraction of GDP just to maintain service quality as the demands on the system increase.

4. *Education*

Education will need to prepare workers for entry into occupations that will involve changing roles. Given the need to learn new skills that this entails, a broad education that emphasises language, communication skills, and science subjects would be better than one that specialises in a small number of related subjects from age 16, as it happens in the UK today. An apprentice system that combines regulated work at a company with formal tuition could also provide a better foundation for the skills that some workers will need to develop in the future. Education up to age 18 needs to prepare students with a more varied knowledge base, which they will then develop at a university, in an apprenticeship, or as full-time workers at a company that offers lifelong learning opportunities. In Britain, the present A-level system needs fundamental reform to reduce the specialisation inherent within it, and to increase both the language and technical training that should be mandatory up to and including sixth form.

5. *Worker transitions*

Given the changing nature of employment, and the increasing complexity of jobs, government has another important role to play, as facilitator of worker transitions. Government needs to provide good social support to workers between jobs, combined with subsidies for approved training that is akin to an apprenticeship system. With increasing specialisation at work, the quality of the match between worker and job become more important than ever. That is the reason why the best kind of practical training is provided at the company level, and not in educational institutions. This role of government is easier to visualise because it is one that has been operating in Sweden and other countries already for several years. The key to the success of these programmes is trust that the government will provide good support accompanied by a strong incentive structure for the worker to learn new skills and find suitable jobs.

But whereas government's role has mainly to do with education before labour force entry, or with the unemployed who are between jobs, the role of companies in the transition is lifelong. As new technology arrives and disrupts production, workers need to adapt their roles within their organisations. To make a success of this they need incentives. Worker talents are diverse, and workers know best how to exploit their special skills. The challenge for companies is how to find management practices that will incentivise their workers to assume the task of evaluating their roles in the company, looking for ways to improve it, and take control of their own lifelong training.

6. *The gig economy*

Modern technologies based on the internet are making it possible to move many transactions online. While the internet has helped many people work flexible hours and operate with more autonomy than in a factory or office environment, it has also created many 'gig' jobs with zero-hour contracts, and no well-defined location in which an employer can offer the facilities and perks that office or factory workers are used to receiving. Typical examples of gig jobs are warehouse jobs, delivery jobs, or drivers that are booked online through a platform. Should government allow such jobs to grow unregulated, or should it step in and offer protection to workers?

Some countries follow a hands-off policy, for example, in the US, but others have tried to regulate by requiring the platform owners to act as employers.[25] There are obvious advantages to the flexibility that gig jobs offer, but on the whole they are dead-end jobs with no prospect of promotion, no sick leave, no pensions, and no paid annual leave. In other words, they are more like casual work, akin to the type that workers used to find in the early years of industrialisation by turning up at the factory gates or the port, and asking if there was work for the day.

Gig work is one of the consequences of the structural transformation that new digital technologies are bringing to the workplace, along with increased inequality and role adjustment. Government could reduce the inequalities between gig work and regular office work, for example, by requiring that the companies regularly using gig workers treat them as regular employees. This appears to be the best solution when it is possible to identify an employer, as, for example, with Uber drivers. Another would be for government to take on the role of the employer in some key services – for example, in the provision of social benefits, such as sick pay and paid annual leave. But this should be seen as a last resort.

V. Conclusions

This chapter has argued that new technologies may demand worker transitions, but do not threaten the end of work. The challenge we face is how to achieve these transitions, which will require workers to learn new skills and adapt to new types of work.

Both companies and government have a role to play. In the case of the latter, this will range from the provision of digital infrastructure that supports the development of new technologies, to strong social support for the workers undergoing job transitions, as well as training support and preparation of the workforce for the jobs of the future through a reformed education system.

The new job tasks that will be created in the digital economy of the future will be of two kinds. On the one hand, technical jobs will require a strong scientific base, as well as data analytics and IT skills. But only a small fraction of workers will need to learn these skills at an advanced level, because new technologies, especially AI, will advance sufficiently to deal with the needs of technical jobs. A basic knowledge of these technologies will be required practically everywhere in the labour market, alongside a good knowledge of English and maths. A century ago, the basic skill requirements were literacy for everyone – the role of literacy then is now being taken over by basic IT knowledge.

Alongside these basic skills, in the majority of jobs the skills required will be closer to the traditional person-to-person skills that are always in demand in a service economy. Good communication, good customer relationships, ability to think critically and make decisions, and generally skills that might be characterised as 'empathy'.

With workers equipped with these skills it becomes easier for companies to offer 'good jobs'. If the jobs are to be good for the workers' wellbeing, managers need to pay more attention to good communication with their workers, so communication skills from the workers will help. Other characteristics of good jobs are more autonomy, more managerial ability within their company roles, and more time flexibility, features which again are better achieved when the workers have the ability to think critically and make decisions. As society advances, the demand for good work will increase and government plays an important role in ensuring that the features for good work are adhered to.

Acknowledgements

I have benefited from funding from the Nuffield Foundation to the Institute for the Future of Work for the Pissarides Review of the Future of Work and Wellbeing, and from the comments and suggestions of the editors, my two discussants, Kirsten Senhbruch and Alan Manning and from others engaged on the Review at the Institute for the Future of Work.

Notes

1 See, for example, AI Index Steering Committee (2022).

2 See Autor and Dorn (2013), Frey and Osborne (2017), Nedelkoska and Quintini (2018) and the McKinsey Global Institute (2017) for estimates in the range 10–20%. Josten and Lordan (2019) use different methodologies and arrive at a much higher figure, 35%, of jobs automated in the next 10 years.

3 López and De Prato (2022).

4 Schumpeter (1942).

5 AI Index Steering Committee (2022).

6 China is on the way to matching them, as it currently installs more robots than the rest of the world put together. See International Federation of Robotics (2022).

7 Graetz and Michaels (2018).

8 Kapetaniou and Pissarides (2025).

9 Capgemini (2018).

10 McKinsey Global Institute (2018).

11 See various publications under the general heading *AI Watch*. A general discussion covering most issues is in the *AI Watch Index 2021*. See López and De Prato (2022).

12 Keynes (1931); Leontief (1983).

13 Writings on the advantages of the four-day week and the results of some pilot trials are proliferating. See Gomes (2021).

14 See for example Freeman and Schettkat (2005) and Ngai and Pissarides (2008).

15 Baumol (1967).

16 See OECD (2021) and López and De Prato (2022).

17 Manpower Group (2025).

18 Dickerson et al. (2023).

19 IFOW (2025).

20 Similar views are expressed by Dani Rodrik in Rodrik (2022). On choosing the direction of technology a good extensive discussion can

be found in the writings of Acemoglu, Johnson, and Robinson, e.g., Acemoglu and Johnson (2023). For a technical review of the literature, see Hémous and Olsen (2021).

[21] See Layard and De Neve (2023), chapter 12. There are also various surveys of workers online, e.g., see the American Psychological Association surveys, American Psychological Association (2022). For other discussions of good work with emphasis on measurement issues and impact on productivity see De Neve and Ward (2023), IFOW (2021), and RSA (2020).

[22] RSA (2020).

[23] American Psychological Association surveys, American Psychological Association (2022).

[24] Mayer (2018).

[25] The first country to do this explicitly was Spain, after starting a long legal process in 2014. See European Transport Safety Council (2018).

References

AI Index Steering Committee (2022) 'The AI Index 2022 Annual Report', Stanford Institute for Human-Centered AI, Stanford University.

Acemoglu, D. and Johnson, S. (2023) *Power and Progress: Our Thousand Year Struggle over Technology and Prosperity*. London: Basic Books.

American Psychological Association (2022) 'Workers Appreciate and Seek Mental Health Support in the Workplace', APA's 2022 Work and Well-being Survey results. https://www.apa.org/pubs/reports/work-well-being/2022-mental-health-support

Autor, D. H. and Dorn, D. (2013) 'The Growth of Low-Skill Service Jobs and the Polarization of the U.S. Labor Market', *American Economic Review*, 103(5): 1533–1597. https://doi.org/10.1257/aer.103.5.1553

Baumol, W. J. (1967) 'Macroeconomics of Unbalanced Growth: The Anatomy of Urban Crisis', *American Economic Review*, 57: 415–426.

Capgemini (2018) *World Fintech Report 2018*, Paris. https://www.capgemini.com/fr-fr/wp-content/uploads/sites/6/2022/04/world-fintech-report-wftr-20181-2.pdf

De Neve, J. and Ward, G. (2023) 'Measuring Workplace Wellbeing', University of Oxford Wellbeing Research Centre Working Paper 2303.

Dickerson, A., Rossi, G., Bocock, L., Hillary, J. and Simcock, D. (2023) 'An Analysis of the Demand for Skills in the Labour Market in 2035', Working Paper 3. Slough: NFER.

European Transport Safety Council (2018) 'Uber Must Be Regulated as a Transport Service Says Top EU Court' [3 Jan]. https://etsc.eu/uber-must-be-regulated-as-a-transport-service-says-top-eu-court/

Freeman, R. and Schettkat, R. (2005) 'Marketization of Household Production and the EU-US gap in Work', *Economic Policy*: 20, 6–50. https://doi.org/10.1111/j.1468-0327.2005.00132.x

Frey, C. B. and Osborne, M. A. (2017) 'The Future of Employment: How Susceptible Are Jobs to Computerisation?' *Technological Forecasting and Social Change*, 114: 254–280. https://doi.org/10.1016/j.techfore.2016.08.019

Gomes, P. (2021) *Friday Is the New Saturday*, London: Flint.

Graetz, G. and Michaels, G. (2018) 'Robots at Work', *The Review of Economics and Statistics*, 100: 753–768. https://doi.org/10.1162/rest_a_00754

Hémous, D. and Olsen, M. (2021) 'Directed Technical Change in Labor and Environmental Economics', *Annual Review of Economics*, 13: 571–97. https://doi.org/10.1146/annurev-economics-092120-044327

Institute for the Future of Work (IFOW) (2021) *The Good Work Monitor*, London: IFOW publications. https://www.ifow.org/resources/the-good-work-monitor

Institute for the Future of Work (IFOW) (2025) *The Pissarides Review into the Future of Work and Wellbeing*. https://pissaridesreview.ifow.org/

International Federation of Robotics (2022) *World Robotics 2022*, Frankfurt Main, Germany. https://ifr.org/downloads/press2018/2022_WR_extended_version.pdf

Josten, C. and Lordan, G. (2020) 'Robots at Work: Automatable and Non Automatable Jobs', in Zimmermann, K. F. (ed), *Handbook of Labor, Human Resources and Population Economics*, Cham: Springer. https://doi.org/10.2139/ssrn.3435395

Kapetaniou, C. and Pissarides, C. A. (2025) 'Productive Robots and Industrial Employment: The Role of National Innovation Systems', *International Economic Review*, 66(1): 25–52. https://doi.org/10.1111/iere.12738

Keynes, J. M. (1931) 'Economic Possibilities for our Grandchildren', in *Essays in Persuasion*, London: Macmillan and Co.

Layard, R. and De Neve, J. (2023) *Wellbeing: Science and Policy*, Cambridge: University Press. https://doi.org/10.1017/9781009298957

Leontief, W. (1983) 'Machines vs. Workers'. Interview with New York Times [8 Feb]. https://www.nytimes.com/1983/02/08/arts/machines-vs-workers.html

López, C. M. and De Prato, G. (eds) (2022) *AI Watch Index 2021*, EUR 31039 EN, Publications Office of the European Union, Luxembourg.

Manpower Group (2025) *The Talent Shortage*. https://go.manpowergroup.com/talent-shortage

Mayer, C. (2018) *Prosperity: Better Business Makes the Greater Good*, Oxford: Oxford University Press.

McKinsey Global Institute (2017) *Jobs Lost Jobs Gained: Worker Transitions in a Time of Automation*, San Francisco, CA: McKinsey and Company.

McKinsey Global Institute (2018) *Notes from the AI Frontier: Modeling the Impact of AI on the World Economy*, San Francisco, CA: McKinsey Global Institute, September.

Nedelkoska, L. and Quintini, G. (2018) 'Automation, Skills Use and Training', OECD Social, Employment and Migration Working Papers, no. 202, Paris: OECD Publishing.

Ngai, L. R. and Pissarides, C. A. (2008) 'Trends in Hours and Economic Growth', *Review of Economic Dynamics*, 11: 239–256. https://doi.org/10.1016/j.red.2007.07.002

OECD (2021) *Health at a Glance 2021*. Paris: OECD. https://doi.org/10.1787/ae3016b9-en

Rodrik, D. (2022) *An Industrial Policy for Good Jobs*. Washington, DC: The Hamilton Project, Brookings.

RSA (2020) 'Can Good Work Solve the Productivity Puzzle?' London: Royal Society of the Arts. https://carnegieuk.org/publication/can-good-work-solve-the-productivity-puzzle/

Schumpeter, J. (1942) *Capitalism, Socialism and Democracy*, New York: Harper and Brothers.

Response to Christopher Pissarides by Kirsten Sehnbruch

I. A new social contract for labour markets?

The former Washington Consensus is often criticised – among other things – for its neglect of the social and institutional underpinnings that are indispensable for achieving both sustained economic growth and both fair and cohesive societies (as the brief for this project highlighted). Political developments over recent decades in the form of a resurgence of both populism and extremism clearly show that populism has flourished in the geographical areas or subgroups of the population that were left behind by de-industrialisation, deregulation, and globalisation.[1] To prevent an exacerbation of these processes, future political responses should be proactive in responding to the inevitable fallout in the labour market that future technologies will generate for both individual workers and their communities.

Pissarides emphasises that governments will inevitably have a bigger role to play in the future labour market and discusses the many important ways in which they can address the polarisation created by these processes and their resulting socio-economic inequalities. In these brief comments, I will take three of his arguments further by asking, first whether our existing social contracts are prepared for the impact of future technologies or whether the latter will undermine their sustainability. Second, I will argue that the premise of our existing social contract is paradoxically at odds with the regulation that underpins it. Third, I will ask whether our existing institutions are equipped for dealing with the challenges ahead. In making these three points I will refer to the example of labour markets in developing economies, which hold many lessons for advanced economies in terms of what segmented labour markets with a few 'good' jobs and many not so good ones look like.

II. Are social contracts based on 'good jobs' sustainable?

Pissarides argues that the impact of future technologies on labour markets depends significantly on whether they will impact good and/or bad jobs, as well as on whether governments can help workers transition into better jobs. In this context, a more precise definition of what constitutes a 'good' – or its counterpart – a 'bad job' would be useful. Defining a good job as one that promotes worker wellbeing, while remaining productive and beneficial to the employer, which treats workers as stakeholders, and includes a fair pay structure chimes with the growing body of literature on how job quality could be defined,[2] but it does not constitute a precise definition.

Conversely, measures of 'bad jobs', are also now being discussed and produced.[3] These studies emphasise that the conditions of poor-quality employment are likely to *exacerbate* each other: workers with low wages, for example, often also have unstable jobs with other negative employment conditions, such as unpredictable hours or income flows. Examples of such employment conditions are frequently found in those sectors, which are unlikely to be automated (e.g., tourism, healthcare, the care economy, as well as the gig economy). Such jobs often trap workers in situations where they rotate between multiple and sometimes overlapping bad jobs with little prospect of upskilling or developing their capabilities.[4] In fact, many of these jobs require additional social or fiscal support from governments to be sustained in the economy. For example, the increased proportion of employed people receiving Universal Credit in the UK, the increased expenditure required on the healthcare of workers in poor-quality employment, or the pension subsidies paid to workers unable to save sufficient resources during their working lives illustrate this point.[5]

If social contracts are built on employment relationships that are formal, stable, linked to identifiable employers, contribute to social security systems, and are productive (i.e., with growing wages), it is important to measure how many jobs do not do so. A precise measure of poor-quality employment is therefore essential.[6]

In an ideal world, future technologies would eliminate such jobs and replace them with good ones that can sustain our social contract. However, based on present evidence, this is not the case: the best example of this trend is the gig economy, which in the UK is estimated to have doubled in only five years.[7] Platform-based jobs (even when they are carried out in addition to other employment) are largely unregulated, draw more workers into self-employment (which contributes less to social protection systems), have unpredictable flows of income, are associated with higher accident risks, and are unlikely to provide basic work–life balance, which is essential to the mental and physical health of workers.[8] In addition, gig workers are unlikely to be viewed as stakeholders by employers, who so far have attempted to prevent their organisation building (unionisation) that would lead to investment in their skills or the kind of 'exchange of ideas' that Pissarides describes.

As Pissarides suggests, the role of the social security systems and their ability to support workers in their transitions between jobs is therefore essential, a concept that is often referred to as 'flexicurity'. This concept has been extremely influential in shaping labour markets in both advanced and emerging economies in recent years, and is viewed positively in many discussions of the social contract.[9] However, analysts often fail to recognise the potential paradox inherent to this model: flexible working arrangements that have flourished in deregulated, technology-driven labour markets require *more* social and fiscal support from governments, while simultaneously contributing *less* (and less consistently) to the social contract. This prompts the question of whether such a social contract is sustainable in the light of labour market frictions generated by technological progress.

One solution put forward by analysts studying this phenomenon is to decouple the social contract from employment, thus building a welfare state based on taxes and other fiscal revenue rather than social security contributions.[10] However, a transition to such a system in an advanced economy is unlikely to be feasible, neither *politically* nor *fiscally*. A significant amount of debate and effort will therefore have to go into strengthening the existing social contract so that it is prepared for dealing with the impact of future technologies.

The following two sections discuss how regulatory and institutional factors can contribute to this process.

III. Regulating for a sustainable social contract

The existing literature provides us with ample evidence that regulation has a significant impact on the types of jobs that are being created that can have both negative or positive consequences for the sustainability of the social contract in both advanced and emerging economies. The widespread deregulation of labour markets in Southern Europe, for example, led to segmented labour markets with high proportions of workers in short-term contracts, who became 'stuck' in a continuous cycle of precarious employment.[11] In Egypt, deregulation of the labour market in 2003 led to a collapse of job quality in the formal sector despite high economic growth rates.[12] Such processes have equally negative implications for both productivity and the sustainability of the social contract.

On the positive side, significant increases of the minimum wage mandated by legislation in Chile, Brazil, and Colombia have decreased the proportion of the working poor.[13] In the UK, pension reform has led to a significant and rapid expansion of the numbers of workers contributing to pension systems.[14]

In a world in which unemployment is no longer the chief concern as even emerging economies battle with skilled labour supply shortages, deregulation and labour market flexibility should no longer be the defining mantra of policymakers. Instead, it is important to recognise that regulation matters and constitutes the foundation of our social contract, as well as of the kind of employment conditions, which attract workers into the labour market. In addition, without regulation, the benefits of economic growth would be spread even more unevenly, especially in a world of stark inequalities in which the proportion of labour income to GDP appears to be in perpetual decline.[15]

In advanced economies, therefore, the key challenge lies in finding a balance between the needs of workers and those of employers, while sustaining the social contract. One possibility would be to permit flexibility in the labour market, but charge for its negative externalities (as do carbon taxes).[16]

For example, it should never be cheaper to hire a worker on a temporary, outsourced, or zero-hours contract than on a permanent one, as the former is associated with more negative externalities that governments ultimately have to support. A progressive way of approaching this issue would be to factor such costs into the national insurance contributions paid on precarious contracts, which would level the playing field between different types of employment relationships.

In developing countries, the defining issue of improving the functioning of the social contract is to incorporate informal workers into the labour market. Governments can use advanced technology in this process to formalise the informal and gig economy workforce by encouraging the use of automated payment systems, such as M-PESA or PIX. Once these systems have been established, this would also allow governments to track transactions and charge VAT, while also encouraging informal workers to contribute to social security systems, for example, by matching contributions with public funds. In the long run, matching contributions would be cheaper than forgoing both taxes and contributions indefinitely as the informal workforce continues to avoid formalisation.

Levelling the regulatory playing field also means that judicial procedures should not shape fundamental employment rights. In the UK, for example, this has led to the absurd situation that Uber drivers are classified as 'workers', while drivers for other platforms (e.g., Bolt or Ola), Uber Eats, or Deliveroo are *not* classified as such, with all the absence of employment rights that this entails. From the socio-economic perspective of development, regulation relying on unpredictable case law outcomes is unproductive. From the practical policy perspective of sustaining a social contract, they can undermine its very foundation. And from a perspective of social justice, it could be described as unethical.[17]

Regulation also plays a significant role when it comes to the distribution of the productivity gains that future technologies could potentially unleash. Profit-driven companies in the private sector may exacerbate inequalities if these gains accrue only to the most qualified workers. This raises the question of how less qualified workers unlikely to benefit from productivity enhancing technologies should be compensated. In this context, it is unlikely that existing minimum wage regulation will sufficiently contain potential inequalities. Moving towards a stakeholder process within companies, as Pissarides suggests, can point to a way forward here. In addition, countries where unions not only represent workers but also participate in the governing boards of firms can serve as an example. In countries where such mechanisms do not exist, this would also require some degree of institutionalisation.

IV. Institution building for sustaining a social contract

One of the key solutions to frictions generated in the labour market by future technologies is the improvement of active labour market policies that help workers transition into new sectors or adapt to changing roles within their companies, as Pissarides emphasises. The risk here is that those sectors in which technological change generates the most friction will again be left behind – as with processes of de-industrialisation – unless such policies are proactive rather than reactive. This is where research analysing and predicting the use and impact of technology, such as The Pissarides Review, can be very helpful.[18]

Being proactive requires strengthening the institutional underpinnings of the social contract. Chiefly, this means *integrating* employment legislation and regulation with social and labour policy, as well as with productive development policies, such as those proposed by Rodrik in this volume. Typically, however, such policy areas are housed in different government departments or ministries, which often operate as isolated policy silos.

Ironically, it is the progress made in technology and machine learning that can help with this; it allows governments to link administrative data that can then be used to estimate and predict frictions in the labour market, including at a very granular local level or across subgroups of the population, which cannot be done with the much smaller sample sizes of surveys. The best-known examples that have made progress in this direction are Scandinavian countries, but even emerging economies, such as Chile, are now fast moving towards such a system.

Second, linked administrative databases facilitate interdepartmental collaboration between government services and can enable governments to coordinate policies in something approaching 'real time' to respond to the accelerated pace of change that technological advances bring with them. This is particularly necessary in labour markets where workers increasingly juggle multiple jobs, unpredictable hours, and/or income flows. For example, at present, a worker on a zero-hour contract does not receive support funding on time when there is a shortfall of work offered.

Third, lessons from using technology in some public services could also be applied in the areas of labour policy. In the UK, for example, the COVID-19 crisis prompted the government to automate many services provided by the NHS (e.g., reminders for health checks, blood tests, or vaccinations) and established online communication with healthcare providers as a matter of routine. The principle of automated prompts reminding or requiring workers to upgrade their skills over the life cycle is already applied in many sectors where workers need to update their qualifications or licences on a regular basis. This mechanism could be extended to the labour force more broadly, especially to those sectors, professions, or companies that are likely to be affected by technological shifts. This would be a proactive policy that would help workers acquire necessary skills *before* they are affected by technological shifts in their roles or jobs.

Finally, although many experts have discussed the potential advantages and disadvantages of basic income floors or universal basic income as policy tools in responding to labour market frictions, many agree that these would be too costly to implement on a large scale.[19] Instead, the role of work sharing has been researched less in this context. Most studies of shortened working hours relate to company response mechanisms in situations of economic crisis.[20] Such mechanisms have been widely applied in Germany since 1957 (*Kurzarbeit*). However, recent studies have also shown that these could constitute more long-term solutions as the non-monetary and wellbeing-related benefits associated with employment already become manifest when workers are employed for relatively few hours per week.[21]

Similarly, recent experiments with the four-day working week, show that this not only increased the wellbeing of workers, but also increased the sales and profits of participating companies as the experiment reduced job rotation (and thus hiring and training costs) and absenteeism, as well as improving productivity overall.[22]

Key to these processes and policy options are the institutions that facilitate social dialogue, both within companies and between the social actors, who must engage with the broader agenda of sustaining the social contract rather than advocating for only their own interests. This includes governmental departments, parliamentary groups, and the expert commissions that inform them.

V. Conclusions

To conclude, recent research on the future of work has helped us understand better the impact of technology. However, further research on the issues raised by Pissarides and in the comments above is undoubtedly necessary because technological progress is not the only driver of labour market change. Demographic changes, such as population (and therefore workforce) ageing, as well as migration flows, are likely to interact with technological trends. Early predictions of the loss of a significant quantity of jobs[23] in advanced economies may not play out as expected if technology helps deal with potential labour supply shortages. At the same time, migration pressures may continue to feed labour into poor-quality jobs, potentially exacerbating inequalities.

In many developing and emerging economies, similar demographic shifts are also changing employment patterns. De-industrialisation, deregulation, and new technologies have frequently increased the proportion of poor-quality employment in the formal sector, while informal sectors have not decreased, in part due to significantly increased intraregional migration patterns. This combination of factors is devastating for emerging social protection systems, not least because it depletes fiscal resources.

Notes

[1] Baccini and Weymouth (2021); Rodrik and Stantcheva (2021); O'Reilly et al. (2016).

[2] Green (2021); Hovhannisyan et al. (2022).

[3] Florisson (2022); Sehnbruch et al. (2020).

[4] See Prieto et al. (2022) for a methodology that measures this.

[5] Joseph Rowntree Foundation (2023).

[6] See Sehnbruch et al. (2020) and Florrison (2022) for methodologies that measures this.

[7] Although the gig economy has attracted much academic attention in recent years (e.g., Woodcock and Graham, 2020), other forms of precarious employment such as zero-hour contracts (in the UK) or mini jobs (in Germany) have equally flourished, while contributing less to social security systems.

[8] Woodcock and Graham (2020).

[9] Shafik (2021).

[10] See Barr's chapter (11) and Levy's response in this volume.

[11] Bendapudi et al. (2003); Bellani and Bosio (2019).

[12] Sehnbruch et al. (2021).

[13] Apablaza et al. (2024).

[14] Cribb and Emmerson (2020).

[15] ILO et al. (2015).

[16] World Bank (2019).

[17] Robeyns (2017).

[18] Pissarides (2022).

[19] Shafik (2021).

[20] Casey and Mayhew (2022).

[21] Wang et al. (2022b).

[22] Wang et al. (2022a; 2022b).

[23] Frey and Osborne (2017).

References

Apablaza, M., Villatoro, P., González, P. A. and Sehnbruch, K., Mancero, X. (2024) 'Índice de mala calidad del empleo: una exploración de la última década en América Latina', *Estudios Estadisticos* 107. Economic Commission for Latin America and the Caribbean, Santiago de Chile.

Baccini, L. and Weymouth, S. (2021) 'Gone For Good: Deindustrialization, White Voter Backlash, and US Presidential Voting', *American Political Science Review*, 115(2), 550–567. https://doi.org/10.1017/S0003055421000022

Bellani, D. and Bosio, G. (2019) 'Knockin' on Heaven's Door? Reframing the Debate on Temporary Employment and Wages: Evidence from Europe', *Socio-Economic Review*, 19(3): 869–907. https://doi.org/10.1093/ser/mwz042

Bendapudi, V., Magnum, S. L., Tansky, J. W. and Fisher, M. M. (2003) 'Nonstandard Employment Arrangements: A Proposed Typology and Policy Planning Framework', *Human Resource Planning*, 26: 24–33.

Casey, B. H. and Mayhew, K. (2022) '*Kurzarbeit*/Short Time Working: Experiences and Lessons from the Covid-induced Downturn', *National Institute Economic Review*, 263: 47–60. https://doi.org/10.1017/nie.2021.46

Cribb, J. and Emmerson, C. (2020) 'What Happens to Workplace Pension Saving When Employers Are Obliged to Enrol Employees Automatically?', *International Tax and Public Finance*, 27: 664–693. https://doi.org/10.1007/s10797-019-09565-6

Florisson, R. (2022) 'The UK Insecure Work Index', https://www.lancaster.ac.uk/work-foundation/publications/the-uk-insecure-work-index

Frey, C. B. and Osborne, M. A. (2017) 'The Future of Employment: How Susceptible Are Jobs to Computerisation?', *Technological Forecasting and Social Change*, 114: 254–280. https://doi.org/10.1016/j.techfore.2016.08.019

Green, F. (2021) 'Decent Work and the Quality of Work and Employment', in Zimmermann, K. F. (ed.), *Handbook of Labor, Human Resources and Population Economics*. Cham: Springer, pp. 1–39. https://doi.org/10.1007/978-3-319-57365-6_218-1

Hovhannisyan, S., Montalva-Talledo, V., Remick, T., Rodríguez-Castelán, C. and Stamm, K. (2022) 'Global Job Quality: Evidence from Wage Employment across Developing Countries', The World Bank. https://documents1.worldbank.org/curated/en/099815508012237346/pdf/IDU09ac855b6033b20401e0b7d20c77cc771201c.pdf

International Labour Organization (ILO), International Monetary Fund (IMF), Organisation for Economic Co-operation and Development (OECD) World Bank Group (2015) 'Income Inequality and Labour Income Share in G20 Countries: Trends, Impacts and Causes', Report for G20 Labour and Employment Ministers Meeting and Joint Meeting with the G20 Finance Ministers, Ankara, Turkey [3–4 September]. https://www.ilo.org/publications/income-inequality-and-labour-income-share-g20-countries-trends-impacts-and

Joseph Rowntree Foundation (2023) 'UK Poverty 2023: The Essential Guide to Understanding Poverty in the UK', Joseph Rowntree Foundation. https://www.jrf.org.uk/uk-poverty-2023-the-essential-guide-to-understanding-poverty-in-the-uk

O'Reilly, J., Froud, J., Johal, S., Williams, K., Warhurst, C., Morgan, G., Grey, C., Wood, G., Wright, M., Boyer, R., Frerichs, S., Sankari, S., Rona-Tas, A. and Le Galès, P. (2016) 'Brexit: Understanding the Socio-Economic Origins and Consequences', *Socio-Economic Review*, 14: 807–854. https://doi.org/10.1093/ser/mww043

Pissarides, C. (2022) 'Introducing the Pissarides Review into the Future of Work and Wellbeing', Institute for the Future of Work. https://pissaridesreview.ifow.org/

Prieto, J., Sehnbruch, K. and Vidal, D. (2022) 'A Dynamic Counting Approach to Measure Multidimensional Deprivations in Jobs', *Applied Economics Letters*, 31(10), 907–912. https://doi.org/10.1080/13504851.2022.2156460

Robeyns, I. (2017) *Wellbeing, Freedom and Social Justice: The Capability Approach Re-Examined,* London: Open Book Publishers. https://doi.org/10.11647/OBP.0130

Rodrik, D. and Stantcheva, S. (2021) 'Fixing Capitalism's Good Jobs Problem', *Oxford Review of Economic Policy*, 37(4): 824–37. https://doi.org/10.1093/oxrep/grab024

Sehnbruch, K., González, P., Apablaza, M., Méndez, R. and Arriagada, V. (2020) 'The Quality of Employment (QoE) in Nine Latin American Countries: A Multidimensional Perspective', *World Development*, 127, 104738. https://doi.org/10.1016/j.worlddev.2019.104738

Sehnbruch, K., Méndez, R. and Atallah, S. (2021) 'Multidimensional Quality of Employment (QoE) Index in Egypt', *Alternative Policy Solutions*, Working Paper, American University of Cairo.

Shafik, M. (2021) *What We Owe Each Other: A New Social Contract*, London: The Bodley Head. https://doi.org/10.1515/9780691220277

Wang, S., Kamerāde, D., Bessa, I., Burchell, B., Gifford, J., Green, M. and Rubery, J. (2022a) 'The Impact of Reduced Working Hours and Furlough Policies on Workers' Mental Health at the Onset of COVID-19 Pandemic: A Longitudinal Study', *Journal of Social Policy*, 53(3): 1–25. https://doi.org/10.1017/S0047279422000599

Wang, S., Kamerāde, D., Burchell, B., Coutts, A. and Balderson, S. U. (2022b) 'What Matters More for Employees' Mental Health: Job Quality or Job Quantity?', *Cambridge Journal of Economics*, 46: 251–274. https://doi.org/10.1093/cje/beab054

Woodcock, J. and Graham, M. (2020) *The Gig Economy: A Critical Introduction*, Cambridge: Polity Press.

World Bank Group (2019) *State and Trends of Carbon Pricing 2019*. Washington, DC: World Bank. https://documents1.worldbank.org/curated/en/191801559846379845/pdf/State-and-Trends-of-Carbon-Pricing-2019.pdf

9. Labour markets and gender inequality

Oriana Bandiera and Barbara Petrongolo

Wide disparities persist in the wages and economic power of men and women in nearly all countries. Women still make different educational decisions to men, are under-represented in high-paying jobs, and suffer the majority of the financial penalty related to having children. Notably, the disproportionate role women play in unpaid work in the home or family businesses more than makes up for the gap in paid work in the labour market, usually leading to less leisure time and possibly lower social prestige. This chapter argues that both justice and efficiency considerations support the case for tackling gender inequalities in the labour market. The chapter reviews evidence on existing disparities, on the mechanisms underpinning them – including related to novel explanations based on group identity and social norms – and on the policies promising to close these persistent gaps.

I. Introduction

Over the course of the last century there has been enormous progress in equalising rights between men and women. Today, women have the same rights to property, credit, and schooling in every country but a few, mostly in North Africa and the Arabian Peninsula. Most countries have also adopted laws against discrimination at work and domestic violence. Nearly every country has outlawed provisions that gave husbands control over household finances and that required women to obey their husbands. But equal rights have not closed gaps in labour market opportunities and outcomes. There is a wide disparity in the wages and economic power of men and women in nearly all countries. Women still make different educational decisions to men, are under-represented in high-paying jobs, and suffer the majority of the financial

---

How to cite this book chapter:

Bandiera, Oriana and Petrongolo, Barbara (2025) 'Labour markets and gender inequality', in: Besley, Tim, Bucelli, Irene and Velasco, Andrés (eds) *The London Consensus: Economic Principles for the 21st Century*, London: LSE Press, pp. 281–309 https://doi.org/10.31389/lsepress.tlc.i

penalty related to having children. Notably, the disproportionate role women play in unpaid work in the home or family businesses more than makes up for the gap in paid work in the labour market, usually leading to less leisure time and possibly lower life satisfaction. These differences raise concerns about social justice related to unequal access to labour market opportunities and life satisfaction, as well as concerns about efficiency that are related to the (mis)allocation of talents to jobs. Gender inequality in labour outcomes is too large to be a manifestation of gender differences in traits and essential preferences. This implies that gender disparity creates misallocation, and policies that encourage gender equality can enhance efficiency.

II. The case for gender equity at work

Gender equity at work is achieved when gender has no bearing on individual occupational choices and rewards. It requires men and women to have access to the same opportunities and have the freedom to choose whichever occupation suits their talents and preferences. At the time of writing, no country in the world has achieved gender equity, and most are quite far from it. In this section we argue that this clashes with basic principles of justice, as well as economic efficiency. In all human societies, the allocation of work inside and outside the home is gendered. This can be clearly seen in the next section in Figure 9.1, which plots the gender gaps in the average daily hours that men and women spend on paid and unpaid work for a selection of OECD countries. Gaps are defined as the difference between male and female time spent on each type of work, relative to male time. Data are drawn from nationally representative time-use surveys and show that in all countries women do more unpaid work within the household than men. Differences in unpaid work range from 4.5 times as much in Japan to 20% more in Sweden. The UK is roughly at the median, with women devoting nearly twice the amount of time to unpaid housework than men do. The figure also shows that the allocation of domestic work is (far) more unequal than that of paid work, which implies that men can enjoy more leisure time than women.

Paid and unpaid work do not convey the same economic power and prestige, which is therefore in breach of distributive justice. In fact, work inside the home is not counted as 'employment', while the same activities would be filed under employment if performed outside the home – like educating children, keeping accounts, or cleaning, to name a few. This inconsistent classification of jobs, depending on whether they are performed inside or outside the home, puts women at a disadvantage by default.

The justice motive per se provides sufficient ground to argue for gender equality. In addition, in a world where resources are increasingly scarce, analysing the efficiency implication of gender inequality is also key to assess the cost of policies needed to foster equality. Indeed, economists are increasingly re-thinking equity-efficiency trade-offs and the zero-sum fallacies that are typically implicit in them. An argument frequently made to support the link between gender equality and economic efficiency is that, by favouring women's work outside the home, labour supply increases and, together with it, output per person increases too. This argument is, however, based on the fallacious notion that women who perform work inside the home are in fact not working. Once one takes into account the fact that women perform several tasks that still need to be performed if a woman works outside the home, the above argument may not hold. If somebody else is hired to perform the tasks that the woman was performing before, then measured labour supply increases but the actual labour supply remains constant. Labour supply only increases if women do both the work inside the home as well as the work outside. However, in this case the increase in efficiency comes to the detriment of women's leisure and welfare.

There is, however, a more valid reason why gender equity can increase efficiency. Assuming that innate talent is equally distributed among men and women, eliminating any restrictions that limit the types of jobs women can do can increase efficiency by assigning the right skills to the right tasks. This redistribution of workers to different roles (both within the home and in the workplace) can have an effect on productivity, i.e., income and output per worker. Specifically, the match between skills and job requirements can be improved in three ways: women taking up work in the market sector; men working in the household instead; and household work being outsourced to the market. Unlike a model in which a woman remains at home and provides services that are not monetised, the market for domestic help has the added advantage of pricing household tasks and potentially improving their allocation.

III. The data

1. *Gender, labour, and economic development*

Gender gaps at work depend on the nature of work as well as economic, institutional, and cultural factors. The measure of female work that is most easily comparable across contexts, and most widely used, is participation in the labour force. The relationship between female participation and gross domestic product (GDP) per head is U-shaped: participation is relatively high at low levels of development, then drops at intermediate levels, before rising again at higher levels. This pattern – which may be observed both in the cross-section of countries and in within-country time series[1] – reflects substantial changes in the nature and the composition of female work.

In extremely poor countries, where most individuals are generally engaged in subsistence agriculture or production for home consumption, labour force participation does not have the same meaning as in high-income countries, where most people work for others and receive a wage in exchange for their labour services. The reason why female participation is especially high at low levels of development is that women are heavily engaged in small-scale agriculture, whether for own subsistence or the family farm.

With modernisation of agriculture and industrialisation, the main locus of production and exchange gradually shifts from the household to the market. Most men leave the home to sell their labour in the market, whereas most women remain at home, where the production of home services is not counted as labour.

Figure 9.1: Paid versus unpaid work by gender/Gender gaps in employment rates (%)

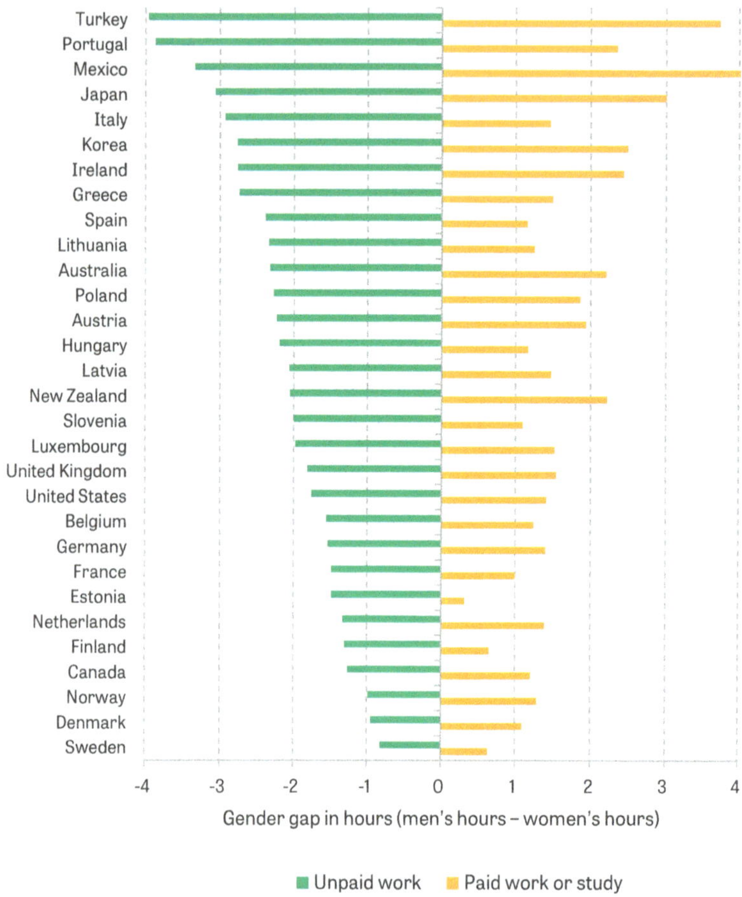

Source: Andrew et al. (2021)[2] Figure 2, reproduced with permission from the authors/IFS.

The process of industrialisation thus creates the first wedge between male and female work. The organisation of labour and capital in firms opens other margins, for example, via differences in the number of hours worked and the hourly wage rate. As development progresses, economies grow more complex and create a wider variety of jobs. Human capital gains and the expansion of white collar jobs attract women into the labour force, due to higher opportunity costs of home making and comparative advantages in white collar occupations. An increasing portion of jobs in the labour market is taken by women, especially in the rising service sector.

2. *Gender gaps in high-income countries*

If we focus on countries that are relatively similar in terms of the organisation of work and production, we can decompose the differences between men and women at work in finer details.

The gender gap in earnings is defined as the difference between the average gross income of men and women, relative to men's earnings. This is a key summary measure of gender differences in labour market outcomes that captures differences in all aspects of working life, including whether and how much men and women work, the types of jobs they do, their experiences and skills, the returns to these, and frictions in wage setting (including discrimination).

Gender gaps in earnings encompass three margins: gaps in participation; gaps in hours, conditional on participating; and gaps in hourly wages. Figure 9.2 shows the overall gap and – where available – its three components: paid employment (in dark blue), hours worked (in red), and hourly wages (in light blue). Gender earnings gaps are large across all OECD countries, from over 20% in Denmark and Sweden, to about 40% in the UK, and over 70% in Korea and Japan.

The first point to note is that, in most countries, all three margins contribute to overall inequality: women are under-represented in the labour force and,

Figure 9.2: The earnings gap and its components

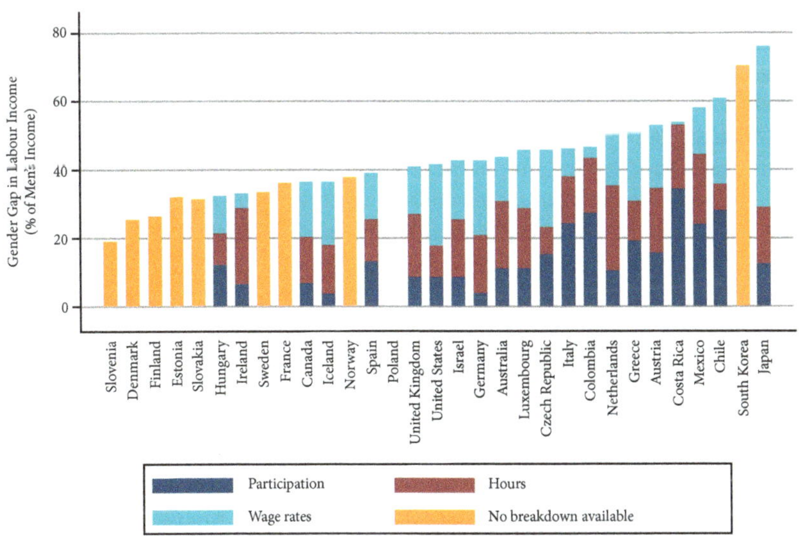

Source: Figure 1 in Andrew et al. (2024)[3], republished under CC BY Licence.

when they participate, they both work fewer hours on average and are paid less per hour. Two further points are noteworthy. First, the gap in hours tends to be larger where the gap in participation is smaller. One possible explanation is that in countries where most women work outside the home, jobs have adjusted to facilitate the combination of home and market work, and part-time work becomes widespread (as it is the case for the Netherlands and, to a lesser extent, the UK). Where fewer women work, most jobs are full time, and gaps in hours, conditional on participation, are smaller (as is the case, for example, in Italy and Greece). Second, the gender gap in participation is also negatively correlated with the wage gap. Olivetti and Petrongolo (2008) highlight that this pattern is consistent with selection on gains, namely in countries where women face high barriers to work outside the home, only those who are exceptionally talented will do so, and they will work similar hours and earn similar wages as men.[4]

IV. The economics of gender inequalities in the labour market

Seminal work on gender inequality in the labour market has emphasised the role of gaps in productivity, reflecting differential investments in human capital. But, by the late 1970s, gender differences in completed schooling or potential work experience already explained a small portion of the overall wage gap, with the bulk of the gap reflecting differences in returns to characteristics typically associated with pay discrimination.[5] Job characteristics like occupation, industry, and part-time status were (and still are) important components of pay gaps, although it was hard to disentangle the roles played by differences in work preferences versus entry barriers in the allocation of men and women to jobs.

Rapid female advances in human capital accumulation, alongside the decline in pay discrimination for equal work, have gradually diverted economists' attention away from first-order factors like human capital differences and discrimination. Indeed, the evidence that remaining earnings gaps in high-income countries were associated with systematic differences in the work done by men and women has naturally steered the research focus towards reasons why men and women tend to specialise in different labour market segments.

Meanwhile, the growing influence of social psychology in economic research has provided economists with novel approaches and data to investigate gender differences in preferences and behavioural nuances, as well as novel explanations based on group identity and social norms.[6] From this, new perspectives on gender have emerged. One strand of work emphasises the role of gender differences in preferences and psychological traits in setting limits to women's labour market involvement. Another strand gives prominence to the role of gender identity and norms in defining appropriate roles for men and women in the household and the labour market.

Work on gender differences in psychological traits has investigated the role of risk aversion, self-confidence, competitiveness, willingness to ask, as well as other-regarding preferences in driving male and female choices of education and career tracks.[7] Recent analyses however show that differences in these essential traits tend to be context-dependent and they typically account for a modest proportion of the gender gap in labour market outcomes.[8] Importantly, there remains an open question on the extent to which differences in traits and preferences are driven by innate gender differences or reflect socially constructed norms.

Most of the recent advances on gender inequalities research are coalescing around the study of differential barriers to labour market success, focusing in particular on the unequal role of family responsibilities and gendered social norms. Evidence on the household origins of gender inequality has contributed to the rekindling of early models of household specialisation and has given prominence to insights from the literature on household economics, which had mostly developed along different approaches without much cross-pollination with the labour literature.

V. Recent ideas

Evidence for several high-income countries has established that much of the remaining gender gaps can be explained by the differential impacts of children on maternal and paternal earnings. While childbirth is largely neutral to the careers of men, it drives a large and persistent drop in women's earnings. After having their first child, women have more intermittent workforce attachment, also associated to subsequent pregnancies and spells on parental leave. When in work, mothers tend to have higher demand for family-friendly working conditions, shorter commutes, remote work opportunities, and other job characteristics that may interfere with financially rewarding careers. Dynamic aspects of the motherhood penalty may also be relevant, including the formation of aspirations, differential job search behaviour, and changing attitudes and norms around birth.

Qualitative findings on the motherhood penalty are remarkably robust across countries, regardless of levels of development and institutional contexts.[9] Importantly, while non-child-related aspects of gender gaps have steadily shrunk over recent decades – mostly via female gains in human capital accumulation and declining discrimination – the child-related component of gender gaps has remained large and persistent. As a consequence, the presence of children currently explains the bulk of remaining gender gaps in earnings.

In most contexts the motherhood penalty is rooted in gender identity and social conservatism. If gender roles within the household were equalised, parenthood would not be any more detrimental to female rather than male careers. While one may argue that different gender roles reflect at least in part gender differences in preferences, the influence of prescriptive norms on behaviour makes it hard to draw a clear distinction between preferences and constraints. Preferences may mostly internalise prescriptive norms whenever group identities induce certain behaviours and choices.

VI. Towards a policy consensus

Consistent with the view that the bulk of remaining inequalities is driven by differential experiences of men and women upon childbirth, all high-income countries have in place targeted support for families as a way to alleviate the impacts of children on the careers of mothers. Job-protected parental leave is the most widespread family-oriented policy, followed – in both timing and diffusion – by public support for childcare. In several countries, firms complement public policies with an array of family friendly practices, including top-up of parental leave, support for childcare, and flexible work arrangements.

To date, there is little evidence of beneficial effects of longer or more generous parental leave on maternal labour supply and earnings, and early evidence on fathers' leave quotas suggests only limited leeway for replacing maternal childcare, mostly because complying fathers rarely take longer than the relatively short, reserved quotas. Existing evidence on childcare support is more encouraging. Policy evaluations for several countries has shown that more generous childcare funding tends to boost female participation whenever take-up is large and subsidised childcare effectively replaces maternal childcare.[10] However, this may not be the case in contexts where conservative norms on gender roles effectively limit the substitutability of maternal childcare during the early childhood years. Moreover, public support tends to be far more limited beyond the early years, when the organisation of the school timetable is hardly compatible with full-time parental employment. In general, policy faces an uphill struggle whenever gendered beliefs and behaviour have deep roots in intrinsically held norms. Norms are hardly malleable and most forms of policy intervention have limited traction on their evolution, at least in the short run.

The outlook for policy is more optimistic in cases of pluralistic ignorance, in which most individuals personally reject a conservative norm, but may abide to it in the incorrect belief that their peers would socially sanction those who do not.[11] In this case, the education system and the media, as well as role models and peer influences, may be especially effective in eroding conformity to stereotypical beliefs and conservative behaviour. Intervention targeted at families may be both less effective and more costly, as shifting norms would require treating a large share of the compliers. Moreover, results from policy pilots would be misleading because policies that could break the norm if implemented at scale would be ineffective in small pilots.

Affirmative action is an additional form of intervention often invoked to encourage female participation in high-earnings careers and leadership roles, especially in politics and the corporate sector. The rationale for intervention in these sectors is to overcome entry barriers to male-dominated professions.

Moreover, by changing the gender composition of decision makers, the effects of quotas may percolate to lower layers of organisations and to general attitudes towards gender roles in society at large. However, the imposition of quotas in contexts in which the availability of specialised female expertise is scarce may distort the meritocratic allocation of talent and possibly entrench gender stereotypes. In this case, the prospect of quotas to be introduced in the future would give institutions a better opportunity to cultivate women's talent than unanticipated constraints on gender composition.

The available evidence on the impact of gender quotas is mixed. A study on India has found that the introduction of gender quotas in political representation has enhanced general perceptions about women's leadership abilities.[12] For Europe, there is instead no evidence of improved promotion prospects for female employees exposed to more gender-balanced company boards.[13]

Modern welfare states and labour regulations contain several instruments that, while not directly aimed at gender equality, would nonetheless have an impact on the relative earnings of women, who tend to be lower earners in their households and workplaces. For example, tax credit systems typically encourage women's employment and hours, especially among single mothers. Similarly, labour regulations that compress the wage distribution tend to result in lower gender differences in pay.[14] Hence, the labour deregulation that OECD countries implemented since the 1980s with the erosion of union coverage and dismissal costs has caused higher wage dispersion overall and may have offset some of the gender convergence in wages. On the other hand, female under-representation in sectors that were highly unionised meant that the bulk of the de-unionisation process has mostly resulted in wider wage dispersion among men.

Finally, further insight is welcome into the political economy dimension of policy adoption, to relate the evolving support for political and economic equality between genders to economic development and societal changes. Throughout the world, there is a clear cross-country correlation between most indexes of gender equality in legal rights and GDP per person, and evidence suggests that changes in legal institutions are often fuelled by economic shocks. For example, Doepke and Tertilt argue that technological change and higher returns to education in 19th-century England and US eased women's economic empowerment thanks to their prominent role in the education of children.[15] Alternatively, economic development may encourage the expansion of women's rights indirectly via cultural change.

But while economic development clearly eases gender convergence in legal rights, progressively higher living standards do not necessarily achieve gender convergence in labour market outcomes. Further steps towards gender equality need therefore to understand and embrace the role of policy in achieving equal labour market opportunities, feeding back into economic growth via the improved allocation of male and female talent to jobs where its value is the greatest.

Notes

[1] Ngai et al. (2022).

[2] Andrew et al. (2021).

[3] Andrew et al. (2024).

[4] Olivetti and Petrongolo (2008).

[5] Altonji and Blank (1999).

[6] Bertrand (2011).

[7] Croson and Gneezy (2009).

[8] Blau and Kahn (2016).

[9] Kleven et al. (2019).

[10] Albanesi et al. (2022).

[11] Bursztyn et al. (2020).

[12] Beaman et al. (2009).

[13] Bertrand et al. (2018).

[14] Blau and Kahn (2003).

[15] Doepke and Tertilt (2009).

References

Albanesi, S., Olivetti, C. and Petrongolo, B. (2022) 'Families, Labor Markets, and Policy', in Lundberg, S. and Voena, A. (eds), *Handbook of the Economics of the Family*, North Holland: Elsevier Science Publishers; 1(5): 255–326. https://doi.org/10.3386/w30685

Altonji, J. G. and Blank, R. M. (1999) 'Race and Gender in the Labor Market', in Ashenfelter, O. and Card, D. (eds), *Handbook of Labor Economics*, North Holland: Elsevier Science Publishers; 3(48): 3143–3259. https://doi.org/10.1016/S1573-4463(99)30039-0

Andrew, A., Bandiera, O., Costa-Dias, M. and Landais, C. (2021) 'Women and Men at Work', IFS Deaton Review of Inequalities. https://ifs.org.uk/inequality/wp-content/uploads/2021/12/IFS-Inequality-Review-women-and-men-at-work.pdf

Andrew., A, Bandiera, O., Costa Dias, M. and Landais, C. (2024) 'Women and Men at Work', *Oxford Open Economics*, Volume 3, Issue Supplement_1, 2024, Pages i294–i322, https://doi.org/10.1093/ooec/odad034

Beaman, L., Chattopadhyay, R., Duflo, E., Pande, R. and Topalova, P. (2009) 'Powerful Women: Does Exposure Reduce Bias?' *The Quarterly Journal of Economics*, 124(4): 1497–1540. https://doi.org/10.1162/qjec.2009.124.4.1497

Bertrand, M. (2011) 'New Perspectives on Gender', in Ashenfelter, O. and Card, D. (eds) *Handbook of Labor Economics*, North Holland: Elsevier Science Publishers; 4b(17): 1543–1590. https://doi.org/10.1016/S0169-7218(11)02415-4

Bertrand, M., Black, S. E., Jensen, S. and Lleras-Muney, A. (2018) 'Breaking the Glass Ceiling? The Effect of Board Quotas on Female Labour Market Outcomes in Norway', *The Review of Economic Studies*, 86(1): 191–239. https://doi.org/10.1093/restud/rdy032

Blau, F. and Kahn, L. (2016) 'The Gender Wage Gap: Extent, Trends, and Explanations', *Journal of Economic Literature*, 55(3): 789–865. https://doi.org/10.1257/jel.20160995

Blau, F. D. and Kahn, L. M. (2003) 'Understanding International Differences in the Gender Pay Gap', *Journal of Labor Economics*, 21(1): 106–144. https://doi.org/10.1086/344125

Bursztyn, L., Gonzalez, A. L. and Yanagizawa-Drott, D. (2020) 'Misperceived Social Norms: Women Working Outside the Home in Saudi Arabia', *American Economic Review*, 110(10): 2997–3029. https://doi.org/10.1257/aer.20180975

Croson, R. and Gneezy, U. (2009) 'Gender Differences in Preferences', *Journal of Economic Literature*, 47(2): 448–74. https://doi.org/10.1257/jel.47.2.448

Doepke, M. and Tertilt, M. (2009) 'Women's Liberation: What's in It for Men?', *The Quarterly Journal of Economics*, 124(4): 1541–1591. https://doi.org/10.1162/qjec.2009.124.4.1541

Kleven, H., Landais, C., Posch, J., Steinhauer, A. and Zweimuller, J. (2019) 'Child Penalties across Countries: Evidence and Explanations', *AEA Papers and Proceedings* 109: 122–126. https://doi.org/10.3386/w25524

Ngai, R., Olivetti, C. and Petrongolo, B. (2022) 'Structural Transformation over 150 of Men's and Women's Work', Mimeo. https://personal.lse.ac.uk/ngai/NgaiOlivettiPetrongolo.pdf

Olivetti, C. and Petrongolo, B. (2008) 'Unequal Pay or Unequal Employment? A Cross-Country Analysis of Gender Gaps', *Journal of Labor Economics*, 26(4): 621–654. https://doi.org/10.1086/589458

Response to Oriana Bandiera and Barbara Petrongolo by Ashwini Deshpande

Gender gaps in labour markets are rife, despite progress in several dimensions of women's rights. While gender gaps in many dimensions are persistent, there have been significant improvements in some, such as the average gap between male and female wages, a reduction in occupational segregation, and types of work contracts. These improvements are global, including in countries like India, where the issue of low and declining female labour force participation is under academic and media spotlights.

Gender equality is important because of equity and social justice, as well as efficiency reasons. Increasing participation of women in work and decision-making is key to ensuring that institutional structures facilitate the best use of individual talents and abilities.

The chapter raises the important issue of the role of gendered social norms in developed countries. This is a refreshing perspective, especially for readers from India and South Asia, where almost the entire onus of gender inequality is placed on adverse social norms by multilateral international agencies[1] and mainstream researchers. So much of the mainstream discussion in the South Asian context is dominated by the social norms discourse that one might think that, elsewhere in the world social norms are gender egalitarian; and that Indian people, and Indian women in particular, are fundamentally unable to respond to standard economic incentives. In other words, even if jobs are available in plenty, Indian women would not enter the labour market because of specific social norms. This chapter reminds us that social norms everywhere are discriminatory towards women.

The chapter shows the variation across countries in the time spent on paid work and on unpaid domestic work. We see that the former variation is far less significant than the latter. Though there has been progress towards gender equality in the arena of paid work, the progress in the arena of unpaid domestic work has been slow and uneven. Figure 9.3 illustrates this in the context of the United States.

Figure 9.3 shows that the gap between men and women in the hours spent on domestic and care narrowed between 1900–1980. The share of hours women spent on housework declined especially between 1950 and 1980, and the time spent doing domestic chores increased steadily from 1920 onwards. However, the narrowing of the gap over eight decades seems to have stalled after 1980. Thus, women continue to spend far more time in home production compared to men, in the US, and indeed, everywhere else in the world.

Figure 9.3: Weekly hours dedicated to home production, US, by gender, 1900–2005

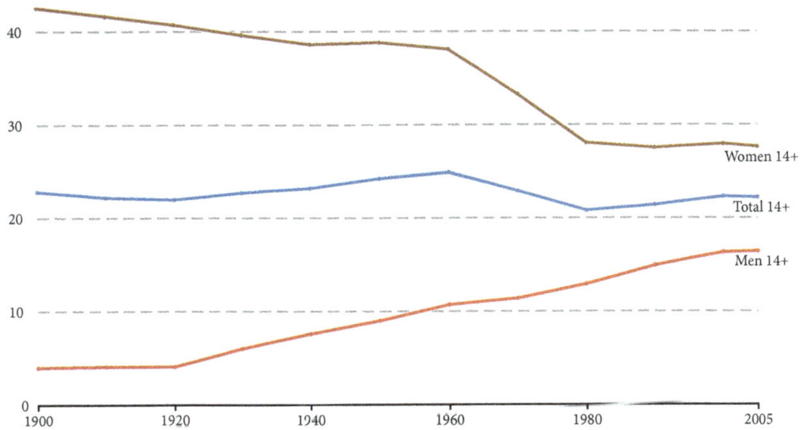

Source: Ramey and Francis (2009) – processed by Our World in Data, reproduced under a CC BY licence.[2]

This inequality came to light during the COVID-19 pandemic when women dropped out of the labour force in the US and many other developed economies, not necessarily because they were retrenched, but because they were predominantly responsible for domestic chores and home schooling of children and found it very difficult to bear the double burden of paid work and domestic chores and childcare.

I. Insights from feminist economics

What economists call 'home production', feminist economists call reproductive labour. Reproductive labour does not refer simply to the physical act of childbearing, but to the whole gamut of domestic chores, including care work.

Here we see a clear difference between the developed and developing countries. In the latter, the quantum of reproductive labour is far higher: cooking, cleaning, house maintenance, buying items for daily food consumption, washing clothes, fetching water, fetching fuel for cooking, and taking care of children and the elderly. These activities are done every day, multiple times a day. For instance, in India, having three freshly cooked meals from scratch is the norm in most homes that can afford it. These tasks are predominantly, even almost exclusively, women's responsibility. They are expected to either do it themselves, or for those who can afford it, get them done through paid help.

This immense pressure of reproductive labour is the real norm that prevents women from participating to their full potential in the arena of paid work.[3] In this context, the argument of the authors about the positive two-way effect of economic growth on gender equality assumes significance. The relationship between economic growth and women's labour is two-sided. Increasing participation of women in paid work will raise economic growth. Equally, economic growth has the potential to free women from the drudgery of everyday labour, as higher family incomes can increase access to labour-saving devices.

Feminist scholars have argued that the reproductive economy, which encompasses the entire gamut of domestic chores and unpaid care work, is essential for the smooth and uninterrupted functioning of the 'productive economy'. First, society needs the next generation of workers to be born and nurtured for the economy to keep running. Second, those in paid work cannot continue to work uninterruptedly without unpaid or reproductive work being taken care of. While women's participation in the productive economy has increased, it has not necessarily reduced the burden of reproductive work substantially or evenly across the globe. This is often referred to as the 'double burden on women': women who are in the productive economy are not necessarily able to avoid the work in the reproductive economy.

This double burden also leads to a double whammy for women, where they are held to higher standards than men. At work, employers suspect them of having a low attachment to their jobs. Thus, they need to work doubly hard to prove they are just as good as their male counterparts. The expectations from them in their domestic roles include, over and above domestic chores, provision of emotional labour, including nurturing, being there as a supportive figure, organising social events, and so forth. Any slippage or suboptimal performance (real or imaginary) in these dimensions is looked down upon as prioritising career over family, or a case of 'wanting to have it all'. Men routinely prioritise career over family, but that is not seen as a negative trait.

II. The 'motherhood penalty' and the 'fatherhood bonus'

In the title of Nancy Folbre's 1994 book, she asked a very important question: 'Who Pays for the Kids?'[4] Everywhere in the world, labour markets penalise women for their reproductive responsibilities. Take the motherhood penalty. Figure 9.4 shows data for six countries including Scandinavian countries known for having the highest levels of gender equality: Denmark, Sweden, US, UK, Austria, and Germany.

Based on earnings data from couples, Figure 9.4 shows that immediately after the birth of the first child, mothers' earnings dip, whereas fathers' earnings either stay the same or increase slightly. This is true even in countries like the UK and Germany, where mothers earned slightly more than fathers prior to the birth of their first child. Bertrand shows how the bulk of the gender wage gap in Denmark is due to the motherhood penalty.[5]

While Figure 9.4 is an example from one paper, the motherhood penalty has been studied fairly widely in the literature on gender gaps. What is getting

Figure 9.4: Motherhood penalty in earnings in three sets of countries, 2015

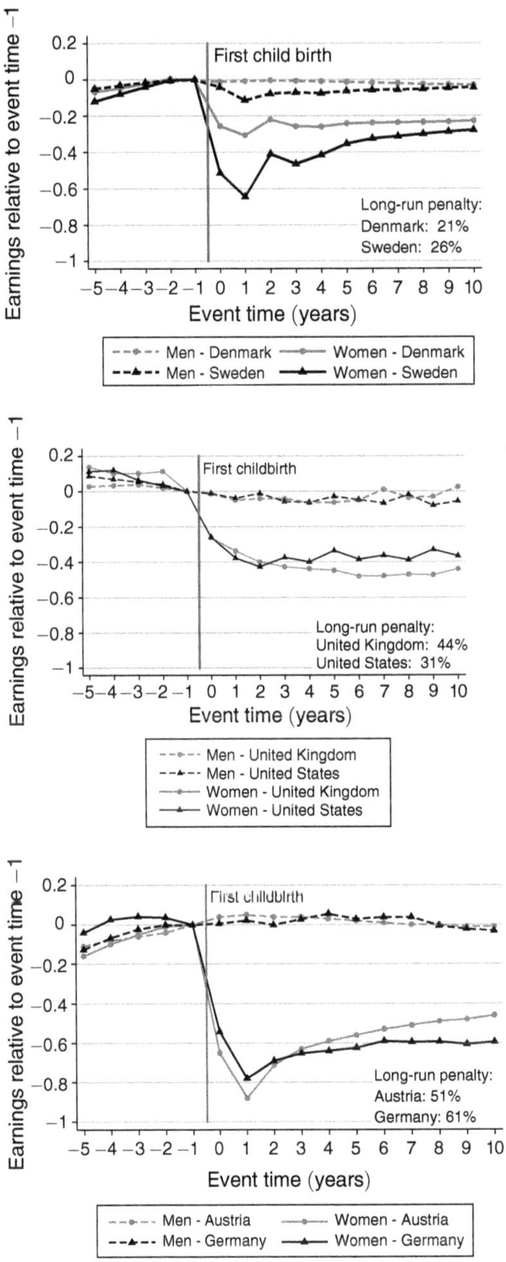

a) Scandinavian countries

b) English-speaking countries

c) German-speaking countries

Source: Figures 1, 2, and 3 in Kleven et al. (2019)[6], reproduced with permission from the authors.

increasing attention is a phenomenon called the 'fatherhood bonus'. There is evidence that fathers get actively rewarded after the birth of the first child.

Why might this happen? Studies have explored if this is due to the fact that fathers put in more hours at work due to an additional child, and women put in fewer hours due to the additional childcare responsibility. This is certainly a plausible mechanism and it partly explains the earnings gap that happens after the birth of the first child. However, there is evidence to show that employers see men as more responsible, committed, and stable after they become fathers.[7] These qualities are rewarded through a wage premium to fathers.

Thus, the structure of rewards and penalties in labour markets, including in highly developed economies committed to gender equality, produce or reinforce gender norms that fix the mother in a caregiving or reproductive role and fathers in the more remunerative productive roles. This has led many women to make a choice between family and career, as pursuing both is very challenging.

III. The way forward: policy solutions

Since the burden of reproductive work keeps gender wage gaps persistent in both developed and developing countries, albeit to different degrees, a common solution for all economies to adopt can be summarised in a simple framework known as the '3 Rs': Recognise, Redistribute, and Reduce women's burden of reproductive work.[8] This does not only relate to provision of affordable childcare but more substantially to shifting the norms around the gendered distribution of domestic tasks.

A recent paper analysing time use in the US shows how mothers are substantially more affected by the school year than are fathers. When school is in session, mothers sleep less, spend more time caring for family members and driving them around, and spend less time on eating, free time, and exercise.[9] Therefore, the 3Rs framework needs to emphasise that unpaid domestic and care work is not a woman's job alone. Some of the tasks need to be replaced by public provision, such as childcare; additionally, intra-family redistribution is essential. The latter, being in the private domain, is not directly amenable to policy intervention. However, a changed structure of labour market incentives has the potential to shift norms and practices inside the home.

Yet, policies can have perverse outcomes. Adopting policies that are supposed to be gender neutral can have perverse outcomes if they are not accompanied by shifts in norms around the division of reproductive and productive work. For example, Antecol et al. analysed data on the assistant professor hires at top-50 economics departments in the US between 1985 and 2004.[10] They show that the adoption of gender-neutral tenure clock stopping policies, e.g., extension of the tenure clock for both parents, substantially reduced female tenure rates and substantially increased male tenure rates. This was because mothers used their maternity leave for childcare, while fathers, on average, used the extension to work on their academic publication, leaving the bulk of the childcare to the mothers.

Finally, we need to note that in developing countries women do unpaid *economic* work as they support family-run income-generating enterprises, such as agriculture, horticulture, dairy farming, fisheries, production and sale of food items, artisanal products, such as mats, baskets, pottery, handwoven cloth, or running small shops. Yet, usually, their contribution is not formally recognised. They are not counted in labour force surveys, are unpaid, and often have no assets in their name, making them ineligible for, say, bank loans.

Thus, unpaid work in the context of developing countries refers to both unpaid economic work as well as unpaid domestic and care work. Here the challenge is to recognise women's unpaid contribution to family enterprises, as well as increase their participation in paid/remunerative work. Additionally, we need to adopt an intersectional lens and recognise the invisibility of the doubly marginalised. For instance, in the context of India, the standard story around why women's labour force participation rate (LFPR) is low and declining is inadequate. It does not sufficiently recognise important differences within the category of 'Indian' women, and is thus unable to capture and account for differential caste, religion, and regional norms. A focus on the intersection of caste and gender reveals that so-called lower-caste women have always had far higher LFPRs compared to their upper-caste counterparts, but have experienced a greater decline. This is indicative of declining work opportunities, rather than restrictive social norms, because the most marginalised caste groups have more egalitarian norms about women's participation in public spaces, compared to upper-caste women. Thus, the decline in their LFPR cannot solely be due to changing norms. The gap between male and female LFPRs is also not due to the lack of education, as education rates are not only converging, but female enrolment has surpassed male enrolment in higher education.

In conclusion, there are several policy responses that would have to be adopted to alter the gendered structure of labour markets and associated rewards and penalties. These policy changes are actively discussed in the context of developing countries. The chapter under review makes a strong case for policy changes in the context of developed countries, underlining an important global truth: when it comes to gender inequalities, countries at various income levels are more similar than different.

Notes

1 Bussolo et al. (2024).

2 'Home production working hours per week in the US, by gender and demographic group (Ramey and Francis (2009))' [dataset]. Ramey and Francis (2009) [original data].

3 Deshpande and Kabeer (2024).

[4] Folbre (1994).

[5] Bertrand (2020).

[6] Kleven et al. (2019).

[7] Cain Miller (2014).

[8] UN Women (2024).

[9] Cowan et al. (2023).

[10] Antecol et al. (2018).

References

Antecol, H., Bedard, K. and Stearns, J. (2018) 'Equal but Inequitable: Who Benefits from Gender-Neutral Tenure Clock Stopping Policies?', *American Economic Review,* 108(9): 2420–41. https://doi.org/10.1257/aer.20160613

Bertrand, M., (2020) 'Gender in the Twenty-First Century', *AEA Papers and Proceedings*, 110: 1–24. https://doi.org/10.1257/pandp.20201126

Bussolo, M. Amarachi Ezebuihe, J., Muñoz Boudet, A. M., Poupakis, S., Rahman, T. and Sarma, N. (2024) 'Social Norms and Gender Disparities with a Focus on Female Labor Force Participation in South Asia', *The World Bank Research Observer*, 39(1): 124–158 https://doi.org/10.1093/wbro/lkad010

Cain Miller, C. (2014) 'The Motherhood Penalty vs. the Fatherhood Bonus', TheUpshot, *New York Times* [6 September]. https://www.nytimes.com/2014/09/07/upshot/a-child-helps-your-career-if-youre-a-man.html

Cowan, B. W., Jones, T. R. and Swigert, J. M. (2023) 'Parental and Student Time Use Around the Academic Year', NBER Working Paper No. 31177. https://doi.org/10.3386/w31177

Deshpande, A. and Kabeer, N. (2024) 'Norms Matter: Exploring the Distribution of Women's Work between Income Generation, Expenditure Saving and Unpaid Domestic Responsibilities in India', *World Development*, 174: 106435. https://doi.org/10.1016/j.worlddev.2023.106435

Folbre, N. (1994) *Who Pays for the Kids? Gender and the Structures of Constraint*, New York, London: Routledge. https://doi.org/10.4324/9780203168295

Kleven, H., Landais, C., Posch, J., Steinhauer, A. and Zweimüller, J. (2019) 'Child Penalties Across Countries: Evidence and Explanations', *AEA Papers and Proceedings*, 109: 122–26. https://doi.org/10.1257/pandp.20191078

Ramey, V. A. and Francis, N. (2009) 'A Century of Work and Leisure', *American Economic Journal: Macroeconomics* 1(2), 189–224. https://doi.org/10.1257/mac.1.2.189

UN Women (2024) 'Transformative Approaches to Recognize, Reduce and Redistribute Unpaid Care Work in Women's Economic Empowerment: Good practices, Lessons Learned and Recommendations from Rwanda, Senegal and South Africa', Economic Empowerment Section, UN WOMEN, New York. https://www.unwomen.org/en/digital-library/publications/2024/12/transformative-approaches-to-recognize-reduce-and-redistribute-unpaid-care-work-in-womens-economic-empowerment#:~:text=This%20document%20compiles%20the%20good,paid%20care%20and%20domestic%20work

Response to Oriana Bandiera and Barbara Petrongolo by Almudena Sevilla

The chapter on gender inequality by Oriana Bandiera and Barbara Petrongolo gives a clear picture of the current consensus in terms of where we stand with respect to gender equality, why it is important, and what the general policy goal is as a result. The chapter recognises both the significant strides made towards gender equality and the substantial challenges that remain, such as persistent earnings disparities, with gaps ranging from 20–80% in different parts of the world. Failing to achieve gender equality has a significant opportunity cost in terms of economic growth, as it leads to the misallocation of female talent. The policy aim should be to reach a stage where gender does not influence individuals' decision-making processes. Here, I reflect on the policy implications and challenges emerging from four paradigm shifts that are relevant to future policymaking in the area of gender equality.

I. The complex and dynamic mechanisms behind the motherhood penalty

The first paradigm shift, as pointed out by Bandiera and Petrongolo, is the growing consensus among economists about the interaction between family life and labour market decisions. We now know that if women's occupations followed the male distribution, a third of the difference in earnings between men and women would be reduced.[1] The other two-thirds of the gender-based difference in earnings comes from factors *within* each occupation. Women's inability to combine work with family seems to account for the lion's share of the pay gap, partly because of women's greater relative demands at home. Data from decades confirms this effect, prompting policies like parental leave and childcare subsidies to address the issue. Yet, after years of policies, gender equality remains elusive. Here I argue that there are two limitations with the existing approach that limit the design of policy. First, the focus on childbirth as the starting point for the widening gender gap in the labour market needs to be reassessed. Second, the mechanisms underlying the dynamics of the so-called child penalty need to be further understood.

First, it is important to note that the establishment of a household, in addition to childbirth, plays a role in the gender disparities seen in household duties and labour market inequalities. Evidence for several countries shows that the formation of a couple leads to an increase in five-and-a-half hours per week for women, whereas the difference in total housework between married men and single men is not statistically significant and amounts to less than a quarter-of-an-hour a week.[2] This finding holds for a wide variety of countries, even for couples that remain childless. Second, as Petrongolo and Bandiera acknowledge, there is still limited understanding of the underlying mechanisms behind the gender gap, which opens upon the arrival of children.

Work hours seem to be part of the explanation for the widening earnings gaps after household formation and childbirth. Goldin et al. show that the earnings penalty for mothers reduces as their children age, and mothers work longer hours, particularly for the less educated.[3] Yet a question remains about why initial levels of employment and work hours are not recovered. One answer derives from 24-hours diary surveys. Table 9.1 shows the hours per day in household-related activities. As has been widely documented, housework and childcare demands fall on mothers significantly more than fathers regardless of children's ages. These demands are also increasing because economic inequality and more competitive college admissions processes are driving parental (particularly maternal) time investments in childcare.[4] Less well known is the fact that housework and childcare time demands remain high even when children enter school, and can be constraining for women who spend on average seven hours a day with children over the age of six, a load that only appears to ease up during the teenage years. A separate answer comes from the unpredictable nature of children's needs, especially as they mature and their lives become more complex, which requires parents to be mentally and emotionally available. Therefore, even if the time required to be with children decreases during teenage years, the need for mothers to remain constantly on-call persists. This expectation, whether self-imposed or external, can create a sense of responsibility and guilt that compels many mothers to maintain a constant readiness to respond to their children's needs.[5] Similarly, grandmothers, like mothers, experience a drop in earnings and work hours upon the arrival of a grandchild, despite minimal childcare time, as they provide on-call support when needed.[6]

II. Gender roles and the technology of work

The insights on gender roles and household duties discussed in section II highlight the potential benefits of a more equitable distribution of domestic responsibilities, especially childcare. By sharing these tasks more evenly, women may have additional opportunities for labour market participation. Such changes might involve support from both men and public policies. Alternatively, reshaping a labour market that acknowledges and values caregivers can be beneficial. Claudia Goldin's research on 'Career and Family' delineates how, in a world where women remain the main caregivers, the tension between the asynchronous demands of the labour market (by greedy jobs) and household labour forms a dichotomy for women, leading to a reduction in labour supply for paid work.[7] The key question arises: Are greedy jobs, characterised by little substitution between workers, inherently

Table 9.1: Hours per day devoted to activities

	(1)		(2)		(3)		(4)		(5)
VARIABLES	Housework		Primary childcare		In care of children		Time with children		Obs
Females	Mean	SD	Mean	SD	Mean	SD	Mean	SD	
Age youngest child 0–5	3.199	(2.550)	2.518	(2.386)	6.339	(4.370)	9.562	(5.067)	24,473
Age youngest child 6–12	3.180	(2.717)	1.227	(1.623)	5.157	(4.520)	7.020	(4.895)	20,369
Age youngest child 13–17	2.696	(2.712)	0.377	(0.990)	0.232	(1.241)	2.564	(3.561)	12,650
Men									
Age youngest child 0–5	1.812	(2.253)	1.302	(1.815)	4.228	(4.333)	6.316	(4.907)	17,509
Age youngest child 6–12	1.771	(2.251)	0.630	(1.215)	3.686	(4.267)	4.927	(4.721)	14,704
Age youngest child 13–17	1.538	(2.166)	0.185	(0.668)	0.110	(0.926)	1.754	(3.123)	10,374

Notes: The sample used in this study consists of household heads who have at least one child under the age of 18 living in their homes. The data is derived from the American Time Use Survey (ATUS) spanning the years 2003–2022. For the sub-sample selection, participants were chosen based on the age of the youngest child in their household. The study focuses on two main categories of activities: 'Housework' and 'Childcare'. 'Housework' includes various tasks, such as cooking, cleaning, shopping, elder care, and other related activities. This definition follows the approach taken by Gimenez-Nadal and Sevilla.[8] 'Primary childcare' refers to the time spent engaging in childcare activities reported as the main or primary activity. 'In care of children' encompasses the time spent in activities where parents are responsible for any children, including 'Primary childcare' when parents report there is a child under their care. 'Time with children' accounts for the time devoted to activities that fall under 'Primary childcare', 'In care of children', and any other activity where a child is present (e.g., household child, grandchild, foster child, etc.). All the time measurements for these activities are reported in hours per day. The values presented in the study include both the mean and standard deviations (in parenthesis).

so because of the production technology function (as she argues) or because of entrenched gender roles?[9] A new paradigm shift is needed that considers the influence of gender roles in the organisation of paid work.

In recent years we have witnessed a decline in self-employment across various high-end professions, attributed in part to reduced flexibility. Even prior to the onset of the COVID-19 pandemic, there was a noticeable uptick in workplace flexibility, driven both by external factors such as the growing scale of operations, and internal shifts towards corporate ownership of businesses.[10] These changes, occurring both from within the workforce and through broader economic trends, were already reshaping the landscape of employment. However, the unprecedented societal disruptions catalysed by the COVID-19 pandemic have further accentuated these dynamics. As we witnessed, there was a swift transition to remote work enabled by rapid change in already quite advanced communication technologies, and we must interrogate why such adaptations were not instituted prior to the pandemic given that a significant portion of the labour force was technologically capable of operating remotely. Both, mothers and fathers worked more from home during the pandemic,[11] and fathers increased the amount of childcare done during this time as a result.[12] The resistance to remote work adaptation may have originated from entrenched norms in the workplace and gender roles rather than technological insufficiencies. In essence, the pandemic may have exposed the extent to which these societal norms and gender roles have been institutionalised in our managing practices and workplaces and have acted as barriers to progressive labour market restructuring.[13]

III. The unchangeable nature of gender roles

Another paradigm shift that has occurred since the 1989 Washington Consensus is the increasing acceptance among economists of the potential malleability and the responsiveness to policy of social norms and gender roles.[14] A relatively recent line of enquiry looks at how long it takes for gender roles to change, under what conditions, and what the mechanisms are that explain the change, such as social contagion and learning.[15] Bandiera and Petrongolo allude to some of this latest line of research that attempts to uncover how gender norms originate and evolve, such as classroom interventions, promoting women's work and control over income, and information programmes – all these interventions have been shown to have made traditional gender norms less entrenched.

Emerging findings underscore that change can be swift. Fernández et al. illuminate a previously underrepresented aspect in literature by highlighting how high-impact events, such as the AIDS epidemic, can lead to significant cultural shifts – in this case, changing views on homosexuality.[16] Their research posits that if every US state had confronted high AIDS rates, we might have seen a surge in acceptance rates of gay individuals by an additional 50% between the 1970s and 1990s. This novel observation about the rapid shift of gender roles in response to shocks offers invaluable insights for policymakers aiming to shape future interventions.

IV. Gender equality as a zero-sum game

The most important paradigm shift that has occurred since the Washington consensus is that the notion of gender equality as a zero-sum game is starting to be challenged actively. The discourse around gender equality is in the process of transcending its initial social justice underpinnings to be increasingly acknowledged as an economic efficiency issue. There is a wider acceptance among economists of the view that as gender equality progresses, it enhances resource allocation, leading towards economic growth and prosperity – potentially expanding the economic 'pie' rather than redistributing a fixed amount.

The journey towards gender equality, while instrumental in fuelling economic growth and enhancing efficiency, instigates important distributive disruption. Bandiera and Petrongolo's work offers a pivotal perspective, yet there is an opportunity to delve deeper into these underlying disruptions. The unveiling of these disruptions has become evident thanks to recent development in the analysis of big data in various format types, such as video, images, text, and other forms of media. Consequently, issues like sexual harassment and violence, once considered anecdotal, are now being researched to uncover layers of systemic discrimination.[17] In our own discipline, economics, a recent paper encompassed recordings from hundreds of research seminars revealing that women presenters faced more, often patronising or hostile, questions than their male counterparts.[18] Recent evidence shows that more than 10% of posts on Economic Job Market Rumors (EJMR), a popular forum among economists, can be classified as potentially 'toxic'.[19] An example of such toxic discourse on EJMR is 'Given women get free spots, blks and latins get free spots, it basically means you need to be far far right tail if u are a yt or azn homegrown American. (2022-12-27)'.[20] This data provides an unprecedented exploration into the dynamics of seminar culture within the field of economics, suggesting a more pervasive bias than initially assumed.

V. Policy implications

Grasping the nuances of household-related demands is crucial for shaping effective policies aimed at counteracting talent depletion, especially when mothers adjust working hours after childbirth and exhibit prolonged absences from the workforce as children age. It is vital for policies to extend beyond child-centric concerns, encompassing the overarching dynamics of household creation and its ramifications on gender equity. Traditional time diaries fall short of encapsulating the emotional readiness associated with child-rearing, signifying a notable void in the extant literature. Addressing this data shortfall presents a valuable opportunity for social science research to steer the prioritisation of certain policy strategies, such as introducing flexible work arrangements, enhancing parental leave provisions for both parents, and promoting an equitable distribution in domestic chores.

It is also imperative to accept that job structures are influenced by beliefs about social norms and gender roles of those in managerial positions. Advancements in information-sharing technologies within the pharmaceutical sector have significantly impacted job structures. Such technologies facilitate seamless communication and coordination, enabling workers to cover for one another more effectively. As a result, the role of individual workers becomes more fluid, making it easier for employees to step in and out of tasks as needed without loss of productivity. This flexibility can reduce the career impact of taking time off for caregiving duties, thereby addressing one of the systemic causes behind gender pay disparities.[21] While policy tools like job-sharing in the UK aim to promote such interchangeability, they face challenges in implementation due to technical constraints. Therefore, policies that encourage technological adoption to enhance worker substitutability in specific sectors might be a more effective approach.[22]

The realisation that cultural values can swiftly adapt following a shock is reshaping policy priorities. In developing countries, gender norms are more likely to be explicitly targeted in policy measures than in wealthier nations, probably because policy is dominated by development agencies.[23] In developed countries, there's a shift from policies supporting gender equality that inadvertently reinforce traditional roles towards ones challenging these norms. While maternity leave and subsidised childcare maintain the status quo, paternity leave, especially promoted in Northern Europe, challenges established gender norms. Yet paternity leave policies remain low in uptake and their effects on changing social norms is mixed. Social contagion indicates young men are more inclined to take leave if influenced by older brothers or co-workers.[24] Farré and González, Patnaik, and Tamm show fathers' increased involvement post-leave, but the influence on gender norms remains mixed in the longer term.[25] The COVID-19 pandemic further highlights entrenched traditional roles in terms of the household division of housework and childcare.[26] Understanding the dynamics of these swift transformations can provide policymakers with valuable insights on how to craft impactful interventions.

The recent recognition that advancing gender equality can boost efficiency and growth, but can also disrupt traditional power structures akin to the effects of globalisation or technological progress, requires policymaking to balance these gains with measures that address the resulting societal disruptions, aiming for a more equitable society. The future focus lies on both promoting gender equality and managing its distributive challenges, preventing potential backlash through inclusive policy design, and fostering dialogue about evolving gender roles.

Acknowledgements

I thoroughly enjoyed reading this chapter and I want to thank the editors, colleagues Tim Besley and Andrés Velasco, and the authors of this chapter for giving me the opportunity to read and to respond to such an interesting piece of work.

Notes

1. Goldin (2021).
2. Borra et al. (2021).
3. Goldin et al. (2022).
4. Doepke and Zilibotti (2017); Ramey and Ramey (2010); Borra and Sevilla (2019).
5. Gimenez-Nadal and Sevilla (2016).
6. Gørtz et al. (2020).
7. Goldin (2021).
8. Gimenez-Nadal and Sevilla (2012).
9. The contrast between sectors like healthcare and banking raises questions about whether gendered social expectations, rather than work technology, drive the differences. Goldin notes that the belated discovery of the contraceptive pill resulted from systemic disinterest in women's issues and suggests that the persistence of greedy jobs may stem from deep-seated gender roles. Goldin underscores this by pointing out the accepted practice in the US and other developed countries where any on-shift ob-gyn can deliver a baby, contrasting this with sectors like law or consulting where clients insist on continuity with a particular professional.
10. Goldin and Katz (2011).
11. Amuedo-Dorantes et al. (2023).
12. Gamage et al. (2020).
13. Sevilla and Giusta (2022).
14. See Sevilla (2020). Answers to attitudinal questions have been widely used in gender economics to assess cultural beliefs on the role of women in society, see Fortin (2005). A quick look at the World Values Survey reflects a substantial change in societal attitudes. In 1990, around 50% of US respondents agreed that 'when a mother works for pay, the children suffer'. By 2017, the agreement with this statement had dropped to just 17%. The malleability of gender roles is promising.

[15] Giuliano (2020).

[16] Fernández et al. (2019).

[17] Folke and Rickne (2022).

[18] Dupas et al. (2021).

[19] Ederer et al. (2024).

[20] Ederer et al. (2024).

[21] Goldin and Katz (2016).

[22] Sevilla (2020).

[23] Lundberg (2022).

[24] Dahl et al. (2014).

[25] Farré and González (2019); Patnaik (2019); Tamm (2019).

[26] Sevilla and Smith (2020).

References

Amuedo-Dorantes, C., Marcén, M., Morales, M. and Sevilla, A. (2023) 'Schooling and Parental Labor Supply: Evidence from COVID-19 School Closures in the United States', *Industrial & Labor Relations Review*, 76(1): 56–85. https://doi.org/10.1177/00197939221099184

Borra, C., Browning, M. and Sevilla, A. (2021) 'Marriage and Housework', *Oxford Economic Papers*, 73(2): 479–508. https://doi.org/10.1093/oep/gpaa026

Borra, C. and Sevilla, A. (2019) 'Competition for University Places and Parental Time Investments: Evidence from the United Kingdom', *Economic Inquiry*, 57(3): 1460–1479. https://doi.org/10.1111/ecin.12761

Dahl, G. B., Løken, K. V. and Mogstad, M. (2014) 'Peer Effects in Program Participation', *American Economic Review*, 104(7): 2049–2074. https://doi.org/10.1257/aer.104.7.2049

Doepke, M. and Zilibotti, F. (2017) 'Parenting with Style: Altruism and Paternalism in Intergenerational Preference Transmission', *Econometrica*, 85(5): 1331–1371. https://doi.org/10.3982/ECTA14634

Dupas, P., Modestino, A. S., Niederle, M. and Wolfers, J. (2021) 'Gender and the Dynamics of Economics Seminars' (No. w28494). *National Bureau of Economic Research*. https://doi.org/10.3386/w28494

Ederer, F., Goldsmith-Pinkham, P. and Jensen, K. (2024) 'Anonymity and Identity Online', NBER Working Paper. https://florianederer.github.io/ejmr.pdf

Farré, L. and González, L. (2019) 'Does Paternity Leave Reduce Fertility?', *Journal of Public Economics*, 122: 52–66. https://doi.org/10.1016/j.jpubeco.2018.12.002

Fernández, R., Parsa, S. and Viarengo, M. (2019) 'Coming out in America: AIDS, Politics, and Cultural Change', (No. w25697). *National Bureau of Economic Research*. https://doi.org/10.3386/w25697

Folke, O. and Rickne, J. (2022) 'Sexual Harassment and Gender Inequality in the Labor Market', *The Quarterly Journal of Economics*, 137(4): 2163–2212. https://doi.org/10.1093/qje/qjac018

Fortin, N. M. (2005) 'Gender Role Attitudes and the Labour-Market Outcomes of Women across OECD Countries', *Oxford Review of Economic Policy*, 21(3): 416–438. https://doi.org/10.1093/oxrep/gri024

Gamage, D. K., Sevilla, A. and Smith, S. (2020) 'Women in Economics: a UK Perspective', *Oxford Review of Economic Policy*, 36(4): 962–982. https://doi.org/10.1093/oxrep/graa048

Gimenez-Nadal, J. I. and Sevilla, A. (2012) 'Trends in Time Allocation: A Cross-Country Analysis', *European Economic Review*, 56(6): 1338–1359. https://doi.org/10.1016/j.euroecorev.2012.02.011

Gimenez-Nadal, J. I. and Sevilla, A. (2016) 'Intensive Mothering and Well-being: The Role of Education and Child Care Activity (No. 10023)', IZA Discussion Papers. https://www.iza.org/publications/dp/10023/intensive-mothering-and-well-being-the-role-of-education-and-child-care-activity

Giuliano, P. (2020) 'Gender and Culture', *Oxford Review of Economic Policy*, 36(4): 944–961. https://doi.org/10.1093/oxrep/graa044

Goldin, C. (2021) *Career and Family: Women's Century-Long Journey toward Equity*, Princeton, NJ: Princeton University Press. https://doi.org/10.1515/9780691226736

Goldin, C. and Katz, L. F. (2011) 'Cost of Workplace Flexibility for Highpowered Professionals', *The Annals of the American Academy of Political and Social Science*, 638(1): 45–67. https://doi.org/10.1177/0002716211414398

Goldin, C. and Katz, L. F. (2016) 'A Most Egalitarian Profession: Pharmacy and the Evolution of a Family-Friendly Occupation', *Journal of Labor Economics*, 34(3): 705–746. https://doi.org/10.1086/685505

Goldin, C., Kerr, S. P. and Olivetti, C. (2022) 'When the Kids Grow Up: Women's Employment and Earnings across the Family Cycle', (No. w30323) *National Bureau of Economic Research*. https://doi.org/10.3386/w30323

Gørtz, M., Sander, S. and Sevilla, A. (2020) 'Does the Child Penalty Strike Twice', (No. 30/20). CEBI Working Paper Series. https://www.econstor.eu/bitstream/10419/258944/1/cebi-wp2030.pdf

Kleven, H., Landais, C., Posch, J., Steinhauer, A. and Zweimüller, J. (2024) 'Do Family Policies Reduce Gender Inequality? Evidence from 60 years of Policy Experimentation', *American Economic Journal: Economic Policy*, 16 (2): 110–49. https://doi.org/10.1257/pol.20210346

Lundberg, S. (2022) 'Gender Economics and the Meaning of Discrimination', *AEA Papers and Proceedings*, 112: 588–91. https://doi.org/10.1257/pandp.20221086

Patnaik, A. (2019) 'Reserving Time for Daddy: The Consequences of Fathers' Quotas', *Journal of Labor Economics*, 37(4): 1009–1059. https://doi.org/10.1086/703115

Ramey, G. and Ramey, V. A. (2010) 'The Rug Rat Race', *Brookings Papers on Economic Activity*, Spring: 129–176. https://doi.org/10.1353/eca.2010.0003

Sevilla, A. (2020) 'Gender Economics: An Assessment', *Oxford Review of Economic Policy*, 36(4): 725–742. https://doi.org/10.1093/oxrep/graa054

Sevilla, A. and Giusta, M. D. (2022) 'Career and Family: Women's Century-Long Journey Toward Equity: by Claudia Goldin', Princeton, NJ: Princeton University Press; 2021. 218 p. *Feminist Economics*, 29(1): 301–305. https://doi.org/10.1080/13545701.2022.2108550

Sevilla, A. and Smith, S. (2020) 'Baby Steps: The Gender Division of Childcare during the COVID-19 Pandemic', *Oxford Review of Economic Policy*, 36(Supplement_1): S169–S186. https://doi.org/10.1093/oxrep/graa027

Tamm, M. (2019) 'Fathers' Parental Leave-Taking, Childcare Involvement and Labor Market Participation', *Journal of Labor Economics*, 59: 184–197. https://doi.org/10.1016/j.labeco.2019.04.007

PART V

COHESION, EQUITY AND SOCIAL POLICY

10. Is there a 'new consensus' on inequality?

Francisco H. G. Ferreira

Thirty years after the Washington Consensus, is there a new policy consensus that addresses the problem of inequality? There is widespread acceptance that multiple, interrelated, and mutually reinforcing inequalities exist – in income, wealth, education, health, power, and recognition – and that these inequalities are generally 'too high'. There has also been a significant shift towards a shared view that these inequalities matter, both intrinsically and because of their detrimental effects on economic efficiency and political institutions. There is much less consensus, perhaps surprisingly, on what the actual levels of income inequality are, and there are common misperceptions about their trends. In policy terms, there is something approaching a consensus regarding the desirability of various 'pre-distribution' policies, ranging from early childhood development to investment in better teaching. In certain quarters, there is also agreement that sharper antitrust regulation, freer labour unions, and more progressive taxation is needed in most countries. But much less is known about how to provide the poor with genuine opportunities to break the cycle of intergenerational transmission of disadvantage in a durable way.

I. Introduction

The word 'inequality' does not appear – even once – in 'What Washington Means by Policy Reform', the 1989 book chapter where John Williamson laid out the 10 topics that he saw as defining a 'Washington Consensus' for policy reform following the Latin American debt crisis.[1] 'Poverty' appears once in the 5,806-word document. Some 30 years later, it is difficult to imagine the same being true of any attempt to summarise a set of policy instruments needed to

---

How to cite this book chapter:

Francisco, H. G. Ferreira (2025) 'Is there a 'new consensus' on inequality?', in: Besley, Tim, Bucelli, Irene and Velasco, Andrés (eds) *The London Consensus: Economic Principles for the 21st Century*, London: LSE Press, pp. 313–350 https://doi.org/10.31389/lsepress.tlc.j

address current problems, in Latin America or anywhere else. Indeed, in the present attempt 'to build a *London Consensus* around which new ideas can coalesce, and which can become a 'user's guide' for leaders and policy makers [...]'[2] an entire chapter – one of only 16 – was commissioned on the topic.

The 1980s probably marked the nadir of attention to distributional issues in both mainstream economics and development policy. The pressing global issues of the day were quintessentially macroeconomic: how to adjust to the dramatic terms of trade shocks arising from the oil price shocks of 1973 and 1979, and the subsequent stagflation in richer countries and debt crises in poorer ones. In the United States and the United Kingdom, Ronald Reagan and Margaret Thatcher held sway. The (first?) Cold War was approaching its conclusion, and inequality had been a concern identified squarely with the losing side. There were individual exceptions in the Western mainstream, of course, but the broad 'consensuses' of the day decidedly did not include a preoccupation with inequality.

This began to change gradually in the 1990s,[3] but it was the Global Financial Crisis of 2007–09 and the rise of the 'Occupy' movements in the US that changed the discourse in the leading Anglophone countries, which, for better or worse, largely set the intellectual and policy agendas in economics. Popular books by leading mainstream economists became major bestsellers.[4] The leading International Financial Institutions, which had played a major role in shaping the Washington Consensus, also incorporated inequality into their discourse: the World Bank's *World Development Report 2006* highlighted the extent and costs of inequality and argued that it was a drag on development. A decade later, the International Monetary Fund (IMF) agreed.[5]

Does any of this mean that there is a new consensus on inequality that could now be summarised, be it in London or elsewhere? In what follows, I briefly examine some of what we now know about the nature, levels, and trends in inequality (section I); the current thinking on whether it matters at all (section II); and some prominent ideas on policy responses (section III). I argue that there is a rising, if as yet incomplete, consensus that inequality matters and that it is a legitimate concern for analysts and policymakers alike. Perhaps surprisingly, there is actually no consensus on many of the basic facts about inequality, largely because different data sources tell different stories and are seldom easy to combine.

In the policy space, I briefly describe three broad policy domains with documented potential in reducing inequalities: pre-distribution (investing in children and youth before they enter the labour market); market regulation (with applications in the product, labour, and capital markets); and redistribution (taxing richer people to redistribute cash or opportunities to poorer ones). I argue that policies in all these areas have important roles to play, and probably more is needed in most countries. But I also suggest that, when one contemplates the depth and intergenerational durability of deprivation around the world, even this rich menu seems vastly inadequate, and that more research and innovation is needed to find truly transformational interventions.

II. The nature, levels and changes in inequality

One thing there is broad agreement on is that inequality is neither a unique nor a unidimensional concept. While most of the discussion focuses on inequality of incomes, there is also inequality in wealth; in educational achievements; and in health outcomes. There are inequalities in political power and participation; in agency and social recognition; and in opportunities for future achievement. These multiple inequalities are interconnected in complex ways, and matter for different reasons. While it is impossible to do justice to that entire landscape here, below are some basic facts on which there is broad agreement – and some issues on which there are not. Specifically, I list three points on which I argue there is a measure of consensus, and two areas where the facts themselves remain contested.

First, there is broad agreement that, with rare exceptions, inequalities in income and wealth are judged to be high in all but a handful of countries. Figure 10.1, drawn from the World Bank's World Development Indicators as captured in 2023, shows the income shares of the richest and poorest deciles of the distribution of income (or consumptions expenditure) for the 50 countries for which data was available.[6] The column of numbers to the right of the country names presents the ratio of one to the other, ranging from 4.7–4.9 in Armenia, Belarus, and Slovenia to 46.4 in Colombia.

Analogous measures for wealth distribution are even more extreme. In a study of 15 advanced economies using data from the Luxembourg Wealth Study, Pfeffer and Waitkus report top 5% net wealth shares ranging from 23% (in Slovakia) to 70% (in the US).[7] The corresponding Gini coefficients[8] are 0.49 and 0.90. The median wealth share was 39%, for Luxembourg, with a Gini of 0.66.

Second, income and wealth inequality do not come alone. They are associated with pronounced inequalities in other life domains, such as education and health. Perhaps the most prominent such association is the so-called wealth gradient of health, which depicts associations between better health outcomes and higher income or wealth. In 1980, for example, the life expectancy of men in the top 5% of the US family income distribution was 25% greater than for those in the bottom 5%.[9] In Latin America, infant mortality is strongly associated with household wealth across various countries.[10]

Educational outcomes are also associated with family background. In 2018, the OECD's Programme of International Student Assessment (PISA) published comparable test results for 15-year-olds from 79 countries. The scores are standardised so that distributions have a mean of 500 and a standard deviation of 100 (for the OECD). In the PISA 2018 dataset, the difference in mathematics test scores between children with at least one parent who completed tertiary education and for children for whom neither parent had completed at least upper secondary school was as high as 79 in Korea, 74 in Peru, 73 in Chile, and 66 in the US.[11]

Figure 10.1: Top and bottom decile income shares for 50 countries in 2020

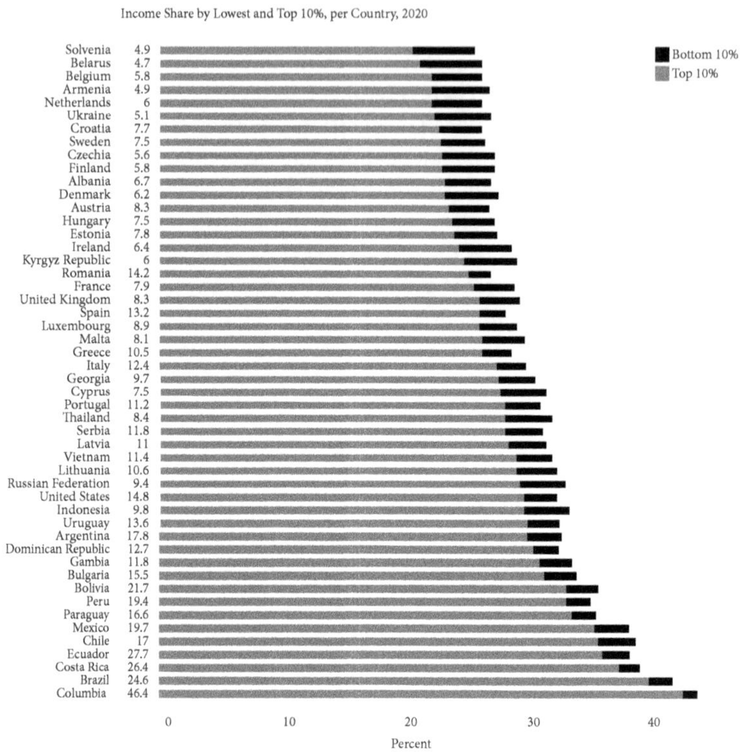

Source: databank.worldbank.org/source/world-development-indicators. Data reproduced from World Bank under a CC BY 4.0 licence.

Less tangible but equally important dimensions of a person's agency and wellbeing are also unequally distributed and correlated with economic status. This is easiest to document for measures of political power and activity, such as voting behaviour. In the United States, voter turnout is strongly associated with family income: in the 2016 presidential election, for example, turnout was 48% for those living in households with annual incomes less than US$5,000 and 86% for those earning more than US$150,000, with the relationship largely monotonic in between.[12] When additional sources of political power, such as the ability to contribute to campaign finance, are taken into account, the association between political and economic power becomes even greater.

Third, it is also widely accepted that some inequalities are more salient than others, such as those between men and women, across different racial groups, or different caste or religious groups. Gender inequalities remain pervasive, although not always in the ways one expects. Across most – if not all – countries, men continue to command a wage premium over women, both unconditionally and conditionally on observed characteristics. In the richer economies of the West, this remains true despite remarkable progress in recent decades, and appears to be increasingly explained by child penalties.[13] In education, on the other hand, the picture is considerably more mixed. In most rich countries – and in many others – access to and completion of tertiary education are now considerably higher for women than for men, and this reflects superior achievement by females in secondary schools as well. This is true in general, despite the fact that boys and men remain overrepresented in science, technology, engineering, and mathematics subjects.[14] Racial inequalities also abound, particularly but not exclusively in countries that experienced long histories of slavery, such as the US, Brazil, or Haiti. As with the broader societal inequalities discussed above, this is true not only for wages and incomes, but also in terms of educational attainment, health outcomes, political participation, incarceration rates, etc. These between-group – or horizontal – inequalities are important because membership in these groups is salient in the formation of individual identity.

Let us now turn to two areas where there is less agreement, and certainly no consensus. Perhaps surprisingly, the first of these concerns the exact levels of income inequality in almost any country. Although I argued earlier that

Figure 10.2: Income share of top 1%, WID vs WIID, by country

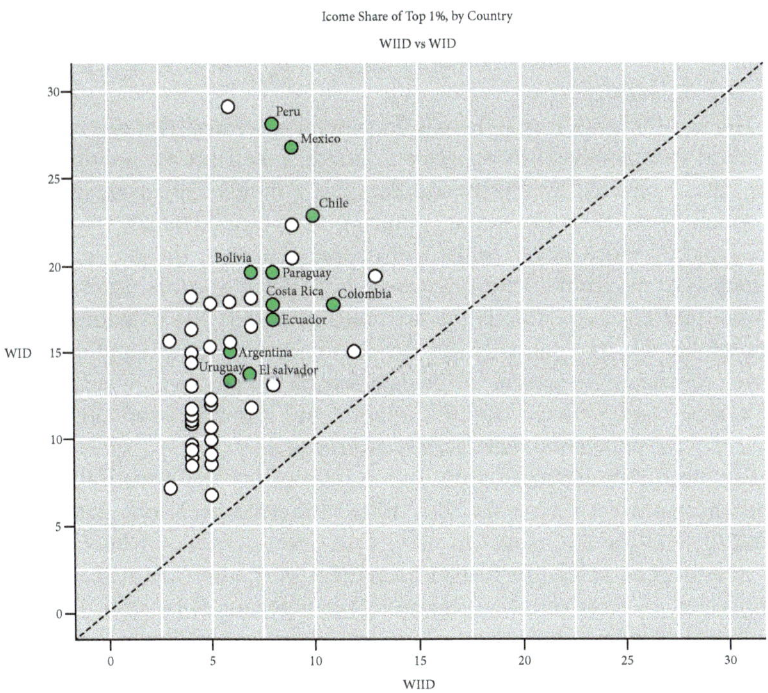

Source: author's elaboration from: World Income Inequality Database (WIID), World Institute for Development Economics Research at the United Nations University (UNU-WIDER) and World Inequality Database (WID), World Inequality Lab (WIL) at the Paris School of Economics.[15]

there is broad agreement that these levels are high, it turns out that different authors and institutions will report different – and sometimes substantially different – indicators of inequality for the same country–year combinations. To illustrate these stark differences, Figure 10.2 plots the income share of the richest 1% of the population for 53 countries in 2020. On the horizontal axis is the share reported in the World Income Inequality Database (WIID) of United Nations University World Institute for Development Economics Research (UNU-WIDER) (in their preferred 'WIID companion' series) while the vertical axis captures the share reported by the WID of the World Inequality Lab at the Paris School of Economics. These are all the countries for which data were available in both series. Green circles denote Latin American countries.

There is a clear and systematic pattern of lower shares for the richest 1% from the WIID than from the WID. The average share of the top 1% reported in the WIID is 5.9, whereas in the WID it is 14.3. For Peru, the WIID sees the top 1% earning 8% of total income, whereas the WID sees the same group earning 28%. These dramatic differences are due largely to the sources from which the original data is obtained. Whereas most of the observations in the WIID come from household surveys of one kind or another, most of the data reported by the WID comes from administrative tax data, although some of it is for tax data combined with survey data. Most importantly, most of the WID data attempts to further incorporate income imputations to match national account aggregates.

The key challenge is that there is no general agreement that one source or method is unambiguously superior to another. Reliance on administrative tax data, pioneered by Piketty and Saez has a number of advantages: (i) it is much better than surveys at capturing very high incomes; (ii) datasets are typically much larger; and (iii) in some countries, the data goes back a long way, permitting long time coverage.[16] But it also has disadvantages: (i) the unit of observation is the tax unit rather than the individual or the household, which are usually the more economically meaningful units; (ii) fewer covariates are present in the data, which is a problem for many kinds of analysis; and, perhaps most importantly, (iii) it is only informative of the subset of the population that declares income taxes.

For many rich countries, with well-developed tax and statistical systems with near-universal coverage, this third disadvantage is not particularly binding, and the advantages of fiscal data over surveys may outweigh the disadvantages – at least in pure measurement work where covariates are less important. In most countries, however, tax reporting is far from universal and highly selective. Across Latin America, Africa, and developing economies in Asia, informal sectors are large, often employing more workers than the formal, tax-paying sector. In these countries, fiscal data alone cannot provide a representative picture of the income distribution or measures of inequality.

Recognising this, researchers have sought to combine information from tax and survey data in order to deliver a more integrated and comprehensive picture.[17] This is ingenious and important work, but it is far from assumption-free. Inequality estimates thus generated come with substantial uncertainty, which is difficult to quantify. This uncertainty only grows when researchers seek to impute income so that survey aggregates (using expansion factors) match those of either the household account or the national income estimates from the system of national accounts, as additional assumptions must then inevitably be made to distribute incomes that are not observationally attached to any household. To be clear, both the expanded use of tax data and attempts to construct distributional national accounts are important innovations that have transformed the field of inequality measurement over the last two decades or so. But, for most countries and certainly those in the developing world, they have not yet reached a point where one can be completely confident of the summary inequality estimates that they generate. On the other hand, these innovations have highlighted serious shortcomings of standard household surveys, particularly on the measurement of top incomes. The result, in these countries, is one of increased uncertainty: We now know that we probably underestimate inequality by looking only at surveys, but may or may not overestimate it through the various incremental assumptions made when combining survey and other kinds of data. The result is a world of 'inequality bands', where it is tempting to take survey-based estimates as lower-bounds, and Distributional National Accounts guidelines-based estimates as (plausible) 'upper bounds', with 'true' inequality somewhere in between.

There is a second, rather unrelated, reason for uncertainty about the actual levels of inequality in our societies, namely the persistent neglect of intra-household inequality in most reported statistics. The reason for this neglect is clear: most household surveys and administrative data sources contain information on individual incomes and/or aggregate household consumption, but information on individually disaggregated consumption is exceedingly rare, leading to the frequent assumption of perfect sharing within households. Although that assumption underpins virtually all national-level statistics mentioned previously, when tested, it has been found to be entirely inadequate. Using one of those rare surveys that collect individual-level information – in this case on food intake in the Philippines – Haddad and Kanbur found that ignoring intra-household differences could lead to underestimates of overall inequality by as much as 30%.[18] Using a collective household model, Lise and Seitz find that overall inequality in the UK could be underestimated by between 25% and 50% if inequality within households is ignored.[19] These are large differences and their frequent omission from the public debate adds to our uncertainty about the true levels of inequality.

A second area where there is perhaps less agreement than meets the eye is the popular assessment of recent inequality trends, particularly within countries. There is, of course, a consensus that inequality has (massively) increased in the US, regardless of the data source. According to the latest WIID estimates (which themselves come from harmonised household survey data from the Luxembourg Income Study), the US Gini coefficient for pre-tax household per capita income has risen from 0.375 to 0.415 between 1987 and 2020. The latest estimates from the WID indicate an increase in the pre-tax national income share of the top 1% from 13% to 18% over the same period. The indicators differ – as would the levels for the same indicator – but the direction is clear. Agreement on trends also holds for most developed countries, whether inequality has recently been rising (as in the UK until 2000–02) or not (as in France). Indeed, if one takes an average across developed countries, inequality has generally been on the rise over the last 30–40 years.

The problem arises when, as often happens, the press and others generalise from this important, but small, set of countries to the rest of the world. Among developing countries, there is much greater heterogeneity in terms of inequality trends, particularly in the 2000s. Of course, inequality rose in a number of poor countries too, but on average, '[t]he available evidence suggests that [...] the levels of national income inequality in the developing world increased in the 1980s and 1990s, and declined in the 2000s'.[20] This was particularly true in Latin America,[21] but not exclusively: looking at 87 countries between 2000 and 2015 and using household survey-based inequality estimates, the World Bank found that inequality rose (by more than one percentage point) in 22 countries and fell (by more than one percentage point) in 45 countries.[22] You would not have guessed this nuanced picture from the inequality coverage in the US and UK press, which frequently extrapolates from the experience of their own countries to the world as a whole.[23]

III. Does inequality matter?

Does any of this matter, whether inequality is high or low, has gone up or down, is measured one way or another? After all, as recently as in 2004, in a much-quoted passage, Robert Lucas, a Nobel Laureate in Economics, wrote that '[of] all the tendencies that are harmful to sound economics, the most seductive, and in my opinion the most poisonous, is to focus on questions of distribution'.[24] It is in the answer to this question that the consensus has shifted the most since the 1980s. While there are always outliers, the dominant view in economics (and among policymakers) today is that excessive inequality is 'a bad thing', for at least three reasons.

First, inequality – and some forms of inequality in particular – matter directly and intrinsically to people. This became clear even to the most hard-nosed economists through the lab experiments on preferences for fairness, conducted by various authors in the 1990s and 2000s. The experiments used games, such as the Ultimatum Game, in which one player is randomly selected for the role of Proposer while a second is the Responder. The players are allocated a sum (S) of (real) money. The Proposer suggests a division of the sum, and the Responder can only accept or reject the offer. If the offer is rejected, both payoffs are zero. If it is accepted, the division is implemented and players keep the payoffs. Players do not know each other's real identities and are told that the game will not be repeated.

The single Nash equilibrium of this game, where each player's strategy is optimal given the decisions of other players, is for the Proposer to suggest a sum that is positive but as small as possible and for the Responder to accept. Yet, several studies found a substantial share of offers far above the minimal amount and, even more importantly, a number of low offers that were rejected. Such rejections are interpreted as 'altruistic punishment', whereby one player gives up real financial resources in order to punish the other for unfair behaviour.[25] Variations of this behaviour have been documented across both 'advanced' and 'traditional' societies.[26] Other studies found that certain animals, such as capuchin monkeys, are also prepared to forgo food that they would normally consume to protest against what they perceive as an unfair allocation by the experimenter.[27] Subsequent work that attempted to distinguish between different sources of inequality – such as luck versus effort – finds that people are likelier to offer compensation for inequalities for which people cannot be held responsible (such as a randomly allocated wage rate), as opposed to those they can control (such as the number of words typed correctly or how long somebody chooses to work on a task).[28]

Second, there is much evidence to suggest that inequality – when combined with various market imperfections – implies that some efficient investment projects are not undertaken, reducing allocative efficiency and, most likely, economic growth. While I would not claim that there is a 'consensus' about this relationship between inequality and investment, I argue that this is now the preponderant view in the profession. The original theoretical arguments go back to Stiglitz[29] and Loury.[30] In the 1990s, a set of influential papers included Galor and Zeira,[31] Banerjee and Newman,[32] and Aghion and Bolton.[33] Hsieh et al. provide convincing empirical support, arguing that the expansion of professional opportunities for women and ethnic minority men in the medical and legal professions in the US accounted for a substantial share of productivity growth in those industries.[34] The argument that inequality in productive opportunities is particularly detrimental to efficiency and growth is also consistent with the finding that inequality of opportunity was negatively associated with economic growth across 26 US states between 1970 and 2000.[35]

Third, there is growing acceptance that high inequality may also hurt a society by lowering the quality of its political institutions – which matter both intrinsically and because of the effects of those institutions on economic outcomes. The basic idea that high wealth inequality may lead to capture of the state and its institutions by a small elite, whose interests may not be aligned with those of the majority and who may, therefore, choose policies that are not optimal from the viewpoint of society more broadly, goes back all the way to Plato's *Republic*. In modern economics, theoretical models linking economic inequality, political inequality, and worse economic outcomes have been put forward by Alesina and Rodrik,[36] Persson and Tabellini,[37] Bénabou,[38] Bourguignon and Verdier,[39] and Acemoglu and Robinson,[40] to name a few. Economic historians, such as Engerman and Sokoloff,[41] have argued that this mechanism underpins the different political and economic outcomes of North and South America: initial factor endowments shaped different degrees of 'initial' wealth inequality, which in turn affected political institutions through, e.g., different paths for the expansion of education and the franchise, and these in turn led to different qualities of economic governance.

IV. What is to be done?

1. *The family curse*

To productively discuss 'policies that address inequality', it is essential first to understand the inequality-perpetuating forces that such policies are up against. After all, if people prefer fairness and inequality can hold societies back and prevent them from reaching their full economic potential, why is inequality nevertheless as ubiquitous as described in section I?

One answer, of course, is the aforementioned interaction between economic and political inequalities. The models discussed by Bourguignon and Verdier[42] and Bénabou[43] are all about stable high-inequality equilibria that will persist, despite the possibility of richer and more egalitarian alternatives. In essence, they are stories of power built on wealth, which are then used to choose policies that preserve such unequal distributions of wealth, even if the potential gains to others in alternative equilibria might exceed the losses of the powerful.

But there is another, possibly even deeper reason why inequality is so persistent or, in Charles Tilly's words, 'durable', and that is the remarkable degree to which families are able to transmit advantage – or disadvantage – across generations.[44] Parents bequeath their genes, so that high-ability parents may be more likely to beget high-ability children. Parents also bequeath human capital directly, during childhood and possibly beyond. At the critical early-childhood phase, between the ages of 0 and 5, families are either the sole or the principal source of human interaction for infants, providing both the nutritional and the stimulation inputs we now know are critical for future brain development.[45] The children of more educated parents develop larger vocabularies and other measures of cognitive skill development earlier than those of their less educated peers.[46]

Given the early advantage conferred upon children by better-off families, one might look to school as the great equaliser, from age 6 or 7 onward. Yet, school quality differs markedly within most countries and, once again, richer families are typically better able to send their children to the best schools, with the best teachers and peers, than poorer families. This mechanism can differ across settings: in the US, it operates through local financing for public schools and residential sorting, whereby house prices rise in the vicinity of better schools, concentrating richer families in the neighbourhood and further raising school funding from local property taxes.[47] In Latin America, it often operates through a Tiebout-style opting out of public services. Rich families are prepared to pay for better private schools, while poor families must send their children to lower-quality public schools. Richer and more powerful families are then less inclined to support higher taxes to fund better quality public education, and the cycle persists.[48]

The cumulative build-up of advantage in the production of both cognitive and socio-emotional skills throughout childhood and adolescence, life's primary formative phases, would likely be sufficient to ensure a great deal of intergenerational transmission of inequality. Yet, it is plainly not the only mechanism at work. Beyond the advantages that superior education affords in the labour market, parents are also able to intervene directly in the job matching process. Richer families will typically have high-value professional networks that facilitate recommendations, internships, and other entryways to employment. Corak and Piraino[49] even document the existence of intergenerational transmission of employers.

So far, this discussion has focused on human capital, perhaps the kind where the advantage of the rich might be expected to be lowest. Through inter-vivo transfers or bequests, the rich are able to transmit a great deal of their wealth to their children as well, perpetuating inequality in that domain. Finally, there is overwhelming evidence that families are often able to bequeath political power to their descendants too. This is true not only in the obvious case of (old and present-day) monarchies. It is also true of great political dynasties, such as the Kennedys or the Bushes in the US, or the Trudeaus in Canada. And the persistence is often very long-lived: Stone[50] documents that 31 presidents and 285 members of parliament in Costa Rica descend directly from Don Juan Vázquez de Coronado y Anaya, born in 1523, who was Spain's main conqueror of the part of Central America that is now Costa Rica.

These mutually reinforcing channels for intergenerational transmission of advantage can be summarised in rather dry intergenerational mobility or inequality of opportunity statistics. Using rank-based measures, Chetty et al.[51] found that a 10 percentile increase in parental income is associated with a 3.4 percentile increase in a child's adult income, a 6.7 percentage point increase in college attendance rates and a 3 percentage point reduction in teenage pregnancies (leading to birth) for girls. Brunori et al.[52] found that 59% of income inequality in a child's generation in Brazil can be accounted for by inherited circumstances such as race, gender, place of birth, and family background.

There is a multitude of such estimates for many countries, which I will not review here. Taken together, though, they point to two facts. First, the various mechanisms previously outlined have a clear and measurable effect on income and wealth: on average, the children of richer and more educated families are themselves richer and more educated than their peers. Second, when one looks at the pattern across a large number of countries, there is a strong positive association between income inequality (measured, say, by the Gini coefficient) and intergenerational persistence (measured, say, by the intergenerational income elasticity). This association, first documented by Corak[53] was named the 'Great Gatsby Curve'. Figure 10.3 – which is an update of a figure from Brunori et al.[54] is a version of such a curve. It plots the share of overall inequality accounted for by pre-determined circumstances, such as family, place of birth, and family background (on the y axis) against the cross-sectional Gini coefficient (on the x axis). Clearly, more unequal places also tend to have less intergenerational mobility and more inequality of opportunity.

2. *Against the family tide*

Those seeking to reduce inequality have often seen the un-equalising forces of 'the market' as the enemy.[55] In my view, the task is even harder: as argued above, the great inequality- reproducing institution is actually the family – simply because everyone wants to provide their children with the best possible opportunities, but families with greater resources do this more successfully than those with fewer resources. As a result, a broadly equal provision of public services to all families – while likely to be an improvement in much of the world – is not enough to fully eliminate the transmission and production of inequality.[56] If one is convinced by the arguments summarised in section II for trying to lower inequality, but remains mindful of potential equity-efficiency trade-offs, is there then a consensus on the policies to be pursued?

Figure 10.3: An inequality of opportunity 'Great Gatsby Curve'

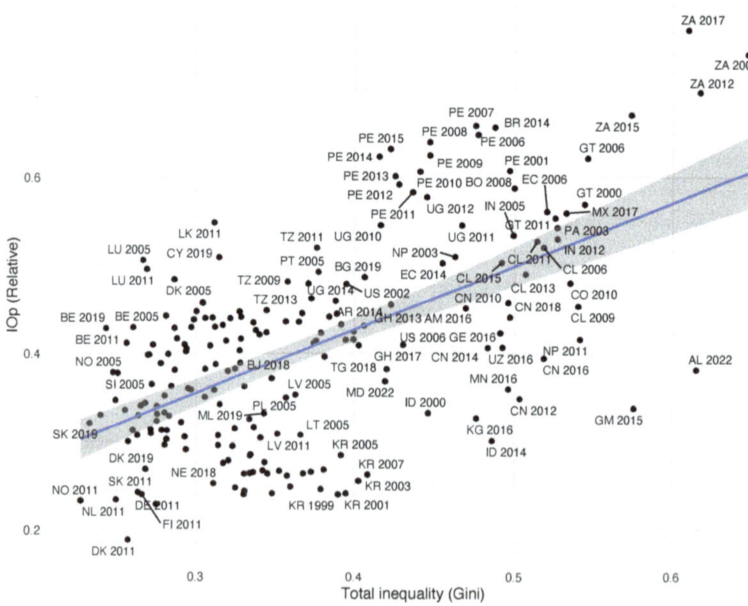

Source: author's elaboration from the Global Estimates of Opportunity and Mobility.

The array of potentially relevant policies is vast since, in general, any policy affecting some people's incomes differently from other's, will affect inequality. It would be impossible to do justice to all of the policy options here. In what follows, I try merely to provide a heroically brief summary of some of the current thinking about policies that might successfully reduce inequality, at low or no efficiency costs. In broad terms, and without any hope of being exhaustive, one could divide the policy space into three large sub-spaces: first, policies that affect people's earning potential before they enter the labour market; second, policies that affect the way product, labour, and capital markets work; and third, policies that redistribute incomes – or wealth – *ex-post*.

My reading is that there is a greater measure of consensus about the first group, often described as *'pre-distribution'* policies. Pre-distribution refers to public investments intended to enhance the human capital accumulation of the least advantaged – in part, to make up for the greater private investments of better off families discussed earlier. The need is not trivial: in a *Lancet* article, Grantham-McGregor et al.[57] estimate that over 200 million children in developing countries were not reaching their development potential, owing to four main causes; stunting, iron deficiency, iodine deficiency, and lack of cognitive and social-emotional stimulation. Pre-distribution policies focus largely – although not exclusively – on education, health, and early childhood development.

Early childhood interventions range from simple nutritional programmes, such as the INCAP programme in Guatemala in the 1970s[58] to centre-based stimulation and intellectual development programmes, such as the Perry Pre-School project in Ypsilanti, Michigan and the Abecedarian programme in North Carolina. Sometimes, they combine both a nutritional and a stimulation component, as in the well-known Jamaican Study of Grantham-McGregor et al.,[59] where stunted children were divided into one control and three treatment groups, all of which were benchmarked against a comparison group of normal-weight children at baseline. One of the treatment arms received only a nutritional supplement, while another one received a stimulation treatment. The third received both the supplement and the stimulation treatment. The latter group almost caught up with the comparison group in terms of cognitive measures 24 months later. Even more impressively, perhaps, their wages were significantly higher than those of the control group, and statistically indistinguishable from the comparison group, 20 years later.[60]

Beyond early childhood, there are innumerable pro-poor education interventions, from busing[61] in the US and school vouchers in Chile or Colombia, to targeted interventions to provide anything from school uniforms to computers and tablets to under-privileged students in Africa. In a comprehensive survey of such interventions in the developing world, Kremer et al. found that complementary input provision interventions had a mixed record at best, and were generally less successful than programmes aimed at improving teaching and pedagogical methods.[62] There is support for the primacy of teaching as the key input into the school-based learning production function from Chetty et al.[63] for the US, and Araujo et al.[64] for Ecuador. If there is an overarching policy message on pre-distribution policies, it is that they *can* work and, when they do, they can make a real difference to the children who benefit from them. However, as is often the case, they are not guaranteed to work, and the details of design and delivery matter a great deal.

There is rather less agreement about the second broad policy category, which consists of interventions directly intended to change the ways markets work.[65] Examples include antitrust regulation, policies towards unions, and minimum wages. Regulation aimed at preventing the excessive concentration of market power has always been important for a well-functioning market economy, but probably never as important as it is now. There is credible evidence that some of the increase in the capital shares of national income that we have observed in recent decades, particularly in developed countries[66] is attributable to a marked rise in pure economic profits arising from market power.[67] This reflects rising monopoly power, particularly among very large firms, which enables them to extract markups above the hypothetical competitive market price. De Loecker et al., for example, estimate that aggregate markups in the US have risen from 21% above marginal cost in 1980, to 61% more recently.[68]

In addition, it seems that market power by dominant firms is not restricted to product markets. Markdowns in wages have been detected increasingly frequently, just as have markups in prices. These markdowns manifest when wages fall below the marginal productivity of workers and reflect the presence of monopsony power in local labour markets. One way to offset such imbalances between large employers and individual employees is to permit or even support the work of labour unions, which have a longstanding record of success in defending the labour share in the economy as a whole.[69] Minimum wages can also support workers' bargaining power by providing an effective floor and, when set at an adequate level, can help reduce inequality. See Engbom and Moser for an analysis of the rise in Brazilian minimum wages between 1996 and 2018.[70]

Finally, the third broad category of anti-inequality policies concerns redistribution through the fiscal system, using taxes, subsidies, and transfers as the main instruments. Such policies have a long history, going back at least to Bismarck and Beveridge in the early- and mid-20th century, respectively.[71] Their fiscal reforms gave rise to the so-called 'welfare states' said to characterise much of Europe today. Countries so described generally have rates of income taxation sufficient to finance not only public schooling but also to subsidise (partially or fully) the costs of healthcare, provide basic old-age pensions, and a variety of other income supplements to those unable to derive sufficient income from employment, either temporarily or more permanently. In addition to public pensions and unemployment insurance, these programmes include child and family benefits, earned income tax credits, food stamps, subsidised school meals, and many others. It would be impossible to do them justice here, and indeed there is an entire chapter in this volume dedicated to the welfare state.[72]

When welfare states have been generous and also succeeded in providing high-quality public schooling, as in Finland and Scandinavia, they have certainly contributed to keeping inequality levels lower than elsewhere. Denmark, Finland, Iceland, and Norway form a cluster of countries closest to the origin in Figure 10.3, with income Gini coefficients below 0.3, and less than 20% of that associated with inequality of opportunity. Just 'North' of them in the graph, the Netherlands, the Czech Republic, Slovakia, and Slovenia, which have similar levels of income inequality but slightly higher measures of inequality of opportunity, also have actively redistributive fiscal systems.

Even in developing countries, where inequality is typically greater and redistribution typically weaker, social protection programmes have contributed to reductions in poverty and inequality, at least during the last 50 years or so.[73] The late 1980s saw the introduction of some non-contributory pension schemes with a greater reach into the informal sectors, such as the *Aposentadorias Rurais* in Brazil. In Asia, public work and food transfer schemes were more common. From the 1990s onward all of these were complemented, in many countries, by conditional cash transfer programmes, which were targeted to the poorest households and provided small payments on condition that children were enrolled in and attending school.[74] These targeted cash transfers often replaced subsidies on specific goods, such as basic foodstuffs or fuel, which were typically both less redistributive and more distortionary.

Obviously, this short discussion does not cover every policy within those three broad areas, nor are the three areas themselves exhaustive. Where should we list agricultural extension services aimed at raising the productivity of poor farmers? Or investments in public transport, which can create new job opportunities for people living far from city centres? Or the supply of solar energy to remote off-grid villages, where children study by candlelight and women collect firewood for cooking? The scope of policies that can help reduce inequality is truly vast, and highly context-dependent.

Nor is it necessarily the case that the policies discussed are those on which there is greater consensus. One can certainly find economists who would argue against minimum wages or any kind of government regulation. But these are at least some of the policies which are (a) potentially quite important, and (b) for which there is growing support in the modern scholarly literature. There is, as previously mentioned, broad agreement that pre-distribution policies, such as early childhood development programmes and investment in better teaching, are socially desirable. The sense is that the combination of the aggregate productivity gains obtained from the additional human capital formed among recipients with whatever value one places in greater equity is likely to outweigh any incentive costs incurred in raising and spending the cash that these programmes cost. There is also growing acceptance, at least in some quarters, that higher and more progressive taxation may have to be part of the solution in large parts of the world, including the US and most of Western Europe. Saez and Zucman,[75] among others, have noted that income tax rates are now considerably less progressive than they were in the 1950s, 1960s, and 1970s, and suggested that a return to higher rates would be advantageous.

Yet, when considering not only the egregious wealth at the top, but also the depth of deprivation at the bottom of the distribution, it is hard to avoid the sense that even this rich policy menu is inadequate. Among the (formerly) coal mining communities of the Appalachians or in the poorest counties of Mississippi (in the US), or among isolated indigenous communities in the Bolivian Andes or the Afro-descendants at Colombia's Pacific Coast, or along Nigeria's northern border with Niger, or among the Adivasi in Jharkhand, the poor and deprived number in the billions. By and large, their predecessors have been in similar positions for generations.

In these places, early childhood stimulation campaigns and new teaching methods financed by higher taxes on the rich will be welcome. But it seems unlikely that they will make a serious dent on the systematic deprivations – relative and absolute – that they live with, within a couple of generations. Unlike those who would fight inequality merely by bringing down the billionaires, those who would also like to see the world's poor raised to a life with dignity and opportunity must do more than raise taxes or train better teachers. There are some promising leads, in remote corners of the public policy space. There is evidence that the so-called Graduation or Ultra-Poor Programmes, sponsored by BRAC in Bangladesh and other poor countries, succeeded not only in raising the incomes of very poor rural self-employed people, but that they raised them above some critical poverty trap, enabling them to access more profitable occupations, so that the gains persisted many years after the programme transfers ended.[76]

More such transformational programmes are needed, but not only in isolated rural settings in the world's poorest countries – where some meaningful progress can arguably be achieved at a relatively low cost; they are needed everywhere else where poverty persists across generations. What would be the equivalent to Graduation programmes that might work in the *villas miseria* around Greater Buenos Aires; in the banlieues of Paris; in inner-city Baltimore; or the poor neighbourhoods of Jakarta or Manila? Even after we have succeeded in returning income tax rates to the levels of the 1960s, or in persuading voters that inheritance taxes are a good idea, how should we spend those resources to break the intergenerational transmission of disadvantage at the bottom of the distribution? I see no consensus – and too little research – on that.

Acknowledgements

I am grateful to Oriana Bandiera, Tim Besley, Raquel Fernández, Ravi Kanbur, Nora Lustig, Barbara Petrongolo, Andrés Velasco, and participants of a workshop at LSE for comments on an earlier draft. I am also grateful to Hillary Vipond for excellent research assistance. All remaining errors are my own.

Notes

1 Williamson (1989).

2 This is an excerpt from the letter by Besley and Velasco introducing the project to invited participants, in 2022.

3 Pfeffer and Waitkus (2021).

4 Stiglitz (2012; 2015); Piketty (2014).

5 World Bank (2005); Berg et al. (2018); Ostry et al. (2019).

6 I follow the common (mis)usage of the word decile, to mean 'tenth' of the distribution.

7 Pfeffer and Waitkus (2021).

8 The Gini coefficient is a common measure of inequality that is based on an (adjusted) aggregation of all income differences in society. It ranges from zero, when all incomes are the same, to one, when all the income is held by a single person.

9 Rogot et al. (1992); Deaton (2002).

10 As shown by Bancalari et al. (2023).

11 Fernández et al. (2023).

12 Akee (2019). See also, Leighley and Nagler (2014) for a more detailed analysis, which confirms that, despite closures in the race and gender voting gaps, the income gradient in voting in the US has persisted at least since the 1970s.

13 Kleven et al. (2019).

14 Reeves (2022).

15 WIID (2020); WID (2020).

16 Piketty (2003); Piketty and Saez (2003).

17 For instance, Blanchet et al. (2022).

18 Haddad and Kanbur (1990).

19 Lise and Seitz (2011).

[20] Gasparini and Alvaredo (2015).

[21] On the decline in inequality in Latin America in the 2000s, see López-Calva and Lustig (2010).

[22] It changed by less than one percentage point (up or down) in the remaining countries (World Bank, 2016).

[23] Nor would you necessarily guess from the broader public debate that global inequality – between all individuals in the world (but still assuming perfect sharing within households) – declined between the 1990s and at least the mid-2010s, although there is relatively little disagreement in the scholarly literature. We have no space to explore that literature in this paper but see Lakner and Milanovic (2016) for a prominent example.

[24] Lucas (2004).

[25] Hoffman et al. (1996); Fehr and Fischbacher (2003).

[26] Henrich et al. (2004).

[27] Brosnan and De Waal (2003).

[28] See Cappelen et al. (2010). There is also plenty of more observational, survey-based evidence that inequality and wellbeing are inversely related, e.g., Alesina et al. (2004) or Luttmer (2005). Yet another research strand argues that certain goods – such as houses or cars – are 'positional', in the sense that there are negative externalities from their consumption simply from direct comparisons (Frank, 2005). Under fairly weak assumptions, such negative externalities tend to rise with inequality.

[29] Stiglitz (1969).

[30] Loury (1981).

[31] Galor and Zeira (1993).

[32] Banerjee and Newman (1993).

[33] Aghion and Bolton (1997).

[34] Hsieh et al. (2019).

[35] Marrero and Rodriguez (2013).

[36] Alesina and Rodrik (1994).

[37] Persson and Tabellini (1994).

[38] Bénabou (2000).

[39] Bourguignon and Verdier (2000).

[40] Acemoglu and Robinson (2000).

41 Engerman and Sokoloff (1997).

42 Bourguignon and Verdier (2000).

43 Bénabou (2000).

44 See Tilly (1998). See also Haveman and Wolfe (1995) for a review of the various paths through which child achievements are influenced by parental characteristics.

45 See Cunha and Heckman (2007) for an influential model of the production function of human capital, which emphasises inter-temporal complementarities and the role of early childhood.

46 Paxson and Schady (2007).

47 Fernández and Rogerson (1998).

48 Ferreira (2001); De la O et al. (2023).

49 Corak and Piraino (2011).

50 Stone (1975).

51 Chetty et al. (2014b).

52 Brunori et al. (2013).

53 Corak (2013).

54 Brunori et al. (2013).

55 Markets can, of course, reinforce inequalities, e.g., by providing high and increasing (i.e., convex) returns to education, or higher financial returns to larger investments. They can also reduce inequalities, e.g., by eliminating monopoly profits through competition.

56 As shown by Heckman and Landersø's (2021) comparison of social mobility in Denmark and the United States.

57 Grantham-McGregor et al. (2007).

58 Maluccio et al. (2009).

59 Grantham-McGregor et al. (1991).

60 Gertler et al. (2014).

61 'Busing', in the United States, is the practice of transporting students to schools within or outside their local school districts as a means of rectifying racial segregation.

62 Kremer et al. (2013).

63 Chetty et al. (2014a).

64 Araujo et al. (2016).

[65] Of course, taxes, subsidies, and transfers also affect the ways markets work, but I will consider the bulk of taxation and redistribution under the third category below.

[66] Karabarbounis and Neiman (2013).

[67] Barkai (2020).

[68] De Loecker et al. (2020).

[69] Young and Zuleta (2018).

[70] Engbom and Moser (2022).

[71] Incipient precursors go back much further, and include, for example, the Poor Laws in England in the early 1600s.

[72] See Barr in this volume (Ch. 11).

[73] See, e.g., Ferreira and Robalino (2011) for the case of Latin America.

[74] The exact nature, extent, and enforcement of conditions varied across countries, but the school enrolment ones were the most common. See Fiszbein and Schady (2009).

[75] Saez and Zucman (2019).

[76] Bandiera et al. (2017).

References

Acemoglu, D. and Robinson, J. (2000) 'Why Did the West Extend the Franchise? Democracy, Inequality and Growth in Historical Perspective', *The Quarterly Journal of Economics*, 115: 1167–1199. https://doi.org/10.1162/003355300555042

Aghion, P. and Bolton, P. (1997) 'A Trickle-Down Theory of Growth and Development with Debt Overhang', *The Review of Economic Studies*, 64(2): 151–172. https://doi.org/10.2307/2971707

Akee, R. (2019) 'Voting and Income', *Econofact Blog Series*. https://econofact.org/voting-and-income

Alesina, A. and Rodrik, D. (1994) 'Distributive Politics and Economic Growth', *The Quarterly Journal of Economics*, 109: 465–490. https://doi.org/10.2307/2118470

Alesina, A., di Tella, R. and MacCulloch, R. (2004) 'Inequality and Happiness: Are Europeans and Americans Different?', *Journal of Public Economics*, 88: 2009–42.

Araujo, M. C., Carneiro, P., Cruz-Aguayo, Y. and Schady, N. (2016) 'Teacher Quality and Learning Outcomes in Kindergarten', *The Quarterly Journal of Economics*, 131(3): 1415–1453. https://doi.org/10.1093/qje/qjw016

Bancalari, A., Berlinski, S., Buitrago, G., Vera-Hernández, M. and De la Mata, D. (2023) 'Health Inequalities in Latin America', Processed, *Latin American and Caribbean Inequality Review*. https://doi.org/10.18235/0005243

Bandiera, O., Burgess, R., Das, N., Gulesci, S., Rasul, I. and Sulaiman, M. (2017) 'Labor Markets and Poverty in Village Economies', *The Quarterly Journal of Economics*: 811–870. https://doi.org/10.1093/qje/qjx003

Banerjee, A. and Newman, A. (1993) 'Occupational Choice and the Process of Development', *Journal of Political Economy*, 101: 274–298. https://doi.org/10.1086/261876

Barkai, S. (2020) 'Declining Labor and Capital Shares', *The Journal of Finance* LXXV(5): 2421–2463. https://doi.org/10.1111/jofi.12909

Barr, N. (2025) 'Welfare State', in Besley, T., Bucelli, I. and Velasco, A. (eds) *The London Consensus: Economic Principles for the 21st Century*, London: LSE Press.

Bénabou, R. (2000) 'Unequal Societies: Income Distribution and the Social Contract', *American Economic Review*, 90(1): 96–129. https://doi.org/10.1257/aer.90.1.96

Berg, A., Ostry, J., Tsangarides, C. and Yakhshilikov, Y. (2018) 'Redistribution, Inequality, and Growth: New Evidence', *Journal of Economic Growth*, 23: 259–305. https://doi.org/10.1007/s10887-017-9150-2

Blanchet, T., Flores, I. and Morgan, M. (2022) 'The Weight of the Rich: Improving Surveys Using Tax Data', *The Journal of Economic Inequality*, 20. https://doi.org/10.1007/s10888- 021-09509-3

Bourguignon, F. and Verdier, T. (2000) 'Oligarchy, Democracy, Inequality and Growth', *Journal of Development Economics*, 62(2): 285–313. https://doi.org/10.1016/S0304-3878(00)00086-9

Brosnan, S. F. and. De Waal, F. B. M. (2003) 'Monkeys Reject Unequal Pay' *Nature*, 25(6955): 297–99. https://doi.org/10.1038/nature01963

Brunori, P., Ferreira F. and Peragine, V. (2013) 'Inequality of Opportunity, Income Inequality, and Economic Mobility: Some International Comparisons', in Paus, E. (ed) *Getting Development Right*, New York: Palgrave Macmillan. https://doi.org/10.1596/1813-9450-6304

Cappelen, A., Sorensen, E. and Tungodden, B. (2010) 'Responsibility for What? Fairness and Individual Responsibility', *European Economic Review* 54(3): 429–441. https://doi.org/10.1016/j.euroecorev.2009.08.005

Chetty, R., Friedman, J. and Rockoff, J. (2014a) 'Measuring the Impact of Teachers II: Teacher Value-Added and Student Outcomes in Adulthood', *American Economic Review*, 104: 2633– 2679. https://doi.org/10.1257/aer.104.9.2633

Chetty, R., Hendren, N., Kline, P. and Saez, E. (2014b) 'Where Is the Land of Opportunity? The Geography of Intergenerational Mobility in the United States', *The Quarterly Journal of Economics* 129(4): 1553–1623. https://doi.org/10.1093/qje/qju022

Corak, M. (2013) 'Inequality from Generation to Generation: the United States in Comparison', in Rycroft, R. (ed) *The Economics of Inequality, Poverty and Discrimination in the 21st Century*, Santa Barbara, CA: ABC-CLIO.

Corak, M. and Piraino, P. (2011) 'The Intergenerational Transmission of Employers', *Journal of Labor Economics* 29(1): 37–68. https://doi.org/10.2139/ssrn.1575852

Cunha, F. and Heckman, J. (2007) 'The Technology of Skill Formation', *American Economic Review*, 97: 31–47. https://doi.org/10.3386/w12840

Deaton, A. (2002) 'Policy Implications of the Gradient of Health and Wealth', *Health Affairs* 21(2): 13–30. https://doi.org/10.1377/hlthaff.21.2.13

De la O, A., Rossel, C. and Manzi, P. (2023) 'The Political Economy of Opting Out from Public Services in Latin America', Processed, *Latin American and Caribbean Inequality Review*. https://doi.org/10.18235/0005329

De Loecker, J., Eeckhout, J. and Unger, G. (2020) 'The Rise of Market Power and the Macroeconomic Implications', *The Quarterly Journal of Economics*, 135(2): 561–644. https://doi.org/10.1093/qje/qjz041

Engbom, N. and Moser, C. (2022) 'Earnings Inequality and the Minimum Wage: Evidence from Brazil', *American Economic Review*, 112(12): 3803–3847. https://doi.org/10.1257/aer.20181506

Engerman, S. and Sokoloff, K. (1997) 'Factor Endowments, Institutions and Differential Paths of Growth among New World Economies: A view from Economic Historians of the United States', in Haber, S. H. (ed) *How Latin America Fell Behind*. Stanford, CA: Stanford University Press. https://doi.org/10.1515/9781503622500-013

Fehr, E. and Fischbacher, U. (2003) 'The Nature of Human Altruism', *Nature*, 425: 785–91. https://doi.org/10.1038/nature02043

Fernández, R. and Rogerson, R. (1998) Public Education and Income Distribution: A Dynamic Quantitative Evaluation of Education-Finance Reform', *American Economic Review*, 88(4): 813–833.

Fernández, R., Székely, M. and Acevedo, I. (2023) 'Education Inequalities in Latin America', Processed, *Latin American and Caribbean Inequality Review*. https://doi.org/10.2139/ssrn.4716691

Ferreira, F. (2001) Education for the Masses? The Interaction between Wealth, Educational and Political Inequalities', *Economics of Transition*, 9(2): 533–552. https://doi.org/10.1111/1468-0351.00087

Ferreira, F. and Robalino, D. (2011) 'Social Protection in Latin America: Achievements and Limitations', in Ocampo, J. A. and Ros, J. (eds) *Oxford Handbook on Latin American Economics,* Oxford: Oxford University Press. https://doi.org/10.1093/oxfordhb/9780199571048.013.0033

Fiszbein, A. and Schady, N. (2009) 'Conditional Cash Transfers: Reducing Present and Future Poverty', Washington, DC: World Bank. https://doi.org/10.1596/978-0-8213-7352-1

Frank, R. (2005) 'Positional Externalities Cause Large and Preventable Welfare Losses', *American Economic Review*, 95(2): 137–141. https://doi.org/10.1257/000282805774670392

Galor, O. and Zeira, J. (1993) 'Income Distribution and Macroeconomics', *The Review of Economic Studies*. 60: 35–52. https://doi.org/10.2307/2297811

Gasparini, L. and Alvaredo, F. (2015) 'Recent Trends in Inequality and Poverty in Developing Countries', in Atkinson, A. B. and Bourguignon, F. (eds) *Handbook of Income Distribution*, chapter 9: 697–805. North Holland. https://doi.org/10.1016/B978-0-444-59428-0.00010-2

Gertler, P., Heckman, J., Pinto, R., Zanolini, A., Vermeersch, C., Walker, S., Chang, S. M. and Grantham-McGregor, S. (2014) 'Labor Market Returns to an Early Childhood Stimulation Intervention in Jamaica', *Science*, 344 (6187): 998–1001. https://doi.org/10.1126/science.1251178

Grantham-McGregor, S. M., Powell, C., Walker, S. P. and Himes, J. H. (1991) 'Nutritional Supplementation, Psychosocial Stimulation, and Mental Development of Stunted Children: The Jamaican Study', *The Lancet*, 338(8758): 1-5. https://doi.org/10.1016/0140-6736(91)90001-6

Grantham-McGregor, S. M., Cheung, Y. B., Cueto, S., Glewwe, P., Richter, L. M. and Strupp, B. J. (2007) 'Developmental Potential in the First 5 Years for Children in Developing Countries', *The Lancet*, 369: 60–70. https://doi.org/10.1016/S0140-6736(07)60032-4

Haddad, L. and Kanbur, R. (1990) 'How Serious Is the Neglect of Intra-household Inequality?', *The Economic Journal*, 100: 866–881. https://doi.org/10.2307/2233663

Haveman, R. and Wolfe, B. (1995) 'The Determinants of Children's Attainments: A Review of Methods and Findings', *Journal of Economic Literature* 33(4): 1829–78.

Heckman, J. and Landersø, R. (2021) 'Lessons from Denmark about Inequality and Social Mobility', *NBER* Working Paper 28543. https://doi.org/10.3386/w28543

Henrich, J., Boyd, R., Bowles, S., Camerer, C., Fehr, E. and Gintis, H. (2004) *Foundations of Human Society: Economic Experiments and Ethnographic Evidence from Fifteen Small-scale Societies*. New York: Oxford University Press. https://doi.org/10.1093/0199262055.001.0001

Hoffman, E., McCabe, K. A. and Smith, V. L. (1996) 'On Expectations and Monetary Stakes in Ultimatum Games', *International Journal of Game Theory*, 25(3): 289–301. https://doi.org/10.1007/BF02425259

Hsieh, C., Hurst, E., Jones, C. and Klenow, P. (2019) 'The Allocation of Talent and U.S. Economic Growth', *Econometrica*, 87(5): 1439–1474. https://doi.org/10.3982/ECTA11427

Karabarbounis, L. and Neiman, B. (2013) 'The Global Decline of the Labor Share', *The Quarterly Journal of Economics*, 129: 61–103. https://doi.org/10.1093/qje/qjt032

Kleven, H., Landais, C. and Sogaard, J. (2019) 'Children and Gender Inequality: Evidence from Denmark', *American Economic Journal: Applied Economics*, 11(4): 181–209. https://doi.org/10.1257/app.2018 0010

Kremer, M., Brannen, C. and Glennerster, R. (2013) 'The Challenge of Education and Learning in the Developing World', *Science*, 340: 297–300. https://doi.org/10.1126/science.1235350

Lakner, C. and Milanovic, B. (2016) 'Global Income Distribution from the Fall of the Berlin Wall to the Great Recession', *World Bank Economic Review*, 30(2): 203–232. https://doi.org/10.1093/wber/lhv039

Leighley, J. and Nagler, J. (2014) *Who Votes Now? Demographics, Issues, Inequality, and Turnout in the United States*, Princeton, NJ: Princeton University Press. https://doi.org/10.1515/9781400848621

Lise, J. and Seitz, S. (2011) 'Consumption Inequality and Intrahousehold Allocations', *The Review of Economic Studies*, 78(1): 328–355. https://doi.org/10.1093/restud/rdq003

López-Calva, L. F., and Lustig, N. (2010) *Declining Inequality in Latin America: A Decade of Progress?* Washington, DC: Brookings Institution and UNDP.

Loury, G. (1981) 'Intergenerational Transfers and the Distribution of Earnings', *Econometrica*, 49(4): 843–867. https://doi.org/10.2307/1912506

Lucas, R. (2004) 'The Industrial Revolution: Past and Future', The Region: Annual Report of the Federal Reserve Bank of Minneapolis: 5–20. https://www.minneapolisfed.org/article/2004/the-industrial-revolution-past-and-future

Luttmer, E. F. P. (2005) 'Neighbors as Negatives: Relative Earnings and Wellbeing', *The Quarterly Journal of Economics*, 963–1002. https://doi.org/10.1093/qje/120.3.963

Maluccio, J., Hoddinott, J., Behrman, J. R., Martorell, R., Quisumbing, A., and Stein, A. (2009) 'The Impact of Improving Nutrition During Early Childhood on Education Among Guatemalan Adults', *The Economic Journal*, 119(April): 734–763. https://doi.org/10.1111/j.1468-0297.2009.02220.x

Marrero, G. and Rodriguez, J. G. (2013) 'Inequality of Opportunity and Growth', *Journal of Development Economics*, 104: 107–122. https://doi.org/10.1016/j.jdeveco.2013.05.004

Ostry, J., Loungani, P. and Berg, A. (2019) *Confronting Inequality: How Societies Can Choose Inclusive Growth,* New York: Columbia University Press. https://doi.org/10.7312/ostr17468

Paxson, C. and Schady, N. (2007) 'Cognitive Development among Young Children in Ecuador: The Roles of Wealth, Health, and Parenting', *The Journal of Human Resources*, 42(1): 49–84. https://doi.org/10.3368/jhr.XLII.1.49

Persson, T. and Tabellini, G. (1994) 'Is Inequality Harmful for Growth?', *American Economic Review*, 84(3): 600–621.

Pfeffer, F. and Waitkus, N. (2021) 'The Wealth Inequality of Nations', *American Sociological Review*, 86(4): 567–602. https://doi.org/10.1177/00031224211027800

Piketty, T. (2003) 'Income Inequality in France, 1901–1998', *Journal of Political Economy,* 111(5): 1004–1042. https://doi.org/10.1086/376955

Piketty, T. (2014) *Capital in the Twenty-First Century,* Cambridge, MA: Harvard University Press. https://doi.org/10.4159/9780674369542

Piketty, T. and Saez, E. (2003) 'Income Inequality in the United States, 1913–1998', *The Quarterly Journal of Economics*, 118(1): 1–41. https://doi.org/10.1162/00335530360535135

Reeves, R. (2022) *Of Men and Boys: Why the Modern Male Is Struggling, Why It Matters, and What to Do about It*, Washington, DC: Brookings Institution Press.

Rogot, E. Sorlie, P. D., Johnson, N. J. and Schmitt, C. (eds) (1992) 'A Mortality Study of 1.3 Million Persons by Demographic, Social, and Economic Factors: 1979–1985 Follow-up'. Bethesda, MD: National Institutes of Health.

Saez, E. and Zucman, G. (2019) *The Triumph of Injustice: How the Rich Dodge Taxes and How to Make Them Pay*, New York: W.W. Norton & Company.

Stiglitz, J. (1969) 'Distribution of Income and Wealth Among Individuals', *Econometrica*, 37(3): 382–397. https://doi.org/10.2307/1912788

Stiglitz, J. (2012) *The Price of Inequality: How Today's Divided Society Endangers Our Future*, New York: W.W. Norton & Company.

Stiglitz, J. (2015) *The Great Divide: Unequal Societies and What We Can Do about Them*, New York: W.W. Norton & Company.

Stone, S. (1975) 'La dinastía de los conquistadores: la crisis del poder en la Costa Rica contemporánea', San José: Editorial Universitaria Centroamericana.

Tilly, C. (1998) *Durable Inequality*, University of California Press. https://doi.org/10.1525/9780520924222

Williamson, J. (1989) 'What Washington Means by Policy Reform', in Williamson, J. (ed) *Latin American Readjustment: How much Has Happened*, Washington, DC: Peterson Institute for International Economics.

World Bank (2005) 'World Development Report 2006: Equity and Development', Washington, DC: The World Bank and Oxford University Press. https://doi.org/10.1596/978-0-8213-6249-5

World Bank (2016) 'Poverty and Shared Prosperity Report 2016: Taking on Inequality', Washington, DC: The World Bank. https://www.worldbank.org/en/publication/poverty-and-shared-prosperity-2016

World Inequality Database (WID) (2020) Database. World Inequality Lab, Paris School of Economics. https://wid.world/data/

World Income Inequality Database (WIID) (2020) Dataset. World Institute for Development Economics Research at the United Nations University (UNU-WIDER). https://www.wider.unu.edu/project/wiid-world-income-inequality-database

Young, A. and Zuleta, H. (2018) 'Do Unions Increase Labor Shares? Evidence from US Industry-Level Data', *Eastern Economic Journal*, 44: 558–575. https://doi.org/10.1057/s41302-016-0086-6

Response to Francisco H. G. Ferreira by Ravi Kanbur

Resisting the drift away from income redistribution

I welcome Francisco H. G. Ferreira's attempt to identify the elements of consensus in the inequality literature and discourse over the past three decades. I agree with him that inequality has gained salience and that the patterns and trends of inequality are more nuanced and open to empirical debate than might appear at first glance from headlines in popular media.[1;2;3]

There are two areas that I believe he could have emphasised more. First, the general neglect of intra-household inequality in our headline numbers on inequality and poverty. In my writings, I have argued that this neglect leads to a significant understatement of inequality and poverty (in the magnitude of about 25%) as well as an overstatement of the growth elasticity of poverty reduction (meaning the responsiveness of poverty to changes in economic growth). Furthermore, it is crucial to consider intra-household inequalities in policy discussions, such as the distributional impact of minimum wages and the targeting of anti-poverty expenditures.[4] Second, I have argued elsewhere that the philosophical and operational implications of the evolution of inequality at the global level, with a decline in between-country inequality greater than the rise in within-country inequality, also requires further exploration and reflection.[5;6]

The focus of my commentary here, however, is an assessment of what I consider a major feature of the discourse on inequality of the last three decades, namely a drift away from directly redistributing income through taxes and transfers towards what has been termed 'pre-distribution' in attempts to reduce the inequality of market incomes even before redistribution takes hold. Paradoxically, I see this emerging consensus in Ferreira's concluding paragraph on a lack of consensus:

> Even after we have succeeded in returning income tax rates to the levels of the 1960s, or in persuading voters that inheritance taxes are a good idea after all, how should we spend those resources to break the intergenerational transmission of disadvantage at the bottom of the distribution? I see no consensus – and too little research – on that.

In this summary of a lack of consensus, Ferreira is in effect reporting a consensus that has emerged, perhaps crept up on us somewhat unthinkingly. A consensus that direct and simple redistribution of income and wealth is not anywhere near enough to address what Ferreira says are 'multiple inequalities interconnected in complex ways'. This is a turn away from what we might call the 'social democratic consensus' of the first four post-war decades, that a direct and vigorous policy of income and wealth redistribution must be at the heart of any strategy for addressing inequalities.

The arguments of the last few decades have steadily eroded this consensus on income and wealth distribution, propelled primarily by anti-egalitarian sentiment, but I would also argue that strands of egalitarian thinking have aided and abetted, perhaps unwittingly, this shift in thinking. Incentive effects, multidimensionality, capability, equality of opportunity, pre-distribution, political economy, etc., are the terms that have frequently been used when arguing for the move away from direct redistribution of market outcomes in income and wealth to addressing inequalities through other means and in other dimensions. These terms, separately or in combination, are underpinned by three types of arguments: (1) that redistribution of income is associated with technical and economic issues, (2) that redistribution can be challenged on moral philosophical grounds, and (3) that political economy has turned against redistribution in favour of pre-distribution.

Before diving into each of these arguments, let me clarify the scope of what we are discussing here. First, what we are discussing is a continuum, not a strict division between two clear-cut policy options. We are observing a drift towards one end of the spectrum, namely a focus on pre-distribution solutions. Second, income redistribution refers not just to direct taxation, but to the full gamut of tax and transfer regimes. It is the combined effect of all of these policy options that we should be discussing. Third, there are indeed incentive effects with income redistribution that we need to take into account.

Let us start then with the argument that redistributing income may not be the best way of, well, redistributing income. Even if redistributing income is the objective, it may be better to aim for a more equal distribution of education, for example. The technical and economic challenges associated with income redistribution through taxes and transfers are well developed in economic analysis and well publicised in policy debates. The framework of the Nobel Prize-winning economic analysis of James Mirrlees, highlights the balance between incentive effects and redistribution in assessing the progressivity of taxation. Economists' focus on incentive effects of progressive taxation have influenced policy and politicians. Atkinson highlights this through an example from the United Kingdom:

> These research findings were factored into the influential review of UK taxation carried out by the Institute for Fiscal Studies and chaired by Sir James Mirrlees. The conclusion of the Mirrlees

> review in turn influenced the UK Chancellor of the Exchequer, George Osborne, when he announced that the top income tax rate in the UK would be cut from 50 percent to 45 percent beginning in 2013…[7]

Atkinson went on to counter the arguments for lowering the top income tax rate on technical grounds. It is worth noting that there is no comparable assessment or discussion of incentive effects on 'redistributing education'. These effects may be smaller or greater. We do not know because such issues have not been researched to the same extent and are not brought to the fore in the public discourse. The incentive effects of income redistribution remain the main focus of academic and popular debates on inequality.

Ferreira recognises and emphasises the role of informational problems and cultural factors in changing educational preferences of parents. However, these considerations are not brought into commensurate comparison with the informational and other challenges associated with income redistribution, which often receive greater attention and focus in policy discussions. Consider the following assessment from Ferreira:

> My reading is that there is a greater measure of consensus about the first group, often described as '*pre-distribution*' policies [than the second and third groups of policies, namely how product, labour and capital markets work, and policies that redistribute incomes – or wealth – *ex-post*]. Pre-distribution refers to public investments intended to enhance the human capital accumulation of the least advantaged – in part to make up for the greater private investments of better-off families…

The irony in this statement needs to be appreciated. The reason for the move from redistribution of income to pre-distribution of education, with its attendant difficulties of 'getting inside the family' as Ferreira highlights, is to make up for inequality of income, which is contributing to inequality of education. Why not just redistribute income?[8;9]

The second argument is that redistribution of income is not a legitimate normative target, at least not to the fullest extent. Income is the result of effort and choice and the portion of the inequality of this outcome, which is not the result of inequality of 'circumstances' or 'opportunity', should not be a target for policy. Over the last four decades even scholars from the egalitarian end of the political spectrum have developed this argument. Marxist philosopher Gerry Cohen lauded Ronald Dworkin for helping egalitarianism by 'incorporating within it the most powerful idea in the arsenal of the anti-egalitarian right: the idea of choice and responsibility'.[10] According to Roemer and Trannoy:

> In the welfarist tradition of social-choice theory, egalitarianism means equality of welfare or utility. Conservative critics of egalitarianism rightly protest that it is highly questionable that this kind of equality is ethically desirable, as it fails to hold persons responsible for their choices, or for their preferences…[11]

I, as many others, have criticised the opportunity perspective on conceptual, empirical, and policy grounds.[12] This is not the occasion to rehearse these arguments (see, for example, Sypnowich's work and the accompanying commentaries in the Boston Review symposium).[13] In my view, the steady march of the opportunity perspective partly explains the turn away from income redistribution in the post-Washington Consensus.

Finally, consider the third argument in favour of the drift away from focusing on income redistribution – that it is supported by the population at large and thus by politicians. This argument from analysts like Claude Fischer and Leah Gordon is stated and then countered by Sypnowich as follows:

> ….Claude Fischer and to a lesser degree Leah Gordon, reflecting on the inhospitable American scene past and present, provide sobering counsel that a focus on outcomes could be political suicide. Given the popular appeal of ideas like merit, private property, and social mobility, it is only prudent for egalitarians to adopt modest goals and focus on equality of opportunity…In my view, if we heed the realists' advice, we risk capitulating to a grudging outlook that is unwilling to remedy disadvantage that, though ostensibly the result of free choices, is mired in unchosen and unjust social conditions.[14;15;16]

It is not clear to what extent and in what precise sense the public supports or does not support equality of outcomes. Hufe et al. argue that evidence supports interventions to redress extreme outcomes like poverty.[17] Kanbur and Levy contend that the social acceptability of tax and transfer schemes is a subtle and nuanced matter, contingent upon various contextual factors and timing.[18] But the fact remains that conceding the case for income redistribution on these grounds right from the outset diminishes the negotiating power of egalitarians in the rough and tumble of policy and political discourse.

Let me conclude by saying that the drift away from income redistribution identified by Francisco H. G. Ferreira, which is definitely part of the current consensus, needs to be challenged. I very much hope that it will not remain, even unthinkingly, as part of any new consensus to replace the Washington Consensus.

Notes

[1] Kanbur (2019).

[2] Kanbur et al. (2021).

[3] Kanbur and Sumner (2012).

[4] Kanbur (2018b).

[5] Kanbur (2019).

[6] Kanbur (2018a).

[7] Atkinson (2015).

[8] Haaparanta et al. (2022).

[9] Tuomala et al. (2022).

[10] Cohen (1989).

[11] Roemer and Trannoy (2016).

[12] Hufe et al. (2022).

[13] Sypnowich (2023b).

[14] Sypnowich (2023a).

[15] Fischer (2023).

[16] Gordon (2023).

[17] Hufe et al. (2022).

[18] Kanbur and Levy (2022).

References

Atkinson, A. B. (2015) *Inequality: What Can Be Done?*, Cambridge, MA and London, England: Harvard University Press. https://doi.org/10.4159/9780674287013

Cohen, G. A. (1989) 'On the Currency of Egalitarian Justice', *Ethics,* 99(4): 906–944. https://doi.org/10.1086/293126

Fischer, C. S. (2023) 'Public Opinion Doesn't Support Equal Outcomes', https://www.bostonreview.net/forum_response/the-american-way/

Gordon, L. (2023) 'History Shows the Risks of a Focus on Outcomes', *Boston Review*. https://www.bostonreview.net/forum_response/equality-of-results-revisited/

Haaparanta, P., Kanbur, R., Paukkeri, T., Pirttilä, J. and Tuomala, M. (2022) 'Promoting Education Under Distortionary Taxation: Equality of Opportunity Versus Welfarism', *Journal of Economic Inequality*, 20: 281–297. https://doi.org/10.1007/s10888-021-09492-9

Hufe, P., Kanbur, R. and Peichl, A. (2022) 'Measuring Unfair Inequality: Reconciling Equality of Opportunity and Freedom from Poverty', *Review of Economic Studies*, 89(6): 3345–3380. https://doi.org/10.1093/restud/rdab101

Kanbur, R. (2018a) 'Citizenship, Migration and Opportunity', *Journal of Human Development and Capabilities*, 18(4): 429–441. https://doi.org/10.1080/19452829.2017.1349088

Kanbur, R. (2018b) 'Intrahousehold Inequality and Overall Inequality', in Ocampo, J. A. and Stiglitz J. E. (eds), *The Welfare State Revisited*, Columbia University Press. https://doi.org/10.7312/ocam18544-009

Kanbur, R. (2019) 'Inequality in a Global Perspective', *Oxford Review of Economic Policy*, 35(3): 431–444. https://doi.org/10.1093/oxrep/grz010

Kanbur, R. and Levy, S. (2022) 'Social Acceptability of Tax and Transfer Schemes', *LSE Public Policy Review*, 2(4): 3, 1–10. https://doi.org/10.31389/lseppr.66

Kanbur, R. and Sumner, A. (2012) 'Poor Countries or Poor People? Development Assistance and the New Geography of Global Poverty', *Journal of International Development*, 24(6): 686–95. https://doi.org/10.1002/jid.2861

Kanbur, R., Wang, Y. and Zhang, X. (2021) 'The Great Chinese Inequality Turnaround', *Journal of Comparative Economics*, 49(2): 467–482. https://doi.org/10.1016/j.jce.2020.10.001

Roemer, J. and Trannoy, A. (2016) 'Equality of Opportunity', in Atkinson, A. and Bourguignon, F. (eds), *Handbook of Income Distribution*, 2A, Amsterdam: Elsevier North-Holland. https://doi.org/10.1016/B978-0-444-59428-0.00005-9

Sypnowich, C. (2023a) 'Equality Matters', *Boston Review*. https://www.bostonreview.net/forum_response/equality-matters/

Sypnowich, C. (2023b) 'Is Equal Opportunity Enough?', *Boston Review*. https://www.bostonreview.net/forum/is-equal-opportunity-enough/

Tuomala, M., Pirttilä, J., Kanbur, R., Paukkeri, T. and Haaparanta, P. (2022) 'Pre-Distribution Requires Redistribution', CEPR, VoxEU. [14 Dec] https://cepr.org/voxeu/columns/pre-distribution-requires-redistribution

Response to Francisco H. G. Ferreira by Nora Lustig

The mistakes that should not be repeated: what can we learn from the Washington Consensus on the inequality front?

The conception and application of the Washington Consensus policies took place in a highly unequal context.[1] The debt crisis that precipitated their emergence stemmed from both the over-lending practices of European and US banks and the over-borrowing of many countries in the developing world. Yet, the borrowing countries bore the brunt of the costs. By controlling access to resources, the governments in rich countries controlled the process. They used their leverage in multilateral organisations – the IMF and the World Bank in particular – to put pressure on debtor countries to generate fiscal and foreign exchange surpluses that were large enough to ensure servicing of their debt, even if this often happened at the expense of the wellbeing of the general population in developing countries, especially among the poor.

Governments in rich countries also used this leverage to make debtor countries implement market-oriented reforms that would presumably result in more efficient productive systems and higher growth rates in the longer run. These policies were part and parcel of the IMF stabilisation packages and the World Bank structural adjustment loans. During the 1980s at least 40 countries had IMF stabilisation programmes each year. Most of them were in Latin America and Sub-Saharan Africa. Access to loans was conditional on following the Washington Consensus policies, which asked countries for drastic devaluations of their currency, sharp reductions in their fiscal deficit, fast-paced trade liberalisation, deregulation of markets, and privatisation of state-owned companies. These policies were not necessarily wrong per se. Fiscal prudence and eliminating egregiously inefficient state interventions were desirable goals. In fact, failure to correct unsound macroeconomic policies proved to be very costly as well.

However, the conditions attached to stabilisation programmes often resulted in overadjustment. Sharp cuts on the fiscal front resulted in larger-than-expected recessions, which in turn led to higher fiscal deficits down the road, ultimately defeating the purpose of the initial austerity measures. The magnitude, speed, and zealousness with which fiscal deficits were forced to adjust, and the economies forced to open up to external competition, had lasting costs on the countries that implemented them. If the burden of the debt overhang had been shared more equally between lending and borrowing countries and market-oriented reforms had been introduced more gradually, the so-called lost decade of the 1980s – a period in which many countries especially in Latin America and Africa experienced sharp declines in living standards, leaving behind persistent scars – could have been avoided.

During the debt crisis, the IMF-led stabilisation programmes were largely insensitive to the social costs. The general view by governments in creditor countries, multilateral organisations, and mainstream academics (especially in the US and Europe) was that these costs were primarily the consequence of mismanagement within the borrowing countries, and not of the adjustment policies designed to fix the self-inflicted imbalances. Regardless, the multilateral organisations should have prioritised shielding the poor. They did not. As it has been well documented, poverty rates rose significantly in the affected countries.[2] The human costs, however, went beyond low-income groups. The human capital of the next generation was damaged.

In 'Adjustment with a Human Face', Richard Jolly, UNICEF's deputy executive director at the time, was among the most influential voices in the global arena to sound the alarm bells, pointing out the human costs in terms of unemployment, child malnutrition, and setbacks in education and health.[3] At the time, rising malnutrition was recorded in Bolivia, Brazil, Chile, Jamaica, the Philippines, Sri Lanka, and in ten African countries.[4] In Latin America, infant mortality rates improved at a slower pace than in the 1970s.[5] After improving systematically in the 1970s, the proportion of low-birthweight infants and undernourished children increased in Chile and infant and preschool mortality caused by nutritional deficiency rose in Mexico throughout the 1980s. School attendance and literacy also took a hit. In Mexico, the proportion of each graduating class that entered the subsequent educational level declined after 1982, particularly for junior high school and high school students. The percentage of children entering primary school out of the total number of children in the relevant age cohort declined. In Venezuela, the literacy rate for people aged 15 to 19 fell in the 1980s.[6]

The slowdown in educational attainment and rise in child malnutrition during the lost decade of the 1980s trapped children in poverty, exacerbated inequality of opportunities, and contributed to the rise in earnings inequality during the 1990s, when the supply of low-skilled workers grew relatively more than the demand for them.[7] Furthermore, to the extent that human capital contributes to economic growth, these setbacks in education, health, and nutrition affected overall welfare as well. But this is not the end of the story. In some countries the Washington Consensus policies were also linked to severe macroeconomic crises down the road. This was the case in Mexico, for example, where a botched privatisation of the banking system was one of the underlying causes of the economic crisis in 1995.[8]

Another disturbing fact is that safety nets were broadly absent from the 1980s stabilisation and structural adjustment programmes and, when implemented, they were (oddly) ill-conceived. While in the aftermath of the debt crisis there was a widespread perception that social investment funds had been created to cushion the impact of the stabilisation policies on the poor, a closer examination revealed that this was not the case. Even though social investment funds may have helped poor workers and communities, they were not designed to create employment opportunities for those hurt by the policies. For instance, when Bolivia created an emergency social fund in the 1980s, only 10% of the workers who benefited from the fund were ex-miners affected by privatisation. And this 10% represented just over 1% of all the miners that had been let go.[9]

The Washington Consensus exacerbated inequality because fiscal cuts did not exempt pro-poor spending or investment in human capital more broadly; compensatory safety nets were absent for the most part; trade liberalisation and other market-oriented reforms frequently resulted in higher demand for skilled workers; and in many countries privatisation of state-owned enterprises produced a new generation of powerful rent-seekers and new forms of crony capitalism.

The fundamentalist nature that characterised Washington-Consensus thinking in many quarters meant that more heterodox approaches to correcting macroeconomic disequilibria and fighting inflation were not given a fair chance for long. The next consensus should not be a consensus that is only crafted among the powerful. Rather, it should keep an open mind regarding which policies can be adopted and it should contemplate ways of protecting the poor and vulnerable in the face of shocks such as crises, natural disasters, and pandemics, as well as policy-induced shocks.

The green agenda is a case in point. Decarbonising societies requires changes in many areas from transportation to home energy use, industrial restructuring, electricity generation, dietary habits, land use regulations, and alternative energy uses. Many of these changes impose a cost or burden that is relatively higher for some groups in society than others, resulting in policies that have a positive impact on the environment, but that are distributionally regressive. Poorer people, for instance, spend a higher share of their income on home energy and tend to use dirtier fuels than richer households. This has an impact both on greenhouse gas emissions and on local air quality in terms of smog and acid rain. Fiscal policies, such as carbon taxes and the elimination or reduction of energy subsidies, have a disproportional impact on poorer households. The green agenda risks hurting the poor disproportionately if the costs of carbon-reducing policies, such as carbon taxes or eliminating electricity and fuel subsidies, are not accompanied by compensatory policies to protect the poor during the transition to cleaner energy.

Notes

[1] The term, Washington Consensus, was first used in 1989 by English economist John Williamson in the context of a conference on Latin American adjustment. See Irwin and Ward (2021). The conference proceedings were published as Williamson (1990).

[2] For Latin America see, for example, Lustig (1995) and Lustig (2000).

[3] Jolly (1991). See also Cornia et al. (1987).

[4] Stewart (1988).

[5] Lustig (2000).

[6] Lustig (2000).

[7] Lustig (1995).

[8] Lustig (1998).

[9] Newman et al. (1991).

References

Cornia, A., Jolly, R. and Steward, F. (1987) *Adjustment with a Human Face, Volumes 1 and 2*, Oxford: Oxford University Press.

Irwin, D. A. and Ward, O. (2021) 'What Is the "Washington Consensus?"', Realtime Economics Blog, Peterson Institute for International Economics. https://www.piie.com/blogs/realtime-economic-issues-watch/what-washington-consensus.

Jolly, R. (1991) 'Adjustment with a Human Face: A UNICEF Record and Perspective on the 1980s', *World Development*, 19(12): 1807–1821. https://doi.org/10.1016/0305-750X(91)90026-E

Lustig, N. (ed) (1995) *Coping with Austerity: Poverty and Inequality in Latin America*, Washington DC: Brookings Institution Press.

Lustig, N. (1998) *Mexico: The Remaking of an Economy*, Washington, DC: The Brookings Institution Press.

Lustig, N. (2000) 'Crises and the Poor: Socially Responsible Macroeconomics', *Economía: The Journal of the Latin American and Caribbean Economic Association*, 1(1), 1–45. Fall 2000. LACEA's Presidential Address. https://doi.org/10.1353/eco.2000.0009

Newman, J., Jorgensen, S. and Pradham, M. (1991) 'Workers' Benefits from Bolivia's Emergency Social Fund', Living Standards Measurement Study. Working Paper 77. Washington: World Bank. https://documents1.worldbank.org/curated/en/332861468740706175/pdf/multi-page.pdf

Stewart, F. (1988) 'Adjustment with a Human Face: The Role of Food Aid', *Food Policy*, 13(1): 18–26. https://doi.org/10.1016/0306-9192(88)90004-8

Williamson, J. (1990) 'What Washington Means by Policy Reform', Chapter 2 from Williamson, J. (ed) *Latin American Adjustment: How Much Has Happened?* Institute for International Economics.

11. Welfare state

Nicholas Barr

Debates about the roles of markets and government are often framed as a binary choice between two polar cases, and often in ideological terms. This chapter recognises a spectrum, ranging from markets with light regulation (weights and measures) to heavy regulation (pharmaceutical drugs). I argue that it is useful to analyse the types and extent of government interventions as a mosaic comprising multiple objectives, multiple ways in which governments can intervene, multiple reasons why markets, including insurance markets may fail, and why governments may fail.

Sections I and II outline the approach. Section III discusses social insurance, including unemployment insurance, medical insurance, and long-term care. Section IV considers pensions and section V outlines a view to the future. The final section offers the main conclusions.

Drawing on findings for which multiple Nobel prizes in economics have been awarded since 1995, the chapter contrasts with the Washington Consensus by suggesting analysis based on a fuller model than the simple competitive market equilibrium. The idea is not to offer a blueprint, but to show how the elements in Boxes 11.1–11.4 offer building blocks for thinking about appropriate interventions. The elements of the mosaic are neither a mechanistic template nor an invitation to random artistry. Instead, they establish a strategic logic for discussing options for intervention. Answers will depend on the good or service in question, on a country's economic and institutional capacity, its demography, and its politics and social attitudes.

How to cite this book chapter:

Barr, Nicholas (2025) 'Welfare state', in: Besley, Tim, Bucelli, Irene and Velasco, Andrés (eds) *The London Consensus: Economic Principles for the 21st Century*, London: LSE Press, pp. 351–390 https://doi.org/10.31389/lsepress.tlc.k

I. Introduction

I often start my course by asking students if they agree with two value judgements: (1) In a civilised society, everyone should have access to adequate nutrition (everyone's hands go up); (2) In a civilised society, everyone should have access to adequate healthcare (ditto). So why, I then ask, does the UK have a National Health Service (NHS), but not a National Food Service? Silence. More generally why, absent war or famine, do people buy food from supermarkets, market traders, and street stalls, with limited or no government intervention, whereas in almost all countries government has significant involvement in healthcare? This chapter explains why those outcomes are not accidental or mistaken, and for the most part not ideological (for fuller discussion see references for advanced countries[1;2], reforming post-communist countries[3] and developing economies[4]). This argument contrasts with the Washington Consensus which argues that: 'government is not the solution to our problem, government is the problem', an argument that implicitly assumes an idealised economic model.

> Most branches of science have special and limiting cases. In physics, there is zero gravity and a perfect vacuum; in engineering, zero friction. These cases provide benchmarks from which to judge what happens when these conditions are relaxed. But it would be useless to build machines or set up experiments by relying on an understanding of what happens only in these special states.[5]

Idealised models are useful for understanding the main driving forces in the economy, but are incomplete and therefore misleading as a basis for policy design. A car designed assuming zero friction would have no lubrication or cooling. A vehicle with a seized-up engine will not get to the shops, let alone to the end of an Amazon delivery round. The analysis in this chapter is based on a fuller model that encompasses ways in which markets can diverge from the theoretical archetype.

In short, the Washington Consensus implies that government intervention should be minimised. In contrast, in the London Consensus, the extent and type of state intervention should be optimised. This chapter presents a framework for choosing whether to intervene and, if so, in what form. Section II outlines the economic theory that underpins later policy discussion – theory that is essential to show that the conclusions for policy are not personal opinions, but rooted in the best of modern economic analysis. Subsequent sections discuss social insurance (including unemployment benefits, healthcare, and long-term care), pensions, and a view to the future. Section VI offers conclusions. This chapter does not discuss education explicitly, on which I refer to Pritchett (this volume) and other references.[6]

The approach of this chapter suggests some core conclusions:

- The welfare state exists not only to assist the poor, but also to cover areas that private markets cover badly or not at all.
- Consumer choice does not always work well, particularly for complex products like pensions and healthcare. In such cases, offering less choice can be a better design.
- Competition does not always produce efficient outcomes.
- Private actuarial insurance[7] is unable to cover some individual risks, including unemployment and important medical risks. Nor can actuarial insurance cover losses created by systemic uncertainties, such as the Great Financial Crisis of 2007-09 and the COVID-19 pandemic, accentuating the role of the state as insurer of last resort.
- The fuller model, supported by international experience, creates a strong case in both efficiency and equity terms for relying mainly on public finance of healthcare, though not necessarily public delivery.
- Changes in the nature of jobs, increased diversity of family types, and the speed of technological change all have implications for the design and finance of the welfare state.

II. Economic underpinnings

Good policy design starts by specifying objectives, of which two are central:

- Efficiency in the use of resources at a point in time (static efficiency), and in pursuit of sustainable economic growth (dynamic efficiency).
- Equity, including redistribution from richer to poorer (vertical equity) and assisting equal treatment of equals (horizonal equity).

Much of the discussion in this chapter is about efficiency because – paradoxically – it turns out that the answer to the efficiency question gives important guidance about how to pursue equity objectives.

While specific institutions vary widely, all advanced and middle-income countries have a welfare state of some sort, i.e., a system of income transfers, old-age pensions, and government involvement in the financing and/or provision of healthcare and education. Low-income countries generally have at least embryonic such institutions.

Government intervention, when it occurs, is of four generic types (Box 11.1).

Box 11.1: Types of government intervention

Regulation of *quality includes* hygiene laws relating to food and regulation of pharmaceutical drugs. Regulation of *quantity* includes mandatory school attendance and social-insurance contributions. *Price* regulation includes minimum wages and rent control.

Public finance involves subsidies or taxes applied to the *prices* of specific goods or to the *incomes* of individuals. Price subsidies can be partial (public housing) or total (free pharmaceutical drugs). Similarly, prices can be affected by a variety of taxes (e.g., on pollution or congestion). Income subsidies raise different issues, discussed shortly.

Public delivery: regulation and finance modify market outcomes but leave the basic mechanism intact. Alternatively, the state can produce goods and services itself, e.g., owning the capital (school buildings) and employing the labour (teachers).

The fundamental distinction between the previous two types of intervention – finance and delivery – is prominent in later discussion.

Income transfers can be tied to particular expenditures (education vouchers) or untied (old-age pensions).

As discussed below, governments intervene to address distributional concerns, assist economic efficiency, promote economic growth, and share risk.

1. *Addressing distributional concerns*

Poverty, although declining globally, remains high. Policy responses include redistributive taxes and transfers, and investment in people's health and skills. For present purposes, the issue is sufficiently well known not to require extended justification of the need for government action.[8] Alongside issues of poverty, equity is also concerned with inequality of income and wealth, which has widened in many countries, and with wider inequalities.[9] Intergenerational distribution embodied in social contracts has recently received more attention.[10] Inequality is further discussed in Ferreira's chapter in this volume and other literature.[11;12]

2. *Assisting economic efficiency*

Less well-realised than its equity role is government intervention to address ways in which markets can be inefficient (generically referred to as market failures). Such inefficiencies have been identified by the award of multiple

Nobel prizes over the past 30 years for research on the economics of information, behavioural economics, search frictions, incomplete contracts, and optimal taxation.

> The welfare state exists not only to protect the poor but because it does things that markets would do badly or not at all. Thus we would need a welfare state even if all poverty could somehow magically be eliminated. It follows that it is mistaken to seek to minimise the welfare state—rather, its scale and scope should be optimised.[13]

As a simple heuristic, Box 11.2 sets out the core conditions under which markets produce efficient outcomes (what economists call a 'first-best' economy).

Box 11.2: Properties of an idealised market

Well-functioning markets require a series of assumptions to hold:[14]

1. Perfect competition in production and distribution.
2. No externalities (e.g., no pollution or congestion), public goods or increasing returns to scale.
3. Well-informed buyers and sellers.
4. Frictionless economic activity, i.e., no search or transactions costs.
5. Rational economic behaviour, i.e., individuals seek to maximise their lifetime wellbeing.
6. Complete markets, e.g., the ability to buy insurance against unemployment or future inflation.
7. No distortionary taxation.

These characteristics apply reasonably well for many products, but can fail as outlined in the following points.

Imperfect competition, externalities, public goods, and increasing returns to scale violate assumptions 1 and 2. External benefits include the social benefits of education and medical interventions against infectious diseases, such as COVID-19 vaccinations. External costs ('the tragedy of the commons') manifest themselves, inter alia, through pollution (a health hazard) and global climate change.

Imperfect information violates assumptions 3 and 4. Buyers and sellers may be poorly informed about the quality and nature of goods or services (the topic of the Nobel Prize in 2001), for instance, about the quality of particular pharmaceutical drugs or a particular fund manager. Imperfect information can also occur for prices, including search theory (i.e., the impact on outcomes when economic activity faces frictions, such as time needed to gather information, the topic of the Nobel Prize in 2010).

Behaviour different from narrow economic rationality[15] violates assumption 5. Literature on behavioural economics (Nobel Prize 2002 and 2017) addresses this problem by drawing on insights from psychology and economics. Two aspects are particularly relevant:

- Bounded rationality questions whether, in the face of complexity, people know what choices will maximise their long-run wellbeing.
- Bounded-willpower arises where a person knows what they ought to do (lose weight, quit smoking), but does not do so.

Missing markets and incomplete contracts violate assumption 6 (Nobel Prize 2016). A missing market arises for pensions because private providers do not offer insurance against the inflation a worker will experience during their retirement. Incomplete contracts arise where aspects of the contract – particularly relating to quality – cannot be fully specified and/or effectively monitored, for example, the quality of teaching or hospital cleaning.

Distortionary taxation, which is necessary to finance redistribution, violates assumption 7. This issue is addressed in the literature on optimal taxation (Nobel Prize 1996). A tax causes distortions if it changes behaviour, for instance, the introduction of a window tax in England in 1696 led to smaller and fewer windows. A tax on earnings will generally affect labour supply, and a tax on interest income is likely to change savings behaviour. A core purpose of the welfare state is to provide poverty relief, which by definition requires redistribution from richer to poorer individuals or households. Thus, the taxes that finance the welfare state inevitably have some distortionary effects. Policy should not seek to minimise distortions, but instead, should aim to limit distortions to those that are necessary to achieve chosen distributional gains.

3. *Promoting economic growth*

The arguments about the centrality of physical infrastructure – roads, bridges, etc. – for economic growth are well known. Recently, there has been increasing awareness of the importance of human capital for inclusive growth. Improving access to healthcare and education adds to a country's stock of skills, and widening access improves opportunities for disadvantaged groups. Well-designed income transfers can assist growth, for instance, the ability to afford a healthy diet improves educational outcomes. Thus, a study by the International Monetary Fund concludes that: '...the combined direct and indirect effects of redistribution—including the growth effects of the resulting lower inequality—are on average pro-growth'.[16]

Studies of Latin America confirm the potential growth benefits of social policy for example, the positive impact of conditional cash transfers on health and education outcomes.[17]

3. *Sharing risk*

In some ways, risk sharing embraces the previous three rationales for intervention.

- Addressing distributional concerns can be regarded as risk sharing behind Rawls' 'Veil of ignorance'.[18]
- As discussed shortly, a second aspect is providing insurance against risks that are poorly covered by private insurance. As noted, governments also have a role as insurer of last resort, exemplified by responses to the COVID-19 pandemic.[19]
- Third, optimal risk sharing contributes to economic growth. Too much risk is bad; with no safety net, people will be reluctant to start a new business. Too little risk is also suboptimal; it can stifle entrepreneurial initiatives, exemplified by the communist economic system.

The simple model of insurance.[20] The business model behind insurance has an easy intuition. Suppose that 100 people are flying to a football match, each with a suitcase worth £500, and that on average 1% of suitcases are lost in transit. The expected loss is the value of the suitcase, L, times the probability, p, that the loss will occur. Thus, the insurer could collect 1% × £500 = £5 from each of the 100 people, i.e., a total of £500 – enough to reimburse the person whose suitcase was lost. Box 11.3 sets out the circumstances in which such an arrangement will work well.

Box 11.3: Properties of an idealised insurance market

Just like markets for goods and services generally, the simple model of insurance rests on a number of assumptions.

1. Probabilities are independent; the probability of the insured event happening to person A is independent of it happening to person B, e.g., having a car accident. In contrast, with systemic risks, if one person suffers a loss, so does everyone else, e.g., inflation.

2. The probability of the insured event occurring is less than 1; the condition can fail, e.g., insurers often do not want to cover patients with a pre-existing medical condition because the probability of the condition recurring is too close to 1.

3. Risk, not uncertainty: the distinction is fundamental. With risk, the probability of an event is known. With uncertainty, it is not,[21] for example, an event a long way in the future. If the probability of the insured event is unknown, the insurer cannot calculate a premium, making probability-based insurance difficult or impossible. A central conclusion is that actuarial insurance can cope with risk but not uncertainty.

4. No adverse selection: the problem arises if an individual knows that they are a bad risk, but can hide the extent of risk from the insurer (e.g., a potential health problem).

5. No moral hazard: the problem arises if the individual who buys insurance can costlessly influence either (a) the probability that the insured event will occur, or (b) the cost to the insurer.

The failure of one or more of these assumptions leads to inefficiencies, discussed in section III.

4. *Limitations of government*

Box 11.4 offers a brief summary of the qualities of effective government.

Box 11.4: Characteristics of an idealised government

Adequate capacity:

- Technical skills that are sufficiently advanced and available in sufficient quantity.
- Sufficient information on which to form policy.
- Adequate resources for financing good-quality public services.
- The ability to align decisions by legislators with actions by administrators.

Appropriate motivation:

- The desire and capacity to resist short-term political pressures in order to take a long-term view, including in situations where incurring political costs today brings benefits mainly in the future.

- An absence of corruption.

Governments may lack key skills or have limited information on which to base policy (e.g., an out-of-date census). Financing high-quality public services involves fiscal, institutional, technical, and political constraints. The tighter the constraints, the more limited the policy options. A clever policy design that exceeds a country's ability to implement it is bad policy design.

Additionally, the links between legislators' political choices and the actions taken by administrators are complex. When operating public agencies, bureaucrats may seek personal benefits (e.g., avoiding time-consuming reforms) because politicians cannot fully monitor their actions (a manifestation of incomplete contracts). Similarly, a government may have other motivations than the welfare of its citizens.

5. *From theory towards policy*

Market failure is not an automatic trigger for intervention. A potential market failure poses three key questions for policymakers:

- Can the market solve the problem itself, e.g., though online reviews?
- If not, would intervention improve matters? Intervention is justified only if cost effective, which depends on (a) the seriousness of market failure(s), (b) government's capacity and motivation, and (c) the relative importance given to efficiency, equity, and other objectives like individual freedom. For a libertarian, a heavy weight for individual freedom may dominate efficiency considerations.
- If intervention is contemplated, which of the interventions in Box 11.1 (regulation, finance, public production, or income transfers) or combination of interventions might improve efficiency?

6. *Wider applications*

Mainly private activities. Food broadly conforms with the assumptions in Box 11.2. Consumers generally know about balanced diets and prices, and the production and distribution of food is competitive. Food, however, does not conform perfectly. Consumers generally do not know how food is produced, nor about its ingredients, hence government imposes regulations about hygiene and labelling. The prevalence of obesity may create additional reasons for regulation and/or taxation, e.g., a sugar tax. Choice and market allocation of food, albeit imperfect, are more efficient than alternative options not least because of great diversity in consumer tastes. It is not surprising that there are no serious advocates of a national food service.

Clothing is less regulated than food because the costs of mistaken choices are lower. The exceptions, e.g., safety clothing and crash helmets, *are* regulated for precisely that reason.

Burglary and car insurance broadly comply with the conditions in Box 11.3; probabilities are independent, known, and less than 1. Bad risks (living in a high-crime area, accident-prone drivers) cannot hide the fact, and inspection of claims can guard against moral hazard.

Applying the same approach to areas such as banking and cars also point to the advantages of market allocation with regulation (a) to protect consumers, e.g., reserve requirements for banks and safety standards for cars, and (b) to ensure proper competition, e.g., anti-trust legislation.

Privatisation. In the 1980s, the UK government rightly privatised telecoms, airlines, and steel. These industries conform with the conditions outlined in Box 11.2 sufficiently well for market allocation with suitable regulation to work better than nationalisation. Other industries, e.g., railways, were privatised even though economic theory correctly predicted problems (in the case of railways the central problem is increasing returns to scale to the fixed cost of the track).

Under the Communist economic system most industries were state-owned, hence a substantial part of the reform agenda concerned large-scale privatisation, the issue being less whether to move to private ownership than the practical challenge of privatising large parts of the economy – banking, agricultures, most manufacturing – in a short time.

Activities with a major role for government. Other areas experience multiple market failures, examples below including unemployment benefits, the finance of healthcare, and pensions. Although all have some private elements, all are substantially public-sector activities.

7. *Financing the welfare state*

When designing policy within a budget constraint two issues are logically separate:

- What is the appropriate *structure* of activity – that is, what public/private mix? This question refers to earlier discussion about which activities are most efficiently privately funded and/or privately delivered.
- What should be the *scale* of government activity, i.e., what should be the size of public spending? The answer partly depends on taxable capacity and partly on political economy considerations: if there are two goods, food (produced privately) and education (produced

publicly), the scale of the public sector will depend in part on preferences between the two.

The distinction between structure and scale is important: a budgetary crisis is *not* a ground for privatisation, but rather a reason to consider the scale of government.

III. Social insurance

1. *The nature of social insurance*

While actuarial insurance covers some risks well, that does not mean that it can be applied uncritically. In a seminal article about medical insurance, Arrow wrote:

> I propose here the view that, when the market fails to achieve an optimal state, society will, to some extent at least, recognize the gap, and nonmarket social institutions will arise attempting to bridge it....[22]

Social insurance is one such institution, where private markets, for technical reasons, provide insurance inefficiently or not at all, and where inability to acquire insurance would create a damaging gap in social policy.

Social insurance differs from private insurance in two fundamental ways. Since membership is generally compulsory, good risks cannot opt out, thereby sidestepping the worst problems of adverse selection, and, consequently, premiums can be related to an individual's earnings rather than to individual risk.

Second, the contract is not fully specified. Thus, benefits and contributions can be changed by legislation, and so can respond to unforeseen events, such as the COVID-19 pandemic and to social changes (e.g., a pension for the surviving partner in an unmarried couple or in same-sex marriages). Unlike actuarial insurance, social insurance can address uncertainty as well as risk.

Thus, social insurance has two mutually reinforcing rationales: as a response to market failure and as a redistributive device. The Washington Consensus ignores the first.

2. *Unemployment insurance*

Unemployment can be high and long-term, with youth unemployment a particular problem in some countries, and underemployment in many low- and middle-income countries (LMICs).

Actuarial insurance is a bad fit for dealing with the unemployment risk.[23] A comparison with the conditions in Box 11.3 shows the contrast with the Washington Consensus:

Independent probabilities. Although private insurance may be able to cope with cyclical unemployment, it cannot address common shocks like mass unemployment in the 1930s or the COVID-19 pandemic.

Probability known and less than one. There is good data on unemployment rates. However, for some groups the probability of being unemployed may be too high for private insurance to be viable, e.g., low-skilled young people or some ethnic minorities.

Adverse selection. A hypothetical private insurer could ask about an applicant's employment history. However, verification is not always possible, not everyone has a previous work history, and individuals may have private information about potential future job loss.

Moral hazard arises because a worker may be able to influence the duration of unemployment. The literature on job search explains how taking time to find a new job can be efficient if it leads to a better match. The problem is that the optimal duration is unmeasurable. If a worker remains unemployed after six months, there are two potential explanations:

- The worker has tried hard to find a job, but failed – continuing unemployment is caused by a lack of jobs.
- The worker may not have looked very hard – continuing unemployment is partly by choice.

The first is an insurable risk; the second is not. The problem is that an insurer cannot tell which one applies. The same is true for publicly provided unemployment benefits, but governments have more tools at their disposal than a private insurer, e.g., requirements to undertake training and/or job search. The Danish 'flexicurity' model provides an example in an OECD context, where the private sector is able to hire and fire workers relatively easily, while the government provides workers with income support and training, hence the idea of 'protect workers, not jobs'.[24] An approximate analogue in LMICs is public works employment (e.g., working on a government road-building project), which makes it difficult for a person to receive benefits while continuing to work unofficially.

It is therefore no accident that there are no private unemployment insurance policies on offer. Benefits have to be financed via social insurance, taxation or a mix, alongside regulation such as a requirement to look for work or undertake training.

3. *Health and long-term care*

Medical spending is rising in the face of population growth and population ageing (increasing demand) and advances in medical technology (increasing what can be offered). Although insurance cover is good in OECD countries, with the major exception of the United States, there are frequently gaps in LMICs. It is necessary to consider medical care and medical insurance separately.[25]

The market for medical care. Since medical treatment is often complex, healthcare raises problems with consumer information (violating assumptions 3 and 4 in Box 11.2), bounded rationality (assumption 5) and incomplete contracts (assumption 6). Individuals often do not know what treatments are available or the pros and cons of different treatments. The patient's information often comes from the provider and some treatment (e.g., of a broken leg) is not repeated, so that what the patient learns may be of little future use.

Similar problems arise for pharmaceutical drugs: consumers may not know whether the product is suitable for their condition, safe, and of high quality – the latter two aspects are especially a problem in LMICs.

There are other areas (e.g., used cars) where the consumer depends on the supplier for information. With medical care, however, information is often complex, and a mistaken choice can have high costs in terms of future health. Sick patients may not have time to shop around for options (in contrast to a car repair), and may lack the information necessary to weigh one doctor's advice against another's.

The market for medical insurance. The purpose of insurance is to protect a person from the risk that a bad thing may happen, which the person cannot stop happening, and which, if it happens, is very expensive. Needing medical attention or long-term care at some point in the future is precisely such a risk. Again, the conditions in Box 11.3 draw out contrasts with the Washington Consensus:

Independent probabilities. This condition generally holds except during epidemics.

Probability less than one. This condition holds for ailments like appendicitis, but fails for chronic medical problems (e.g., diabetes) that arise before an insurance policy has been bought. This condition will also be violated as developments in genetic screening, by improving knowledge about future health problems, create more uninsurable conditions.[26]

Known probability. Although it is generally possible to estimate the relevant probabilities, problems arise for health problems a long time in the future.

Adverse selection. Akerlof's classic article asks why Americans over 65 cannot easily buy medical insurance, and concludes that:

> …as the price [of insurance] rises, the people who insure themselves will be those who are increasingly certain that they will need the insurance; for error in medical check-ups, doctors' sympathy with older patients and so on make it much easier for the applicant to assess the risks involved than the insurance company.[27]

Similarly, if workers know better than employers that they are likely to have high medical bills, firms providing good medical benefits will tend to attract workers with health problems.

At its simplest, adverse selection causes inefficiency because there is an incentive for the worst risks to buy insurance and for the best risks to opt out. Where the problem is serious, the market may fail entirely. A partial solution is to restrict the range of choice, for instance, making membership compulsory to prevent low risks from opting out.

Moral hazard. An insured person might take fewer precautions. In addition, some healthcare is a matter of choice. Generally, elective medical care is not well covered by voluntary insurance, which is not a problem for interventions like cosmetic surgery, but matters greatly for an event like pregnancy. Moral hazard can also arise if all costs are paid by the insurer, so that the provider is not constrained by the patient's ability to pay. This point is not new:

> That any sane nation, having observed that you could provide for the supply of bread by giving bakers a pecuniary interest in baking for you, should go on to give a surgeon a pecuniary interest in cutting off your leg, is enough to make one despair of political humanity.[28]

Figure 11.1 Life expectancy and health expenditure 1970–2022[29]

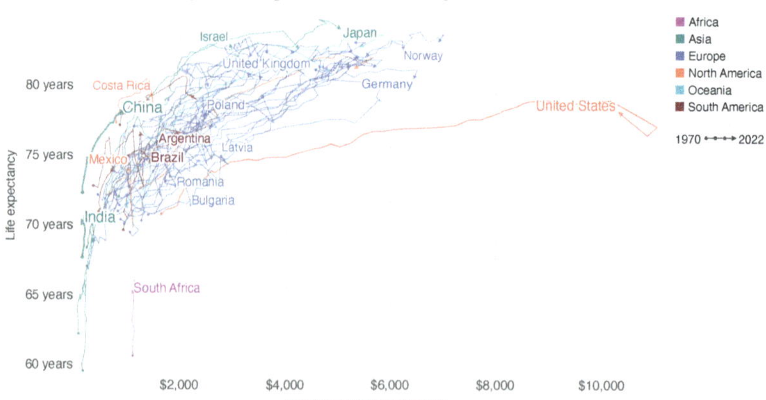

Source: Ortiz-Ospina and Roser (2017) – Our World in Data, published under a CC-BY licence.

One result of moral hazard is excessive medical treatment, as seen in the United States, where medical spending is considerably higher than in comparable countries, yet, with lower life expectancy. Figure 11.1 shows (a) that those outcomes are not a random deviation and (b) that the difference with other countries is increasing.

An array of policy options. What do these problems imply for policy design? Information failures justify regulation; the externality of treating communicable disease, coupled with incomplete insurance; may justify public finance; and bounded rationality and incomplete contracts create a strong (although not overriding) argument for a significant public role in allocating resources.

Earlier discussion highlighted the fundamental distinction between finance (how healthcare is paid for) and delivery (who provides the services). Economic theory and international experience point to two conclusions:

- There is a strong case in both efficiency and equity terms for relying mainly on public finance.
- There is no similarly strong conclusion about delivery: there are successful healthcare systems with mainly public production, mainly private production or with a mix.

Public finance in the UK and Nordic countries is organised through taxation. Finance can also be arranged through social insurance; although usually organised by government, it can be administered by the private sector acting as agents of the state, e.g., German sickness funds. The Stanford Plan, designed to address the problems of actuarial insurance within a mainly private system, offers a third approach.

The Stanford Plan. The design has five components:

1. The university contracts with a small number of insurers.
2. As a condition of joining Stanford's 'club', each insurer offers a policy with three elements: an agreed core package of services; premiums that can differ with family size, etc., but must be unrelated to a person's medical risk; and agreement to accept all applicants.
3. The university operates a redistributive pooling arrangement so that plans with a higher-than-average risk group receive transfers.
4. Employees can choose which plan to join.
5. The university contributes a fixed sum to each person's package, broadly equal to the cost of the cheapest approved plan.

Under 1 and 2, the university acts as agent for badly informed consumers, ensuring that the insurance policy contains no hidden snags. Element 2 ensures that nobody is excluded, and 2 and 5 ensure that everyone can afford cover. Element 3 protects insurers from adverse selection. Element 5 assists with cost containment since the individual faces the full marginal cost of joining a more expensive plan.

Thus, the arrangement is a genuine strategy,[30] but the interesting question is what sort of strategy? From a US perspective, this is a private plan with regulation and transfers carefully chosen to address the main market failures. But the arrangement can equally be described as decentralised social insurance, since nobody is excluded, and premiums are unrelated to individual risk.

What emerges is an important conclusion: that intervention on the scale necessary to address the many and major technical problems faced by actuarial medical insurance leads to an arrangement which, though it may be private, is de facto social insurance.

No single best system. In broad terms, countries have adopted one of three stylised strategies: mainly public finance plus public delivery (the UK, Sweden); mainly public finance plus mainly private delivery (Canada); or mainly private finance plus mainly private delivery, the US being the only OECD example. Each strategy has different but predictable strengths and stress points – there is no such thing as a perfect healthcare system.

Policy should avoid two errors. First, the failure to distinguish finance from delivery. The strong arguments against major reliance on private finance should not inappropriately spill over into debates about delivery, which can be successful in either public or private sectors. A second error is that the 'grass is always greener', i.e., 'public finance and provision has problems, therefore, the answer is private insurance'. It is essential to diagnose accurately whether a problem is the result of a faulty strategy, a fixable design problem, or bad implementation.

Long-term care. Many of the same issues arise for long-term care, i.e., residential or nursing care, or care in the home. As populations age, more people become incapable of caring for themselves, creating a rising demand for long-term care. As with medical care, the ability to buy insurance would raise wellbeing, but such insurance faces market failures similar to medical care. Perhaps the most serious is uncertainty: insurers do not know the probability that someone aged 35 today will need care in old age, nor the cost of that care.[31] As a result, private insurance, where it exists, is priced conservatively and includes many restrictions. As with medical insurance, market failures point to finance mainly from taxes and/or social insurance. Germany, for example, finances long-term care through an add-on to social insurance contributions.

IV. Pensions

Many countries face upward pressure on pension spending, often combined with significant pensioner poverty. The problem is partly caused by a pincer movement of rising life expectancy and lower birth rates. Without adjustments, projected trends in longevity, fertility, and economic growth suggest that pension spending in some countries could double as populations age.[32;33;34]

One response to longer life expectancy is a combination of later retirement and improved options for flexible retirement. An important response to lower fertility is to increase saving: declining fertility will lead to a smaller workforce than otherwise; a rational response is to make each individual in that smaller workforce more productive through increased investment in human and physical capital, and to that end, higher saving is important provided (and the proviso is crucial) that it leads to investment in productive assets.[35]

Problems with a voluntary approach. In the simple economic model, individuals save the optimal amount over their working life, retire at the optimal time, and convert an optimal fraction of their savings into an annuity (i.e., a monthly or annual pension payment for life).[36]

In the face of complexity, many individuals make bad choices (violating conditions 3 and 4 in Box 11.2) and behave in ways that are at odds with economic rationality (condition 5). Individuals often do not save enough, retire too early, delay choice or make no choice, choose an unsuitable advisor, and/or choose an unsuitable portfolio.[37]

It is a major policy error to assume widespread good financial literacy. An international survey of financial literacy asked respondents three questions.[38] The first was: 'If you have $100 in a bank account and the interest rate is 2%, how much money would you have in your account after five years: $102, less than $102, or more than $102?' Although the other two questions were equally simple, only about 35% of respondents in the US answered all three questions correctly, and in Japan and New Zealand only 25%. Additionally, financially literate people may not devote sufficient time and energy to making complex choices – we may think of these twin problems as 'Can't' and 'Won't'.

Problems also arise on the supply side because firms may exploit asymmetric information through high charges and/or biased advice. In addition, though often overlooked, administrative charges matter greatly: if a pension fund charges 1% of a worker's accumulation per year, over a full career the worker's accumulation (and hence their pension) will be 20% smaller than without the administrative charge.[39] That figure is not opinion but simple arithmetic fact.

These problems contrast sharply with the view that government involvement should be minimised.

Different responses to rising pension spending. Government responses include:

- Reducing benefits.
- Increasing contributions.
- Raising pension age over time.
- Reinforcing incentives to save, intended to increase national output.
- Adopting a mix of these policies.
- Leaving painful reform to later governments.

Ways of organising pensions. In a *funded plan*, pensions are paid out of a fund built over a period of years from member contributions. Thus, funding is a method of accumulating financial assets that are exchanged for goods at a later date. In a *Pay-As-You-Go* plan, pensions are paid out of current contributions, relying on the state's ability to tax the working population to pay the pensions of retired workers.

A separate dimension is the relationship between a worker's contribution history and their resulting benefit:

- In a *defined-contribution plan*, the worker accumulates a set of assets which finance their consumption in retirement, either by drawing down capital or through an annuity.
- In a *defined-benefit plan*, a worker's pension is based on a measure of length of service and the worker's final pay or some form of career average. The pension takes the form of an annuity covering the individual and frequently also their partner.

The relative merits of Pay-As-You-Go and funding have been debated widely, with questions about the right economic model, empirical magnitudes (e.g., life expectancy in 2050), the quality of a country's government, and the political economy of reform and ideology.[40]

No single best system.[41] Pensions have multiple objectives, including consumption smoothing (e.g., redistributing from ones younger to ones older self), insurance, poverty relief, and redistribution. The pursuit of those objectives faces a series of constraints, including fiscal capacity, institutional capacity, behavioural parameters, and the shape of the income distribution (a heavier lower tail increases the need for poverty relief).

There is no single best system because (a) across countries and over time policymakers will attach different relative weights to the objectives, and (b) the pattern of economic, institutional, and political constraints will differ. If the objectives differ and the constraints differ, the optimum will generally also differ.

Resulting policy directions. Pension systems vary considerably:

- Chile has a system which comprises a tax-financed non-contributory pension for low- and middle-income workers complemented by a defined-contribution plan organised through mandatory contributions to individual funded accounts from competing regulated providers. Australia has a similar strategy.
- Canada has a national partially-funded defined-benefit plan, supplemented by a tax-financed non-contributory pension for low- and middle-income workers.
- Sweden has a partially-funded national plan paying benefits that have a broadly actuarial relation to a worker's total contribution record (known as a notional defined-contribution plan[42]), supplemented by a tax-financed pension guarantee for low earners.
- The Netherlands has a non-contributory tax-financed pension along with fully-funded occupational plans.

The range of options widens with increasing fiscal and institutional capacity.[43] Thus, a low-income country may be able to offer only a small income-tested benefit, perhaps with subsidies of some basic commodities. With greater capacity, a country could offer a non-contributory pension or a simple Pay-As-You-Go contributory pension, though noting that the reach of a contributory plan is reduced by informal labour-market activity.

V. A view to the future

Labour market relations are changing.[44] In 1950, the main labour market connection in OECD countries was long-term, full-time, formal employment. Today, portfolio careers are common, including spells of employment, part-time employment, self-employment, unemployment, and time outside the paid labour force. In addition, precarious employment, like zero-hour contracts and work in the gig economy, are common.

Levy argues that employment-related social insurance contributions fail to cover all workers in OECD countries because labour market relations have become more diverse in the ways described in the previous paragraph, and in LMICs because they discourage formal employment.[45;46] Thus, there is some convergence between advanced economies with their historical archetype of formal employment, and developing economies with continuing informality and movements of workers between formal and informal work.

Levy therefore suggests a move away from employment-related finance. Clearly, benefits aimed at consumption smoothing, such as an earnings-related pension, require an explicit contribution. However, benefits whose primary aim is poverty relief (e.g., basic pensions) or insurance (e.g., healthcare) are better financed from broadly-based taxation.

Looking into the future, pension contributions could be based on consumption spending rather than income, for example, as a percentage top slice of a person's credit or debit card payments, as illustrated by an experimental programme in Mexico.[47;48]

VI. Some takeaways

1. *Analytical conclusions*

Conclusion 1: *The Washington Consensus adopts an over-simplified economic model.* As noted, a series of Nobel prizes since 1995 have been awarded for fundamental research published in the 1970s and 1980s that identifies multiple potential market failures. The Washington Consensus reflects economic theory that pre-dates those findings. The fuller economic model facilitates policy based more closely on the world as it is, not a world as some people might imagine it.

Conclusion 2: *Well-designed policy should be a thoughtfully assembled mosaic.* The elements of the mosaic in Boxes 11.1–11.4 are neither a mechanistic template nor an invitation to random artistry. Instead, they establish an agenda for discussion of options based on a strategic logic. The mosaic can show more complex patterns than a binary market-state classification. Food, although mostly provided by the market, is not a pure market activity, partly because of extensive regulation on hygiene and labelling. Equally, the UK National Health Service is not fully public; the service has never grown its own food for hospital patients, and it buys much of its equipment and pharmaceutical drugs from the private sector.

Within the elements of the mosaic, different intellectually honest people could reach different conclusions because of:

- Differences in ideology, for example, about the role of the state or about the relative weights accorded poverty relief and other objectives, e.g., a greater weight to poverty relief leads to increased distributional activity.
- Different views about the appropriate theory, e.g., how to model individual behaviour in the face of uncertainty.
- Different empirical views, for example about a country's fiscal or institutional capacity, or about the extent of market failures, e.g., whether financial education could empower better choices about pensions and retirement, or the extent to which compliance with contracts (e.g., for hospital cleaning) can be monitored and enforced.
- Different views about political economy, for example, whether citizens regard their pensions as safer based on a Pay-As-You-Go promise by government or as owners of capital.

Conclusion 3: *Ideology in the right place.* The distinction between the *objectives* of a policy and the *mechanisms* for achieving it, i.e., between the 'What' and the 'How', is central. The primary place for ideology is the choice of objectives, but, once objectives have been agreed, the choice of mechanism has a substantial technical dimension. Whether a particular good or service is provided publicly or privately should be based on which mechanism more nearly achieves the chosen objectives. Thus, market versus state provision should be regarded as a contingent matter rather than an item of dogma. Okun presents a classic defence of the mixed economy on broadly similar grounds.[49]

How, then, should we choose between different methods? If the assumptions in Boxes 11.2 and 11.3 broadly hold, private markets, with regulation where appropriate, are likely to be more efficient, and distributional objectives generally better served by *income* transfers.

In contrast, where the assumptions fail, intervention in the form of public production and allocation may increase efficiency, and equity can be enhanced by *in-kind* transfers, e.g., free or heavily subsidised education or healthcare.

The differences between the Washington Consensus and the London Consensus are clear. Instead of adopting a solution – market allocation – as the default, the approach is to adopt a process for deciding which mosaic pattern to use in pursuit of given objectives, ranging from largely unconstrained individual choice and market allocation (e.g., clothes) through models that constrain choice (e.g., by nudges, such as automatic enrolment in a pension plan), through models with mainly public finance (e.g., healthcare) and/or mainly public finance and public delivery (e.g., school education).

2. *Policy conclusions*

Conclusion 4: *Practical experience confirms the theory.* Institutions that ignore market imperfections face predictable problems. Private unemployment insurance is not offered. Private medical insurance faces predictable gaps in coverage and upward pressures on medical spending. Workers and pensioners often do not behave as predicted by the simple model. Instead, they often make poor choices about saving and retirement and respond sluggishly, if at all, to differences in administrative charges by different funds. An infamous example of policy based on the simple economic model was the ill-fated UK mini-budget of September 2022.[50] In contrast, institutions that go with the grain of economic theory, such as social insurance, have broadly stood the test of time. The literature on social investment fits into the fuller model as a discussion about the balance between spending on income transfers and investment in health and skills.[51;52;53]

Conclusion 5: *Insurance matters – arguably more than ever.* There are good reasons for thinking that government as the insurer of last resort will become increasingly important. Risk and uncertainty are likely to intensify: economic (another economic crisis), political (instability and war), environmental (accelerating effects of climate change), technical (artificial intelligence, nuclear safety) and social (the multiple effects of a changing age structure).[54;55] Critically, these are (a) mostly uncertainties and (b) are mostly systemic. Those twin problems reinforce the centrality of the welfare state – not only a device to address individual risk but also to protect against systemic uncertainties. Actuarial insurance cannot address problems like the 2008 economic crisis, COVID-19 and war in Europe in the 2020s.

Conclusion 6: *There are good but no perfect solutions*. Earlier discussion outlined cases where industries were rightly privatised, but they may still face problems as private firms. The same is true for activities that are rightly in the public sector. Social insurance covers risks where private policies would leave gaps, but publicly organised unemployment insurance faces similar problems of moral hazard as hypothetical private policies, but governments have greater powers to impose checks; and different strategies for healthcare will have different and predictable pressure points. The same is true for pension systems.

The conclusion that there are no perfect solutions is not mere logic chopping, but important for correct diagnosis and, hence, sound policy prescriptions. A common fallacy is that 'X does not work well, therefore the answer is Y'. That the UK National Health Service has imperfections does not automatically translate into an argument for privatisation. The issue for policy design is whether the strategy is sound. If so, the implication is to keep the strategy and work within it to improve outcomes either by fixing correctable design flaws or by improving implementation. It is important that the best does not become the enemy of the good. Only if the strategy is flawed, is there on that account a strong case for radical reform.

Conclusion 7: *A wider range of policy tools*. The mosaic of potential interventions that emerges from the fuller economic model offers a wider range of policy designs and types of intervention. Examples include recognition of:

- Less choice, e.g., of pension options, as a deliberate part of good design.
- Nudges such as automatic enrolment in a default pension plan, or simply for a cafeteria to have smaller plates.
- A greater role for quality assurance where (a) consumers are not well-enough informed to do their own quality assurance *and* (b) the costs of getting it wrong are high, for example, hospital cleaning.

It should now be clear why the UK has a National Health Service but not a National Food Service. Food, subject to some regulation, broadly conforms with the assumptions in Box 11.2. On the demand side, healthcare faces major problems of imperfect consumer information, and the supply side of the market for medical insurance fails badly to comply with the conditions in Box 11.3.

Thus, if we want to protect grandma against malnutrition, the efficiency arguments point to income transfers, with grandma using her pension to buy food in the same shops as the rest of us, at the same prices. In contrast, to ensure that grandma has good access to medical care, the efficiency arguments point to provision at a zero or below market price. Counterintuitively, the answer to the question of how best to pursue distributional objectives is given largely by the answer to the efficiency question.

Acknowledgements

I am grateful for helpful comments from Paul Johnson, Santiago Levy, participants at a symposium at the London School of Economics, and the editors. The views expressed and remaining errors are my responsibility.

Notes

1 Barr (2020).

2 Barr (2001).

3 Barr (2005).

4 Levy (2008).

5 Woolley (2014).

6 Barr (2020).

7 As explained more fully in section II, an actuarial insurance premium is based on (a) the probability that the individual buying insurance will experience the loss in question (e.g., a car accident), and (b) the size of the loss against which they are insuring.

8 Ravallion (2016).

9 UK Equalities Review (2007).

10 Shafik (2021).

11 Atkinson and Bourguignon (2015).

12 Lustig (2018).

13 Barr (2020).

14 Barr (2020).

15 Thaler (2015).

16 Ostry et al. (2014).

17 Stampini et al. (2023).

[18] Rawls (1971). The Veil of Ignorance is a hypothetical construct by the philosopher John Rawls in which rational individuals negotiate a just constitution for a country in which they will have to live, but without knowing who they will be (i.e., whether they will be a chief executive or a sharecropper).

[19] Velasco (2020).

[20] Barr (2020).

[21] Kay and King (2020).

[22] Arrow (1963).

[23] Barr (2020).

[24] OECD (2021).

[25] Barr (2020).

[26] Barr (2001).

[27] Akerlof (1970).

[28] Shaw (2011).

[29] Ortiz-Ospina and Roser (2017).

[30] This is not surprising, since Alain Enthoven, a Stanford faculty member and one of America's leading health economists, chaired the committee that designed the plan. For further details, see Stanford Medicine Health Care (2025).

[31] Barr (2010).

[32] Barr (2020).

[33] Barr and Bosch (forthcoming).

[34] Barr (2023).

[35] Barr (2021).

[36] For discussion of the analytical errors in applying a first-best approach to pensions see Barr and Diamond (2010); on limits to choice, see Barr (2022a).

[37] Barber and Odean (2013).

[38] Lusardi and Mitchell (2014).

[39] Barr and Diamond (2010), Box 7.2.

[40] Barr (2023); Orenstein (2011).

[41] Barr and Diamond (2010), Ch. 2.

[42] Barr and Diamond (2010), Ch. 2.

[43] Barr and Diamond (2009).

[44] Packard et al. (2019); or more briefly, Barr (2018).

[45] Levy (2008).

[46] Levy (2021).

[47] Hernández et al. (2020).

[48] Walker (2018).

[49] Okun (1975).

[50] Barr (2022b).

[51] Shafik (2021).

[52] Hemerijck (2013).

[53] Hemerijck (2017).

[54] OECD (2003).

[55] Reis and Velasco, chapter 6 in this volume.

References

Akerlof, G. A. (1970) 'The Market for "Lemons": Qualitative Uncertainty and the Market Mechanism', *The Quarterly Journal of Economics*, 84: 488–500. https://doi.org/10.2307/1879431

Arrow, K. F. (1963) 'Uncertainty and the Welfare Economics of Medical Care', *American Economic Review*, 53: 941–73.

Atkinson, A. B. and Bourguignon, F. (eds) (2015) *Handbook of Income Distribution*, Volume 2A–2B, North-Holland: Elsevier.

Barber, B. M. and Odean, T. (2013) 'The Behavior of Individual Investors', in Constantinides, G., Harris, M. and Stulz, R. (eds) *Handbook of the Economics of Finance*, Elsevier: 1533–1569. https://doi.org/10.1016/B978-0-44-459406-8.00022-6

Barr, N. (2001) *The Welfare State as Piggy Bank: Information, Risk, Uncertainty, and the Role of the State*, Oxford and New York: Oxford University Press. https://doi.org/10.1093/0199246599.001.0001

Barr, N. (ed) (2005) *Labor Markets and Social Policy in Central and Eastern Europe: The Accession and Beyond*, Washington, DC: The World Bank. https://openknowledge.worldbank.org/server/api/core/bitstreams/490f9f70-5063-52bb-8bfb-fedcd051e0f4/content

Barr, N. (2010) 'Long-term Care: A Suitable Case for Social Insurance', *Social Policy and Administration*, 44(4): 359–374. https://doi.org/10.1111/j.1467-9515.2010.00718.x

Barr, N. (2018) 'Shifting Tides', *Finance and Development*, 55(4): 16–19. https://doi.org/10.5089/9781484386194.022

Barr, N. (2020) *The Economics of the Welfare State*, 6th edn., Oxford and New York: Oxford University Press.

Barr, N. (2021) 'Pension Design and the Failed Economics of Squirrels', *LSE Public Policy Review*, 2(1): 5, 1–8. https://doi.org/10.31389/lseppr.40

Barr, N. (2022a) 'Pensions: How Much Choice?', CENIE International Centre on Ageing [21 April]. https://cenie.eu/en/pensions-how-much-choice

Barr, N. (2022b) 'Trussonomics for Dummies', *LSE Politics and Policy* [28 September]. https://blogs.lse.ac.uk/politicsandpolicy/trussonomics-for-dummies/

Barr, N. (2023) 'Individual Funded Pension Accounts and the World Bank: Evolving Views', *Social Insurance, Theory and Practice*, 158 (3): 63–75. https://doi.org/10.5604/01.3001.0053.8834

Barr, N. and Bosch, M. (forthcoming) 'Pensions in Low- and Middle-Income Countries', in Hanna, R. and Olken, B. (eds) *The Handbook of Social Protection: Evidence and New Directions for Low- and Middle-Income Countries*, Cambridge: MIT Press.

Barr, N. and Diamond, P. (2009) 'Reforming Pensions: Principles, Analytical Errors and Policy Directions, *International Social Security Review*, 62(2): 5–29. https://doi.org/10.1111/j.1468-246X.2009.01327.x

Barr, N. and Diamond, P. (2010) *Pension Reform: A Short Guide*, New York and Oxford: OUP. https://doi.org/10.1093/acprof:oso/9780195387728.001.0001

Hemerijck, A. (2013) *Changing Welfare States*, Oxford: Oxford University Press.

Hemerijck, A. (2017) *The Uses of Social Investment*, Oxford: Oxford University Press. https://doi.org/10.1093/oso/9780198790488.003.0035

Hernández, A., Galindo, F., López, J. and Salas, F. (2020) 'Saving with Gusto', *Journal of Applied Business and Economics*, 22(13). https://doi.org/10.33423/jabe.v22i13.3899

Kay, J. and King, M. (2020) *Radical Uncertainty: Decision-making for an Unknowable Future*, New York: W. W. Norton.

Levy, S. (2008) *Good Intentions, Bad Outcomes: Social Policy, Informality, and Economic Growth in Mexico*, Washington DC: The Brookings Institution.

Levy, S. (2021) 'Informality – Addressing the Achilles Heel of Social Protection in Latin America', WIDER Annual Lecture 23, UNU-WIDER. https://www.wider.unu.edu/publication/informality-%E2%80%93-addressing-achilles-heel-social-protection-latin-america

Lusardi, A. and Mitchell, O. S. (2014) 'The Economic Importance of Financial Literacy: Theory and Evidence', *Journal of Economic Literature*, 52(1): 5–44. https://doi.org/10.1257/jel.52.1.5

Lustig, N. (ed) (2018) *Commitment to Equity Handbook: Estimating the Impact of Fiscal Policy on Inequality and Poverty*, Washington, DC: The Brookings Institution.

Okun, A. M. (1975) *Equality and Efficiency: The Big Tradeoff*, Washington, DC: The Brookings Institution.

OECD (2003) *Emerging Risks in the 21st Century: An Agenda for Action*, Paris: OECD.

OECD (2021) *OECD Economic Surveys: Denmark*. OECD Publishing, Paris. https://www.oecd.org/content/dam/oecd/en/publications/reports/2021/12/oecd-economic-surveys-denmark-2021_76fa110a/86f7b2d9-en.pdf

Orenstein, M. A. (2011) 'Pension Privatization in Crisis: Death or Rebirth of a Global Policy Trend?', *International Social Security Review*, 64(3): 65–80. https://doi.org/10.1111/j.1468-246X.2011.01403.x

Ortiz-Ospina, E. and Roser, M. (2017) 'Healthcare Spending', Published online at Our World in Data. https://ourworldindata.org/financing-healthcare

Ostry J., Berg, A. and Tsangarides, C. G. (2014) *Redistribution, Inequality, and Growth*, Washington, DC: IMF. https://doi.org/10.5089/9781484352076.006

Packard, T., Gentilini, U., Grosh, M., O'Keefe, P., Palacios, R., Robalino, D. and Santos, I. (2019) Protecting All: Risk Sharing for a Diverse and Diversifying World of Work, Washington, DC: The World Bank. https://doi.org/10.1596/978-1-4648-1427-3

Ravallion, M. (2016) *The Economics of Poverty: History, Measurement, and Policy*, Oxford: Oxford University Press. https://doi.org/10.1093/acprof:oso/9780190212766.001.0001

Rawls, J. (1971) *A Theory of Justice*, Cambridge, MA: Belknap Press.

Reis, R. and Velasco, A. (2025) 'Fiscal Policy and Public Debt', in Besley, T., Bucelli, I. and Velasco, A. (eds) *The London Consensus: Economic Principles for the 21st Century*, London: LSE Press.

Shafik, M. (2021) *What We Owe Each Other: A New Social Contract*, London: The Bodley Head. https://doi.org/10.1515/9780691220277

Shaw, B. G. (2011) *The Doctor's Dilemma*, London: Constable.

Stampini, M., Medellín, N. and Ibarrarán, P. (2023) 'Cash Transfers, Poverty, and Inequality in Latin America and the Caribbean', III Working Papers (116). International Inequalities Institute, London School of Economics and Political Science, London, UK. https://doi.org/10.18235/0005235

Stanford Medicine Health Care (2025) *Benefits Guide 2025. Choose You, Live Better.* https://cdn.phenompeople.com/CareerConnectResources/SHCAUS/documents/2025SHCBenefitsGuide_NonRep_SEIUFINAL-1731683516891.pdf

Thaler, R. H. (2015) *Misbehaving: The Making of Behavioral Economics*, New York: W. W. Norton & Co.

UK Equalities Review (2007) *Fairness and Freedom: The Final Report of the Equalities Review*. https://justice.org.uk/equalities-review/#:~:text=The%20Equalities%20Review%20was%20set,the%20Commission%20for%20Equality%20and

Velasco, A. (2020) 'Are We All Keynesians Again?' CGTN Opinion [16 August]. https://news.cgtn.com/news/2020-08-26/Are-we-all-Keynesians-again--Tgxckqpv6U/index.html

Walker, O. (2018) 'How Millennials and Savings Apps are Making Asset Managers Wake up and Smell the Coffee', *Financial Times* [14 October]. https://www.ft.com/content/567f4684-8084-3f5b-82b0-9a150de7b3a6?desktop=true&segmentId=7c8f09b9-9b61-4fbb-9430-9208a9e233c8

Woolley, P. (2014) 'The Fallibility of the Efficient Market Theory: A New Paradigm', *CFA Institute Conference Proceedings Quarterly*, Second Quarter, 1–4. https://www.fmg.ac.uk/sites/default/files/2021-02/Woolley-CFA-April-2014-cp.v31.n2.6.pdf

Response to Nicholas Barr by Santiago Levy

Professor Barr provides an excellent review of the theoretical justifications for the welfare state, highlighting two central messages. First, contemporary economic theory strongly supports the need for a welfare state, yet its exact contours should depend on objectives and context, recognising that a uniform solution will not work across very diverse circumstances. Second, policy prescriptions should be based on specific objectives and the nature of the problem/market and on considerations of government incentives and administrative capabilities.

I largely concur with Barr's arguments. My value added in this comment is to focus on their implications for Latin America, while noting that my insights may be useful to other regions with similar characteristics.

I. No welfare in the Washington Consensus

Recall the 10 dictums of the Washington Consensus:[1]

1. Reduce national budget deficits.
2. Redirect spending from politically popular areas towards neglected fields with high economic returns.
3. Reform the tax system.
4. Liberalise the financial sector with the goal of market-determined interest rates.
5. Adopt a competitive single exchange rate.
6. Reduce trade restrictions.
7. Abolish barriers to foreign direct investment.
8. Privatise state-owned enterprises.
9. Abolish policies that restrict competition.
10. Provide secure, affordable property rights.

These dictums were inspired by the failures of Latin America during the 'lost decade', a period in the 1980s characterised by economic stagnation and debt crises in the region. They were mostly focused on issues of macroeconomic stabilisation, and international trade and foreign investment, while they said nothing about social insurance, pensions, inequality, or poverty. Certainly, there was no mention of a welfare state.

With the benefit of hindsight, it is clear that as a development model the Washington Consensus was incomplete and, ultimately, flawed. There was an expectation that macroeconomic stability combined with competitive product markets would lead to better functioning labour markets. Greater coverage of social insurance and reduced inequality would follow (aided by investments in human capital). As we now know, by-and-large countries in Latin America achieved macroeconomic stability and all of the countries in the region invested in human capital. Some opened to trade more than others, and a few achieved notable export success. However, few, if any at all, experienced socially inclusive growth (exhibit 1: Mexico).

II. The evolution of social protection in Latin America

Countries in Latin America began constructing their welfare states long before the Washington Consensus, in the 1920s and 1930s in South America, and in the 1940s and 1950s everywhere else in the region.[2] Throughout the region, the cornerstone of the welfare state was the 'Bismarckian model', made up of three components:

1. A bundle of pensions, health and other programmes like day care, housing, and labour training for salaried (or dependent) workers paid from an earmarked wage-based tax.
2. Protection against the loss of employment mostly through stringent firing conditions, supplemented by unemployment insurance in some cases.
3. Minimum wages, sometimes set relatively high in the wage distribution.

In the early 1990s, coverage of the Bismarckian model was far from universal. Though it varied across countries, for the region as a whole coverage was less than 50% of the labour force. Thus, in parallel to the implementation of the Washington Consensus, and very much linked to the pressures for greater redistribution associated with the transition to democracy, most countries expanded the coverage of social protection. However, expansion did not follow any over-arching view. It took place through a series of 'scheme-by-scheme' piecemeal additions of programmes on an ad-hoc basis, mostly through a mix of:

- Targeted income transfers to redistribute income to the poor, often through Conditional Cash Transfer programmes (a Latin American innovation), but sometimes through transfers in-kind.
- Parallel social insurance programmes, mostly for health and pensions, financed from general revenues, like income, trade and value-added taxes.

In practice, programme combinations and targeting criteria varied substantially, and the insurance and redistribution objectives were conflated. General principles, like the ones laid out in Barr's chapter as to when and how to intervene, were de facto set aside and superseded by a desire to increase the coverage of social protection to those excluded from the Bismarckian model, but an unwillingness to reform the underlying tax, labour, and social insurance regulations that limited its coverage.

Figure 11.2 provides a stylised description of the resulting welfare state for the 'typical' country in the region. The columns refer to the insurance objective and divide the working-age population between those covered by the Bismarckian model (A + B), commonly referred to as formal workers, and those receiving some form of insurance through parallel programmes; informally employed workers, the unemployed and those outside the labour force (C + D). In turn, the rows refer to the redistribution objective, with individuals divided by an exogenously determined poverty line. Those below it (B + D) receive income transfers from targeted programmes, sometimes with behavioural conditions (like in Conditional Cash Transfer programmes); those above it (A + C) do not.

Ignoring targeting errors, in this 'Latin American welfare state' everybody receives some social protection, although the scope of insurance provided to formal workers is wider as it includes coverage against disability, death, and loss of employment. The quality of protection is usually also better, although differences in health services between formal and informal workers or those who are unemployed or outside the labour force have narrowed, and in some countries like Colombia even disappeared.

Figure 11.2: A stylised description of the Latin American welfare state

Insurance

Redistribution		Formal	Informal + unemployed + out of labour force
	Non-poor	A	C
	Poor	B	D

A + B + C + D = working age population

Source: created by author.

Most countries in the region have more individuals in group C than in D; and, in parallel, more in D than B. In other words, most informal workers are not poor, although the majority of the poor are informal. As a result, countries allocate anywhere between 2–4% of gross domestic product (GDP) to social insurance programmes for individuals in groups C + D, but around 0.5% to targeted poverty programmes for individuals in groups B + D.

Critically, and contrary to what is often assumed, individuals move between the columns. Throughout their lifetime, they transit from formal to informal employment, or to unemployment, and in and out of the labour force. Indeed, two facts are well established (for countries where data is available): first, the average individual is formally employed only about 50% of the time that they work. Second, time spent in formality is positively correlated with incomes.

III. Challenges of the Latin American welfare state

Given these labour market dynamics, the welfare state described in Figure 11.2 has two substantive problems. The first problem is that it is ineffective. Protection against risks is erratic because workers are protected against disability, death, or loss of unemployment only half of the time that they work, while they and their families bear risks on their own the other half of the time. Moreover, when workers are formal, they contribute to a retirement pension (defined benefit or defined contribution plans), but the majority of them will not get one, because they will not accumulate the required years of contributions; instead, they will bear the risks associated with longevity on their own. Lower-income workers will also be relatively less protected than higher-income workers because they spend less time in formality.

The ineffectiveness of the type of welfare state depicted in Figure 11.2 is reflected in its weak impact on income inequality. While there is some country heterogeneity, for the region as a whole, the difference in the Gini coefficients (a measure of income inequality, ranging from 0 to 1 where 0 denotes perfect equality and 1 denotes perfect inequality) between incomes before and after taxes and transfers is very small, from 0.51 to 0.49. In the OECD, the difference is much larger, from 0.47 to 0.30.

The second problem is that it punishes productivity. When workers are formal, they and their employer contribute to a pension that half of the workers will eventually not get access to, or they contribute to health services that are often of low quality. For these and other reasons, contributions are undervalued. De facto, formality is taxed. Furthermore, high minimum wages sometimes create entry barriers and firms that hire workers formally bear large contingent costs of firing, which ultimately result in less formal hiring.

Meanwhile, informal employment is subsidised because workers receive some benefits – health services, a pension, maybe day care services – that neither they nor the firm they are associated with will have to pay for. Sometimes even illegal behaviour by firms is subsidised, particularly when the firm is small and enforcement of labour and social insurance laws is proportional to firm size: their salaried workers receive benefits even if they do not enrol them in the Bismarckian scheme.

In some countries, targeted poverty programmes create poverty or informality traps, depending on the inter-phase between targeting rules and social insurance programmes; exactly the opposite of what is needed to incorporate poor workers into higher productivity jobs and break the intergenerational transmission of poverty.

The incentive structure implicit in the overall scheme depicted in Figure 11.2 affects occupational choices, the distribution of firms and firm dynamics. Self-employment or employment in firms with a maximum of five workers is often close to half or more of all employment. The patterns of firm exit, entry, and survival are distorted, as small informal firms are subsidised while larger formal ones are taxed. Needless to say, this hurts aggregate productivity because it is well established that the productivity of capital and labour is substantially higher in the formal sector.

Of course, many other factors impact occupational choices and firm behaviour. However, the patterns of resource misallocation that we observe in the region are consistent with the ones induced by the taxes, subsidies, and regulations that are part of the dual nature of its welfare state.

IV. Concluding remarks and next steps

Since the onset of the Washington Consensus, Latin America has made significant efforts to increase the coverage of social protection. Between 1990 and 2020 (before the COVID-19 pandemic), the average country in the region increased public spending on social protection from 7–15% of GDP. Nevertheless, Latin America continues to be one of the most unequal regions in the world and has poverty rates that are high relative to countries' per capita income. At the same time, total factor productivity has stagnated and even decreased in some Latin American countries. While many other factors can explain part of these outcomes, a welfare state that is relatively ineffective in pursuing its own aims and generates persistent misallocation of resources is certainly an important part of the explanation.

What is next? First, we need to recognise that socially inclusive growth is impossible with dysfunctional welfare states and that it is time (in fact, long overdue) to give up on the Bismarckian model. Second, we need to recognise that the goal of universal coverage of social protection often expressed by governments in the region should not be pursued through an ever-expanding combination of social protection programmes, each with its own sources of finance, rules, and targeting criteria. Third, we need to recognise that social protection programmes affect the behaviour of firms and workers, and that if productivity stagnates the welfare state will be fiscally unsustainable.

Looking forward, Latin America needs a new vision of its welfare state, with universalism at its core. This does not mean that redistribution and social insurance programmes should be the same across all countries. In fact, the principles laid out in Barr's chapter would advise against this. Barr argues, and I agree with him, that one size does not fit all. Policy prescriptions should be based on specific objectives and constraints. Because these vary across countries, so should the design of the optimal welfare state.

A new consensus, labelled the London Consensus or something else, should not be about specific policy recommendations for all; it should be about principles. Social protection policy needs to adapt to a context where labour market dynamics imply that individuals have different labour status throughout their life cycle; it should facilitate rather than hinder productivity growth; and it should be fiscally sustainable. Reaching a consensus about the urgent need to renovate the welfare state in Latin America and about the principles that should guide this endeavour would be a significant achievement.

Notes

1 Williamson (2004).

2 Levy and Cruces (2021).

References

Levy, S. and Cruces, G. (2021) 'Time for a New Course: An Essay on Social Protection and Growth in Latin America', United Nations Development Program, Latin American and Caribbean Bureau, Working Paper Series 24, New York.

Williamson, J. (2004) *A Short History of the Washington Consensus*, Washington, DC: Peterson Institute for International Economics.

Response to Nicholas Barr by Paul Johnson

Barr's conclusions that the Washington Consensus is 'oversimplified', that 'well-designed policy should be a thoughtfully assembled mosaic', and that there are 'good but no perfect solutions', should be obvious to anyone who has looked at the design, theory, or practice of the welfare state. Clearly, the market alone cannot adequately address the needs for healthcare or pensions, let alone for unemployment insurance or poverty relief. That does not mean the private sector has no role to play. Barr's statements are all descriptive of the welfare state in most developed countries, as well as prescriptive. But economics does not support simply minimising state involvement, nor ruling out the private sector. It is much more complicated than that. Optimisation depends on the extent of market and government failures, the degree of concern for redistribution, the need for insurance, and a range of other factors.

In practical terms, where does this stance lead us? For a start, it takes us one step further than the ideologues on either end of the spectrum. A publicly-funded, and largely publicly-provided, universal healthcare system may be anathema to proponents of the Washington Consensus. *Any* use of the private sector within that system appears to be anathema to the opposite side of the ideological spectrum in the United Kingdom. One side ignores the well-known market failures in health insurance and the extraordinary experience of the United States in overprovision of healthcare at exorbitant costs. The other side dismisses the idea that public management can ever fail and ignores the fact that significant elements of healthcare provision are run privately in all countries, for good reasons. The ideas that the UK's National Health Service should be either fully privatised or should make no use of the private sector at all are both patently absurd.

But how and where do we place the boundaries to construct the mosaic of policies advocated by Barr? How do we find the good but imperfect solutions? Barr provides a series of general guidelines as to where markets are likely to be more or less effective, and where government failure is more or less likely. These will be familiar to any student of welfare economics. We generally know when insurance markets will fail, when moral hazard and adverse selection are likely to be problematic, and when governments are likely to lack the information or the ability to replicate incentives that make markets function. However, I want to illustrate some of those difficulties and trade-offs by reference to three aspects of welfare policy specific to the UK: pensions, student finance, and healthcare.

I. Pensions

The perspective on the state's role in pension provision in the UK has undergone significant changes over the past 80 years. Beginning in 1945, we had a flat-rate state pension, set close to subsistence level, funded by flat-rate contributions, creating an actuarially 'fair' social insurance system. The flat-rate contributions quickly gave way to earnings-related contributions, and in the late 1970s a substantial earnings-related pension was added on top. This adjustment acknowledged the importance of private sector occupational defined benefit schemes, allowing individuals to opt out of the state earnings-related pension. During the 1980s, those opt-out rights were extended to personal, defined contribution pensions as a broader role was recognised for the private sector. Mis-selling resulted in huge compensation schemes. The escalating costs of state earnings-related pensions, coupled with changing ideological perspectives, gradually led to the demise of the state earnings-related scheme, leaving just a flat-rate basic pension, amounting to slightly below 30% of median earnings. In part because of excess regulation, virtually all private sector employer-sponsored defined benefit schemes ceased to accept new members. A combination of complexity, cost, and short-sightedness meant that many private sector employees had no pension provision beyond their state pension. In response, auto-enrolment into private pensions was successfully introduced in the 2010s, with coverage now exceeding 80%. These private pension pots are tax privileged but come with no annuitisation requirement – they serve as a savings vehicle rather than guarantee a stream of income in retirement.

This thumbnail sketch of the development of UK pension policy lays bare some of the trade-offs and complexities inherent in designing policy, each component contributing to the mosaic.

Across most developed countries, there is consensus that it is the state's responsibility to provide a minimum income in retirement. That can be means-tested, as in Australia, universal, or contribution-based, or some combination thereof, each carrying its own set of advantages and drawbacks. Where disagreements often arise is in defining the state's role beyond this minimum provision, particularly in providing earnings replacement. While the state is capable of providing such replacement, doing so requires high levels of taxation, significant redistribution between generations, and a sustained cross-generational consensus. Simply leaving it to the private sector can lead to substantial under-saving and, in a complex market rife with information asymmetries, could result in considerable consumer detriment. Thus, careful and intelligent regulation is necessary. The success of auto-enrolment underscores the power of inertia and default options. State action, or inaction, is not neutral. Indeed, with so little opt out from auto-enrolment the difference between state compulsion and a strong default is less than might initially appear.

It is possible to rely largely on the state or the private sector for earnings replacement in retirement. The appropriate mix will depend to some extent on a country's political economy. In the UK, trust in the state to provide, and willingness to pay the level of taxes required, seemed to wane in the 1980s. No subsequent government has been willing to contemplate the increase in taxation that a return to state-provided earnings-related pensions would require. Belief in the social insurance system and a willingness to accept higher levels of taxation seems to run deeper in many other European systems. The economics are the same; the political choices have been different. Not that reliance on the private sector releases the state from responsibility. Such reliance still requires a central role for careful and appropriate state engagement and regulation to set boundaries for how the market works. This is complex, and can go wrong.

A central choice is about risk sharing. State provision allows risk sharing across and within generations. This principle is also evident in employer-sponsored defined benefit schemes, where the employer – and hence some combination of shareholders and current employees – assumes much or all of the risk. However, when these risks appeared too great, employers withdrew. In contrast, within individual defined contribution schemes there is no risk sharing in the accumulation phase and, without annuitisation, none during drawdown either. Consequently, beyond the basic state pension, there is no risk sharing in the UK pension system. All risks, whether pertaining to investment returns or longevity, are borne by the actor least able to bear it – the individual.

A similar risk burden is evident in our social care system, where state support is entirely means-tested. Individuals bear the risk of high care costs that cannot be mitigated through private insurance.

These situations underscore the need for state intervention through social insurance. In the case of pensions, the state used to compel annuitisation, hence sharing longevity risk, but has stepped back even from that. People can choose to annuitise, but market failures, including adverse selection and underestimation of life expectancy, persist. There is a case for more, rather than less, state involvement in pensions.

Finally, it is worth mentioning how the value of the basic pension and other state benefits for pensioners has changed over time. Nearly 30 years of consensus that the basic pension should grow only in line with prices was replaced by a 15-year consensus that it should grow each year by the higher of price inflation, earnings growth, or 2.5%. Once a trajectory is set, it proves exceedingly challenging to deviate from it. Under the current trajectory, benefits for those over pension age consistently rise relative to those for younger cohorts. Politicians feel unable to move away from this equilibrium. It is hard to take away something once it has been provided, even if we are talking about an indexation rule. The design of the welfare state is highly path-dependent, and any changes to it need to consider that.

II. Student finance

Decisions about risk allocation are also central to the design of student finance policies. When higher education tuition is free, it is tax-financed. The students bear no risk – they gain the full benefit of higher earnings, and suffer no penalty for doing poorly in the labour market. Alternatively, a graduate tax concentrates the risk among graduates, but shares it among them. While graduates generally would pay more than under a pure tax-financed arrangement, high earners pay back more than the cost of their course and low earners less – resulting in risk sharing between them. A pure loan system gets rid of the redistribution and risk sharing. The incentive to earn well to pay back the loan is strong, but the unlucky and unsuccessful face high repayments as a fraction of their lifetime income.

The UK's student finance system is a hybrid of these models. Repayments are limited to the amount borrowed, albeit subject to the interest rate charged), and low earners pay back less than they borrowed, partly because there is an earnings threshold below which no repayments are required, and partly because debt is forgiven after a certain period. Adjusting these parameters can move the system closer to either a graduate tax or a pure loan. Until 2023, with a positive real interest rate, a 30-year repayment limit, and a relatively high earnings threshold, the system resembled a graduate tax. High earners paid back more than they borrowed, low earners much less. The majority was set not to pay back in full. By reducing the real value of the threshold, extending the repayment period to 40 years, and setting the interest rate equal to inflation, a set of reforms have moved the system much closer to a loan-based model. Most graduates will repay their loans in full, with high earners not repaying more than they borrowed or more than most modest earners.

These are all plausible choice parameters. A degree of cost and risk sharing between graduates and the population as a whole, and between high and low earning graduates, seems appropriate. Many possible designs would fit within a 'thoughtfully assembled mosaic'.

Most of these parameters have proven remarkably easy to adjust. The notion that the current system will endure 40 years is unrealistic. But one parameter will not shift – the tuition fee itself. Perceived as a loan, it has proven almost impossible to increase the fee even in line with inflation, and the real value of tuition fees has dropped precipitously since they were introduced, creating financial management problems for universities. Similar problems of policy stickiness are evident in other parts of the welfare state, such as the long periods of generous indexation of state pensions, as previously mentioned, as well as the persistent challenges in reforming social care funding.

The design of any aspect of the welfare state needs to consider these political economic constraints. Incorporating automatic indexation from the outset might help in cases like this. Mosaics, however thoughtfully assembled, can either become rigid and resistant to change or subject to constant meddling. We have residual elements in our pension system that hark back decades, including a £10 Christmas bonus. At age 80 the pension payment rises by 25 pence. What has been given is hard to take away. In other areas, like the structure of tuition fee repayments the only constant is change. You could say the same for the system of vocational education post-16, but absolutely not for the apparently unchangeable system of academic A levels.

III. Healthcare

The political and the economic perhaps butt up against one another more in the design of healthcare funding than anywhere else. Reform of the US system has been notoriously difficult. In the UK, former chancellor Nigel Lawson famously described the NHS as more akin to a national religion than a public service. Whatever the theoretical attractions of changing the funding model for the NHS, the benefits of doing so would be far outweighed by the costs associated with such an attempt. Given its reliance on public funding and the widespread support for a system that offers care that is free at the point of use, there are infinite options for the organisation of the system and the use of private provision within it. Many of the upheavals in the decades since the NHS was founded have been experiments with different ways of organising it, the use of internal markets, greater or lesser central control, and the use of private providers.

Barr effectively outlines the rationale for public funding of healthcare, highlighting multiple market failures and equity concerns that have made public provision the dominant model in affluent countries. Instead of getting lost in the details of optimal design – which in healthcare presents a far more complex mosaic than in any other part of the welfare state – I want to explore two different, but related issues: the scale of healthcare spending, and what happens when things start to go wrong.

One cannot consider the design of welfare systems – and healthcare systems – without grappling with their scale. In 2023–2024, the UK is projected to spend around 150 billion GBP on benefits for pensioners and over 120 billion GBP on benefits for children and those of working age. The Department of Health and Social Care (DHSC) will consume another 180 billion GBP. Together, these expenditures account for a fifth of national income. The proportion of current public services spending attributable to the DHSC has surged from around a quarter of the total at the start of the century to more than 40% by the mid-2020s, with further increases anticipated. Just accounting for planned increases in the workforce, spending will rise by a further 2% of national income by the mid-2030s. The UK's expenditure levels are not uncommon from an international perspective.

From the perspective of a rational economist, these trends are both understandable and predictable. Not only is the population ageing, medical salaries must also keep pace with salaries in the rest of the workforce. Additionally, technology is making more treatments available. Since healthcare is a superior good, as we get richer, we want more of it. There is no point being better off if you are either sick or dead. But that does not mean that persuading the electorate to cough up more money to pay for it, or to accept greater cuts in other areas of public spending, will be easy. The only alternative is increased rationing. No amount of welfare economics is going to provide an answer to how those trade-offs should pan out.

Currently, we are going down all three routes. Healthcare spending is rising, putting pressure on both taxes, which are increasing, and spending on other public services, which is being squeezed. The increase in spending has not been enough to prevent serious additional rationing as evidenced by prolonged waiting times. Moreover, this is leading to more private spending, both through health insurance and out-of-pocket spending.

The design of the welfare state should consider political constraints on available resources for public spending. Such constraints can lead to behavioural responses, including more opting out of public provision by those who can afford it. Given the shortcomings of the private market, this could reduce overall efficiency. If there is also a constraint on total resources, such as medical personnel, at least some of that additional private spending may either further reduce public capacity or increase the prices the public sector has to pay.

IV. Conclusions

Examining just these three areas of the welfare state suggests some additional guiding principles for action.

All analyses stress the role of the welfare state in creating mechanisms for risk sharing. In the UK, occupational pensions once facilitated significant risk sharing between different workers and generations. But these no longer exist, partly as a result of poorly designed regulation. The end of compulsory annuitisation has taken another big chunk of risk sharing out of the pension system. A few apparently minor tweaks to the system of student finance have substantially reduced the risk sharing within that system. Once lost, risk sharing can be hard to put back together.

We must not overlook the stickiness of policy and the importance of political economy. England's dysfunctional social care system exists as an accidental consequence of decisions made in the 1940s. Change, when it costs money, is hard. Some decisions quickly become part of the policy architecture in ways that can be difficult to alter. The nominal level of student loans has been raised only once in more than a decade, putting pressure on university finances in a way that was never initially intended. Concessions to one group, for example, generous indexation of the state pension, can become impossible to undo.

Ultimately, it all boils down to resources. The design of the welfare state will be increasingly constrained by the willingness of the population to pay for it. This may compel us to adopt solutions that deviate considerably from the optimal course.

12. Addressing the learning crisis: an emergent consensus

Lant Pritchett

Success can make a previous consensus not so much wrong as just irrelevant. The Washington Consensus joined in a broader consensus that governments need to spend on education in order to reach universal schooling to create human capital. But 'spend to expand access' has been so successful there is less and less space for additional improvements in education outcomes – the skills and competencies children need to acquire in school – through 'access'. Global, national, and local actors agree on the need to increasingly focus on improving learning outcomes. Moreover, there is an emergent consensus that improving learning will require much more than just 'more spend' and that a substantial re-alignment of education systems from 'expansion of access' to 'increased learning' is needed. And, while there is not yet a consensus on the granular details (and may never be as success tends to be home-grown and adapted to context), there is increasing agreement around a set of principles that will drive sustained gains in improving learning outcomes.

I. Introduction

The world needs to move on from something many believe John Williamson's original 1990 Washington Consensus got right. In the section under 'public expenditure priorities' in Williamson's paper, Williamson said that 'Washington' loves spending on education and health. 'Education and health', he argued, 'are regarded as quintessentially proper objects of government expenditure. They have the character of investment (in human capital) as well as consumption. Moreover, they tend to help the disadvantaged'.[1] Government expenditure in education was deemed particularly useful when focused on primary school.

How to cite this book chapter:

Pritchett, Lant (2025) 'Addressing the learning crisis: an emergent consensus', in: Besley, Tim, Bucelli, Irene and Velasco, Andrés (eds) *The London Consensus: Economic Principles for the 21st Century*, London: LSE Press, pp. 391–432 https://doi.org/10.31389/lsepress.tlc.l

The consensus that primary education is essential to development, a key governmental responsibility, and a 'proper object' of spending is not new, not a consensus of economics alone, nor particular to 'Washington', but rather it is long-standing and broad, across the globe, across the political spectrum, and across academic disciplines. Just as one example, in 1990, one year after Williamson's essay, the 1,500 assembled delegates of governmental, non-governmental, and inter-governmental organisations at the Education For All conference in Jomtien, Thailand made a similar case for state spending on education. The Jomtien Declaration asserted that every person has the right to educational opportunities that equip them with basic literacy, numeracy, and problem-solving skills, in order 'to live and work in dignity', among other goals.[2]

Yet this consensus did not go nearly far enough to actually achieve its objectives. Though primary education has become nearly universal, learning outcomes are poor, and this leaves most students badly equipped either for future education or to compete in the labour market. We need a new, post-Washington, post-Jomtien consensus that focuses on the *quality* of education in preparing students with the learning, skills, and competencies students will need in their adult lives, rather than just intermediate goals like increasing spending and expanding years of schooling to complete. The first consensus was successful in that it did lead to universal primary schooling (and more). The second must go deeper and improve learning systems and lead to the universal education outcomes the world needs.

This chapter is organised as follows: in the first section, I review the successes and shortcomings of the expansion of primary schools since the end of World War II. Though access to education has massively increased, learning results are lacklustre, children are learning less than they should for their age, and in many developing countries learning results have either stagnated or became worse in recent decades, in an alarming reversal. In the second section, I propose five deep and broad actions policymakers can take to improve learning systems. For years, most approaches conflated spending on schools with providing a quality education. But the problem today is not a lack of access to education. Rather, learning *in* schools is radically inadequate. To solve the learning crisis, we need a new approach grounded in a new consensus.

II. The successes and failures of the first consensus

In the past 70 years the expansion of schooling, both primary and 'basic' (which can be flexibly defined to include junior or full secondary), has been enormous. The completed schooling of the median youth aged 25 to 34 in the developing world increased from only 2.9 years in 1960 to 9.8 years in 2015. By 2015, nearly all children around the world had completed primary schooling – and most completed several years beyond primary. Young people in most developing countries, even very poor ones, today have more years of schooling than their counterparts in advanced countries did in 1960. By 2015, the typical 25 to 34 year old had completed 9.2 years of schooling in Bangladesh, and 7.2 years in Zambia, compared with 6.7 years of schooling completed for youth in Denmark in 1960.

Basic schooling, the physical act of being enrolled and attending school, is a necessary condition for basic education, but schooling and education are not – even though this elision is distressingly common – synonyms. Basic education refers to outcomes, the gains in the wide variety of learning, skills, ideas, competencies, dispositions, and behaviour that are the object of schooling. Because of the impressive success of the 'first consensus' in facilitating the expansion of schooling, there is increasingly limited progress possible in reaching universal basic education by further expanding schooling.

Even as basic schooling vastly expanded, there were fears that the quality of the education being provided was not fit for purpose. Education experts knew that there needed to be both *more* and *better* schooling. Yet, understandably, the priority was first to expand access. If we think of a global cohort of 15-year-olds as represented by 20 youth, in 1960 only 2 out of 20 were reaching a goal of foundational learning, defined as having reached modest levels of literacy and numeracy, and most of this was lack of schooling as 10 of the 18 children not getting to foundational learning were not completing primary school.[3] Expansion was the clear priority. In 1990 it was still the case that of the 15 children out of 20 who were not reaching foundational learning, 6 were not completing primary school and hence it was hard to shift away from the expansion agenda.

However, because of the success in expanding schooling we have now reached the point where further expansion cannot alone lead to major gains in expanding education. Hence it is now essential to focus on improving the pace of learning of those in school. In 2023 it was still the case that most of the world's youth, 12 of 20, did not reach foundational learning – but only 2 of those 12 without foundational learning are failing to complete primary schooling. The 'learning crisis' is the name for the fact that in many developing countries youth are completing basic schooling without achieving even basic learning, which includes at a minimum literacy and numeracy, as articulated in 1990 at Jomtien. The pace of learning in schools is too slow (especially in the early years) and the learning acquired is too 'thin', based on rote memorisation. This means that even those who complete basic schooling enter adulthood ill-equipped for the complex and changing world they face.

An understanding that basic education needs to be more focused on learning outcomes is already emerging. While in 2000 the Millennium Development Goal for education was merely 'completion' of primary school, the education aspirations in Goal 4 of the Sustainable Development Goals in 2015 emphasised that all youth should achieve literacy and numeracy (a specific competence goal) as well as completing 'free, equitable and quality primary and secondary education leading to relevant and Goal-4 effective learning outcomes'.[4] Many global supporters of education have adopted the goal to eliminate 'learning poverty' by ensuring that, at a minimum, all children can read fluently by grade 4 – while *The State of Global Learning Poverty: 2022 Update,* a joint report of six major global supporters[5] of education, estimates that currently 70% of children are not reaching even that very modest education goal.

III. 'Schooling ain't learning'

The strong evidence that learning outcomes are insufficient is the result of an enormous expansion in assessment of student skills and capacities in previous decades. These assessments fall under six types.

First, there are assessments of enrolled students, typically in later grades near completion of basic education, that probe students' understanding and ability to apply curricular cognitive learning in concrete ways. These include both assessments with global participation (although participation is voluntary and much higher by richer countries) and regional assessments in Latin America and Africa.

Second, there are citizen-led assessments of the literacy and numeracy abilities of children through household surveys. These have the advantage of including children both in and out of school and cover children of different ages, not just a specific grade.

Third, simple questions about literacy or numeracy have increasingly been included in large-scale, multi-module, household surveys, carried out in many countries, like the Demographic and Health Surveys (DHS) and the Multiple Indicator Cluster Surveys (MICS). For instance, the DHS have implemented (nearly) identical survey instruments in over 80 developing countries, repeated in multiple rounds since the 1980s. Since 2000 the standard DHS survey instrument measures a respondent's ability to read by asking them to read a simple sentence in their preferred language. This allows direct comparisons across and large number of countries and, even more importantly, over time.[6]

Fourth, there has been a proliferation of assessments for the youngest children. These assess early skills in literacy and numeracy orally, such as Early Grade Reading Assessments and early assessments of numeracy, which have the advantage of allowing very early grade assessments without the conflation of the subject matter assessment with the ability to take a 'pen and paper' test.

Fifth, there are individual country assessments of learning that happen in various grades, but which are not internationally comparable.

Sixth, there are assessments constructed as part of research endeavours, such as impact evaluations of specific interventions.

The results of these various types of assessments lead to four robust conclusions about learning in many developing countries:

- Learning of those near the end of basic school is too *low*.
- Learning in the early years is too *slow*.
- Learning is too *thin*.

- Learning is (mostly) not getting better; it is either staying the same or getting *worse*.

Learning is too low. In most developing countries the levels of learning of enrolled students at age 15 – the age at which the Programme of International Student Assessment (PISA) is completed – is often far below reasonable and achievable thresholds. Table 12.1 shows the results from the most recent study of whether youth aged 15 are reaching a level of basic skills in maths and science (where the level defined as 'basic' roughly corresponds to the global standard for 'basic' adopted in the Sustainable Development Goals), by combining a number of existing assessments.[7] The researcher's findings are that 94.1% of youth in Sub-Saharan Africa (SSA) are not reaching basic skills in maths and science, defined as the ability to apply maths to solve simple problems. Of the one-third of the 15-year-olds who are enrolled in school, 89.3% are not reaching these basic skills. This implies that, while almost two-thirds of students in SSA are not in school at age 15, even if all those students were in school and had the same learning as those now in school, the fraction of the youth cohort lacking basic maths and science skills would only drop 5 percentage points, from 94.1% to 89.3%.

In Latin America, learning outcomes are much better, but it is still the case that 61.2% of enrolled students are not reaching basic skills. Again, even if all students were in school it would raise the fraction reaching basic skills at most by 4 percentage points.

Table 12.1: In many developing regions the majority of students enrolled in school at age 15 have not reached basic skills in maths and science

Region	Fraction of enrolled students in secondary education *not* reaching basic skills	Fraction of youth *not* enrolled in secondary education	Fraction of youth *not* reaching basic skills
Sub-Saharan Africa	0.893	0.665	0.941
South Asia	0.850	0.402	0.892
Middle East and North Africa	0.639	0.195	0.679
Latin America and Caribbean	0.612	0.210	0.652
Central Asia	0.400	0.094	0.421
East Asia & Pacific	0.252	0.219	0.291
Europe	0.259	0.102	0.284
North America	0.222	0.069	0.239

Source: Gust et al. (2022)[8] Table 2.

Learning is too slow. Unlike in-school, late-age assessments, the ASER-style[9] assessments pioneered by the non-governmental organisation (NGO) Pratham in India, cover all children and hence can show the progress from grade to grade in achieving basic skills, like the ability to read a simple story or do simple addition. These assessments show that a proximate cause of the low learning levels in later grades, and likely the cause of much drop-out,[10] is that many students are arriving at grades 3 and 4 still unable to read simple stories or handle simple arithmetic operations. A recent analysis of foundational numeracy skills from UNICEF's MICS surveys found that by 3rd grade, 60% of Thai children had reached foundational numeracy, while less than 20% had in Pakistan and less than 10% in Ghana.[11] Even before the COVID-19 pandemic hit in 2020, more than half of children in the world were unable to read fluently by grade 4.[12]

Learning is too thin. While test scores, even in a single domain like reading or mathematics, are reported as a single number, the score has at least two dimensions. With assessment of cognitive skills there is a 'breadth' of coverage but also an assessment of the 'depth' of understanding. There are different ways of describing this depth of understanding, as a move from rote memorisation to 'procedural/algorithmic' (e.g., able to do multiple digit addition following a rule, without necessarily a conceptual understanding of why the procedure produces correct answers) to 'conceptual understanding' (e.g., being able to explain to others) to 'non-routine application' (e.g., the ability to apply skills in new circumstances). Assessments that probe the depth of understanding often reveal that even the learning that is present is 'thin'. Most students can answer questions that can be answered in a rote or purely procedural way. But they usually struggle to answer questions that probe their conceptual understanding of material. Students also generally lack the ability to apply their rote skills to novel applications.

For instance, the India Education Initiatives assessment asked children: '29×28 is more than 28×28 by how much?'[13] There are three paths to the answer to this question. One, if a person understands that multiplication is repeated addition, then the answer is easy and requires no computations. 29×28 is adding up 28, 29 times and 28×28 is adding up 28, 28 times, so the difference is adding up 28 one less time, hence the answer is 28. Two, if one can write the question as an equation and apply the distributive law then again the answer is easy: 29×28-28×28=(29-28) ×28=1×28=28. Three, even without any conceptual understanding of multiplication or the ability to apply the distributive law, one could get to the right answer by carrying out the two 2-digit multiplications and subtracting. But the study found that even children who could answer the multiplications when asked in a standard way, such as: '29×28=?', could not answer this question, even though, with a modicum of conceptual understanding this question is actually easier.

In another example, in 2017 the Pratham/ASER study surveyed rural Indian youth aged 14 to 18 on their ability to apply literacy and numeracy to simple practical tasks.[14] One question (not displayed here) showed a key with the base aligned on a ruler at zero and the tip on 4cm and asked 'Using the scale shown, measure the length of the key. Give the answer in centimetres'. Since this is exactly how measurement is taught in Indian textbooks, 94.1% of those youth enrolled in tertiary education answered this question correctly. But when the base of a pencil was displaced, and started at 2cm on the ruler, with the tip on 8cm, only 60.1% of youth enrolled in tertiary education answered correctly. It seems that about a third of students who appeared to understand measurement were actually just giving rote answers that reflected no conceptual understanding. Similarly, the results in Table 12.2 suggest that just over half of rural Indian youth who had successfully completed secondary education and were enrolled in tertiary education could correctly calculate the passage of time.

Table 12.2: Even rural Indian youth enrolled in tertiary education had limited skills in simple practice tasks like calculation of time or measurement with a ruler

Task: Calculating Time	
Current Level of Enrolment	Correct in %
Not enrolled	20.6
Enrolled in grade 12 or less	40.5
Enrolled in undergraduate or other	**54.4**
Task: Measurement (hard)	
Current Level of Enrolment	Correct in %
Not enrolled	19.0
Enrolled in grade 12 or less	41.7
Enrolled in undergraduate or other	**60.1**

Source: ASER (2018), Beyond Basics.[15]

The 'thinness', or lack of conceptual understanding of foundational skills, explains how and why the results of many developing country students on international assessments can be so low. For instance, the PISA carried out by the OECD was designed for OECD 15-year-olds and hence asks very few questions to probe purely procedural skills in arithmetic but rather asks questions that probe higher/deeper levels of understanding. But when this same PISA instrument is applied in low-performing developing countries one realises the ability to answer questions that go beyond rote/procedural is almost completely absent. So, while 54% of OECD 15-year-olds score at levels 3, 4, 5, and 6 (of a six-step ladder of proficiency in mathematics) – and in a high-performing system like Singapore 80% reach this level – only 1.7% of youth from six developing countries that participated in a PISA for Development exercise reached that level.

Learning outcomes are not getting better – and in many developing countries they have been getting worse (and in some, much worse). I recently heard a famous development economist recommend 'patience' as a strategic response to the learning crisis in developing countries. This might be good advice if you are waiting for a caterpillar to emerge from a cocoon as a butterfly, or responding to a child who has asked repeatedly 'are we there yet?' but patience is good advice only if the existing dynamics are working in the right direction. There is, however, powerful evidence that many countries' learning outcomes are headed in the wrong direction, in which case patience is terrible, and tragic, advice.

Le Nestour, Moscoviz, and Sandefur used the DHS, which surveyed people of a wide range of ages in each round and had multiple rounds to examine cohort effects in learning, allowing for age.[16] Figure 12.1 shows that for the 87 countries with data on women (the DHS primary respondents are women of child-bearing age), they found that the likelihood a woman born in the first cohort (usually in the 1950s) could read if they had attended five years of schooling was 85.1%, whereas the women born in the last cohort (who started school in the 2000s) with five years of schooling had only a 68.2% chance of being able to read. So, over a roughly 30 to 40 year period (depending on the country survey timing) there was an almost 17 percentage point decline in the likelihood that primary schooling (five years) resulted in any literacy at all. This varied massively across countries. For instance, in India a child born in 1958 (who would have reached age 6 in 1964) who attended five years of schooling had a likelihood of 90.7% of being able to read when surveyed as an adult (adjusted for age), whereas a child born in 1995 (who would have reached age 6 in 2001) and attended exactly five years of schooling had only a 53.8% chance of being able to read. But in Indonesia, a person born in 1997 and completing exactly five years of schooling had a 91.7% chance of being able to read a sentence, higher than a child born in 1954. (While the reader may raise the obvious objection that the expansion in enrolments caused those in school and completing exactly five years to have very different characteristics over time, this obvious 'selection effect' does not seem to be the main cause of these observed facts, as there is no correlation at all across countries between the magnitude by which schooling expanded and the extent of improvement deterioration in learning performance).

These long-term results are consistent with more recent examinations of pre-COVID-19 trends in learning in Indonesia, which showed a modest decline in learning outcomes.[17] ASER results in India also showed a steep decline and then stagnation in learning outcomes pre-COVID-19.[18] They are also consistent with the general tenor of the PISA results, where a comparison of results from 2000 to 2019 finds mixed outcomes, with some countries improving and others deteriorating. (I do not take up the issue of learning losses during COVID-19 at all, as I am concerned with the long-term trends).

These studies are important, in three ways.

First, they reveal that the current level of low performance in producing basic skills like literacy in primary school is typically not the result of lack of progress from a low base, but rather is commonly a significant *deterioration* from a much higher level. If we only compared the current results for the most recent cohorts we would find that both Nigeria and Ghana had similarly low levels of learning in primary school (26.2% of the 1998 cohort in Nigeria; 18.5% of the 1999 cohort in Ghana). But this is not because the two countries have had similar trajectories, but rather because Nigeria's collapsed from quite a high level for their 1955 cohort of 61.9% of grade 5 completers able to read *downwards* towards Ghana's consistently low level.

Figure 12.1: The likelihood an adult in the developing world with five years of schooling could read a sentence (in any language) *declined* substantially for both men and women – with large variations across countries

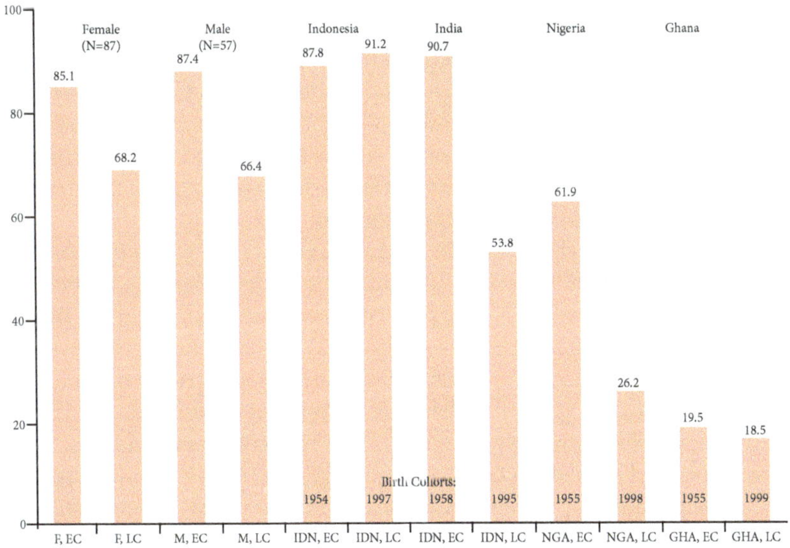

Source: author's calculations using data from le Nestour et al. (2021),[19] Table A.4.

These facts that current low levels are the result of long-term trends of decline rule out a variety of explanations for poor performance, like a general lack of pedagogical knowledge of how to teach; both Indonesia and India achieved very high levels of reading of primary school graduates in the 1960s and so, demonstrably, had all of the technical knowledge needed to produce those learning results over 70 years ago. These trends also cast doubt on claims that better 'inputs', such as the formal qualification of teachers, class size, and expenditures per pupil, are key to improving learning *outcomes*, since most inputs improved over the same period in which learning outcomes have deteriorated. Similarly, there are many claims that technology will make education better, but access to technology has significantly improved over the period in which learning outcomes have deteriorated in many countries.

Second, the studies reveal that maintaining very high levels of reading results of primary school leavers, even while moving to universal schooling, is possible. In the 57 countries with results for men and women, there are eight where the reading of grade 5 completers in the most recent birth cohort is over 80% (achieved near universality in schooling) and the fraction of the cohort with five or more years of schooling is also over 80% (achieved near universality in reading). A number of countries had significant improvements in literacy of grade 5 completers even as enrolments expanded. Vietnam has data only for women and their data shows literacy at grade 5 increasing from 72% to 94%, even while completion of grade 5 or higher increased from 76% to 89%. In Peru, women's completion of grade 5 or higher rose from 72% to 94% from the birth cohort of 1952 to that of 1992, and the ability to read of those completing just grade 5 also rose from 69% to 85%. While India and Nigeria appear to be deteriorating, the success cases of Vietnam and Peru demonstrate that the learning crisis can be solved.

Third, all this data can help us understand the driving forces behind changes in learning outcomes, and how policymakers can begin to address them. Analysts often cite cultural obstacles, the availability of resources, or the rapid expansion of schooling as reasons for poor learning results. But reading outcomes for Indian women who completed grade 5 in the early cohort were much better than in Peru. In 1952 Peru was at 69% versus 90% for the 1958 cohort in India. Superficial explanations of these learning differences might have explained Peru's poor performance as the result of the social gap between the indigenous and non-indigenous populations, or focused on Peru's mineral dependent economy, or on the heritage of Spanish colonialism, or other factors over which Peru has little control. But the difference in favour of India has been completely reversed. In the 1992 cohort in Peru those with five years of school completed who could read reached 85% (and with 95% completing grade 5 or higher) – a significant improvement over its historical level of 69%. In contrast, in India for the 1995 female birth cohort reading of those with five years of schooling complete was only 51.4% in India, a significant deterioration from its historical level of 90%. Learning outcomes are a destination to be worked towards that can be achieved, not a destiny fixed by fate.

IV. Five actions to address the learning crisis

From 2014 to 2023 I was the research director of a large-scale, long-term, many-country, multi-disciplinary research programme called Research on Improving Systems of Education (RISE). The goal of this research programme was to understand how to address the learning crisis by reforming education systems. RISE, which finished in March of 2023, cumulatively produced over

500 written works, including over 150 research papers, many review papers, two books, and hundreds of technical blogs. The information we gleaned in the project is highly relevant to addressing the learning crisis. First, there was a consensus that global, national, and local stakeholders in education policy must move from what is known as a 'proximate determinants' approach to a 'system' approach (explained shortly). Second, the RISE team boiled down the research and experiences into five key principles to guide efforts to reform education systems.[20]

I am not articulating these specific five actions as a new 'consensus'. Other organisations and individuals describing paths to successful education system reform, such as the World Development Report 2018 'Learning to Realize Education's Promise' or the 2024 McKinsey Global Institute report 'Spark and Sustain' come to different lists.[21] And different global organisations, from large to small, will necessarily adopt their own tactics and strategies, each with their own focus. My title does not declare or attempt to amalgamate the many voices into a single consensus, or even an 'emerging' consensus, but something different, an 'emergent' consensus: a large number of actors moving in a new and broadly similar direction are creating a wave that can drive action not by agreement on a rigid doctrine or by complete agreement but just by moving, fluidly and adaptively, in the same direction.

1. *'System' versus 'proximate determinants' approaches*

Now that there is increasing consensus that improving learning outcomes needs to be the focus of any future educational reform, the debate hinges on what kind of reform can improve results. Researchers generally support one of two educational approaches. The 'proximate determinants' approach looks at the elements that need to be in place in order for a child to have a successful learning experience in school, such as a physical space conducive to learning, adequate learning materials, enough time to complete tasks, a curriculum that specifies what is to be learned at every stage of school, and a teacher who knows what and how to teach. Researchers who subscribe to this approach believe that these proximate determinants can create quality schools. Recommendations that follow the proximate determinant approach focus on expanding children's exposure to schools with better inputs.

The 'system approach' starts from the premise that whether or not a child has access to a quality school that produces effective learning for that child is the *outcome* of the current education system. Every country already has an extensive (and expensive) education system: a collection of individuals working in and around education, public and private organisations in the field, laws, policies, and programmes concerning education, and a collection of institutions that structure and condition the ways in which educational organisations behave. The system question is: 'Why does the existing education system not already produce quality schools?'

Answering this question requires an understanding of how education systems currently function. While proximate determinant recommendations seem concrete and easily applicable across contexts, this is superficial as the approach has deep and significant conceptual and practical limitations as a guide to action. It cannot provide a causal explanation of the observed facts about learning outcomes, either across countries, over time within countries, or even across schools within countries. A recent study used the data from the Young Lives study that tracked children aged 2 to 12 in Vietnam and Andhra Pradesh, a state in India.[22] With this data the researchers could observe not just their learning at a specific age (like nearly all other studies) but could also observe a child's history, including health and nutrition outcomes as a young child and tests of cognitive ability at pre-school ages. They found massive differences between the learning of Vietnamese and Indian children at age 12, consistent with the evidence from other studies. More importantly, using detailed panel data, they found that essentially none of the differences in learning could be explained by differences in the children (including the measures of child pre-school ability – not that these were not important for explaining the learning of each child but since they were roughly equal across the countries at pre-school age they could not explain the differences across the countries). Only one of the school 'proximate determinant' variables helped to explain the learning gap, namely 'math teacher pedagogical skills'. Even this is an endogenous outcome of a system rather than simply an 'input' (like class size, expenditures, or formal qualifications of teachers).

This is why the facts about the cross-national differences and the evolution over time in learning outcomes is so important. Teaching children to read is something that many countries have been doing quite successfully since the 1950s or 1960s (or even earlier). Therefore, a lack of knowledge or understanding about how to teach children cannot explain why some countries are doing badly now. Moreover, many countries with low levels of reading proficiency today (e.g., India) had much higher levels of learning in the past. On standard measures of 'proximate determinants', countries like India are doing much better while, at the same time, learning performance appears to be getting considerably worse. Despite the fact that the proximate determinants approach has been dominant for decades it actually does not provide an empirically adequate explanation of the main learning differences across schools, across countries, or over time.[23]

The system approach starts from root causes. Better trained or higher paid teachers, better textbooks, a better curriculum, and the appropriate use of technology are subsumed as the result of the outcome of a well-functioning education system, which is therefore the relevant cause of differences in learning outcomes.

2. *A new approach to addressing the learning crisis*

A system approach to addressing the learning crisis suggests countries need to take five actions to re-orient their existing systems and make sustained progress in improving learning:[24]

- *Commit* to learning results, and in particular, early universal conceptual and procedural mastery of foundation skills.
- *Measure* learning outcomes in ways that provide information that is regular, reliable, and relevant to the key actors within the system, including much more use of formative assessment.
- *Align* the system around learning, moving from a focus on expansion to a focus on learning.
- *Support* teaching, moving the emphasis from a bureaucratic approach to creating the possibility that teachers consistently engage in effective teaching and learning practices.
- *Adapt* what is adopted so that, even when copying lessons from successful places, these are adapted to existing contexts and capabilities.

Action 1. Commit to universal, early foundational learning

Vietnam is an outlier in learning performance. In the 2012 and 2015 rounds of PISA the 15-year-old Vietnamese youth had astoundingly good learning results, with higher average scores in mathematics in 2015 than youth in France, the United States, or Britain. One key research question for RISE was 'how and why does Vietnam achieve these learning results at levels of resources (GDP per capita) and spending per student that is so low?'

Three studies probing this question were particularly interesting. One used PISA data to see whether the factors measured in PISA (which includes many 'proximate determinant' features of systems, schools, and teachers) could explain Vietnam's performance. The clear answer was no. Dang et al. show that Vietnam's success is not associated with better characteristics of students or their households.[25] Another study used the Young Lives data from four countries, which assessed children first in 2002 at young ages (two groups, at age 1 and age 5) with surveys in rounds every three to four years until 2017.[26] This study showed that, first, on all measures, Vietnamese children looked similar to those from Peru and India at age 5, including on measures of cognitive ability. This means that the learning gains happened because they learned more in school. Second, of the school-specific factors, only 'maths teacher pedagogical skills' seemed to matter at all, and hence the upshot was that only about 10% of the enormous learning gaps between India and Vietnam could be explained by any of the available measures.

Third, a study of the politics of education in Vietnam detailed that the success in Vietnam was *not* the result of some central plan masterfully implemented by a tightly controlled, top-down, bureaucracy.[27] Vietnam is a federal system and the states are mainly responsible for the implementation of basic education. Local provinces compete against each other to achieve the best learning outcomes, as the central government conveys ambitious learning targets while many of the resources needed to fund the system are collected locally. Vietnam's success is not the result of a clear, orderly, top-down, 'command and control' as one might imagine from a one-party (Communist) state. Rather, success was the emergent result of a messy and muddy process of local contestations within provincial and federal government structures of pressures.

This is a frustrating set of outcomes as it told us what the source of Vietnam's success *wasn't*, but did not tell us what *was*. Finally, one of the key researchers on the Vietnam study said, 'Let's face it, Vietnam succeeded because they *wanted* to'. That answer, while perhaps seeming simplistic or naïve, is actually wise.

Creating an education system that makes sustained progress in learning outcomes requires a commitment to learning. This commitment must not only come from the education ministry but from all stakeholders involved, including the government, parents, students, the business community, and thought leaders.

The commitment that will most likely lead to progress has three elements:

Putting learning at the centre. Education systems must commit to learning as their central purpose, and learning must animate all decisions in the system. Practically, this means having direct, concrete goals for learning outcomes.

One way in which education systems have managed to sustain their legitimacy without actually delivering on learning has been to set and achieve other goals, on the premise that these goals were themselves necessary and sufficient to improve learning. Many education systems have focused on (i) expanding schooling, (ii) enforced some degree of compliance with some processes, such as hiring teachers according to some criteria deemed merit-based, and (iii) expanding inputs, such as reducing class size and providing better physical infrastructure and more learning materials. These three elements of an education system are desirable, and certainly some levels of these are necessary, but, without the additional characteristic of being driven by an overarching shared *purpose* that is clearly understood as providing children with the needed skills and capabilities, these are clearly not *sufficient* to sustain effective teaching and learning practices.[28] Unless they are motivated by purpose, education systems can gain legitimacy through 'isomorphism'. Just as many animals gain survival by camouflage that makes them look like something they are not, the sociologists DiMaggio and Powell described the process of 'isomorphism' for organisations of gaining survival (and continued flow of resources) but looking like other effective organisations, even when they were not effective, and this use of 'isomorphic mimicry' is especially for public organisations with contested and hence ill-defined purposes.[29] Just as weak education systems are plagued by rote learning, they also suffer from rote implementation, in which the means (used by effective systems) – like examinations to hire teachers – are substituted for ends, and hence are disconnected from a drive for outcomes.

A recent impact evaluation of a large-scale programme of school improvement in Madhya Pradesh in India illustrates what can happen in the absence of a commitment to improving learning outcomes.[30] In 2014–16 the state government introduced a programme, modelled on one implemented in Britain, that required each school to create its own school improvement plan. The idea was that each school would do a diagnostic of its own strengths and weaknesses and then, based on that diagnostic, devise a plan for how to improve things. The state's education bureaucracy would then support the school in the implementation of that plan. This approach was explicitly designed to avoid the defects of the one-size-fits-all and top-down approaches of previous decades. The study found that the school diagnostics were completed in detail, and that school plans were created based on those diagnostics. But after that, nothing improved. Teacher practices did not change, supervision or support from the bureaucracy did not change, and, given that, student outcomes did not change at all.

This example is just one of a long list of studies that shows that, without a clear, system-wide (where the notion of 'system' extends beyond the education ministry) commitment to the purpose of learning, it will be impossible to implement effective teaching and learning practices at scale. Here is a partial list, just from RISE research (or related researchers):

- Banerji on scaling the practice of 'teaching at the right level' (TaRL), the adoption of teaching methods that adopt teaching to the student's current level of competence and focus on improvements from that level, in Bihar.[31]
- de Ree et al. showing that doubling teacher wages in Indonesia has no impact on learning.[32]
- Bold et al. on the failed scaling by the Kenyan government[33] of an intervention that was 'proven' to be effective of using contract teachers to reduce early grade class size (in Kenya).[34]
- Aiyar et al. on the implementation of TaRL in Delhi.[35]
- Bano on the government's tactical use of isomorphism, in adopting school-based management committees in Nigeria in a way designed to deflect external and donor pressure but without any commitment to success.[36]
- Siddiqi on the contestation between bureaucracy (insisting on process compliance) and local government (wanting actual performance in practice) in defining what makes 'good teachers' in Khyber Pakhtunkhwa province in Pakistan.[37]
- Revina et al. review four decades of in-service teacher training in Indonesia, detailing how contested purposes within the ministry led to the many different approaches to teacher training adopted over the decades to all fail to significantly improve teaching practices.[38]

Focusing first on foundational skills. Systems must commit to building foundational skills so that children are prepared for subsequent learning. This is not advocating for 'back to basics' or rote memorisation but rather the opposite: a focus on building a deep, conceptual understanding of reading, mathematics, and other foundational skills in the short term so that children can achieve the high aspirations we hold for them in the long term. Children first learn to read; only then children can read to learn.[39] As shown above, in existing weak systems learning is often too 'thin', in that students never acquire sufficient command over ideas, concepts, and skills they are exposed to in school to apply and deploy them in concrete and novel situations. Hence even capabilities acquired are not retained or utilised in practice.[40]

Foundational learning needs to be a clear and urgent priority both politically and socially. Case studies tracing out the recent history of the politics of education in a dozen countries as part of the RISE research agenda reveal that an education system actually focused on learning is far from a given, and that it is hard to shift education systems in a positive direction.[41] Moreover, political commitment is necessary, but the commitment has to go beyond politics. It must extend throughout society, encompassing a shared understanding among families, schools, bureaucracies, and different branches of government.[42]

Often recommendations from global actors for improving learning outcomes are based on the technocratic premise that national education ministries have sufficient authorisation to adopt and implement education reforms when they have evidence that these reforms could improve learning. But in reality, education ministers are often politically weak actors, the education ministry often has little or no autonomy to act, and the ministry itself can often be focused more on educational expansion and process compliance than on learning-oriented reforms. Moreover, resistance to implementation is widespread. The case of Indonesia shows how national, government-wide reforms pushed by the education ministry often fail because of the entrenched interests of local elites.[43] Studies about reforms to improve teaching practices in Ecuador[44] and in Peru[45] reveal that successful reforms cannot rely on pre-existing support but rather need to assemble and actively sustain political authorisation.[46] This is a challenge as education reforms, particularly those that affect teachers, will be contested by teacher unions, and, while the political costs are immediate, the benefits take time to bear fruit.

Qualitative studies from contexts as different as India, Nigeria, Malawi, Pakistan, South Africa, and Indonesia all reveal that generating local support for learning is also not a given but rather depends on how local communities perceive the relationship between the school, the bureaucracy, and their own power. Studies of the local dynamics of education reform in specific districts in Indonesia found that different social and economic conditions produced very different demands from parents for the priorities of education.[47] Qualitative research in Malawi revealed that, by and large, local communities did not see the local government schools as 'theirs' or as being responsive to their needs.[48]

Ethnographic research in northern Nigeria revealed that the long-standing reluctance of parents to enrol their children in government schools was, in part, based on the perception that the schools were ineffective at conveying skills and yet were conveying attitudes and values hostile to their own.[49]

As part of Action 2, the four actions that policymakers can take to improve learning outcomes all begin with a commitment to improving these. The 'proximate determinant' or 'quality schools' approaches, reflected in the Washington Consensus, implicitly assume that the system is, broadly speaking, fit for the purpose of improving learning outcomes, and that all that is needed is more money or a technocratic tweak or a 'best practice' reform. But this approach alone, without system reform, has proven radically insufficient for decades. Doing the same thing and expecting a different outcome will not work.

Action 2. Measure learning regularly, reliably, and relevantly

Many education systems around the world collect detailed data on school enrolments and inputs – yet many do not use data on student learning to inform policy and improve instruction. Educational systems should follow the 'three Rs' of useful learning assessments:

- *Relevant.* Assessments must be designed to measure learning and must include measures of conceptual and procedural mastery of foundational skills. This is not current practice, as many existing assessments are designed as tools for selection, and mainly measure pass rates or student rankings, and are often passable with cramming and rote learning.[50]
- *Regular.* Systems should measure learning over time, beginning in the early grades of primary school. This allows decision makers to track the pace of learning and to see when children start to fall behind and, therefore, what additional classroom or learning interventions are needed.[51] Expanding the use of formative assessment is particularly important.
- *Reliable.* In many systems, especially where assessments are high-stakes for the student, widespread cheating distorts the results.[52] Assessments must be reliable to serve as useful feedback on the system's progress.

Figure 12.2: There is often misalignment among curricula, exams, and classroom teaching, shown here for primary school English class in Uganda

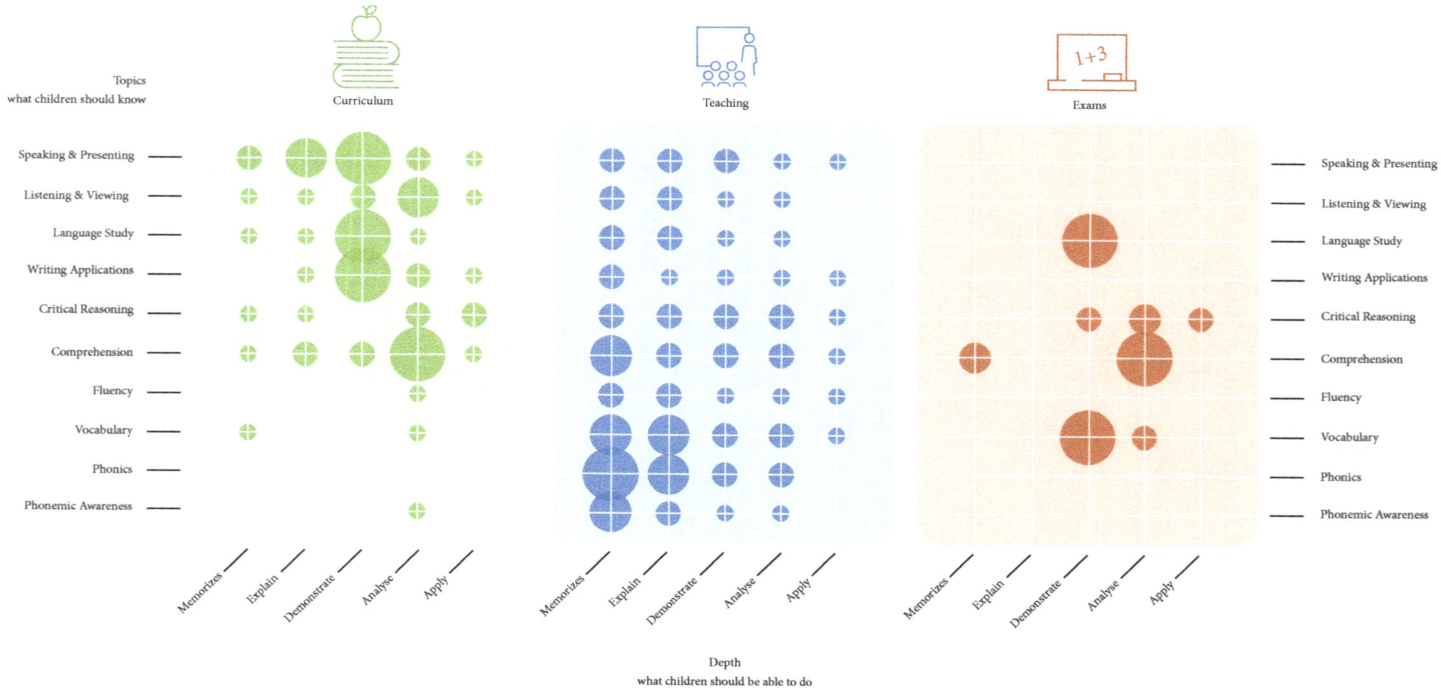

Source: adapted by the author from Atuhurra and Kaffenberger (2022).[53]

Action 3. Align education systems and instruction around learning commitments

Education systems deliver learning when all of their different parts are aligned with each other. This is not typically the case as the relationships of accountability in education systems are often badly structured and incoherent for producing good learning outcomes.[54] This system incoherence is both within relationships of accountability and across relationships of accountability. Even within a principal–agent relationship (say, management to employee) there can be incoherence between the elements of an accountability relationship: a disconnect between what is asked from the agent by the principal, what is measured to assess agent performance, and what actions are actually rewarded. Moreover, as the analysis above has stressed again and again, an education system is not reducible to just the primary organisations of the government, such as the education ministry, but has to include politics, the relationship between political leadership and the ministry, parents, and communities. This creates incoherence across these various relationships of accountability within a system (so, for instance, teachers are under very different pressures from the hierarchy of their bureaucracy than from the students and parents they work with).

There is also technical incoherence in the approach to instruction. A prominent example of a lack of alignment is that in many systems the curriculum standards, the content of examinations, and the actual instructional practices are completely out of sync. Figure 12.2, adapted from a 'survey of the enacted curriculum' in Uganda,[55] shows both the expected *coverage* of topics (vertical axis) and the *depth* of mastery of those topics (horizontal axis) with the emphasis represented by the size of the circle. The curriculum (first panel) expects very sophisticated concepts to be covered and high levels of mastery of those topics to be attained, with large circles for 'language study' and 'writing applications' and 'speaking and presenting' at the 'demonstrate to others' level. In contrast, the actual classroom instruction is predominantly in the lower left (simple concepts, simple understanding, e.g., 'memorise').

This misalignment of the curriculum, moving at a very fast pace with lack of effective instruction, often leaves children very far behind. Muralidharan and Singh show that the typical child in Rajasthan, India, in grade 8 actually only mastered the grade 4 curriculum (and at a shallow level) – with many students only at grade 2 or grade 3 comprehension. Almost no students were actually at grade 8 level.[56] Misaligned, over-ambitious curricula can lead to very low levels of learning[57] and recent efforts at TaRL and 'structured pedagogy' are attempts to remedy and improve student learning by addressing this mismatch.[58]

Action 4. Support teaching

Education systems must change their focus from *teachers* – including a narrow focus on manpower and rewards for seniority and formal qualifications – to effective *teaching* – with a focus on teaching and learning practices. At a minimum this means:

- Refocusing professional development on the craft of teaching. Teachers need to understand and experience what effective teaching looks like, and they must receive ongoing support to build specific content and pedagogical skills associated with student learning.[59]
- Reforming teacher careers to attract, retain, and motivate quality teaching. For example, this could mean using more nuanced hiring criteria beyond degrees earned – which have little relationship to teacher quality – and being more selective, with offers of long-term employment during the early phases of a teacher's career.[60]

Action 5. Adapt what you adopt as you implement

A growing number of success stories show that education systems with low learning outcomes can be reoriented to deliver higher learning outcomes.[61] However, the transition from a low- to higher-performing system is really hard. There is no single blueprint for transforming an education system. Rather, *adaptation* and *iteration* – learning while doing and doing what you learn – are the keys to success. When programmes are adopted without enough adaptation to local problems and context, even a well-designed and well-implemented programme that may have improved learning elsewhere or that was successfully implemented by NGO in the same context, may have no impact at all when scaled.[62] Alongside understanding 'what works', it is equally important to understand 'how it works' in a particular place, with its unique history, society, and politics.[63]

V. Conclusion

The goal expressed in the 1948 Universal Declaration of Human Rights that 'Everyone has the right to education (Article 26.1)', and the consensus expressed in 1990 in both the Washington Consensus and the Jomtien Declaration created the basis for the expansion of education systems worldwide. This impulse was necessary, since universal schooling is a precondition for universal education. It was correct to see spending on basic education as a proper use of government funds and to acknowledge that reaching universal basic schooling would require substantial fiscal commitments. Yet precisely because of the success of the previous consensus in expanding schooling, so that nearly every child does enrol in school and nearly all complete primary, and most are now completing some or all of secondary, we need a new consensus today. The main obstacle to universal education is no longer lack of schooling, but rather the learning crisis – children *in* school are not learning enough. Ample and compelling evidence has accumulated that simply spending more in existing education systems will not, in and of itself, solve the learning crisis. It has become clear that technocratic changes at the margin are not enough. There needs to be a shift from education systems fit for the purpose of expansion to education systems fit for the purpose of learning.

Notes

[1] Williamson (1990).

[2] UNESCO (1990).

[3] Pritchett et al. (2022).

[4] Global Goals (2015).

[5] World Bank (2022), UNESCO Institute of Statistics, UNICEF, UK Foreign, Commonwealth, and Development Office, USAID, Gates Foundation, all in partnership with UNESCO.

[6] lele Nestour et al. (2021).

[7] Gust et al. (2022).

[8] Gust et al. (2022).

[9] ASER is both an acronym (Annual Status of Education Report) and means 'impact' in Hindi.

[10] Kaffenberger and Pritchett (2021).

[11] Silberstein (2021).

[12] World Bank (2022).

[13] Educational Initiatives (2009).

[14] ASER (2018).

[15] ASER (2018).

[16] le Nestour et al. (2021).

[17] Beatty et al. (2021).

[18] ASER (2015).

[19] Le Nestour et al. (2021).

[20] The structure of 'five actions' and much of the material below draws on the RISE policy brochure (Pritchett et al. 2022).

[21] World Bank (2018); McKinsey (2024).

[22] Glewwe et al. (2021).

[23] Pritchett (2013).

[24] Pritchett et al. (2022).

[25] Dang et al. (2020).

[26] Glewwe et al. (2021).

[27] London and Duong (2023).

[28] London and Duong (2023).

[29] DiMaggio and Powell (1983); Andrews et al. (2016).

[30] Muralidharan and Singh (2020).

[31] Banerji (2015).

[32] de Ree et al. (2017).

[33] Bold et al. (2018).

[34] Duflo et al. (2015).

[35] Aiyar et al. (2023).

[36] Bano (2022).

[37] Siddiqi (2022).

[38] Revina et al. (2020).

[39] Belafi et al. (2020).

[40] ASER (2018); Beatty et al. (2021).

[41] Gershberg and Spindelman (2023).

[42] Levy et al. (2018); Levy (2022).

[43] Rosser et al. (2022).

[44] Schneider et al. (2019).

[45] Bruns et al. (2023); Saavedra (2023).

[46] Schneider et al. (2019).

[47] Bano and Dyonisius (2022); Arif et al. (2022); Nihayah et al. (2020).

[48] Watkins and Kaler (2016); Watkins and Ashforth (2019).

[49] Bano (2022).

[50] Stern et al. (2022); Burdett (2017).

[51] Bau et al. (2021); Beatty et al. (2021); Kaffenberger and Pritchett (2021); Crouch et al. (2021).

[52] Johnson and Parrado (2021); Singh (2020); Berkhout et al. (2020).

[53] Atuhurra and Kaffenberger (2022)

[54] Banerji (2015); Crouch (2020); Pritchett (2015); Kaffenberger and Spivack (2022); Mbiti (2016); Mbiti et al. (2019).

[55] Atuhurra and Kaffenberger (2020).

[56] Muralidharan and Singh (2020).

[57] Pritchett and Beatty (2012).

[58] Piper et al. (2018).

[59] Cilliers et al. (2022); Yusrina et al. (2022); Filmer et al. (2021); Revina et al. (2020); DeJaeghere et al. (2021).

[60] Hwa and Pritchett (2021); Bau and Das (2020); Siddiqi (2022).

[61] Crouch (2020); Stern et al. (2022); Kaffenberger (2022).

[62] de Ree et al. (2017); Muralidharan and Singh (2020); Hwa and Pritchett (2021); Bold et al. (2018); Angrist and Meager (2022); Kerwin and Thornton (2021).

[63] Barjum (2022); McNaught (2022); Moore and Spivack (2023); Samji and Kapoor (2022); Matthew (2021).

References

Aiyar, Y., Davis, V., Govindan, G. and Kapoor, T. (2023) *Rewriting the Grammar of the Education System: Delhi's Education Reform (a Tale of Creative Resistance and Creative Disruption)*, Oxford: Oxford University Press.

Andrews, M., Pritchett, L. and Woolcock, M. (2016) *Building State Capability: Evidence, Analysis, Action*, Oxford, UK: Oxford University Press. https://doi.org/10.1093/acprof:oso/9780198747482.001.0001

Angrist, N. and Meager, R. (2022) 'The Role of Implementation in Generalisability: A Synthesis of Evidence on Targeted Educational Instruction and a New Randomised Trial', CEDIL Syntheses Working Paper 4. https://cedilprogramme.org/publications/synthesis-of-evidence-on-targeted-educational-instruction-and-new-randomised-trial/

Arif, S., Nihayah, R. W., Rarasati, N., Revina, S. and Usman, S. (2022) 'Of Power and Learning: District Heads, Bureaucracy, and Education Policies in Indonesia's Decentralised Political System', RISE Working Paper 2022/111. https://dx.doi.org/doi.org/10.35489/BSG-RISE-WP_2022/111

ASER (2015) 'Trends over Time 2006–2014 (a Supplement to the Aser 2014 Report)', [13 Jan] Delhi: ASER Centre. http://img.asercentre.org/docs/Publications/ASER%20Reports/ASER%20TOT/fullasertrendsovertimereport.pdf

ASER (2018) Annual Status of Education Report (Rural) 2017 'Beyond Basics', [16 Jan] ASER Centre. https://img.asercentre.org/docs/Publications/ASER%20Reports/ASER%202017/aser2017fullreportfinal.pdf

Atuhurra, J. and Kaffenberger, M. (2020) 'System (In)Coherence: Quantifying the Alignment of Primary Education Curriculum Standards,

Examinations, and Instruction in Two East African Countries', RISE Working Paper 20/057. https://doi.org/10.35489/BSG-RISE-WP_2020/057

Atuhurra, J. and Kaffenberger, M. (2022) 'Measuring Education System Coherence: Alignment of Curriculum Standards, Examinations, and Teacher Instruction in Tanzania and Uganda', *International Journal of Educational Development*, vol. 92, 102598, https://doi.org/10.1016/j.ijedudev.2022.102598.

Banerji, R. (2015) 'How Do Systems Respond to Disruptive Pedagogic Innovations? The Case of Pratham in Bihar', RISE Working Paper 15/002. https://riseprogramme.org/publications/how-do-systems-respond-disruptive-pedagogic-innovations.html

Bano, M. (2022) 'International Push for SBMCS and the Problem of Isomorphic Mimicry: Evidence from Nigeria', RISE Working Paper 2022/102. https://dx.doi.org/doi.org/10.35489/BSG-RISE-WP_2022/102

Bano, M. and Dyonisius, D. (2022) 'The Role of District-Level Political Elites in Education Planning in Indonesia: Evidence from Two Districts', RISE Working Paper 22/109. https://doi.org/10.35489/BSG-RISE-WP_2022/109

Barjum, D. (2022) 'PDIA for Systems Change: Tackling the Learning Crisis in Indonesia', [Sept] RISE Insight Note 2022/046, RISE Programme. https://riseprogramme.org/publications/pdia-systems-change-tackling-learning-crisis-indonesia.html

Bau, N. and Das, J. (2020) 'Teacher Value-Added in a Low Income Country', *American Economic Journal: Economic Policy*, 12(1): 62–96. https://doi.org/10.1257/pol.20170243

Bau, N., Das, J. and Chang, A. (2021) 'New Evidence on Learning Trajectories in a Low-Income Setting', *International Journal of Educational Development,* 84. https://doi.org/10.1016/j.ijedudev.2021.102430

Beatty, A., Berkhout, E., Bima, L., Pradhan, M. and Suryadarma, D. (2021) 'Schooling Progress, Learning Reversal: Indonesia's Learning Profiles between 2000 and 2014', *International Journal of Educational Development*, 85: 102436. https://doi.org/10.1016/j.ijedudev.2021.102436

Belafi, C., Hwa, Y., and Kaffenberger, M. (2020) 'Building on Solid Foundations: Prioritising Universal, Early, Conceptual and Procedural Mastery of Foundational Skills', RISE Programme Insight Note, RISE Programme. https://riseprogramme.org/publications/building-solid-foundations-prioritising-universal-early-conceptual-and-procedural.html

Berkhout, E., Pradhan, M., Rahmawati, Suryadarma, D. and Swarnata, A. (2020) 'From Cheating to Learning: An Evaluation of Fraud Prevention on National Exams in Indonesia', RISE Working Paper 20/046. https://doi.org/10.35489/BSG-RISE-WP_2020/046

Bold, T., Kimenyi, M., Mwabu, G. and Sandefur, J. (2018) 'Experimental Evidence on Scaling up Education Reforms in Kenya', *Journal of Public Economics*, 168: 1–20. https://doi.org/10.1016/j.jpubeco.2018.08.007

Bruns, B., Schneider, B. R. and Saavedra, J. (2023) 'The Politics of Transforming Education in Peru: 2007–2020', RISE Working Paper Series. 23/135 RISE Programme. https://riseprogramme.org/publications/politics-transforming-education-peru-2007-2020.html

Burdett, N. (2017) 'Review of High Stakes Examination Instruments in Primary and Secondary School in Developing Countries', RISE Working Paper 17/018, RISE Programme. https://riseprogramme.org/sites/default/files/publications/RISE_WP-018_Burdett_0.pdf

Cilliers, J., Fleisch, B., Kotze, J., Mohohlwane, N., Taylor, S. and Thulare, T. (2022) 'Can Virtual Replace in-Person Coaching? Experimental Evidence on Teacher Professional Development and Student Learning', *Journal of Development Economics*, 155: 102815. https://doi.org/10.1016/j.jdeveco.2021.102815

Crouch, L. (2020) 'Systems Implications for Core Instructional Support Lessons from Sobral (Brazil), Puebla (Mexico), and Kenya', RISE Insight Note 2020/020. https://doi.org/10.35489/BSG-RISE-RI_2020/020

Crouch, L., Kaffenberger, M. and Savage, L. (2021) 'Using Learning Profiles to Inform Education Priorities: An Editors' Overview of the Special Issue', *International Journal of Educational Development*, 86: 102477. https://doi.org/10.1016/j.ijedudev.2021.102477

Dang, H., Glewwe, P., Lee, J. and Vu, K. (2020) 'What Explains Vietnam's Exceptional Performance in Education Relative to Other Countries? Analysis of the 2012 and 2015 Pisa Data', RISE Working Paper Series 20/036. https://doi.org/10.35489/BSG-RISE-WP_2020/036

de Ree, J., Muralidharan, K., Pradhan, M. and Rogers, H. (2017) 'Double for Nothing? Experimental Evidence on an Unconditional Teacher Salary Increase in Indonesia', *The Quarterly Journal of Economics*, 133(2): 993–1039. https://doi.org/10.1093/qje/qjx040

DeJaeghere, J., Duong, B. and Dao, V. (2021) 'Teaching Practices That Support Thinking and Promote Learning: Qualitative Evidence from High and Low Performing Classes in Vietnam', RISE Insight Note 2021/024. https://doi.org/10.35489/BSG-RISE-RI_2021/024

DiMaggio, P. J. and Powell, W. W. (1983) 'The Iron Cage Revisited: Institutional Isomorphism and Collective Rationality in Organizational Fields', *American Sociological Review*, 48(2): 147–60. https://doi.org/10.2307/2095101

Duflo, E., Dupas, P. and Kremer, M. (2015) 'School Governance, Teacher Incentives, and Pupil–Teacher Ratios: Experimental Evidence from Kenyan Primary Schools', *Journal of Public Economics*, 123(C): 92–110. https://doi.org/10.1016/j.jpubeco.2014.11.008

Educational Initiatives (2009) 'Student Learning Study: Status of Student Learning across 18 States of India in Urban and Rural Schools', https://www.semanticscholar.org/paper/Status-of-Student-Learning-across-18-States-of-in/97861b3d6dc6f260d2f3691e7b37f7a5c8940c0e

Filmer, D., Nahata, V. and Sabarwal, S. (2021) 'Preparation, Practice, and Beliefs: A Machine Learning Approach to Understanding Teacher Effectiveness', [8 Dec] RISE Working Paper Series. 21/084, RISE Programme. https://riseprogramme.org/publications/preparation-practice-and-beliefs-machine-learning-approach-understanding-teacher.html

Gershberg, A. I. and Spindelman, D. (2023) 'Politics, Accountability, and Learning: Insights from the RISE Programme's Political Economy Case Studies', RISE Programme. https://riseprogramme.org/publications/politics-accountability-and-learning-insights-rise-programmes-political-economy-case.html

Glewwe, P., James, Z., Lee, J., Rolleston, C. and Vu, K. (2021) 'What Explains Vietnam's Exceptional Performance in Education Relative to Other Countries? Analysis of the Young Lives Data from Ethiopia, Peru, India and Vietnam', RISE Working Paper Series 21/078. https://doi.org/10.35489/BSG-RISE-WP_2021/078

Global Goals (2015) 'Quality Education', https://www.globalgoals.org/goals/4-quality-education/

Gust, S., Hanushek, E. A. and Woessmann, L. (2022) 'Global Universal Basic Skills: Current Deficits and Implications for World Development', National Bureau of Economic Research Working Paper Series 30566. https://doi.org/10.3386/w30566

Hwa, Y. and Pritchett, L. (2021) 'Teacher Careers in Education Systems that Are Coherent for Learning: Choose and Curate toward Commitment to Capable and Committed Teachers (5Cs)', RISE Primer 2021/02. https://doi.org/10.35489/BSG-RISE-Misc_2021/02

Johnson, D. and Parrado, A. (2021) 'Assessing the Assessments: Taking Stock of Learning Outcomes Data in India', *International Journal of Educational Development*, 84: 102409. https://doi.org/10.1016/j.ijedudev.2021.102409

Kaffenberger, M. (2022) 'The Role of Purpose in Education System Outcomes: A Conceptual Framework and Empirical Examples', RISE Working Paper 22/18. https://doi.org/10.35489/BSG-RISEWP_2022/118

Kaffenberger, M. and Pritchett, L. (2021) 'A Structured Model of the Dynamics of Student Learning in Developing Countries, with Applications to Policy', *International Journal of Educational Development*, 82: 102371. https://doi.org/10.1016/j.ijedudev.2021.102371

Kaffenberger, M. and Spivack, M. (2022) 'System Coherence for Learning: Applications of the RISE Education Systems Framework', RISE Working Paper 22/086. https://doi.org/10.35489/BSG-RISEWP_2022/086

Kerwin, J. T. and Thornton, R. L. (2021) 'Making the Grade: The Sensitivity of Education Program Effectiveness to Input Choices and Outcome Measures', *The Review of Economics and Statistics*, 103(2): 251–64. https://dx.doi.org/10.1162/rest_a_00911

le Nestour, A., Moscoviz, L. and Sandefur, J. (2021) 'The Long-Term Decline of School Quality in the Developing World', Center for Global Development, Consultation draft. https://www.cgdev.org/sites/default/files/consultation-draft-le-nestour-et-al-school-quality-decline.pdf

Levy, B. (2022) 'How Political Contexts Influence Education Systems: Patterns, Constraints, Entry Points', RISE Working Paper 22/122. https://dx.doi.org/10.35489/BSG-RISE-WP_2022/122

Levy, B., Cameron, R., Hoadley, U. and Naidoo, V. (2018) *The Politics and Governance of Basic Education: A Tale of Two South African Provinces*, Oxford: Oxford University Press. https://doi.org/10.1093/oso/9780198824053.001.0001

London, J. and Duong, B. H. (2023) 'The Politics of Education and Learning in Vietnam: Contributions to a Theory of Embedded Accountabilities', RISE Political Economy Papers. RISE Programme. https://riseprogramme.org/publications/politics-education-and-learning-vietnam-contributions-theory-embedded-accountabilities.html

Matthew, A. (2021) 'Getting Real About Unknowns in Complex Policy Work', [Nov]. RISE Working Paper 2021/083, RISE Programme. https://riseprogramme.org/sites/default/files/2021-11/Getting_Real_about_Unknowns_Complex_Policy_Work.pdf

Mbiti, I. (2016) 'The Need for Accountability in Education in Developing Countries', *Journal of Economic Perspectives* 30(3): 109–32. https://dx.doi.org/10.1257/jep.30.3.109

Mbiti, I., Muralidharan, K., Romero, M., Schipper, Y., Manda, C. and Rajani, R. (2019) 'Inputs, Incentives, and Complementarities in Education: Experimental Evidence from Tanzania', *The Quarterly Journal of Economics*, 134(3): 1627–73. https://doi.org/10.1093/qje/qjz010

McKinsey Global Institute (2024) 'Spark & Sustain: How All of the World's School Systems Can Improve Learning at Scale', [12 Feb] San Francisco,

CA: McKinsey and Company. https://www.mckinsey.com/industries/education/our-insights/spark-and-sustain-how-school-systems-can-improve-learning-at-scale#/

McNaught, T. (2022) 'A Problem-Driven Approach to Education Reform: The Story of Sobral in Brazil', [2 Mar] RISE Insight Note 2022/039. RISE Programme. https://riseprogramme.org/publications/problem-driven-approach-education-reform-story-sobral-brazil.html

Moore, M. and Spivack, M. (2023) 'A Public Value Approach to Analyzing and Intervening in National Educational Systems', [31 Jan] RISE Essay, RISE Programme. https://riseprogramme.org/publications/public-value-approach-analyzing-and-intervening-national-educational-systems.html

Muralidharan, K. and Singh, A. (2020) 'Improving Public Sector Management at Scale? Experimental Evidence on School Governance in India', RISE Working Paper 20/056. RISE Programme. https://riseprogramme.org/publications/improving-public-sector-management-scale-experimental-evidence-school-governance-india.html

Nihayah, R., Revina, S. and Usman, S. (2020) 'Sociocultural Drivers of Local Educational Innovations: Findings from Indonesia', RISE Working Paper Series. 20/043. RISE Programme. https://riseprogramme.org/publications/sociocultural-drivers-local-educational-innovations-findings-indonesia

Piper, B., Simmons Zuilkowski, S., Dubeck, M., Jepkemei, E. and King, S. J. (2018) 'Identifying the Essential Ingredients to Literacy and Numeracy Improvement: Teacher Professional Development and Coaching, Student Textbooks, and Structured Teachers' Guides', *World Development,* 106: 324–36. https://doi.org/10.1016/j.worlddev.2018.01.018

Pritchett, L. (2013) 'The Rebirth of Education: Schooling Ain't Learning', Washington, DC: Center for Global Development. https://www.cgdev.org/sites/default/files/rebirth-education-introduction_0.pdf

Pritchett, L. (2015) 'Creating Education Systems Coherent for Learning Outcomes: Making the Transition from Schooling to Learning', [Dec] RISE Working Paper Series 15/005. https://riseprogramme.org/sites/default/files/inline-files/RISE_WP-005_Pritchett.pdf

Pritchett, L. and Beatty, A. (2012) 'The Negative Consequences of Overambitious Curricula in Developing Countries', *Center for Global Development* Working Paper 293. https://doi.org/10.2139/ssrn.2235869

Pritchett, L., Newman, K. and Silberstein, J. (2022) 'Focus to Flourish: Five Actions to Accelerate Progress in Learning. Research on Improving Systems of Education', RISE Policy Paper. https://doi.org/10.35489/BSG-RISE-Misc_2022/07

Revina, S., Pramana, R. P., Fillaili, R. and Suryadarma, D. (2020) 'Systemic Constraints Facing Teacher Professional Development in a Middle-Income Country: Indonesia's Experience over Four Decades', RISE Working Paper 2020/054. https://dx.doi.org/doi.org/10.35489/BSG-RISE-WP_2020/054

Rosser, A., King, P. and Widoyoko, D. (2022) 'The Political Economy of the Learning Crisis in Indonesia', Research on Improving Systems of Education (RISE), PE01. https://doi.org/10.35489/BSG-RISE-2022/PE01

Saavedra, J. (2023) *Estamos Tarde: Una Memoria Para Recobrar La Education En El Peru*. Lima, Peru: Penguin Random House Grupo Editorial.

Samji, S. and Kapoor, M. (2022) 'Funda Wande through the Lens of PDIA: Showcasing a Flexible and Iterative Learning Approach to Improving Educational Outcomes', [14 Jan] RISE Insight Note 2022/036, RISE Programme. https://riseprogramme.org/publications/funda-wande-through-lens-pdia-showcasing-flexible-and-iterative-learning-approach.html

Schneider, B. R., Cevallos Estarellas, P. and Bruns, B. (2019) 'The Politics of Transforming Education in Ecuador: Confrontation and Continuity, 2006–2017', *Comparative Education Review*, 63(2): 259–80. https://doi.org/10.1086/702609

Siddiqi, S. (2022) 'Contested Identities; Competing Accountabilities: The Making of a 'Good' Public Schoolteacher in Khyber Pakhtunkhwa, Pakistan', RISE Political Economy Papers. https://doi.org/10.35489/BSG-RISE-2022/PE02

Silberstein, J. (2021) 'Measuring, Visualising, and Simulating Solutions to the Learning Crisis: New Evidence from Learning Profiles in 18 Countries', RISE Programme Insight Note. https://doi.org/10.35489/BSG-RISE-RI_2021/029

Singh, A. (2020) 'Myths of Official Measurement: Auditing and Improving Administrative Data in Developing Countries,' RISE Working Paper 20/042. https://doi.org/10.35489/BSG-RISE-WP_2020/042

Stern, J., Dubeck, M., Piper, B. and Jukes, M. (2022) 'Instructional Support for Effective Large-Scale Reading Interventions', Learning at Scale Study. https://shared.rti.org/author/stern-j?page=1

UNESCO (1990) 'World Declaration on Education for All and Framework for Action to Meet Basic Learning Needs', World Conference on Education for All. https://unesdoc.unesco.org/ark:/48223/pf0000127583

Watkins, S. and Ashforth, A. (2019) 'An Analysis of the Political Economy of Schooling in Rural Malawi: Interactions among Parents, Teachers, Students, Chiefs and Primary Education Advisors', RISE Working Paper 19/031. https://doi.org/10.35489/BSG-RISE-WP_2019/031

Watkins, S., and Kaler, A. (2016) 'Pivoting to Learning: A Puzzle with Many Pieces Usan Watkins and Amy Kaler Rise-Wp-16/006', RISE Working Paper 16/006. https://riseprogramme.org/sites/default/files/2020-11/RISE_WP-006-Watkins-Kaler.pdf

Williamson, J. (1990) 'What Washington Means by Policy Reform', Chapter 2 from Williamson, J. (ed) *Latin American Adjustment: How Much Has Happened?* Institute for International Economics.

World Bank (2018) *World Development Report 2018: Learning to Realize Education's Promise*. Washington, DC: World Bank.

World Bank (2022) 'The State of Global Learning Poverty: 2022 Update' [June]. https://thedocs.worldbank.org/en/doc/34035a49acb5700ce8b118aeda81a5cb-0510022023/original/TheStateOfLearningPoverty-Feb2023Update-03-08-23.pdf

Yusrina, A., Alifia, U., Revina, S., Putri Pramana, R. and Bima, L. (2022) 'Is the Game Worth the Candle? Examining the Effectiveness of Initial Teacher Education in Indonesia', [Aug]. RISE Working Paper Series. 22/106, RISE Programme. https://riseprogramme.org/publications/game-worth-candle-examining-effectiveness-initial-teacher-education-indonesia.html

Response to Lant Pritchett by Pedro Carneiro

In this volume, Lant Pritchett paints a bleak picture of the state of learning in the developing world, in what he calls *The Learning Crisis*. The case he makes is compelling: the learning crisis is real, and its magnitude is scandalous. There is now widespread evidence from multiple data sources of staggering knowledge disparities between students of poor and rich countries. This is true even when we compare students with similar levels of schooling.

Pritchett stresses that the issue is not so much the quantity of schooling, but the quality. Across many countries in the developing world, students' learning does not improve even as they stay longer in education. Statistics based on the quantity of education, such as years of schooling, are woefully inadequate as measures of human capital in many countries because so little learning takes place in schools. Yet these statistics are still frequently used as a guide to policy.

According to Pritchett, knowing about the best practices for promoting children's learning is not really the issue. More than finding out which interventions do and do not work in schools in different settings, the central issue faced by many poor countries is one of implementation, and it is primarily a systemwide issue (or set of issues). This is important because addressing the learning crisis requires primarily addressing systemwide failures in public education.

One typical criticism of Pritchett's argument is that systemwide changes are incredibly hard to achieve, and so resources could be better suited to interventions that attempt to bypass the system, and operate at a more micro level, such as schools. Pritchett would argue that, even if apparently sensible, there is substantial evidence that such an approach is doomed to fail. It is difficult for interventions to be successful on a large scale without being fully integrated in a working public education system. He goes on to lay out a set of principles that should guide systemwide reforms in the developing world.

This is an excellent chapter. We cannot afford to continue to ignore the picture it paints and its proposals. Here I present three (modest) complementary reflections.

I. Gaps in circumstances vs gaps in learning

Learning depends on multiple factors, of which schools are only one. One reaction to Pritchett's article could be that it demonstrates that the learning crisis is real and very serious, but not that its main determinants are in the school system. Children in poor families face multiple challenges to development, such as poor health and nutrition, home environments that are not optimal for learning and exposure to violence, among many others. Such challenges could be so overwhelming that they would severely dampen the impact even of the best school system. So, to what extent is the learning crisis a consequence of education systems, and to what extent is it a consequence of other country-level deficiencies?

Multiple non-schooling factors surely play a large role in learning, and addressing the learning crisis adequately requires engaging with them. It is difficult to know exactly how much can be changed by moving one factor alone (even a big one), in this case, the provision of public education.

Pritchett is convinced that substantial improvements can be made even if the sole intervention is on the school systems. In fact, as he points out, it is striking that the learning crisis is also evident among children from high socioeconomic status in poor countries. Such a comparison controls for many of the other barriers to learning that could be afflicting most children in the developing world, suggesting that low-quality schooling bears substantial responsibility for this problem.

In support of Pritchett's view, in a recent paper, Singh provides convincing evidence that country-level differences in student performance could be substantially driven by differences in the productivity of schools between countries. He compares the performance of students across countries in the Young Lives Study: Ethiopia, India, Peru, and Vietnam.[1] He shows that although there are some early (pre-school age) differences in children's test scores, they grow substantially during the first eight years of school. Vietnam far outperforms the other three countries in this sample, and one can attribute most of the cross-country differences in learning rates in this study to cross-country differences in school productivity. This would suggest that Pritchett is indeed right, and that although other factors matter for learning, cross-country differences in student performance could in large part be a consequence of cross-country differences in school systems. It would be important to investigate to what extent this applies beyond the comparison of Vietnam with these other three countries.

Vietnam is indeed well known for its incredible performance in PISA tests. Dang et al. document this fact, although they struggle to explain Vietnam's outstanding results relative to other countries based on student, household, and school variables observed in the dataset.[2] It is possible that the main difference lies in features of the school system that Pritchett emphasises, and which are not easily observed in the type of surveys that accompany the administration of PISA tests.

In spite of the learning crisis emphasised by Pritchett, returns to formal education remain large across the world, even in countries where not much learning seems to be taking place during the schooling years.[3] Obviously, we do not know what counterfactual returns would be if school systems worked better: it is likely that returns would be even higher. That said, there appears to be a substantial payoff to schooling in very poor countries with little learning, which is at least as large or even larger in percentage terms than that observed in advanced economies, where students appear to have a much higher level of knowledge. It would be interesting to further investigate why this is the case if students do not learn too much in school. It is possible that schools in places like Sub-Saharan Africa are still imparting important knowledge to students that is not easy to capture through simple standardised tests.

II. Private schools

Disappointed with the services offered by public schools, many families in developing countries are turning to low-cost private schools.[4] The market has increased dramatically. When measured, test scores of students in private schools are as high or higher than those of students in public schools, and fees are typically low. The effectiveness of such schools has been questioned by some researchers,[5] but there have been others who have presented much more optimistic results.[6]

Private schools may have an important role to play, especially in systems with dysfunctional public schools. Parents seem to value them substantially.[7] Enrolment in private schools is quite high in a variety of countries, and surprisingly, in very poor contexts. For example, in Pakistan 39% of children are now enrolled in a private school. Similar levels of private enrolment are observed in several other developing countries.[8] Therefore, it is no longer possible to discuss the issues addressed in Pritchett's chapter without considering the role of what is, in many cases, an unregulated low-cost private sector.

III. The implementation of systemwide changes

Pritchett's diagnostic and ideas are sensible, and the problem is indeed dramatic and urgent. He makes a passionate case for systemwide changes, in contrast to more micro interventions. He provides a set of principles that should guide such changes.

But how can one achieve such widescale changes? The case usually made for micro-level interventions is precisely that it is not feasible to change the whole system, but it may be feasible and worthwhile to intervene in some of its components.

This is not a problem only of poor countries. Even in rich countries systemwide changes are rare, in many cases not because they are undesirable, but because they are so difficult to implement. Pritchett's view is that systemwide changes are a necessary condition for any noticeable improvement in standards, and he is probably correct. But his proposals risk falling flat if not accompanied by a realistic discussion about implementation.

In sum, Pritchett rightly emphasises one of the most important problems in education in poor countries: the quality of schools is low, and there is little or no learning occurring in many settings. He presents a proposal for systemwide changes, which is well articulated, sensible, and has very concrete recommendations. It is hard to argue against what Pritchett writes.

In this discussion I raise three small points. First, there are many other non-school factors that are central determinants of learning. While there is evidence that the school system can in fact make a huge difference in the performance of students, as argued by Pritchett, it may not be possible to produce significant and long-lasting changes without addressing many of the other dramatic challenges faced by students and their families in the poorest countries in the world. Furthermore, while student knowledge appears to be very low in many developing countries, returns to schooling remain stubbornly high, suggesting that students are indeed getting something valuable out of their years in school.

Second, private school enrolment has exploded in the developing world. There are several countries where private enrolment accounts for almost half of total enrolment in basic education. This growth has been fuelled by an expansion of low-cost private schools, in what is often a very unregulated sector. With such high – and growing – levels of private school enrolment one cannot conceive of a plan to increase student learning in poor countries without incorporating the role of private schools.

Third, Pritchett's proposal is very ambitious, and its implementation is daunting. His ambition is understandable given the scale of the problem and the paucity of available solutions. But a subsequent discussion of the process through which one can achieve the needed reforms is required, without which it is difficult, if not impossible, to make progress.

Notes

1 Singh (2020).

2 Dang et al. (2023).

3 Patrinos and Psacharopoulos (2020).

4 Tooley (2021).

5 Akmal et al. (2019).

6 Andrabi et al. (2021).

7 Carneiro et al. (2024).

8 Baum et al. (2014).

References

Akmal, M., Crawfurd, L. and Hares, S. (2019) 'Low-Cost Private Schools: What Have We Learned in the Five Years since DFID Rigorous Review' Centre for Global Development. https://www.cgdev.org/blog/low-cost-private-schools-what-have-we-learned-five-years-dfid-rigorous-review

Andrabi, T., Bau, N., Das, J. and Khwaja, A. (2021) 'Private Schools, Learning and Civic Values in a Low-Income Country', Working Paper. https://www.hks.harvard.edu/centers/cid/publications/private-schooling-learning-and-civic-values-low-income-country

Baum, D., Lewis, L., Lusk-Stover, O. and Patrinos, H. (2014) 'What Matters Most for Engaging the Private Sector in Education: A Framework Paper Systems Approach for Better Education Results', (SABER) Working Paper, Washington, DC: World Bank. https://documents.worldbank.org/en/publication/documents-reports/documentdetail/600511468126896866/what-matters-most-of-engaging-the-private-sector-in-education-a-framework-paper

Carneiro, P., Das., J. and Reis, H. (2024) 'The Value of Public Schools: Evidence from Pakistan', *Review of Economics and Statistics*, 106(5): 1301–1318. https://doi.org/10.1162/rest_a_01237

Dang, H., Glewwe, P., Lee, J. and Vu, K. (2023) 'What Explains Vietnam's Exceptional Performance in Education Relative to Other Countries? Analysis of the 2012, 2015 and 2018 PISA Data', *Economics of Education Review*, 96, October. https://doi.org/10.1016/j.econedurev.2023.102434

Patrinos, H. and G. Psacharopoulos (2020) 'Returns to Education in Developing Countries', in Bradley, S. and Green, C. (eds) *The Economics of Education*, 2nd Edition, Academic Press. https://doi.org/10.1016/B978-0-12-815391-8.00004-5

Singh, A. (2020) 'Learning More with Every Year: School Year Productivity and International Learning Divergence', *Journal of the European Economic Association*, 18(4): 1770–1813. https://doi.org/10.1093/jeea/jvz033

Tooley, J. (2021) Really Good Schools: Global Lessons for High-Caliber, Lowcost Education, Oakland: Independent Institute. https://doi.org/10.1007/s11138-022-00577-w

Response to Lant Pritchett by Miguel Urquiola

Research on the Economics of Education has made real strides since the days of the Washington Consensus (circa 1990). This comment reviews five lessons such research has produced. It uses these lessons to frame comments on Lant Pritchett's paper.

The lessons provide a contrast. Namely, 1990s observers would find some of them intuitive and expected; others they would find quite surprising. The lessons are:

1. Raising school value-added is crucial to educational policy.
2. One can measure (close to) causal school value-added in many settings.
3. The public sector, left to its own devices, may not improve school value-added.
4. The private sector, left to its own devices, may not improve school value-added.
5. System design can affect school value-added.

I. Lesson 1: Raising school value-added is crucial

School value-added is the impact that attending a given school has on a student's outcomes, for example, her skills. All else equal, a school with high value-added enhances a student's skills more than one with low value-added – i.e., it teaches her more.

Economists typically analyse school value-added with respect to achievement as measured by test scores. One can consider value-added with respect to other outcomes, such as labour market earnings. Research suggests that schools' value-added in different dimensions are positively correlated. For example, Chetty et al. show that value-added measured using test scores is correlated with school value-added in terms of college attendance and later earnings.[1]

It is not surprising that value-added garnered attention in the economics of education – it is closely related to the concept of productivity, which is salient in all of economics. Value-added is also closely related to Pritchett's learning profiles (Figure 12.2). Countries with steep learning profiles have school systems with high average school value-added. Further, as Pritchett notes, there is enormous variation in value-added – much of it within as to opposed to between countries. The same holds regarding many countries' public and private sectors; each can contain both high and low value-added schools, with significant overlap.[2]

In short, consistent with Pritchett's conclusions, raising school value-added is crucial to effective education policy.

II. Lesson 2: (Close to) causal school value-added can be observed in many settings

If one could time travel and tell 1990 education economists that value-added would gain salience in their field, they would not be surprised. However, the fact that a concept is salient does not mean it is easy to measure. What would surprise 1990 researchers is that in many settings, their successors have succeeded at estimating *causal* school value-added – that is, at capturing the impact of a school independent of other factors that influence a child's progress.

To elaborate, around 1990, pessimism about measuring school value-added arose from two sources. First, few countries had representative data on outcomes like test scores or labour market earnings.

Second, the 'credibility revolution' was getting underway – a consensus was emerging that policy should be based on causal estimates. With that came the realisation that obtaining such estimates often called for experiments or quasi-experiments. Economists realised that finding/running such experiments would be a tall order with respect to school value-added. An essential fact about education is that families do not choose schools randomly, e.g., some schools are more likely to have wealthier students than others. In the presence of such non-random sorting, it should be challenging to estimate schools causal value-added. For example, children in a given school might make good progress in reading, but that might have more to do with their household wealth than with how well that school teaches reading.

Yet, two things have happened since then. First, as researchers emphasised the importance of school value-added, many governments began to collect data on outcomes like test scores. Today, Pritchett can produce a figure like Figure 12.1 covering many countries.

Economists also found that using appropriate methodologies, causal school value-added can be reasonably approximated even in the absence of true experiments or quasi-experiments.[3]

In short, measuring school value-added is more feasible than 1990s observers might have expected.

III. Lesson 3: The public sector, left to its own devices, may not improve school value-added

Another lesson is that the public sector left to its own devices – or, as Pritchett says, operating 'business as usual' – may not improve value-added.

A 1990 observer would not be shocked by this lesson. By then, Hanushek was making the case, albeit with non-experimental evidence, that public school spending could increase substantially with little impact on outcomes like skills.[4] Pritchett illustrated that this finding held in multiple developed countries.[5]

Further, it was already apparent that many public schools face few incentives to improve their value-added. And that public teacher unions resist experimentation (and recently displayed a striking enthusiasm for COVID-19 school-closures, with substantial adverse impacts on children's skills).

In recent years, experimental studies in Indonesia and Tanzania confirmed that even large increases in public expenditure can fail to improve skills.[6] Further, in Pakistani public schools, the link between parental demand and school value-added is tenuous.[7]

Nonetheless, recent studies consider US school finance reforms and find a clear link between public spending and student skills.[8]

The bottom line is that one cannot systematically rely on the public sector, operating under its usual rules, to raise school value-added. That might happen at times, but not as a general rule.

IV. Lesson 4: The private sector, left to its own devices, may not improve school value-added

Another lesson would be more surprising to 1990s observers: the private sector cannot be relied upon to raise value-added either.

To elaborate, since Friedman, many economists have argued that the way to address low public school value-added was to give families vouchers to attend private schools.[9] This idea has natural appeal because it extends standard results from markets for consumer goods to education.[10]

The idea was implemented in Chile by the 'Chicago Boys', economists partially trained by Friedman himself.[11] They presided over a large expansion of the private sector. Chile's average school value-added should have taken off. But Hsieh and Urquiola presented early non-experimental evidence that this had not happened.[12] The main effect of vouchers was greater student sorting (along traits like family income) rather than greater student learning.

More recent experimental studies find that vouchers' effects on skills can be highly positive,[13] highly negative,[14] or modest.[15]

Recent years have also seen theoretical and empirical work that helps explain why Friedman's intuition did not hold. The short story is that consumers – the source of demand and many incentives in a market system – do not always prefer higher value-added schools. This may be for two reasons. First, value-added is challenging to compute/interpret, even for researchers; thus, families may lack information on it. Second, households may rationally value school attributes other than value-added, such as peer quality, networks, and proximity.[16] If these are not highly correlated with value-added, households will not always demand/reward school productivity.

The bottom line is that one cannot systematically rely on the private sector, operating under its usual rules, to raise school value-added. That might happen at times, but not as a general rule.

V. Lesson 5: System design can affect value-added

Research since the 1990s shows that other ways in which the school system is configured (beyond the public/private division) can affect average school value-added. To cite one example, inequality was not a central concern in the Washington Consensus, but it has gained salience since then. As a result, many observers call for school systems that are less segregated by ability or income. Related, many also wish to reduce/reform the use of standardised test scores in admissions.

Yet rigorous research shows that each of these policies could lower average school value-added – it is possible that they could *reduce* almost all students' learning.[17]

In short, one must be mindful that as elsewhere, trade-offs rather than 'free lunches' characterise policy in education.

VI. Conclusion

Consistent with Pritchett's paper, raising school value-added is urgent but unlikely to happen without deliberate/focused attention. In particular, post-1990s research shows that school value added is central and easier to measure than expected. But that does not mean that it can be improved by 'easy' measures like increasing public funding or distributing vouchers.

Notes

1 Chetty et al. (2014). See also Riehl et al. (2019); Ainsworth et al. (2023); Beuermann et al. (2023).

2 Andrabi et al. (2023).

3 Angrist et al. (2017); Ainsworth et al. (2023); Andrabi et al. (2023).

4 Hanushek (2003).

5 Pritchett (2003).

6 de Ree et al. (2018); Mbiti et al. (2019).

7 Andrabi et al. (2023).

8 Jackson (2020).

9 Friedman (1955).

[10] MacLeod and Urquiola (2019).

[11] Edwards (2023).

[12] Hsieh and Urquiola (2006).

[13] Bettinger et al. (2017).

[14] Abdulkadiroğlu et al. (2018).

[15] Muralidharan and Sundararaman (2015).

[16] MacLeod and Urquiola (2015); Allende (2019); Andrabi et al. (2023); Neilson (2021); Ainsworth et al. (2023).

[17] Duflo et al. (2011); Riehl (2023).

References

Abdulkadiroğlu, A., Pathak, P. and Walters, C. R. (2018) 'Free to Choose: Can School Choice Reduce Student Achievement?', *American Economic Journal Applied Economics*, 10(1): 175–206. https://doi.org/10.1257/app.20160634

Ainsworth, R., Dehejia, R., Pop-Eleches, C. and Urquiola, M. (2023) 'Why Do Households Leave School Value Added on the Table? The Roles of Information and Preferences', *American Economic Review,* 113(4): 1049–1082. https://doi.org/10.1257/aer.20210949

Allende, C. (2019) 'Competition under Social Interactions and the Design of Education Policies', Stanford Economics Working Paper No. 3979. https://www.gsb.stanford.edu/faculty-research/working-papers/competition-under-social-interactions-design-education-policies

Andrabi, T., Bau, N., Das, J. and Khwaja, A. (2023) 'Heterogeneity in School Value-Added and the Private Premium', Mimeo, Harvard University. https://doi.org/10.35489/BSG-RISEWP_2022/116

Angrist, J. D., Hull, P. D., Pathak, P. A. and Walters, C. A. (2017) 'Leveraging Lotteries for School Value-Added: Testing and Estimation', *The Quarterly Journal of Economics*, 132(2): 871–919. https://doi.org/10.1093/qje/qjx001

Bettinger, E., Kremer, M., Kugler, M., Medina, C., Posso, C. and Saavedra, J. E. (2017) 'Can Educational Voucher Programs Pay for Themselves?', Unpublished manuscript, Harvard University. https://www.bc.edu/content/dam/bc1/schools/mcas/economics/pdf/seminars/private_school_scholarships_august15_2017-CLEAN%20(1).pdf

Beuermann, D. W., Jackson, C. K., Navarro-Sola, L. and Pardo, F. (2023) 'What Is a Good School, and can Parents Tell? Evidence on the

Multidimensionality of School Output', *Review of Economic Studies*, 90(1): 65–101. https://doi.org/10.1093/restud/rdac025

Chetty, R., Friedman, J. N. and Rockoff, J. (2014) 'Measuring the Impacts of Teachers II: Teacher Value-Added and Student Outcomes in Adulthood', *American Economic Review*, 104(9): 2633–2679. https://doi.org/10.1257/aer.104.9.2633

de Ree, J., Muralidharan, K., Pradhan, M. and Rogers, H. (2018) 'Double for Nothing? Experimental Evidence on an Unconditional Teacher Salary Increase Indonesia', *The Quarterly Journal of Economics*, 133(2): 993–1039. https://doi.org/10.1093/qje/qjx040

Duflo, E., Dupas, P. and Kremer, M. (2011) 'Peer Effects, Teacher Incentives, and the Impact of Tracking: Evidence from a Randomized Evaluation in Kenya', *American Economic Review*, 101(5): 1739–1774. https://doi.org/10.1257/aer.101.5.1739

Edwards, S. (2023) *The Chile Project: The Story of the Chicago Boys and the Downfall of Neoliberalism*, Princeton, NJ: Princeton University Press. https://doi.org/10.1353/book.112152

Friedman, M. (1955) 'The role of Government in Education', in Solo, R. A. (ed), *Economics and the Public Interest*, New Brunswick, NJ: Rutgers University Press: 124–44.

Hanushek, E. A. (2003) 'The Failure of Input-Based Schooling Policies', *The Economic Journal*, 113(485): F64–F98. https://doi.org/10.1111/1468-0297.00099

Hsieh, C. T. and Urquiola, M. (2006) 'The Effects of Generalized School Choice on Achievement and Stratification: Evidence from Chile's School Voucher Program', *Journal of Public Economics*, 90: 1477–503. https://doi.org/10.1016/j.jpubeco.2005.11.002

Jackson, C. K. (2020) 'Does School Spending Matter? The New Literature on an Old Question', in Tach, L., Dunifon, R. and Miller, D. L. (eds), *Confronting Inequality: How Policies and Practices Shape Children's Opportunities*,. American Psychological Association: 165–186. https://doi.org/10.1037/0000187-008

MacLeod, W. B. and Urquiola, M. (2015) 'Reputation and School Competition', *American Economic Review*, 105(11): 3471–88. https://doi.org/10.1257/aer.20130332

MacLeod, W. B. and Urquiola, M. (2019) 'Is Education Consumption or Investment? Implications for School Competition', *Annual Review of Economics*, 11: 563–589. https://doi.org/10.1146/annurev-economics-080218-030402

Mbiti, I., Muralidharan, K., Romero, M., Schipper, Y., Manda, C. and Rajani, R. (2019) 'Inputs, Incentives, and Complementarities in Education: Experimental Evidence from Tanzania', *The Quarterly Journal of Economics*, 134(3): 1627–73. https://doi.org/10.1093/qje/qjz010

Muralidharan, K. and Sundararaman, V. (2015) 'The Aggregate Effect of School Choice: Evidence from a Two-Stage Experiment in India', *The Quarterly Journal of Economics*, 130: 1011–66. https://doi.org/10.1093/qje/qjv013

Neilson, C. (2021) 'Targeted Vouchers, Competition among Schools and the Academic Achievement of Poor Students', Mimeo, Yale University. https://christopherneilson.github.io/work/documents/Neilson_JMP/Neilson_SEP Vouchers2021.pdf

Pritchett, L. (2003) 'Educational Quality and Costs: A Big Puzzle and Five Possible Pieces', Mimeo, Harvard University.

Riehl, E. (2023) 'Do Less Informative College Admission Exams Reduce Earnings Inequality? Evidence from Colombia', *Journal of Labor Economics*, 42(4): 1009–1047. https://doi.org/10.1086/725167

Riehl, E., Saavedra, J. and Urquiola, M. (2019) 'Learning and Earning: An Approximation to College Value-Added in Two Dimensions', in Hoxby, C. M. and Stange, K. (eds), *Productivity in Higher Education*, University of Chicago Press: 105–32. https://doi.org/10.7208/chicago/9780226574615.003.0005

13. Towards resilient and sustainable universal healthcare coverage

Alistair McGuire, Joan Costa-i-Font and Ranjeeta Thomas

Over the past three decades, health systems have made significant strides towards achieving universal health coverage. However, household out-of-pocket payments for medical care still remain high, and disparities in financial risk protection and healthcare quality continue to give rise to pervasive health inequalities, and some Western countries exhibit a slowdown in life expectancy. The COVID-19 pandemic has shown that global health systems need to be both (i) resilient to shocks and (ii) sustainable in their ability to provide for basic healthcare needs. However, the challenge that health systems in ageing societies face today include how to overcome staffing shortages, waste of resources, and poor regulation, as well as the incomplete integration of long-term care programmes into the main insurance package. Interventions include the expansion of the fiscal space, more efficient allocation of public funding, designing policies to provide high-quality care, and institutions to regulate the diffusion of new, generally costly, healthcare technologies and drugs, and limiting expenditures on waste and corruption.

I. Introduction

During the past three decades, health systems have experienced significant transformations with many systems undergoing major reforms to progress towards the 2030 United Nations Sustainable Development Goals (UN SDGs) of achieving universal health coverage (UHC) and hence improving individuals' financial healthcare risk protection.[1] While care insurance packages vary greatly across countries, both in terms of services covered and quality delivered, Figure 13.1 shows evidence of significant achievements at a global scale. However,

How to cite this book chapter:

McGuire, Alistair, Costa-i-Font, Joan and Thomas, Ranjeeta (2025) 'Towards resilient and sustainable universal healthcare coverage', in: Besley, Tim, Bucelli, Irene and Velasco, Andrés (eds) *The London Consensus: Economic Principles for the 21st Century*, London: LSE Press, pp. 433–471 https://doi.org/10.31389/lsepress.tlc.m

progress has mostly taken place in high- and upper middle-income countries (UMICs), and there remains much room for improvement in low- and low middle-income countries (LMICs).

Evidence from past reforms illustrates that achieving financial risk protection requires significant public financing of healthcare. This is true even in primarily private healthcare systems, such as the United States, where public financing funds about half of health spending. As discussed in Barr's chapter (14) in this volume on the welfare state, private insurance fails for various reasons and only social insurance schemes, or tax-based financing can provide the base for sustainable healthcare funding for the entire population. Consequently, most of the countries that have achieved high levels of financial risk protection are financed primarily through social insurance, tax-based schemes, or a mix, with private insurance playing a complementary or supplementary role. Even with notable progress towards UHC, out-of-pocket expenditure on healthcare remains high in a significant part of the globe, as Figure 13.2 illustrates. Finally, catastrophic spending is not confined to low-income countries alone; it is significant in many middle-income and high-income countries, particularly the US, where around 4.6% of the population spend more than 10% of their household budget on healthcare.

The gradual improvement in UHC and associated benefits of financial security have taken place alongside significant improvements in life

Figure 13.1: Progress towards universal health coverage: service coverage index for low- to high-income countries, 2000–2017

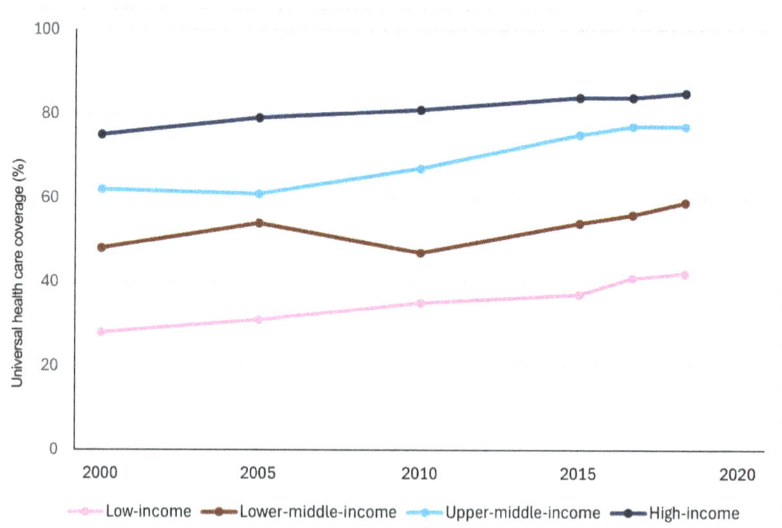

Source: created by the authors based on data by the Global Health Observatory, World Health.

Figure 13.2: Out-of-pocket expenditure (% of current health expenditure), for low- to high-income countries, 2000–2020

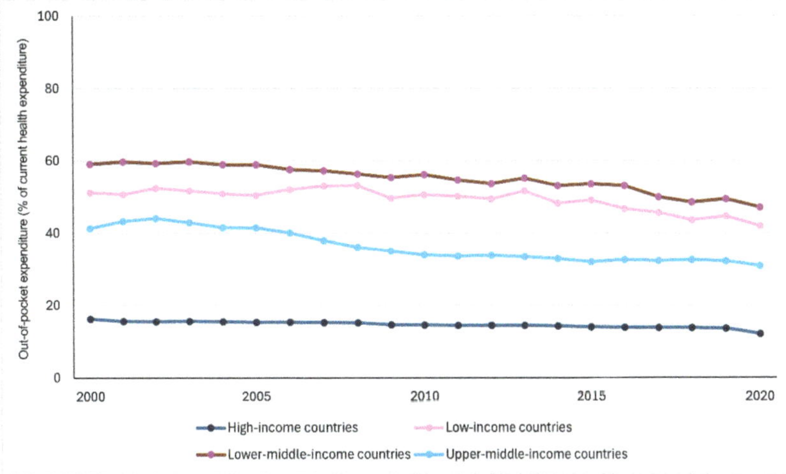

Source: created by the authors based on data from 'Our World in Data'.

expectancy, especially in low-income countries, but has recently fallen as a result of the COVID-19 pandemic, as Figure 13.3 shows.

However, such improvements are far from universal. In fact, Figure 13.4 reveals that life expectancy at birth has recently declined generally in high-income countries, even after accounting for global downturns related to the COVID-19 pandemic. Life expectancy has either levelled off or decreased after decades of improvement, mostly due to behavioural factors related to wider social determinants of health that are not fully under the control of the health system. Comorbidities have increased markedly in the elderly, particularly in high-income countries, where healthcare systems in these countries are now struggling to maintain universal, high-quality delivery in an equitable manner.[2]

This chapter assesses the role of healthcare funding, delivery and investment in promoting global health, wellbeing and growth. In section II, we consider the impact of social determinants and progress in equity of health. Section III considers the various approaches taken to address common global issues of (i) financing healthcare, (ii) delivery of healthcare, (iii) access to effective healthcare, (iv) healthcare workforce and (v) provision of long-term care. We argue that UHC requires building resilient and sustainable healthcare systems and the best approaches to UHC are context-specific and depend on the political context and economic trajectory of each country. Policy lessons from countries that have made the transition to UHC can serve as a roadmap for others. In the final section, we summarise these as policy recommendations.

Figure 13.3: Life expectancy at birth (years) across countries

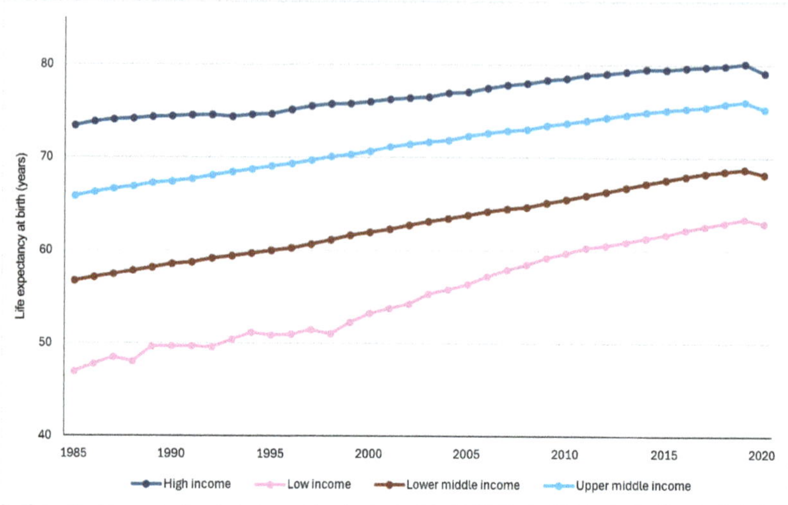

Source: created by the authors based on data from the World Development Indicators, World Bank.

Figure 13.4: Life expectancy at birth (years) in G7 countries

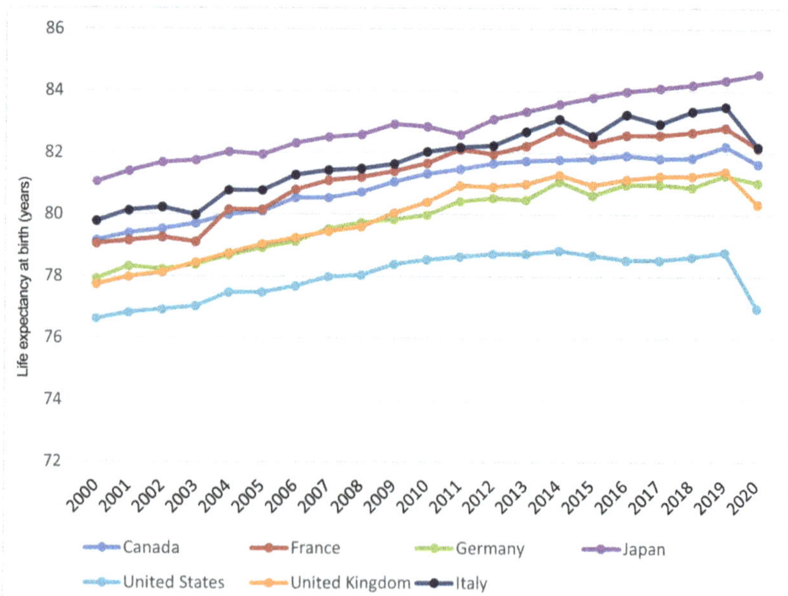

Source: created by the authors based on data from the World Development Indicators, World Bank.

II. Progress towards health equity and social determinants of health

The COVID-19 pandemic became an example of the Hobbesian remark that life can be 'nasty, brutish, and short'. The pandemic showed that health disparities endure even when contagious diseases level the playing field. The COVID-19 experience was extremely different in wealthy and less developed nations. Although over 5.55 billion people (72% of the world's population) have received at least one dose of the COVID-19 vaccine, access to vaccinations has been markedly unequal both between and within countries. In many African countries vaccination rates remain around 30%, while in high-income countries poor and ethnic minorities had higher levels of disease exposure, due to the nature of their work and lower vaccine uptake rates.

The persistence of health inequalities reflects inequalities in the access to healthcare, but also the impact of social determinants of health. The World Health Organization (WHO) Commission on Social Determinants of Health highlighted the importance of poverty, education, employment, gender inequality, and social exclusion as contributors to health inequalities and as issues that must be addressed across the world.[3] For instance, the poorest 1% in the US die 10–15 years earlier than the richest 1%; in England there is a growing life expectancy gap of more than eight years between those living in the most and least deprived areas; in India, there is an eight-year gap in male life expectancy between those in the wealthiest and poorest quintile. These disparities hold both within and across countries. Current global life expectancy is 73 years (71 for males and 76 for females), ranging from 57.7 in Western Africa to 87.2 in Western Europe,[4] even with African life expectancy increasing by over 10 years between 2000 and 2016. Adjusting for healthy life expectancy gives rise to even greater inequalities (for example, life expectancy in the US was 78.5 years in 2019, but healthy life expectancy was 66.1 years). United Nations projections on world population ageing suggest that in the next three decades, the number of older people (age 65 and above) will double globally, increasing from 0.7 billion in 2019 to 1.5 billion in 2050.[5] Healthy ageing requires immediate investment in health and social care over the life course.

While the importance of social determinants is widely accepted, it is difficult to establish causal evidence of its effects. For instance, health inequalities are both a cause and consequence of income inequality. Income and health are highly correlated with a strong negative gradient. Ill health impacts income, for instance, by constraining investments in educational and non-cognitive skills, which has a detrimental impact on later life outcomes.[6;7;8;9;10;11] Existing evidence confirms that adult health is determined early in life and is further shaped through social determinants.[12;13] While it is true that poorer children are less healthy in high-income countries, it is difficult to establish why based on existing evidence.[14;15;16;17] Evidence from middle- and low-income countries that considers the impact of unconditional cash transfers supports that poor people have improved birth outcomes as their income increases,[18] but this is not always the case, as several findings record no health impact from such schemes.[19] Consequently, policy implications from this work are weak.

One explanation for the mixed evidence on the relationship between income and health is that once patterns of health inequality have been documented, individuals with higher incomes generally enagage in healthier behaviours with lower likelihood to smoke, drink heavily, become obese, or use illicit drugs.[20;21] The role of education is particularly important, as education rather than income per se could mediate healthy behaviour (as first set out in the seminal work by Grossman).[22] Generally, wider social determinants of health can partly explain the emergence of a widespread obesity epidemic that implies higher later-life comorbidities and doubles the costs of an individual's healthcare.[23] The literature supports a robust, strong positive correlation between education and health, even across generations, as maternal education correlates with their children's health.[24;25]

Up to 2010, life expectancy at birth was increasing in all high-income countries. But since then, increases in life expectancy have stalled or even fallen in some countries. This tendency is not explained by the COVID-19 pandemic, but appears to have other underlying causes which have resulted in increased mortality rates in specific population groups with low-incomes. Recent work by Case and Deaton on rising deaths by despair (mortality linked to illicit drugs, drink and suicides) in poor middle-aged, uneducated white non-Hispanics in the US clearly supports the impact of wider social determinants on health outcomes.[26;27] Although the evidence is not universal, similar trends appear in Australia, Ireland, the United Kingdom, and Spain. The impact of concentrated increased mortality rates in sections of high-income country populations, attributable to specific lifestyle behaviours, cardiovascular diseases, and cancers, and compounded by COVID-19 mortality, have led to significant decreases in life expectancy in some high-income countries. This decrease can also be linked directly to commercial influences on health, such as corporate sector priorities shifting health systems away from health improvement goals. A recent study found that climate change, the COVID-19 pandemic and four industrial sectors (tobacco, ultra-processed food, fossil fuel, and alcohol) are responsible for approximately one-third of global deaths.[28]

Paying attention to social determinants tends to promote the role of public health, particularly the role of prevention over treatment seems to be increasingly more relevant. For example, McGinnis et al. highlight the limited role of healthcare in reducing mortality, with less than 15% of gains in US mortality rates in the early 2000s directly attributable to healthcare, and over half of US deaths involving a behavioural cause.[29] A clearer understanding of causal relationships is needed in order to change health behaviour.[30] Regardless, shifting attention towards prevention, with its upfront costs and delayed benefits, and increasing reliance on individual responsibility for health improvements is unlikely to be sufficient to replace stuttering health gains even in high-income countries, particularly in a context of limited government resources given high levels of public debt. Consequently, it is important to consider healthcare financing, production, and delivery.

III. What can the health system do?

1. *Healthcare financing*

Health financing arrangements are core to the functioning of any health system. They determine the volume of revenues raised, the extent of financial risk pooling that is feasible, the coverage and quality of health services, and the level of financial protection for the population. Most countries with high levels of UHC have some form of collective financing mechanism through mandatory public funding, such as taxation (direct and indirect) or social insurance. Since the late 1980s, most European health systems have shifted towards mixed modes of mandatory public financing. Many Western European health systems that were predominantly financed by social insurance are now complemented with large governmental transfers from taxation to cover non-working population groups or health sector deficits. In 2018, government transfers accounted for between 25–35% of social insurance revenues in Belgium, France, and Greece; and around 40% in Luxembourg.[31] Starting in 1990, several Central and Eastern European countries (re)introduced social insurance schemes to complement universal schemes financed through government budgets. The latter were efforts to increase public investment in health through earmarked contributions and a return to schemes that had been dismantled under the Soviet Union.[32] Studies analysing equity in financing of healthcare in high-income countries suggest that social insurance contributions are proportionate or moderately regressive, while predominantly tax-financed health systems vary from mainly progressive to moderately regressive.[33;34]

Other voluntary private contributions such as private health insurance (PHI), medical savings accounts (MSAs), or out-of-pocket payments (OOPs) form the basis of health financing in several countries. PHI is the primary source of finance among working people in the US or Switzerland. Although PHI has been shown to be highly regressive, it may be a complementary and supplementary source of coverage to public contribution in order to cater to heterogeneous preferences and needs.[35;36] In Ecuador, Peru, and Uruguay, PHI plays a supplementary role, covering healthcare services that are not covered by public contribution mechanisms. In other countries, such as Brazil and Chile, PHI is complementary, covering cost-sharing for health goods and services covered by public contribution mechanisms.[37]

MSAs involve voluntary contributions by individuals to their own savings accounts earmarked for healthcare costs. Employers often contribute to these individual accounts although there is a cap on annual contributions. In Singapore, MSAs (called MediSave) were launched in 1984 and are the primary source of health finance. They are complemented by MediShield, a voluntary, high-deductible, catastrophic insurance plan, with direct subsidies to hospitals and the Medical Endowment Fund (MediFund), a safety net for poorer people. By 2011, most healthcare was paid for out-of-pocket, while MediSave withdrawals and MediShield claims only accounted for about 5.5 and 2.1% of national health expenditure, respectively.[38] MSAs were introduced in the US in 2003 under the term Health Savings Accounts. While MSAs enable individuals to level risks over time, they do not involve risk pooling across the wider population, tend to be inequitable and, consequently, have not provided universal financial protection.[39]

OOPs are typically direct payments to providers for services either in the absence of a statutory benefits package or as cost sharing for services covered by the benefits package. OOPs form a large part of healthcare financing in many LMICs. On average more than 40% of health spending in LMICs (and nearly 60% if only low-income countries are considered) are OOPs.[40] Many LMICs have implemented direct charges to health services users since the 1980s, as part of the structural adjustment policies of the World Bank and the International Monetary Fund. Various studies have looked at the effects of user charges and conclude: (i) user fees impede access to health disproportionately for the poor; (ii) waivers and exemption policies are administratively difficult to implement effectively; and (iii) user fees can result in catastrophic health expenditures driving households into poverty.[41;42] OOPs are more regressive than any other method of healthcare financing, capturing a higher proportion of income among poor households than wealthier ones.[43] In contrast, tax-financed schemes are largely progressive and reduce inequities in health financing. In practice, there are barriers that may limit the adoption of these financing approaches.

A major barrier in LMICs is inadequate generation of revenues from public financing sources.[44;45] This is often due to several factors: (i) low public spending on health as a share of gross domestic product, even in countries that have witnessed rapid economic growth; (ii) taxation systems where capacity to enforce tax and contribution collection is weak; and (iii) large informal sectors in LMICs that limit contributions to social insurance schemes and tax revenues.

The age-mix of the world population is also changing. While many LMICs have relatively young, growing populations (e.g., Indonesia and much of sub-Saharan Africa), many high-income countries have a large proportion of older individuals. Changes in the age-mix affects countries' ability to generate revenues from all the aforementioned approaches. Mandatory contributions are typically low in young adults, and they increase and correlate closely with working ages, declining as people reach retirement. For countries with young populations, ageing can present an opportunity to expand the fiscal space by generating more revenues for health and other public services. However, these countries are often characterised by large informal sectors and less-developed tax systems, and to improve fiscal sustainability they must reduce the informal sector and invest in improving the tax system.

Countries with an ageing population or a large share already in older age groups rely primarily on the labour market (through social insurance) to raise revenues for health, which can result in a declining revenue base over time. Some sources of indirect taxation, such as consumption, property, and wealth taxes, may be more resilient to changes in the population age-mix and can contribute to diversification of revenue sources. But in the long term such diversification is unlikely to generate adequate revenues and may be politically unpopular (e.g., in the cases of property or wealth taxes). Therefore, regulators should prioritise reorienting the share of public revenue allocated to healthcare.

Recent studies of national health insurance schemes in LMICs show that raising funds from social insurance is unlikely to raise sufficient revenues to provide coverage for financial risk protection.[46;47] To expand the fiscal space, countries could diversify the public revenue base to include indirect taxes, e.g., by earmarking revenue generated by increasing taxes on unhealthy products, such as tobacco and alcohol or reducing subsidies for fossil fuels. Studies show that when earmarked revenues are channelled directly into an autonomous fund dedicated to public health, they successfully add funding for health, and in LMICs it adds revenues from the informal economy. Yet they tend to be regressive.[48] Some countries have diversified the public revenue base to stimulate employment while maintaining or increasing public health spending. For example, in 2009 Germany moved to a unified national contribution rate of 15.5% of wages, but then used general tax revenue to reduce this contribution to 14.9% as part of an economic stimulus package. Further budget subsidies were channelled through these rate subsidies.

Reducing fragmentation in health financing

Pooling revenues enables the sharing of health risk across individuals and over time. Equity of access to healthcare is further improved when healthy individuals subsidise the costs of those in need of healthcare. Most health systems that rely on mandatory public contributions employ some degree of pooling even when funds are at times heterogenous. However, over the last two decades, several European countries have implemented reforms to reduce fragmentation. In 2006, the Netherlands created a national health insurance fund, by removing the dividing line between statutory cover for 63% of the population and substitutive private cover for the remaining 37%. A major administrative reform in Denmark in 2007 led to a merging of health schemes by lowering the number of municipalities from 275 to 98. This reform also removed the responsibility for raising tax revenue for healthcare from regional and local governments to the central government.[49]

Latin American countries have adopted different approaches to financing UHC, resulting in varying levels of coverage and financial protection. Brazil and Costa Rica adopted a unified health system approach, where funds from different sources are pooled to limit user fees and cover the entire population. Countries like Argentina, Chile, Mexico, and Peru developed parallel health insurance, service delivery systems, and correspondingly different benefits for different population groups within a country. Over time, the latter group of countries have moved to a 'semi-integrated' approach, where contributory schemes coexist with parallel pooling arrangements funded by tax revenues that subsidise enrolment for the poor.[50] Overall, expanding UHC has resulted in reduced catastrophic health expenditures among the poor. However, OOP expenditures remain high in Latin America, varying from 16% of health expenditure in Uruguay to 43% in Ecuador. The main reasons for high OOPs are high levels of private healthcare coverage and reliance on demand-side cost-sharing to control volumes.[51]

The ability to pool revenues in LMICs remains constrained by external funding for the health system. In the provision of many public health interventions, diagnosis and treatment of communicable diseases is typically vertically arranged with limited integration with other healthcare services. Vertical arrangements are typically the result of reliance on external financing. Particularly in low-income countries, the contribution of external assistance to health expenditures is large (~33% on average in 2015), with competing objectives among donors. Funding from bilateral, multilateral, and philanthropic organisations typically target specific disease areas or priority populations.[52] Vertical financing arrangements offer health systems little flexibility in pooling resources across population groups or in planning at an aggregate level. Greater cooperation between donors and countries can facilitate integration of funding into more comprehensive health benefits plans, ensuring key populations and specific diseases are not excluded from coverage, particularly as countries transition away from donor aid.[53;54]

2. *Delivery*

All health systems employ some form of purchasing of health services from health providers. We consider below such purchasing decisions in terms of the role of technology, improvements in procurement strategies, priority setting as it relates to UHC, the degree of integration between primary and specialist providers, and issues relating to diagnosis and personalised medicine.

Strategic purchasing

Health systems employ some form of purchasing of health services from healthcare providers. Traditional ways of paying healthcare providers, such as salary, fee-for-service, bundled payments, and capitation, do not explicitly reward providers for delivering better and more efficient quality care. Strategic purchasing intends to improve allocative efficiency (maximise health gains from available resources), improve quality by introducing incentives for providers, and improve technical efficiency through pay-for-performance and competition between providers and purchasers. Consequently, several countries have implemented provider payment models that seek to align payment incentives with the quality and efficiency of services provided by linking rewards to the achievement of performance measures.

Models that directly link worker renumeration to performance targets have generally been termed 'pay-for-performance' in high-income countries and performance-based financing in LMICs. The pay-for-performance schemes have been implemented to augment existing payment schemes and typically involve incentives for achieving specific objectives, such as higher quality, processes of care that follow evidence-based guidelines, increased coverage of preventive services, better management of chronic diseases, and better patient outcomes. In LMICs performance-based financing typically includes performance-based incentives for health workers and performance-linked financing for health facilities. They have primarily been applied to purchasing provisions of maternal and child health services.

Evidence from high-income countries suggests pay-for-performance can lead to improvements in the quantity and quality of care, while effects on health outcomes are mixed and inconclusive.[55;56;57] It is unclear what design elements of pay-for-performance work best under which conditions. Recently, US pay-for-performance schemes have evolved to value-based purchasing, where cost-based reimbursement is combined with incentives (e.g., see Medicare's Hospital value-based purchasing programme). There is limited evidence on the success of value-based purchasing programmes in improving quality and outcomes.[58;59]

The use of performance pay within performance-based financing has successfully increased institutional deliveries and quality in LMICs, particularly in primary care settings.[60] But beyond institutional deliveries, performance-based financing shows mixed results.[61] In contrast to performance-based financing interventions that provide an unconditional core budget and additional financial incentives conditional on performance, direct facility financing interventions only provide additional unconditional financing. In both approaches, additional funding is usually accompanied by autonomy over the budget and supportive supervision. In direct facility financing, the purchasing of services is based on bundled output-based payments like primary healthcare service per capita and case-based hospital payment schemes, including diagnostic-related groups (defined shortly).[62] Evidence suggests performance-based financing may be no more effective than direct facility financing (or not even better than no intervention) across a range of reproductive, maternal, and child health indicators.[63] In addition, direct facility financing has lower administration costs and is generally more cost-effective than performance-based financing, as it does not involve verification of quantity and quality for payment.[64] Direct facility financing could improve frontline service delivery, but it requires investment in strengthening facility financial management.

To improve the quality of services delivered, in some tax-financed, centrally regulated high-income countries (UK, Nordic countries, Spain, Portugal, and Italy), UHC has happened alongside the introduction of competition between suppliers. For example, the UK has offered patients a greater choice in healthcare providers since the 2000s. Evidence suggests that even with regulated fixed prices, introducing choice increased competition among hospitals, and patients increasingly chose hospitals deemed as having better clinical care before competition was introduced. Patients were also more likely to choose a hospital that was not their local hospital (the default provider under the no-choice setup) post-introduction of choice.[65;66]

Price regulation within the hospital sector has increasingly become associated with diagnostic-related group (DRG) pricing, first introduced by Medicare (the US social insurer for people above 65 years of age). With DRG payments, heterogeneous hospital activities classify patients into groups that exhibit similar medical conditions and resource-use pairings, allowing comparable outcomes to be defined across the hospital sector. Reimbursement is based on prices regulated at the average treatment cost level for each condition–resource pairing. If reimbursement prices are fixed, hospitals can only increase revenue by attracting a higher volume of patients. To do this, it is assumed, they will increase their quality of treatment. However, the impact of such reforms on quality is mixed.[67] Some studies find evidence of lower mortality and improved quality of heart surgery in hospitals that faced greater choice, while patients became more selective based on quality for their choice of hospital for hip replacement surgery.[68;69] Yet, another study found no effect on mortality, and the effects seem heterogenous.[70] Evidence from the US shows that improving quality is an important lever for hospitals to attract patients when prices are regulated, but these effects are less clear where prices are determined by markets.[71;72]

Role of technology

Technological improvements are partly responsible for the rises in life expectancy, particularly in the area of cardiovascular medicine.[73] Technology explains a large share of health spending and is regarded as the main driver of health expenditure growth. Expanding the scope of treatments and diagnostics technology uptake and diffusion accounts for between 30–50% of health expenditure growth in high-income countries.[74;75] Technological improvements may be associated with cost reduction but still lead to expenditure growth, as patient treatment volume expands. Cutler and Huckman[76] document that angioplasty in the treatment of heart disease displaced open heart surgery, as it was as effective and a third of the cost. However, overall expenditures rose for this treatment as higher-risk patients could now be operated upon with the less invasive technique. This is no doubt true for laparoscopic, or minimally invasive, surgery generally.

Technological uptake and diffusion and its influence on healthcare expenditure depends on the institutional and regulatory environment. Health systems with lower price regulation and less centralised control tend to have faster diffusion rates.[77;78;79] However, the effect of new technology on outcome quality is far less clear. Some technologies come with similar costs and higher quality,[80] while others merely entail costs and have little impact on outcomes. These technologies can be classified based on their cost effectiveness in three categories: (i) inexpensive 'low-tech' technologies'; (ii) technologies that are effective in some indications alone; and (iii) technologies that are clearly cost-effective across the board.[81] Health technology assessment agencies, discussed shortly, play a crucial role in incorporating the cost of new technologies into hospital reimbursements and the coupling of health technology assessments with DRG-based hospital reimbursement is seen across the globe. Health technology assessments are also used to evaluate general technology efficiencies, not always with complete success.

Improving procurement strategies

The COVID-19 pandemic highlighted the importance of delivering a safe, effective, and timely supply of vaccines and medicines. Weaknesses in the procurement processes in many LMICs have become evident. Even prior to COVID-19, the 50 poorest countries in the world spent approximately US$63 billion on health products (comprising spending by governments, donors, and the private sector).[82;83] Health product markets in LMICs are characterised by high proportionate spending on expensive branded generics compared to unbranded generics. Unbranded generics account for only 5% by volume and 3% by value in LMICs compared to 80% of the pharmaceutical market by volume (and 30% by value) in the US and the UK.[84]

Reducing fragmentation through centralised and/or pooled procurement can lower costs and limit supply shortages. Centralised procurement of drugs substantially lowers prices in LMICs.[85] Globally, the benefits of pooled procurement have been demonstrated by initiatives, such as GAVI, the Vaccine Alliance, and the Global Fund to Fight AIDS, Tuberculosis, and Malaria. Such initiatives use global tenders and bulk purchasing to shape markets for specific health products and enhance availability of high-quality generics in LMICs.

Priority-setting for UHC

In all health systems, achieving UHC implies trade-offs between the population covered, the quality of services provided, and the number of services included in the health benefit package. Decision makers in LMICs often face severe resource limitations compared to decision makers in high-income countries. Their challenge is to choose safe, effective, good quality, and affordable health technologies, medicines, and vaccines. Policymakers can mitigate some of the political challenges associated with priority-setting by making the process of defining health benefit packages transparent, based on scientific evidence on the safety and cost-effectiveness of different interventions and products, and by considering criteria such as equity and financial protection.

Many countries, particularly in Europe, have established health technology assessment agencies to examine short- and long-term health and resource-use consequences of healthcare treatments. Health technology assessment agencies play a vital advisory or regulatory role in making reimbursement or pricing recommendations, informing the development of clinical guidelines and supporting healthcare purchasing and disinvestment decisions.[86;87] The agencies typically focus on maximising value for money with the aim of improving financial sustainability. Since new healthcare technology is largely introduced through the hospital sector in high-income countries, health technology assessment agencies also work to ensure that the fixed DRG hospital pricing does not impede the uptake and diffusion of technologies.

Health technology assessment, including cost-effectiveness analysis, can help LMICs with their priority-setting. This requires countries (with international donor support) to establish health technology assessment agencies with clear responsibility for reimbursement and pricing decisions, invest in capacity building to generate evidence on local cost-effectiveness and equity implications of key technologies and interventions, and focus on disinvestment of cost-ineffective technologies as much as on the assessment of new technologies. In some cases, international donors could support interventions that are marginally cost-ineffective, i.e., subsidising key cost-ineffective interventions to make them cost-effective for a given country's threshold.[88] For example, treatments for high burden diseases that are not cost-effective for a country to implement given its budget constraint.

Improving integration between primary and specialised care

A major difference across health systems lies in the extent of their reliance on or integration of general practitioners (GPs) as gatekeepers responsible for access to specialist care for non-emergency cases. So far, we know that GP-based systems are more expensive[89] but tend to prioritise the health of communities and enhance equitable access as they can target people with lower socio-economic status by prioritising care continuity.[90;91] Challenges remain with regards to the coordination of primary care with public health, specialist- and hospital-based care, as integration does not necessarily lead to improved cooperation.

Diagnosis and personalised medicine are being revisited

The expansion of diagnostic techniques adds to the traditional models of sick patients demanding access to care to include 'patients-in-waiting', where individual information on genetic variants or other biomarkers and self-tracked lifestyles are subject to ongoing monitoring. Probabilistic diagnosis relies heavily on access to individual data collection and collation, which raises issues about data privacy and how to incorporate genetic information into existing insurance schemes. Meanwhile, we can expect a greater push towards non-probabilistic-based social insurance to counter insurance exclusion. Physicians in such a setting may also see an expansion of primary care move beyond gatekeeping roles towards increasing screening and health surveillance.[92]

3. *Workforce*

The healthcare sector is heavily service-oriented and staff costs generally account for over 60% of provider spending. Any global shortage of healthcare workers directly impacts the attainment of UHC. The UNSDG identified a lower limit of 4.45 doctors, nurses, and midwives per 1,000 population as the basic minimum required to achieve its health goals by 2030. Even prior to the COVID-19 pandemic, which increased shortages due to staff burnout, there was an estimated needs-based shortfall of around 17.5 million healthcare workers globally, including 2.6 million doctors and 9 million nurses.[93] Of the nurse shortage, 90% is concentrated in LMICs.[94] The WHO predicts a continuing shortfall of 14.5 million healthcare workers globally by 2030, with the largest shortfalls in LMICs.

An adequate, sustainable health and care workforce is one that will be able to meet the needs of the population both immediately and in the foreseeable future. However, this does not merely mean increasing supply, but also ensuring adequate quality of supply and a distribution that is accessible to the defined population. To deliver a sustainable and appropriately skilled health and care workforce, countries need a long-term workforce strategy, which should be informed by workforce planning models that consider the necessary mix of skills to meet the changing health and care needs, and aspires to develop a self-sufficient supply of staff, rather than an ongoing reliance on foreign-trained staff. The strategy needs to consider technological developments that have the potential to improve quality of care and productivity.

To ensure the delivery of adequate planning, workforce estimates require significant coordination across educational and funding bodies. Most fiscal cycles are aligned with political cycles and last, at most, for five years. It generally takes at least four years to incorporate a trained nurse into the workforce and five to eight years to train doctors, depending on their specialty. Both figures are towards or beyond the upper end of many countries' fiscal cycles. Thus, unless there is adequate discussion between fiscal and healthcare bodies to plan workforce supply, lack of coordination will be inevitable. Already difficult in high-income countries, low-income countries suffer additional workforce shortages arising from significant migration.

The highest levels of physician migration are experienced by LMICs, particularly in the Caribbean and Africa (Liberia, Ghana, Congo, Zimbabwe, and Ethiopia). The Caribbean saw migration rates of approximately 19% in 1990 rising to 28% by 2014, partly explained by proximity to the US, but also due to increased acceptance of foreign students within medical schools. In Sub-Saharan Africa, there was a slight decline in emigration rates, attributable to increasing training centres, over the period 2004–14, but 18% of trained doctors still emigrate. Not surprisingly, the biggest winners in terms of physician migration were the US, the UK, and EU-15. Germany, France, Sweden, and Switzerland have become emerging, important gainers of migrants. Overall, low-income countries had an average emigration rate of over 10% during 1990 to 2014, while UMICs had emigration rates of around 3% over this period. Accompanying analysis in Andovor et al. shows a strongly positive pull of high gross domestic product (GDP) levels in attracting migrant physicians. [95] This is reinforced when destination countries operate a points-based, skilled migrant system and permanent residency controls are lax.

Migration within countries is also an issue, with inequitable distribution across rural and urban areas being a common problem that impedes universal access to healthcare and response rates to specific health concerns (e.g., Ebola). While this imbalance affects almost all countries, it is most noticeable in low-income countries. Approximately half of the world's population lives in rural areas and tends to be poorer and less healthy, while most health workers are concentrated in urban settings. Several studies suggest that if medical students attend a rural campus or spend time training in rural areas, they are more likely to remain in practice in these settings.[96]

4. *Integration of long-term care*

With population ageing, the need for long-term care has increased. Programmes have been introduced at national and local levels to increase the subsidisation and integration of services that are typically designed for older age individuals in need of support, e.g., nursing care, personal care services, assistance services, and social services.[97] In the US, approximately half of adults reaching the age of 65 can expect to use long-term services and support before they die, and in the absence of insurance either the family or Medicaid end up self-financing care.[98] Such issues are not confined to high-income countries alone and affect many LMICs and emerging economies, partly due to declining fertility rates.[99] According to projections from the European Union's Economic Policy Committee,[100] associated public-sector-financed long-term care spending is estimated to increase from 1.6% to 2.2% of GDP between 2016 and 2040.

A greater increase may come from private funding, as long-term care is associated with high out-of-pocket spending. Across 26 OECD countries, reported total costs of long-term care range between one-half and five times the median disposable income of individuals of retirement age or older.[101]

Costa-Font and Raut show that the proportion of individuals who use savings to pay for health and care expenditure has increased significantly between 2004 and 2010 in most countries.[102] Recognising private insurance failures in this area, several high-income countries have developed public long-term care systems, starting with the Netherlands in 1968 and in more recent years Israel, Austria, Germany, Luxembourg, Japan, Scotland, Spain, and China have implemented such systems too.

In Japan, long-term care is paid through a mandatory insurance premium for the over 40s (the age at which individuals tend to face some old age care need in their household), which is matched with similar tax revenue funding and a 10% user co-payment. Entitlement to services is needs-tested by a medical doctor. Several countries have developed forms of social insurance for long-term care, e.g., South Korea supports the expenditures of elderly individuals in nursing home and home care, and Uruguay and Costa Rica support expenditures for home care and home-based care. Long term care services have been particularly prone to spending cuts, which has led to a rise in cost shifting, with increasing private contributions and inadequate supply.

Long-term care delivery models range from highly integrated systems reliant on public provision with limited private alternatives to systems with considerable family involvement that complement a fragmented and residual public system.[103] The separation of funding, delivery, and organisation of long-term care and healthcare creates problems in coordination across health and social care, even when systems are integrated.[104] The organisational separation of health services and care is one of the main causes of coordination failures (a phenomenon whereby services are organised and financed by different organisations that are subject to different rules) in the provision of health and social services. This raises concerns over the development of adequate integration of services. A consequent issue arising from ageing populations and lack of fully funded long-term care in health systems is the over-utilisation of healthcare services due to bed blocking and subsequent unnecessary use of healthcare given the lack of alternative support for individuals of older age.

IV. Conclusions

Healthcare systems are one of the determinants of health, but not the only one. Health inequality remains a fundamental and persistent policy challenge despite progress in universalising healthcare. Financial insecurity related to healthcare needs remains substantial, and out-of-pocket payments and private healthcare continue to play an important, regressive role in health (and social service) care financing. Many countries rely solely on externally set health benefits packages, such as the WHO's essential medicines list, rather than a locally defined, publicly funded health benefits package that reflects local population needs to allocate available resources. This overcomes problems that result from aggregating multiple donor objectives in low-income countries, for example, but does not aid structural, system-level reform. Regulating and monitoring quality of healthcare remains a core challenge for many countries. The incentives associated with payment structures are critical. While the use of fixed-price, hospital-based reimbursement and the use of health technology assessment agencies to set priorities have become increasingly prevalent, ensuring quality provision remains a problem. Achieving such sustainability requires adequate funding for the health system and investments in the workforce. It also requires integration of different levels of care to improve prevention and management of chronic conditions, and the expansion of long-term care to avoid inefficient use of hospital and other healthcare services.

V. Policy lessons

Progress towards UHC requires building a sustainable health system that is resilient to shocks, offers financial risk protection, and is well prepared to meet changing population needs. Building such a system requires sustained political and financial commitment from countries. Rather than one-size-fits all, the best approaches to UHC are context-specific and depend on the institutional, political, and economic context of each country. Thus, each country will have a different starting point and trajectory towards UHC. However, policymakers can draw on several lessons from countries that have made the transition.

Improving health system sustainability and financial risk protection requires expanding public funding for healthcare through a mix of progressive financing approaches to minimise regressive out-of-pocket payments. Regardless of the size of the available healthcare budget, sustainability requires maximising allocative efficiency and optimising the mix of services through explicit priority-setting. This implies setting up and relying on health technology assessment agencies or similar institutions to define a health benefits package that reflects population health needs and available resources. It also means expanding the use of health technology assessments to standardise and regulate quality of care and to regulate the diffusion of new, generally costly healthcare technologies and drugs. Thus, the health benefits package must be designed with the budget in mind, but it will generally be accompanied by rising overall health expenditure. Reaching and maintaining financial sustainability also requires effective governance of the health system, limiting expenditures due to waste and corruption.

However, progress will first require countries to overcome several political economy barriers. Defining a publicly financed health benefits package makes priority-setting a political issue. Some individuals may consider any reductions in their access to services unacceptable; pharmaceutical companies and medical technology manufacturers may perceive priority-setting as a barrier to market access; and healthcare providers may perceive governance as restrictive of their autonomy. The ethical principles of priority-setting may also be difficult to convey to the public. This may lead to the emergence of complementary private insurance catering to heterogenous population preferences. Consistent regulation must be developed to ensure that any two-tier system remains efficient, while limiting inequalities.

Health systems must prioritise workforce planning to avoid shortages and ensure realignment of the fiscal and workforce planning cycles, as well as identifying the best ways to integrate different levels of care and giving patients a stronger role in choices, which may increase with the proliferation of new diagnostic tools. Care integration calls for expanding the public funding of long-term care, reducing reliance on informal caregivers, and improving integration between health and social care sectors to minimise inefficiencies, and take advantage of the development of telemedicine. The most effective health system structure that can achieve these objectives will differ from country to country given different social preferences and institutions. Each country must devise the best level of centralisation or decentralisation depending on the scale and spillovers of each responsibility, which might even encompass supranational decision-making in some parts of the world (e.g., Europe). Similarly, countries ought to optimally utilise the network of existing private providers in the delivery of public healthcare where possible, finding the best balance between public and private providers to achieve its own objectives of universal healthcare coverage.

Notes

1 Sustainable Development Goal 3.8 is a target to provide all people with access to essential high-quality health services, including safe, effective, and affordable medicines and vaccines, while ensuring financial risk protection by providing care regardless of a person's ability to pay for it.

2 Chowdhury et al. (2023).

3 Marmot et al. (2008).

4 United Nations (2022).

5 United Nations (2020).

6 Almond et al. (2018).

7 Conti et al. (2010).

8 Cunha and Heckman (2007).

9 Heckman (2007).

10 Heckman et al. (2006).

11 Currie (2009).

12 Marmot et al. (2008).

13 Marmot and Wilkinson (2006).

[14] Propper et al. (2007).

[15] Burgess et al. (2004).

[16] Currie and Lin (2007).

[17] Apouey and Geoffard (2013).

[18] Amarante et al. (2016).

[19] Paxson and Schady (2010).

[20] Cutler et al. (2011).

[21] Cutler and Lleras-Muney (2010).

[22] Grossman (1972).

[23] Cawley et al. (2021).

[24] Currie (2009).

[25] Currie and Moretti (2003).

[26] Case and Deaton (2020).

[27] Case and Deaton (2015).

[28] Gilmore et al. (2023).

[29] McGinnis et al. (2002).

[30] Patel et al. (2018).

[31] World Health Organization (2021).

[32] World Health Organization (2021).

[33] Wagstaff et al. (1999).

[34] Wagstaff and van Doorslaer (1992).

[35] Wagstaff et al. (1999).

[36] Wagstaff and van Doorslaer (1992).

[37] Lorenzoni et al. (2019).

[38] Wouters et al. (2016).

[39] Wouters et al. (2016).

[40] World Health Organization (2020a).

[41] James et al. (2006).

[42] Xu et al. (2003).

[43] Wagstaff et al. (1993).

[44] Marten et al. (2014).

[45] Atim et al. (2021).

[46] Barasa et al. (2021).

[47] Gheorghe et al. (2019).

[48] World Health Organization (2017).

[49] Thomson et al. (2009).

[50] World Bank (2015).

[51] Kanavos et al. (2019).

[52] Atun et al. (2008).

[53] Global Fund (2020).

[54] Herberholz (2020).

[55] Doran and Roland (2010).

[56] Mendelson et al. (2017).

[57] Damberg et al. (2014).

[58] Damberg et al. (2014).

[59] Figueroa et al. (2016).

[60] de Walque et al. (2022).

[61] Diaconu et al. (2021).

[62] World Health Organization (2022).

[63] de Walque et al. (2022).

[64] Zeng et al. (2021).

[65] Gutacker et al. (2016).

[66] Gaynor et al. (2013).

[67] Moscelli et al. (2021).

[68] Gaynor et al. (2016).

[69] Gutacker et al. (2016).

[70] Moscelli et al. (2016).

[71] Gaynor et al. (2015).

[72] Gaynor and Town (2012).

[73] Marino and Lorenzoni (2019).

[74] Smith et al. (2009).

[75] Chernew and Newhouse (2011).

[76] Cutler and Huckman (2003).

[77] Bech et al. (2009).

[78] Cockburn et al. (2016).

[79] Costa-Font et al. (2014).

[80] Cutler and McClellan (2001).

[81] Chandra and Skinner (2012).

[82] Silverman et al. (2019).

[83] Rosen et al. (2017).

[84] Kaplan et al. (2013).

[85] Kaplan et al. (2013).

[86] Sorenson and Chalkidou (2012).

[87] Sorenson et al. (2008).

[88] Morton et al. (2018).

[89] Kringos et al. (2015).

[90] Gravelle et al. (2010).

[91] van Gool et al. (2021).

[92] Eyal et al. (2019).

[93] World Health Organization (2016).

[94] World Health Organization (2020b).

[95] Adovor et al. (2021).

[96] Farmer et al. (2015).

[97] Costa-Font et al. (2015).

[98] Favreault et al. (2015).

[99] Bloom and Eggleston (2014).

[100] European Commission (2021).

[101] OECD (2020).

[102] Costa-Font and Raut (2022).

[103] Lundsgaard (2005).

[104] Barber et al. (2021).

References

Adovor, E., Czaika, M., Docquier, F. and Moullan, Y. (2021) 'Medical Brain Drain: How Many, Where and Why?', *Journal of Health Economics*, 76: 102409. https://doi.org/10.1016/j.jhealeco.2020.102409

Almond, D., Currie, J., Duque, V. (2018) 'Childhood Circumstances and Adult Outcomes: Act II', *Journal of Economic Literature*, 56(4): 1360–446. https://doi.org/10.1257/jel.20171164

Amarante, V., Manacorda, M., Miguel, E. and Vigorito, A. (2016) 'Do Cash Transfers Improve Birth Outcomes? Evidence from Matched Vital Statistics, and Program and Social Security Data', *American Economic Journal Economic Policy*, 8(2): 1–43. https://doi.org/10.1257/pol.20140344

Apouey, B. and Geoffard, P. Y. (2013) 'Family Income and Child Health in the UK', *Journal of Health Economics*, 32(4): 715–27. https://doi.org/10.1016/j.jhealeco.2013.03.006

Atim, C., Bhushan, I., Blecher, M., Gandham, R., Rajan, V., Davén, J. and Adeyi, O. (2021) 'Health Financing Reforms for Universal Health Coverage in Five Emerging Economies', *Journal of Global Health*, 11: 16005. https://doi.org/10.7189/jogh.11.16005

Atun, R., Bennett, S. and Duran, A. (2008) 'When Do Vertical (Stand-Alone) Programmes Have a Place in Health Systems?', World Health Organization. https://iris.who.int/handle/10665/107977

Barasa, E., Kazungu, J., Nguhiu, P. and Ravishankar, N. (2021) 'Examining the Level and Inequality in Health Insurance Coverage in 36 Sub-Saharan African Countries', *BMJ Global Health*, 6(4). https://doi.org/10.1136/bmjgh-2020-004712

Barber, S. L., van Gool, K., Wise, S., Woods, M., Or, Z., Penneau, A., Milstein, R., Ikegami, N. Kwon, S., Bakx, P., Schut, E., Wouterse, B., Flores, M. and Lorenzoni, L. (2021) *Pricing Long-term Care for Older Persons*. World Health Organization (Centre for Health Development) and OECD. https://iris.who.int/bitstream/handle/10665/344505/9789240033771-eng.pdf

Bech, M., Christiansen, T., Dunham, K., Lauridsen, J., Lyttkens, C. H., McDonald, K., McGuire, A. and TECH Investigators (2009) 'The Influence of Economic Incentives and Regulatory Factors on the Adoption of Treatment Technologies: A Case Study of Technologies Used to Treat Heart Attacks', *Health Economics*, 18(10): 1114–32. https://doi.org/10.1002/hec.1417

Bloom, D. E. and Eggleston, K. N. (2014) 'The Economic Implications of Population Ageing in China and India: Introduction to the Special Issue', *The Journal of the Economics of Ageing*, 4: 1–7. https://doi.org/10.1016/j.jeoa.2014.10.002

Burgess, S., Propper, C. and Rigg, J. A. (2004) 'The Impact of Low Income on Child Health: Evidence from a Birth Cohort Study', Centre for Analysis of Social Exclusion, London School of Economics and Political Science. https://eprints.lse.ac.uk/6305/1/The_Impact_of_Low_Income_on_Child_Health_Evidence_from_a_Birth_Cohort_Study.pdf

Case, A. and Deaton, A. (2015) 'Rising Morbidity and Mortality in Midlife among White Non-Hispanic Americans in the 21st Century', *Proceedings of the National Academy of Sciences – PNAS*, 112(49): 15078. https://doi.org/10.1073/pnas.1518393112

Case, A. and Deaton, A. (2020) *Deaths of Despair and the Future of Capitalism*, Princeton, NJ: Princeton University Press. https://doi.org/10.1515/9780691217062

Cawley, J., Biener, A., Meyerhoefer, C., Ding, Y., Zvenyach, T. and Smolarz, B. G. (2021) 'Direct Medical Costs of Obesity in the United States and the Most Populous States', *Journal of Managed Care & Specialty Pharmacy*, 27(3): 354–66. https://doi.org/10.18553/jmcp.2021.20410

Chandra, A. and Skinner, J. (2012) 'Technology Growth and Expenditure Growth in Healthcare', *Journal of Economic Literature*, 50(3): 645–80. https://doi.org/10.1257/jel.50.3.645

Chernew, M. E. and Newhouse, J. P. (2011) Health Care Spending Growth, in *Handbook of Health Economics* (Vol. 2, pp. 1–43). Elsevier. https://www.sciencedirect.com/science/article/abs/pii/B9780444535924000013

Chowdhury, S. R., Chandra Das, D., Sunna, T. C., Beyene, J. and Hossain, A. (2023) 'Global and Regional Prevalence of Multimorbidity in the Adult Population in Community Settings: A Systematic Review and Meta-analysis', *EClinicalMedicine*, 57: 101860. https://doi.org/10.1016/j.eclinm.2023.101860

Cockburn, I. M., Lanjouw, J. O. and Schankerman, M. (2016) 'Patents and the Global Diffusion of New Drugs', *The American Economic Review*, 106(1): 136–64. https://doi.org/10.1257/aer.20141482

Conti, G., Heckman, J. J. and Urzua, S. (2010) 'The Education-Health Gradient', *The American Economic Review*, 100(2): 234–8. https://doi.org/10.1257/aer.100.2.234

Costa-Font, J. and Raut, N. (2022) 'Global Report on Long-Term Care Financing', *LSE*, Kobe, Japan. https://www.lse.ac.uk/business/consulting/reports/global-report-on-long-term-care-financing

Costa-Font, J., McGuire, A. and Varol, N. (2014) 'Price Regulation and Relative Delays in Generic Drug Adoption', *Journal of Health Economics*, 38(C): 1–9. https://doi.org/10.1016/j.jhealeco.2014.04.004

Costa-Font, J., Courbage, C. and Swartz, K. (2015) 'Financing Long-Term Care: Ex Ante, Ex Post or Both?', *Health Economics*, 24(S1): 45–57. https://doi.org/10.1002/hec.3152

Cunha, F. and Heckman, J. (2007) 'The Technology of Skill Formation', *The American Economic Review*, 97(2): 31–47. https://doi.org/10.1257/aer.97.2.31

Currie, J. (2009) 'Healthy, Wealthy, and Wise: Socioeconomic Status, Poor Health in Childhood, and Human Capital Development', *Journal of Economic Literature*, 47(1): 87–122. https://doi.org/10.1257/jel.47.1.87

Currie, J. and Moretti, E. (2003) 'Mother's Education and the Intergenerational Transmission of Human Capital: Evidence from College Openings', *The Quarterly Journal of Economics*, 118(4): 1495–532. https://doi.org/10.1162/003355303322552856

Currie, J. and Lin, W. (2007) 'Chipping Away at Health: More on the Relationship Between Income and Child Health', *Health Affairs*, 26(2): 331–44. https://doi.org/10.1377/hlthaff.26.2.331

Cutler, D. M. and Huckman, R. (2003) 'Technological Development and Medical Productivity: The Diffusion of Angioplasty in New York State', *Journal of Health Economics*, 22(2): 187–217. https://doi.org/10.1016/S0167-6296(02)00125-X

Cutler, D. M. and Lleras-Muney, A. (2010) 'Understanding Differences in Health Behaviors by Education by education', *Journal of Health Economics*, 29(1): 1–28. https://doi.org/10.1016/j.jhealeco.2009.10.003

Cutler, D. M. and McClellan, M. (2001) 'Is Technological Change in Medicine Worth It?', *Health Affairs*, 20(5): 11–29. https://doi.org/10.1377/hlthaff.20.5.11

Cutler, D. M., Lange, F., Meara, E., Richards-Shubik, S. and Ruhm, C. J. (2011) 'Rising Educational Gradients in Mortality: The role of Behavioral Risk Factors', *Journal of Health Economics*, 30(6): 1174–87. https://doi.org/10.1016/j.jhealeco.2011.06.009

Damberg, C. L., Sorbero, M. E., Lovejoy, S. L., Martsolf, G. R., Raaen, L. and Mandel, D. (2014) *Measuring Success in Healthcare Value-Based Purchasing Programs: Findings from an Environmental Scan, Literature Review, and Expert Panel Discussions*. Santa Monica, CA: RAND Corporation. https://www.rand.org/content/dam/rand/pubs/research_reports/RR300/RR306/RAND_RR306.pdf

de Walque, D., Kandpal, E., Wagstaff, A., Friedman, J., Adam, N., Piatti-Fünfkirchen, M., Sautmann, A., Shapira, G. and Van de Poel, E. (2022) 'Improving Effective Coverage in Health: Do Financial Incentives Work?. Washington, DC: World Bank. http://hdl.handle.net/10986/37326

Diaconu, K., Falconer, J., Verbel, A., Fretheim, A. and Witter, S. (2021) 'Paying for Performance to Improve the Delivery of Health Interventions in Low- and Middle-Income Countries', *Cochrane Database of Systematic Reviews*, 5. No.: CD007899. https://doi.org/10.1002/14651858.CD007899.pub3

Doran, T. and Roland, M. (2010) 'Lessons from Major Initiatives to Improve Primary Care in the United Kingdom', *Health Affairs*, 29(5): 1023–9. https://doi.org/10.1377/hlthaff.2010.0069

European Commission (2021) 'The 2021 Ageing Report: Economic and Budgetary Projections for the EU Member States (2019–2070)'. https://economy-finance.ec.europa.eu/publications/2021-ageing-report-economic-and-budgetary-projections-eu-member-states-2019-2070_en

Eyal, G., Sabatello, M., Tabb, K., Adams, R., Jones, M., Lichtenberg, F. R., Nelson, A., Oschner, K., Rowe, J., Stiles, D., Sivaramakrishnan, K. and Underhill, K. (2019) 'The Physician–Patient Relationship in the Age of Precision Medicine', *Genetics in Medicine*, 21(4): 813–5. https://doi.org/10.1038/s41436-018-0286-z

Farmer, J., Kenny, A., McKinstry, C. and Huysmans, R. D. (2015) 'A Scoping Review of the Association between Rural Medical Education and Rural Practice Location', *Human Resources for Health*, 13(1): 27. https://doi.org/10.1186/s12960-015-0017-3

Favreault, M. M., Gleckman, H. and Johnson, R. W. (2015) 'Financing Long-Term Services And Supports: Options Reflect Trade-Offs for Older Americans And Federal Spending', *Health Affairs*, 34(12): 2181–91. https://doi.org/10.1377/hlthaff.2015.1226

Figueroa, J. F., Tsugawa, Y., Zheng, J., Orav, E. J. and Jha, A. K. (2016) 'Association between the Value-Based Purchasing Pay for Performance Program and Patient Mortality in US Hospitals: Observational Study', *BMJ*, 353: i2214. https://doi.org/10.1136/bmj.i2214

Gaynor, M. and Town, R. J. (2012) 'Competition in Healthcare Markets', in Pauly, M. V., McGuire, T. G. and Barros, P. P. (eds) *Handbook of Health Economics, 2,* The Netherlands: Elsevier Science & Technology. https://doi.org/10.3386/w17208

Gaynor, M., Moreno-Serra, R. and Propper, C. (2013) 'Death by Market Power: Reform, Competition, and Patient Outcomes in the National Health Service', *American Economic Journal: Economic Policy*, 5(4): 134–66. https://doi.org/10.1257/pol.5.4.134

Gaynor, M., Ho, K. and Town, R. J. (2015) 'The Industrial Organization of Health-Care Markets', *Journal of Economic Literature*, 53(2): 235–84. https://doi.org/10.1257/jel.53.2.235

Gaynor, M., Propper, C. and Seiler, S. (2016) 'Free to Choose? Reform, Choice, and Consideration Sets in the English National Health Service', *American Economic Review*, 106(11): 3521–57. https://doi.org/10.1257/aer.20121532

Gheorghe, A., Straehler-Pohl, K., Nkhoma, D., Mughandira, W., Garand, D., Malema, D., Murray-Zmijewski, A., Kardan, A. and Lievens, T. (2019) 'Assessing the Feasibility and Appropriateness of Introducing a National Health Insurance Scheme in Malawi', *Global Health Research and Policy*, 4: 13. https://doi.org/10.1186/s41256-019-0103-5

Gilmore, A. B., Fabbri, A., Baum, F., Bertscher, A., Bondy, K., Chang, H. J., Demaio, S., Erzse, A., et al. (2023) 'Defining and Conceptualising the Commercial Determinants of Health', *Lancet*, 401(10383): 1194–213. https://doi.org/10.1016/S0140-6736(23)00013-2

Global Fund (2020) 'Technical Evaluation Reference Group: Thematic Review on Sustainability, Transition and Co-financing (STC) Policy: Global Fund to Fight Tuberculosis, AIDS and Malaria' [Jan]. https://archive.theglobalfund.org/media/9269/archive_terg-sustainability-transition-co-financing_report_en.pdf

Gravelle, H., Sutton, M. and Ma, A. (2010) 'Doctor Behaviour under a Pay for Performance Contract: Treating, Cheating and Case Finding', *The Economic Journal* (London), 120(542): F129–F56. https://doi.org/10.1111/j.1468-0297.2009.02340.x

Grossman, M. (1972) 'On the Concept of Health Capital and the Demand for Health', *Journal of Political Economy*, 80(2): 223–55 https://doi.org/10.1086/259880

Gutacker, N., Siciliani, L., Moscelli, G. and Gravelle, H. (2016) 'Choice of Hospital: Which Type of Quality Matters?', *Journal of Health Economics*, 50: 230–46. https://doi.org/10.1016/j.jhealeco.2016.08.001

Heckman, J. J. (2007) 'Economics, Technology, and Neuroscience of Human Capability Formation', *Proceedings of the National Academy of Sciences – PNAS*, 104(33): 13250–5. https://www.pnas.org/doi/10.1073/pnas.0701362104

Heckman, J. J., Stixrud, J. and Urzua, S. (2006) 'The Effects of Cognitive and Noncognitive Abilities on Labor Market Outcomes and Social Behavior', *Journal of Labor Economics*, 24(3): 411–82. https://doi.org/10.1086/504455

Herberholz, C. (2020) 'The Role of External Actors in Shaping Migrant Health Insurance in Thailand', *PLOS One*, 15(7): e0234642. https://doi.org/10.1371/journal.pone.0234642

James, C. D., Hanson, K., McPake, B., Balabanova, D., Gwatkin, D., Hopwood, I., Kirunga, C., Knippenberg, R., Meessen, B., Morris, S. S., Preker, A., Souteyr, Y., Tibouti, A., Villeneuve, P. and Xu, K. (2006) 'To Retain or Remove User Fees? Reflections on the Current Debate in Low- and Middle-Income Countries', *Applied Health Economics Health Policy*, 5(3): 137–53. https://doi.org/10.2165/00148365-200605030-00001

Kanavos, P., Parkin, G. C., Kamphuis, B. and Gill, B. (2019) *Latin America Healthcare System Overview: A Comparative Analysis of Fiscal Space in Healthcare*. London, UK: London School of Economics and Political Science.

Kaplan, W. A., Wirtz, V. J. and Stephens, P. (2013) 'The Market Dynamics of Generic Medicines in the Private Sector of 19 Low and Middle Income Countries between 2001 and 2011: A Descriptive Time Series Analysis', *PLOS One*, 8(9): e74399-e. https://doi.org/10.1371/journal.pone.0074399

Kringos, D. S., Boerma, W. G. W., Hutchinson, A. and Saltman, R. B. (eds) (2015) 'Building Primary Care in a Changing Europe: Case Studies'. Copenhagen: European Observatory on Health Systems and Policies. PMID: 29064645. https://pubmed.ncbi.nlm.nih.gov/29064645/

Lorenzoni, L., Marino, A., Morgan, D. and James, C. (2019) *Health Spending Projections to 2030: New Results Based on a Revised OECD Methodology*, Paris: OECD Publishing.

Lundsgaard, J. (2005) 'Consumer Direction and Choice in Long-Term Care for Older Persons, Including Payments for Informal Care: How Can it Help Improve Care Outcomes, Employment and Fiscal Sustainability?', *OECD Health Working Papers*, No. 20, Paris: OECD Publishing. https://doi.org/10.1787/616882407515

Marino, A. and Lorenzoni, L. (2019) *The Impact of Technological Advancements on Health Spending: A Literature Review*, Paris: OECD Publishing.

Marmot, M. and Wilkinson, R. G. (2006) *Social Determinants of Health*, Second edition. Oxford: Oxford University Press.

Marmot, M., Friel, S., Bell, R., Houweling, T. and Taylor, S. (2008) 'Closing the Gap in a Generation: Health Equity through Action on the Social Determinants of Health', *The Lancet* (British edition), 372(9650): 1661–9. https://doi.org/10.1016/S0140-6736(08)61690-6

Marten, R., McIntyre, D., Travassos, C., Shishkin, S., Longde, W., Reddy, S. and Vega, J. (2014) 'An Assessment of Progress towards Universal Health Coverage in Brazil, Russia, India, China, and South Africa (BRICS)', *The Lancet*, 384(9960): 2164–71. https://doi.org/10.1016/S0140-6736(14)60075-1

McGinnis, J. M., Williams-Russo, P. and Knickman, J. R. (2002) 'The Case for More Active Policy Attention to Health Promotion', *Health Affairs* (Millwood), 21(2): 78–93. https://doi.org/10.1377/hlthaff.21.2.78

Mendelson, A., Kondo, K., Damberg, C., Low, A., Motúapuaka, M., Freeman, M., O'Neil, M., Relevo, R. and Kansagara, D. (2017) 'The Effects of Pay-for-Performance Programs on Health, Healthcare Use, and Processes of Care: A Systematic Review', *Annals of Internal Medicine*, 166(5): 341–53. https://doi.org/10.7326/M16-1881

Morton, A., Arulselvan, A. and Thomas, R. (2018) 'Allocation Rules for Global Donors', *Journal of Health Economics*, 58: 67–75. https://doi.org/10.1016/j.jhealeco.2018.02.003

Moscelli, G., Gravelle, H. and Siciliani, L. (2016) 'Market Structure, Patient Choice and Hospital Quality for Elective Patients', Contract No.: Centre for Health Economics Research Paper No. 139, Lay Summary, *Economics of Social and Health Care Unit*. https://www.york.ac.uk/media/che/documents/papers/researchpapers/RP139_Lay_summary.pdf

Moscelli, G., Gravelle, H. and Siciliani, L. (2021) 'Hospital Competition and Quality for Non-emergency Patients in the English NHS', *RAND Journal*, 52(2): 382–414. https://doi.org/10.1111/1756-2171.12373

OECD (2020) *Affordability of Long-term Care Services among Older People in the OECD and the EU*, Paris: OECD Publishing.

Patel, M. S., Volpp, K. G. and Asch, D. A. (2018) 'Nudge Units to Improve the Delivery of Health Care', *New England Journal of Medicine*, 378(3): 214–6. https://doi.org/10.1056/NEJMp1712984

Paxson, C. and Schady, N. (2010) 'Does Money Matter? The Effects of Cash Transfers on Child Development in Rural Ecuador', *Economic Development and Cultural Change*, 59(1): 187–229. https://doi.org/10.1086/655458

Propper, C., Rigg, J. and Burgess, S. (2007) 'Child Health: Evidence on the Roles of Family Income and Maternal Mental Health from a UK Birth Cohort', *Health Economics*, 16(11): 1245–69. https://doi.org/10.1002/hec.1221

Rosen, D., Chalkidou, K. and Keller, J. M. (2017) 'An Initial Estimation of the Size of Health Commodity Markets in Low- and Middle-Income Countries', *Centre for Global Development* [13 Dec]. https://www.cgdev.org/publication/initial-estimation-size-health-commodity-markets-low-and-middle-income-countries

Silverman, R., Keller, J. M., Glassman, A. and Chalkidou, K. (2019) *Tackling the Triple Transition in Global Health Procurement*. Washington, DC: Centre for Global Development. https://www.cgdev.org/sites/default/files/better-health-procurement-tackling-triple-transition.pdf

Smith, S., Newhouse, J. P. and Freeland, M. S. (2009) 'Income, Insurance, And Technology: Why Does Health Spending Outpace Economic Growth?', *Health Affairs*, 28(5): 1276–84. https://doi.org/10.1377/hlthaff.28.5.1276

Sorenson, C. and Chalkidou, K. (2012) 'Reflections on the Evolution of Health Technology Assessment in Europe', *Health Economics, Policy and Law*, 7(1): 25–45. https://doi.org/10.1017/S1744133111000296

Sorenson, C., Drummond, M. and Kanavos, P. (2008). *Ensuring Value for Money in Healthcare: The Role of Health Technology Assessment in the European Union*. Belgium: World Health Organization.

Thomson, S., Foubister, T. and Mossialos, E. (2009) 'Financing Healthcare in the European Union: Challenges and Policy Responses', World Health Organization on Behalf of the European Observatory on Health Systems and Policies. https://iris.who.int/bitstream/handle/10665/326415/9789289041652-eng.pdf

United Nations (2020) 'World Population Ageing 2019'. New York: United Nations. https://doi.org/10.18356/b564c742-en

United Nations (2022) 'World Population Prospects 2022 Summary of Results'. New York: United Nations. https://doi.org/10.18356/9789210014380

van Gool, K., Mu, C. and Hall, J. (2021) 'Does More Investment in Primary Care Improve Health System Performance?', *Health Policy* (Amsterdam), 125(6): 717–24. https://doi.org/10.1016/j.healthpol.2021.03.004

Wagstaff, A. and van Doorslaer, E. (1992) 'Equity in the Finance of Healthcare: Some International Comparisons', *Journal of Health Economics*, 11(4): 361–87. https://doi.org/10.1016/0167-6296(92)90012-P

Wagstaff, A., Rutten, F. and Doorslaer, E. K. (1993) *Equity in the Finance and Delivery of Healthcare: An International Perspective*, Oxford: Oxford University Press.

Wagstaff, A., van Doorslaer, E., van der Burg, H., Calonge, S., Christiansen, T., Citoni, G., Gerdham, U-G., Gerfin, M., et al. (1999) 'Equity in the Finance of Healthcare: Some Further International Comparisons', *Journal of Health Economics*, 18(3): 263–90. https://doi.org/10.1016/S0167-6296(98)00044-7

World Bank (2015) 'Toward Universal Health Coverage and Equity in Latin America and the Caribbean: Evidence from Selected Countries'. Washington, DC: World Bank. https://openknowledge.worldbank.org/entities/publication/63f3c978-0996-56b9-884b-7657b43202d8

World Health Organization (2016) 'Health Workforce Requirements for Universal Health Coverage and the Sustainable Development Goals', (Human Resources for Health Observer, 17). World Health Organization. https://iris.who.int/handle/10665/250330

World Health Organization (2017) 'Earmarking for Health: From Theory to Practice', Health Financing Working Paper N.5. https://www.who.int/publications/i/item/9789241512206

World Health Organization (2020a) 'Global Spending on Health: Weathering the storm', Geneva: WHO. https://www.who.int/publications/i/item/9789240017788

World Health Organization (2020b) 'State of the World's Nursing 2020: Investing in education, jobs and leadership', Geneva: WHO. https://www.who.int/publications/i/item/9789240003279

World Health Organization (2021) 'Spending on Health in Europe: Entering a new era', Copenhagen: WHO. https://www.who.int/europe/publications/i/item/9789289055079

World Health Organization (2022) 'Direct Facility Financing: Concept and Role for UHC'. Geneva: WHO. https://www.who.int/publications/i/item/9789240043374

Wouters, O., Cylus, J., Yang, W., Thomson, S. and McKee, M. (2016) 'Medical Savings Accounts: Assessing their Impact on Efficiency, Equity and Financial Protection in Health Care', *Health Economics Policy and Law*, 11(3): 321–335. https://doi.org/10.1017/S1744133116000025

Xu, K., Evans, D. B., Kawabata, K., Zeramdini, R., Klavus, J. and Murray, C. J. L. (2003) 'Household Catastrophic Health Expenditure: A Multicountry Analysis', *The Lancet* (British edition), 362(9378): 111–117. https://doi.org/10.1016/S0140-6736(03)13861-5

Zeng, W., Pradhan, E., Khanna, M., Fadeyibi, O., Fritsche, G. and Odutolu, O. (2021) 'Cost-Effectiveness Analysis of the Decentralized Facility Financing and Performance-Based Financing Program in Nigeria', *Journal of Hospital Management and Health Policy*, 6: 13. https://doi.org/10.21037/jhmhp-20-82

Response to Alistair McGuire, Joan Costa-i-Font and Ranjeeta Thomas by Carol Propper

McGuire et al. analyse how to progress towards the goal of resilient and sustainable healthcare coverage. The need for resilience is clear, as highlighted by events like the COVID-19 pandemic and the Russian invasion of Ukraine, as well as the need for sustainability in the face of population ageing, increased migration, and economic cycles. As McGuire et al. note, progress has been made towards both resilience and sustainability in healthcare in richer countries, but far less so in poorer countries, and even in high-income countries, substantial health inequalities remain (and in some cases, have even been growing as GDP increases).

Against this backdrop, McGuire et al. identify the main challenges as being the expansion of public financing for meaningful universal coverage, the design of policies to deliver quality care to populations, and the design of institutions to increase the take-up of innovation and to reduce waste. With this focus, the chapter provides an excellent discussion of the key building blocks of healthcare systems – finance, delivery, access, workforce – and they add to this list the need to consider the provision of long-term care, which is often not treated as an integral part of a healthcare system. They provide evidence on what has worked (in some contexts) and what has not (in other contexts), and they make a series of mostly technical recommendations.

The chapter provides an impressive review of the healthcare issues and literature by covering a lot of countries, and it is excellent reading for someone seeking to understand what the basic building blocks of a healthcare system comprise and existing evidence on these.

My comments focus on the following observations:

- Healthcare is not the only (nor the most important) determinant of health and, relatedly, inequalities in health are strongly associated with other inequalities that are not orthogonal to each other. Other important determinants of health include income, education, where they work and live, and their genetic inheritance.
- Healthcare policy has objectives that relate to fairness, implicitly or explicitly embodied, and healthcare reform is very political. For example, countries may have explicit statements about fairness in access to healthcare. Others may have fairness in access as one of the principles that guides policy on who should pay for healthcare.

- The healthcare sector is characterised by both innovation, as well as many examples of practices which are harmful to patients and not cost-effective.

In terms of my first bullet point, the authors rightly begin their analysis by pointing out that the persistence of health inequalities partly reflects inequalities in the access to healthcare, but also reflects the impact of social determinants of health. This is an important message for policymakers to hear: the impact of healthcare on inequalities in health may be limited, and governments targeting the latter may well want to make choices to allocate funds towards other domains (the design of cities, employment, education, the reduction of income inequality) rather than healthcare. Too often in the healthcare reform space, too much attention is given to healthcare expenditure and not enough attention to how we can improve health and reduce health inequalities through non-healthcare public expenditure, non-healthcare social programmes and changes in individual and collective behaviour. This is particularly pertinent in periods of high levels of public debt and shocks to economic growth when there are significant limits to public expenditure. While the authors note this, after their initial discussion about inequalities in health, they implicitly assume that the goal of a healthcare system should be universal healthcare coverage. While this may be something that rich countries can afford, it is not something that low- or lower middle-income countries are likely to be able to achieve. Thus, it is necessary to make trade-offs between reforms to the healthcare system and other reforms. While this may be somewhat beyond the scope of this present chapter, it is worth noting these trade-offs are real and will be made, usually implicitly.

My second observation is related. Precisely because one of the goals of healthcare reform is often to improve fairness or equity in the payment for and access to healthcare, it is also often very political. With limited public budgets, it often involves denying public coverage or access to some groups in order to allow greater coverage/access for others. I would have liked for the authors to unfold this a bit more; technical recommendations of best practices may flounder because of political opposition and vested interests (the limited success of some of the key planks of the Obama administration Affordable Care Act in the United States seems like a good example of this), and it would have been useful to provide some examples of where this issue has been addressed successfully within the domain of healthcare reform (Taiwan is an example that springs to mind).

Third, I would have liked to see more discussion of incentives for innovation. As countries grow richer and their demand for healthcare increases, there is a need to increase the amount of innovation that takes place in the sector too. The authors rightly stress the need for health technology assessments to make sure that innovations are cost-effective and decisions are transparent. However, there is also a need to embrace the promises of the digital age and in some cases to use reforms to leapfrog over older methods of production and thereby encourage innovation that makes better use of the scarce labour that the authors highlight as a limiting factor. It would have been good to draw out general lessons around innovation to a greater extent in this chapter.

Fourth, the authors could have devoted more discussion to ways of curbing expenditure on practices that are not cost-effective, or even may be harmful to individuals.

The authors' discussion of the separate building blocks is very comprehensive and useful. However, it would have been helpful to have more discussion of successful reform packages: system reforms that address issues of financing, delivery, access, and workforce all together. For many countries, this may be the only way the system would be able to make substantial progress towards sustainable financing and provision of healthcare.

Finally, it would have been good to see more discussion of the limits to appetite for extensions of public financing and the trade-offs that this involves, both within healthcare policy and between other investments and healthcare investments. Although health policy analysts recognise increased public financing as a good way of achieving a sustainable and resilient healthcare system, taxpayers – and the politicians that they vote for – may not think the same. Greater discussion of the importance of the political economy and healthcare reform would have been refreshing and useful.

Response to Alistair McGuire, Joan Costa-i-Font and Ranjeeta Thomas by Michael Marmot

Social determinants and health equity – arguing against premature dismissal

McGuire, Costa-Font, and Thomas's chapter is about the important and much-discussed issue of healthcare financing. They seek to clear social determinants of health and prevention out of the way, so that they can get to their topic. They are aware that some authorities think healthcare is not the most important determinant of population health, but they dismiss the evidence as weak and conclude that:

> … shifting attention towards prevention, with its upfront costs and delayed benefits, and increasing reliance on individual responsibility for health improvements is unlikely to be sufficient for stuttering health gains even in high-income countries, particularly in a context of limited government resources given high levels of public debt.

Ergo, let's focus on healthcare. I need no convincing of the importance of universal health coverage. When people get sick they need access to healthcare. Such access should be universal and independent of people's ability to pay. This chapter from McGuire et al. adds to the important literature on how to organise and finance universal healthcare. My concern is their unnecessary dismissal of prevention and the social determinants of health. Apart from questions of cost, I argue that if given the choice, people would rather not suffer from cancer or heart disease, dysentery, or tuberculosis in the first place – i.e., people prefer prevention over waiting to get ill and then hopefully being treated. In other words, the authors dismiss a valuable natural human preference. It is worth having a critical look at why and how they discarded a whole body of evidence.

I have been here before with other economists. In 2010, my colleagues and I, at what became the University College London Institute of Health Equity, published *Fair Society Healthy Lives, the Marmot Review.*[1] I had led the WHO's Commission on Social Determinants of Health and was invited by the British government to conduct a review to answer how the findings and recommendations of the global commission could be adapted to England.[2] Although we had already reviewed the global evidence on social determinants of health in the WHO Commission, we convened nine task groups with approximately 80 experts to review the evidence relevant to the United Kingdom. We – a group of experienced commissioners – synthesised the evidence into six recommendations:

1. Give every child the best start in life.
2. Enable all children, young people and adults to maximise their capabilities and have control over their lives – a focus on education.
3. Create fair employment and good work for all.
4. Ensure a healthy standard of living for all.
5. Create and develop healthy and sustainable places and communities.
6. Strengthen the role and impact of ill health prevention.

Following publication of the Marmot Review, *Social Science and Medicine*, a journal, commissioned eight comments on our review. Six of them were what you would expect from fellow academics: this looks fine, but a bit more emphasis on this, a little less emphasis on that, be more political. All very helpful and constructive. The other two commentaries said Marmot and colleagues got the model wrong: that there is no evidence for social determinants of health. The social gradient in health is related to lack of access to healthcare, and ill-health leads to low income, not low income leads to ill-health.

It should not come as a surprise that the dissenting two commentaries were written by economists. Our response was robust.[3] We said that these two commentaries were tapping into a long-standing debate. In the past, I had a screening test for economists: if you show someone the social gradient in health – for example, the link between deprivation and ill-health – when the person says that ill-health causes deprivation, that person is an economist. It is a matter of ideology parading as empirical rigour. For reasons that are slightly obscure, economists are taught that health leads to income; public health professionals are taught that income leads to health. But this is changing. I argue that when economists start to grapple with the overwhelming evidence of social causation, as good scientists they should change their view. Case and Deaton's *Deaths of Despair and the Future of Capitalism* is a good example.[4] These two distinguished economists examined the evidence on the rise in mortality of middle-aged Americans without a four-year college degree, and blamed deaths from opioid poisonings, suicide, and alcohol not primarily on failures of the healthcare system – although it played a role – but on the conditions of these people's lives related to social circumstances. The subtitle of their book was *The Future of Capitalism*.

I had been reading Dickens's 19th-century novel *Hard Times* at the time of the exchange in *Social Science and Medicine* and addressed the selection argument, which is the notion that it is health that leads to social conditions, not social conditions that lead to health. Were these economists seriously suggesting that the link between Dickensian living and working conditions and ill-health arose because sick people choose to live in noxious places and work in dark satanic mills? That bad conditions at home and at work did not damage health? And that all the improvements in health from the 19th to the 20th century had come about with the development of the healthcare system and had nothing to do with improved sanitation or nutrition? If, on the other hand, there was acceptance that sub-standard living conditions could lead to ill-health in Victorian times, why a priori rule it out now?

Given this, it is perhaps understandable that when I read in McGuire et al.'s chapter that the argument for social determinants of health is based on a weak evidence base, it has familiar echoes. There is a second part of their dismissal of social determinants of health and prevention: it relies on changes in the behaviours of individuals.

To keep it simple, I will base my argument on evidence from the UK. In stating that the evidence for social determinants of health is weak, did the authors look at the six domains of recommendations in 'Fair Society Healthy Lives', examine the evidence, and find it wanting? Did they go back to read the 589 references to the literature in the Marmot Review and remain unconvinced that there is any evidence for social determinants of health? If their critique is that they did not need to read the papers because most of this evidence is likely to be based on correlations without using economists' more sophisticated econometric techniques, then the critique might have some merit. I emphasise *some* merit.

In a complex system, with multiple potential causes, it is true that we base much of our evidence on causal reasoning rather than on complex econometric modelling. Look at our first recommendation: give every child the best start in life. A measure of good child development, readiness for school at age five, predicts school performance that, in turn, predicts the level of qualifications an individual gains. Educational level, in turn, predicts occupation, income, level of deprivation – all associated with living and working conditions, which are in turn associated with health. Therefore, early childhood is likely to be important for health inequalities in adulthood.

There are two types of influence on early child development: positive and negative. Parenting, including playing, talking, and hugging children, is associated with positive child development. Adverse childhood experiences have negative effects on children's development. Both of these – lack of the positive influences and presence of the negative – are increasingly more common the greater the deprivation. A body of evidence shows why child poverty should have adverse effects on health and health inequalities through the life course (here, I am ignoring those behavioural geneticists who claim that everything worth bothering about is genetically determined). We should then add that growing up in a cold home damages children's lungs and their mental health; air pollution has further detrimental effects. Low income is associated with food insecurity that, in turn, is linked to childhood obesity; energy-dense food is cheaper per calorie than more nutritious alternatives.

All of this paints a picture of the social determinants of health. If the criterion of causation was one huge econometric model with all the relevant variables thrown into it, then it is true that no causation has been established. But to argue that therefore we can ignore child poverty and focus on funding of healthcare is a step too far.

A second plank of the argument is that prevention depends on behaviour change, which is both difficult to achieve and expensive. Look again at our six domains of recommendations; by and large improvements in the first five of these recommendations do not depend on individual behaviours. Reduction of child poverty, subsidising childcare, and spending on pre-school education will all improve early child development. Improvement of schools by spending on teachers, facilities, and capital will improve education, and similarly for the other recommendations. Even for the sixth recommendation, which involves lifestyle changes, attention to social determinants is crucial. For example, to follow the healthy eating advice, people in the poorest quintile of household income would have to spend 50% of their income on food. A prime reason for not following the healthy eating advice is poverty rather than reluctance to change behaviour.

The blithe dismissal of prevention and social determinants of health is unwarranted. The authors really did not need to do it in order to focus on the healthcare system. If the aim is to improve population health and reduce avoidable health inequalities, we need universal health coverage *and* a clear and sustained focus on the social determinants of health.

Notes

1 Marmot (2010).

2 Commission on the Social Determinants of Health (2008).

3 Marmot et al. (2010).

4 Case and Deaton (2020).

References

Case, A. and Deaton, A. (2020) *Deaths of Despair and the Future of Capitalism*, Princeton, NJ: Princeton University Press. https://doi.org/10.1515/9780691217062

Commission on the Social Determinants of Health (2008) 'Closing the Gap in a Generation: Health Equity through Action on the Social Determinants of Health. Final Report of the Commission on Social Determinants of Health'. Geneva: World Health Organization. https://www.who.int/publications/i/item/WHO-IER-CSDH-08.1

Marmot, M. (2010) 'Fair Society, Healthy Lives: the Marmot Review'; Strategic Review of Health Inequalities in England Post-2010. Institute of Health Equity. https://www.instituteofhealthequity.org/resources-reports/fair-society-healthy-lives-the-marmot-review

Marmot, M., Allen, J., Goldblatt, P. (2010) 'A Social Movement, Based on Evidence, to Reduce Inequalities in Health', *Social Science & Medicine*, 71(7): 1254–8. https://doi.org/10.1016/j.socscimed.2010.07.011

Part VI

ENVIRONMENT AND CLIMATE CHANGE

14. Climate and environment: what we know and what we need to know

Robin Burgess and Tim Dobermann

Expanding welfare in a world with climate change requires meeting two fundamental challenges. First, economic growth must properly account for the damaging effects of environmental externalities. Secondly, societies need to build resilience and adapt to the changes in climate that are already upon us. In this chapter, we summarise the existing evidence on how countries can undertake these two necessary transitions. Rich or poor, big or small, these transitions apply to all countries across the world. At the same time, climate justice is pertinent, as countries or individuals most vulnerable to climate change and environmental decline are likely to have contributed least to the problem. We argue that innovation is the path through these challenges. Technological and institutional innovations can help overcome the trade-offs that make political action on the environment so difficult. While much is known, a great deal remains unclear. We lay out where researchers can support policymakers by addressing knowledge gaps that can form a new research agenda for sustainable growth.

I. Introduction

Our impact on the world's climate and biosphere is 'unequivocal'.[1] Any combination of social, economic, and moral arguments justifies a sharp departure from the status quo. Two concurrent transitions need to happen. First, expanding wellbeing while rebalancing our relationship with nature requires a fundamental overhaul in how we harness energy, produce goods, and manage natural capital. Second, those in harm's way – often the poorest – must change occupations, locations, or adopt new technologies to protect themselves. Rich or poor, big or small, these transitions apply to all countries

---

How to cite this book chapter:

Burgess, Robin and Dobermann, Tim (2025) 'Climate and environment: what we know and what we need to know', in: Besley, Tim, Bucelli, Irene and Velasco, Andrés (eds) *The London Consensus: Economic Principles for the 21st Century*, London: LSE Press, pp. 475–506 https://doi.org/10.31389/lsepress.tlc.n

across the world. In this chapter we argue that innovations, broadly defined, are the path through these two goals.

Unless our method of expanding economic activity changes, our actions will increasingly have harmful impacts in ways that we are only beginning to understand. Thus, sustainable growth, which we define as the path that delivers the maximum possible gains in human welfare after properly accounting for the damaging effects of environmental externalities, is paramount. This is especially true for today's low- and middle-income countries (LMICs), which house the majority of the world's poor, as well as those most vulnerable to climate change. Economic growth remains a political and moral imperative in these countries – but climate change and environmental degradation can slow down future economic growth and threaten essential amenities, severely reducing the potential to improve human welfare. To deliver on the promise of radically increasing the standards of living across the world, these externalities must be addressed.

Sustainable growth will need systemwide changes in how we obtain energy, produce goods, and manage our natural capital (Figure 14.1). A core component of this change involves shifting to clean sources of energy for electricity generation, such as solar or wind. More of the energy used for consumption or production also needs to be from electricity, which, in turn, should be derived from clean sources. Industrial production releases greenhouse gases (GHG) both from its energy-intensive nature, as well as the materials and inputs used in its various processes. Firms will need to switch to cleaner inputs and production processes. Lastly, we need to preserve and restore our natural capital by limiting emissions from agriculture and by lowering the stress placed on land and other natural ecosystems in the process of growth. This is especially pertinent for rapidly developing low-income countries.

The fundamental challenge, in our view, is that many of the standard economic solutions to these environmental externalities – such as carbon taxes, emission quotas, or deforestation bans – face enormous political opposition. These policies typically generate well-defined groups of losers who can organise and effectively lobby governments to block their implementation. Further, these policies are often perceived to be detrimental to economic growth or unjust in the face of historical emissions. No government will support an anti-growth agenda. Likewise, for the most vulnerable countries – often among the least developed – an adaptation imperative may take precedence over goals to minimise externalities.

We argue that innovations, be they technological or institutional, can help solve this gridlock. This is chiefly because innovation can ease the trade-offs that make political action on the environment so difficult. A clear example of this is the recent development of cheap solar energy, which makes low-emissions growth not only viable but also financially attractive. Innovation, however, will not address every tension between growth and environmental conservation, and some difficult trade-offs are likely to remain. For these, governments need to find effective ways to respond to environmental externalities.

Figure 14.1: Global greenhouse emissions by sector

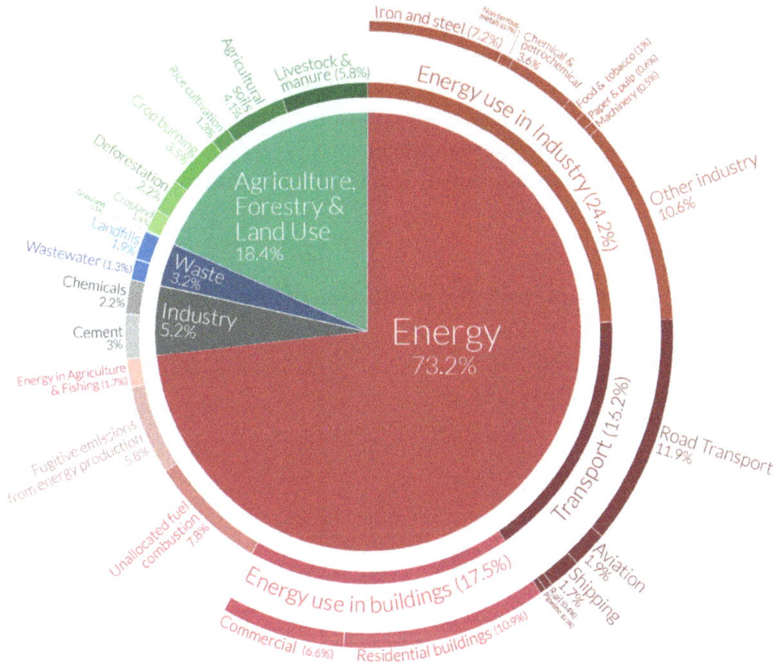

Source: Hannah Ritchie (2020)[2] 'Sector by sector: where do global greenhouse gas emissions come from?' Our World in Data. Reproduced under CC-BY licence.
Notes: Global greenhouse gas emissions are shown for the year 2016, when they were 49.4 billion tonnnes CO_2eq.

In this chapter, we summarise the existing evidence on how countries can undertake the two necessary transitions of sustainably expanding living standards, while adapting to a world with climate change. Achieving this rests on technological and institutional innovations that (i) enable clean energy; (ii) foster clean growth; (iii) preserve and restore our natural capital; and (iv) facilitate adaptation to a warming world in a just manner. The breadth of such topics naturally creates important omissions; we focus on what we think may be some of the leading issues that have universal relevance. Within these issues, we pay special attention to today's developing economies, for both reasons of climate justice and the fact that they will be the largest drivers of future emissions.

A central theme throughout our chapter is that, while much is known, a great deal remains unclear. In each section we lay out where researchers can support policymakers by generating more evidence. We make no claims of exhaustiveness, but taken together these knowledge gaps can form a new research agenda to understand the key market failures preventing innovation for sustainable growth.

II. Clean energy

Energy use, be it for consumption, production or transportation, is the single largest source of externalities. Two facts frame the following discussion: (i) the demand for energy, particularly in emerging economies, will continue to grow aggressively; and (ii) this energy must be produced cleanly if we are to minimise environmental externalities. Electricity will play an ever greater role in the global primary energy supply and is thus a central focus.

1. *What we know*

Figure 14.2: Historical costs and production of key energy supply technologies

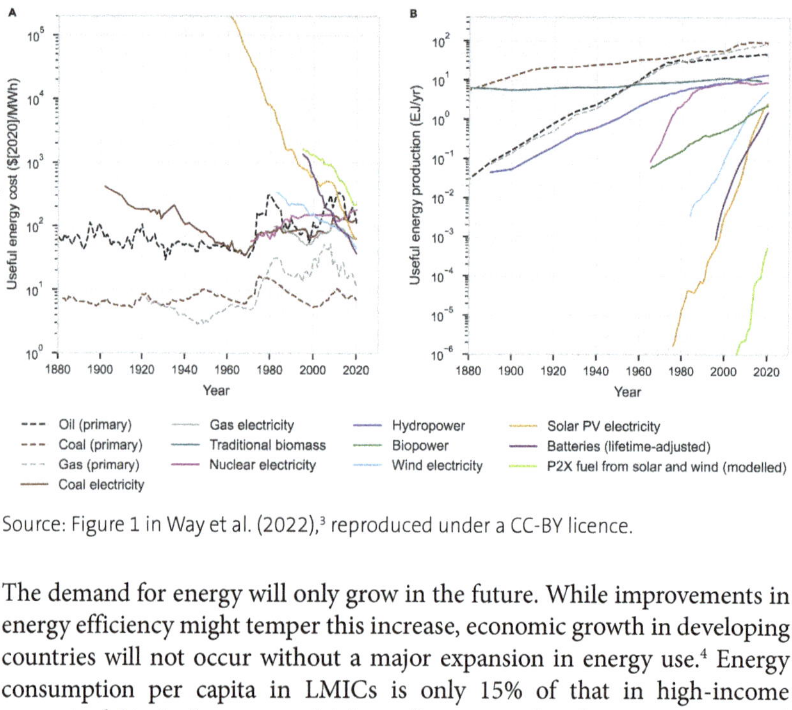

Source: Figure 1 in Way et al. (2022),[3] reproduced under a CC-BY licence.

The demand for energy will only grow in the future. While improvements in energy efficiency might temper this increase, economic growth in developing countries will not occur without a major expansion in energy use.[4] Energy consumption per capita in LMICs is only 15% of that in high-income countries.[5] Limited access to high-quality energy has large economic and social costs in the form of lower levels of employment, firm entry, and human development outcomes, especially in the long run.[6] Expanding energy use is thus a first-order priority for developing countries.

In 2021, 71% of global electricity production was sourced from fossil fuels including oil, coal, and gas.[7] If that percentage remains the same, any great expansion in energy use will generate substantial environmental externalities. Today, however, innovation in clean energy technology has fundamentally changed the nature of this trade-off. The costs of key green technologies have fallen according to a power law based on their greater deployment

– the so-called Wright's Law.[8] Accounting for full system costs, renewables like solar or wind are now the cheapest sources of electricity ever known.[9] This makes it possible, in principle, to produce low-emissions electricity at a large scale, resulting in substantial net savings once appropriate cost declines are modelled.[10] How quickly the transition can be made towards these new technologies will determine whether we are able to mitigate emissions in time to prevent even more severe climate change.

The significant recent advances in clean energy still do not imply that the overall direction of innovation is optimal. Higher energy prices have been associated with more innovation in energy efficiency.[11] The predominant role of fossil fuels, plus the minimal pricing of negative externalities from their use, skew innovation away from clean energy.[12] Engineering breakthroughs in the extraction of shale gas, for instance, brought short-run benefits by lowering coal use but likely reduced the speed and direction of green innovation.[13] Overall, these innovation distortions are quantitatively meaningful.[14]

In the long run, the energy transition requires electrifying almost all activities that rely on combustion for energy – be it wood for cooking, fuel for cars, or coal for boilers – and producing this electricity cleanly.[15] Along the way, improvements in energy efficiency, like adopting more efficient cook stoves or LED lighting, can make significant contributions towards flattening the trade-off between emissions and growth. Even for activities that do not require electricity, new technologies are allowing individuals to consume more while polluting less. For example, clean fuels for cooking and heating substantially improve household air quality, lowering morbidity and mortality, and curb deforestation.

A broad class of constraints slow down the diffusion of clean energy: (i) weak incentives resulting from distorted price mechanisms; (ii) poor information; (iii) adoption risks (including leakage) and high cost of capital; (iv) lack of a trained workforce; (v) infrastructure; and (vi) other legal and regulatory hurdles, for example, regarding land acquisition or permitting.

Poor transmission infrastructure and intermittency can slow the uptake of renewables. This is amplified in countries that have large swings between peak and off-peak electricity consumption. Intermittency becomes a larger challenge as the penetration of renewables in the electricity mix grows.[16] Handling these issues will require significant investments to expand grid capacity and interconnections, improve grid management systems, and introduce new incentive mechanisms to ensure timely dispatch. Over time, as battery prices fall, grid storage systems can be connected.

Furthermore, clean energy is often produced in scarcely populated areas, such as deserts, which are not currently connected to the grid.[17] The locations of generation, such as offshore wind, do not typically overlap with main demand centres, which can create congestion within the transmission system. A commensurate expansion in the transmission network – both in terms of reach and capacity – will be required to realise the gains in clean energy innovation.[18]

Fortunately, policies and investments can help lift these barriers. Where private actors are involved in energy generation, there must be clear economic returns to expanding clean energy generation capacity. This may involve subsidies that compensate private actors for start-up and infrastructure costs, and feed-in-tariffs that limit the risks of adoption. Feed-in-tariffs were a key part of Germany's policy to foster the development of solar electricity, while China used production and innovation subsidies to support its nascent solar energy sector.[19] The Inflation Reduction Act marked an initial foray into channelling large amounts of subsidies and support relating to energy and climate change in the US, though recent political changes make its future increasingly uncertain. The state may also have a key role to play in training the workforce with non-general skills, and those specific to the large-scale adoption of clean energy technologies.[20] The familiar economic ideas of gains from trade arising from enhanced market access and integration apply to the diffusion of energy: in Chile, for example, the expansion of transmission infrastructure sparked considerable private entry in upstream production markets, especially in renewables.[21]

Well-performing energy markets can also speed up the diffusion of new innovations. However, in most low and middle-income countries, genuine markets for producing and selling electricity do not exist. Instead, there is a reliance on fixed long-term contracts for procuring energy. While playing an important role in risk reduction, such contracts are often not competitively awarded, which risks locking in disadvantageous terms. Neither can they be easily exited, complicating the path for cheaper and cleaner alternatives like solar or wind to enter. The movement towards wholesale markets for electricity production, where plants bid against each other to supply power at frequent intervals (e.g., daily), opens up more opportunities for new technologies to displace old ones.

Lastly, energy usage is fundamentally misallocated in several countries.[22] The core source of misallocation is the disconnect between prices and social marginal costs. Where energy retail is organised by the state, this may require lifting some indiscriminate subsidies, while providing some additional support for the poorest households. In low- and middle-income countries, additional complications of non-payment and outright theft of energy arise. The presence of high subsidies and weak enforcement of payments, coupled with political pressure, keeps energy prices far below costs in much of the world. This forces utilities to run at a loss and makes it impossible to fund investment in a high-quality diffusion infrastructure.[23] Overall, energy is not systematically allocated to those who have the highest marginal willingness to pay for it. Where energy retail has been privatised, fostering competition among private retailers is also essential to unleash the full benefits from privatisation. Even with private competition, independent regulators are necessary to ensure consumers are not unduly affected.

2. *What we need to know*

Continued innovation in clean energy will further drive down costs and help diffuse these technologies. But, at the same time, continued investments into exploration and innovation in fossil fuels is taking place. Will the market process get the direction of innovation right?[24] Understanding where and how state intervention is needed (beyond the standard subsidising of research and development (R&D) to account for positive knowledge externalities) remains an important area of research. There is some evidence that policies aimed at curbing emissions, such as an emissions trading scheme, increase low-carbon patenting.[25] However, we still need more direct evidence on what types of policies best encourage innovation in clean energy. This can build on top of the wider literature on the impact of innovation policies.[26]

Next, we need a better grasp of the dual challenges of intermittency and grid infrastructure in inhibiting the uptake of clean energy. Even accounting for system costs from intermittency, wind power in Spain generated an increase in consumer welfare.[27] The gains, however, are heterogenous, and negatively impact non-wind power producers. More evidence on the impacts of intermittency on consumers, producers, grid stability, market outcomes, and investment is critical as penetration rates increase. Likewise, disparate and limited grid networks pose an immediate block on expanding clean energy. In some areas of the US, for example, wholesale electricity prices are now negative for 20% of all hours as excess power generation is trapped in a constrained grid.[28] We need to know more about how grid investments can be financed, but also how policies and regulations need to be adjusted to allow for more integrated networks and the timely construction of new lines.

It is also important to consider how fossil fuel energy production will respond to the expansion of renewables. There is a risk, in particular, that clean energy will displace gas proportionally more than coal. As burning coal produces more emissions than burning gas, it may be possible to obtain further gains in emission reductions by providing incentives for energy producers to discontinue coal rather than gas. Auctions for phasing out coal plants, such as those seen in Germany, are being looked at as possible mechanisms for ensuring a timely exit from coal.[29] These auctions, or any policy aimed at the same outcome, will have to be careful in their design to ensure additionality – that they result in greater carbon reductions than would otherwise have been the case.

Reforming energy markets and introducing more wholesale competition is a complex institutional endeavour that takes years or decades of planning. This includes setting up markets for emissions. An important area of research is how markets for electricity production can help deliver welfare gains for society through cheaper costs, as well as the adoption of the latest and cleanest forms of production. While these gains may seem obvious on paper, they may be limited in practice by the emergence of monopoly power or collusion. For example, recent evidence from Colombia exposes how the prevalence of collusive practices between energy producers in a privatised market drove up consumer prices.[30]

III. Clean growth

1. *What we know*

Figure 14.3: The decline of externalities from manufacturing production in the United States

a) Trends in manufacturing pollution emissions and real output

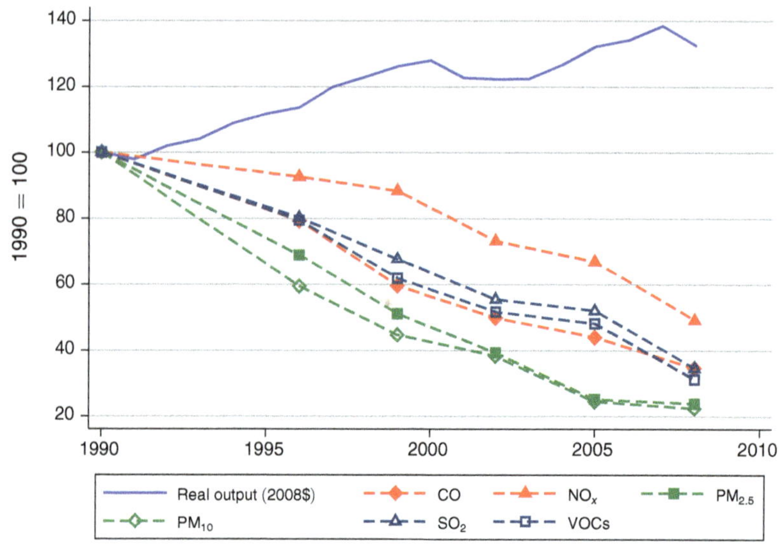

b) Nitrogen oxides emissions from manufacturing

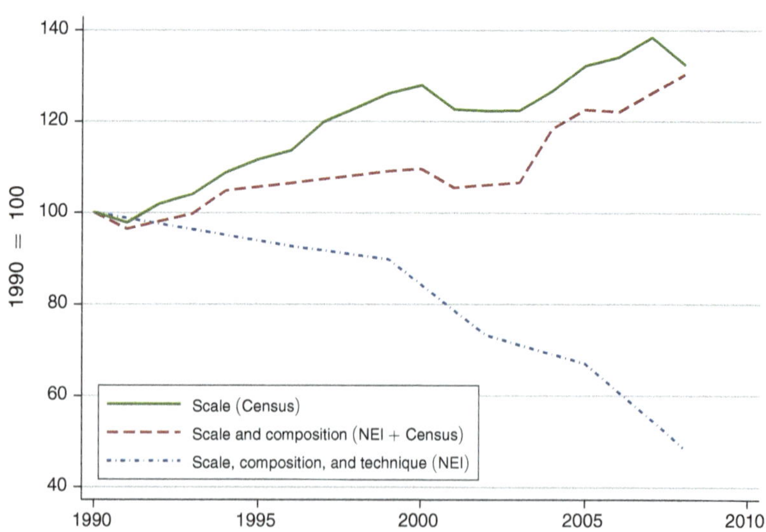

Source: Figures 1 and 3 in Shapiro and Walker (2018).[31] Copyright American Economic Association; reproduced with permission of the *American Economic Review.*

As economies grow, firms expand and adopt new technologies. Wage labour in complex organisations becomes increasingly predominant. Better technologies and better workers raise productivity, boosting their earnings and living standards. During this process, however, many firms also generate substantial environmental externalities. This is the challenge that must be overcome.

A combination of technological innovations in production and regulation have lowered pollution from manufacturing without lowering production.[32] However, while GHG emissions have been declining or plateauing in the European Union, they are on the rise in LMICs.[33] Industries such as cement manufacturing are massive emitters: by one estimate, cement manufacturing alone contributes 8% of global emissions.[34] China's cement production emits around 850 million tonnes of CO2 each year; the total of all low-income country emissions is a mere 200 million tonnes. All of Africa emits 1.4 billion tonnes.[35] Firms are also responsible for a significant amount of air and water pollution. Approximately 40% of PM2.5, the finest form of particulate matter with a diameter smaller than 2.5 micrometers, in Sub-Saharan Africa can be attributed to the combustion of fossil fuels for energy and industry, while the misuse of nitrogen-based fertiliser by agricultural firms has driven freshwater eutrophication.[36]

The development of large, technologically advanced firms offers several sustainable growth opportunities. First, these firms are better placed to mitigate environmental externalities through innovation compared to smaller, less productive firms. For example, large firms can more easily electrify production and adopt other effective pollution reduction measures. Smaller firms face more constraints in making these investments. Second, larger firms, especially those with multinational linkages, are likely to be more resilient to environmental shocks. This protection can be both physical – e.g., when jobs are performed indoors in safe environments – and economic. Since these firms are better integrated with markets, they can easily access credit, and are potentially less sensitive to climatic shocks. Their multinational linkages may also make them yield to pressure to green their own supply chains.

The market failures that inhibit innovation in clean energy also stymie green innovation in production. The standard optimal policy combines two separate tools: R&D subsidies to spur green innovation, and a tax on the negative environmental externality, e.g., a carbon tax. As of 2023, 37 carbon tax schemes exist around the world, covering only about 6% of global GHG emissions.[37] Note that these schemes extend beyond electricity generation and touch large-emitting industries. However, in many cases such policies are not feasible. Instead, alternative policies and broader interventions will be necessary. One alternative is a cap-and-trade system, where the government caps the total amount of emissions allowed by a sector or geography, but lets firms trade emissions permits. Cap-and-trade systems are attractive as they do not require governments to commit to a particular price for emissions. However, they are often more complex to establish than a tax set by the government, and, in the case of CO_2 emissions, they have not been able to deliver carbon prices anywhere near the estimated social cost of carbon.[38] Industrial policy for strategic sectors or activities that have the potential to generate clean growth has also garnered recent attention, especially given the lower public aversion to the policy.[39]

The regulation of production is another central tool to address externalities. Governments can regulate externalities by setting standards or individual quotas on pollution or emissions. Examples of this include fuel efficiency standards in automobiles and pollution quotas. The global nature of the externality, however, alters not only private actors' incentives to pollute but also governments' incentives to regulate the externalities from production. Economists have examined various potential solutions to the collective action problem facing regulators. Some have investigated whether trade policy can curb environmental degradation, or whether climate clubs can induce emission abatement by imposing trade penalties on non-members.[40] Others have considered the role of the contractability of green investments, or the role of intellectual property rights for green technologies and the duration and stringency of climate agreements in facilitating cooperation.[41]

Unilaterally implementing green regulation does, however, raise concerns about carbon leakage: businesses transferring production to countries with laxer emission constraints. That said, empirical studies have yet to find significant evidence of leakage, perhaps because key industrial sectors are often shielded by policymakers.[42] This may not be the case in the future. A final concern is that uncoordinated policies designed to mitigate emissions in developed countries may have adverse consequences for production in less developed economies.

Trade may have a particularly important role in moderating the damages from climate change, as the impacts of climate change are projected to be highly heterogeneous across locations and sectors. The literature has produced a set of nuanced findings on this point, and it remains an active area of investigation. Trade can lower the price volatility of agricultural goods following weather shocks; when combined with risk mitigation technologies, this can raise overall farmer welfare. One paper argues that, due to high trade barriers, the low-income countries that will be most affected by climate change will specialise more in food production, despite the fact that climate change will decrease the productivity of agriculture by more than it will affect the productivity of manufacturing.[43] Their model suggests that increasing trade openness will result in a major reduction in the cost of climate change in poor economies. A separate analysis showed that, while climate change will alter the relative productivity of different crops across space, trade will play an important role in the reallocation of plots to the most productive crops.[44] Exploiting this 'evolving comparative advantage' can greatly diminish the aggregate welfare effects of climate change.

2. *What we need to know*

The primary question is how production can be made cleaner without harming economic performance. Answering this requires more evidence on at least three complementary policy areas: promoting green innovation in firms; skills and matching policy as climate change intensifies and during the green transition; and trade policy to maximise the benefits from green comparative advantage.

Concerning green innovation, a fundamental question is whether carbon taxes, or something like them, are politically viable, especially if they harm growth, have negative distributional effects, or if they may be unjust with respect to historical emissions. A related question is over whether to target innovation subsidies to specific sectors or technologies, even within green sectors or technologies, especially if there are knowledge or technological spillovers. Lastly, it remains valuable to consider how policy should change in a dynamic world where there are first-mover advantages (e.g., 'winning the green race') or where a clear end date to an industry is mandated (e.g., net zero by 2050). Understanding how such policies can be designed or communicated in a palatable way is a crucial area for more evidence.

More evidence on the important ingredients for successful industrial policy is required. For example, China provided local demand subsidies to support its solar sector, but these were less effective compared to production and innovation subsidies.[45] India introduced local content requirements to boost demand for local firms involved in the solar energy value chain, but the policy failed to ignite domestic growth in the sector due to its flawed design.[46] Both shortcomings require explanation.

It is unclear to what extent economies lack the skills to adopt green innovations in production. If a lack of skills keeps individuals in occupations that damage the environment, skills programmes may also have positive benefits for the environment. In addition to skills in sectors that reduce emissions, more thought should be given to the role of training and other skills programmes in creating opportunities for adaptation and resilience, such as providing skills that create more opportunities for non-agricultural work. More generally, as climate change intensifies there may be a growing mismatch between the supply of human capital entering a local labour market and the demand for it. Left unaddressed, these imbalances could impede the ability for individuals to find suitable opportunities. In fact, job search and matching is an area where policy intervention may be beneficial. Firms face significant search frictions, especially in developing countries, when trying to hire the workers they need. Such issues are pertinent if we expect large-scale reallocation of labour across occupations, sectors, and locations due to climate change and the accompanying green transition. The ability of an area or sector to absorb additional labour matters for evaluating the opportunities for local adaptation and to better understand the welfare effects of policies aimed at curtailing environmental externalities.

Finally, we require more evidence on the extent of and remedies to carbon leakage as governments implement more ambitious mitigation policies. Aside from avoiding leakage, international cooperation could in fact further facilitate achieving emissions reductions as efficiently as possible: since LMICs offer particularly cost-effective opportunities to save GHG emissions, financing climate projects in developing countries could accelerate mitigation efforts at current spending levels. More research on how this cooperation can be organised and designed effectively, as well as on how climate change mitigation projects can boost development, is urgently needed. Concerning trade policy, LMICs will also have to adapt to changes in trade policy implemented in rich economies, in particular via mechanisms such as carbon border adjustments. The EU has recently developed a plan for a regional carbon border adjustment mechanism, which would require importers without equivalent carbon prices to buy carbon credits to cover the carbon cost of goods procured.[47] Understanding the full impacts of border carbon adjustment policies in developing countries is a research area of first-order importance.

IV. Natural capital

1. *What we know*

Natural capital is vital for continued economic development. Consider vultures: a keystone species in India, their population collapse led to an increase in water-borne diseases, producing mortality impacts on the same order of magnitude as those expected from excess heat by the end of the century.[48] Allowing the stock of natural capital to collapse, as it has been doing in recent decades, is exposing us to myriad risks that we are only just beginning to understand.[49]

The collapse is happening along multiple dimensions. We are witnessing the sixth great historical extinction of species on Earth.[50] Global coverage of living coral has fallen by more than half since the mid-20th century, greatly compromising the services they provide to society, such as food and coastal protection.[51] The diminishing quality of soil, water resources, and forest ecosystems is well documented.[52] Deforestation continues at an alarming pace: subtropical forest loss doubled during the 21st century, and the rate of global forest cover loss increased in every region (except Brazil) from 2000 to 2012.[53]

Advances in monitoring technologies have provided greater resolution and precision on the scale of natural capital loss. Remote-sensing products can now detect land use changes at very fine levels of aggregation.[54] Such techniques have been employed to assess the use of fire for land clearing and its associated negative externalities in Indonesia.[55] Likewise, they have been used to document both the improvement and subsequent reversal of deforestation rates over the past two decades in the Brazilian Amazon as policy regimes changed.[56]

Figure 14.4: Tropical forest loss in the past two decades

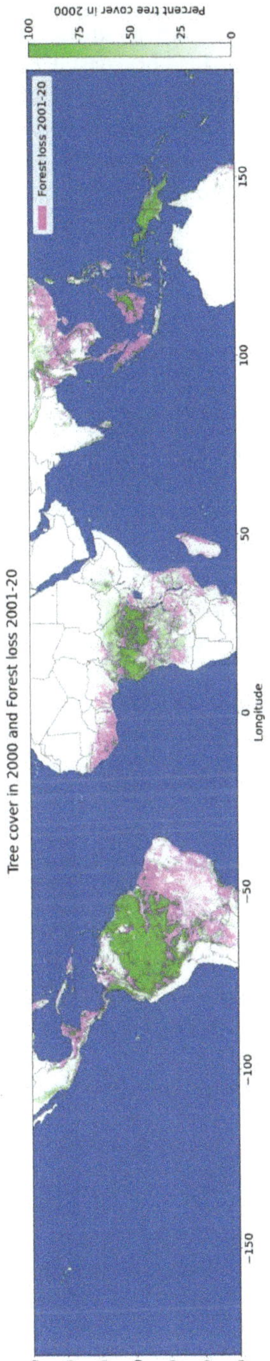

Source: Figure 2 in Balboni et al. (2023),[57] reproduced under a Creative Commons Attribution 4.0 International License.

Conservation policies have been the traditional go-to policy for reducing environmental degradation. This includes, for example, the creation of protected areas for old growth forests, savannahs, or coastal wetlands. Conservation efforts are designed to maintain the critical functions of these ecosystems – habitat provision, carbon sequestration, adaptive benefits, and other environmental services. But the efficacy of conservation programmes continues to be a contested topic in both environmental management and economics literature. Focusing on the economics, evidence on whether conservation programmes reduce poverty at both the local and macro-level is inconclusive.[58]

Several other policies have been deployed but with mixed results, or without rigorous assessment. Take payments for ecosystem services: they have shown clear benefits, for example, in the case of deforestation, but overall, the evidence on their performance is mixed.[59] Another set of policies focuses on strengthening property rights, for example, through land titling: they too have had mixed results.[60] Meanwhile conservation interventions, such as rewilding, may hold promise to protect biodiversity, but rigorous evidence on their impact is largely missing.

Lastly, a clear grasp of economic and political incentives remains critical to design feasible policies for natural capital management. For example, consider the central tension between government, firms, and citizens to exploit forests and convert land for other uses: a global imperative (climate change) may compel the national government to preserve the forest; local firms may be driven by a desire for rent extraction; and individuals may lack attractive economic alternatives that disincentivise deforestation. Indeed, for countries like Indonesia, Brazil, and the Democratic Republic of Congo, the exploitation of forest land is critical to national development. Thus, there is an urgent need to devise effective policies that balance local development and global conservation objectives.

Overall, the knowledge of scientists and local communities is essential for designing and implementing policies to bolster natural capital. The former can help identify priorities in the face of highly complex systems by pointing to the relevant keystone species, threshold effects, or emissions contributions. The latter will know about their local ecology and the importance of different natural resources in their daily lives. Economists can contribute by bringing the two together.

2. *What we need to know*

While the problem is clear, there is still a substantial evidence gap on how best to integrate natural capital into policy. Evidence is needed in two overarching areas. The first relates to improving our measurements of natural capital and the benefits and costs of conservation. Central to this is the continued efforts of scientists to capture the drivers and impacts of natural capital loss. The second relates to designing and evaluating policies to manage natural capital, taking into account how the distribution of costs and benefits overlaps between stakeholders and geographies.

Conserving natural capital generates winners and losers. A large portion of the benefits of these resources are external to the populations that live close to them and can profit from their depletion. This creates bottlenecks. How these conflicts or coordination failures can be overcome is a key area for more evidence. An element of this relates to better measuring the economic and environmental impacts of proposed interventions. In most cases, the benefits are not restricted to local users, nor spread evenly in an area, and the threats can come from inside as well as outside. These are the instances where careful research on the design and evaluation of markets, institutions, and transfers for managing natural capital is still needed.

Understanding the value of natural capital and who benefits from it does not guarantee sustainable use. Institutions and markets must create the right conditions and incentives for conservation. Even for relatively well-tested programmes, such as PES (payments for ecosystem services), there is still a need for more evidence on when and why these interventions generate additionality and sustained impacts. Identifying alternative incentive schemes that ensure cost-effective natural capital protection in local communities remains a priority.

Many of the world's natural resources are in settings that are governed under limited state capacity. It is therefore likely that some will have to be given priority over others. Services can be derived from a number of environmental assets including biodiversity, forests, and water, all of which have high economic value with low substitutability. More research is needed on valuing natural resources using accurate methods, especially those that are well-suited for LMICs, to help prioritise interventions.

V. Adaptation and climate justice

1. *What we know*

Climate change and extreme weather events will have large negative effects on outcomes like income and mortality. These effects can transmit across space via supply relationships or migration, and persist across time, including in some instances for decades.[61] While households and firms benefit from a variety of adaptation measures – financial products, new technologies, mobility, and government policies – these are seldom able to mitigate the impacts of climate change completely, indicating that policies to facilitate adaptation will likely have large welfare gains. Innovative policies and strategies, both public and private, to enhance adaptation to climate change are thus urgently needed.

The central premise is that occupations, technologies, and locations of residence and work all need to shift to account for a world with climate change. Numerous dimensions, from institutions to geography to income, determine a community's exposure to climate change. Hence, there are

Figure 14.5: Mortality effects of climate change

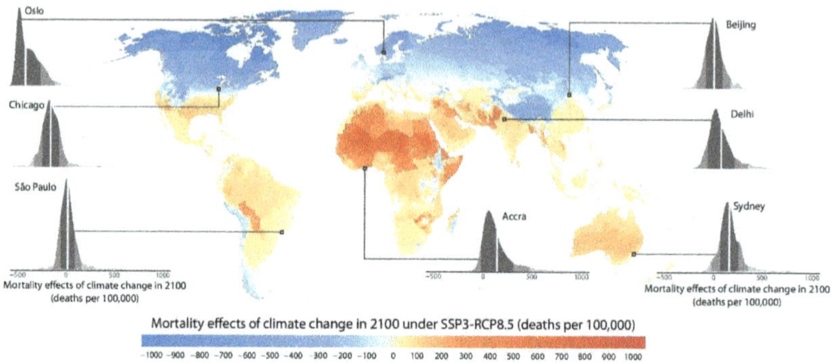

Source: Figure IV in Carleton et al. (2022); © The Author(s) 2022. Reproduced with permission from the Oxford University Press.

Figure 14.6: Percentage of individuals living below $2.15 a day, 2023

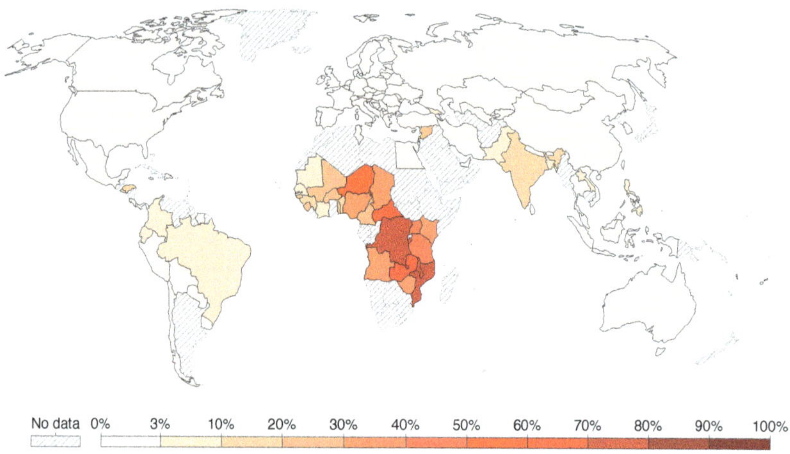

Source: Hasell et al. (2022), reproduced under a CC BY licence.

multiple, overlapping barriers to adaptation. For some households and firms, the absence of insurance may be a key constraint. In other cases, access to liquidity may be the most important barrier, especially in the aftermath of a major shock, or to cover upfront adaptation costs. A lack of information about new technologies and practices, such as how improved seed varieties offer higher yields and greater tolerance to droughts or floods, may hinder climate resilience. Funds flowing into communities to assist in climate adaptation need to be curated towards relaxing the tightest local constraints. For some settings, the primary challenge may be obvious, e.g., sea level rise in small-island states. For most, however, it is far less clear what the most impactful intervention point is.

The problem of measuring and enhancing climate adaptation is complicated by the fact that climate change manifests not only via a 'falling floor' (e.g., the gradual increase in global temperatures causes lower crop yields and lower firm and worker productivity), but it also brings an increase in the likelihood of uncommon, but extremely costly events.[62] Take, for example, the devastation wrought by Hurricane Katrina in the southern United States in 2005, or the 2004 Boxing Day tsunami in southeast Asia. Such environmental damages can reverse welfare gains. In the long run, capital will migrate out of climate-impacted areas if they are unable to insure against climate shocks.[63] This calls for a major expansion and reform of support for policies and investments to deal with the new risks that climate change poses. The principal idea underpinning climate adaptation is the adoption of innovations that increase productivity and reduce the risk for households and firms. Only in this way can we continue to expand welfare and confront climate change.

Social programmes can also protect individuals against shocks. Cash transfers, unemployment insurance, ultra-poor graduation, and work guarantees have been shown to boost consumption and psychological wellbeing, especially in the face of shocks. Today, these programmes cover an estimated 2.5 billion people worldwide.[64] In LMICs, 46% of the population receives some form of social assistance. However, coverage remains limited in low-income countries, where only 15% of the population receive social protection.[65] Environmental externalities and climate hazards make the expansion of social protection more urgent. This applies to both low-income countries and vulnerable groups in richer countries. Agricultural, health, and job-loss risks are all likely to become more pronounced due to climate change. Climate change could slow down progress towards poverty elimination. In the face of these challenges, an expanded social assistance system will be essential. For example, a study in Nicaragua shows that augmenting a conditional cash transfer with either a business loan or a vocational training product enabled beneficiary households to diversify their income streams and to become more resilient to climate shocks.[66]

Climate justice is also a central issue for adaptation. The uneven distribution of pollution and damages is a major concern. The least developed countries have made minimal contributions to global externalities, yet remain highly vulnerable and are also least able to prepare for, and respond to, natural disasters. This creates an ethical imperative to redistribute resources from high-income to LMICs for adaptation and resilience. Middle-income countries can use a combination of international financing and local public–private financing to cover adaptive investments.

International coordination on climate finance for adaptation and loss and damage is at the heart of climate justice. This should be additional to, and separate from, the necessary financing to support mitigation in these contexts. Important progress has recently been made in this area: for example, COP28 initiated the long-awaited operationalisation of a loss and damage fund.[67]

Climate justice issues also occur within countries. For example, there are significant disparities in exposure to environmental externalities like water or air pollution in the US.[68] Understanding the source of these disparities requires uncovering how exposure correlates with socioeconomic factors like income, occupation, and location. As a result, regulations designed to limit overall pollution levels may have unequal impacts on different subgroups. The Clean Air Act in the US helped lower the racial gap in PM2.5 exposure through its greater impacts in larger urban areas.[69] This speaks to the need for targeted policies and investments for environmental justice even within advanced economies.

Economic research is already contributing to such investigations, for example, by pointing out pitfalls of spending and adaptation policies in the face of rising sea levels.[70] Similarly, estimates of the costs inflicted by natural disasters can inform the timing and amount of funds to be disbursed.[71] Finally, an ample literature investigates how public policy can effectively target the poor and vulnerable.[72]

2. *What we need to know*

We need more evidence on the relative effectiveness of different programmes in reducing vulnerability to environmental externalities. The key challenge will be to develop interventions that complement rather than substitute individual and community efforts to adapt to climate change. For example, social protection programmes with non-portable benefits implicitly incentivise individuals to remain in areas affected by climate shocks. Improving portability will unlock further benefits by allowing individuals to use social protection to fund migration towards less vulnerable areas. Additionally, it may be useful to design programmes that are conditional on certain kinds of behaviour that generate long-term adaptation gains (in the same way that conditional cash transfers have been used to promote human capital accumulation). The timing of assistance may also be crucial: support ahead of a predicted shock may enable households to engage in a host of adaptive responses that would not be possible if support was only given after the event. We also know very little about how adaptation constraints interact with one another. Often, multiple market failures inhibit migration from climate vulnerable areas or induce sub-optimal crop choices. For many local communities, it is therefore unclear what the most immediately effective set of interventions for protecting against climate change would be. Broad principles, such as enhancing productivity while minimising risks, can still guide the search for these points, but the need for greater empirical evidence on promising innovations remains.

Even once constraints are identified, there is much we can learn on how best to deliver support. Relative to past efforts targeting the poor, in this case the set of affected individuals may be far higher, making scalable methods critical. Future research could build on the insights of the literature on policy targeting, exploring which mechanisms best channel funding to the most vulnerable communities. Existing literature has provided evidence on the effectiveness of specific targeting mechanisms, such as proxy means testing, community targeting, and self-selection methods.[73] It will be important to understand whether these methods succeed in identifying those individuals that are most vulnerable to climate shocks. Once identified, the modality of support needs to be considered: in kind, cash, vouchers, etc. Cash has higher fungibility, but may generate inflation in communities poorly integrated with outside markets, and may expose households to considerable consumption risk determined by price volatility – a point that will become more salient in the future due to climate change. Whether this affects the ultimate balance of costs and benefits of the different support modalities is currently unclear.

The literature has emphasised the importance of general equilibrium effects, and climate hazards have major negative equilibrium impacts on affected localities.[74] Whether social protection programmes, rolled out at scale, can counteract these negative equilibrium impacts remains a key open question.

How we can effectively address climate justice concerns requires more evidence. Research can continue to play a role in providing evidence for the design of financing mechanisms to support the vulnerable, for example, by identifying effective adaptive measures for slow-onset events, or by improving measurements of the magnitude of local climate damages. To keep donors convinced of the utility of providing climate finance, implementers will need to document the use and impact of these funds. Governments should pilot, refine, test, and evaluate investments to make the case to donor countries that climate spending can support climate adaptation and mitigation.

Finally, the international dimension of climate change complicates policy and represents an important area of research. We need innovative approaches to break deadlocks in international climate diplomacy, especially on issues related to adaptation finance and loss and damage. Advances in attributing particular weather events to climate change have been helpful in laying a factual base for discussions on compensation. Much more evidence and thinking will be needed to quantify just or adequate compensation for particular events and to determine on whom, and to what degree, the burden of compensation falls.

VI. Conclusion

Expanding welfare in a world with climate change requires meeting two fundamental challenges. First, economic growth must liberate itself from generating harmful environmental externalities. Based on the composition of environmental externalities today, this will require the rapid uptake of clean energy, the introduction of green production processes, and a systematic rebalancing of how we manage natural capital. Second, societies need to build resilience and adapt to the changes in climate that are already upon us. The countries or individuals most vulnerable to climate change and environmental decline are typically those in the lowest income deciles. They are also likely to have contributed least to the problem. These factors make climate justice a pertinent aspect of the adaptation problem and call for substantial outside financing and support.

The path through these two challenges is innovation. New technologies, policies and regulatory frameworks are opening opportunities for sustainable growth that were previously deemed out of reach. Technological innovations have slashed the costs of renewable energy. Institutional innovations have enabled markets for emissions to emerge, creating incentives for firms to internalise environmental damages. Innovations in the design of social protection programmes are better equipping the most vulnerable to be resilient in the face of worsening shocks. We therefore know that there are promising innovations that can make sustainable growth a reality.

The existence of such innovations does not guarantee their timely diffusion. Classic market failures slow down the rate of innovation. Coordination problems distort investments to adopt new technologies. Incomplete information and imperfect enforcement weaken our ability to manage our natural capital. On several dimensions, such as clean energy, the diffusion of existing innovations is on par with the need for further breakthrough innovation. Markets may eventually guarantee their spread, but governments can play an active role in speeding up their deployment around the world.

While there is much that we do know, there is as much that we still need to learn. The precise way our global climate is changing, and how these changes will affect our daily economic lives, is still evolving. How we can coordinate investments to transform the existing paradigm for producing energy and goods within a condensed timeline is an open question. We also need greater insights into how we can design incentives for conserving and restoring nature in a just way, especially involving international transfers.

These unknowns have created an important space for research and evidence. The systemwide changes in question call for widespread interaction across disciplines and the fields within them. Economists, engineers and ecologists can all bring valuable tools and methods to help identify and implement innovations for sustainable growth.

Notes

1. Pörtner et al. (2022).
2. Ritchie (2020).
3. Way et al. (2022).
4. Steinbuks and Foster (2010); Lee et al. (2020).
5. Ritchie et al. (2022).
6. Dinkelman (2011); Allcott (2018); Lipscomb et al. (2013); Fried and Lagakos (2023).

[7] Ritchie et al. (2022).

[8] Wright (1936/2012).

[9] Way et al. (2022).

[10] Popp (2010); Itskos et al. (2016); IRENA (2017); Burgess et al. (2023).

[11] Popp (2002).

[12] Acemoglu et al. (2012); Acemoglu et al. (2016); Aghion et al. (2016).

[13] Acemoglu et al. (2023).

[14] Acemoglu (2023).

[15] For the subset of hard-to-decarbonise sectors, such as producing steel or cement, other technologies may be necessary.

[16] For countries with minimal existing renewable electricity generation, this may pose a challenge only in the future.

[17] Fowlie and Reguant (2018); Gonzales et al. (2023).

[18] Davis et al. (2023).

[19] Banares-Sanchez et al. (2023).

[20] Wasmer (2006).

[21] Gonzales et al. (2023).

[22] Burgess et al. (2020).

[23] McRae (2015); Allcott et al. (2016); Fried and Lagakos (2023).

[24] Acemoglu (2023).

[25] Calel and Dechezleprêtre (2016).

[26] Bloom et al. (2019).

[27] Petersen et al. (2024).

[28] Davis et al. (2023).

[29] Jewell et al. (2019).

[30] Bernasconi et al. (2023).

[31] Shapiro and Walker (2018).

[32] Shapiro and Walker (2018).

[33] Ritchie et al. (2020).

[34] Lehne and Preston (2018).

[35] Friedlingstein et al. (2022).

[36] Brauer (2022); Damania et al. (2019).

[37] Metcalf (2021); Timilsina (2022).

[38] Metcalf (2021).

[39] Rodrik (2014).

[40] Hsiao (2024); Farrokhi and Lashkaripour (2022).

[41] Battaglini and Harstad (2016).

[42] Branger and Quirion (2013); Grubb et al. (2022).

[43] Nath (2025).

[44] Costinot et al. (2016).

[45] Banares-Sanchez et al. (2023).

[46] Harrison et al. (2017).

[47] Grubb et al. (2022).

[48] Frank and Sudarshan (2023).

[49] Pörtner et al. (2022).

[50] Kolbert (2014).

[51] De'ath et al. (2012); Eddy et al. (2021).

[52] Dasgupta (2021).

[53] Feng et al. (2022); Hansen et al. (2013).

[54] Hansen et al. (2013).

[55] Balboni et al. (2023).

[56] Burgess et al. (2022).

[57] Balboni et al. (2023).

[58] Adams et al. (2004); Andam et al. (2010); Naidoo et al. (2019).

[59] Pattanayak et al. (2010); Jayachandran (2022).

[60] BenYishay et al. (2017); Jayachandran (2022); Holland et al. (2022).

[61] Kala et al. (2023).

[62] Weitzman (2011).

[63] Albert et al. (2021).

[64] Banerjee et al. (2022).

[65] Division, United Nations Statistics (2020); Parekh and Bandiera (2020).

[66] Macours et al. (2012).

[67] Abnett et al. (2023).

[68] Fowlie et al. (2020).

[69] Currie et al. (2023).

[70] Balboni (2019); Hsiao (2023).

[71] Anttila-Hughes and Hsiang (2013).

[72] For example, Hanna and Olken (2018); Alatas et al. (2012); Alderman (2002); Alatas et al. (2016a); Banerjee et al. (2018).

[73] For example, Alatas (2011); Alatas et al. (2012; 2016b); Premand and Schnitzer (2020); Blattman and Ralston (2015).

[74] For example, Muralidharan et al. (2023); Imbert and Papp (2015); Egger et al. (2019); Bustos et al. (2016); Jedwab et al. (2021).

References

Abnett, K., El Dahan, M. and Volcovici, V. (2023) 'COP28 Kicks Off with Climate Disaster Fund Victory', *Reuters* [30 Nov]. https://www.reuters.com/business/environment/cop28-summit-opens-with-hopes-early-deal-climate-damage-fund-2023-11-30/

Acemoglu, D. (2023) 'Distorted Innovation: Does the Market Get the Direction of Technology Right?', *AEA Papers and Proceedings*, 113 (1): 1–28. https://doi.org/10.1257/pandp.20231000

Acemoglu, D., Aghion, P., Bursztyn, L. and Hemous, D. (2012) 'The Environment and Directed Technical Change', *The American Economic Review*, 102 (1): 131–166. https://doi.org/10.1257/aer.102.1.131

Acemoglu, D., Akcigit, U., Hanley, D. and Kerr, W. (2016) 'Transition to Clean Technology', *Journal of Political Economy*, 124 (1): 52–104. https://doi.org/10.1086/684511

Acemoglu, D., Aghion, P., Barrage, L. and Hemous, D. (2023) 'Climate Change, Directed Innovation, and Energy Transition: The Long-Run Consequences of the Shale Gas Revolution', *Working Paper*. https://economics.mit.edu/sites/default/files/2023-08/Climate%20Change%2C%20Directed%20Innovation%2C%20and%20Energy%20Transistion%20-%20The%20Long-run%20Consequences%20of%20the%20Shale%20Gas%20Revolution.pdf

Adams, W. M., Aveling, R., Brockington, D., Dickson, B., Elliott, J., Hutton, J., Roe, D., Vira, B. and Wolmer, W. (2004) 'Biodiversity Conservation and the Eradication of Poverty', *Science*, 306 (5699): 1146–1149. https://doi.org/10.1126/science.1097920

Aghion, P., Dechezleprêtre, A., Hémous, D., Martin, R. and Van Reenen, J. (2016) 'Carbon Taxes, Path Dependency, and Directed Technical Change: Evidence from the Auto Industry', *Journal of Political Economy*, 124 (1): 1–51. https://doi.org/10.1086/684581

Alatas, V. (2011) 'Program Keluarga Harapan: Main Findings from the Impact Evaluation of Indonesia's Pilot Household Conditional Cash Transfer Program', *World Bank Technical Report*. https://clear.dol.gov/Study/Program-Keluarga-Harapan-Main-findings-impact-evaluation-Indonesia%E2%80%99s-pilot-household-0

Alatas, V., Banerjee, A., Hanna, R., Olken, B. A. and Tobias, J. (2012) 'Targeting the Poor: Evidence from a Field Experiment in Indonesia', *American Economic Review*, 102 (4): 1206–40. https://doi.org/10.1257/aer.102.4.1206

Alatas, V., Banerjee, A., Chandrasekhar, A. G., Hanna, R. and Olken, B. A. (2016a) 'Network Structure and the Aggregation of Information: Theory and Evidence from Indonesia', *American Economic Review*, 106 (7): 1663–1704. https://doi.org/10.1257/aer.20140705

Alatas, V., Purnamasari, R., Wai-Poi, M., Banerjee, A., Olken, B. A. and Hanna, R. (2016b) 'Self-Targeting: Evidence from a Field Experiment in Indonesia', *Journal of Political Economy*, 124 (2), 371–427. https://doi.org/10.1086/685299

Albert, C., Bustos, P. and Ponticelli, J. (2021) 'The Effects of Climate Change on Labor and Capital Reallocation', Technical Report, National Bureau of Economic Research 7. [28 October]. https://abfer.org/media/abfer-events-2023/annual-conference/papers-trade/AC23P4005-The-Effects-of-Climate-Change-on-Labor-and-Capital-Reallocation.pdf

Alderman, H. (2002) 'Do Local Officials Know Something We Don't? Decentralization of Targeted Transfers in Albania', *Journal of Public Economics*, 83 (3): 375–404. https://doi.org/10.1016/S0047-2727(00)00145-6

Allcott, H. (2018) 'Evaluating Energy Efficiency Policies', *NBER Reporter*, 8–11. https://www.nber.org/reporter/2017number2/evaluating-energy-efficiency-policies

Allcott, H., Collard-Wexler, A. and O'Connell, S. D. (2016) 'How Do Electricity Shortages Affect Industry? Evidence from India', *American Economic Review*, 3 (106): 587–624. https://doi.org/10.1257/aer.20140389

Andam, K. S., Ferraro, P. J., Sims, K., Healy, A. and Holland, M. B. (2010) 'Protected Areas Reduced Poverty in Costa Rica and Thailand', *Proceedings of the National Academy of Sciences*, 107 (22): 9996–10001. https://doi.org/10.1073/pnas.0914177107

Anttila-Hughes, J. and Hsiang, S. (2013) 'Destruction, Disinvestment, and Death: Economic and Human Losses Following Environmental Disaster', SSRN. https://doi.org/10.2139/ssrn.2220501

Balboni, C. (2019) 'In Harm's Way? Infrastructure Investments and the Persistence of Coastal Cities', PhD dissertation, London School of Economics and Political Science. https://etheses.lse.ac.uk/3910/1/Balboni__In-harm%27s-way.pdf

Balboni, C., Berman, A., Burgess, R. and Olken, B. A. (2023) 'The Economics of Tropical Deforestation', *Annual Review of Economics*, 15: 723–754. https://doi.org/10.1146/annurev-economics-090622-024705

Banares-Sanchez, I., Burgess, R., László, D., Simpson, P., Van Reenen, J. and Wang, Y. (2023) 'Ray of Hope? China and the Rise of Solar Energy', Working paper. [18 July]. https://www3.nd.edu/~nmark/Climate/Ray%20of%20Hope.pdf

Banerjee, A., Hanna, R., Kyle, J., Olken, B. A. and Sumarto, S. (2018) 'Tangible Information and Citizen Empowerment: Identification Cards and Food Subsidy Programs in Indonesia', *Journal of Political Economy*, 126 (2): 451–491. https://doi.org/10.1086/696226

Banerjee, A., Hanna, R., Olken, B. and Sverdlin-Lisker, D. (2022) 'Social Protection in the Developing World', *Journal of Economic Literature*. Working paper: https://economics.mit.edu/sites/default/files/2023-08/Social_Protection_paper_manuscript.pdf

Battaglini, M. and Harstad, B. (2016) 'Participation and Duration of Environmental Agreements', *Journal of Political Economy*, 124 (1): 160–204. https://doi.org/10.1086/684478

BenYishay, A., Heuser, S., Runfola, D. and Trichler, R. (2017) 'Indigenous Land Rights and Deforestation: Evidence from the Brazilian Amazon', *Journal of Environmental Economics and Management*, 86: 29–47. https://doi.org/10.1016/j.jeem.2017.07.008

Bernasconi, M., Espinosa, M., Macchiavello, R. and Suarez, C. (2023) 'Relational Collusion in the Colombian Electricity Market', Working Paper, No. 10384, Center for Economic Studies and ifo Institute (CESifo), Munich. https://www.econstor.eu/bitstream/10419/272028/1/cesifo1_wp10384.pdf

Blattman, C. and Ralston, L. (2015) 'Generating Employment in Poor and Fragile States: Evidence from Labor Market and Entrepreneurship Programs', [19 July]. https://papers.ssrn.com/sol3/papers.cfm?abstract_id=2622220

Bloom, N., Van Reenen, J. and Williams, H. (2019) 'A Toolkit of Policies to Promote Innovation', *Journal of Economic Perspectives*, 33 (3): 163–184. https://doi.org/10.1257/jep.33.3.163

Branger, F. and Quirion, P. (2013) 'Climate Policy and the 'Carbon Haven' Effect', *Wiley Interdisciplinary Reviews: Climate Change*, 5 (1): 53–71. https://doi.org/10.1002/wcc.245

Brauer, M. (2022) 'The State of Air Quality and Health Impacts in Africa', Technical Report 2578–6881, State of Global Air Institute. https://www.stateofglobalair.org/resources/report/state-air-quality-and-health-impacts-africa

Burgess, R., Greenstone, M., Ryan, N. and Sudarshan, A. (2020) 'The Consequences of Treating Electricity as a Right', *Journal of Economic Perspectives*, 12(34): 145–169. https://doi.org/10.1257/jep.34.1.145

Burgess, R., Dobermann, T. and Sharma, N. (2022) 'Sustainable Growth for a Changing Climate', Technical Report, International Growth Centre 11. [Sept]. https://www.theigc.org/sites/default/files/2023-01/Burgess-et-al-Growth-brief-September-2022.pdf

Burgess, R., Greenstone, M., Ryan, N., and Sudarshan, A. (2023) 'Demand for Electricity on the Global Electrification Frontier', Technical Report, Warwick Economic Research Papers 1. https://wrap.warwick.ac.uk/id/eprint/152572/1/WRAP-demand-electricity-global-electrification-frontier-Sudarshan-2023.pdf

Bustos, P., Caprettini, B. and Ponticelli, J. (2016) 'Agricultural Productivity and Structural Transformation: Evidence from Brazil', *American Economic Review*, 6 (106): 1320–1365. https://doi.org/10.1257/aer.20131061

Calel, R. and Dechezleprêtre, A. (2016) 'Environmental Policy and Directed Technological Change: Evidence from the European Carbon Market', *Review of Economics and Statistics*, 98 (1): 173–191. https://doi.org/10.1162/REST_a_00470

Carleton, T., Jina, A., Delgado, M., Greenstone, M., Houser, T., Hsiang, M., Hultgrun, A., Kopp, R. E., et al. (2022) 'Valuing the Global Mortality Consequences of Climate Change Accounting for Adaptation Costs and Benefits', *The Quarterly Journal of Economics*, 137 (4): 1–69. https://doi.org/10.1093/qje/qjac020

Costinot, A., Donaldson, D., and Smith, C. (2016) 'Evolving Comparative Advantage and the Impact of Climate Change in Agricultural Markets: Evidence from 1.7 Million Fields Around the World', *Journal of Political Economy* vol. 124, no. 1, pp.205–248

Currie, J., Voorheis, J. and Walker, R. (2023) 'What Caused Racial Disparities in Particulate Exposure to Fall? New Evidence from the Clean Air Act and Satellite-based Measures of Air Quality', *American Economic Review*, 113 (1): 71–97. https://doi.org/10.1257/aer.20191957

Damania, R., Desbureaux, S., Rodella, A. Russ, J. and Zaveri, E. (2019) *Quality Unknown: The Invisible Water Crisis,* Washington DC: World Bank. https://doi.org/10.1596/978-1-4648-1459-4

Dasgupta, P. (2021) 'The Economics of Biodiversity: The Dasgupta Review', Technical Report, HM Treasury. [Feb] https://assets.publishing.service.gov.uk/media/602e92b2e90e07660f807b47/The_Economics_of_Biodiversity_The_Dasgupta_Review_Full_Report.pdf

Davis, L., Hausman, C. and Rose, N. (2023) 'Transmission Impossible? Prospects for Decarbonizing the US Grid', *Journal of Economic Perspectives*, 37 (4): 155–180. https://doi.org/10.1257/jep.37.4.155

De'ath, G., Fabricius, K. E., Sweatman, H. and Puotinen, M. (2012) 'The 27 Year Decline of Coral Cover on the Great Barrier Reef and Its Causes', *Proceedings of the National Academy of Sciences*, 109 (44): 17995–17999. https://doi.org/10.1073/pnas.1208909109

Dinkelman, T. (2011) 'The Effects of Rural Electrification on Employment: New Evidence from South Africa', *American Economic Review*, 12 (101): 3078–3108. https://doi.org/10.1257/aer.101.7.3078

Division, United Nations Statistics (2020) 'Proportion of Total Population Effectively Covered by at Least One Social Protection Benefit and Vulnerable Persons Covered by Social Assistance, by Income-Level of Country'. https://unstats.un.org/sdgs/report/2022/goal-01/

Eddy, T. D., Lam, V., Reygondeau, G., Cisneros-Montemayor, A. M., Greer, K., Palomares, M., Bruno, J., Ota, Y. and Cheung, W. (2021) 'Global Decline in Capacity of Coral Reefs to Provide Ecosystem Services', *One Earth*, 4 (9): 1278–1285. https://doi.org/10.1016/j.oneear.2021.08.016

Egger, D., Haushofer, J., Miguel, E., Niehaus, P. and Walker, M. (2019) 'General Equilibrium Effects of Cash Transfers: Experimental Evidence from Kenya', NBER Working Papers 26600, National Bureau of Economic Research, December. https://doi.org/10.3386/w26600

Farrokhi, F. and Lashkaripour, A. (2022) 'Can Trade Policy Mitigate Climate Change?', *STEG Working Paper Series*. https://steg.cepr.org/publications/can-trade-policy-mitigate-climate-change

Feng, Y., Zeng, Y., Searchinger, T. D., Ziegler, A. D., Wu, J., Wang, D., He, X., Elsen, P. R., et al. (2022) 'Doubling of Annual Forest Carbon Loss over the Tropics During the Early Twenty-first Century', *Nature Sustainability*, 5 (5): 444–451. https://doi.org/10.1038/s41893-022-00854-3

Fowlie, M. and Reguant, M. (2018) 'Challenges in the Measurement of Leakage Risk', *AEA Papers and Proceedings*, 108: 124–29. https://doi.org/10.1257/pandp.20181087

Fowlie, M., Walker, R. and Wooley, D. (2020) 'Climate Policy, Environmental Justice, and Local Air Pollution', *Brookings Economic Studies*. https://www.brookings.edu/wp-content/uploads/2020/10/ES-10.14.20-Fowlie-Walker-Wooley.pdf

Frank, E. and Sudarshan, A. (2023) 'The Social Costs of Keystone Species Collapse: Evidence from the Decline of Vultures in India', *Social Science Research Network*. [26 June] https://www.aeaweb.org/articles?id=10.1257/aer.20230016

Fried, S. and Lagakos, D. (2023) 'Electricity and Firm Productivity: A General-Equilibrium Approach', *American Economic Journal: Macroeconomics*, 7. Working paper. https://www.nber.org/system/files/working_papers/w27081/w27081.pdf

Friedlingstein, P., O'Sullivan, M., Jones, M. W., Andrew, R. M., Gregor, L., Hauck, J., Le Quéré, C., Luijkx, I. T., et al. (2022) 'Global Carbon Budget 2022', *Earth System Science Data*, 14 (11): 4811–4900. https://doi.org/10.5194/essd-14-4811-2022

Gonzales, L. E., Ito, K. and Reguant, M. (2023) 'The Dynamic Impact of Market Integration: Evidence from Renewable Energy Expansion in Chile', Technical Report, National Bureau of Economic Research. https://doi.org/10.3386/w30016

Grubb, M., Jordan, N. D., Hertwich, E., Neuhoff, K., Das, K., Bandyopadhyay, K. R., van Asselt, H., Sato, M., Wang, R., Pizer, W. and Oh, H. (2022) 'Carbon Leakage, Consumption, and Trade', *Annual Review of Environment and Resources*, 9 (47): 753–795. https://doi.org/10.1146/annurev-environ-120820-053625

Hanna, R. and Olken, B. A. (2018) 'Universal Basic Incomes versus Targeted Transfers: Anti-Poverty Programs in Developing Countries', *Journal of Economic Perspectives*, 32 (4): 201–26. https://www.aeaweb.org/articles?id=10.1257/jep.32.4.201

Hansen, M. C., Potapov, P. V., Moore, R., Hancher, M., Turubanova, S. A. Tyukavina, A., Thau, D., Stehman, S. V., et al. (2013) 'High-Resolution Global Maps of 21st-Century Forest Cover Change', *Science*, 2013, 342 (6160), 850–853. https://doi.org/10.1126/science.1244693

Harrison, A., Martin, L. A. and Nataraj, S. (2017) 'Green Industrial Policy in Emerging Markets', *Annual Review of Resource Economics*, 9 (1): 253–274. https://doi.org/10.1146/annurev-resource-100516-053445

Hasell, J., Rohenkohl, B., Arriagada, P., Ortiz-Ospina, E. and Roser, M. (2022) 'Poverty', *Our World in Data*. https://ourworldindata.org/poverty

Holland, M., Masuda, Y. and Robinson, B. (2022) *Land Tenure Security and Sustainable Development*, London: Palgrave MacMillan. https://doi.org/10.1007/978-3-030-81881-4

Hsiao, A. (2023) 'Sea Level Rise and Urban Adaptation in Jakarta', *Working Paper* https://allanhsiao.com/files/Hsiao_jakarta.pdf

Hsiao, A. (2024) 'Coordination and Commitment in International Climate Action: Evidence from Palm Oil', *Econometrica*. Working paper: https://allanhsiao.com/files/Hsiao_palmoil.pdf

Imbert, C. and Papp, J. (2015) 'Labor Market Effects of Social Programs: Evidence from India's Employment Guarantee', *American Economic Journal: Applied Economics*, 7 (2): 233–63. https://doi.org/10.1257/app.20130401

IRENA (2017) Renewable Power: Sharply Falling Generation Costs', Technical Report, IRENA. https://www.irena.org/-/media/Files/IRENA/Agency/Publication/2017/Nov/IRENA_Sharply_falling_costs_2017.pdf?rev=b76f4fa771764bf8bca23a52f5e52ccd&hash=11059F07972F2C719C8A5270A6DD4B58

Itskos, G., Nikolopoulos, N., Kourkoumpas, D. S., Koutsianos, A., Violidakis, I., Drosatos, P. and Grammelis, P. (2016) 'Energy and the Environment', in *Environment and Development Basic Principles, Human Activities, and Environmental Implications*, 363–452, Elsevier. https://doi.org/10.1016/B978-0-444-62733-9.00006-X

Jayachandran, S. (2022) 'How Economic Development Influences the Environment', *Annual Review of Economics*, 14 (1): 229–252. https://doi.org/10.1146/annurev-economics-082321-123803

Jedwab, R., Haslop, F., Zarate, R., Masaki, T. and Rodríguez Castelán, C. (2021) 'The Real Effects of Climate Change in Poor Countries: Evidence from the Permanent Shrinking of Lake Chad', Technical Report 2, World Bank. https://openknowledge.worldbank.org/server/api/core/bitstreams/7ce4d8ef-8170-532a-be1e-c4ef63eabf0b/content

Jewell, J., Vinichenko, V., Nacke, L. and Cherp, A. (2019) 'Prospects for Powering Past Coal', *Nature Climate Change*, 9 (8): 592–597. https://doi.org/10.1038/s41558-019-0509-6

Kala, N., Balboni, C. and Bhogale, S. (2023) Climate Adaptation', Technical Report 7(1). [28 June]. https://voxdev.org/sites/default/files/2023-09/Climate_Adaptation_Issue_1.pdf

Kolbert, E. (2014) *The Sixth Extinction: An Unnatural History*, London: Bloomsbury Publishing.

Lee, K., Miguel, E. and Wolfram, C. (2020) 'Experimental Evidence on the Economics of Rural Electrification', *Journal of Political Economy*, 128(4): 1535–1565. https://doi.org/10.1086/705417

Lehne, J. and Preston, F. (2018) 'Making Concrete Change: Innovation in Low-Carbon Cement and Concrete', Chatham House Report. [June]. https://www.chathamhouse.org/sites/default/files/publications/2018-06-13-making-concrete-change-cement-lehne-preston-final.pdf

Lipscomb, M., Mushfiq Mobarak, A. and Barham, T. (2013) 'Development Effects of Electrification: Evidence from the Topographic Placement of Hydropower Plants in Brazil', *American Economic Journal: Applied Economics*, 4 (5), 200–231. https://doi.org/10.1257/app.5.2.200

Macours, K., Schady, N. and Vakis, R. (2012) 'Cash Transfers, Behavioral Changes, and Cognitive Development in Early Childhood: Evidence from a Randomized Experiment', *American Economic Journal: Applied Economics*, 4 (2): 247–73. https://doi.org/10.1257/app.4.2.247

McRae, S. (2015) 'Infrastructure Quality and the Subsidy Trap', *American Economic Review*, 105 (1): 35–66. https://doi.org/10.1257/aer.20110572

Metcalf, G. E. (2021) 'Carbon Taxes in Theory and Practice', *Annual Review of Resource Economics*, 13 (1): 245–265. https://doi.org/10.1146/annurev-resource-102519-113630

Muralidharan, K., Niehaus, P. and Sukhtankar, S. (2023) 'General Equilibrium Effects of (Improving) Public Employment Programs: Experimental Evidence from India', *Econometrica*, 91 (4), 1261–1295. https://doi.org/10.3982/ECTA18181

Naidoo, R., Gerkey, D., Hole, D., Pfaff, A., Ellis, A. M., Golden, C. D., Herrera, D., Johnson, K. et al. (2019) 'Evaluating the Impacts of Protected Areas on Human Well-Being Across the Developing World', *Science Advances*, 5(4): eaav3006. https://doi.org/10.1126/sciadv.aav3006

Nath, I. (2025) 'Climate Change, the Food Problem, and the Challenge of Adaptation through Sectoral Reallocation', *Journal of Political Economy*. Published ahead of print. https://doi.org/10.1086/734725

Parekh, N. and Bandiera, O. (2020) 'Poverty in the Time of COVID: The Effect of Social Assistance', CPI Technical Report. [Jan] https://climatepolicyinitiative.org/wp-content/uploads/2014/01/Finance-Mechanisms-for

-Lowering-the-Cost-of-Clean-Energy-in-Rapidly-Developing-Countries .pdf

Pattanayak, S., Wunder, S. and Ferraro, P. (2010) 'Show Me the Money: Do Payments Supply Environmental Services in Developing Countries?', *Review of Environmental Economics and Policy*, 4 (2): 254–274. https://doi.org/10.1093/reep/req006

Petersen, C., Reguant, M. and Segura, L. (2024) 'Measuring the Impact of Wind Power and Intermittency', *Energy Economics*, 129, 107200. https://www.sciencedirect.com/science/article/pii/S0140988323006989

Popp, D. (2002) 'Induced Innovation and Energy Prices', *American Economic Review*, 92 (1): 160–180. https://doi.org/10.1257/000282802760015658

Popp, D. (2010) 'Innovation and Climate Policy', *Annual Review of Resource Economics*, 10 (2): 275–298. https://doi.org/10.1146/annurev.resource.012809.103929

Pörtner, H., Roberts, D. C., Poloczanksa, K., Mintenbeck, M., Tignor, A., Alegría, A., Craig, M., Langsdorf, S., et al. (2022) Climate Change 2022: Mitigation of Climate Change, Contribution of Working Group III to the Sixth Assessment Report of the IPCC, United Nations https://www.ipcc.ch/report/ar6/wg2/downloads/report/IPCC_AR6_WGII_FullReport.pdf

Premand, P. and Schnitzer, P. (2020) 'Efficiency, Legitimacy, and Impacts of Targeting Methods: Evidence from an Experiment in Niger', *The World Bank Economic Review*, 35 (4): 892–920. https://doi.org/10.1596/40834

Ritchie, H. (2020) 'Sector by Sector: Where Do Global Greenhouse Gas Emissions Come From?', *Our World in Data*. https://ourworldindata.org/ghg-emissions-by-sector?

Ritchie, H., Roser, M. and Rosado, P. (2020) 'CO_2 and Greenhouse Gas Emissions', *Our World in Data*. https://ourworldindata.org/co2-and-greenhouse-gas-emissions

Ritchie, H., Roser, M. and Rosado, P. (2022) 'Energy', *Our World in Data*. https://ourworldindata.org/energy

Rodrik, D. (2014) 'Green Industrial Policy', *Oxford Review of Economic Policy*, 30 (3): 469–491. https://doi.org/10.1093/oxrep/gru025

Shapiro, J. and Walker, R. (2018) 'Why Is Pollution from US Manufacturing Declining? The Roles of Environmental Regulation, Productivity, and Trade', *American Economic Year*, 108 (12): 3814– 3854. https://doi.org/10.1257/aer.20151272

Steinbuks, J. and Foster, V. (2010) 'When Do Firms Generate? Evidence on In-house Electricity Supply in Africa', *Energy Economics*, 32 (3): 505–514. https://doi.org/10.1016/j.eneco.2009.10.012

Timilsina, G. R. (2022) 'Carbon Taxes', *Journal of Economic Literature*, 60 (4): 1456–1502. https://doi.org/10.1257/jel.20211560

Wasmer, E. (2006) 'General versus Specific Skills in Labor Markets with Search Frictions and Firing Costs', *American Economic Review*, 96 (3): 811–831. https://doi.org/10.1257/aer.96.3.811

Way, R., Ives, M. C., Mealy, P. and Doyne Farmer, J. (2022) 'Empirically Grounded Technology Forecasts and the Energy Transition', *Joule*, 6 (9): 2057–2082. https://doi.org/10.1016/j.joule.2022.08.009

Weitzman, M. (2011) 'Fat-Tailed Uncertainty in the Economics of Catastrophic Climate Change', *Review of Environmental Economics and Policy*, 5 (2): 275–292. https://doi.org/10.1093/reep/rer006

Wright, T. P. (1936/2012) 'Factors Affecting the Cost of Airplanes', *Journal of the Aeronautical Sciences*, 3 (4), 122–128. https://doi.org/10.2514/8.155

15. Tackling climate change in low- and middle-income countries

Elizabeth Robinson and Chukwumerije Okereke

Designing and implementing action to address climate change is one of the most important public policy challenges of our time – and particularly acute for low- and middle-income countries (LMICs) around the world. One aspect of that challenge is to tackle climate change without exacerbating poverty. Although there is widespread agreement that LMICs need economic growth to reduce poverty and build resilience to climate change, there are few – if any – precedents on how to achieve this kind of development at scale, and still less agreement on how to go about it. In this chapter we highlight the importance of providing access to low-carbon energy, ensuring food security, protecting nature and biodiversity, and improving adaptation and resilience. We also recognise that any action to tackle climate change needs to be considered within the principles of equity and climate justice. As such, we frame our exploration of 'what works' within a sensitivity to national political economy dynamics and the need for effective national institutions. LMIC policymakers must also contend and engage with international political and economic structures and institutions. All told, while there are several promising initiatives around the world, the reality is that we still lack shining examples of countries that have successfully achieved low-carbon and resilient development. Evidence of 'what works' in LMICs is sparse.

I. Introduction and context

In 1989, atmospheric carbon dioxide was 352 ppm (parts per million), compared to pre-industrial levels of around 280 ppm, and although the drivers and likely impacts of climate change were already clearly understood, tackling climate change was not a priority for LMICs, nor was it addressed

How to cite this book chapter:

Robinson, Elizabeth and Okereke, Chukwumerije (2025) 'Tackling climate change in low- and middle-income countries', in: Besley, Tim, Bucelli, Irene and Velasco, Andrés (eds) *The London Consensus: Economic Principles for the 21st Century*, London: LSE Press, pp. 507–532 https://doi.org/10.31389/lsepress.tlc.o

by the Washington Consensus. Fast forward to 2025 and it is clear that climate change is one of the most pressing public policy issues of our time. Atmospheric carbon dioxide has exceeded 420 ppm, and the diverse impacts of climate change, ranging from glacial melt to sea-level rise, droughts, cyclones and wildfires, now pose significant challenges to global livelihoods, and human and natural systems.

The Washington Consensus focused on economic growth, and critics urged a greater focus on poverty reduction. Today, a different perspective is needed – one that recognises the continued importance of economic growth and poverty reduction, but focuses on building climate-resilient societies along growth pathways compatible with global net-zero. However, with few if any precedents of low-carbon development at scale, there is little clarity or agreement on what works and how the sometimes conflicting objectives of economic growth and climate change mitigation can best be reconciled.

LMICs are home to approximately 6.82 billion people, or around 85% of the world's total population. These countries, including China, are responsible for less than half of historical carbon emissions, but around 66% of current emissions, driven primarily by China and a handful of other countries, and this share of emissions is increasing.[1] While some LMICs already have emissions considerably higher than the global per capita average, others barely register, mainly due to a lack of access to energy. Indeed, low-income countries account for 9% of the global population but just 0.6% of emissions.[2] As such, how LMICs prioritise efforts to tackle climate change will differ considerably.

Pursuing economic growth in the context of climate change is a global policy priority, but one that is particularly challenging for LMICs, many of which have limited institutional, technical, and financial resources and capabilities, as well as weak adaptive capabilities and often a high dependence on rain-fed agriculture. If LMICs follow economic growth paths similar to those taken by today's high-income countries, which were driven in no small part by the burning of fossil fuels, it will be impossible to limit global warming to less than 2°C with dire consequences for all nations. As a result, a central challenge of climate policy is how to effectively tackle climate change while allowing for accelerated economic development in LMICs, which brings issues of equity and justice to the centre of international politics and diplomacy.[3]

Despite the appeal of concepts like green growth and low-carbon development, the challenge of decoupling economic growth from greenhouse gas (GHG) emissions is daunting. According to the Sixth Assessment Report of the Intergovernmental Panel on Climate Change (IPCC), only a few countries have achieved a sustained decoupling of their economies. Other researchers doubt that such decoupling exists at all.[4]

Under the banner of 'degrowth' scholarship, a growing number of academics argue that economic growth can never be consistent with the emissions reductions required to meet the goal of limiting climate change to 1.5°C, as stated in the Paris Agreement.[5] But even degrowth scholars make exceptions for development and GHG emissions growth in the 'Global South'. Particularly for lower-income countries, economic growth is considered necessary to enable countries to adapt and build resilience to the increasing negative impacts of climate change. While climate vulnerability is a complex concept, it retains a strong correlation with economic development. Some of the most climate vulnerable countries in the world, such as the Central African Republic, the Democratic Republic of the Congo, Chad, Nigeria, and South Sudan, are also some of the poorest countries in the world.

Given the current global emissions trajectory, the reality is that limits to adaptation will almost certainly be breached and urgent action on climate change is required from all countries to limit the potential.[6] It is also evident that climate change is already making growth in LMICs, and any associated poverty reduction, more challenging. It is reducing labour supply, affecting labour productivity, compromising crop yields, increasing food insecurity, and harming health, particularly of the poorest and most vulnerable.[7]

In the next section we set out the climate policy landscape in LMICs. Section III then presents a framework for improving climate policy in LMICs, which addresses what might be considered the core fundamentals, such as political will and leadership, and national institutions and capacities. There follows a section on national plans and strategies, which brings us to some of the practical actions individual LMICs can take to tackle climate change. It would be remiss of us not to also address the global context, and in particular why the principles of global climate and economic justice matter if LMICs, and the world more broadly, are to be able to tackle climate change. Indeed, in the context of globalisation and international cooperation for climate action and sustainable development, it is clear that action will be required at national, continental, and global scales.

II. Climate policy landscape in LMICs

There are currently few if any precedents on how to do low-carbon development at scale. However, across the many LMICs there are certain climate institutions and policies that offer examples of good practice for policymakers. There is certainly no lack of climate policy initiatives. Indeed, the IPCC Report shows that climate laws and targets grew exponentially in lower-income countries between 2010 and 2020 (Figure 15.1).

In recognition of their economic circumstances, the climate policy approach of most LMICs has tended to focus on adaptation and mitigation, while attempting to achieve development. Nevertheless, the characteristics and emphases differ significantly depending on local and national priorities.

In low-income countries, issues of social justice and poverty reduction are key thrusts of climate policy, while for higher and middle-income countries the key pillars are low-carbon innovation and emissions reduction.[8] The focus on poverty reduction resonates with the Washington Consensus, which supported reorienting public expenditure towards pro-poor priorities.[9]

Figure 15.1: Number of countries with national climate emission targets in 2010, 2015 and 2020

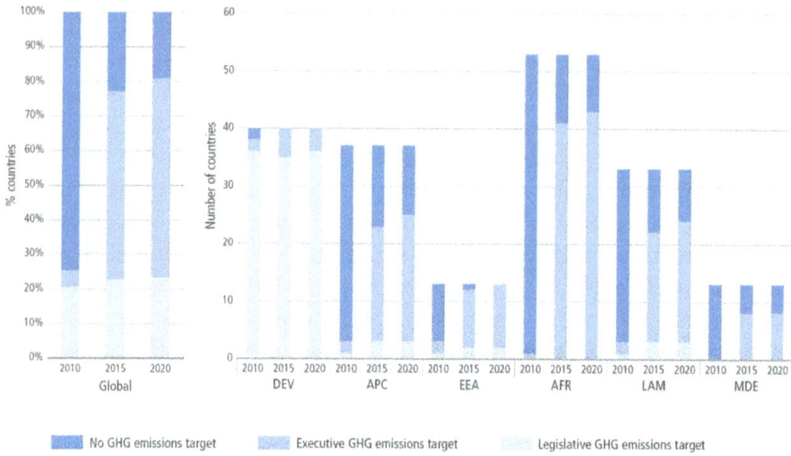

Source: Figure 13.2 (b) in IPCC (2022)[10] reproduced with permission.
DEV = Developed countries; APC = Asia and developing Pacific; EEA = Eastern Europe and West-Central Asia; AFR = Africa; LAM = Latin America and the Caribbean; MDE = Middle East.

Indeed, given that the poorest countries tend to be the most affected by climate change and the least able to adapt, tackling climate change in LMICs will require increased attention to pro-poor policies. The OECD has suggested that the best way for LMICs to adapt to climate change is to integrate adaptation responses into development planning, and to explicitly link this planning with finance.[11] But what this means in practice is not always clear. Suggestions include that development and adaptation funds should be coordinated, which requires institutions and mechanisms to enable such coordination. One way some countries have sought to address this is through 'national funding entities', which now exist in more than a dozen countries.[12] Other suggestions include that, where there are either synergies or trade-offs between development and climate change, these need to be addressed and understood explicitly; and that adaptation will be more successful if people are empowered and participate in determining national plans.[13]

But there is great variation among LMICs when it comes to climate policy. One recent study described some of the highest emitters among LMICs, such as Brazil, Indonesia, Mexico, Vietnam, India, and China, as 'climate developmentalists', whose approach to climate policy comprises 'a mixed set of attempts at incorporating climate mitigation measures into broader schemes for state-led development whether through regulation or industrial policy for emerging clean technologies'.[14] These countries are further characterised as having medium-to-high state capacity and institutionalisation of scientific expertise. The same study also coined the term 'carbon centralist' for countries like Iran, Turkey, and Saudi Arabia, whose approach to climate policy is claimed to be more tokenistic, with greater emphasis on energy security and only marginal greening of their growth.

It may be that the expansion of climate policy in LMICs is motivated less by a desire to mitigate climate change and more by the pursuit of co-benefits – that is, the indirect influence of climate policy on a non-climate objective, such as diminished air pollution or energy security.[15] In the case of India, for example, researchers have emphasised the importance of energy security and social justice for climate development.[16] And in Vietnam, economic restructuring, energy security, and access to finance and technology have been cited as motivations.[17] In many cases, LMICs might establish national climate policy frameworks to signal credibility and attract climate finance.[18] There may also be subtle coercion and diplomatic pressure from international development partners.[19]

But while it is encouraging to see LMICs actively announcing and implementing climate action, there remains ample opportunity for further acceleration in the robust implementation of their climate initiatives, highlighting the potential for even greater positive impact on a global scale. There is a need, therefore, to understand the drivers and barriers of climate policy – and to understand what works.

III. Framework for design, implementation and improvements in climate policy in LMICs

The literature offers a variety of different frameworks for studying efforts by higher and lower-income countries to design and implement climate policy.[20] They focus variously on institutions and governance, structural factors, such as economic wealth and natural resources, or sociocultural dimensions including lifestyle, behaviour, and norms.

Based on a literature review and our own experience working with stakeholders on climate policy development in the Global South, we suggest the framework in Figure 15.2 as a basis for the design, implementation, and improvement of climate policy in LMICs. The rest of the chapter uses the framework to explain some of the most important innovations and challenges in tackling climate change in the Global South.

1. *Material endowment, geopolitics, domestic and international political economy*

Some of the key factors that shape LMIC climate policies are resource endowments and geographical location – and the related political economy dynamics that come with them. As such, it is important to situate climate policy in the context of multiple policy objectives for sustainable development.[21]

Figure 15.2: A framework of the key drivers and barriers of climate action in LMICs

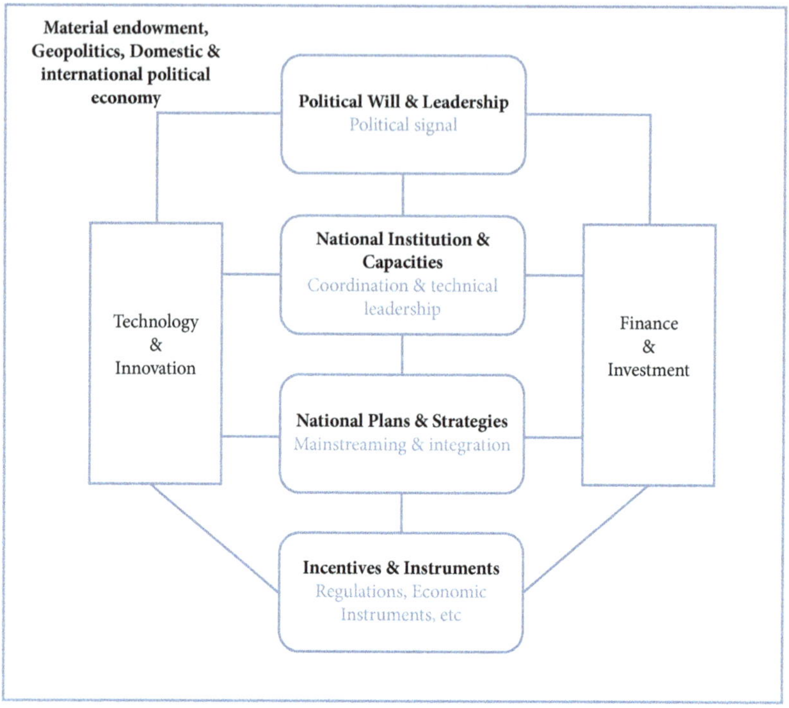

Source: authors.

Fundamental reform of the global economic system

Reform of the World Trade Organisation (WTO) and international trade regimes that disempower poor countries is needed to promote greater equity between the prices of raw materials and primary commodities exported by developing countries and the high-value goods, capital goods, and equipment that they import. Evidence from countries like Mali, Mozambique, Nicaragua, and Ethiopia show the difference that fair trade can make to the incomes and livelihoods of farmers around the world and provide an indication of how fairer terms of trade could help increase economic growth and resilience to climate change in poor countries. (However, these non-governmental organisation-led initiatives are no substitutes for fundamental reforms at the level of WTO rules.)

Reform of intellectual property rights regimes will also be needed to ensure that poor countries benefit from the global innovation that is driving the green transition. Recent IPCC reports have found, for example, that while the prices of many renewable technologies have fallen dramatically in the last five years, in some cases to levels that make them competitive with fossil fuels, access to these technologies remains a major challenge for low-income countries. Alongside such reform, there is a need for investment to build the research and innovation capabilities in lower-income countries to enable them to develop manufacturing capabilities for the technologies that are driving the green transition.

The need for changes to international political economy dynamics

Some critical political economy and postcolonial scholars argue that low-income countries will struggle to take radical climate action unless there is a fundamental change in both global economic structures and models of international cooperation to emphasise climate justice.[22] Any discussion of how to tackle climate change in LMICs must consider the historical context.

In the past, rich countries tended to focus on giving poor countries aid and loans that enable these countries barely to subsist, rather than removing the structural barriers that hold these countries from achieving self-reliant economic growth.[23] The great majority of LMICs depend on the export of raw materials for their economic growth. In return, they must import high-value goods from advanced countries, the consequence of which includes large trade deficits and weak currencies.[24] Often, the policy recommendation from institutions, such as the World Bank, has been for lower-income countries to export more, to undergo structural adjustment programmes, and to stabilise their exchange rates by issuing more dollar and euro-denominated debt. But these prescriptions have resulted in more external debt and more poverty – the so-called 'poverty trap'.[25] The persistence of this dynamic between richer and poorer countries has denied many LMICs the ability to achieve the food and energy sovereignty that is fundamental to self-reliant economic development, and ever more important for building resilience in the context of climate change.

Another aspect of the global economic system is debt, which sees some indebted LMICs pressured to invest in fossils fuels in order to enable repayment. If oil and gas prices subsequently fall, this can actually increase debt, or even result in stranded assets. New research shows that the world's poorest countries are spending an average of 16.3% of their revenue on debt service – the highest level for 25 years. Previously, the United Nations revealed that 54 of the world's poorest countries are on the brink of default, with several LMICs having debt of up to 42% of their gross national income. This means that poor countries are having to sacrifice investment in infrastructure, energy, and food security in order to pay debt – precisely when such investments are needed to address climate change.

Compounding these issues is a trade system that reinforces unequal levels of consumption by shifting resources from poorer, low-consuming countries to richer, high-consuming countries. Several LMICs are still struggling under unfair resource extraction contracts and terms of trade inherited from colonial relations.[26] Globalisation, while providing some benefits to LMICs, has broadly enabled rich countries to use cheap labour from poor countries to produce goods, to flood the markets of poor countries with manufactured and processed products, and to make it difficult for low-income countries to develop the manufacturing capabilities they need for self-reliant growth. One example of this is how, in part because of agricultural subsidies in Europe, beef and milk imported from the Netherlands can be cheaper than the equivalent produced in Botswana, Zimbabwe, or The Gambia. In the same vein, it is striking that that the Democratic Republic of the Congo holds large deposits of some of the critical minerals like lithium and cobalt needed to manufacture solar panels and electric cars but has no local facility to produce solar panels and or lithium batteries.

2. *Political will and leadership*

While leadership is important in any form of collective decision-making and implementation, it is particularly needed for the urgent and complex challenge of societal transformation demanded by climate change. This will not only require rallying resources and stakeholders, but also implies managing potential winners and losers from the transition. Strong leadership is needed to build coalitions and address resistance that can be expected from entrenched interests.

Commentators on green growth in Africa have emphasised the role of government leadership.[27] For example, Carlos López, then Executive Secretary of the UN's Economic Commission for Africa, said it is futile to expect green industrialisation to happen spontaneously in Africa without bold measures by governments.[28] Top-level leadership is required to map pathways to green industrialisation if a country is to progress from tweaking at the margins to achieving lasting structural transformation. Such articulation would, without a doubt, require redesigning national growth strategies, formulating and implementing clear, coherent and consistent long-term policies, mobilising resources, and investing in relevant innovation and infrastructure.

Effective vision articulation and framing is a core aspect of leadership. This entails clear identification of the problem to be solved, the identification of plausible alternatives and the means of achieving them, then formulating narratives that will focus the mind. To give one example, political leadership from China's Premier Xi Jinping has been identified as instrumental in China's engagement with climate action.

3. *National institutions and capacities*

National institutions structure the process of climate mitigation policymaking and shape its ambition and performance. They need to have policies in place that are not only national in scope, but also specifically address regional and local climate challenges. At the same time, however, their remit extends beyond national borders, fostering collaboration and cooperation with other countries and international organisations to ensure a coordinated response to climate change.

Many LMICs have what are termed 'weak institutions', which make any efforts to mitigate and adapt to climate change less likely to be effective. Improving these institutions will be central. That requires not just reform of institutions, but improvement on the rule of law, greater ease of doing business, increased transparency, and the elimination of inefficient subsidies. Such reforms might well be needed anyway – but facing climate change, the need is still greater.

The challenges faced by national institutions in climate policy implementation are significant. They include the need to adapt institutional systems to handle new situations and changing climate conditions, the allocation of adequate financial and human resources for policy implementation, the coordination of efforts across government departments and agencies, and the engagement of stakeholders at all levels of society.

4. *National plans and strategies*

Low-carbon energy security, affordable low-carbon transport, food security, nature and biodiversity, investment in adaptation and resilience – all of these are essential for net zero compatible growth in LMICs. To achieve them, countries will need climate finance and debt reduction, and the international community will need to provide cooperation and confront historical structures. Though context specific, climate and development will need to be addressed in an integrated way, with adaptation responses incorporated into development planning. We provide some concrete examples of policy areas before returning to the remaining categories in the framework.

Energy security through efficient low-carbon development

Energy, as a driver of growth, is central to economic development in LMICs. It is also inseparable from discussions of climate change. Although energy was not a focal area for the Washington Consensus, a critical question for the 21st century is how countries can generate the energy to power economic growth while transitioning away from fossil fuels. In LMICs, policies will need to focus on efficient low-carbon development: reducing the use of fossil fuels, rapidly expanding renewable energy, and improving energy efficiency.

Enabling the green transition is the falling cost of renewable energy. But LMICs face many challenges if they are to take part in the renewable energy 'revolution'. These include access to finance, vested interests, and valid concerns over the tax base. Perhaps unsurprisingly just 1.4% of the electricity in low human development index (HDI) countries is produced from renewables, compared with 9.5% in very high HDI countries.[29] As a consequence, many oil-producing and oil-importing countries continue to follow – and even subsidise – fossil-fuel economic development pathways, despite the fact they may be suboptimal over the longer run and have immediate negative health impacts on top of the global implications for climate change.

Given that many African countries in particular have an urgent need for energy for economic development and poverty reduction, and a high dependence on biomass, there is a compelling, if controversial, argument for some African countries to exploit natural gas reserves in the short-to-medium term. Yet the evidence on the benefits of fossil-fuel growth is mixed. Experiences from countries such as Nigeria, Libya, Ghana, and Mozambique make clear that exploiting fossil fuels does not necessarily translate into greater economic growth.[30] Meanwhile, there is evidence showing that fossil fuel exploitation can both slow economic growth and increase environmental degradation in many countries. Rent seeking, Dutch disease,[31] and increasing potential for corruption are frequently given as explanations. One study found that, 'across LMICs real income per capita falls as proved oil and natural gas reserves increase. For all developing countries that have experienced an increase in reserves over 1980 levels … real GDP per capita is lower'.[32]

This question is perhaps particularly pertinent for new oil producer countries, such as Senegal and Guyana, the latter having discovered recoverable crude oil reserves in excess of 8 billion barrels since 2015. It is an open question as to whether oil discoveries will 'transform Guyana from a small irrelevant economy to one of the most dynamic in South America', especially given that Guyana lacks strong governance.[33] Cautionary tales come from neighbouring Venezuela, and more distant Angola and Nigeria. More promising tales – for economic growth if not the climate – come from the US, Canada, and Norway.

Recently, a number of countries have called for a Fossil Fuel Non-Proliferation Treaty. There have even been calls for a global fund to support LMICs that commit to keep fossil fuels in the ground.[34] Such discussions around supply-side climate policy will be central to an orderly and just transition away from fossil fuels.[35] LMICs interested in restricting fossil fuel supply can look to the governments of Belize and Costa Rica, which have put in place partial or total bans or moratoria on the exploration and extraction of oil and gas. Research suggests such efforts are more likely to be successful when the rationale combines the protection of biodiversity and ecosystem services, rather than simply climate conservation; when the local benefits are clearly articulated, and not simply the global ones; and, somewhat surprisingly, when external compensation is not sought.[36] This latter observation has troubling implications for a just transition, particularly for lower-income countries.

Beyond the matter of energy production, energy efficiency in LMICs also tends to be lower than in high-income countries. Improving this has the potential to reduce energy bills for consumers and commercial enterprises – but could also lead to demand rebound, again emphasising the importance of investing in low-carbon energy sources in parallel. Areas where the scope for energy expenditure savings has been demonstrated include transitioning from kerosene to solar lighting, which in one study in Kenya saw savings of 42%, and switching to more efficient cookstoves, which saw savings of 40%.[37]

However, there are many barriers to efficient energy investment that need to be overcome. Detailed roadmaps can be used to help target where and how energy use can be made more efficient for a specific country. Relevant policies include removing energy subsidies; metering consumption; improving reliability of energy supplies; and increasing access to credit. Where electricity consumption is reliable, with regular and enforced billing, energy efficiency revolving funds have been shown to aid countries' efforts to increase energy efficiency, though there is to date insufficient assessment of their effectiveness.[38]

Decarbonising transportation

Globally, the transport sector contributes around a quarter of CO2 emissions.[39] Decarbonising public transport could therefore contribute to global mitigation efforts, and has national level health co-benefits through improved air quality. What's more, the policies and technologies needed already exist.

Because reliable access to low-carbon electricity is a prerequisite to decarbonise public transport,[40] an intermediate strategy is to invest in mass transit systems that reduce emissions by encouraging people out of their cars. Improving fuel efficiency and electrification of public transportation can then reduce emissions further. Bus rapid transport (BRT) systems have the advantage of being relatively quick to implement compared with light rail transit and can be decarbonised over time through the introduction of electric buses, as is being planned in Mexico City, for example. Places that have successfully introduced BRT include Bogota, Colombia, where, even if the primary rationale for introducing a BRT system was to ensure lower-income urban households had cost-effective transport, once the BRT was implemented air pollutants were found to have fallen by 40%. Brazil, Chile, and India are in the process of electrifying their bus fleets, facilitated by innovative finance and improved procurement practices.[41]

A number of complementary policies can speed up the transition to a decarbonised transport sector. These include tax reforms to support the purchase of low-carbon vehicles, waiving of import fees, congestion pricing for internal combustion engine vehicles, and emissions standards, in addition to public awareness campaigns.[42] That said, lower-income countries may face both financial constraints and infrastructure limitations.

Sustainable agriculture

Agriculture accounts for around a third of all GHG emissions, and is central to the livelihoods of the rural poor in many LMICs. Any efforts to tackle climate change must therefore address the agricultural sector. Climate-smart agriculture, a catch-all phrase, refers to approaches that aim to increase agricultural productivity, reduce vulnerability, increase resilience, and reduce emissions.[43] Approaches variously include agroforestry, cover cropping, crop rotation, and regenerative agriculture to improve soil health. Better water management will be essential, whether through the adoption of new technologies that monitor soil moisture, or a switch away from water-thirsty crops.

Each lower-income country will need its own adaptation roadmap for its agricultural sector. These will likely need to involve diversification and the development and introduction of climate-resilient crop varieties as a starting point. Thereafter, climate information services and climate-smart technologies and practices have the potential to transform food systems, particularly in African countries, making them more resilient and reducing emissions.[44] In terms of financial policy, there is evidence that weather-indexed crop insurance can help farmers adapt to climate change[45] – however, index insurance schemes tend to be heavily subsidised and do not necessarily endure.[46]

Meanwhile, as the climate changes, safety nets will become increasingly important, whether cash or in kind, to buttress food security.[47] Ethiopia's extensive experience with safety nets has demonstrated that efforts to protect food security and livelihoods can also reduce GHG emissions, and as such can be an important element of a country's nationally determined contributions (NDCs).[48]

Sustainable and resilient nature and biodiversity

LMICs can increase resilience to climate change through nature and biodiversity. Part of this will be achieved through the agriculture sector, as already discussed. Many LMICs also have considerable forests and conservation areas, which help protect critical habitats, biodiversity, and threatened species and ecosystems. However, the reality for many lower-income countries is that demands for improved food security may be at least partially at odds with protecting the natural resource base. Any trade-offs in this regard can be minimised in part through a better understanding of the spatial distribution of biodiversity and broader ecosystem services, combined with well-defined and enforced land-use planning.[49]

Ecosystem-based adaptation is defined by the Convention on Biological Diversity as 'the use of biodiversity and ecosystem services as part of an overall adaptation strategy to help people to adapt to the adverse effects of climate change'.[50] Guidelines include the need to involve relevant stakeholders, to ensure a local context while linking to national frameworks, and to safeguard local communities against risks and costs.

5. *Incentives and instruments*

There is evidence that creating an environment for investors that is sufficiently stable, low risk, and profitable can produce results for climate action. Take Uruguay's success in decarbonising its electricity generation, which points to the importance of 'clear decision making, a supportive regulatory environment and a strong partnership between the public and private sector', with an emphasis on ensuring investors have a secure environment.[51] Uruguay's Ministry of Finance played a central role, providing fiscal incentives, based on a 1998 law, that included 'value added tax exemption for specific renewable energy equipment; income tax reduction for renewable energy generation, energy efficiency initiatives and equipment, and net metering generation; and import duty exemptions for wind equipment and a reduction in duty for solar equipment'.[52]

Where such stability has not been achieved, multilateral development banks (MDBs) have an important role to play in de-risking climate-linked projects. The idea that MDBs, instead of financing projects outright, can use their capital to de-risk projects is not new. Such an approach can avoid the possibility of MDBs crowding out private investment, and indeed can conversely crowd in that investment.[53]

It is now frequently observed that renewable energy sources are lower cost than fossil fuels – and yet LMICs continue to invest in fossil fuels. One reason for this is that, in LMICs, the upfront investment costs and the cost of capital are high. De-risking these investments – shifting risk away from the private sector investor – has the potential to enable LMICs to follow low-carbon growth pathways.[54] In Chile, for example, the Green Climate Fund provided the Espejo de Tarapaca low-carbon power project with $60 million of direct 'anchor' equity to cover the last stage of development expenses and crowd in private investment.[55] For some countries, this de-risking can been seen as a substitute for a more stable domestic policy environment.

Carbon pricing is an important policy tool for tackling climate change, designed to address a clear market failure. With respect to energy, carbon pricing can play a role in both encouraging investment in renewable energy and in increasing energy efficiency. It also provides a source of revenue for governments and can ensure that businesses aligned with net zero are not at a disadvantage. Carbon pricing can be implemented through a carbon tax or an emissions trading scheme. Such schemes may be harder for LMICs to introduce as they are complex to design and implement.[56] But even carbon taxes, favoured by economists as an efficient solution to the climate crisis, may prove tricky to implement, due to potential impacts on vulnerable populations, regulatory capacity and political feasibility.

Some LMIC countries that have successfully introduced carbon pricing have hypothecated revenues to be reinvested in clean energy and emissions reduction more broadly. South Africa was the first African country to introduce a carbon tax, in June 2019, which covers around 90% of the country's GHG emissions not related to agriculture, forest, land use, or waste. To make the tax more politically acceptable, the country phased it in gradually and included an array of tax-free allowances and exceptions for low-income households.[57] This transition phase appears to have helped with the feasibility of a more stringent cap or price. In Chile, the political economy was seen as central; a pragmatic low tax rate was chosen, in part as a signalling device;

and health co-benefits were linked to the tax to boost acceptance.[58] Mexico implemented a carbon tax in 2014, followed by an emissions trading scheme in 2017, but these efforts have been described as being somewhat ineffective, due to the low tax rate and emissions caps being based on reported historical emissions.[59]

6. *Technology and innovation*

Technology and innovation are at the heart of efforts to address climate change in both higher and lower-income countries. Indeed, many of the national plans and strategies addressed in the previous section require new or improved technologies. For example, investments in renewable energy will require solar photovoltaic panels and wind turbines. More efficient energy solutions may require LED lighting or retrofitting. Climate-resilient agriculture will require new crop varieties, remote sensing, and data analytics to optimise the use of scarce resources.

Access to technology and the quality of technology innovation systems are some of the major differences between lower and higher-income countries. Lower-income countries will need to build local expertise and knowledge while formulating international collaborations. Evidence from Kenya has shown the impact of focused policy in driving local innovation. Innovations, such as solar-powered milk storage systems mounted on motorbikes, solar-powered portable kiosks that combine an integrated battery-charging station with a software platform, and pay-as-you-go cooking services, have revolutionised commerce in Kenya and helped the country in its quest for universal energy access by 2038. However, the vast majority of LMICs still lack access to technologies that are crucial to achieve decarbonisation at scale.

7. *Finance and investment*

Finance is central to tackling climate change in LMICs. Indeed, the question of how LMICs can access the finance they need has long been central to international discussion on climate governance and justice, although how this might best be done remains contentious and under-researched.

The idea of a just transition, following the principle of 'common but differentiated responsibility and respective capabilities', has been part of the climate narrative since at least as far back as the Kyoto Protocol and the Paris Agreement.[60] And it is clear that a just transition cannot occur without the provision of climate finance – but novel financing mechanisms are needed.

Recent research highlights the potential role of ministries of finance in driving climate action in both higher and lower-income countries. For example, Rwanda's Ministry of Finance and Economy attracted almost US$1.5 billion in climate finance, guided by its NDC, which addresses mitigation, adaptation, and resilience together.

Debt financing has long been a central element of 'development', and indeed reducing the debt burden through relief was an important element of the Washington Consensus. The poorest countries – those that are eligible to borrow from the World Bank's International Development Association (IDA) – are currently spending on average over 10% of their export revenues on servicing long-term public and publicly-guaranteed external debt.[61] Perhaps unsurprisingly, cutting the debt burden of LMICs has been shown to have the potential to boost growth and reduce poverty.[62] Moreover, debt and debt repayments, including those of the poorest IDA-eligible countries, are emerging as an important area where the imperatives for economic growth and climate justice overlap. High levels of debt and debt servicing reflect how past borrowing is exacerbating inequalities and making it harder if not impossible for LMICs to tackle climate change, whether that be tackling the negative impacts of climate change that are already harming these countries, adapting to ongoing climate change, or following a low-carbon growth pathway. Therefore, novel approaches to tackling debt are needed – and there is already evidence of how these might work.

Debt-for-nature swaps have long been advocated as a form of climate finance in lower-income countries, with the potential to increase investments in sustainable development.[63] In 2021, Belize completed a US$364 million debt-for-nature swap that lowered its debt by 12% of GDP; in exchange, it committed to protect 30% of its ocean and created $180 million of sustainable financing for marine conservation. These types of swaps are likely to be most effective for climate-vulnerable LMICs that are fiscally constrained due to high debt burdens.[64]

In 2015, the Nature Conservancy purchased roughly US$22 million of the debt of Seychelles, and in exchange Seychelles used money that would have been earmarked to pay off debt to invest in the 'blue economy', primarily in fishing and tourism. This investment has the potential to increase blue carbon sequestration and grow important economic sectors. Funding was used in part to create new marine protected areas, which protect corals and help fish stocks recover. Investment in mangrove protection can also enhance breeding grounds for marine animals, protect coastlines from storms, and capture blue carbon.

Such arrangements require a degree of conditionality, which some argue goes against sovereignty. Nonetheless, experiences with, for example, debt cancellation, suggest that conditionality can nudge countries to more effective outcomes – though the extent to which conditionality leads to better outcomes has been contested.[65]

IV. Conclusion

A number of lessons stand out for 'what works' with respect to tackling climate change in LMICs. Many are not new. For example, investment from the private sector is more forthcoming if risk and uncertainty are lowered;

meanwhile the extreme levels of debt that many LMICs find themselves in today, requiring high levels of serving, make it virtually impossible for these countries to invest in any type of development, low-carbon resilient or otherwise.

That said, there are specific domestic policy areas where actions that were not considered in the original Washington Consensus are clearly needed. And in these cases, there is not always sufficiently granular detail on 'what works'. They include the energy sector, where all countries need to transition to low-carbon energy sources and improve efficiency; agri-food systems, which need to be more resilient to the changing climate, while also taking into account their own emissions; and the broader natural environment, which can increase a country's resilience to climate change, generate revenues, and contribute to mitigation. Furthermore, for many countries, implementing climate policies may be more feasible where the rationale for a policy is focused on something other than climate, such as biodiversity; or where there are clear co-benefits, such as the health benefits of reduced air pollution, that accrue to the individual country.

However, it is increasingly clear that a new narrative is emerging, driven primarily by scholars, policymakers, and practitioners based in or from lower-income countries, which emphasises justice, equity, radical reforms and institution building, and LMIC empowerment – and as such reflects a shift in the centre of gravity of power and decision-making. Many of the lowest income countries are struggling with decades of debt and structural adjustment programmes, imposed on them by powerful countries, which have weakened their economies and made them more dependent on foreign assistance and aid. Therefore, international political economic dynamics, and in particular the reform of international structures of trade and models of cooperation, may be even more important than national reforms if one wishes to see climate-resilient development in LMICs. Reframing the discussion of how LMICs can best tackle climate change within this new narrative brings into focus a new perspective on 'what works', and underlines where the driving force behind solutions needs to lie.

Notes

1 Global Carbon Budget (2023) – with major processing by Our World in Data.

2 Ritchie (2023).

3 Roberts and Parks (2006); Okereke (2019).

4 Parrique et al. (2019).

5 Kallis et al. (2018); Buch-Hansen and Carstensen (2021); Dunlap and Laratte (2022).

[6] Dow et al. (2013); Mechler et al. (2020).

[7] Antonelli et al. (2021); Dasgupta et al. (2021).

[8] Urban and Nordensvärd (2013).

[9] Archibong et al. (2021).

[10] IPCC (2022).

[11] Abeygunawardena et al. (2004).

[12] Smith et al. (2011).

[13] Halsnæs and Verhagen (2007).

[14] Guy et al. (2023).

[15] Karlsson et al. (2020).

[16] Dubash (2013).

[17] Zimmer et al. (2015).

[18] Fisher et al. (2017).

[19] Okereke et al. (2019).

[20] Grubb et al. (2022).

[21] Dubash et al. (2022).

[22] Krause (2018); Harris (2009); Warlenius (2018); Roberts and Parks (2009); Okereke (2010); Eckersley (2016).

[23] Moyo (2009).

[24] Rogoff and Reinhart (2003); Atta-Mensah and Ibrahim (2020).

[25] Sachs et al. (2004).

[26] Johnson et al. (2021).

[27] Okereke and Agupusi (2015); Okereke et al. (2019).

[28] United Nations Economic Commission for Africa (2016).

[29] Romanello et al. (2022).

[30] Henri (2019); Dwumfour and Ntow-Gyamfi (2018).

[31] Dutch disease, referencing the natural resource boom experienced by the Netherlands in the 1950s and 1960s that led to the decline of the country's manufacturing sector, occurs when one sector, often the extraction of natural resources, 'booms', resulting in an increase in demand for complementary resources such as labour, additional spending, and strengthening of the country's currency, to the detriment of other exporting sectors.

[32] Barbier (2007).

[33] Panelli (2019).

[34] Larrea and Murmis (2018).

[35] van Asselt (2021).

[36] Tudela (2020).

[37] Fowlie and Meeks (2021).

[38] Fowlie and Meeks (2021).

[39] Romanello et al. (2022).

[40] Environment for Development (2023).

[41] Briceno-Garmendia et al. (2022).

[42] Environment for Development (2023).

[43] Chandra et al. (2018).

[44] Zougmoré et al. (2021).

[45] Mullins et al. (2018).

[46] Loboguerrero Rodriguez et al. (2018).

[47] Dasgupta and Robinson (2022).

[48] Loboguerrero Rodriguez et al. (2018).

[49] Griffiths et al. (2022).

[50] Midgley et al. (2012).

[51] Stern (2015).

[52] Coalition of Finance Ministers for Climate Action (2022).

[53] Uzsoki (2017).

[54] Steckel and Jakob (2018).

[55] Choi et al. (2022).

[56] Black et al. (2022).

[57] Qu et al. (2023).

[58] Pizarro (2019).

[59] Climate Action Tracker (2022).

[60] Chowdhury and Jomo (2022).

[61] World Bank (2022).

[62] Dijkstra and Hermes (2001).

[63] Thomas and Theokritoff (2021).

[64] Kyriakopoulou (2023).

[65] Kanbur (2000).

References

Abeygunawardena, P., Vyas, Y., Knill, P., Foy, T., Harrold, M., Steele, P., Tanner, T., Hirsch, D., et al. (2004) 'Poverty and Climate Change: Reducing the Vulnerability of the Poor through Adaptation (English)', Washington, DC: World Bank. http://documents.worldbank.org/curated/en/534871468155709473

Antonelli, C., Coromaldi, M., Dasgupta, S., Emmerling, J. and Shayegh, S. (2021) 'Climate Impacts on Nutrition and Labor Supply Disentangled–An Analysis for Rural Areas of Uganda', *Environment and Development Economics*, 26(5–6): 512–537. https://doi.org/10.1017/S1355770X20000017

Archibong, B., Coulibaly, B. S. and Okonjo-Iweala, N. (2021) 'How Have the Washington Consensus Reforms Affected Economic Performance in Sub-Saharan Africa?', *Brookings Papers Commentary*. [19 Feb]. https://www.brookings.edu/blog/africa-in-focus/2021/02/19/how-have-the-washington-consensus-reforms-affected-economic-performance-in-sub-saharan-africa/

Atta-Mensah, J. and Ibrahim, M. (2020) 'Explaining Africa's Debt: The Journey so Far and the Arithmetic of the Policymaker', *Theoretical Economics Letters*, 10(2): 409–441. https://doi.org/10.4236/tel.2020.102027

Barbier, E. B. (2007) 'Frontiers and Sustainable Economic Development', *Environmental and Resource Economics*, 37(1): 271–295. https://doi.org/10.1007/s10640-007-9120-9

Black, S., Parry, I. and Zhunussova, K. (2022) 'More Countries Are Pricing Carbon, but Emissions Are Still Too Cheap', *IMF Blog* [21 Jul]. https://www.imf.org/en/Blogs/Articles/2022/07/21/blog-more-countries-are-pricing-carbon-but-emissions-are-still-too-cheap

Briceno-Garmendia, C., Foster, V. and Qiao, W. (2022) *The Economics of Electric Vehicles for Passenger Transportation*, Washington, DC: World Bank. https://doi.org/10.1596/38265

Buch-Hansen, H. and Carstensen, M. B. (2021) 'Paradigms and the Political Economy of Ecopolitical Projects: Green Growth and Degrowth Compared', *Competition & Change*, 25(3–4): 308–327. https://doi.org/10.1177/1024529420987528

Chandra, A., McNamara, K. E. and Dargusch, P. (2018) 'Climate-Smart Agriculture: Perspectives and Framings', *Climate Policy*, 18(4): 526–541. https://doi.org/10.1080/14693062.2017.1316968

Choi, E., Zhou, L. and Laxton, V. (2022) 'How to De-risk Low-Carbon Investments', *Insights (blog), World Resources Institute*, [July]. https://www.wri.org/insights/de-risking-low-carbon-investments.

Chowdhury, A. and Jomo, K. S. (2022) 'The Climate Finance Conundrum', *Development*, 65(1): 29–41. https://doi.org/10.1057/s41301-022-00329-0

Climate Action Tracker (2022) Mexico. [23 October 2023]. https://climateactiontracker.org/countries/mexico/policies-action/

Coalition of Finance Ministers for Climate Action (2022) 'Strengthening the Role of Ministries of Finance in Driving Climate Action: A Framework and Guide for Ministers and Ministries of Finance', Synthesis Report: Consultation Draft. [July]. https://www.financeministersforclimate.org/sites/cape/files/inline-files/Synthesis%20Strengthening%20the%20Role%20of%20Ministries%20of%20Finance.pdf

Dasgupta, S. and Robinson, E. J. Z. (2022) 'Attributing Changes in Food Insecurity to a Changing Climate', *Scientific Reports*, 12(1): 4709. https://doi.org/10.1038/s41598-022-08696-x

Dasgupta, S., van Maanen, N., Gosling, S. N., Piontek, F., Otto, C. and Schleussner, C. F. (2021) 'Effects of Climate Change on Combined Labour Productivity and Supply: An Empirical, Multi-model Study', *The Lancet Planetary Health*, 5(7): e455–e465. https://doi.org/10.1016/S2542-5196(21)00170-4

Dijkstra, G. and Hermes, N. (2001) *The Uncertainty of Debt Service Payments and Economic Growth of HIPCs: Is There a Case for Debt Relief?* (No. 2001/122). WIDER Discussion Paper. https://www.wider.unu.edu/sites/default/files/dp2001-122.pdf

Dow, K., Berkhout, F., Preston, B. L., Klein, R. J., Midgley, G. and Shaw, M. R. (2013) 'Limits to Adaptation', *Nature Climate Change*, 3(4): 305–307. https://doi.org/10.1038/nclimate1847

Dubash, N. K. (2013) 'The Politics of Climate Change in India: Narratives of Equity and Co-benefits' *Wiley Interdisciplinary Reviews: Climate Change*, 4(3): 191–201. https://doi.org/10.1002/wcc.210

Dubash, N. K., Mitchell, C., Boasson, E. L., Córdova, M. J. B., Fifita, S., Haites, E., Jaccard, M., Jotzo, F., Naidoo, S., Romero-Lankao, P., et al. (2022) 'National and Sub-national Policies and Institutions', in *Climate Change 2022: Mitigation of Climate Change. Contribution of Working Group III to the Sixth Assessment Report of the Intergovernmental Panel on Climate Change*. Cambridge: Cambridge University Press.

Dunlap, A. and Laratte, L. (2022) 'European Green Deal Necropolitics: Exploring "Green" Energy Transition, Degrowth & Infrastructural Colonization', *Political Geography*, 97: 102640. https://doi.org/10.1016/j.polgeo.2022.102640

Dwumfour, R. A. and Ntow-Gyamfi, M. (2018) 'Natural Resources, Financial Development and Institutional Quality in Africa: Is There a Resource Curse?', *Resources Policy*, 59: 411–426. https://doi.org/10.1016/j.resourpol.2018.08.012

Eckersley, R. (2016) 'Responsibility for Climate Change as a Structural Injustice', in Gabrielson, T., Hall, C., Meyer, J. M. and Schlosberg, D. (eds) *The Oxford Handbook of Environmental Political Theory*, Oxford: Oxford University Press; 346–361. https://doi.org/10.1093/oxfordhb/9780199685271.013.37

Environment for Development (2023) 'Policy instruments for an Inclusive Green Economy. Experiences from the East African Region on Policy Instruments to Reduce the Use of Fossil Fuels, Plastic Pollution, and Forest Loss', Gothenburg: Environment for Development. https://www.efdinitiative.org/sites/default/files/publications/WS-Report_IGE_2023_TA_Final.pdf

Fisher, E., Scotford, E. and Barritt, E. (2017) 'The Legally Disruptive Nature of Climate Change', *The Modern Law Review*, 80(2), 173–201. https://doi.org/10.1111/1468-2230.12251

Fowlie, M. and Meeks, R. (2021) 'The Economics of Energy Efficiency in Developing Countries', *Review of Environmental Economics and Policy*, 15(2): 238–260. https://doi.org/10.1086/715606

Global Carbon Budget (2023) 'Cumulative CO_2 emissions – GCB' [dataset]. Global Carbon Project. https://ourworldindata.org/grapher/cumulative-co-emissions

Griffiths, G., Adolph, B., Chapman, A., Davies, J., Devenish, A., Jellason, N. P., Kanja, K., Kwenye, J. M., et al. (2022) 'Future Trade-offs to 2050: Land Cover Change, Biodiversity and Agriculture in Zambia', Sentinel, London; IIED, London.

Grubb, M., Okereke, C., Arima, J., Bosetti, V., Chen, Y., Edmonds, J., Gupta, S., Koberle, A., et al. (2022) 'Introduction and Framing', in Shukla, P. R., Skea, J., Slade, R., Al Khourdajie, A., van Diemen, R., McCollum, D., Pathak, M., et al. (eds) *IPCC, 2022: Climate Change 2022: Mitigation of Climate Change. Contribution of Working Group III to the Sixth Assessment Report of the Intergovernmental Panel on Climate Change*. Cambridge, UK and New York, NY: Cambridge University Press.

Guy, J., Shears, E. and Meckling, J. (2023) 'National Models of Climate Governance among Major Emitters', *Nature Climate Change*, 13(2): 189–195. https://doi.org/10.1038/s41558-022-01589-x

Halsnæs, K. and Verhagen, J. (2007) 'Development Based Climate Change Adaptation and Mitigation—Conceptual Issues and Lessons Learned in Studies in Developing Countries', *Mitigation and Adaptation Strategies for Global Change*, 12: 665–684. https://doi.org/10.1007/s11027-007-9093-6

Harris, P. G. (2009) *World Ethics and Climate Change: From International to Global Justice,* Edinburgh: Edinburgh University Press.

Henri, P. A. O. (2019) 'Natural Resources Curse: A Reality in Africa', *Resources Policy*, 63: 101406. https://doi.org/10.1016/j.resourpol.2019.101406

IPCC (2014) 'Mitigation of Climate Change', *Working Group III Contribution to the IPCC Sixth Assessment Report.* Cambridge: Cambridge University Press.

IPCC (2022) 'Summary for Policymakers', *Climate Change 2022: Mitigation of Climate Change. Contribution of Working Group III to the Sixth Assessment Report of the Intergovernmental Panel on Climate Change* [P.R. Shukla, J. Skea, R. Slade, A. Al Khourdajie, R. van Diemen, D. McCollum, M. Pathak, S. Some, P. Vyas, R. Fradera, M. Belkacemi, A. Hasija, G. Lisboa, S. Luz, J. Malley, (eds)]. Cambridge, UK and New York, NY: Cambridge University Press.

Johnson, O. E. A., Zalik, A., Mollett, C. S., Sultana, F., Havice, E., Osborne, T., Valdivia, G., Lu, F. and Billo, E. (2021) 'Extraction, Entanglements, and (Im)materialities: Reflections on the Methods and Methodologies of Natural Resource Industries Fieldwork', *Environment and Planning E: Nature and Space*, 4(2): 383–428. https://doi.org/10.1177/251484862090 7470

Kallis, G., Kostakis, V., Lange, S., Muraca, B., Paulson, S. and Schmelzer, M. (2018) 'Research on Degrowth', *Annual Review of Environment and Resources*, 43(1): 291–316. https://doi.org/10.1146/annurev-environ-102 017-025941

Kanbur, R. (2000) 'Aid, Conditionality and Debt in Africa', in Kanbur, R. and Venables, A. J. (eds) *Foreign Aid and Development,* Abingdon: Routledge; 335–345. https://www.taylorfrancis.com/chapters/edit/10.4324/97802034 61761-32/aid-conditionality-debt-africa-ravi-kanbur

Karlsson, M., Alfredsson, E. and Westling, N. (2020) 'Climate Policy Co-benefits: A Review', *Climate Policy*, 20(3): 292–316. https://doi.org/10 .1080/14693062.2020.1724070

Krause, D. (2018) 'Transformative Approaches to Address Climate Change and Achieve Climate Justice', in Jafry, T. (ed) *Routledge Handbook of Climate Justice*, Routledge. https://doi.org/10.4324/9781315537689-37

Kyriakopoulou (2023) 'Finance Stands at the Frontier of Nature', LSE Business Review. [21 April]. https://blogs.lse.ac.uk/businessreview/2023/04/21/finance-stands-at-the-frontier-of-nature/

Larrea, C. and Murmis, M. R. (2018) 'Unburnable Carbon and Biodiversity: A Global Fund for Keeping Fossil Fuels in the Ground in Biodiversity Hotspots of Developing Countries', *Paper presented at the Second International Conference on Fossil Fuel Supply and Climate Policy – The Queen's College, Oxford [24–25 September 2018]*. https://www.researchgate.net/publication/316841935_Unburnable_Carbon_and_Biodiversity_A_Global_Fund_for_Keeping_Fossil_Fuels_in_the_Ground_in_Biodiversity_Hotspots_of_Developing_Countries_Conference_Paper_Fossil_Fuel_Supply_and_Climate_Policy_Conferen

Loboguerrero Rodriguez, A. M., Birch, J., Thornton, P. K., Meza, L., Sunga, I., Bong, B. B., Rabbinge, R., Reddy, M., et al. (2018) 'Feeding the World in a Changing Climate: An Adaptation Roadmap for Agriculture'. Rotterdam and Washington, DC: The Global Commission on Adaptation. https://cgspace.cgiar.org/items/f274fb67-1520-49f3-830e-ba9aeab19a72

Mechler, R., Singh, C., Ebi, K., Djalante, R., Thomas, A., James, R., Tschakert, P., Wewirinke-Singh, T., et al. (2020) 'Loss and Damage and Limits to Adaptation: Recent IPCC Insights and Implications for Climate Science and Policy', *Sustainability Science*, 15:1245–1251. https://doi.org/10.1007/s11625-020-00807-9

Midgley, G., Marais, S., Barnett, M. and Wågsæther, K. (2012) 'Biodiversity, Climate Change and Sustainable Development – Harnessing Synergies and Celebrating Successes', Technical Report. [Jan]. https://unfccc.int/sites/default/files/biodiversity_climate_change_sustainable_development_technical_report.pdf.

Moyo, D. (2009) *Dead Aid: Why Aid Is Not Working and How There Is a Better Way for Africa*, New York: Macmillan.

Mullins, J., Zivin, J. G., Cattaneo, A., Paolantonio, A. and Cavatassi, R. (2018) 'The Adoption of Climate Smart Agriculture: The Role of Information and Insurance under Climate Change', in Lipper, L., McCarthy, N., Zilberman, D., Asfaw, S., and Branca, G. (eds) *Climate Smart Agriculture: Building Resilience to Climate Change*, Springer; 353–383. https://doi.org/10.1007/978-3-319-61194-5_16

Okereke, C. (2010) 'Climate Justice and the International Regime', *Wiley Interdisciplinary Reviews: Climate Change*, 1(3): 462–474. https://doi.org/10.1002/wcc.52

Okereke, C. (2019) 'North-South Inequity and Global Environmental Governance', in Kalfagianni, A., Fuchs, D. and Hayden, A. (eds) *Routledge Handbook of Global Sustainability Governance*, Routledge; 65–179. https://doi.org/10.4324/9781315170237-14

Okereke, C. and Agupusi, P. (2015) *Homegrown Development in Africa: Reality or Illusion?* New York: Routledge. https://doi.org/10.4324/9781315715940

Okereke, C., Coke, A., Geebreyesus, M., Ginbo, T., Wakeford, J. J. and Mulugetta, Y. (2019) 'Governing Green Industrialisation in Africa: Assessing Key Parameters for a Sustainable Socio-technical Transition in the Context of Ethiopia', *World Development*, 115: 279–290. https://doi.org/10.1016/j.worlddev.2018.11.019

Panelli, L. F. (2019) 'Is Guyana a New Oil El Dorado?', *The Journal of World Energy Law & Business*, 12(5): 365–368. https://doi.org/10.1093/jwelb/jwz022

Parrique, T., Barth, J., Briens, F., Kerschner, C., Kraus-Polk, A., Kuokkanen, A. and Spangenberg, J. H. (2019) 'Decoupling Debunked – Evidence and Arguments against Green Growth as a Sole Strategy for Sustainability', A study edited by the European Environment Bureau (EEB). [8 Jul]. https://eeb.org/library/decoupling-debunked/

Pizarro, R. (2019) 'Lessons from the Carbon Tax in Chile', Presentation for the Coalition of Ministers of Finance for Climate Action, Stockholm, Sweden. [3 October]. https://www.financeministersforclimate.org/sites/cape/files/inline-files/Lessons%20from%20the%20Carbon%20Tax%20in%20Chile.pdf

Qu, H., Suphachalasai, S., Thube, S. D. and Walker, S. (2023) 'South Africa Carbon Pricing and Climate Mitigation Policy', *Selected Issues Papers*, 2023(040). https://doi.org/10.5089/9798400247620.018

Ritchie, H. (2023) 'Global inequalities in CO2 Emissions', Published online at OurWorldInData.org. https://ourworldindata.org/inequality-co2

Roberts, J. T. and Parks, B. C. (2006) *A Climate of Injustice: Global Inequality, North-South Politics, and Climate Policy*, Cambridge, MA: MIT Press.

Roberts, J. T. and Parks, B. C. (2009) 'Ecologically Unequal Exchange, Ecological Debt, and Climate Justice: The History and Implications of Three Related Ideas for a New Social Movement', *International Journal of Comparative Sociology*, 50(3–4): 385–409. https://doi.org/10.1177/0020715209105147

Rogoff, M. K. and Reinhart, M. C. (2003) *FDI to Africa: The Role of Price Stability and Currency Instability*, International Monetary Fund Working Paper. https://doi.org/10.2139/ssrn.879085

Romanello, M., Di Napoli, C., Drummond, P., Green, C., Kennard, H., Lampard, P., Samman, D., Arnell, N., et al. (2022) 'The 2022 Report of the Lancet Countdown on Health and Climate Change: Health at the Mercy of Fossil Fuel', *The Lancet*, 400(10363): 1619–1654. https://doi.org/10.1016/S0140-6736(22)01540-9

Sachs, J., McArthur, J. W., Schmidt-Traub, G., Kruk, M., Bahadur, C., Faye, M. and McCord, G. (2004) 'Ending Africa's Poverty Trap', *Brookings Papers on Economic Activity*, 35(1): 117–240. https://doi.org/10.1353/eca.2004.0018

Smith, J. B., Dickinson, T., Donahue, J. D., Burton, I., Haites, E., Klein, R. J. and Patwardhan, A. (2011) 'Development and Climate Change Adaptation Funding: Coordination and Integration', *Climate Policy*, 11(3): 987–1000. https://doi.org/10.1080/14693062.2011.582385

Steckel, J. C. and Jakob, M. (2018) 'The Role of Financing Cost and De-risking Strategies for Clean Energy Investment', *International Economics*, 155: 19–28. https://doi.org/10.1016/j.inteco.2018.02.003

Stern, N. (2015) 'Uruguay Makes Dramatic Shift to Nearly 95% Electricity from Clean Energy', *The Guardian* [3 December 2015]. https://www.theguardian.com/environment/2015/dec/03/uruguay-makes-dramatic-shift-to-nearly-95-clean-energy

Thomas, A. and Theokritoff, E. (2021) 'Debt-for-Climate Swaps for Small Islands', *Nature Climate Change*, 11(11): 889–891. https://doi.org/10.1038/s41558-021-01194-4

Tudela, F. (2020) 'Obstacles and Opportunities for Moratoria on Oil and Gas Exploration or Extraction in Latin America and the Caribbean', *Climate Policy*, 20(8): 922–930. https://doi.org/10.1080/14693062.2020.1760772

United Nations Economic Commission for Africa (UN ECA) (2016) 'Economic Report on Africa 2016: Greening Africa's Industrialization'. Addis Ababa: UN ECA https://repository.uneca.org/handle/10855/23017

Urban, F. and Nordensvärd, J. (2013) 'Low Carbon Development: Origins, Concepts and Key Issues', in Urban, F. and Nordensvard, J. (eds) *Low Carbon Development*, Routledge. https://doi.org/10.4324/9780203108628-11

Uzsoki, D. (2017) 'Financing Infrastructure–How Can Multilateral Development Banks Avoid Crowding out Institutional Investors?', *International Institute for Sustainable Development*. [5 April]. https://www.iisd.org/articles/insight/financing-infrastructure-how-can-multilateral-development-banks-avoid-crowding-out

van Asselt, H. (2021) 'Governing Fossil Fuel Production in the Age of Climate Disruption: Towards an International Law of "Leaving it in the Ground"', *Earth System Governance*, 9: 100118. https://doi.org/10.1016/j.esg.2021.100118

Warlenius, R. (2018) 'Decolonizing the Atmosphere: The Climate Justice Movement on Climate Debt', *The Journal of Environment & Development*, 27(2): 131–155. https://doi.org/10.1177/1070496517744593

World Bank (2022) 'Debt-Service Payments Put Biggest Squeeze on Poor Countries since 2000', Press Release. World Bank. [6 Dec]. https://www.worldbank.org/en/news/press-release/2022/12/06/debt-service-payments-put-biggest-squeeze-on-poor-countries-since-2000

Zimmer, A., Jakob, M. and Steckel, J. C. (2015) 'What Motivates Vietnam to Strive for a Low-Carbon Economy?—On the Drivers of Climate Policy in a Developing Country', *Energy for Sustainable Development*, 24: 19–32. https://doi.org/10.1016/j.esd.2014.10.003

Zougmoré, R. B., Läderach, P. and Campbell, B. M. (2021) 'Transforming Food Systems in Africa under Climate Change Pressure: Role of Climate-Smart Agriculture', *Sustainability*, 13(8): 4305. https://doi.org/10.3390/su13084305

PART VII

POLITICAL ECONOMY AND STATE CAPACITY

16. From liberal economic policies to liberal political institutions? Democracy, development clusters and wellbeing

Tim Besley and Torsten Persson

The period since the Washington Consensus has seen a gradual, though sometimes stuttering, growth in liberal political institutions that support free speech, open contests for power, and constraints on the arbitrary use of power. Meanwhile, economists and other social scientists have studied the interplay of economics and politics along alternative paths of development – paths associated with more or less solid underpinnings for a market economy and more or less peaceful resolutions of domestic conflict. Our chapter explores whether this research supports a consensus around the kind of political institutions, values, and norms that can produce flourishing economies and societies.

By development I mean the movement upward of the entire social system, ... besides the so-called economic factors, ... the distribution of power in society; and more generally economic, social, and political stratification; broadly speaking, institutions and attitudes. The dynamics are determined by ... circular causation, ... if one [endogenous condition] changes, others will change in response, and those secondary changes in their turn cause new changes ...[1]

(W)hen people look back at what happened in this century, they will find it difficult not to accord primacy to the emergence of democracy as the preeminently acceptable form of governance. [2]

How to cite this book chapter:

Besley, Tim and Persson, Torsten (2025) 'From liberal economic policies to liberal political institutions? Democracy, development clusters, and wellbeing', in: Besley, Tim, Bucelli, Irene and Velasco, Andrés (eds) *The London Consensus: Economic Principles for the 21st Century*, London: LSE Press, pp. 535–572 https://doi.org/10.31389/lsepress.tlc.p

I. Introduction

When the Washington Consensus was formulated in 1989, a great deal was different in both the real and the academic worlds.[3] The Consensus advocated a set of liberal economic policies to promote development, but was immediately criticised for not paying enough attention to the institutional foundations of a market economy. In the intervening years, research in the field of political economics has flourished and singled out political institutions – together with the norms and values that sustain them – as fundamental drivers of peace and prosperity. In this chapter, we try to assess whether that body of research, which tries to bring insights from political science into our understanding of economic issues, can support a new consensus that highlights the importance of liberal political institutions rather than liberal economic policies.

In the initial quote, from more than half a century ago, Gunnar Myrdal argues that paying greater attention to institutions and attitudes will foster a more nuanced view of development as a process of circular causation among multiple drivers of economic, social, and political change. Above all, Myrdal understood that economic analysis alone would not suffice to understand development processes and policies. Even if the architects of the Washington Consensus were right in their policy prescriptions, they had a blind spot regarding how these policy prescriptions could be introduced and sustained, given the political and institutional incentives faced by real-world policymakers. On a similar note, the architects paid scant attention to social and political dynamics, contributing to a commonly held critique of economics as a narrow and inward-looking discipline.

These oversights were somewhat paradoxical, as they came at the tail end of a major global debate about economic systems, which juxtaposed (mostly) democratic capitalism and (mostly) authoritarian communism. The ideological rift of the Cold War was thus both political and economic. Moreover, when the Consensus was formulated, the Berlin Wall was falling and China's economic model was seemingly changing. On top of this, the 1990s saw a 'third wave of democratisation' in many parts of the developing world. These events unleashed a new wave of globalisation and a new liberal economic order. In retrospect, it seems impossible to understand these global trends without appealing to the underlying institutional forces that helped reshape policies.

In parallel to these real-world events, academics came to emphasise how institutions could foster more inclusive forms of policymaking.[4] More specifically, they recognised that state capacities are vital pre-conditions for effective intervention by the state.[5] We also saw systematic efforts to go beyond formal institutions and incorporate values and norms into dynamic analyses of state effectiveness.[6]

In short, forces that shape politico-institutional change penetrated both the real world and academic thinking over the past few decades. An important question is whether we can use what has been learned to forge insights into the making of an effective state. We will argue that modern research on the political economics of development provides a useful starting point. In particular, it may help us formulate a consensus around certain liberal principles for building effective states by exploring the institutional and social bases of cohesive policy formation.

II. Background

1. *Why politics is key*

Politics is central because it aggregates conflicting interests and, thereby, affects who gets what when the state exercises its power to tax, spend, and regulate. Generally speaking, the political-economics literature has developed a wide variety of models to study how power is acquired and used.[7] To understand how political forces shape development, it is essential to study how they impact incentives to invest.[8]

Research in this tradition has stressed how sub-optimal government policies stem from dynamic political failures, most often due to a lack of policy commitment – for example, governments being unable to offer credible long-term investment-friendly policies.[9] A case in point is the classical time-consistency problem in capital taxation: once it is in place, capital is easily taxed.[10] However, classic redistributive motives in policymaking are also key to recognising how investment incentives are shaped, and to understanding how politics affects development.

2. *Which democratic institutions?*

Debates in political-economics are often framed around the consequences of different constellations of institutions, especially democratic institutions. But 'democracy' is an elastic concept, with multiple dimensions.

We and others have previously argued – from first principles – that it is essential to distinguish two distinct dimensions of democratic institutions.[11]

The first is openness in access to power, particularly in executive recruitment: determining who holds office and whether their position is contestable. Hereditary monarchy lies at one end of the spectrum, and competitive elections at the other. We often refer to the latter end as democracy, as it vests power in the 'people' to choose who governs. Indeed, many equate democracy with a wide franchise in mass elections.

The second dimension of democracy concerns constraints on the exercise of power once it has been acquired. This puts the spotlight on the checks and balances that different political and state actors can impose on each other. At one extreme, leaders possess unconstrained powers; at the other, they are subject to strong checks by legislatures and/or independent judiciaries. This aspect of democracy stresses limits on absolute power even if that power is acquired in a (legitimate and competitive) election. Strong executive constraints also make it more likely that rulers exercise their power in the wider public interest.[12]

The idea is that openness in recruitment allows different groups to alternate in power – but without strong executive constraints, each group may simply govern in its own interest, which might damage the motives for investing in an efficient state and in physical and human capital. In such a situation, institutions could either impose restrictions on access to power, to induce more stability, or impose some constraints on executives, with the purpose of inducing less self-interested policies. Constraints on power also help preserve democratic institutions, by preventing rulers from watering down political rights as a means of staying in power.

3. *Measures of democratic institutions*

Well-established data bases, produced by different research consortia, can be used to classify political institutions along the two dimensions discussed. Here, we largely rely on the Polity-IV project, which scores the political institutions of all independent nations with more than half a million people, going back for more than two centuries. Over that period, getting the top Polity score for strong executive constraints has been a good deal rarer than getting the top score for open executive recruitment.[13] Effective constraints on power may require a stronger political culture, which accepts and enforces such constraints when those in power try to undermine them. Misusing political office in this way may also be less visible to citizens than cancelling or undermining an election.[14]

Figure 16.1 offers a birds-eye view of how the two dimensions of democratic institutions have trended since 1989 – the publication year of the Washington Consensus. Over these three decades, the fraction of countries with open executive recruitment and the fraction with strong executive constraints have both increased, reflecting a general trend towards democratisation. But – as in the historical backdrop mentioned – strong executive constraints are clearly lagging behind.

Figure 16.1: Executive constraints and openness over time

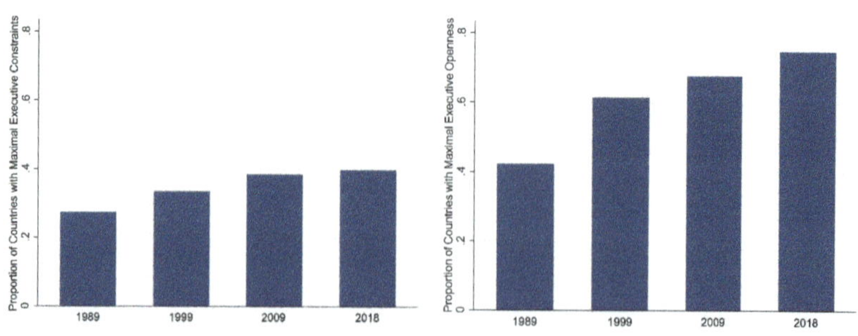

Source: authors' calculations based on The Polity Project data (https://www.systemicpeace.org/polityproject.html).[15]

4. *Development clusters*

We now turn to our central question: how can one build an effective state, all things considered? In the spirit of Myrdal's multidimensional approach, we seek answers guided by theoretical arguments and empirical evidence. However, these will not invoke a single driver but a range of common attributes that underpin clusters of states. We begin by investigating prospective drivers of success or failure in promoting peace, prosperity, and wellbeing. We then show that the data support three distinct 'development clusters', which – in line with the theoretical framework – we label as common-interest, special-interest, and weak states.

5. *Building blocks*

Following on from our previous research, we argue that development clusters are likely to form across two dimensions: the extent of political violence and the build-up of state capacities.[16] These ideas are anchored in two strands of social science research on the history of states, which we trace back to the work of political sociologists Max Weber and Charles Tilly.

6. *The Weber doctrine*

To be effective, a state must limit violence to its own legitimate use of force. This idea goes back, at least, to early social-contract theory, such as Thomas Hobbes's *Leviathan*, but was articulated in a more modern context by Weber.[17] It is now widely accepted that an effective state has a monopoly of coercion in its own territory. Such a monopoly rules out coercion by non-state actors, as in civil wars or in situations where militias contest parts of a territory.

Civil wars where control of the state is at stake remain a common phenomenon.[18] The frequency of such wars increased in the post-World War II period peaked in the 1980s and 1990s, and steadily declined thereafter. The annual prevalence of civil war has now levelled out at around 10% of countries.[19] Of the 172 countries for which both conflict and income data are available, 39 had a violent conflict between 1989 and 2016, of which 24 are classified as low income, 13 as middle income, and only 2 as high income.[20] That is, we see a clear pattern when it comes to civil war and level of economic development.

Mainstream research began to emphasise political violence and peace – as a cause as well as a consequence of development – only after the formulation of the Washington Consensus.[21] But, nowadays, debates about the causes and consequences of internal conflicts underpin a vast body of research in both economics and political science. This work stresses that low income can be both a cause and consequence of conflict. It also studies the role of political institutions, especially legislative and judicial constraints on executive powers. These institutions constrain incumbent behaviours that may provoke conflict, such as encroachments on minority rights. In line with this observation, Polity IV's measure of strong executive constraints shows that 27 of the 39 countries with a civil war between 1989 and 2016 did not have a single instance of strong executive constraints over that period.

However, focusing on civil war is only a partial approach, as not being in civil war does not necessarily imply a society where political violence is absent. States that stave off outright conflict by repressing their populations – for example, by locking up opposition groups and coercively stamping out protests – still engage in violence, although the violence is closer to being 'one-sided' than 'two-sided'.[22]

Throughout human history, coercion and repression have been more common tools for sustaining political power than winning elections. These tools remain prevalent today; even in the third wave of democracy since 1989, 79 countries have sometimes been ruled by regimes classified as repressive. Although the share of countries engaging in repression fell from 30–40% in the 1950s to near zero by the late 1990s/early 2000s, repression has increased since 2006, with close to 10% of states carrying out political purges, including Brazil, the Philippines, Russia, Thailand, Turkey, and Venezuela.[23]

7. *Peace as a condition for an effective state*

Establishing peace is an essential part of establishing social order, which plays an important role in building an effective state. Beyond its direct importance, limiting the use of political violence often improves incentives to invest in physical and human capital. Conversely, civil conflict may hurt incomes through lower earnings, deterred investments, or widespread disruption of vital infrastructures.

Endemic repression may certainly increase political stability – China and the Middle-East monarchies are examples of repressive versions of peace. But unchecked power is also a source of risk that may prevent development. Absence of the rule of law can raise fears of expropriation and deter investment. Repressive regimes often foster corruption, as personal relationships substitute for open access to economic opportunities. This can restrict welfare-enhancing entrepreneurial entry, or entrench welfare-reducing monopolies. Meanwhile, if educational opportunities expand, an aspirational middle class that demands political rights may also pose risks to autocrats. Thus, even stable autocracies face a difficult balancing act, which can result in crackdowns on freedoms with negative economic consequences. When is a state more likely to realise a peaceful and legitimate monopoly on violence? We delineate three conditions.

The first is limited opportunities for using the state to promote the interests of a ruling elite. When state power faces few constraints, it is attractive to capture the state or retain control of the spoils of office. By contrast, when rulers are constrained by courts and parliaments, this reduces the incentives to use violence to acquire or maintain power at all cost. So, executive constraints are key.

The second condition is cross-cutting economic, political, and social cleavages in society. Researchers have stressed how the incentives for conflict, rather than cooperation, go up when groups defined by income, classes, ethnicities, or religions coincide and reinforce each other.[24] In such cases, groups that are competing to be in power are more sharply delineated, so using violence to capture the state is more attractive. On the other hand, when political cleavages are cross-cutting, they foster incentives to build alternative broad-based coalitions for cooperation. Such latent coalitions with common interests across groups may weaken the motives for each group to invest in violence to acquire political power. So, cross-cutting cleavages are key.

A third, related, condition is a developing economy that helps pacify the polity. If many citizens perceive strong gains from economic cooperation, this can help underpin a peaceful society, which feeds back to prosperity through stronger investment incentives. This idea – that economic relations provide a civilising force – is often labelled the 'doux commerce hypothesis'.[25] Thus, peaceful political settlements can be reinforced by an economic peace dividend.

8. *The Tilly doctrine*

The term 'state capacity' has its roots in historical sociology and was popularised by Charles Tilly, who principally used it to describe the power to tax.[26] Nowadays, state capacity is used to describe the general infrastructure that allows a state to deliver a wider range of policies – and to do so at a low cost. The concept of state capacity allows a degree of consensus around public intervention, by cutting through ideologically loaded debates about the size of the state. Thus it appeals to proponents of government intervention, who see building state capacity as a road to wider intervention – say, a greater array of industrial strategies. But the term also appeals to sceptics of state intervention, who see building state capacity as a road to narrower intervention – emphasising more effective regulation but on a smaller scale.[27]

In a previous paper, we described three key state capacities.[28] *Fiscal capacity* refers to the power to tax, which requires investing in systems for compliance with broad-based income taxes and collection of social-security contributions. High fiscal capacity allows the state to raise more tax revenues at lower cost. *Legal capacity* refers to the power to implement laws and regulations, which requires investments in legal institutions, courts, and regulatory bodies to protect property rights and enforce contracts that encourage trade and investment. *Collective capacity* refers to the power to deliver a range of public services, which requires investing in organisational structures to provide infrastructure, and investing in services like health and education.

State capacities can thus be thought of as different forms of public capital – not just physical structures, but digital structures. Such capacities are the bedrock for state intervention: spending money will rarely achieve positive results without the ability to identify and deliver public projects. Moreover, they are inherently dynamic: states can shift the dial by enhancing capacities in times of need – in order to, say, administer vaccinations in a pandemic, or raise new taxes in a war.

We now argue that the very same forces that help constrain investments in political violence help stimulate investments in state capacity. The incentive to invest in a capable state is strongest when current and future rulers use the state to further common interests. For example, the incentive to invest in a broad-based tax system is greater if the proceeds largely finance universal programmes, and such programmes are most effective when backed by organisations that help raise the returns on public spending. A state intent on raising tax revenues will also have stronger motives to build legal capacity to promote a market economy.

Such motives are sustained by political institutions that constrain rulers from spending on narrowly defined group interests. Furthermore, a sense of common purpose – such as defending a country against a common enemy – will help sustain the working of such institutions. As Tilly argues, external warfare has been a key force in building tax capacity throughout history.[29] Similarly, many states reviewed their public-health systems following the pandemic.

Building legal capacity to make the market system work better will provide a boost to productivity and thus stimulate economic development. Indeed, the state can be a source of endogenous growth. With collective capacity, the fruits of growth can also be shared more broadly. This may create a powerful constituency for the development of the state which, in turn, may support the maintenance of peaceful domestic relations.

9. *Three kinds of states – development clusters*

The motives to create different forms of state capacity are complementary, in the sense that they reinforce each other. Moreover, many drivers of investment in state capacities are helpful in creating a peaceful state. In this way, state capacities and peace tend to become symbiotic, which fits nicely with Myrdal's notion of circular causation. In previous publications, we have stressed precisely how, in theory, economic, political, and social outcomes mutually reinforce each other.[30] When operating for a period of time, a process of mutual reinforcement can create three archetypical state structures.

Common-interest states

As the name suggests, taxes raised by such states are largely spent for the common good. Political institutions largely constrain the power of political elites and weaken the motives to use political violence, making common-interest states largely peaceful. Institutions also encourage investments in state capacities. Common-interest states thus tend to have effective systems of revenue collection with broad-based taxation to fund collective provision of universal programmes for health, education, and retirement. They also have legal and regulatory systems, which lay the foundations for a strong market economy.

Special-interest states

Special-interest states are run to favour political elites that become de facto ruling groups, such as dynasties in stable monarchies, or oligarchic party elites in single-party states. Ruling elites are only weakly constrained by institutions, and often resort to repression to maintain a hold on power. Taxes may be used extractively, and public spending may be used to head off political opposition. Being entrenched in power does, however, allow elites to take a long-term view that can spur them to build certain state capacities. Moreover, elites can benefit from economic development if it does not threaten their hold on power – though the latter constraint may hold back the emergence of an educated middle class. Greater control over the economy, limiting competition, often makes sense to the ruling elite.

Weak states

Weak states are prone to internal conflicts and have limited state capacities. In contrast to special-interest states, no group has found a way to maintain a long-term hold on power. Moreover, such states tend to have weak constraints on the exercise of power, which makes it attractive to use the state to serve the short-term interest of the ruling group at any point in time. This rarely means investing in state effectiveness, as the benefits of such investments are likely to be reaped by future governments. As state capacities are low and conflict is endemic, incentives for private investment are limited, and in the worst cases this may result in a vicious cycle of poverty and conflict.

10. *Taking stock*

Given the complexity of today's world, it is a crude simplification to classify countries into three stylised types. Moreover, even within this, there is heterogeneity within types, not least among special-interest states and weak states. Indeed, some countries – Syria being but one example – have cycled between periods of repressive autocracy and conflict. We have previously described this heterogeneity as the 'Anna-Karenina principle', riffing on the opening lines of Leo Tolstoy's eponymous novel:

> 'Happy countries are happy in the same way. But unhappy countries are unhappy in different ways'.[31]

Above all, the principle stresses that – as in other syndromes with multiple and interdependent causes – there are no simple remedies.[32] Nonetheless, below we try to draw some practical lessons based on the patterns we observe in the data.

While our three-way classification of states draws on a specific analytical frame, it has much in common with a large body of research in political economics that examines the underpinnings of economic success. Thus, our classification parallels the celebrated work of Daron Acemoglu and James A. Robinson, who juxtaposed extractive and inclusive institutions in their analysis of why nations succeed or fail.[33] Their work, in turn, drew on established ideas about institutions as a fundamental cause of development, as stressed in the work by Douglass North.[34] Indeed, strong statements about the overall importance of institutions are now widespread in economics.[35]

Understanding the forces behind political violence also chimes with a great deal of research in economics and political science. Researchers have argued persuasively that limits on violence play a central role in effective states, and that the challenge is to build societies with 'open access orders', where transitions to power are competitive in both political and economic terms.[36] In political science, researchers have stressed how survival motives for holding onto power matter crucially for how the state is used.[37] Meanwhile, others emphasise that political violence can also be important in high-capacity countries, where governing factions deliberately weaken and collude with non-state violent actors to maintain power.[38]

The ideas that we have discussed also create a bridge to the extensive research on state failure. The work of Robert Bates is a key reference for problems when it comes to building effective states in Africa.[39] Indeed, it is common to use the term 'state fragility' to describe the challenges of development in the poorest parts of the world.[40] In their practical work, many international organisations and donors look for distinctive ways of engaging with weak and fragile states.

Our notion of building collective capacity is in tune with an extensive literature in recent years on what does and does not work in reducing poverty. Much of this research is associated with the use of randomised controlled trials (RCTs) in development.[41] Increasingly, such field experiments focus on alternative institutions and their consequences, with the aim of learning how government performance can be improved and how complementary investments in state capacities can further enhance this performance.[42]

Many of the conceptual ideas we have discussed have been around for a while. But the acknowledgement of their central importance has grown since the Washington Consensus was formulated. Any attempt to forge a consensus around the preconditions for development must thus take into account the lessons we have learned about institutional conditions that may simultaneously contain political violence and create more effective states.

III. Evidence

In this subsection, we gauge how the dimensions of state effectiveness suggested by our theoretical discussion match up with the empirical evidence. Thus, we searched for development clusters in the data, based on a statistical classification that draws on some of the key concepts that we have discussed so far, namely state capacities, peacefulness, and income. We compute the resulting classifications in a sample of 64 countries for which we have reliable data for long enough a time period.

1. *Measurement*

Measuring state capacities is not straightforward.[43] To capture the main ideas, we use three crude measures, one for each aspect of state capacity. For fiscal capacity, we record the share of total taxes that was raised in the form of income taxes in 2016, using data from the International Centre for Taxation and Development Government Revenue Dataset. The idea is that, compared to, say, border taxes, income taxes require much more extensive bureaucratic infrastructures to be collected. For legal capacity, we collect the 2016 value of the World Bank's contract enforcement index from the Doing Business Project. This is just one, but a key, aspect of supporting market activity by judicial structures. Finally, for collective capacity we construct a basic index that takes the average of educational attainment, from Roberto Barro and Jong Wha Lee's dataset, and life expectancy, from the World Development Indicators.[44]

These three indicators are positively correlated with each other and co-determined with income, rather than causally related to it. The correlation reflects the various feedback loops from economic development to state capacity stressed in our theoretical discussion. One example is when growing formal employment, facilitated by higher legal capacity, enables a state to collect more taxes and firms to produce at a greater scale.

In addition to state capacity measures, we gauge the share of years from 1975 to 2016 that a country was in civil war, according to the UCDP/PRIO Armed Conflict dataset.[45] We also record the share of years when the country was not in civil war but engaged in acts of repression, according to the data on political purges from the Banks Cross-National Time-Series dataset. Finally, we measure income per capita at real international prices in 2016, as defined in the Maddison Project Database.[46]

2. *Real-world development clusters*

We now look for clusters of these six indicators in the data. Specifically, we let a machine-learning algorithm classify countries into distinct groups.[47]

In a first step, the algorithm identifies two dimensions of heterogeneity. Dimension 1 broadly captures differences in state capacity and income, with positive numbers indicating high values and negative numbers low values.

Dimension 2 captures political violence, with positive numbers indicating frequent civil wars, negative numbers frequent acts of repression, and numbers around zero the absence of both violence types.[48]

In a second step, the algorithm picks out distinct clusters of countries. These are illustrated in Figure 16.2, which plots each country's Dimension-1 value on the *x*-axis and its Dimension-2 value on the *y*-axis. We also shade the area behind the countries that belong to each cluster.

Figure 16.2: Three clusters of states

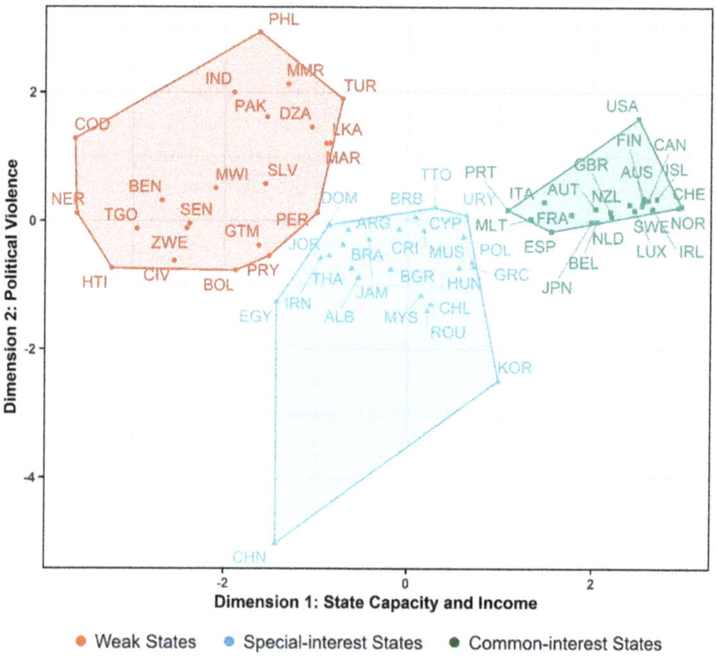

Source: authors' calculations based on the Pillars of Prosperity database (Besley and Persson, 2021).[49]

This procedure picks out three groups of countries, which turn out to quite neatly match the three groups predicted by our conceptual approach to state effectiveness. Weak states in the figure are shaded in red and located at negative values in state capacity/income Dimension 1 and positive values in conflict Dimension 2. This echoes the idea that weak states have high levels of civil war and low levels of state capacity and income. Special-interest states are shaded in blue and have middling levels of state capacity and income. Moreover, many have high repression levels (negative *y*-axis values), China being a notable outlier with its long history of political repression. Finally, common-interest states are shaded in green and form a particularly tight cluster, scoring positively on state capacity/income and around zero on political violence.

Of course, the data is noisy and the boundaries between clusters sensitive to different measures and time periods. But the tight cluster of common-interest states is still remarkable. Arguably, the goal of development efforts is to elevate countries to this cluster, a goal often cheekily referred to as 'making everyone like Denmark'. In retrospect, one way to interpret the Washington Consensus is thus as a recipe to move all countries into the common-interest state cluster. But it would be hard to argue that the recipe has worked.

3. *Subjective wellbeing and development clusters*

This discussion – and our analysis more generally – entails a ranking of states, with common-interest states at the top. While this is an explicit normative judgement, there are good reasons to expect higher levels of wellbeing in states where political violence is largely absent and state capacities are generally high. To explore this assertion, we use a common empirical measure of wellbeing. In the Cantril ladder of the Gallup World Poll, a representative sample of individuals in each country is asked to subjectively score their own lives from 0 to 10, where 0 is the worst and 10 the best. Figure 16.3 plots average country-level scores, holding constant the individual characteristics known to shape individual wellbeing, such as age, income, gender, health, employment, and marital status.

Figure 16.3: States and wellbeing

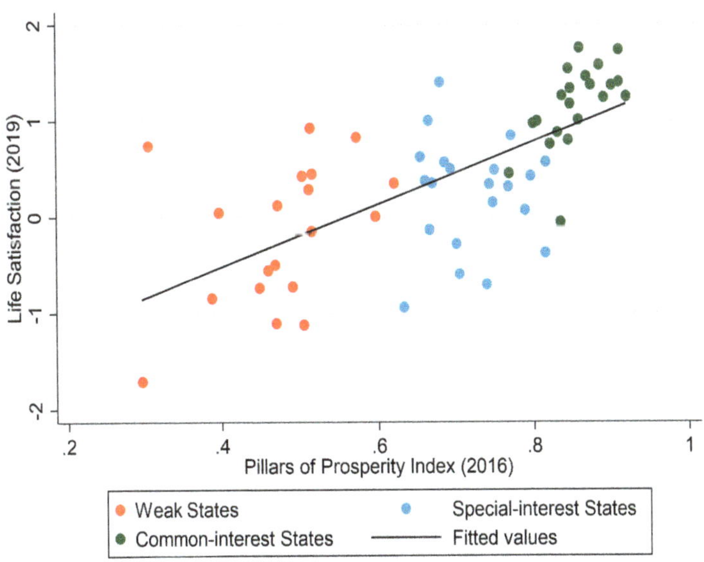

Source: authors' calculations based on the Pillars of Prosperity database (Besley and Persson, 2021) and life satisfaction data from the Gallup World Poll (Gallup, 2019).[50]

The figure relates the national wellbeing scores to an index of state effectiveness, peace, and income, which we constructed and updated several years ago.[51] In Figure 16.3, each dot colours each country according to its cluster in Figure 16.2: red for weak states, blue for special-interest states, and green for common-interest states. The figure shows a tight partial correlation between average subjective wellbeing levels and development clusters, which lends further support to the idea that a set of interrelated country-level factors are an emblem of state effectiveness.[52]

4. *Institutions and development clusters*

As a final exploration, it is interesting to consider how development clusters relate to the two measures of democratic political institutions stressed in section II, open executive recruitment and strong executive constraints. Figure 16.4 plots the average Polity IV scores for these two institutional measures against the three state clusters displayed in Figure 16.2.[53]

Figure 16.4: State types, executive constraints and openness

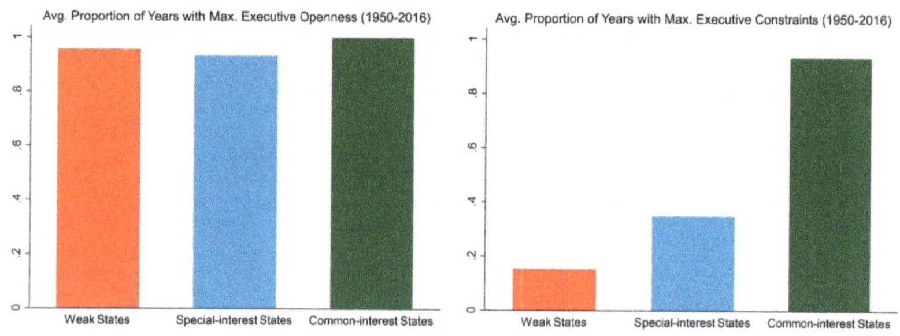

Source: authors' calculations based on the Pillars of Prosperity database (Besley and Persson, 2021) and The Polity Project data (Centre for Systemic Peace, 2021).[54]

The left panel shows that openness does not correlate with development clusters. A more open process of executive recruitment is thus no guarantee for peace or for high state capacity. However, as we stress in the next section, political freedom is not just a means to an end, but also has an intrinsic value. A way to interpret the null relation in the left panel is that incentives to invest in political violence or in state capacities do not reflect how power is acquired, but rather how it is used. This interpretation is consistent with the right panel, which displays a strong relation between state development clusters and the strength of executive constraints.

Of course, Figure 16.4 does not reflect a simple causal chain. Moreover, each country will have to carve out its own development path. But the correlation still gives a useful backdrop to debates about state effectiveness and peace as preconditions for development.

IV. A liberal political consensus?

We now consider how an approach rooted in political economics may frame a consensus around how to support peace, prosperity, and wellbeing. In the spirit of Myrdal, this approach recognises the dynamics of circular causation. We acknowledge that the task of framing such a consensus could easily be seen as foolhardy, given the abundance of political philosophies and the heterogeneity in existing forms of government, some of which appear extremely stable. That said, Figure 16.1 illustrates that the last 30 years have seen enough institutional change to reject the idea that political institutions are set in stone. We also see value in offering a reasoned defence of certain core principles, that are informed by a logical framework and by patterns in the data.

Our approach draws on a broad 'liberal' line of thought that goes back to the enlightenment. It is grounded in a political and social philosophy that emphasises individual rights, civil liberties, and democratic institutions, along with open access to markets that facilitate free enterprise. While these features can be derived from philosophical principles alone, we believe that the evidence also supports the case for a liberal political consensus.

We express our case with three propositions.

1. *Proposition 1 – Intrinsic values*

A liberal society based on principles of basic economic, political, and civil rights has intrinsic value.

The key here is direct 'intrinsic value' – as opposed to indirect instrumental benefits like higher incomes. To us, a liberal polity – where it is right for all citizens to exercise control over government, but wrong for a single elite to dominate others – is a valuable arrangement regardless of its consequences. With a few exceptions, this argument is unusual among economists, most of whom have argued for political liberalism based on its consequences.[55] However, a polity can raise the wellbeing of its citizens and contribute to human flourishing beyond the consumption of material goods. Societies that repress certain freedoms in pursuit of material gains cannot be given the same status as those that both pursue material gains *and* preserve freedoms.

Political equality as a value underpins the idea of a liberal political order where freedom of association and expression, and equality before the law, are central.[56] As many societies do not adhere to such values, actors who support them should try to work out how the intrinsic value of liberal societies affects evaluations of specific policies. This is a largely unresolved challenge for many international organisations. But the European Bank of Reconstruction and Development (EBRD)[57] set a precedent for making public such intrinsic values. As stated in Article 1 in the Incorporation of the EBRD:

> In contributing to progress and reconstruction, the purpose of the Bank shall be to foster transition towards open market-oriented

> economies and to promote private and entrepreneurial initiative in the Central and Eastern European Countries committed to and applying principles of multiparty democracy, pluralism and market economics.

The term 'pluralism' is certainly open to interpretation, even though a standard definition would refer to a setting where people of different beliefs, backgrounds, and lifestyles can co-exist in the same society and participate equally in the political process. Of course, this article is a legacy of the particular circumstances after the fall of the Berlin Wall, but it remains to this day. The EBRD's founders were committed to supporting the transition from communism towards more liberal political ideals. Taken seriously, the article means that policy approaches, project support, and engagement should also promote liberal values where possible.

Whether individual donors and international organisations can and should promote liberal values certainly raises hard choices. Colonial history makes it problematic to externally impose institutions and values. On the one hand, championing certain causes at home and forgetting the same causes abroad can appear hypocritical. But on the other, failing to defend liberal values abroad could end up eroding support for them at home.

2. *Proposition 2 – Instrumental benefits*

Used with caution, the large evidence base on the economic outcomes associated with alternative institutional arrangements does allow us to draw conclusions about their merits.

Compared to the time when the Washington Consensus was formulated, the research about how and why political institutions might matter is now vast. Moreover, this research is being extended from macro to micro evidence, based on RCTs and investigations of sub-national differences, and draws lessons from both historical experiences and contemporary outcomes.[58]

An active strand of work has explored how democratic governance is related to growth. Making the instrumental case for democracy has had mixed success, although some researchers have claimed to find persuasive causal evidence.[59] Though it is always challenging to establish causality in the ebb and flow of institutional histories, such analyses are still useful to discuss the instrumental value of different political institutions.

However, for a nuanced discussion it is vital to go beyond one-dimensional measures of success, such as economic growth rates or levels of income per capita, as well as one-dimensional measures of political institutions, such as democracy. Even for standard economic measures, a quick look at the data reveals heterogenous performance within simple categories. For example, in data since 1989, the average annual growth rate in democracies stands at 2.3%, compared to 2.5% in autocracies.[60] But the standard deviation of growth is very different: 4.7% in democracies versus 8.9% in autocracies.

This reminds us about issues around different forms of democracy: presidential versus parliamentary forms of government, or majoritarian versus proportional electoral systems.[61] 'Democracy' as a common label ignores such differences. Similarly, autocracies display great variation – for example, whether a well-defined 'selectorate' can hold a despotic executive to account and/or regulate succession.[62]

Used judiciously, the accumulated evidence on performance across different institutions can contribute to the debate about the value of liberal political institutions. There are indeed empirical regularities in the data.[63] This evidence base has been used to underpin discussions of why nations succeed and fail.[64] It can also be used as an empirically-based argument in favour of liberal political institutions. This argument, about instrumental benefits, reinforces that of Proposition 1, which was about intrinsic values.

3. *Proposition 3 – Practical policymaking*

When designing practical policy and development assistance, actors should focus on increasing cohesion in public action to support the building and maintenance of an effective state.

This proposition effectively argues that we ought to discount the common idea that access to finance is the main constraint on development. While public and private capital may be scarce in developing countries, it is even more important to find better ways of deploying any existing resources. In our view, 'building effective states' has three related elements.

First, the notion of a 'state' refers to a nation state. For practical purposes, centrally determined policies remain vital to the wellbeing of most countries' inhabitants. Moreover, while support from external actors certainly can make a difference, we see no credible alternative to nations building cohesive states on their own. Only common-interest states can systematically fulfil the needs of their citizens and secure peace within their borders, without one group dominating over others.

Second, the notion of an 'effective' state entails expanding fiscal, legal, and collective state capacities. It also means encouraging a market economy. A state incapable of enforcing property rights will discourage private investment, as will a state without the capacity to deploy public capital to areas with high collective benefits. Such states will have limited impact on development.

Unfortunately, there is no silver bullet. Many states inherited systems of bureaucratic selection and control from a colonial past, a heritage that cannot be ignored when deciding how to build cohesive states. Using external actors, even those with local roots, thus creates accountability challenges. More generally, how far non-state actors can contribute to state building is an open issue. Many RCTs rely on collaborations with non-governmental organisations (NGOs), to avoid working with dysfunctional governments. NGOs may thus draw scarce skilled workers away from state employment or generally avoid systems of state accountability and responsiveness. Because of this, temporary responses to immediate needs by non-state actors may yield immediate collective benefits, but also compromise long-term strategies needed to build effective states. The co-generation of knowledge by researchers working together with governments in evaluating public policies therefore holds more promise for strengthening long-term public service delivery.[65]

Another way that RCTs can help is to shed light on the drivers of state capacity in weakly institutionalised environments.[66] This is consistent with approaches to investigate sources of trust and legitimacy in state action that have been pursued by political scientists. One idea is to link tax payments to tangible benefits from state action.[67] The World Bank and other organisations now pay far greater attention to governance issues and building state effectiveness.[68]

Third, 'building' effective states entails more than just getting institutions right. That idea that norms play a key role in shaping social action is key within the social sciences – and one that is gaining acceptance in economics. A related idea is that prosocial behaviour reflects social values, as well as reactions to the behaviour of others. Formal institutions and rules can create strong incentives, but how people act under these institutions also depends on culture and norms.[69] Social context can thus shape how well people comply with formal rules, whether these rules prescribe that people pay their taxes or abstain from expropriation. While it is not always possible to 'engineer' values, one should be aware of the importance of intrinsic motivation and ways of incorporating it in public organisations.[70]

Furthermore, over the longer term, formal institutions and values may interact as they evolve. In particular, institutions and culture may be complementary and thus reinforce good or bad societal outcomes by gradually strengthening each other. This idea has recently been applied to show how the interplay between democratic electoral institutions and democratic values can help explain the long-run stability of democratic and autocratic societies.[71] Likewise, the interplay between executive constraints and the weight the prevailing culture puts on others in society can help explain the long-run stability of non-corrupt and corrupt societies.[72]

To put this last point differently: cohesive states are embedded in cohesive societies. In practical terms, policy interactions should be viewed as 'teachable moments', with externalities tied to the norms and values of participants. Policymakers should only attempt to implement new policies – or put in place new institutions – that will succeed under realistic assumptions about these norms and values. This can lead to reinforcement learning that builds further prosocial incentives. How to enforce stronger standards to limit corruption, how to increase transparency about the allocation of public resources, and how to administer sanctions all have to be part of concrete policy discussions.

V. Final comments

Development is increasingly studied with a blend of economic, political, and social considerations. In this chapter, we have tried to articulate a political–economics consensus about the roots of societal success. We have stressed that a liberal polity may enjoy an advantage in securing peace and prosperity. We have also stressed multiple outcomes, as well as multiple drivers of these outcomes. Thus, we have discussed how economic success is built on political and social foundations, a discussion which is quite different from the largely technocratic agenda that motivated the Washington Consensus. Hence our stress on a liberal *political* consensus, rather than a liberal *economic* consensus.

But we have also cautioned against an uncritical mantra of 'getting institutions right'. Bringing cohesion to the use of state resources may be done in several ways, and which one will work the best likely reflects a country's heritage, traditions, and history. Put differently, the norms and values that influence policymaking transcend formal institutional rules. A strong civic culture not only helps institutions work for the common good but also makes the institutions more robust in the face of efforts to undermine them. Liberal-governance norms and values are sometimes violated and ultimately citizens must be prepared to stand up and defend democracy against such violations. This, in turn, helps to build strong democratic values.[73]

Labels like democracy and liberalism may be blunt. However, liberal societies and democracies broadly go hand in hand, with one tradition that sees democracy as a universal value and another that sees liberal political institutions as a means to consensual policymaking. When liberal democratic institutions and values combine with greater cohesion in the population, this creates incentives for political leaders to build a strong state and abstain from violent resolution of conflict. This, in turn, makes it more attractive for private actors to invest in the future, which boosts economic outcomes. In such situations, we are more likely to see cohesive societies – common-interest states, as we call them – and the benefits they bring: high incomes, peace, and a rich menu of government services. A range of common-interest states with these characteristics have indeed emerged over the past two centuries.

So, the crucial question becomes how liberal political values and institutions can be built. Given the complex issues, no manual is available. Where and when critical junctures arise to strengthen institutions, these should certainly be taken.[74] Outright external interventions – like the Marshall Plan or membership demands from the European Union – may have been important to help sustain democracy in fragile contexts. External influence – as seen in Japan, South Korea, and Taiwan – may also have helped nurture self-sustaining democratic societies in the wake of existential threats. We have seen how the creators of the EBRD statutes were able to include a political mandate, alongside an economic one, at the critical moment after the fall of communism.

We are not formulating a utopian vision. For all their imperfections and limitations, some common-interest states have been created and sustained. They reflect arguments by political philosophers who identified the freedoms of association, expression, and participation as building blocks for better government. Historically, emerging democracies denied political rights to women, but over time this imperfection has largely been resolved within the system through a process of changing values and legal-cum-political change. Thus, we should think about common-interest states as evolving systems that respond to ongoing shocks and challenges. But their resilience should never be taken for granted, and it remains to be seen how robust they will be in the face of attacks on liberal values by left- and right-wing populist groups.

In conclusion, we return to our two opening quotes, on development as a process of circular causation and on democracy as a universal value.[75] The two visions agree on putting societal values at the heart of the political economics of change. Indeed, when we consider humanity's greatest challenges – climate change, conflict, poverty, and state fragility – it is hard to see solutions that do not involve changing values.[76] To analyse such issues, we need to combine institutional, cultural, and economic dynamics. Although some building blocks are already in place, this remains a huge challenge, not just for economics but social science more generally.

Acknowledgments

We are grateful to Jake Fazzio and Joe Marshall for excellent research assistance, as well as to Andrés Velasco and Margaret Levi for useful feedback both at the conference and in writing. We also thank Leonard Wantchekon, and conference participants for comments.

Notes

1 Myrdal (1974).

2 Sen (1999).

3 Williamson (1990).

4 Acemoglu and Robinson (2012); Bates (2009); North et al. (2009).

5 Besley and Persson (2009); Besley and Persson (2011); Levi (1989); Tilly (1990).

6 Persson and Tabellini (2009); Acemoglu and Robinson (2019).

7 Persson and Tabellini (2000).

8 Alesina and Rodrik (1994); Persson and Tabellini (1994).

9 Acemoglu (2003); Besley and Coate (1998).

[10] Kydland and Prescott (1977); Fischer (1980).

[11] Besley and Persson (2011); Mukand and Rodrik (2020).

[12] Besley and Persson (2011).

[13] This is not unique to data from the Polity Project (Center for Systemic Peace, 2021), but also true for data from the V-Dem project (V-Dem, 2025).

[14] Fearon (2011).

[15] Center for Systemic Peace (2021).

[16] Besley and Persson (2011).

[17] Weber (1919).

[18] There are large literatures on the determinants of civil war in both economics and political science, see Blattman and Miguel (2009) and Walter (2004).

[19] See Figure 9 in Besley et al. (2021).

[20] The latter two (according to the UCDP/PRIO data) are Israel and the US. UCDP/PRIO (2023).

[21] Key early contributions include Collier (1999) and Fearon and Laitin (2003). Blattman and Miguel (2009) review the early literature.

[22] For background discussion see, for example, Davenport (2007).

[23] See Figure 9 in Besley et al. (2021).

[24] Lipset and Rokkan (1967).

[25] Hirschman (1982).

[26] Common references are Tilly (1985), Tilly (1990). We are unsure when the term 'state capacity' became common currency, but Google Ngrams suggests that its usage took off in the English language in the 1980s. However, in the 1950s the term was used in various US government documents in a way that is consistent with Tilly's definition. Mann (1984) also talks about the capacity of the state but in a wider sense than the power to tax.

[27] See, for example, Niskanen Center (2023).

[28] Besley and Persson (2014).

[29] Tilly (1985); Tilly (1990).

[30] Besley and Persson (2011).

[31] Besley and Persson (2011).

[32] Of course, there are differences within states that we classify as common interest. Moreover, many common-interest states face significant challenges, like polarisation and the rise of divisive forms of identity politics, which may lead to a deterioration of norms and institutions.

[33] Acemoglu and Robinson (2012).

[34] North (1990).

[35] Rodrik et al. (2004).

[36] North et al. (2009).

[37] Bueno de Mesquita et al. (2003).

[38] For example, Kleinfeld and Barham (2018).

[39] Bates (2009).

[40] International Growth Centre (2018).

[41] Duflo and Banerjee (2011).

[42] Callen et al. (2023).

[43] For an extensive discussion of the measurement challenges see Hanson and Sigman (2021).

[44] Barro and Lee (2013).

[45] UCDP/PRIO (2023).

[46] Banks et al. (2024).

[47] For details see Besley et al. (2021). We use a two-step clustering method based on so-called principal components: (i) use the raw data to create principal components, (ii) use an agglomerative hierarchical clustering algorithm to identify clusters based on these principal components.

[48] By construction, repression is a substitute for civil war. While the positive orthant captures civil war, the negative orthant captures repression, so that zero represents countries without either type of political violence.

[49] Besley and Persson (2021).

[50] Besley and Persson (2021); Gallup (2019).

[51] For details see Besley et al. (2021).

[52] For a discussion of the links between state effectiveness and wellbeing, including the dispersion of subjective wellbeing, see Besley et al. (2023).

[53] It is important to recall that neither of the two institutional measures appear (directly or indirectly) in any of our six measures of state effectiveness.

54 Besley and Persson (2021); Center for Systemic Peace (2021).

55 Sen (1999).

56 See Sen (1999) and Verba (2001). Beramendi et al. (2022) also argue that the essence of political equality is trying to give every citizen equal consideration.

57 EBRD (2013).

58 Callen et al. (2023); Cantoni and Yuchtman (2021).

59 Persson and Tabellini found mixed success, see Persson and Tabellini (2006); Persson and Tabellini (2008). Acemoglu et al. (2019) claimed to find persuasive causal evidence.

60 As is standard, we define democracies and autocracies as countries with average Polity scores of more or less than 5, on a scale from -10 to 10 between 1989 and 2018. GDP growth data is from the Maddison Project Database. Groningen Growth and Development Centre (2020).

61 See, for example, Taagepera and Shugart (1989); Persson and Tabellini (2003).

62 See, for example, Besley and Kudamatsu (2008).

63 Persson and Tabellini (2003); Acemoglu et al. (2005).

64 Acemoglu and Robinson (2012).

65 Ashraf et al. (2020).

66 Weigel (2020).

67 Levi and Sacks (2009); Levi et al. (2007).

68 For example, the World Bank now has a dedicated Bureaucracy Lab and promotes work on Community Driven Development based on social cohesion and social capital.

69 Levi (1989); Putnam et al. (1993).

70 Ashraf et al. (2014).

71 Besley and Persson bring together insights from two earlier literatures that tried to understand long-run drivers of stable democracies: one on democratic values in political science, going back to Lipset, and one on democratic institutions in economics, going back to Acemoglu and Robinson. See Besley and Persson (2019); Lipset (1959); Acemoglu and Robinson (2000).

72 Persson and Tabellini (2021).

73 Besley and Persson (2019).

[74] Acemoglu and Robinson (2012).

[75] Myrdal (1974); Sen (1999).

[76] For an articulation of this view in the context of climate change see Besley and Persson (2023).

References

Acemoglu, D. (2003) 'Why Not a Political Case Theorem? Social Conflict, Commitment, and Politics', *Journal of Comparative Economics,* 31: 620–652. https://doi.org/10.1016/j.jce.2003.09.003

Acemoglu, D. and Robinson, J. A. (2000) 'Why Did the West Extend the Franchise? Democracy, Inequality, and Growth in Historical Perspective', *The Quarterly Journal of Economics,* 115: 1167–99. https://doi.org/10.1162/003355300555042

Acemoglu, D. and Robinson, J. A. (2012) *Why Nations Fail*, New York, NY: Crown Publishers.

Acemoglu, D. and Robinson, J. A. (2019) *The Narrow Corridor: States, Societies, and the Fate of Liberty,* Penguin Publishing Group.

Acemoglu, D., Johnson, S. and Robinson, J. A. (2005) 'Institutions as a Fundamental Cause of Long-run Growth', in Aghion P. and Durlauf, S. (eds) *Handbook of Economic Growth,* Volume 1, Amsterdam: Elsevier: 385–472, https://doi.org/10.1016/S1574-0684(05)01006-3

Acemoglu, D., Naidu, S., Restrepo, P. and Robinson J. A. (2019) 'Democracy Does Cause Growth', *Journal of Political Economy,* 127: 47–100. https://doi.org/10.1086/700936

Alesina, A. and Rodrik, D. (1994) 'Distributive Politics and Economic Growth', *The Quarterly Journal of Economics,* 109: 465–490. https://doi.org/10.2307/2118470

Ashraf, N., Bandiera, O. and Jack, B. K. (2014) 'No Margin, No Mission? A Field Experiment on Incentives for Public Service Delivery', *Journal of Public Economics,* 120: 1–17. https://doi.org/10.1016/j.jpubeco.2014.06.014

Ashraf, N., Bandiera, O., Davenport, E. and Lee, S. S. (2020) 'Losing Prosociality in the Quest for Talent? Sorting, Selection, and Productivity in the Delivery of Public Services', *American Economic Review,* 110(5): 1355–1394. https://doi.org/10.1257/aer.20180326

Banks, A. S. and Wilson, K. A. (2024) Cross-National Time-Series Data (CNTS). Databanks International. Jerusalem, Israel. https://www.cntsdata.com/

Barro, R. J. and Lee, J. W. (2013) 'A New Data Set of Educational Attainment in the World, 1950–2010', *Journal of Development Economics,* 104: 184–198. https://doi.org/10.1016/j.jdeveco.2012.10.001

Bates, R. H. (2009) *The Logic of State Failure: Learning from Late-Century Africa. Dealing With Failed States*, London, UK: Routledge.

Beramendi, P., Besley, T. and Levi, M. (2022) 'Political Equality: What Is It and Why Does It Matter?', Background Paper for the IFS Deaton Review. https://ifs.org.uk/inequality/political-equality-what-is-it-and-why-does-it-matter/

Besley, T. and Coate, S. (1998) 'Sources of Inefficiency in a Representative Democracy: A Dynamic Analysis', *American Economic Review,* 88: 139–156. https://www.jstor.org/stable/116822

Besley, T. and Kudamatsu, M. (2008) 'Making Autocracy Work', in Helpman, E. (ed), *Institutions and Economic Performance,* Cambridge, MA: Harvard University Press. https://doi.org/10.2307/j.ctv21hrgnz.15

Besley, T. and Persson, T. (2009) 'The Origins of State Capacity: Property Rights, Taxation, and Politics', *American Economic Review,* 99: 1218–44. https://doi.org/10.1257/aer.99.4.1218

Besley, T. and Persson, T. (2011) *Pillars of Prosperity: The Political Economics of Development Clusters*, Princeton, NJ: Princeton University Press. https://doi.org/10.23943/princeton/9780691152684.001.0001

Besley, T. and Persson, T. (2014) 'The Causes and Consequences of Development Clusters: State Capacity, Peace, and Income', *Annual Review of Economics,* 6: 927–949. https://doi.org/10.1146/annurev-economics-080213-041128

Besley, T. and Persson, T. (2019) 'Democratic Values and Institutions', *American Economic Review: Insights,* 1: 59–76. https://doi.org/10.1257/aeri.20180248

Besley, T. and Persson, T. (2021) 'Pillars of Prosperity'. STICERD, *London School of Economics and Political Science.* https://sticerd.lse.ac.uk/_new/publications/books/pillars-of-prosperity/data/)

Besley, T. and Persson, T. (2023) 'The Political Economics of Green Transitions', *The Quarterly Journal of Economics,* 138: 1863–1906. https://doi.org/10.1093/qje/qjad006

Besley, T., Dann, C. and Persson, T. (2021) 'Pillars of Prosperity: A Ten Year Update', CEPR Discussion Paper No. 16256, CEPR Press.

Besley, T., Marshall, J. and Persson, T. (2023) 'Well-being and State Effectiveness', *World Happiness Report*, 11th ed. Ch.3. Sustainable Development Solutions Network. https://worldhappiness.report/ed/2023/well-being-and-state-effectiveness

Blattman, C. and Miguel, E. (2009) 'Civil War', *Journal of Economic Literature,* 48: 3–57. https://doi.org/10.3386/w14801

Bueno de Mesquita, B., Smith, A., Siverson, R. and Morrow, J. (2003) *The Logic of Political Survival,* Cambridge, MA: MIT Press. https://doi.org/10.7551/mitpress/4292.001.0001

Callen, M., Weigel, J. L. and Yuchtman, N. (2023) 'Experiments about Institutions', NBER Working Paper No. w31964. https://doi.org/10.3386/w31964

Cantoni, D. and Yuchtman, N. (2021) 'Historical Natural Experiments: Bridging Economics and Economic History', in Bisin, A. and Federico, G. (eds) *Handbook of Historical Economics*, Amsterdam: Elsevier. https://doi.org/10.3386/w26754

Center for Systemic Peace (2021) 'The Polity Project', https://www.systemicpeace.org/polityproject.html

Collier, P. (1999) 'On the Economic Consequences of Civil War', *Oxford Economic Papers,* 51, 168–183. https://doi.org/10.1093/oep/51.1.168

Davenport, C. (2007) 'State Repression and Political Order', *Annual Review of Political Science,* 10: 1–23. https://doi.org/10.1146/annurev.polisci.10.101405.143216

Duflo, E. and Banerjee, A. (2011) *Poor Economics: A Radical Rethinking of the Way to Fight Global Poverty*, New York: Public Affairs.

European Bank of Reconstruction and Development (2013) 'Political Aspects of the Mandate of the European Bank for Reconstruction and Development'. https://www.ebrd.com/content/dam/ebrd_dxp/assets/pdfs/multiparty-democracy-and-pluralism/Procedures%20to%20implement%20the%20political%20aspects%20of%20the%20mandate%20of%20the%20EBRD.pdf

Fearon, J. (2011) 'Self-enforcing Democracy', *The Quarterly Journal of Economics,* 126: 1661–1708. https://doi.org/10.1093/qje/qjr038

Fearon, J. and Laitin, D. (2003) 'Ethnicity, Insurgency and Civil War', *American Political Science Review,* 97: 75–90. https://doi.org/10.1017/S0003055403000534

Fischer, S. (1980) 'Dynamic Inconsistency, Cooperation, and the Benevolent Dissembling Government', *Journal of Political Economy,* 85: 163–190. https://www.sciencedirect.com/science/article/abs/pii/0165188980900536

Gallup (2019) Gallup World Poll. Gallup Global Analytics. https://www.gallup.com/analytics/318875/global-research.aspx

Groningen Growth and Development Centre (2020) Maddison Project Database 2020. Faculty of Economics and Business. https://www.rug.nl/ggdc/historicaldevelopment/maddison/releases/maddison-project-database-2020

Hanson, J. K. and Sigman, R. (2021) 'Leviathan's Latent Dimensions: Measuring State Capacity for Comparative Political Research', *The Journal of Politics*, 83(4): 1495–1510. https://doi.org/10.1086/715066

Hirschman, A. O. (1982) 'Rival Interpretations of Market Society: Civilizing, Destructive, or Feeble?', *Journal of Economic Literature*, 20: 1463–1484.

International Growth Centre (2018) 'Escaping the Fragility Trap' [April]. https://www.theigc.org/sites/default/files/2018/04/Escaping-the-fragility-trap.pdf

Kleinfeld, R. and Barham, E. (2018) 'Complicit States and the Governing Strategy of Privilege Violence: When Weakness Is Not the Problem', *Annual Review of Political Science*, 21: 215–238. https://doi.org/10.1146/annurev-polisci-041916-015628

Kydland, F. E. and Prescott, E. C. (1977) 'Rules Rather than Discretion: The Inconsistency of Optimal Plans', *Journal of Political Economy*, 85: 473–492. https://doi.org/10.1086/260580

Levi, M. (1989) *Of Rule and Revenue*, Berkeley, CA: University of California Press.

Levi, M. and Sacks, A. (2009) 'Legitimating Beliefs: Sources and Indicators', *Regulation & Governance*, 3: 311–333. https://doi.org/10.1111/j.1748-5991.2009.01066.x

Levi, M., Sacks, A. and Tyler, T. (2007) 'Conceptualizing Legitimacy, Measuring Legitimating Beliefs', *American Behavioral Scientist*, 53: 354–375. https://doi.org/10.1177/0002764209338797

Lipset, S. M. (1959) 'Some Social Requisites of Democracy: Economic Development and Political Legitimacy', *American Political Science Review*, 53: 69–105. https://doi.org/10.2307/1951731

Lipset, S. M. and Rokkan, S. (1967) 'Cleavage Structures, Party Systems and Voter Alignments: An Introduction', in Lipset, S. M. and Rokkan, S. (eds) *Party Systems and Voter Alignments: Cross-National Perspectives*, New York: Free Press.

Mann, M. (1984) 'The Autonomous Power of the State: Its Origins, Mechanisms and Results', *European Journal of Sociology*, 25: 185–213. https://doi.org/10.1017/S0003975600004239

Mukand, S. W. and Rodrik, D. (2020) 'The Political Economy of Liberal Democracy', *The Economic Journal*, 130: 765–792. https://doi.org/10.1093/ej/ueaa004

Myrdal, G. (1974) 'What Is Development?', *Journal of Economic Issues* VIII(4): 729–36. https://doi.org/10.1080/00213624.1974.11503225

Niskanen Center (2023) 'State Capacity'. https://www.niskanencenter.org/policy/state-capacity/

North, D. C. (1990) *Institutions, Institutional Change and Economic Performance*, Cambridge, UK: Cambridge University Press. https://doi.org/10.1017/CBO9780511808678

North, D. C., Weingast, B. and Wallis, J. (2009) *Violence and Social Orders: A Conceptual Framework for Interpreting Recorded Human History*, Cambridge, MA: Cambridge University Press. https://doi.org/10.1017/CBO9780511575839

Persson, T. and Tabellini, G. (1994) 'Is Inequality Harmful for Growth?', *American Economic Review*, 84: 600–621. https://www.jstor.org/stable/2118070

Persson, T. and Tabellini, G. (2000) *Political Economics: Explaining Economic Policy*, Cambridge, MA: MIT Press.

Persson, T. and Tabellini, G. (2003) *The Economic Effects of Constitutions*, Cambridge, MA: MIT Press. https://doi.org/10.7551/mitpress/2591.001.0001

Persson, T. and Tabellini, G. (2006) 'Democracy and Development: The Devil in the Details', *American Economic Review*, 96: 319–324. https://doi.org/10.1257/000282806777212396

Persson, T. and Tabellini, G. (2008) 'The Growth Effect of Democracy: Is It Heterogenous and How Can It Be Estimated?', in Helpman, E. (ed), *Institutions and Economic Performance*, Cambridge, MA: Harvard University Press. https://doi.org/10.2307/j.ctv21hrgnz.17

Persson, T. and Tabellini, G. (2009) 'Democratic Capital: The Nexus of Political and Economic Change', *American Economic Journal: Macroeconomics*, 1: 88–126. https://doi.org/10.1257/mac.1.2.88

Persson, T. and Tabellini, G. (2021) 'Culture, Institutions, and Policy', in Bisin, A. and Federico, G. (eds), *Handbook of Historical Economics*, Amsterdam: Elsevier. https://doi.org/10.1016/B978-0-12-815874-6.00023-X

Putnam, R., Leonardi, R. and Nanetti, R. Y. (1993) *Making Democracy Work: Civic Traditions in Modern Italy*, Princeton, NJ: Princeton University Press. https://doi.org/10.1515/9781400820740

Rodrik, D., Subramanian, A. and Trebbi, F. (2004) 'Institutions Rule: The Primacy of Institutions Over Geography and Integration in Economic Development', *Journal of Economic Growth*, 9: 131–165. https://doi.org/10.1023/B:JOEG.0000031425.72248.85

Sen, A. (1999) 'Democracy as a Universal Value', *Journal of Democracy*, 10: 3–17. https://doi.org/10.1353/jod.1999.0055

Taagepera, R. and Shugart, M. S. (1989) *Seats and Votes: The Effects and Determinants of Electoral Systems*, New Haven, CT: Yale University Press.

Tilly, C. (1985) 'War Making and State Making as Organized Crime', In Evans, P., Rueschemeyer, D. and Skocpol, T. (eds) *Bringing the State Back In*, pp. 169–87, Cambridge, UK: Cambridge University Press. https://doi.org/10.1017/CBO9780511628283.008

Tilly, C. (1990) *Coercion, Capital and European States, AD 990-1992*, Oxford, UK: Blackwell.

Uppsala Conflict Data Program (UCDP) and Peace Research Institute in Oslo (PRIO) (2023) UCDP/PRIO Armed Conflict Dataset. https://ucdp.uu.se/downloads/

Varieties of Democracy (V-Dem) (2025) 'V-Dem Project'. https://v-dem.net/

Verba, S. (2001) 'Political Equality: What Is It? Why Do We Want It?', Russell Sage Foundation Report. [Jan.] https://www.russellsage.org/research/reports/political-equality

Walter, B. F. (2004) 'Does Conflict Beget Conflict? Explaining Recurring Civil War', *Journal of Peace Research*, 41: 371–388. https://doi.org/10.1177/0022343304043775

Weber, M. (1919) 'Politics as a Vocation', Reprinted in Gerth, H. and Mills, C. W. (eds) *From Max Weber*, New York, NY: Free Press.

Weigel, J. L. (2020) 'The Participation Dividend of Taxation: How Citizens in Congo Engage More with the State when It Tries to Tax Them', *The Quarterly Journal of Economics*, 135: 1849–1903. https://doi.org/10.1093/qje/qjaa019

Williamson, J. (ed) (1990) *Latin American Adjustment: How Much Has Happened*? Washington, DC: Institute for International Economics.

Response to Tim Besley and Torsten Persson by Margaret Levi

What I most appreciate about this interesting chapter is its efforts to be a work of *political* economy. Besley and Persson take seriously politics and political institutions, as well as the norms and values that are the oil and glue of such institutions. They deserve applause for recognising the intrinsic value of 'a liberal society based on principles of basic economic, political, and civil rights has intrinsic value'. While going far beyond what most economists do by acknowledging intrinsic value, they also marshal evidence for the instrumental benefits of such a society.

That said, this is still very much an economics chapter, and it would benefit from being even more inclusive of the politics – both the science and the practice. Although Besley and Persson acknowledge the work of political scientists in this chapter, the need for more political analysis becomes most apparent in their argument for focusing '…on increasing cohesion in public action to support the building and maintenance of an effective state'. Cohesion, for them, rests on a society-wide consensus that '...emphasises individual rights, civil liberties, and democratic institutions, along with open access to markets that facilitate free enterprise'. It is this cohesion that allows for institutional reforms to achieve the aims of a liberal society as circumstances change and as countries attempt to attain more inclusive political and economic development. Thus, it is imperative that their theory address the political sources of institutional change.

Besley and Persson are relatively persuasive about the three development clusters and the factors that contribute to them, particularly the role of state capacity. This is hardly surprising, given that they are the authors of the paradigm-shifting *Pillars of Prosperity*. But when it comes to societal cohesion, they tend to assume its existence rather than explain its emergence and maintenance. Although they acknowledge it might not be easy to achieve, they nonetheless proceed as if it is.

Besley and Persson recognise that institutional reform is often a product of changes in incentives that encourage powerful actors to accept reform as the best alternative, and they certainly recognise the threat of violence to both cohesion and stability. It is worth further exploration of the politics of cohesion. One way to start is with the kind of political economics they favour. For example, as Barry Weingast argues in his well-known 1997 paper and Acemoglu and Robinson in their 2005 book, fear of popular reaction is one source of incentive change.[1] It can also be a source of stability if there is a well-grounded belief that certain moves towards special interest politics or revocation of a cherished reform or benefit might provoke electoral push back and mobilised opposition. This was the case with the National Labor Relations Act in the United States in 1935, the federal legislation that gave workers the right to unionise, engage in collective bargaining, and strike legally. The possibility of violence and even a revolution in the country was one reason corporations and legislators were willing to consider significant labour reform, and the likelihood of union pushback helped keep the reforms in place. On the other hand, as union power waned, Congress enacted amendments that undercut labour's rights.[2] The same happened with welfare benefits, which expanded and contracted in response to the electoral power and urban rebellions of the relatively poor.[3]

To get at what sustains 'common-interest states' also requires considering the relationship between citizens and states, or at least their governments. What are the conditions under which people peacefully comply with or withdraw their compliance from governments? Or to put the question another way: what are the conditions under which citizens believe government is trustworthy? This comes up in the chapter but largely in relationship to how RCTs might be used in formulating policy.

The conditions for trustworthiness include:[4]

- That the government uphold the social/fiscal contract to provide promised goods and services to its population.
- That the provision of these goods and services is done in a way that is relatively fair according to the standards of the day.
- That government demonstrate it can and will catch and punish free riders, thus reassuring those who would like to comply with government laws that they are not suckers and that there is good reason to believe there will be sufficient contributions to the public good.

As Pablo Beramendi, Tim Besley, and I argue in our work on political equality,[5] social cohesion may also require arrangements to mitigate conflicts that create problems for democratic practice and public policies by undermining cohesion. Class, ethnic, religious, racial, ideological, and gender divides are often sources of intense disagreement in a polity, as Besley and Persson note. To inhibit violence and achieve a minimal level of consensus requires institutions that facilitate deliberation and mutual respect. Political scientists have long grappled with these questions, as Besley and Persson note, but a new generation of political theorists and philosophers are suggesting new approaches to citizen engagement and social connectedness.[6]

Another way to think about this issue is in terms of an expanded and inclusive community of fate – those with whom our destinies are entwined. We all have some small community of fate, usually with members of our family and close friends. The question is whether it is possible to develop a broader, more encompassing community of fate among those with whom there are no close pre-existing relationships or indeed any personal relationships at all. John Ahlquist and I were able to provide a proof of the possible in our investigation of certain American and Australian longshore worker unions.[7] These are organisations whose primary aims are economistic: to improve wages, hours, and working conditions. Yet, their members chose to engage in costly political actions on behalf of distant others who are unlikely to reciprocate directly. They closed ports despite loss of salary and possible loss of jobs and imprisonment.

What we observed was built on but distinctive from the solidarity necessary for a union. It was solidarity, yes, but for prosocial ends. The mechanism for deciding whom to help and how was a form of participatory democracy. There were personal relationships among those making the decision but on behalf of strangers they would probably never meet. Crucial to an expanded and inclusive community of fate is the existence of some mutually shared values and norms. The value these labour actions embodied was the old union motto, 'An injury to one is an injury to all', with the ensuing commitment to prevent and to mitigate those injuries. Besley and Persson argue that policies must be consistent with prevailing norms if they are to succeed, but there is also reason to believe that institutions are a source of norm creation. The abolition of slavery in Britain, the US and elsewhere reflected the norms of some but not all. Yet, over time the illegality of slavery came to also make it largely unthinkable. In other instances, institutions and laws may facilitate the establishment of new norms. The development of welfare states both reflected and created norms about who is deserving of help and under what conditions. Moreover, those norms – and welfare state institutions – vary widely across countries, reflecting differences in the values that form the basis of cohesion in those polities.

Besley and Persson appropriately emphasise the importance of a liberal consensus and cohesive society for political and economic development. Moreover, they provide us the beginnings of an important road map for how to achieve such a society. The next step is to fill in more of the details. This is a mammoth project for political economists that will depend on drawing from the research of multiple disciplines and their plurality of approaches and methods.

Notes

1 Weingast (1997); Acemoglu and Robinson (2005).

2 Levi et al. (2017); Cuéllar et al. (2020).

3 Piven and Cloward (1993 [1971]).

4 For a fuller summary of this argument and the literature and evidence that informs it, see Levi (2019).

[5] Beramendi et al. (2022). IFS (February 2022). We also have a book in progress.

[6] See, e.g., Allen (2023); Schwartzberg and Knight (2024).

[7] Ahlquist and Levi (2013).

References

Acemoglu, D. and Robinson, J. A. (2005) *Economic Origins of Dictatorship and Democracy*, Cambridge: Cambridge University Press. https://doi.org/10.1017/CBO9780511510809

Ahlquist, J. S. and Levi, M. (2013) *In the Interest of Others: Organizations and Social Activism*, Princeton, NJ: Princeton University Press. https://doi.org/10.23943/princeton/9780691158563.001.0001

Allen, D. S. (2023) *Justice by Means of Democracy*, Chicago: University of Chicago Press. https://doi.org/10.7208/chicago/9780226777122.001.0001

Beramendi, P., Besley, T. and Levi, M. (2022) 'Political Equality: What It Is and Why Does It Matter?', in Deaton, A. (ed) *Inequality: The IFS Deaton Review*, Institute for Fiscal Studies. https://ifs.org.uk/inequality/wp-content/uploads/2022/01/Political-Equality-What-is-it-updated.pdf

Cuéllar, M., Levi, M. and Weingast, B. (2020) 'Twentieth-Century America as a Developing Country: Conflict, Institutions, and the Evolution of Public Law'. *Harvard Journal on Legislation*, 57(1): 25-66.

Levi, M. (2019) 'Trustworthy Government, Legitimating Beliefs', In Knight, J. and Schwartzberg, M. (eds), *Nomos*, New York: New York University Press: 361–82.

Levi, M., Melo, T., Weingast, B. and Zlotnick, F. (2017) 'Opening Access, Ending the Violence Trap: Labor, Business, Government, and the National Labor Relations Act', in Lamoreaux, N. R. and Wallis, J. (eds) *Organizations, Civil Society, and the Roots of Development*, Chicago: University of Chicago Press: 331–336. https://doi.org/10.7208/chicago/9780226426532.003.0009

Piven, F. F. and Cloward, R. (1993 [1971]) *Regulating the Poor*, New York: Pantheon.

Schwartzberg, M. and Knight, J. (2024) *Democratic Deals: A Defense of Political Bargaining*, Cambridge, Mass: Harvard University Press. https://doi.org/10.4159/9780674297012

Weingast, B. R. (1997) 'The Political Foundations of Democracy and the Rule of Law', *The American Political Science Review*, 91(2): 245–263. https://doi.org/10.2307/2952354

Response to Tim Besley and Torsten Persson by Leonard Wantchekon

The chapter by Besley and Persson revisits the evolution of development thinking within academia and policy circles over the past 35 years, starting from the Washington Consensus. This consensus was a blueprint for market-oriented state reforms believed to be essential for helping underdeveloped countries catch up economically with their wealthier counterparts. A notable omission from the Washington Consensus was its lack of focus on the social and political dynamics within nations, which significantly influence the implementation of economic policies. The authors highlight a shift in thinking among policy and academic communities towards recognising institutional and social dynamics as crucial to development. This shift emphasises the importance of institutional foundations, state capacity, and the values and norms that underpin economic growth.

In the theoretical section, Besley and Persson outline the institutional prerequisites for development, including the establishment of a peaceful order through the state's monopoly on legitimate violence. They also emphasise the development of state capacities such as taxation, law enforcement, and public goods provision. These elements are more likely to emerge in nations that impose constraints on rulers, have cross-cutting cleavages, and share economic growth.

The authors categorise countries into three 'development clusters' based on the attributes of effective states. The first cluster, 'common-interest states', features strong constraints on the executive, leading to effective revenue collection and broad-based taxation that supports common good expenditures. The second, 'special-interest states', has weaker executive constraints and some state capacity, allowing for taxation and redistribution to appease opposition and benefit the elite. The third, 'weak states', is marked by unstable leadership, lack of constraints on rulers, ineffective or exploitative taxation, and minimal investment and redistribution.

The empirical section presents evidence supporting these state clusters. Using development indicators from various sources and a clustering algorithm, the authors demonstrate that the data align well with the described development clusters. This classification correlates with an index of state effectiveness, subjective wellbeing, and the strength of executive constraints.

The chapter concludes with a discussion of a new consensus in development thinking that prioritises liberal governance principles. This consensus values liberal institutions both for their intrinsic worth in providing a framework for individual freedom and for their instrumental value, as research shows a correlation between economic performance and democracy. Additionally, it suggests that reforms should extend beyond market policies to bolster state capacity and foster prosocial values and norms that support state functions, marking a significant evolution from the Washington Consensus.

This review and the London Consensus as a whole are both important and timely. The review captures very well the recent evolution of development research, marked by a renewed focus on political institutions and state capacity.

I find the emphasis on liberal and prosocial values very interesting as it both departs from a more 'technocratic' approach to state capacity and invites a more explicit role for social cohesion, citizen empowerment, and autonomy in building state capacity.

I have three main comments to the authors.

I. A liberal consensus?

Is there truly a consensus on liberal institutions as the 'correct' path towards development? While post-war international bodies like the World Bank and the International Monetary Fund champion political and economic liberal institutions, an alternative model has been gaining traction in developing nations. This model is exemplified by China and Vietnam, politically non-liberal regimes that have achieved significant economic growth and poverty reduction through industrialisation and technological innovation.

China's development strategy is characterised by a 'regionally decentralised authoritarian system', which, despite central political control, fosters regional economic innovations via a blend of experimentation and patronage networks. Unlike the Washington Consensus and the authors' proposed 'liberal democratic consensus', China and its financial institutions offer developing countries new financing avenues without demanding liberal economic or political reforms. This alternative financing avenue has led to stronger economic ties between China and Sub Saharan Africa, helping China to surpass North American and European countries and become the primary economic partner for many African countries. For instance, China has overtaken France as the main trade partner of Francophone Africa. There are similar trends in East Africa with China being the dominant infrastructure investment partner.

Given China's unique trajectory and developing countries' long-standing reluctance to adopt liberal institutions, it's worth questioning who upholds the authors' proposed consensus and how the liberal model is being challenged with Chinese influence. I would suggest a discussion of the non-liberal development path (e.g., Rwanda, Vietnam, Ethiopia) with large investment in infrastructure and education, a top-down approach building social cohesion, and a one-party state with internal factions.

The authors might find the SCRIPTS project of interest, which conducted a survey on perceptions of liberal models in various countries.[1]

II. From a typology of states to institutional diagnostics

Transitioning from a state typology to institutional diagnostics raises another point of contention. While categorising countries by similarities and ideal institutional models is insightful, labelling a country merely as a bundle of undifferentiated institutions is limiting.

Consider the United States, positioned at the right-most corner of the cluster analysis. Despite being labelled a 'common-interest state', this designation oversimplifies the complexities of its political and social landscape, marked by a gerontocratic elite, special interest-dominated politics, a highly polarised public, and limited distribution and social welfare.

This critique extends beyond the US; most nations display a mix of liberal and non-liberal institutions. The focus should shift from broad state assessments to detailed diagnostics identifying underperforming institutions, setting normative and empirical benchmarks for their operation, and charting pathways to improvement. This approach, which I term an analysis of 'political distortions', delves into the political incentives hindering optimal economic institution performance.[2]

This perspective is vital, as it not only reveals the current institutional equilibrium but also illuminates potential paths for transition. Encouraging institutional experimentation, as the authors acknowledge, may offer a more feasible route to reform than sweeping state overhauls, which are typically rare in history.

One challenge with the authors' conceptualisation of development clusters emerges when considering policy interventions. After all, political violence and state capacity co-evolve. Indeed, as they suggest, taxation and the protection of property rights may require peace, yet developing institutions that favour such rights also affect the likelihood of civil wars. Hence, which reforms should one target to affect both dimensions of development, when they are endogenous? One possible approach could target the initial sources of such disparities, including endowments or the prevalence of local information. Both affect local state capacity.[3] However, another approach could take the existing frictions (i.e., political distortions due to the historical, institutional and informational past) as given, and then consider which reforms may improve long-run development in this second-best world. These may include bureaucratic reform to merit-based appointments, information provision, or procurement reform.

The discussion above suggests another limitation of the authors' classification approach: it is based on an *ex-post* labelling. Like any clustering method, it is based on the similarity of observed data along multiple dimensions. However, the meaning of the groups is typically given after the classification, and might not remain if more clusters were considered, or if new data were to arise. Indeed, small changes to the data or measures used could significantly alter the groupings in Figure 16.1. There may even be alternative groupings that would be more useful for both policy purposes and classification.

III. From technocratic power to power to the people

Finally, the chapter's emphasis on the importance of norms and values in shaping effective institutions misses an opportunity to fully explore its implications. If cultural factors are crucial for state capacity, then we must scrutinise the often technocratic nature of capacity-building interventions. Development is unlikely to be a top-down process, akin to the Washington Consensus approach, but rather should incorporate institutional experiments that reflect and utilise local power dynamics, fostering state capacity from the ground up.

To sum up, the chapter by Besley and Persson rightly documents the massive transformation in development thinking across academic and policy circles in the last 35 years. Three main challenges stem from the authors' proposal to move forward. First, while liberalism is one natural candidate, alternative paths like that of China threatens its pre-eminence. Second, the interactions between capacity, the maintenance of order, and constraints to power seem to co-evolve, with very few nations able to advance in each one from a liberal path. Finally, while the fields of development and political economy have followed a micro trend (for example, Institutional Experiments), it remains to be seen how we could integrate results from a collection of studies to broader macro models and to actual state reform. All these topics remain an active field of research – one which the authors contextualise in this chapter.

Notes

1 Giebler et al. (2023).

2 Canen and Wantchekon (2022).

3 See de la Sierra (2020); Balán et al. (2022); Aman-Rana et al. (2023).

References

Aman-Rana, S., Minaudier, C. and Sukhtankar, S. (2023) 'Informal Fiscal Systems in Developing Countries', NBER Working Papers 31793, National Bureau of Economic Research. https://doi.org/10.3386/w31793

Balán, P., Bergeron, A., Tourek, G. and Weigel, J. L. (2022) 'Local Elites as State Capacity: How City Chiefs Use Local Information to Increase Tax Compliance in the Democratic Republic of the Congo', *American Economic Review*, 112(3): 762–97. https://doi.org/10.1257/aer.20201159

Canen, N. and Wantchekon, L. (2022) 'Political Distortions, State Capture, and Economic Development in Africa', *Journal of Economic Perspectives*, 36(1): 101–24. https://doi.org/10.1257/jep.36.1.101

de la Sierra R. S. (2020) 'On the Origins of the State: Stationary Bandits and Taxation in Eastern Congo', *Journal of Political Economy*, 128(1): 32–74. https://doi.org/10.1086/703989

Giebler, H., Antoine, L., Ollroge, R., Gerhards, J., Zürn, M., Giesecke, J. and Humphreys, M. (2023) 'The "Public Attitudes towards the Liberal Script" (PALS) Survey. Conceptual Framework, Implementation, and Data', SCRIPTS Working Paper No. 33. https://www.scripts-berlin.eu/publications/working-paper-series/Working-Paper-33-2023/SCRIPTS_Working_Paper_33.pdf

17. State capacity

Dan Honig, Adnan Khan and Joana Naritomi

The Washington Consensus had little to say regarding the internal functioning of the state beyond recognising the importance of securing property rights and general policies, such as 'broadening the tax base'. The past decades have seen significant advances towards understanding the determinants of state capacity. In this chapter we do not attempt to provide universal prescriptions, but identify a few general principles that we believe apply in all countries, irrespective of wealth or level of development. Effective governance requires more than merely setting correct policies; it demands a state's ability to implement, adapt, and learn over time. Drawing from historical and political economy perspectives, as well as contemporary managerial approaches, we examine the evolution and variation of state capacity, focusing on sectors like tax administration and health. State capacity is a process, not an event; hence medium-term commitment is critical, as is acting in the understanding of long-term constraints and environment. That process should begin with diagnostics of a particular place and goal, not universal prescriptions. Building state capacity involves a continuous process of, adaptation, and systemic learning; empowered agents, citizen-state trust, and iterative improvements are often key components of success. Ultimately, enhancing state capacity requires not only technical solutions but also alignment with political incentives and stakeholder motivations, recognising that a capable state is foundational to enabling citizens and markets to thrive.

How to cite this book chapter:

Honig, Dan, Khan, Adnan and Naritomi, Joana (2025) 'State capacity', in: Besley, Tim, Bucelli, Irene and Velasco, Andrés (eds) *The London Consensus: Economic Principles for the 21st Century*, London: LSE Press, pp. 573–614 https://doi.org/10.31389/lsepress.tlc.q

I. Introduction

The state matters for all policy outcomes of concern; however, the state's capacity to realise its objectives is frequently taken for granted. The Washington Consensus had little to say regarding the internal functioning of the state beyond recognising the importance of securing property rights and general policies, such as 'broadening the tax base'.[1] Getting the prices and policies right is indeed critical but their success depends on the ability of the state to implement and course-correct, to (re)organise and (re)adapt and innovate, and to alleviate constraints that hold back delivery by its own agents, the public servants, and by other actors, including citizens and private sector actors.

The ends that states have set themselves – and their capacity to achieve these – have co-evolved over time, responding to external and internal challenges (e.g., wars, pandemics, etc,) and changing preferences (e.g., delivering the range and quality of services comprising a modern, welfare state). Institutions, norms, and politics have influenced the decisions of states to invest in building capacities with longer-term payoffs, turning themselves into more cohesive entities that govern more effectively in all spheres: taxing, regulating, enforcing laws, organising and providing infrastructure, and delivering public goods and services.

Our analysis is informed by a literature that has made significant progress in the past decades towards understanding the determinants of state capacity. We note, in particular, work on the political economy of state building and development of state capacities.[2] This literature suggests that inclusive political institutions can help build an environment conducive to investing in state capacities. We are also aware of the literature on short-term managerial approaches and policy options that focus simply on results. We see much value in both these historical political economies and current managerial perspectives – and indeed, have variously contributed to these strands. We focus here on short-term policy prescriptions informed by long-term structural constraints (e.g., institutional features and incentive structures).

We begin this chapter by discussing the nature and variation of state capacity. We then turn to some stylised cases of state capacity strengthening, focusing variously on tax administration and the health sector. Drawing from these cases, we articulate a set of diagnostic principles and frameworks for understanding the nature of the state's abilities and how they might be strengthened in a particular place, for a particular end. We see this diagnosis as best conducted at the beginning, not the end, of the policymaking process.

While there are no universal prescriptions, we come up with a few general principles that we believe apply in all countries, irrespective of wealth or level of development. First, that state capacity is a process, not an event; hence medium-term commitment is critical, as is acting in the understanding of long-term constraints and environment. Second, cycles of learning, improvement, and iteration are also critical. The first attempt is unlikely to be perfect, and so designing a process for learning what is working, and for continuous improvement over time that incorporates system-level interactions, is essential. Third, every attempt to build capacity should begin with a diagnosis of the issue, organisations, state agents, citizens, and broader context – and only thereafter prescribe means of improvement. Finally, key to improving state capacity is not just action, but also agency. Who should have power over what is a question that must be asked. And this applies not just to implementing plans, but to adjusting and formulating them. In the end, state capacity can be understood as the state's ability to deliver 'to' citizens – but also its ability to enable markets and work with citizens to realise and support citizens' ends.

II. 'Capacities', not capacity: the state's abilities vary widely within states

State capacity, broadly defined, is the ability of the state to achieve its ends, for example, providing public services, enforcing laws, and regulating economic activity. In our view, this capacity to implement is not simply something to turn to after choosing the technically appropriate policy – the choice of *what* to do should begin with an understanding of state capacities and constraints. This will indicate the policy choices that will achieve the most at present given these constraints, and also the actions that will relieve some of these constraints in future, to enable the undertaking of more ambitious tasks. Capacity includes 'hard' capacity, such as tangible skills, know-how, and technical inputs. But it also encompasses 'soft' capacity – that is, management systems, bureaucrats' motivation and orientation, the abilities of (and state relations with) private and/or nonprofit contractors, and the state's relations with its citizens.[3] This includes citizens and state agents' trust of one another, and citizens' responsiveness or compliance with state requests.

Politics is inextricably bound up in what the state can, and in fact will, do. It is by no means always the case that political leaders *wish* for the state to develop capacity. The dysfunction in many states is by design – and not only in developing countries under kleptocratic regimes, such as in Mobutu's Zaire. 'American public bureaucracy is not designed to be effective', as Terry Moe put it; legislatures, executives, and other stakeholders may be unable to prevent a proposal they oppose from becoming policy, but still undermine its implementation.[4] In India, China, the US, Russia, and well beyond, we have myriad examples suggesting that in some cases degree of state incapacity may be due to interest groups not wishing to see that capacity exist.[5]

Inasmuch as capacity is the ability to execute, and not necessarily the actual use of that ability, it is also perfectly possible for the state to have capacities that political actors choose not to exercise. However, it is also possible for politics to serve as an enabler of changes that strengthen capacity. For example, new political configurations, or relations between citizens and state agents that enhance trust in the state can also unlock capacities previously thought beyond the scope of the possible.[6]

State capacity is in part a function of historical legacies that may be beyond the ability of even the most senior leaders to shape in the short term. State capacity is accumulated, and in some cases undermined, over time, because investments in acquiring such capacities have a long-term payoff. For instance, the ability of modern states to tax a large fraction of national income and provide the range of services required in a welfare state has been gradually built over the 20th century, with structural changes in the economy, politics, and the development of information and third-party reporting systems. The enforcement capacity of the state has gone hand in hand with enhanced compliance by citizens.[7]

That said, certain ingredients of state capacity are tractable to shorter-term intervention by current leadership. This includes both 'managerial' improvements, technology adoption, addressing market failures that hinder the private sector, and establishing deeper changes in relations between the state and its citizens. The capacity of governments to deliver welfare-enhancing public goods and services depends on how it employs labour and capital in its production function – but it also depends on interactions among and between state agents, politicians, citizens, and private and non-profit entities implementing on the government's behalf. If we want to improve the welfare of citizens, we must take this complexity seriously.

A given government does not so much have 'capacity' as it has 'capacities': different abilities, resources, dispositions, and strategies in service of different ends.[8] Improving state capacity requires engaging with specificity and thinking through particular challenges and contexts, including the tools available to the state to induce certain behaviours by bureaucrats, firms, and citizens.

These capacities vary not just across countries, but also within a given state, and even a given sector. This parallels variation in the constraints, the objectives, and in the people who act in the state's name – how they are managed, their orientation, their training, their oft-unobservable actions. Capacities vary to some extent all the way down to the smallest observable 'unit' of the state, the individual.[9] The state's ability to deliver is therefore a product of multiple factors, including: contextual factors, which include the implementation environment, technology and structural constraints; organisational factors, which encompass managerial practices and authority structures; and task factors, by which we mean the nature of the tasks themselves – their complexity, transaction intensiveness, and monitorability.

The internal workings of the state and its bureaucrats have become salient topics of research in social sciences in recent decades. See, for instance, work on the personnel economics of the state.[10] This growing body of work, often conducted in collaboration with governments through field experiments, has focused on incentive structures, selection, and monitoring. It has broadly validated the importance of incentives and selection in public sector settings, showing that public servants are responsive to incentives if they are well-designed, and that effective monitoring mechanisms can boost the ability of the state to deliver.

Prior research has also highlighted the importance of motivated bureaucrats and of harnessing their prosocial motivations in order to build mission-driven organisations. Effective public organisations work best when employees are devoted to the cause: where employees have internalised the organisational mission.[11] Contexts where this internalisation has not worked often produce dysfunctional organisations, marked by entrenched cultures of malfeasance and inefficiency that prove hard to shift as the identity, narratives, and norms around the dysfunction are mutually supportive, generating a locally stable belief system that undermines public welfare.[12]

Bureaucracies are complex organisations that ultimately comprise individuals but also capture how individuals and the units/organisations they operate in interact with each other, thus bringing in systems-level issues of organisational mission, coordination, and aggregation.

But the ability of the state to achieve its ends does not necessarily mean delivering through a central bureaucracy. Decentralisation to empower local and state governments can often improve the quality of governance, develop citizen trust in government, and promote local innovation – but it can also backfire by opening the door to elite capture. Literature suggests that whereas functions like infrastructure planning, financial regulation, and governance controls are a better fit for the central government, the transfer of certain functions to local units with upward accountability can work better for areas like local service delivery and community policing.

Monitoring of bureaucrats, citizens, and contractors is a key tool used by the state for effective enforcement. Where clear summary outcomes are available for the task in question, measuring those targets and providing rewards or penalties can be an effective strategy for inducing desired behaviour by citizens or those implementing work. In fact, a great majority of efforts to strengthen state capacity rely on improving monitoring and oversight, often mediated by technology.[13] However, this approach is limited when tasks are not fully monitorable by their nature, when monitoring systems are otherwise incomplete, or when sanctions are difficult or impossible to enforce *in situ*. In such cases, those seeking to bolster state capacity will often benefit from considering channels that do not rely exclusively on monitoring and enforcement.

At least in terms of the state's own personnel, it is clear that greater use of monitoring and incentives does not always achieve the best possible performance by bureaucrats. Importantly, there could be trade-offs between bureaucratic efficiency and curbing misuse of public funds that vary by contexts. In countries of varying income and corruption levels, and across a wide range of tasks, we have examples of improvements in state capacity stemming from management that seeks to grant autonomy and support, rather than monitor and control.[14] Much, of course, depends on the nature of what precisely the state wishes to accomplish; tasks that are more uncertain and harder to monitor see greater returns to this managerial approach.[15]

For some tasks, in some contexts, a key feature of state capacity is developing the ability to deliver through markets. Private sector firms have in many countries increasingly taken on activities once reserved for the state, such as transportation, communication, and sanitation infrastructure. As and where states engage private actors in the delivery of services, states must develop capacities for effective market development, financing, and regulation. The rise of private schooling and healthcare has also become one of the most important developments in service delivery in many developing countries, often in response to failures in public provision. In many cases, governments can respond productively by taking a systems-perspective and investing in public provision, while also lifting the market constraints that hold back better-quality private provision.[16]

Overall, building state capacity is a matter of both ability and will. It is not just a technical challenge because the question of ability is deeply enmeshed with the underlying incentive structures of the system. Thus, progress can be made when technical solutions are aligned with the incentives and capabilities of the stakeholders. For example, one case study of air pollution in Gujarat, India, found that it took independent backchecks to prove that the existing system of environmental auditors was corrupt.[17] This became the basis for a revised policy that addressed the underlying agency issues between the monitors and factory owners and was adopted at scale by the Pollution Control Board. In this case, capacity development was led by internal reform champions, and was supported by external pressure (judicial and civil society activism) and by collaboration with independent researchers.[18]

Sometimes the pathway for strengthening state capacity is clear: we know technologies exist that can reliably improve the functioning of the state in a given area, even if there are implementation challenges borne of, for example, information and monitoring problems, as well as political economy constraints. At other times, however, even the pathway via which improvement in state capacity might occur is unclear, or new problems emerge in implementing even known technologies. In such cases, attention should focus not on implementing a solution, but on building processes and environments in which constraints to better implementation can be identified and addressed.

III. How best to build state capacity – a complex and contingent question

In the past few decades, there have been significant advancements in our understanding of the micro and macro factors that play a critical role in shaping state capacity. In this section, we examine insights from recent research that apply to raising money, spending money, and delivering social services. These areas raise different challenges, and collectively highlight just some of the diverse range of tasks for which a state may seek to build capacity.

1. *Raising money*

Building fiscal capacity is at the heart of state capacity. Beyond raising revenue to fund policies, it can trigger a broader process of state building as it requires investments in bureaucracy and budgetary management and can lead to a governance dividend as citizens demand more from the government as a result.[19]

To establish a strong tax system, one must prioritise tax administration and make it a core component of policy discussions. A government's ability to generate revenue and the economic implications of the tax structure hinge heavily on tax compliance. Lower-income countries (LICs) tax a much smaller share of their gross domestic product (GDP) than higher-income countries, with the former taxing around 15% and the latter around 35%. This disparity may be attributed to weak state capacity, which affects enforcement levels, and the expectations of citizens towards the state. Countries that score high in government trust and tax morale typically tax a larger share of their GDP, reflecting a stronger social contract between the state and its citizens. Since this is seemingly absent or broken in many LICs, engaging with citizens on (re)building this social contract is complementary to building the enforcement capacity of the state.

The contrast between low- and high-income countries goes beyond differences in the levels of taxation over GDP: it also extends to the types of tax instruments that are used. Under weak enforcement, income taxes – the backbone of modern governments – can be difficult to implement. In the case of corporate income tax, the evidence suggests that costs are adjusted more easily than revenue.[20] Thus, a turnover tax could be preferable – especially for smaller firms – if there are concerns about cost adjustments eroding a tax on profits. For personal income, information trails from third-party reporting (e.g., from employers or the financial sector) have been shown to be crucial to prevent tax evasion across different contexts. Importantly, verifiable information on taxable transactions tends to increase with development.[21] In the case of Denmark, the structure of the economy, where well above 90% of income is third-party reported, could explain why there is so little income tax evasion. Indeed, the small share of income that is solely self-reported has an evasion rate above 40%.[22] Therefore, even the high-capacity Danish tax authority falls short from ensuring tax compliance in 'hard-to-tax' sectors that are a much larger share of the economy in lower-income countries. This highlights the commonality of the capacity challenges that countries face, which frequently differ in degree (or in this case, sectoral composition), not kind.

More broadly, the available evidence indicates that generating compliance depends on a crucial combination of traceable information on the tax base and a credible enforcement threat by the tax authority. The Value-Added Tax is possibly one of the best examples of how this combination can be powerful when it generates self-enforcing incentives along the supply chain.[23] It has also been shown that improving the credibility of enforcement can generate more revenue than increasing tax rates.[24] In fact, the evidence also suggests that better enforcement can change the Laffer curve – the inverted U-shape relationship between tax rates and tax revenue – by reducing the non-compliance margin. This can increase the highest tax rate than can be applied before entering the 'wrong side' of the Laffer curve, where revenues drop with higher tax rates.[25]

To enhance tax capacity, though, it is important to look beyond law enforcement efforts and consider the broader contextual constraints that can affect compliance rates. One of these constraints is the compliance cost incurred by taxpayers, particularly those who lack the necessary skills or resources needed to navigate complex tax legislation or adopt new technologies in tax filing or receipts issuance. Recent evidence has shown that in LICs, small taxpayers often leave money on the table by not fully utilising available deductions or exemptions. Instead, small taxpayers rely on compliance heuristics, where taxpayers with poor record-keeping declare taxable income that keeps them under the radar of the tax authority, even if it means paying more taxes than necessary.[26] Deductions or exemptions often exist due to efficiency or equity reasons, and educating taxpayers on how to take up benefits and reduce compliance costs is also a contribution to building tax capacity.

Another important aspect of tax capacity is how the tax system is specialised across levels of government. Decentralising tax collection can help leverage local information on the tax base that subnational entities may possess, and it can also strengthen the social contract and improve efficiency through a tax-benefit link, i.e., a virtuous cycle of tax compliance and the demand for and delivery of public goods. However, local governments in developing countries vary a great deal in terms of their ability to administer tax collection, and there is typically less decentralisation on the revenue side than on the spending side.[27]

Such contextual factors should be carefully considered for policy design. To some extent, this is exactly what many developing country governments already do: the limited use of modern tax tools, such as personal income taxation, could reflect the lack of information governments have about individual income. There is still room for policy advice and improvement, but understanding the local rationale for a 'bad tax' is an important first step to better optimise under constraints.

Similarly, contextual changes can affect the fiscal capacity of a government. Structural transformations in the economy – such as urbanisation, a change in employment across different income brackets, and advances in information technology can lead to changes in the information environment and enforcement capacity of the government. Furthermore, these changes can alter the demand for government assistance, as modern economies tend to invest more resources in social protection programmes and rely less on informal or community-based assistance schemes. Indeed, the increased presence of the state alone can change expectations and foster political participation.

It is also essential to note that improvement in tax capacity is not inevitable. Despite efforts to strengthen tax systems, several factors can hinder progress, such as political instability, corruption, weak institutional capacity, and lack of public trust in the government. Therefore, continuous and sustained efforts are necessary to build tax capacity and improve revenue collection.

A crucial part of this effort is to focus on the inner workings of the state. Effective taxation systems have gradually dealt with informality, capacity constraints, and low tax morale on the side of taxpayers, and have reformed tax administration over time by, among other things, monitoring and rewarding better performance, and in some cases by establishing specialised institutions like Large Taxpayer Units, which are dedicated to law enforcement for larger taxpayers, aiming to harness administrative efficiency.

2. *Public spending*

Once funds have been raised they must, of course, be spent to have any positive impact on citizens' welfare. Similarly to taxation, government spending capacity is also constrained by contextual factors. Low-income country governments operate in challenging environments, especially when it comes to implementing effective social transfer programmes. One of the main challenges is the scarcity of information on targeted beneficiaries, making it difficult to determine their income, employment status, and other indicators of need. Additionally, poor information systems and a lack of accountability can result in wasted resources. As a result, contextual constraints can restrict policy adoption and increase the likelihood of leakages in social transfer programmes.

These contextual factors, though, are dynamic and can change. Modern states not only raised their levels of spending but also its composition, provision, and quality. They also establish fiscal instruments to better assess public spending through fiscal rules and robust internal checks (e.g., Spending Reviews conducted by the United Kingdom Treasury), quasi-independent checks (e.g., the Office of Budget Review in the United Kingdom), and external checks (e.g., the Institute for Fiscal Studies in the United Kingdom, and other think-tanks).[28]

In all countries, government spending gives rise to concerns regarding inefficient management of public funds and the risk of waste and fraud. There is often an assumption that efficient public spending requires external monitoring and top-down control to make things better. This will often be true: monitoring efforts (e.g., audits of politicians' spending decisions) can and often do reduce fraud, particularly where the key features of the task are tractable to monitoring.[29]

One prominent recent example comes from the employment guarantee programme in India (NREGA), where reforms introducing electronic fund flow, reducing administrative tiers, and replacing advance payments with 'just-in-time' payments generated a substantive reduction in leakages.[30] The introduction of biometrically authenticated payments infrastructure delivered a faster, more predictable, and less fraud-prone NREGA.[31]

However, monitoring and control do not always produce the best possible public outcomes, nor even necessarily maximise value for money in government spending. The NREGA example is one in which monitorable outputs were tractable to technology-enabled top-down monitoring, with substantial welfare benefits.[32] But this is not always the case.

Indeed, more control is not always the best way to ensure better spending. In one study, providing procurement officers with greater authority and less monitoring in Punjab, Pakistan, was found to outperform attempts to tighten monitoring and reward those who met delivery targets with performance bonuses.[33] This is because many procurement officers are in fact more oriented towards achieving value for money for the state than their supervisors, who previously held greater authority.[34] Another study on public procurement of generic goods in Italy found that over 80% of all waste was passive – benefiting no one at all.[35] Moreover, a good deal of this passive waste was in fact the product of attempts to reduce active waste – side effects of a prescription to attack the disease of corruption with external controls and accounting-based monitoring.

That said, attempting to minimise active waste – corruption – while ensuring that the 'cure' is not causing more negative effects than the 'disease' is often a good starting point. The misuse of public funds for private ends undermines not just the state's ability to deliver, but also citizens' trust in the state and its agents.

3. *Delivering critical services: building capacity in the health sector*

There is a huge literature on health sector capacity, and we cannot do justice to it here. That said, one of the key things that emerges from examinations of health sector capacity building with broader applicability is the differential monitorability, and thus best routes to capacity strengthening, for different goals.

Vaccine delivery is one particularly easily observable and monitorable health task. Information and communications technology (ICT)-enabled tracking of vaccines and the health workers delivering them can assist in ensuring that vaccines are delivered. This is highly likely to lead to the public health outcome of individual and community immunity: the observable 'output' (i.e., a health worker delivering a jab in someone's arm) is very tightly coupled to the desired 'outcome' (someone is in fact vaccinated/resistant to the pathogen).

Other health tasks have almost none of these features. Take, for example, childhood wasting and stunting. A complex set of inputs – including nutrition, prenatal care for mothers, care during and immediately after childbirth, and antenatal care – plays an important part in a child's growth. Very few of these occur at only one point in time, which means they cannot be 'solved' in the same way a vaccination can be 'delivered'. The observable bits of what the state can do – for example, growth monitoring by doctors or community health workers – is only very weakly coupled with improved childhood thriving, as the desired result of those visits is often caregiver behaviour change over the days and weeks to come, which is far from guaranteed.

Both wasting and stunting and lack of access to vaccinations are the product of many contextual factors, some of which apply to both these health challenges. Two examples would be poverty and the long-term history of state development. Recent evidence shows the long shadow of colonial legacy in Central Africa; French health campaigns from that time still feed modern-day mistrust in health interventions, such as vaccination.[36] These contextual factors are difficult to change and should be considered carefully as part of the implementation process: the demand side for vaccines may not be there even if the state manages to deliver them. But when it comes to organisational factors that are amenable to short- or medium-term intervention – such as managerial changes and staff training – the differences in the nature of these two tasks suggest very different approaches.

Vaccine delivery capacity can be strengthened by 'accounting-based accountability': an accountability system focused on what can be observed and monitored.[37] Perhaps as a result, we have seen remarkable global progress in vaccine uptake and delivery, even in some of the world's poorest countries.

We have seen much less global progress on wasting and stunting. This is, perhaps, because conventional approaches to improving state capacity through monitoring are less well-suited to these types of interventions. Monitoring healthcare workers' attendance and rewarding them with financial incentives does not work in situations where it is hard to monitor healthcare workers' actions well enough, as in Rajasthan, India.[38] Or, as in Karnataka, India, it can simply displace fraud and waste from the limited range of tasks that can be well-monitored to those which cannot, resulting in little net performance improvement.[39]

Indeed, a study on community health workers in Khyber Pakhtunkhwa, Pakistan, showed that a pay-for-performance scheme was outperformed by an approach that focused on increasing the salience of their mission in ways plausibly linked to reducing stunting and wasting. The pay-for-performance scheme catalysed a greater number of home visits but achieved less in terms of child health outcomes – and did so at higher cost than the other approach, which focused on the people delivering the care and what drives them.[40]

4. *Different prescriptions for different policy domains and cases*

Fiscal capacity is one domain where the route to performance improvement is relatively clear, albeit challenging. While 'broadening the tax base' may still be sound advice, how to do it will hinge on reliable information on taxable transactions – preferably covered by third-party reporting – and on the extent to which government enforcement is a credible threat.

Enforcement capacity depends on the organisational structure of the state, such as the number of tax auditors, the incentives they face, and the technology that is used for collection.

Policy advice should, thus, consider that the tax structure of lower-income countries could reflect contextual constraints, such as labour market structure, informality, and the lack of financial intermediation, and that improvements in tax administration can often be more powerful than changes in the tax law. ICTs are rapidly changing the availability of information on the tax base and enforcement tools. For instance, evidence suggests that e-filing taxes can reduce evasion and extortion opportunities by tax collectors.[41]

There are clear pathways e.g., for improving tax enforcement, based on known technologies. In the health and education sectors, by contrast, a lack of state capacity may be a result in part of the fact that there are many possible pathways to address a given problem. We could begin with the observation that, in a given country, children in rural schools are learning very little, facilities are inadequate, and teachers are rarely in the classroom. It is far from obvious what the best way to address this challenge is; we believe a diagnostic step is necessary before proceeding to policy prescriptions.

Perhaps teachers are broadly unmotivated and will perform better if they are more tightly monitored and incentivised to show up in the classroom.[42] But perhaps the precise opposite is true, with teachers' non-attendance largely a consequence of inadequate facilities and an inability to do their job; they may not be unmotivated, but rather *de*-motivated. In the latter case providing teachers with greater autonomy, resources, and support may prove more effective in building state capacity and improving educational performance. This approach also has the advantage of not simply focusing on what can be easily monitored (e.g., attendance), perhaps at the expense of what cannot be so easily monitored (e.g., teaching quality conditional on attendance). It is also possible that state capacity can be more effectively built in other ways, for example, by empowering citizen oversight, or by building more trusting relationships between school officials and citizens. Over time, personnel management policies can differentially recruit, cultivate, and retain those public servants most oriented towards students' learning and holistic development.[43] The best way forward depends on the specifics of the case.

Relatively speaking, fiscal capacity building by its nature can be more easily addressed with a policy and decision structure that leaves control in the hands of senior leaders to diagnose difficulties and prescribe solutions. By contrast in other cases, as we have seen, improving performance may require more authority in the hands of those closest to the action, not simply to execute on policy but even to diagnose what is likely to work in a particular case. Sometimes capacity will be built best not from the top down, but rather from the bottom up. Sometimes capacity will be built not by increasing the state's ability to deliver, but rather the state's ability to empower citizens to make welfare-enhancing choices. Our view is that states are more capable where they facilitate citizens living lives those citizens prefer, which may include citizens choosing non-state provision of some services.[44]

While individual performance matters for service delivery, and we have made some progress towards understanding how to influence it, the bureaucracy and the public sector are a system and not just a collection of individuals. Thus, a systems perspective that captures system-level relationships between different tasks, units, and organisations provides a more solid underpinning to consider state capacity. Such a perspective deals with issues of complementarities across different inputs, coordination across agents, units and organisations, and aggregation of individual performance into organisational capability. A systemic perspective sometimes leads to counter-intuitive lessons. For example, enhancing individual capacities, say, through training, may undermine policy when organisational capability is weak. On the other hand, creating more rules to check the performance of front-line staff may backfire when the supervisors it empowers face greater agency issues.[45]

5. *The role of external actors*

State capacity is essentially an internal undertaking, though there is a legitimate role in supporting capacity strengthening by governments for external actors like foundations, bilateral development funding, and multilateral development organisations. But while there is a role for international expertise, it must be exercised with caution. It has now become obvious in theory, though not yet fully in practice, that state capacity cannot be built by copying 'best practices' from outside. There is much evidence that externally influenced institutional reforms frequently have limited effects due to poor fit with local context, perverse incentives, unrealistic timelines, and an excessive reliance on a narrow set of high-level champions.[46]

The political economy of external actors' provision of services is part of the problem, with purveyors of 'products' to improve state capacity, from IT systems to frameworks, looking to sell their services with the promise of quick, easy, general solutions to capacity strengthening challenges. In some circumstances donors and non-governmental organisations (NGOs) seeking to deliver services build parallel systems, in so doing undermine the very state they claim to be supporting. These parallel systems often have detrimental effects on state capacity by hiring away the most talented public servants.[47] And if roads, schools, and health clinics are provided by well-intentioned parallel systems, this may also undermine the social contract between citizens and the state.

The need for external actors is most clear in fragile states where state capacity breaks down and there is a need to build domestic security and governance with international support. Aid can help when it strengthens a legitimate, domestic government and when it is used to support private investment for job creation. What is critical is acknowledging existing constraints and avoiding long lists of unachievable targets based on over-ambitious expectations about current capacity. A step-by-step process is more likely to stabilise and catalyse capacity development in fragile states that have limited capacity and legitimacy to begin with, and where yielding quick, visible wins on popular initiatives can gain the legitimacy for undertaking more ambitious reforms. In such environments, focusing on processes is as important as on outcomes. However, such environments also present opportunities for capitalising on pivotal moments, such as a change of leadership or a major event, when transformative change is possible by resetting citizen expectations, building trust, and taking difficult decisions.[48]

Experts and researchers are another type of external actor that can have mixed effects on state capacity. These actors can add value when they study simple interventions that are tractable to clear empirical analysis, but also when they engage in longer-term engagements with policy actors that involve the diagnosis of problems, and that help build local academic and policy capacity. However, experts and consultants also run the risk of providing no useful insight on state functioning, while consuming what is in many countries arguably the scarcest of resources: the energy and attention of reform-minded policymakers and mission-driven bureaucrats.

NGOs, donors, and external experts can absolutely play useful roles. These actors do not *always* focus narrowly or on short-term results rather than the broader interests of the state; and even where these actors do focus on the short-term, the visible, and the empirically tractable, that *can* sometimes be aligned with what the state needs, and a useful part of a domestically led effort to strengthen capacity.

In particular, approaches that can align external actors in the position of supporting the diagnosis and problem solving of others show promise in building capacity. The UK National Endowment for Science, Technology, and the Arts' (Nesta's) 'People Powered Results' and the Harvard Building State Capability programme's 'Problem Driven Iterative Adaptation' are two prominent examples of such approaches.[49] That the Nesta offering targets domestic (UK) actors and the Harvard effort developing countries also highlights the broad potential applicability of approaches that centre the agency and knowledge of those already embedded in the system. Such efforts can potentially also put external actors in the position of supporting the agency of others, rather than – as is too often the case – providing particular prescriptions without a full understanding of context and constraints. The road of the past few decades is strewn with the remnants of Potemkin villages: capacity development programmes that ultimately accomplished little because they attempted to replicate structures, not address organisational and operational challenges *in situ*.[50] More can be done by domestic and international policymakers to build relevant capacities if they start with a careful diagnosis of contextual constraints and the state's current capacity. Thereafter, policy pilots and impact evaluations can be powerful aids to improve capacity.

External actors looking to help states deliver public goods might do well to begin not simply from an understanding of the gap between current and desired outcomes, but also an understanding of the current and potential future capacity of states and markets. This requires particular attention to the organisational structures, incentives, motivations, and relationships within state agencies, and between those agencies and the citizens they serve. The lack of such diagnostics is, in our view, one of the greatest shortcomings in building state capacity.

IV. Towards a state that serves its citizens better

The preceding sections underscore how the particular manner in which capacity can best be strengthened, which is contingent and contextual, depending on particular features of the context, task, and environment. This does not mean there are no general principles to be drawn, however. Here we articulate four such principles that emerge from the previous discussion and lie at the heart of how best to approach capacity development.

1. *Begin with diagnosis*

The changes that are likely to improve capacity are, as we have seen earlier, deeply contingent on context, task, and situation. Sometimes raising salaries or otherwise altering recruitment to attract more talented personnel is an excellent way to improve performance;[51] sometimes it is not. Sometimes monitoring clear summary targets and rewarding staff for meeting them will improve the performance of an agency; sometimes it is substantially inferior to simply giving frontline personnel more decision-making power, and even reducing monitoring.[52]

That there are no universal prescriptions underlines the importance of diagnosis that is specific to the place, task, function, and organisation/team whose performance one seeks to improve. Depending on what the reform seeks to achieve, there are a number of key elements that need to be understood in crafting specific reform efforts:

Human resources

- *Selection:* How are public agents currently being selected? What do the actors in the system *want,* and what might other actors recruited into the system want? How can the prosocial motivation of public agents be harnessed or encouraged to build mission-oriented organisations?
- *Incentives:* What are workers currently being rewarded for, and how well aligned is that with the full range of actions and behaviours they are meant to engage in?

- *Monitorability:* Is the information needed for effective monitoring easily accessed? Can the task be summarised in measures you can monitor effectively? Is monitoring likely to lead to distortions of effort? Are there other ways of monitoring or redistributing the tasks to separate out the monitorable and unmonitorable goals we may wish to accomplish?[53]

Interactions of actors, markets, constraints

- *Power and autonomy*: Who holds power over whom and what, and in what ways does that need to change? Who is driving improvement and reform processes? Who ought to hold control over what? On what timescale do results need to be achieved? What are the time horizons of current reform leaders?
- *Accountability:* What is the current accountability regime – who is accountable, to what authorities, and in what manner? Can the direction of accountability be productively shifted towards other actors, such as peers or citizens? Can different accountability tools, such as technology-enabled monitoring or managerial/reporting approaches that allow the exercise of greater judgement and agency, increase capacity and improve performance?
- *State-citizen relations:* What kinds of interactions with citizens exist, or could exist, which are likely to improve performance?[54]
- *Political constraints, enablers, and context:* What are the bounds of the politically possible? If they do not incorporate actions that seem necessary for capacity strengthening, can they be shifted?

These are only a subset, of course, of the relevant dimensions we may wish to think through before moving forward.

Sometimes those seeking to craft reforms will face trade-offs. For example, a pay-for-performance scheme may yield harder working agricultural extension personnel, but at the cost of intrinsic motivation, camaraderie, and some distortions of effort towards the monitorable. At other times there will be no such trade-offs; it may be that agricultural extension's best available performance flows from a managerial approach that focuses on attracting and retaining mission-motivated personnel, with fewer target-induced distortions.

Optimal reform flows from context-specific considerations and assessments. There are no general answers, only general questions – which may apply in London, UK, just as they do in Lilongwe, Malawi.

2. *Capacity building is a process nested in long-term constraints*

Whatever reform a diagnosis suggests, it is rare that it will succeed in precisely the way anticipated or will not lead to new challenges. This requires continuous investments and medium-term commitment to improvement. This is true even for those changes that can be implemented and have effects relatively quickly. It is all the more true for the many possible paths to state capacity improvement that will only see results in the medium term. It is thus important to be realistic about the time horizon.

Such paths might involve changing structural, institutional or political constraints, but also may include improving skills training or altering citizens' expectations and understanding of their roles vis-à-vis the state, for example, regarding tax compliance, or whether police can be trusted with sensitive information. Measures to build information systems that enable better enforcement and greater efficiency and equity, and measures to enable markets for public provision to function, for example, in education and health, are also a part of the process.

Importantly, capacity building is neither an inevitable nor a linear process. It has been shown, for instance, that changes of political leadership in the electoral cycle generate bureaucratic turnover leading to substantive disruptions in public service delivery.[55] Thus, politics can help or hinder investments in state capacity, as discussed in Chapter 16 of this volume.

3. *Engage in continuous learning and adaptation, and leverage systemic interactions*

Following the first two principles on the importance of diagnostics and process, this principle highlights the need to do all of the above on a continuous basis, with the lessons incorporated through adaptations to organisational practices and structure. We must learn as we go. Sometimes this will mean the use of pilots and formal studies, including, where possible, randomised controlled trials. At others, it will be much more informal and rapid, closer to 'agile' management principles of rapidly cycling through different possible solutions and improving them, usually with a central team of frontline employees and, where possible, citizens operating with support from higher-level political authorities. The key is to learn and improve. Undertaking systematic impact evaluations can wield significant power in enhancing capacity.

This learning needs to go beyond fixing determinants of individual performance. A systemic perspective captures issues of complementarities, coordination, aggregation, and unintended consequences. As an attempt at improvement takes hold, the diagnosis upon which it was initially designed will also shift. Citizens, politicians, bureaucrats, and others will change their behaviour, and as such thinking of how to create virtuous cycles of improvement is worth consideration. Whatever is attempted, a learning and adjustment process ought to accompany it. This requires building institutional memory of policies and evaluations, gathering data, and investing in a bureaucracy with analytical skills.

4. *Empower actors and build trust*

Attempts to build capacity often begin and end with what behaviours need to be altered by whom. But if capacity building is cumulative, then careful consideration is needed regarding who it is that drives change. This goes beyond simply who should have the right to make decisions on delivery, for example, granting more or less autonomy to frontline actors, and cuts to the issue of who ought to hold power over the reform *process*.

While external actors have a role, building state capacity must be led by internal actors. It is *only* the leaders and citizens of a country that can legitimately lead this process. Genuine ownership by national leaders is critical because transformational change depends on the actions they choose, and their ability to ensure citizen compliance. But it is equally critical not to over-emphasise the role of top-down leadership. Indeed, the best possible configuration for driving reform is not for it to flow down from a donor or executive office at the top of government, but rather for it to incorporate all those who have a role to play in improving the desired function. This will almost always include frontline bureaucrats and the citizens with whom they interact. While it helps to gather information from these groups, frequently the best possible configuration will involve shifting power and agency to them, so that they themselves can drive and own the reform.[56]

V. Conclusion

The COVID-19 pandemic pointed up the importance of rethinking our approach to capacity – and indeed highlighted a fundamental and global misunderstanding of what capacity actually is. The response and performance of different countries in the event did not in many cases match the various measures and indicators of their preparedness for a pandemic.[57]

We cannot simply wish away the current constraints to reforms. These have persisted for a reason. But optimising what is feasible and setting up an organic, adaptive approach helps gradually relax those constraints so that more ambitious policies become possible. Timing matters, because unrealistic expectations about the pace of progress can make the process all the more fragile.

Implementation is not a residual item to be handled as an afterthought – a gap to be traversed only after choosing the proper policy – but rather as an integral part of the policy process. An understanding of the state's current and possible future capacities is in our view the place from which policymaking should begin; the soil in which the seeds of a better tomorrow might be planted.

There are no universal answers on how to proceed in building capacity, but this does not mean there is nothing to be learned. In this chapter, we have described what we believe represents a consensus of principles and approaches, not one of discrete policy prescriptions.

Capacity is ultimately held by individuals and the systems that organise them. These humans and their agency and motivations have often been treated as a 'bug', not a 'feature' of attempts to strengthen state capacity. If there is one clear takeaway from the past decades of attempts and failures to strengthen state capacity, it is that we should start with an understanding of the individuals who make up the state. Consider empowerment, not just monitoring, of those individuals when you seek to strengthen the state. Personnel are policy – they are also capacity. Ultimately, the state will only be as strong as the actions they take.

Building state capacity *is* possible. Sometimes desired reforms will be beyond the boundary of the politically possible; but often, in our collective experience and reading of the literature, they are not. Much can be done to improve the state's abilities to deliver to its citizens, with reality often far short of the frontier of what it is politically and technically possible to achieve. But improvement requires a careful and critical understanding of the particulars of the terrain. For any actor seeking to galvanise reform, the road ahead is a long one; but it is one worth traversing, one which has a fair chance of improving the functioning of the state. A better world is possible – and it begins in no small part with improving the state's capacities, in working with and for citizens to call that better world into existence.

Acknowledgements

We are grateful to many for comments which informed this draft, particularly Matt Andrews, Ernesto Dal Bo, Pavithra Suryanarayan, Martin Williams, and participants at a conference at LSE in May 2023.

Notes

[1] Our contribution to the London Consensus seeks to explore insights that we believe may be relevant for developing and developed countries alike. We neither believe in the necessity of a new 'consensus' to replace the Washington Consensus where the Global North 'solves' problems for the Global South, nor do we consider ourselves to be articulating one.

[2] For example, Acemoglu and Robinson (2012), Besley and Persson (2011) and in this volume.

[3] In other work, one of the authors (Honig) explored the nature and impacts of 'Relational State Capacity', the nature of a state's interactions and broader relations with its citizens; see Honig et al. (2024).

[4] Moe (1989).

[5] See Suryanarayan (2024) for an overview of this literature.

[6] See for example the work of Ostrom (2000), or Tendler (1997).

[7] Levi (1988) terms this as 'quasi-voluntary compliance'.

[8] As Williams (2021) puts it, 'capacity is a convenient shorthand term [which] achieves this convenience by abstracting away from the mechanisms that determine bureaucratic performance and policy implementation'.

[9] e.g., Best et al. (2023) uncover massive variation in prices paid and spending quality in Russian procurement by individual and organisation. The Global Survey of Public Servants (GSPS); Fukuyama et al. (2022) finds substantial variation by country and agency in orientation and workplace experience of public servants; Honig (2021) finds systematic features of these relationships, with e.g., bureaucrats' motivation seemingly a function of managerial environment.

[10] Finan et al. (2017); Besley et al. (2022).

[11] e.g., Honig et al. (2025). In the economics literature, this has echoes of 'mission match' in the sense of Besley and Ghatak (2005).

[12] Collier (2016); Khan and Roy (2022).

[13] Honig et al. (2025); McDonnell (2020).

[14] Bandiera et al. (2021); Grindle (1997); Khan (2023); McDonnell (2020); Tendler (1997). Some of these document high state capacity in equilibrium, rather than improvements in capacity. See Honig et al. (2025) for a fuller discussion.

[15] Honig (2018); Rasul and Rogger (2018).

[16] Andrabi et al. (2022).

[17] Duflo et al. (2013).

[18] Pande and Datla (2016).

[19] See Besley and Persson (2009); Weigel (2020); Gadenne (2017); Martinez (2023).

[20] See Best et al. (2015); Bachas and Soto (2021); Carrillo et al. (2017).

[21] Jensen (2022).

[22] Kleven et al. (2011).

[23] Pomeranz (2015); Naritomi (2019).

[24] Basri et al. (2021).

[25] Bergeron et al. (2024).

[26] Tourek (2022); Almunia et al. (2022).

[27] Gadenne and Singhal (2014).

[28] See e.g., Berwick and Christia (2018) for a review of the literature on this as it relates to state capacity.

[29] Ferraz and Finan (2011).

[30] Banerjee et al. (2020).

[31] Muralidharan et al. (2016).

[32] Even in this case, there is some dispute; Honig et al. (2025) has an illustrative case of an NREGA auditor who discusses how process compliance undermines the social purpose of the work, as distinct from the process of delivering payments.

[33] Bandiera et al. (2021).

[34] On 'honest principals' higher up the hierarchy, see e.g., Rothstein (2021); on agents' orientation towards the public good see e.g., Besley and Ghatak (2005); Honig et al. (2025); Perry (2021).

[35] The paper in question is Bandiera et al. (2009).

[36] Lowes and Montero (2021).

[37] Honig and Pritchett (2019).

[38] Banerjee et al. (2008).

[39] Dhaliwal and Hanna (2017).

[40] Khan (2023).

[41] Okunogbe and Pouliquen (2022).

[42] Duflo et al. (2012).

[43] See Aiyar et al. (2021) for an example in this spirit; Duflo et al. (2012) and Aiyar et al. (2021)'s implicitly contrasting policy prescriptions are set in Indian schools.

[44] This view is informed by work on schooling in Pakistan, e.g., Carneiro et al. (2024); Andrabi et al. (2020; 2022).

[45] Pritchett et al. (2012); Bandiera et al. (2021).

[46] Pritchett et al. (2012).

[47] Deserranno et al. (2024).

[48] LSE-Oxford Commission on State Fragility, Growth and Development (2018).

[49] 'People Powered Results' is an initiative of Nesta, a UK foundation. 'Problem Driven Iterative Adaptation' is a toolkit developed by the Harvard Kennedy School.

[50] Andrews (2013); Andrews et al. (2017).

[51] Ashraf et al. (2020); Dal Bó et al. (2013).

[52] Bandiera et al. (2021).

[53] e.g., task clustering as a response to multitask problems; Dewatripont et al. (1999) in light of Holmstrom and Milgrom (1991).

[54] e.g., by providing implementation-relevant information; feedback on performance; co-creation and implementation of policy; via interaction with front-line workers sources of motivation and/or accountability for public servants.

[55] Akhtari et al. (2022) show that political party transitions generate higher rates of personnel turnover in schools in Brazil hurting academic performance as reflected in lower test scores.

[56] This follows from Aghion–Tirole's Real vs. Formal Authority (Aghion and Tirole, 1997) and has plenty of empirical support in capacity improvement contexts; see e.g., Andrews et al. (2017); Honig (2018); Tendler (1997).

[57] e.g., the Global Health Security Index (2019) did not do a great job at performance during the pandemic perhaps because it focused on quantifiable and visible indicators and not on measures of citizen compliance. Besley and Dray (2021) explore the role of government and private action during the COVID-19 pandemic. Also see Golden et al. (2023) for results of a prediction competition with the best performing model combining both physical measures and citizen-state relationships.

References

Acemoglu, D. and Robinson, J. A. (2012) *Why Nations Fail: The Origins of Power, Prosperity and Poverty* (pp. 45–47), London: Profile.

Aghion, P. and Tirole, J. (1997) 'Formal and Real Authority in Organizations', *Journal of Political Economy*, 105(1): 1–29. https://doi.org/10.1086/262063

Aiyar, Y., Davis, V., Govindan, G., and Kapoor, T. (2021) 'Rewriting the Grammar of the Education System: Delhi's Education Reform. A Tale of Creative Resistance and Creative Disruption', RISE Programme. [25 Nov]. https://riseprogramme.org/publications/rewriting-grammar-education-system-delhis-education-reform-tale-creative-resistance.html

Akhtari, M., Moreira, D. and Trucco, L. (2022) 'Political Turnover, Bureaucratic Turnover, and the Quality of Public Services', *American Economic Review*, 112(2): 442–493. https://doi.org/10.1257/aer.20171867

Almunia, M., Hjort, J., Knebelmann, J. and Tian, L. (2022) 'Strategic or Confused Firms? Evidence from "Missing" Transactions in Uganda', *Review of Economics and Statistics*, 106(1): 256–265. https://doi.org/10.1162/rest_a_01180

Andrabi, T., Das, J., Khwaja, A.I., Özyurt, S. and Sing, N. (2020) 'Upping the Ante: The Equilibrium Effects of Unconditional Grants to Private Schools', *American Economic Review*, 110(10): 3315–3349. https://doi.org/10.1257/aer.20180924

Andrabi, T., Bau, N., Das, J. and Khwaja, A. I. (2022) 'Heterogeneity in School Value-Added and the Private Premium', RISE Working Paper 22/116, RISE Programme. [Nov]. https://riseprogramme.org/sites/default/files/2022-11/Heterogeneity_School_Value-Added_Private_Premium.pdf

Andrews, M. (2013) *Limits of Institutional Reform in Development: Changing Rules for Realistic Solutions*, Cambridge: Cambridge University Press. https://doi.org/10.1017/CBO9781139060974

Andrews, M., Pritchett, L. and Woolcock, M. (2017) *Building State Capability: Evidence, Analysis, Action*, Oxford: Oxford University Press. https://doi.org/10.1093/acprof:oso/9780198747482.001.0001

Ashraf, N., Bandiera, O., Davenport, E. and Lee, S. S. (2020) 'Losing Prosociality in the Quest for Talent? Sorting, Selection, and Productivity in the Delivery of Public Services', *American Economic Review*, 110(5): 1355–94. https://doi.org/10.1257/aer.20180326

Bachas, P. and Soto, M. (2021) 'Corporate Taxation under Weak Enforcement', *American Economic Journal: Economic Policy*, 13(4): 36–71. https://doi.org/10.1257/pol.20180564

Bandiera, O., Prat, A. and Valletti, T. (2009) 'Active and Passive Waste in Government Spending: Evidence from a Policy Experiment', *American Economic Review*, 99 (4): 1278–1308. https://doi.org/10.1257/aer.99.4.1278

Bandiera, O., Best, M. C., Khan, A. Q. and Prat, A. (2021) 'The Allocation of Authority in Organizations: A Field Experiment with Bureaucrats', *The Quarterly Journal of Economics*, 136(4): 2195–2242. https://doi.org/10.1093/qje/qjab029

Banerjee, A., Duflo, E. and Glennerster, R. (2008) 'Putting a Band-aid on a Corpse: Incentives for Nurses in the Indian Public Healthcare System', *Journal of the European Economic Association*, 6(2-3): 487–50. https://doi.org/10.1162/JEEA.2008.6.2-3.487

Banerjee, A., Duflo, E., Imbert, C., Mathew, S. and Pande, R. (2020) 'E-Governance, Accountability, and Leakage in Public Programs: Experimental Evidence from a Financial Management Reform in India', *American Economic Journal: Applied Economics*, 12(4): 39–72. https://doi.org/10.1257/app.20180302

Basri, M. C., Felix, M., Hanna, R. and Olken, B. O. (2021) 'Tax Administration versus Tax Rates: Evidence from Corporate Taxation in Indonesia', *American Economic Review*, 111(12): 3827–71. https://doi.org/10.1257/aer.20201237

Bergeron, A., Tourek, G. and Weigel, J. (2024) 'The State Capacity Ceiling on Tax Rates: Evidence from Randomized Tax Abatements in the DRC', *Econometrica*, 92(4): 1163–1193. https://doi.org/10.3982/ECTA19959

Berwick, E. and Christia, F. (2018) 'State Capacity Redux: Integrating Classical and Experimental Contributions to an Enduring Debate', *Annual Review of Political Science*, 21: 71–91. https://doi.org/10.1146/annurev-polisci-072215-012907

Besley, T. and Dray, S. (2021) 'Institutions, Trust and Responsiveness: Patterns of Government and Private Action During the COVID-19 Pandemic', *LSE Public Policy Review*, 1(4): 1–11. https://doi.org/10.31389/lseppr.30

Besley, T. and Ghatak, M. (2005) 'Competition and Incentives with Motivated Agents', *American Economic Review*, 95(3): 616–636. https://doi.org/10.1257/0002828054201413

Besley, T. and Persson, T. (2009) 'The Origins of State Capacity: Property Rights, Taxation, and Politics', *American Economic Review*, 99(4): 1218–1244. https://doi.org/10.1257/aer.99.4.1218

Besley, T. and Persson, T. (2011) *Pillars of Prosperity: The Political Economics of Development Clusters*, Princeton, NJ: Princeton University Press. https://doi.org/10.23943/princeton/9780691152684.001.0001

Besley, T., Burgess, R., Khan, A. and Xu, G. (2022) 'Bureaucracy and Development', *Annual Review of Economics*, 14: 397–424. https://doi.org/10.1146/annurev-economics-080521-011950

Best, M., Brockmeyer, A., Kleven, H., Spinnewijn, J. and Waseem, M. (2015) 'Production vs Revenue Efficiency with Limited Tax Capacity: Theory and Evidence from Pakistan', *Journal of Political Economy*, 123(6): 1311–1355. https://doi.org/10.1086/683849

Best, M. C., Hjort, J. and Szakonyi, D. (2023) 'Individuals and Organizations as Sources of State Effectiveness', *American Economic Review*, 113(8): 2121– 2167. https://doi.org/10.1257/aer.20191598

Carneiro, P., Das, J. and Reis, H. (2024) 'The Value of Private Schools: Evidence from Pakistan', *Review of Economics and Statistics*, 105(6): 1301–1318. https://doi.org/10.1162/rest_a_01237

Carrillo, P., Pomeranz, D. and Singhal, M. (2017) 'Dodging the Taxman: Firm Misreporting and Limits to Tax Enforcement', *American Economic Journal: Applied Economics*, 9(2): 144–164. https://doi.org/10.1257/app.20140495

Collier, P. (2016) 'The Cultural Foundations of Economic Failure: a Conceptual Toolkit', *Journal of Economic Behavior & Organization*, 126(Part B), 5–24. https://doi.org/10.1016/j.jebo.2015.10.017

Dal Bó, E., Finan, F. and Rossi, M. A. (2013) 'Strengthening State Capabilities: The Role of Financial Incentives in the Call to Public Service', *The Quarterly Journal of Economics*, 128(3): 1169–1218. https://doi.org/10.1093/qje/qjt008

Deserranno, E., Nansamba, A. and Qian, N. (2024) 'The Impact of NGO-Provided Aid on Government Capacity: Evidence from Uganda', *Journal of the European Economic Association*. 361–395. https://doi.org/10.1093/jeea/jvae029

Dewatripont, M., Jewitt, I. and Tirole, J. (1999) 'The Economics of Career Concerns, Part II: Application to Missions and Accountability of Government Agencies', *The Review of Economic Studies*, 66(1): 199–217. https://doi.org/10.1111/1467-937X.00085

Dhaliwal, I. and Hanna, R. (2017) 'The Devil Is in the Details: The Successes and Limitations of Bureaucratic Reform in India', *Journal of Development Economics*, 124: 1–21. https://doi.org/10.1016/j.jdeveco.2016.08.008

Duflo, E., Hanna, R. and Ryan, S. P. (2012) 'Incentives Work: Getting Teachers to Come to School', *American Economic Review*, 102(4): 1241–1278. https://doi.org/10.1257/aer.102.4.1241

Duflo, E., Greenstone, M., Pande, R. and Ryan, N. (2013) 'Truth-Telling by Third-Party Auditors and the Response of Polluting Firms: Experimental Evidence from India', *The Quarterly Journal of Economics*, 128(4): 1499–1545. https://doi.org/10.1093/qje/qjt024

Ferraz, C. and Finan, F. (2011) 'Electoral Accountability and Corruption: Evidence from the Audits of Local Governments', *American Economic Review*, 101(4): 1274–1311. https://doi.org/10.1257/aer.101.4.1274

Finan, F., Olken, B.A. and Pande, R. (2017) 'The Personnel Economics of the Developing State', in Banerjee, A., Duflo, E. (eds) *Handbook of Economic Field Experiments*, Vol. 2, Amsterdam: North-Holland: 467–514. https://doi.org/10.1016/bs.hefe.2016.08.001

Fukuyama, F., Rogger, D. Hasnain, Z., Bersch, K., Mistree, D., Schuster, C., Mikkelsen, K., Kay, K., et al. (2022), Global Survey of Public Servants Indicators,. www.globalsurveyofpublicservants.org/indicators

Gadenne, L. (2017) 'Tax Me, But Spend Wisely: Sources of Public Finance and Government Accountability', *American Economic Journal: Applied Economics*, 9(1): 274–314. https://doi.org/10.1257/app.20150509

Gadenne, L. and Singhal, M. (2014) 'Decentralization in Developing Economies', *Annual Review of Economics*, 6(1): 581–604. https://doi.org/10.1146/annurev-economics-080213-040833

Global Health Security Index (2019) 'GHS Index: Building Collective Action and Accountability'. https://ghsindex.org/wp-content/uploads/2019/10/2019-Global-Health-Security-Index.pdf

Golden, M., Slough, T., Zhai, H., Scacco, A., Humphreys, M., Vivalt, E., Diaz-Cayeros, A., Dionne, K. Y., et al. (2023) 'Gathering, Evaluating, and Aggregating Social Scientific Models of COVID-19 Mortality', Working Paper. https://doi.org/10.2139/ssrn.4570855

Grindle, M.S. (1997) 'Divergent Cultures? When Public Organizations Perform Well in Developing Countries', *World Development*, 25(4): 481–495. https://doi.org/10.1016/S0305-750X(96)00123-4

Holmstrom, B. and Milgrom, P. (1991) 'Multitask Principal–Agent Analyses: Incentive Contracts, Asset Ownership, and Job Design', *The Journal of Law, Economics, and Organization*, 7(special_issue): 24–52. https://doi.org/10.1093/jleo/7.special_issue.24

Honig, D. (2018) *Navigation by Judgment: Why and When Top-down Management of Foreign Aid Doesn't Work*, Oxford, UK: Oxford University Press. https://doi.org/10.1093/oso/9780190672454.001.0001

Honig, D. (2021) 'Supportive Management Practice and Intrinsic Motivation Go Together in the Public Service', *Proceedings of the National Academy of Sciences*, 118(13): e2015124118. https://doi.org/10.1073/pnas.2015124118

Honig, D. (2024) *Mission Driven Bureaucrats. Empowering People To Help Government Do Better*, Oxford, UK: Oxford University Press. https://doi.org/10.1093/oso/9780197641194.001.0001

Honig, D. and Pritchett, L. (2019) 'The Limits of Accounting-Based Accountability in Education (and Far Beyond): Why More Accounting Will Rarely Solve Accountability Problems', Working Paper 510, Center for Global Development. https://www.cgdev.org/sites/default/files/limits-accounting-based-accountability-education-and-far-beyond-why-more-accounting-will.pdf

Honig, D., Krishnamurthy, M. and Sharma, K. R. (2025) 'Relational State Capacity: Conceiving of Relationships as a Core Component of Society's Ability to Achieve Collective Ends', Working paper. https://snfagora.jhu.edu/wp-content/uploads/2025/01/SNF-Agora-Working-Paper-01_Relational-State-Capacity-2.pdf

Jensen, A. (2022) 'Employment Structure and the Rise of the Modern Tax System', *American Economic Review*, 112(1): 213–234. https://doi.org/10.1257/aer.20191528

Khan, M. and Roy, P. (2022) 'Making Anti-corruption Real: Using a 'Power Capabilities and Interest Approach' to Stop Wasting Money and Start Making Progress', Synthesis Report 001. SOAS University of London and SOAS-ACE (Anti-Corruption Evidence). [Jun]. https://ace.soas.ac.uk/wp-content/uploads/2022/06/ACE-SynthesisPaper001-MakingAntiCorruptionReal-1.pdf

Khan, M. Y. (2023) 'Mission Motivation and Public Sector Performance: Experimental Evidence from Pakistan', Working Paper. [23 Oct]. https://y-khan.github.io/yasirkhan.org/muhammadyasirkhan_jmp.pdf

Kleven, H. J., Knudsen, M. B., Kreiner, C. T., Pedersen, S. and Saez, E. (2011) 'Unwilling or Unable to Cheat? Evidence from a Tax Audit Experiment in Denmark', *Econometrica*, 79(3): 6516–92. https://doi.org/10.3982/ECTA9113

Lowes, S. and Montero, E. (2021) 'The Legacy of Colonial Medicine in Central Africa', *American Economic Review*, 111(4): 1284–1314. https://doi.org/10.1257/aer.20180284

Levi, M. (1988) *Of Rule and Revenue*, Berkeley and Los Angeles, CA: University of California Press.

LSE-Oxford Commission on State Fragility, Growth and Development (2018). https://www.bsg.ox.ac.uk/research/commission-state-fragility-growth-and-development

Martínez, L. R. (2023) 'Natural Resource Rents, Local Taxes, and Government Performance: Evidence from Colombia', *Review of Economics and Statistics*, 1–28. https://doi.org/10.1162/rest_a_01324

McDonnell, E. M. (2020) *Patchwork Leviathan: Pockets of Bureaucratic Effectiveness in Developing States*, Princeton, NJ: Princeton University Press. https://doi.org/10.23943/princeton/9780691197364.001.0001

Moe, T. M. (1989) 'The Politics of Bureaucratic Structure', in Chubb, J. and Peterson, P. (eds) *Can the Government Govern?* Washington, DC: Brookings.

Muralidharan, K., Niehaus, P. and Sukhtankar, S. (2016) 'Building State Capacity: Evidence from Biometric Smartcards in India', *American Economic Review*, 106(10): 2895–2929. https://doi.org/10.1257/aer.20141346

Naritomi, J. (2019) 'Consumers as Tax Auditors', *American Economic Review*, 109(9): 3031–3072. https://doi.org/10.1257/aer.20160658

Okunogbe, O. and Pouliquen, V. (2022) 'Technology, Taxation, and Corruption: Evidence from the Introduction of Electronic Tax Filing', *American Economic Journal: Economic Policy*, 14(1): 341–72. https://doi.org/10.1257/pol.20200123

Ostrom, E. (2000) 'Collective Action and the Evolution of Social Norms', *The Journal of Economic Perspectives*, 14(3), 137–158. http://www.jstor.org/stable/2646923

Pande, R. and Datla, A. (2016) 'Fighting Pollution with Data: Environment Audits and the Gujrat Pollution Control Board', HKS Case 2054. Harvard Kennedy School. https://www.hks.harvard.edu/sites/default/files/centers/mrcbg/programs/sustsci/files/Pande_2016_Gujarat_HKS_Case_2054.pdf

Perry, J. L. (2021) *Managing Organizations to Sustain Passion for Public Service*, Cambridge, UK: Cambridge University Press. https://doi.org/10.1017/9781108915236

Pomeranz, D. (2015) 'No Taxation without Information: Deterrence and Self-Enforcement in the Value Added Tax', *American Economic Review*, 105(8): 2539–69. https://doi.org/10.1257/aer.20130393

Pritchett, L., Woolcock, M. and Andrews, M. (2012) 'Looking Like a State: Techniques of Persistent Failure in State Capability for Implementation', *The Journal of Development Studies*, 49(1): 1–18. https://doi.org/10.1080/00220388.2012.709614

Rasul, I. and Rogger, D. (2018) 'Management of Bureaucrats and Public Service Delivery: Evidence from the Nigerian Civil Service', *The Economic Journal*, 128(608): 413–46. https://doi.org/10.1111/ecoj.12418

Rothstein, B. (2021) *Controlling Corruption: The Social Contract Approach*, Oxford: Oxford University Press. https://doi.org/10.1093/oso/9780192894908.001.0001

Suryanarayan, P. (2024) 'Endogenous State Capacity', *Annual Review of Political Science*, 27(1): 223–243. https://doi.org/10.1146/annurev-polisci-061621-084709

Tendler, J. (1997) *Good Government in the Tropics*, Johns Hopkins University Press. https://doi.org/10.56021/9780801854521

Tourek, G. (2022) 'Targeting in Tax Behavior: Evidence from Rwandan Firms', *Journal of Development Economics,* 158(3): 102911. https://doi.org/10.1016/j.jdeveco.2022.102911

Weigel, J. L. (2020) 'The Participation Dividend of Taxation: How Citizens in Congo Engage More with the State When It Tries to Tax Them', *The Quarterly Journal of Economics,* 135(4): 1849–1903. https://doi.org/10.1093/qje/qjaa019

Williams, M. J. (2021) 'Beyond State Capacity: Bureaucratic Performance, Policy Implementation and Reform', *Journal of Institutional Economic,* 17(2): 339–357. https://doi.org/10.1017/S1744137420000478

Response to Dan Honig, Adnan Khan and Joana Naritomi by Matthew Andrews

I. Optimism, and my comments

Dan Honig, Adnan Khan, and Joana Naritomi (hereafter HKN) provide the most important chapter in this venerable volume. It reminds us that states are central to everything that other authors in the book propose, and that the consensuses these other authors identify as key to addressing the world's problems depend on having states with the capacity needed to get things done. HKN are also optimistic about building such states, exclaiming that, 'Building state capacity *is* possible', and that, 'A better world is possible – and it begins substantially in improving the state's capacities, in working with and for citizens to call that better world into existence'.

This conclusion comes from a discussion of themes HKN identify about state capacity in the political economy and public management literatures, mostly after the Washington Consensus was proposed, in the early 1990s. They argue that this consensus did not suggest a specific approach to state capacity, and that work since then also offers no hard prescriptions about what state capacity is or how it can or should be developed. They do suggest, however, that emergent thinking has yielded 'a few general principles' that apply 'in all countries'. According to these principles:

1. States require multiple capacities.
2. These capacities are contingent on many factors, such as the type of challenges that states face, and the political and administrative space they must inhabit.
3. They need to be built through iterative and contextual discovery processes.
4. And they must emphasise local agency, with local people – including politicians, technocrats, street-level bureaucrats, and citizens – driving the discovery process, benefiting from all discoveries, and owning and building on the capacities that emerge.

This perspective – and the optimism evident throughout HKN – inspired me. It also got me thinking about how much the ideas they propose really influence state building activities across the world. This commentary captures such thoughts. It is not intended as a research piece and does not therefore provide traditional citations or methodological references. It also does not try to synthesise or otherwise refer to existing literature, and should not be seen as a contribution to the literature. It does, however, reflect my thoughts on the state of state capacity building work after three decades of practice, research, and observation.

II. An emergent 'Contingent Capacities Consensus'

When combined, I see the principles HKN identify informing a particular logic or way of thinking about state capacity. In the spirit of this volume, I will label this logic the 'Contingent Capacities Consensus'. I suspect that this is a much more formal moniker than HKN would probably accept; but I am personally excited to recommend it. I subscribe to the way this consensus suggests we should think about state capacity. And I do see it gaining traction.

I observe first that it offers a strong explanation of prominent state capacity building initiatives that appear to have led to sustained performance improvements, such as Singapore's economic miracle of the 1970s, and Rwanda's more recent success in developing its primary healthcare system. These stories involve the kinds of discovery processes HKN allude to, where local agents worked with the grain of local politics (no matter how messy) and with and through local administrative mechanisms (no matter how weak) to create new and more effective ways of getting things done.

Like HKN, I have also observed that local people are central to building state capability. Leadership stories are at the heart of all the cases I study about states that built their capacities to do great things. This leadership is seldom about just one leader, but instead involves many agents taking risks to effect change, often – or even always – against the odds. Such leadership typically spans time, space, and interests – crossing generations, sectors, professions, political affiliations, and the many other differences that can thwart change. As HKN imply, mobilising agency of this kind is hard but possible and seems vital to the process of building state capacity.

And I believe that HKN are right to note that state capacity comes – of necessity – in many forms; and that these forms are contingent on many things. My research regularly shows, for instance, that states considered to have higher capacity often look quite different from one another, exhibiting various ways of doing similar things because of their unique historical, political, and administrative realities. These varying realities make different forms of working, deciding, and delivering not just possible but necessary.

My research also shows that states need the capacity to tightly manage certain tasks or activities they face, such as technical and procedural aspects of monetary policy and service delivery work, but must also be able to foster more flexible creativity in others – particularly those that involve novelty, such as attracting investors to new sectors of economic engagement. Indeed, I often observe that states get into trouble when they either tightly or flexibly manage everything they do – exhibiting a one-best-way approach to building capacity – or when they match the wrong management style to the wrong task.

Finally, I agree with HKN that this kind of 'Contingent Capacities Consensus' is a source of optimism. Such thinking is not only useful in explaining past success stories. It is also helping structure current and future-focused strategies to build state capacities. I have been developing such a strategy with colleagues like Lant Pritchett, Michael Woolcock, and Salimah Samji for over a decade. It is based on an approach to capacity or capability building called Problem Driven Iterative Adaptation and has proved effective in helping many actors build capacities needed to better address their challenges. A host of related approaches have been deployed to help do similar things in other contexts, including adaptive management practices, such as Rapid Results, Human Design Thinking, and Agile. These approaches show that the emergent 'Contingent Capacities Consensus' is not just a way of thinking or talking about building state capacity – it is also a way of doing the capacity building itself!

III. A competing 'Copy-Ready Capacity Consensus'

I find that many people working in states (and on state building) around the world are very receptive to versions of the Contingent Capacities Consensus. However, I also find that the most influential entities in this space do not adhere to or promote such thinking in their work – or support the discovery approaches it implies as central to building state capacities. Instead, their understanding about state capacity and state building derives from a competing logic or consensus of thought. I call this the 'Copy-Ready Capacity Consensus'. This holds that a state's capacity depends on the formal rules, mechanisms and procedures it follows – and that there are generally applicable good or best practices that all states can and should copy. According to such thinking, we can evaluate a state's capacity by assessing its uptake of internationally accepted best practices. And we can improve a state's capacity by increasing its uptake of these practices.

As I see it, this way of thinking about state capacity emerged at about the same time as the Washington Consensus. It was influenced by the New Institutional Economics emphasis on formal institutions, the New Public Management focus on adopting private sector management practices in the public sector, and a growing best practice movement in the world economy, seen clearly in management schools, development organisations, and consultancies.

I observe this consensus in the many indicators now commonly used to measure government effectiveness and capacity. These indicators are applied both at the level of states as a whole and also for parts of states, for example, in the tax, budgeting, and health examples discussed by HKN. The indicators usually ask if and to what extent governments have adopted generally accepted good or best formal practices (like whether a tax bureau is independent or if a budget covers multiple years). The evidence of adoption (or lack thereof) is then used to reflect the government's capacity, quality or effectiveness. This reinforces the view that capacity can be defined by the degree to which a state's formal structures comply with 'copy-ready' 'best' practices.

Connected to the focus on indicators, I also observe this consensus in the common nature of best practice reforms and processes in governments across the world. In keeping with the sectors that HKN review, my research has shown that many governments have taken steps to adopt generic best practice solutions like independent revenue agencies, large taxpayer bureaus, electronic revenue systems, programmatic policymaking processes, multi-year budgets, health management information systems, and more. These governments seem to believe the narrative that state capacity is about the mechanisms they adopt, and that the best practice mechanisms on offer from development organisations, and public sector consultancies will give them the capacity they need. Accordingly, the governments continue adopting these practices even when evidence shows that the practices often do not work.

IV. A battle of state capacity consensuses

I see the dominance of the Copy-Ready Capacity Consensus in the high rates of best practice adoption in governments across the world. For example, a few years ago I investigated the extent to which a sample of 60 national governments used formal programmatic policy tools in allocating finances to policy alternatives in budgeting and implementation. Drawing on surveys of a highly varied set of countries, I found the legal uptake was between 70% and 90%, meaning that the great majority of countries had laws requiring that the same tools be used. I followed up by surveying 240 officials working in different parts of the same governments, asking if they used the required tools when doing their policy work. Over 70% of the responses affirmed this was the case, and all responses showed an awareness of the language associated with such tools.

This evidence suggests that the same best practice policy and budgeting process is formally required across a wide set of highly different countries – and that the Copy-Ready Capacity Consensus has significant influence over the way governments think about doing policy work, which is itself a key state capacity. It is not what one would expect if a version of the Contingent Capacities Consensus were to influence how governments build their policy capacities. Rather, such thinking would have led me to expect different ways of doing this work across different governments and even within governments, given the contingent nature of effective capacity.

My survey of the 240 officials also asked if the best practice programmatic policy tools they were required to use were actually useful – and whether the officials departed from using these tools in any routine manner. Answers to these questions were illuminating, with over two-thirds answering that the formal procedures were of moderate to no use and describing significant and routine departures from their use. Over 60% of the officials noted that they departed from using the tools because of political pressures. Over 40% said that they did not have the necessary competence, information, or time to use the tools properly. Over 30% said that the tools required a level of certainty in planning and budgeting that was not possible for the kind of work they were doing.

Such evidence suggests – at least to me – that the budgeting and policy capacities needed to do actual policy work differ by place and activity. People need to navigate their way through contextually peculiar challenges to do this work, discovering the necessary capacities as they progress. This seems to support the thinking implied in the Contingent Capacities Consensus. By contrast, it seems at odds with the Copy-Ready Capacity Consensus that state capacity can be built by formally adopting a one-size-fits-all set of best practices.

This example points to what I believe is a battle between competing ways of thinking about state capacity, and how it can and should be built. HKN identify an emergent way of thinking in the Contingent Capacities Consensus that I believe aptly describes how states really work in practice, and how capacities are really built. But the more dominant Copy-Ready Capacity Consensus continues to influence how most governments and development organisations actually try to build capacity. To really have a positive impact, the Contingent Capacities Consensus will have to overcome the Copy-Ready Capacity Consensus. Until that happens, I fear the world will still struggle with states that look like they should have more capacity than they do.

Response to Dan Honig, Adnan Khan and Joana Naritomi by Ernesto Dal Bó

The policy recommendations of the Washington Consensus were not contingent on national circumstances, such as state capacity. This was a serious drawback, because low state capacity limits the ability to design and implement policy.

The search for a new consensus must grapple with two issues. One is to characterise more precisely how state capacity constrains policy. The other is how to increase state capacity. Dan Honig, Adnan Khan, and Joana Naritomi (henceforth, HKN) offer a valuable perspective on the second problem, based on a wealth of personal experience and research.

I will briefly summarise their main messages, and then argue that those messages put political economy considerations centre stage. To make my argument, I will identify three trade-offs studied in political economy in connection to policymaking broadly understood. Once we take HKN's messages seriously, those trade-offs will be seen to apply to the process of building state capabilities.[1]

I. HKN's main messages

The authors emphasise four aspects of how state capabilities are developed.

First, state capabilities are not developed through a single foundational event, but through a process of steady improvement of everyday practices.

Second, the capability-building process is iterative, so it not only takes time, but is 'alive' in that it involves learning and adaptation. This message may seem to simply restate the idea that learning-by-doing is important. But I will argue that in policymaking (and capability building more specifically) learning and doing are often in conflict.

Third, in developing state capabilities we must pay attention to agency and power. State agents and citizens have their own goals and the ability to affect outcomes. This message matches the tradition in political economy of paying attention to the incentives and profiles of public servants. I will argue this focus highlights two additional trade-offs as particularly relevant for the process of capacity building.

Fourth, the authors recommend starting with a diagnosis. But how to diagnose? I trust that the trade-offs I highlight provide a useful checklist of what to watch out for.

II. Three trade-offs

1. *Learning vs doing*

If learning matters for state capacity, policymaking should produce actionable evidence about what works, and adjust policy accordingly. Two problems will stand in the way. First, policymakers may not want to adjust policy based on evidence because doing so is politically costly. Costs may arise from constituencies that were created or empowered by the policy. Or they may arise if adjustment suggests the officials in charge were wrong the first time around. The career concerns of bureaucrats and politicians have motivated a robust literature suggesting that officials acting strategically may alter their effort or policy choice.[2]

The second problem arises from intertemporal considerations. Most initiatives to strengthen capabilities come with different mixes of immediate effects and future learning returns. The temporal mismatch separates what is optimal from what officials consider attractive. Officials will prefer projects that promise quick wins before the next election or round of promotions – especially if these wins are easily attributable to the policymaker even if the learning returns are low. Conversely, projects that yield valuable learning may be passed over when their lessons would mainly benefit the policymaker's successor.

The political economy literature has long studied how policymaking distortions arise from intertemporal strategic motives, and how they can affect investments in state capacity.[3] Such motives appear to be empirically relevant. A large literature has documented the existence of political budget cycles and the fact that term limits affect policy choices and corruption.[4] Research I contributed to has shown that, as effort resembles an investment with delayed yields, longer legislative terms *raise* legislative effort.[5]

HKN do well to emphasise the value of learning, but the trade-off between learning and doing highlights the need to pay attention to the delayed arrival of evidence and the costs of acting on it. One promising aspect of integrating learning and attention to evidence into capacity building is that positive evidence may insulate good programmes politically – and this is something non-clientelistic programmes often need.

2. *Accountability vs insulation (or autonomy) – and why it is important to select the right people*

HKN's third message underscores the importance of incentives and authority among agents in the public sector. One solution to incentive problems is intense scrutiny. Classic models of electoral accountability show that politicians can be disciplined through frequent elections, and empirical evidence supports the usefulness of elections coupled with monitoring.[6] The bureaucracy, in turn, can be placed under tight legislative control, and thus be held indirectly accountable to voters.

These forms of accountability come with costs. As mentioned above with regard to politicians, longer term lengths imply looser accountability but actually raise legislative effort. When it comes to the bureaucracy, limiting the scope for political control can also be beneficial. For example, civil service protections reduce the scope for congress to discipline bureaucrats, but also insulate state personnel against political interference.[7] When such protections are absent, political cycles can harm service delivery.[8] At a more qualitative level, a recent review of case studies on developing state capabilities in Latin America suggested that successful experiences went hand in hand with insulation from politics.[9] Such insulation likely helped in at least two ways. One, by allowing better control over resources and lengthening effective time horizons. And two, by producing a less politicised working environment that helped attract better personnel.

When it is difficult to evaluate performance, one way to curb incentive problems is to track inputs and procedures. But this can lead bureaucrats to become unduly concerned with compliance, as they avoid being caught in unjustifiable positions. A self-regarding bureaucrat will seek to maximise justifiability, not policy impact.

For that reason, it may not be surprising that a study of management practices in the public sector in Nigeria found that more autonomy is associated with higher project completion rates, while the opposite is true under stronger incentives and monitoring.[10] Work in progress by Fernandez et al. shows that tighter procedural controls harm public sector performance in Brazil.[11] These tensions are relevant in the developed world as well. Observers of state functioning in the United States argue that internal compliance requirements hinder effectiveness.[12]

Incentive problems create a strong tension between accountability and insulation. This tension can be alleviated by selecting better people. A literature in political economy studies the determinants and implications of selection in politics and the bureaucracy.[13] Selecting high-ability personnel improves state capacity directly by improving the quality of labour. Selecting personnel with integrity and concern for organisational mission improves state capacity indirectly by relaxing the accountability versus insulation trade-off.

3. *Top-down vs bottom-up – from state capacity to citizen capacity*

HKN's emphasis on process, learning, and agency may suggest de-emphasising top-down approaches to developing capabilities. But developing capabilities demands coordination, which is more easily done from the top, and taking advantage of human capital, which may also be more available at the top.

The top-down approach promises accountability by placing policy implementation (e.g., by agencies) under the supervision of a political authority that is accountable to voters (e.g., congress). A bottom-up approach is more direct: it enlists lower-tier managers, end-users, and other private actors in implementation and evaluation. There is evidence that lower-level public sector managers hold valuable information about how to deploy resources, although they may have less than perfect information and possibly biased preferences.[14] That said, decentralisation will present challenges when the gradient of human capital along the state hierarchy is steep, especially if a mismatch with that of private actors facilitates abuse or state capture.

The scope of citizen engagement may also have to be carefully delimited. A theoretical literature on pandering showed that whenever voters hold the wrong priors about policy, the choices of officials will be distorted.[15] And research in political economy suggests that voters can hold the wrong priorities when they learn with mis-specified models, have trouble engaging in hypothetical thinking, or under-appreciate equilibrium effects.[16]

Bottom-up approaches create more direct channels of accountability and increase decentralisation. There are gains to reap—but bottom-up approaches also raise coordination challenges and make state capabilities more dependent on the capabilities of lower-tier agents and citizens.

III. Conclusion

HKN highlight aspects of state capabilities that present challenges shared with other policy domains. Future reflection should engage in the complementary exercise of identifying aspects that are distinct to building state capabilities. An advantage of the approach taken by HKN is that we can use established knowledge in political economy to identify critical tensions in the process of strengthening state capabilities. This should help build the diagnostic tools that the authors call for.

Notes

1 I will use the terms 'capacity' and 'capabilities' interchangeably. The meanings are distinct, but they do not matter for the purposes of this note.

2 See, for example, Dewatripont et al. (1999); Alesina and Tabellini (2007); Canes-Wrone et al. (2001); Maskin and Tirole (2004); Prat (2005); Besley and Smart (2007); Smart and Sturm (2013).

3 See, for example, Persson and Svensson (1989); Alesina and Tabellini (1990); Besley and Coate (1998); and Besley and Persson (2011).

4 See Alesina et al. (1992) for an early contribution regarding political budget cycles. The effect of term limits on policy choices and corruption has been highlighted by Besley and Case (1995) and Ferraz and Finan (2011), respectively.

5 Dal Bó and Rossi (2011).

6 See Barro (1973); Ferejohn (1986); and Avis et al. (2018).

[7] Foy (2024).

[8] Akhtari et al. (2022).

[9] Cornick et al. (2018).

[10] Rasul and Rogger (2018).

[11] Fernandez et al. (2022).

[12] Pahlka (2023).

[13] See Besley (2005); Dal Bó and Finan (2018); Finan et al. (2017); and Besley et al. (2022) for reviews.

[14] Duflo et al. (2018); Dal Bó et al. (2021).

[15] See Canes-Wrone et al. (2001); Maskin and Tirole (2004); and Prat (2005).

[16] See Esponda and Pouzo (2016); Esponda and Vespa (2014); and Dal Bó et al. (2018).

References

Akhtari, M., Moreira, D. and Trucco, L. (2022) 'Political Turnover, Bureaucratic Turnover, and the Quality of Public Services', *American Economic Review*, 112(2): 442–93. https://doi.org/10.1257/aer.20171867

Alesina, A. and Tabellini, G. (1990) 'A Positive Theory of Fiscal Deficits and Government Debt', *The Review of Economic Studies,* 57(3) 403–414. https://doi.org/10.2307/2298021

Alesina, A. and Tabellini, G. (2007) 'Bureaucrats or Politicians? Part I: A Single Policy Task', *American Economic Review,* 97(1): 169–179. https://doi.org/10.1257/aer.97.1.169

Alesina, A., Cohen, G. and Roubini, N. (1992) 'Macroeconomic Policy and Elections in OECD Democracies', *Economics & Politics*, 4: 1–30. https://doi.org/10.1111/j.1468-0343.1992.tb00052.x

Avis, E., Ferraz, C. and Finan, F. (2018) 'Do Government Audits Reduce Corruption? Estimating the Impacts of Exposing Corrupt Politicians', *Journal of Political Economy,* 126(5): 1912–1964. https://doi.org/10.1086/699209

Barro, R. (1973) 'The Control of Politicians: An Economic Model', *Public Choice*, 14: 19–42. https://doi.org/10.1007/BF01718440

Besley, T. (2005) 'Political Selection', *Journal of Economic Perspectives*, 19(3): 43–60. https://doi.org/10.1257/089533005774357761

Besley, T. and Case, A. (1995) 'Does Political Accountability Affect Economic Policy Choices? Evidence From Gubernatorial Term Limits' *The Quarterly Journal of Economics,* 110(3): 769–98. https://doi.org/10.2307/2946699

Besley, T. and Coate, S. (1998) 'Sources of Inefficiency in a Representative Democracy: A Dynamic Analysis', *American Economic Review*, 88(1): 139–56. https://www.jstor.org/stable/116822

Besley, T. and Persson, T. (2011) *Pillars of Prosperity*, Princeton, NJ: Princeton University Press. https://doi.org/10.1515/9781400840526

Besley, T. and Smart, M. (2007) 'Fiscal Restraints and Voter Welfare', *Journal of Public Economics* 91(3–4): 755–773. https://doi.org/10.1016/j.jpubeco.2006.09.009

Besley, T., Burgess, R., Khan, A. and Xu, G. (2022) 'Bureaucracy and Development', *Annual Review of Economics,* 14: 397–424. https://doi.org/10.1146/annurev-economics-080521-011950

Canes-Wrone, B., Herron, M. and Shotts, K. (2001) 'Leadership and Pandering: A Theory of Executive Policymaking', *American Journal of Political Science*, 45(3): 532–550. https://doi.org/10.2307/2669237

Cornick, J., Dal Bó, E., Fernández-Arias, E., Rivas, G. and Stein, E. (eds) (2018) 'Building Capabilities for Productive Development', Inter-American Development Bank https://publications.iadb.org/en/building-capabilities-productive-development

Dal Bó, E. and Finan, F. (2018) 'Progress and Perspectives in the Study of Political Selection', *Annual Review of Economics,* 10: 541–575. https://www.annualreviews.org/content/journals/10.1146/annurev-economics-080217-053221

Dal Bó, E. and Rossi, M. (2011) 'Term Length and the Effort of Politicians', *The Review of Economic Studies*, 78(4): 1237–1263. https://doi.org/10.1093/restud/rdr010

Dal Bó, E., Dal Bó, P. and Eyster, E. (2018) 'The Demand for Bad Policy when Voters Underappreciate Equilibrium Effects', *The Review of Economic Studies,* 85(2): 964–998. https://doi.org/10.1093/restud/rdx031

Dal Bó, E., Finan, F., Li, N. and Schechter, L. (2021) 'Information Technology and Government Decentralization: Experimental Evidence from Paraguay', *Econometrica,* 89(2): 677–701. https://doi.org/10.3982/ECTA17497

Dewatripont, M., Jewitt, I. and Tirole, J. (1999) 'The Economics of Career Concerns, Part II: Application to Missions and Accountability of Government Agencies', *The Review of Economic Studies,* 66(1): 199–217. https://doi.org/10.1111/1467-937X.00085

Duflo, E., Greenstone, M., Pande, R. and Ryan, N. (2018) 'The Value of Regulatory Discretion: Estimates from Environmental Inspections in India', *Econometrica*, 86(6): 2123–2160. https://doi.org/10.3982/ECTA12876

Esponda, I. and Pouzo, D. (2016) 'Berk–Nash Equilibrium: A Framework for Modeling Agents with Misspecified Models', *Econometrica,* 84(3): 1093–1130. https://doi.org/10.3982/ECTA12609

Esponda, I. and Vespa, E. (2014) 'Hypothetical Thinking and Information Extraction in the Laboratory', *American Economic Journal: Microeconomics,* 6(4): 180–202. https://doi.org/10.1257/mic.6.4.180

Ferejohn, J. (1986) 'Incumbent Performance and Electoral Control', *Public Choice,* 50: 5–25. https://doi.org/10.1007/BF00124924

Fernandez, G., Martínez, S., Moreira, D., Naritomi, J. and Leite, B. (2022) 'State Paralysis: The Impact of Compliance Uncertainty on Government Effectiveness'. https://www.socialscienceregistry.org/trials/9821

Ferraz, C. and Finan, C. (2011) 'Electoral Accountability and Corruption: Evidence from the Audit of Local Governments', *American Economic Review*, 101: 1274–1311. https://doi.org/10.1257/aer.101.4.1274

Finan, F., Olken, B. and Pande, R. (2017) 'The Personnel Economics of the Developing State', in Banerjee, A. and Duflo, E. (eds) *Handbook of Economic Field Experiments*, Vol 2, Elsevier; 467–514. https://doi.org/10.1016/bs.hefe.2016.08.001

Foy, M. (2024) 'When Individual Politics Become Public: Do Civil Service Protections Insulate Government Workers?', *American Economic Journal: Applied Economics*, 16(3): 292–322. https://doi.org/10.1257/app.20220723

Maskin, E. and Tirole, J. (2004) 'The Politician and the Judge: Accountability in Government', *American Economic Review,* 94(4): 1034–1054. https://doi.org/10.1257/0002828042002606

Pahlka, J. (2023) *Recoding America: Why Government is Failing in the Digital Age and How We Can Do Better*, Abingdon: Macmillan.

Persson, T. and Svensson, J. (1989) 'Why a Stubborn Conservative would Run a Deficit: Policy with Time-Inconsistent Preferences', *The Quarterly Journal of Economics,* 104(2): 325–34. https://doi.org/10.2307/2937850

Prat, A. (2005) 'The Wrong Kind of Transparency', *American Economic Review*, 95(3): 862–877. https://doi.org/10.1257/0002828054201297

Rasul, I. and Rogger, D. (2018) 'Management of Bureaucrats and Public Service Delivery: Evidence from the Nigerian Civil Service', *The Economic Journal,* 128: 413–446. https://doi.org/10.1111/ecoj.12418

Smart, M. and Sturm, D. (2013) 'Term Limits and Electoral Accountability', *Journal of Public Economics*, 107: 93–102. https://doi.org/10.1016/j.jpubeco.2013.08.011

Afterword

Pranab Bardhan

The following comments are a response to the London Consensus as a whole but focus on a select set of relatively neglected topics, mainly involving different types of governance issues that are of particular interest to me. Instead of a detailed analysis I shall here only indicate the broad themes and some of the relevant literature.

I. Local commons, not just global commons

The issue of global climate change has been rightly emphasised. This will affect vast numbers of people, particularly in poorer parts of the world that have little financial capacity to cope with such problems, which are mainly not of their own making. However, there is a whole range of other environmental problems that affect their daily lives and livelihoods and in which the local community has somewhat more direct responsibility. I have in mind problems involving local forests and fisheries, irrigation and drinking water, grazing lands, local air pollution, and soil erosion, etc. While none of these problems is entirely local or unconnected from global environmental problems, it is worth highlighting that some of them may arise from local failures of community organisations and accountability processes.

To understand why such local failures are prominent in some parts of the world, while in others there are successful community efforts, one has to delve deep into socio-economic and cultural factors. I have, for example, empirically studied the question of why in irrigation communities in south India some communities succeed in resolving water conflicts and others do not. In my statistical study[1] of 48 irrigation communities I find that the underlying inequality in land distribution and the prevalence of what I call 'exit options' (i.e., the opportunity to move, say to urban areas, out of the prevailing norms and conventions of cooperation in the village) negatively affect the ability to resolve conflicts in the management of local environmental issues.[2] Many such management issues have been discussed in the context of both rich and poor countries, showing that the 'tragedy of the commons' is not an inevitable outcome, and that there are also cases of happy endings, as analysed in the collection of essays put together by Ostrom et al.[3] The manifold relation between local inequality and environmental sustainability in the context mainly of developing countries has been explored in Baland et al.[4]

II. Decentralisation of governance and local civic organisations

The importance of local governance and civic management has also been demonstrated by the failures of centralised governance to handle the growing complex of problems arising in our polity, economy, and society – often precisely because it neglects to tap the reservoir of local information, initiative, and ingenuity.

In recent populist movements against distant bureaucracies 'take back control' has been a common refrain; decentralisation of governance is one way local people can try to achieve this. But the debate on decentralised governance goes back decades. Even apart from the widely debated issues of subsidiarity and devolution in the European Union, and of states' rights in the United States, decentralised governance has been at the centre of policy experiments in many developing countries.[5]

To give one example, Brazil had introduced a participatory budgetary process (with citizens' direct input in budgeting and investment priorities) in a substantial fraction of municipalities. Sónia Gonçalves subsequently showed, using data from all Brazilian municipalities between 1990 and 2004, that municipalities adopting such a budgetary process increased spending on health and sanitation significantly more than those that did not, and that this had sizeable effects on outcomes like infant mortality.[6] Many agree that this is an innovative and potentially empowering process that could be replicated elsewhere. It is not, however, easy to undertake. New York sought to establish its own participatory budgeting programme, but its achievements were limited by lack of voter participation and knowledge. Technology can help here, as in the city of Reykjavik, Iceland, where an online platform allows residents to suggest how money should be spent, and the majority of them participate. At its best, this kind of local programme has feedback effects on democracy itself: citizens participate more in civic affairs when they see they can have an effect. Estonia and Taiwan are often cited as good examples of 'digital democracy'.

Yet, as the decentralisation literature makes abundantly clear, much depends on the structures of power at the local level and the opportunities for democratic participation among common people. Even in rich countries there is often too much insider control in local bodies for zonal restrictions or professional licensing, resulting in 'not in my backyard'-type resistance to new projects. There are many cases, in rich and poor countries alike, where it is easier for the elite or the oligarchs to capture the local than the central government, and where corruption and malfeasance can proliferate. As the underlying socioeconomic conditions vary from one area to another, chances of elite capture of local governments vary accordingly. One may think of possible institutional safeguards in the form of various accountability mechanisms, such as: contested local elections; transparency of budgeting procedures; public provision of information; and oversight by citizen councils, judicial authorities, auditors, or media.

Local governments in poor countries are also afflicted by a lack of finance and administrative capacity. Many federal or provincial governments are unwilling to devolve powers and funds to local governments, leaving a gap between decentralisation on paper and in reality it is not uncommon for higher-level governments to devolve responsibilities for social services to the lower level without a corresponding devolution of funds or personnel – the notorious 'unfunded mandates'. Given the low taxable capacity at the local level in many poor countries, substantial financial devolution from above is thus imperative.[7] In financial devolution it is often recommended that unconditional grants to local governments – with random audits after the fact – may be the best way to ensure enough local autonomy and flexibility and yet some external discipline. And in addition to local public finance reform, one needs an overhaul of local democratic processes, and administrative and police reform.

III. Restoring trust in institutions of representation and governance

In recent years, distrust of institutions of representative government has grown. This has led to proposals to improve democratic deliberation by choosing at least one chamber of the legislature through 'sortition', i.e., random selection of lay citizens. Such proposals have emerged in Australia, the United Kingdom, Belgium, Iceland, and elsewhere. In their book, John Gastil and Erik Olin Wright bring together a range of ideas about implementing sortition, without obscuring its limitations, and examine its potential for reshaping modern politics of representation.[8] On a smaller scale, a citizens' assembly was used effectively in Ireland in 2016–17 to deliberate on controversial issues such as abortion rights and come to some sort of resolution.

In developing countries, the loss of public trust in democratic institutions is associated with rampant corruption and widespread cynicism about the possibility of doing anything about it. There is a large literature on corruption. Analysts have distinguished between grand corruption and petty corruption. Grand corruption involves large-scale political deals in which substantial sums of money are exchanged between politicians (and their official accomplices) and those who seek their favour, often in the business world (and including organised crime in some countries). Petty corruption refers to smaller-scale malfeasance mostly involving clerks, inspectors, or policemen. Such corruption often arises from the monopoly power of the official involved, and there are various technological solutions for reducing that monopoly by dispersing the provision of service, for example, making it available online or outsourcing to various agencies.

In the case of grand corruption, cleaning up systems of election funding for politicians is essential. Julia Cagé's book discusses many such reforms.[9] It will be similarly important to reform procedures of bidding, auctions, and auditing in cases of large government procurement deals or purchases (e.g., in the case of military aircrafts or hardware), and the allocation of public resources that are highly valued (e.g., land or mineral resources or segments of the telecommunications spectrum). Technology is playing an increasingly important role in such reform.

Several countries have anticorruption investigative agencies, but more often than not they are not quite independent of powerful political leaders. Nonetheless, independent investigative agencies with enough clout to follow through are crucial. If they can unearth and publicise egregious cases involving the corrupt and well connected, and start the process of public indictment, then people may move away from the cynical conviction that nothing can be done.

IV. Improving the voice of labour organisations and other associations that enrich democracy

Traditional trade unions are in decline across much of the world. We need to restructure labour organisations and redefine their goals, such that they are not just wage bargaining institutions, but also play a larger role in corporate governance and provide, in collaboration with other community institutions, an anchor for the shared identity of workers and citizens. Currently, workers are fragmented in terms of professional and blue-collar workers, or formal and informal workers (particularly in developing countries, where the large majority of workers are informal). One has to think in terms of universal policies that can bridge the gulfs between the different segments of workers. These include minimum wages, social insurance, the reduction of capital subsidies and higher taxes on the rich, universal health care, universal access to vocational training, and, in the context of large masses of informal workers in poor countries, some form of universal basic income supplement. The list goes on.

'German works councils' provide an example of how to boost the voice of labour in the top governing boards of companies, in a way that can improve productivity and industrial relations without hurting long-run profits. A stronger voice for labour in corporate governance can positively influence the company's research and development (R&D) decisions, and therefore the pattern of future innovations, in a more labour-friendly rather than labour-replacing direction.[10] Such a voice may also increase the influence of labour in international negotiations on trade and investment rules, which are currently dominated by the corporate lobbies of rich countries – and this may restore some of the loss of trust among rank-and-file labour in globalisation.

The role of unions in fostering democracy is part of a larger discussion of democratic institutions that goes beyond the state and the market. The late sociologist Erik Olin Wright had a whole project of what he called 'Real Utopias' – ideals grounded in the real potential for social change and exploring concrete institutional alternatives to status-quo capitalism. (As Wright noted, some examples already exist, from Wikipedia and open-source technologies to the Mondragon federation of worker cooperatives in Spain.) In the first volume of Wright's project, *Associations and Democracy*, Joshua Cohen and Joel Rogers suggest ways of strengthening secondary associations mediating between individual citizens and the state and thus enhancing democracy. Such associations could include unions, works councils, neighbourhood associations, parent-teacher groups, and women's societies.[11]

V. Democratising the sphere of capital

In view of excessive corporate concentration, many now argue for vigorous anti-monopoly policies. Such policies are needed not just on the grounds of promoting competition, efficiency, and growth, but also to improve labour power in the face of monopsony in labour hiring, and to control the influence of corporate lobbies in legislation, regulation, and the election of pliant politicians. These policies must also be accompanied by the demand for 'Big Tech' to give more back for the profits it extracts using the massive amounts of private data it collects from its users. The state is in a better position to bargain with Big Tech than isolated, private users; it might, for example, demand on their behalf a share of the digital dividend be earmarked for a public fund (some have suggested a large tax on digital advertisement). However, others believe that control of data should be in the hands of the local community rather than the state. The city of Barcelona has implemented a civic data trust so that citizens have greater say over data collection and the purposes for which data are used. This is just one way that data capital might be democratised.

Notes

1 See Chapter 11 in Bardhan (2004).

2 See Chapter 11 in Bardhan (2004).

3 Ostrom et al. (2002).

4 Baland et al. (2007).

5 Much of the empirical literature, particularly the local-level evidence on developing countries, has been reviewed by Bardhan and Mookherjee (2015) and by Mansuri and Rao (2013).

6 Gonçalves (2014).

[7] One reason for low taxable capacity at the local level in developing countries is that the current system of taxation of local property is highly deficient. (In Latin America, for example, local property taxes collect only around 0.5% of gross domestic product, whereas in Europe it is about 3%. In India the percentage is even lower, more like 0.15%.)

[8] Gastil and Wright (2019).

[9] Cagé (2020).

[10] The importance of this has been stressed by Acemoglu and Restrepo (2020).

[11] Cohen and Rogers (1995).

References

Acemoglu, D. and Restrepo, P. (2020) 'The Wrong Kind of AI? Artificial Intelligence and the Future of Labor Demand', *Cambridge Journal of Regions, Economy and Society*, 13(1): 25–35. https://doi.org/10.1093/cjres/rsz022

Baland, J. M., Bardhan, P. and Bowles, S. (2007) *Inequality, Cooperation, and Environmental Sustainability*, Princeton, NJ: Princeton University Press. https://doi.org/10.1515/9780691187389

Bardhan, P. (2004) *Scarcity, Conflicts, and Cooperation*, Cambridge, MA: MIT Press.

Bardhan, P. and Mookherjee, D. (2015) 'Decentralization and Development: Dilemmas, Trade-offs and Safeguards', in Ahmad, E. and Brosio, G. (eds), *Handbook of Multi-Level Finance*, Edward Elgar. https://doi.org/10.4337/9780857932297.00026

Cagé, J. (2020) *The Price of Democracy: How Money Shapes Politics and What to Do About It*, MA Cambridge, Harvard University Press. https://doi.org/10.4159/9780674246133

Cohen, J. and Rogers, J. (1995) *Associations and Democracy*, Verso Books.

Gastil, J. and Wright, E. O. (2019) *Legislature by Lot: Transformative Designs for Deliberative Governance*, Verso Books.

Gonçalves, S. (2104) 'The Effects of Participatory Budgeting on Municipal Expenditures and Infant Mortality in Brazil', *World Development*, 53(C): 94–110. https://doi.org/10.1016/j.worlddev.2013.01.009

Mansuri, G. and Rao, V. (2013) *Localizing Government: Does Participation Work?* World Bank. https://doi.org/10.1596/978-0-8213-8256-1

Ostrom, E., Dietz, T., Dolšak, N., Stern, P. C., Stonich, P. and Weber E. U. (eds) (2002) *The Drama of the Commons*, National Research Council.

List of figures and tables

Figures

2.1 Real GDP (in US$) per capita of India, Indonesia and Egypt on a logarithmic scale, 1950–2020 71

2.2 Growth rates, in GDP, GDP per hour worked, and TFP for OECD countries, 1960–2020 72

2.3 US establishment entry and exit rates (%), 1980–2020 73

3.1 Remedies for prosperity and inequality 81

3.2 Traditional welfare state model 82

3.3 Traditional growth model 82

3.4 The productivist 'good-jobs' model 83

5.1 Purchasing power parity adjustment factor and GDP per capita at PPP, 2021 151

5.2 Exports of goods and services per capita, and GDP per capita 2019, logs 153

5.3 Presence and absence of products in the export basket of countries (2019) 154

5.4 (a) Average income per capita by quintile of growth; and (b) Change in the rankings of the Economic Complexity Index by quintile of growth 155

5.5 Relationship between real price of the economy and GDP (per capita) 186

5.6 Relationship between trade and exports 187

5.7 Relationship between income (GDP per capita) and trade (per capita) 188

5.8 Relationship between trade (per capita) and population size 189

5.9 Relationship between GDP (per capita) and population size 190

5.10 Relationship between GDP (per capita) and economic complexity 190

7.1 The global financial cycle 221

7.2 Federal reserve and risk on, risk off 222

7.3 Pass-through of monetary policy 224

7.4	Debt in emerging markets	246
7.5	Macro facts	247
9.1	Paid versus unpaid work by gender/Gender gaps in employment rates (%)	284
9.2	The earnings gap and its components	285
9.3	Weekly hours dedicated to home production, US, by gender, 1900–2005	293
9.4	Motherhood penalty in earnings in three sets of countries, 2015	295
10.1	Top and bottom decile income shares for 50 countries in 2020	316
10.2	Income share of top 1%, WID vs WIID, by country	317
10.3	An inequality of opportunity 'Great Gatsby Curve'	324
11.1	Life expectancy and health expenditure 1970–2022	364
11.2	A stylised description of the Latin American welfare state	381
12.1	The likelihood an adult in the developing world with five years of schooling could read a sentence (in any language) declined substantially for both men and women – with large variations across countries	399
12.2	There is often misalignment among curricula, exams, and classroom teaching, shown here for primary school English class in Uganda	408
13.1	Progress towards universal health coverage: service coverage index for low- to high-income countries, 2000–2017	434
13.2	Out-of-pocket expenditure (% of current health expenditure), for low- to high-income countries, 2000–2020	435
13.3	Life expectancy at birth (years) across countries	436
13.4	Life expectancy at birth (years) in G7 countries	436
14.1	Global greenhouse emissions by sector	477
14.2	Historical costs and production of key energy supply technologies	478
14.3	The decline of externalities from manufacturing production in the United States	482
14.4	Tropical forest loss in the past two decades	487
14.5	Mortality effects of climate change	490
14.6	Percentage of individuals living below \$2.15 a day, 2023	490

15.1 Number of countries with national climate emission targets in 2010, 2015 and 2020 510

15.2 A framework of the key drivers and barriers of climate action in LMICs 512

16.1 Executive constraints and openness over time 538

16.2 Three clusters of states 546

16.3 States and wellbeing 547

16.4 State types, executive constraints and openness 548

Tables

5.1 The evolution of development gaps vis-à-vis the United States since 1990 149

9.1 Hours per day devoted to activities 302

12.1 In many developing regions the majority of students enrolled in school at age 15 have not reached basic skills in maths and science 395

12.2 Even rural Indian youth enrolled in tertiary education had limited skills in simple practice tasks like calculation of time or measurement with a ruler 397

Boxes

11.1 Types of government intervention 354

11.2 Properties of an idealised market 355

11.3 Properties of an idealised insurance market 357

11.4 Characteristics of an idealised government 358

About the editors and contributors

Editors

Tim Besley is School Professor of Economics and Political Science and W. Arthur Lewis Professor of Development Economics at the London School of Economics (LSE). His main research interests are in studying how governments can more effectively design and deliver economic policies. He has extensive policy experience advising the World Bank, International Monetary Fund (IMF) and European Bank for Reconstruction and Development, and, from 2006 to 2009, he served on the Bank of England Monetary Policy Committee. He is also a member of the UK's National Infrastructure Commission and was an academic convenor of the Oxford-LSE Commission on State Fragility, Growth and Development, and joint Chair of the LSE Growth Commission. He is a past President of the European Economic Association (EEA), Econometric Society and Royal Economic Society (RES).

Irene Bucelli is Research Officer at the School of Public Policy and the Centre for Analysis of Social Exclusion at LSE. Her research focuses on the relationship between multidimensional inequality and poverty, exploring both theoretically and empirically the interplay between different forms of disadvantage and their implications for policy. She coordinates the LSE Public Policy Review programme at the School of Public Policy and is managing editor of the *LSE Public Policy Review* journal.

Andrés Velasco is Professor of Public Policy and Dean of the School of Public Policy at LSE. Between 2006 and 2010 he served as Minister of Finance of Chile. He is also an Associate Fellow at Chatham House, the Royal Institute of International Affairs, and a Research Fellow at the Centre for Economic Policy Research (CEPR). In 2023–24 he served on the Task Force on Fiscal Policy for Health; during 2021–23 he was part of the High-Level Advisory Group to the IMF and the World Bank; in 2017–18 he was a member of the G20 Eminent Persons Group on Financial Governance; during 2015–16 he co-chaired the Global Panel on the Future of the Multilateral Lending Institutions; in 2013–16 he was a member of the Global Oceans Commission. Before coming to LSE, he held professorial appointments at the Harvard Kennedy School (HKS), Columbia School of International Public and Affairs (SIPA) and the New York University Economics Department. His research has been published in leading academic journals including the *American Economic Review*, the *Journal of Political Economy*, the *Quarterly Journal of Economics* and the *Journal of Economic Theory*. In 2006 he received the Inter-American Development Bank Award for Excellence in Economic Research.

Contributors

Philippe Aghion is a Professor at the College de France, Institut européen d'administration des affaires, the London School of Economics, and a fellow of the Econometric Society and of the American Academy of Arts and Sciences. His research focuses on the economics of growth. With Peter Howitt, he pioneered the so-called Schumpeterian growth paradigm, which was subsequently used to analyse the design of growth policies and the role of the state in the growth process. Much of this work is summarised in their joint book *Endogenous Growth Theory* (MIT Press, 1998) and *The Economics of Growth* (MIT Press, 2009), in his book with Rachel Griffith on *Competition and Growth* (MIT Press, 2006), and in his recent book *The Power of Creative Destruction* (Harvard University Press, 2021, joint with C. Antonin and S. Bunel). In 2001, Philippe Aghion received the Yrjö Jahnsson Award of the best European economist under age 45, in 2009 he received the John Von Neumann Award, and in March 2020 he shared the Banco Bilbao Vizcaya Argentaria Frontier of Knowledge Award with Peter Howitt for 'developing an economic growth theory based on the innovation that emerges from the process of creative destruction'.

Matt Andrews is the Edward S. Mason Senior Lecturer in International Development at Harvard's Kennedy School of Government. He is also the faculty director of the Building State Capability programme at Harvard, which is where he has developed – with a team – a policy and management method to address complex challenges. This method is called problem driven iterative adaptation (PDIA) and was developed through over a decade of applied action research work by Matt and his team. It is now used by practitioners across the globe.

Oriana Bandiera is the Sir Anthony Atkinson Professor of Economics at LSE, and an honorary foreign member of the American Economic Association, a fellow of the British Academy, the Econometric Society, CEPR, Bureau for Research and Economic Analysis of Development (BREAD), and the Institute of Labor Economics (IZA). She is director of the Hub for Equal Representation at LSE and of the Gender, Growth and Labour Markets in Low-Income Countries (G^2LM|LIC) programme at the IZA. She serves on the council of the Econometric Society, on the board of the International Growth Centre (IGC) and of the Barcelona Graduate School of Economics. Her research has been awarded the IZA Young Labor Economist Prize (2008), the Carlo Alberto Medal (2011), the Ester Boserup Prize (2018), the Yrjö Jahnsson

Award (2019), the Arrow Award (2021) and an Honorary Doctorate in Economics from the University of Munich (2021). At LSE she teaches the undergraduate Development Economics course, for which she won a Student Union Award in 2020.

Pranab Bardhan is Distinguished Professor Emeritus of Economics at University of California (UC), Berkeley. He had been at the faculty of Massachusetts Institute of Technology (MIT), Indian Statistical Institute and Delhi School of Economics before joining Berkeley. He has done theoretical and field studies research on rural institutions in poor countries, on the political economy of development policies, and on international trade. He is the author of 17 books and editor of 14 other books, and the author of more than 150 journal articles. A part of his work is in the interdisciplinary area of economics, political science and social anthropology. He was chief editor of the *Journal of Development Economics* for 1985–2003. He was the co-chair of the MacArthur Foundation-funded Network on the Effects of Inequality on Economic Performance for 1996–2007. His latest two books are *A World of Insecurity: Democratic Disenchantment in Rich and Poor Countries* (Harvard University Press, 2022) and a memoir titled *Charaiveti: An Academic's Global Journey* (Harper Collins India, 2023).

Nicholas Barr is Professor of Public Economics at LSE, the author of numerous articles, and the author or editor of over 20 books, including *The Economics of the Welfare State* (6th edition, 2020), *Financing Higher Education: Answers from the UK* (with Iain Crawford, 2005), and *Pension Reform: A Short Guide* (with Peter Diamond, 2010, also in Spanish). The heart of his work is an exploration of how market failures both explain and justify the existence of welfare states. He is a member of the Editorial Board of the *International Social Security Review* and associate editor of *CESifo Economic Studies*, the *Australian Economic Review* and the *Journal of the Economics of Ageing*. Alongside academic writing is wide-ranging policy work, including spells at the World Bank and IMF, and as a member of the World Economic Forum's Global Agenda Councils on Demographic Shifts and on Ageing Society. He has advised governments in post-communist countries, and in the UK, Australia, Chile, China, Hungary, New Zealand and South Africa. He was a member of a small group advising the government of China on pension reform, presenting their findings to the premier in 2004. In Chile he was a member of the Bravo Commission. He has also been active in the debate on higher education finance, and he and his colleague Iain Crawford have been described as the architects of the 2006 reforms in England.

Olivier Blanchard, senior fellow and former C. Fred Bergsten Senior Fellow at the Peterson Institute for International Economics, is the Robert M. Solow Professor of Economics emeritus at MIT. A citizen of France, Blanchard has spent most of his professional life in the United States. After obtaining his PhD in economics from MIT in 1977, he taught at Harvard University and returned to MIT in 1982. He was chair of the economics department from 1998 to 2003. In 2008, he took a leave of absence to serve as economic counsellor and director of the research department at the IMF, where he stayed until 2015. He then joined the Peterson Institute.

Timo Boppart is Professor at University of Zurich and Associate Professor at the Institute for International Economic Studies (IIES) Stockholm University. He is interested in macroeconomics, broadly defined with a special focus on growth, firm dynamics, development and labour supply. Boppart is an associate editor of *Econometrica* and *Quantitative Economics*, as well as on the editorial board of *Review of Economics Studies*.

Robin Burgess is a Professor of Economics, Co-Founder and Director of the IGC and Director of the Economics of Environment and Energy Research Programme, all at LSE. He is Co-Director (with Michael Greenstone) of the Coase Project on the Economics of Climate, Energy and Environment, was the past President of BREAD, serves on the board of VoxDev and Center for Effective Global Action and is an Affiliate of Abdul Latif Jameel Poverty Action Lab (J-PAL) and Yale Research Initiative on Innovation & Scale, a Research Fellow in CEPR and Center for Economic Studies and ifo Institute (CESifo) and a Fellow of the British Academy and the Econometric Society. His main interests are in the areas of environmental economics, development economics and political economy. He has published on a variety of topics – natural disasters, political accountability, mass media, deforestation and forest fires, access to electricity, renewable energy, marine protection zones, poverty traps, bureaucracy, youth unemployment, rural banks, land reform, labour regulation, industrial policy, taxation, poverty, and growth.

Pedro Carneiro is a Professor of Economics at University College London (UCL) and an economist in the Institute for Fiscal Studies (IFS) Centre for Microdata Methods and Practice (cemmap). His research interests include development economics, labour economics, the economics of education, and microeconometrics. In the past he has examined issues such as the returns to education, human capital policy, and labour regulation in developing countries. He has studied poverty and education programmes in several countries in Latin America, Africa, and Eastern Europe.

Joan Costa-i-Font is an academic and policy-oriented economist currently working as a Professor of Health Economics at LSE, where he co-leads the Ageing@LSE group. He is a faculty associate at the International Inequalities Institute, and LSE Health, where he leads the Ageing and Health Incentives Lab. He is affiliated with prominent global economics research networks including the IZA and CESifo and holds a PhD in Economics, yet has an interdisciplinary background, which includes undergraduate degrees in Law,

Politics, and Sociology. He has authored numerous articles in leading journals covering debates in health and behavioural economics, as well as political economy, and general interest journals. He has authored and edited books for both Cambridge University Press and Oxford University Press, and he has held prestigious fellowships and visiting positions at Harvard University, Princeton University, and Columbia University, as well as Sciences Po Paris. He has served as a consultant for the World Bank, the European Commission, the World Health Organization (WHO), and the Inter-American Development Bank. In the UK, he has contributed to National Institute for Health and Care Research research committees, advised the Cabinet Office and various House of Lords committees, served on the scientific board of the LSE Press, some NHS Trusts, the Nuffield Council on Bioethics and the Ada Lovelace Institute, among others.

Diane Coyle is Bennett Professor of Public Policy at the University of Cambridge, and author of *The Measure of Progress* (Princeton University Press, 2025). She has served in many policy roles, most recently as an advisor to the Competition and Markets Authority and member of the UK Government's New Towns Taskforce.

Ernesto Dal Bó is the Phillips Girgich Professor of Business and Public Policy at the Haas School of Business, UC, Berkeley. A political economist, he is interested in the origin and development of states, political selection, conflict, and democratic governance. He holds a DPhil in Economics from the University of Oxford, is the founding co-director of the Berkeley Center for Economics and Politics, a Research Associate at the National Bureau of Economic Research, and a member of the IGC and the J-PAL.

Ashwini Deshpande is Professor and Head at the Department of Economics, and Academic Director at the Centre for Economic Data and Analysis at Ashoka University, India. Her PhD and early publications were on the international debt crisis of the 1980s. Subsequently, she has been working on the economics of discrimination and affirmative action, with a focus on caste and gender in India. She has published extensively in leading scholarly journals. She is the author of *Grammar of Caste: Economic Discrimination in Contemporary India*, Oxford University Press, New Delhi, 2011 (Hardcover) and 2017 (Paperback), and *Affirmative Action in India*, Oxford University Press, New Delhi, Oxford India Short Introductions Series, 2013. She has edited several volumes, the latest of which is *Handbook on Economics of Discrimination and Affirmative Action* (Springer Major Reference Works, 2023). She is a Fellow of the International Economic Association (IEA). She received the EXIM Bank award for outstanding dissertation (now called the IERA Award) in 1994, the 2007 VKRV Rao Award for Indian economists under 45 and SKOCH Award for Gender Economics in 2022.

Tim Dobermann is the Director of Research for the IGC and a Research Fellow in Environmental Economics at LSE. His research focuses on how climate change impacts those in poverty and how energy sectors in developing countries can be made more effective. He has advised several governments in Asia and Africa on energy, public finance, and sustainable growth issues. He holds a PhD in Economics from LSE.

Dave Donaldson is the Class of 1949 Professor of Economics in the Economics Department at MIT. A native of Toronto, Canada, he obtained an undergraduate degree in Physics from Oxford University and a PhD in Economics from LSE. His research focuses on trade, both international and intranational, with applications in the fields of international economics, development economics, urban economics, economic history, environmental economics, and agricultural economics. He has studied, among other topics, the welfare and inequality effects of market integration, the impact of improvements in transportation infrastructure, how trade can mitigate and exacerbate the effects of climate change, and how economists can quantify market failures and the interventions (such as industrial policy) that attempt to fix them. He was awarded the 2017 John Bates Clark Medal as well as an Alfred P. Sloan Research Fellowship and several grants from the National Science Foundation. He has served as a co-editor at *Econometrica* and the *American Economic Journal: Applied Economics*, and is a fellow of the Econometric Society and a member of the American Academy of Arts and Sciences.

Francisco H. G. Ferreira is the Amartya Sen Professor of Inequality Studies and Director of the International Inequalities Institute at LSE. Francisco works on the measurement, causes, and consequences of inequality and poverty in developing countries. His work has been published widely and awarded various prizes. He is a Research Fellow of the IZA; an Affiliated Scholar with the Stone Center at City University of New York; a former President of the Latin American and Caribbean Economic Association and a former editor-in-chief of the *Journal of Economic Inequality*. Prior to joining the faculty at LSE, he had a long career at the World Bank but also taught at Pontifical Catholic University of Rio de Janeiro (PUC-Rio) and at the Paris School of Economics. He was born in São Paulo, Brazil, and holds a PhD in Economics from LSE.

Pierre-Olivier Gourinchas is the Economic Counsellor and the Director of Research of the IMF. He is on leave from UC, Berkeley where he is the S.K. and Angela Chan Professor of Global Management in the Department of Economics and at the Haas School of Business. He was the editor-in-chief of the *IMF Economic Review* from its creation in 2009 to 2016, the managing editor of the *Journal of International Economics* between 2017 and 2019, and a co-editor of the *American Economic Review* between 2019 and 2022. He is on leave from the National Bureau of Economic Research, where he was director of the International Finance and Macroeconomics programme, a Research Fellow with the Centre for Economic Policy Research (CEPR) London and a Fellow of the Econometric Society. He is the laureate of the 2007 Bernácer Prize for best European economist working in macroeconomics and finance under the age of 40, and of the 2008 Prix du Meilleur Jeune Économiste for best French economist under the age of 40. He attended École Polytechnique and received his PhD in Economics in 1996 from MIT.

Chryssi Giannitsarou is a Professor of Macroeconomics and Finance at the University of Cambridge. With postgraduate degrees from LSE and London Business School (LBS), her research spans a wide range of topics, such as financial decision-making, macroeconomic dynamics, economic networks, international finance, and she has been published in many leading economic journals. She is a fellow of King's College Cambridge and a research fellow of the CEPR.

Ricardo Hausmann is the founder and Director of Harvard's Growth Lab and the Rafik Hariri Professor of the Practice of International Political Economy at HKS. His scholarly contributions have had a significant impact on the study and practice of economic growth policies. These include the development of the Growth Diagnostics and Economic Complexity methodologies, as well as several widely used economic concepts, such as Dark Matter, Original Sin, and Self-discovery and have been cited over 53,000 times. Since launching the Growth Lab in 2006, Hausmann has served as principal investigator for more than 50 research initiatives in over 30 countries, including the US, informing development policy, macroeconomic stabilisation, growth strategies and diversification agendas at the national, regional, and city levels. Before joining Harvard University, he served as the first Chief Economist of the Inter-American Development Bank (1994–2000), where he founded the Research Department. He has served as Minister of Planning of Venezuela (1992–93) and as a member of the Board of the Central Bank of Venezuela. He also served as Chair of the IMF-World Bank Development Committee. He was Professor of Economics at the Instituto de Estudios Superiores de Administración (1985–91) in Caracas, where he founded the Center for Public Policy. He holds a PhD in Economics from Cornell University.

Dan Honig is an Associate Professor at UCL's Department of Political Science and Georgetown University's McCourt School of Public Policy. His research focuses on the organisational bits of government's role in enhancing citizens' welfare – particularly organisational structure, bureaucrats' motivation, and relations between citizens and state agents.

Paul Johnson has been Director of the IFS since 2011. He is a columnist for *The Times*, and is a regular contributor to other broadcast and print media. He is a Visiting Professor in the UCL Policy Lab and at the UCL Department of Economics. He was for 10 years a member of the UK Climate Change Committee, and has served on the council of the Economic and Social Research Council and of the RES. Paul led reviews of pension auto-enrolment and of inflation measurement for the UK Government, and of fiscal devolution for the Northern Ireland Executive. Previous roles have included time as chief economist at the Department for Education and as director of public spending at HM Treasury, where he also served as deputy head of the Government Economic Service. Paul published the Sunday Times bestseller *Follow the Money* in 2023. He was appointed CBE in the 2018 birthday honours.

Şebnem Kalemli-Özcan is Schreiber Family Professor of Economics at Brown University and the Director of the Global Linkages Lab. She is a Research Associate at the National Bureau of Economic Research (NBER) and a Research Fellow at the CEPR. Currently, she is the co-editor of *American Economic Journal: Macroeconomics*. She also serves at the economic advisory panels of the Federal Reserve Bank of New York and the Bank of International Settlements. Formerly, she was the Duisenberg Fellow at the European Central Bank, Lead Economist for the Middle East and North Africa Region of the World Bank, Houblon-Norman Fellow of Bank of England, Senior Policy Advisor at the IMF and the International Fellow of Council of Foreign Relations, where she is also an elected member. She is the first Turkish social scientist who has received the 2008 Marie Curie IRG prize aimed to reverse brain drain for her research on European financial integration. Her research focuses on the impact of global trade and financial linkages on economic fluctuations and growth.

Ravi Kanbur researches and teaches in development economics, public economics and economic theory at Cornell University. He has served on the senior staff of the World Bank including as Chief Economist for Africa. He has also published in leading economics journals. He has served as Co-Chair of the Food System Economics Commission, Chair of the Board of United Nations University-World Institute for Development Economics Research (UNU-WIDER), is a member of the Organisation for Economic Co-operation and Development High Level Expert Group on the Measurement of Economic Performance, President of the Human Development and Capability Association, President of the Society for the Study of Economic Inequality, member of the High Level Advisory Council of the Climate Justice Dialogue, Co-Chair of the Scientific Council of the International Panel on Social Progress, and member of the Core Group of the Commission on Global Poverty.

Adnan Khan is a Professor in Practice at the LSE School of Public Policy, currently on secondment as Chief Economist to the Foreign, Commonwealth and Development Office of the UK. He has spent 30 years in the research and policy worlds – as a researcher, teacher, a catalyser of other people's research, and as a practitioner and policymaker. His areas of interest include economic development, state capacity and fragility, political economy and taxation, and geoeconomics.

Margaret Levi is Emerita Professor of Political Science, Senior Fellow of Freeman Spogli Institute for International Studies, and faculty fellow and former Sara Miller McCune Director of the Center for Advanced Study in the Behavioral Sciences, Stanford University. She is co-director of the Stanford Ethics, Society, and Technology Initiatives. She is the winner of the 2019 Johan Skytte Prize and the 2020 Falling Walls Breakthrough. She has been elected to the National Academy of Sciences, the British Academy, the American Academy of Arts and Sciences, the American Philosophical Society, and the American Academy of Political and Social Sciences, and she served as president of the American Political Science Association (APSA). The most recent of her many books are *In the Interest of Others* (Princeton, 2013), co-authored with John Ahlquist, and *A Moral Political Economy: Present, Past, Future* (Cambridge University Press, 2021), co-authored with Federica Carugati. She writes about what makes for trustworthy governance in states and organisations and what evokes citizen compliance, consent, and dissent. She is currently engaged in projects to reconceptualise political equality, to reimagine property rights, and to develop a social science of care and caregiving.

Santiago Levy is currently a Senior Fellow at The Brookings Institution and member of the board of various development organisations. Before that, he was Vice-President at the Inter-American Development Bank, General Director of Mexico's Social Security Institute, Deputy Minister at Mexico's Ministry of Finance, and President of Mexico's Federal Competition Commission. In academia, he was President of the Latin American and Caribbean Economic Association (LACEA), Associate Professor of Economics and Director of the Institute for Economic Development at Boston University, Visiting Researcher at Cambridge University and Professor of Economics at the Instituto Tecnológico Autónomo de México. At the Ministry of Finance, he was the main architect of Progresa-Oportunidades. At the Social Security Institute, he promoted legal changes to reform pensions and extend coverage to rural workers. He has published on social policy, informality, education, tax policy, trade and competition policy, and policies for poverty alleviation. He has received First Place, National Research Prize in Economics (Banco Nacional de México); First Place, Latin American Economics Prize (El Trimestre Económico); and Distinguished Alumni Award, Boston University. His current work focuses on the challenges of socially inclusive growth in Latin America.

Nora Lustig is Samuel Z. Stone Professor of Latin American Economics and the founding Director of the Commitment to Equity Institute at Tulane University. She is also a Non-resident Senior Fellow at the Brookings Institution, Georgetown University Americas Institute, the Center for Global Development, the Inter-American Dialogue, and the Paris School of Economics. Lustig's research is on economic development, inequality, and social policies with emphasis on Latin America. Her recent publication *Commitment to Equity Handbook: Estimating the Impact of Fiscal Policy on Inequality and Poverty* is a step-by-step guide to assessing the impact of taxation and social spending on inequality and poverty in developing countries. Lustig is the President of the Society for the Study of Economic Inequality and President Emeritus of the LACEA. She serves on the editorial board of the *Journal of Economic Inequality*. In November 2021, she was recognised with the Tulane University Innovation Award. She received her doctorate in Economics from UC, Berkeley.

Isabela Manelici joined the Department of Economics at LSE in the autumn of 2021 as an Assistant Professor. Isabela's current research lies at the intersection of International Trade and Development Economics. A citizen of Romania, Isabela received her BA in Civil Engineering from École Nationale des Ponts et Chaussées (Paris), her MA in Economics and Finance from Centro de Estudios Monetarios y Financieros Madrid, and her PhD in Economics from UC, Berkeley in 2020. For the 2020–2021 academic year, Isabela Manelici was an International Economics Section Postdoctoral Research Associate in the Department of Economics at Princeton University. Prior to her graduate studies in Economics, she has worked as a Junior Professional Associate at the World Bank in Washington, DC.

Sir Michael Marmot has been Professor of Epidemiology at UCL since 1985, and is Director of the UCL Institute of Health Equity. He is the author of *The Health Gap: The Challenge of an Unequal World* (Bloomsbury, 2015), and *Status Syndrome* (Bloomsbury, 2004). Marmot is a Distinguished Visiting Professor at Chinese University of Hong Kong (CUHK) (2019–), and Co-Director of the CUHK Institute of Health Equity. He is the recipient of the WHO Global Hero Award; the Harvard Lown Professorship (2014–17); the Prince Mahidol Award for Public Health (2015), and 20 honorary doctorates. Marmot has led research groups on health inequalities for nearly 50 years. He chaired the WHO Commission on Social Determinants of Health, several WHO Regional Commissions, and reviews on tackling health inequality for governments in the UK. He served as President of the British Medical Association in 2010–11, and as President of the World Medical Association in 2015. He is President of Asthma + Lung UK. He is a Fellow of the Academy of Medical Sciences and Honorary Fellow of the American College of Epidemiology and of the Faculty of Public Health; an Honorary Fellow of the British Academy; and of the Royal Colleges of Obstetrics and Gynaecology, Psychiatry, Paediatrics and

Child Health, and General Practitioners. He is an elected member of the US National Academy of Medicine (NAM), the National Academy of Medicine of Mexico and the Brazilian Academy of Medicine. He was knighted by Queen Elizabeth II, for services to epidemiology and the understanding of health inequalities. He was appointed a Companion of Honour in recognition of his services to public health in the King's 2023 New Year Honours.

Alistair McGuire is Head of Department and Chair of Health Economics at the Department of Health Policy. Prior to this he was Professor of Economics at City University, London, after being a tutor in Economics at the University of Oxford. McGuire has also been a Visiting Professor at Harvard University, the University of Sydney, the University of York, and the Universitat Pompeu Fabra, Barcelona. He has acted as an advisor to a number of governments and governmental bodies, including the UK Government, the UK Competition Commission, the UK Medical Research Council, the German Institut fur Qualität Wirtschaftlichkeit im Gesundheitswesen, as well as for a number of international bodies (including the World Bank, the WHO, and the IMF) and pharmaceutical and healthcare insurance companies.

Joana Naritomi is an Associate Professor and the Academic Director of the LSE School of Public Policy. She is a Research Affiliate in BREAD, the CEPR Public Economics and Development Economics programmes, STICERD Public Economics, IFS, IGC, and a J-PAL Latin America and the Caribbean Invited Researcher. Her research lies at the intersection of Public Economics and Development Economics, focusing on taxation, social protection, and state capacity.

Chukwumerije Okereke is Professor of Global Climate Governance and Public Policy at the School of Policy Studies at the University of Bristol. He is a Visiting Professor at LSE and Co-Director of the Center for Climate Change and Development (CCD) in Alex Ekuweme Federal University, Nigeria. He was formerly Co-Director of the Centre for Climate and Justice and of the Leverhulme Doctoral Scholarship Programme, both at the University of Reading. He was also previously Director of the Centre for Climate Change and Development at the Smith School of Enterprise and the Environment at the University of Oxford. A globally recognised leading scholar on global climate governance and international development, Okereke was the Coordinating Lead Author of the UN's Intergovernmental Panel on Climate Change Sixth Assessment Report, Working Group 3.

Torsten Persson is a Swedish Research Council Distinguished Professor at the IIES, Stockholm University, and a Centennial Professor at LSE. His research often involves issues at the boundary between economics and other fields, mostly political science but also other social and medical sciences. Persson has experience of evaluating policies in deep crises – he was part of Sweden's

Economics Commission in the early 1990s and its Corona Commission in the early 2020s. He has served as the President of the Econometric Society and the EEA, and is currently a member of the European Research Council's Scientific Council.

Barbara Petrongolo is a Professor of Economics at the University of Oxford and a Professorial Fellow at Nuffield College. She is Fellow of the British Academy, Director of the CEPR Labour Economics Programme, and Research Associate at the Centre for Economic Performance of LSE. She previously held positions at Queen Mary University of London, LSE, the Paris School of Economics and the University of Carlos III (Madrid). Her primary research interests are in labour economics. She has worked extensively on the performance of labour markets with job search frictions, with applications to unemployment dynamics, welfare policy, and monopsony. Her work also researches the causes of gender inequalities in labour market outcomes, in a historical perspective and across countries, with emphasis on the role of employment selection mechanisms, structural transformation, and parenthood.

Jean Pisani-Ferry is a Senior Fellow at Bruegel, the European think tank, and a Non-Resident Senior Fellow at the Peterson Institute (Washington, DC). He sits on the supervisory board of the French *Caisse des Dépôts* and serves as non-executive chair of I4CE, the French Institute for Climate Economics. He served from 2013 to 2016 as Commissioner-General of France Stratégie, the ideas lab of the French government.

Sir Christopher Pissarides is the Regius Professor of Economics at LSE, the Professor of European Studies at the University of Cyprus and the co-chair of the Institute for the Future of Work. He specialises in the economics of labour markets, economic growth, and structural change, especially as they relate to market imperfections, where his work has been internationally influential. He has recently worked extensively on the employment implications of automation and artificial intelligence for the future of work. In 2010 Sir Christopher was awarded the Nobel Prize for his work on the labour market, sharing it with Dale Mortensen of Northwestern University and Peter Diamond of MIT. He has since been honoured with several other awards, prizes, and society fellowships. He was knighted by Queen Elizabeth II in 2013.

Lant Pritchett is a development economist from Idaho. He graduated from Brigham Young University in 1983 and received his PhD in Economics from MIT in 1988. He worked for the World Bank from 1988 to 2007, living in Indonesia 1998–2000 and India 2004–07. He taught at the HKS from 2000 to 2019, and from 2018 to 2023 he was the Research Director of the Research on Improving Systems of Education Programme at Oxford's Blavatnik School of Government. He is currently a Visiting Professor at LSE in the School of

Public Policy and the co-founder and Research Director of Labor Mobility Partnerships. His work spans a range of development topics including basic education, economic growth, state capability, labour mobility, development assistance (and more).

Carol Propper is Professor of Economics at Imperial College. Her research focuses on the impact of incentives on the quality of healthcare delivery and health system productivity and, more widely, on the design and consequences of incentives within the public sector and the boundary between the state and private markets. She was made a Dame in the 2021 New Year's Honours in recognition of her public services to health and economics. She is a Fellow of the British Academy, an International Fellow of the NAM and Fellow of the Association for Social Sciences and a Life-Vice President of the RES. Carol is currently a non-executive director of the UK Statistics Authority and was a member of the Prime Minister's Council of Science and Technology 2023–24. She was Associate Dean for Faculty and Research at Imperial Business School 2016–19, Co-Director and Director of the Centre for Market and Public Organisation at the University of Bristol 1998–2009 and Co-Director of the Centre for the Analysis of Social Exclusion at London School of Economics 1997–2007. From 2016 to 2023 she was Deputy Editor of VoxEU.

Danny Quah is Li Ka Shing Professor in Economics, National University of Singapore. He works on world order, economic growth and development, and inequality and income mobility. In his research on world order, Quah analyses the supply and demand of international systems, contrasting the goals of the Great Powers and the needs of the global community. Quah's work on income mobility challenges conventional narratives on inequality, highlighting the broad diversity of economic experiences across nations. Through academic research, public commentary, and as a member of World Bank President's Economic Advisory Panel and other public commissions, as well as in advisory roles at WEF, United Nations Development Programme, government agencies and ministries, and elsewhere, Quah seeks to help shape global economic and geopolitical discourse. He is the author of 'The Global Economy's Shifting Centre of Gravity' (2011) in the journal *Global Policy*.

Ricardo Reis is the A.W. Phillips Professor of Economics at LSE. He was elected a Fellow of the British Academy, the Academia de Ciências de Lisboa, and the Econometric Society. Recent honours include the 2022 Carl Menger prize, the 2021 Yrjö Jahnsson Award, the Banque de France and the Toulouse School of Economics 2017 BdF/TSE junior prize, and the 2016 Bernácer prize. Reis is an academic consultant at the Bank of England, the Riksbank, the Federal Reserve Bank of Richmond, and the European Stability Mechanism. He directs the Centre for Macroeconomics at LSE, and he serves on the council and is an advisor of multiple organisations. He has published widely on macroeconomics, including both monetary and fiscal policy, inflation, and business cycles. Reis received his PhD from Harvard University, and was previously on the faculties at Columbia University and Princeton University.

Hélène Rey OBE, FBA is Lord Bagri Professor of Economics at London Business School. Formerly, she was Professor of Economics at Princeton University. Her research focuses on external imbalances, monetary policy and the financial sector, and the international monetary system. She introduced the idea of a global financial cycle and qualified the idea of the Mundellian Trilemma. She received numerous prizes including the Bernácer Prize, the Yrjö Jahnsson Award and the inaugural Birgit Grodal and Carl Menger Awards. She is a Fellow of the Econometric Society, a Foreign Member of the American Academy of Arts and Sciences and Foreign Honorary Member of the American Economic Association. She is an editor of the *Annual Review of Economics* and a vice president of CEPR. She is a member of the Bellagio Group, the Group of Thirty and of the external advisory group to the managing director of the IMF. She is on the Board of the Haut Conseil de Stabilité Financière. She is elected President of the EEA.

Elizabeth Robinson is Professor of Environmental Economics in the Department of Geography and Environment, and is currently Acting Dean of LSE and Political Science's Global School of Sustainability, seconded from her role as Director of the Grantham Research Institute on Climate Change and the Environment. Her research focuses on climate change and health, particularly food security and undernutrition, and heat and worker rights. She was on the UK Defra Economic Advisory Panel for five years; Specialist Advisor to the UK House of Lords Select Committee on Food, Poverty, Health, and Environment; Working Group 1 lead for the Lancet Countdown on Health and Climate Change from 2016 to 2024; and is currently Chair of the Economics Advisory Group for CCRA4 for the UK's Climate Change Committee, and is on the Scientific Committee of the Regenerative Society Foundation. Elizabeth previously worked at the University of Reading, the University of Oxford as a Lecturer in the Economics Department and Tutorial Fellow at St Hugh's College, the Boston Consulting Group, the World Bank, Rockefeller Foundation, and Natural Resources Institute. She has a first class degree in Engineering, Economics, and Management from Oxford University, and a PhD in Applied Economics from Stanford University.

Dani Rodrik is Ford Foundation Professor of International Political Economy at the HKS. He has published widely in the areas of economic development, international economics, and political economy. His current research focuses on employment and economic growth, in both developing and advanced economies. He is the recipient of numerous awards, including the inaugural Albert O. Hirschman Prize of the Social Science Research Council (SSRC) and the Princess of Asturias Award for Social Sciences. Rodrik is Co-Director of the Reimagining the Economy Program at the HKS and of the Economics for Inclusive Prosperity network. He was President of the IEA during 2021–23 and helped found the IEA's Women in Leadership in Economics initiative. His most recent books are *Combating Inequality: Rethinking Government's Role* (2021, edited with Olivier Blanchard) and *Straight Talk on Trade: Ideas for a Sane World Economy* (2017). He is also the author of *Economics Rules: The Rights and Wrongs of the Dismal Science* (2015), *The Globalization Paradox: Democracy and the Future of the World Economy* (2011) and *One Economics, Many Recipes: Globalization, Institutions, and Economic Growth* (2007).

Thomas Sampson is an Associate Professor of Economics at LSE. He is also an Associate in the Trade programme at the Centre for Economic Performance, where he has worked extensively on the implications of Brexit for the UK economy. Thomas has a PhD in Economics from Harvard University and previously worked as an Overseas Development Institute Fellow at the Bank of Papua New Guinea.

Kirsten Sehnbruch is a Global Professor of the British Academy and a Distinguished Policy Fellow at the International Inequalities Institute at LSE. Previously, she was a Research Fellow at the Universidad de Chile, and a Senior Lecturer at UC, Berkeley. Kirsten works on conceptualising and measuring poor-quality employment in both developing and advanced economies, particularly in Latin America and European countries. Her work has been replicated by the World Bank's study on Global Job Quality, and by the UN's study on poor-quality employment in Latin America. Her current work focuses on how the intensity of employment deprivations determines the extent to which workers in poor-quality employment get stuck in 'bad jobs'. She further argues that the most vulnerable workers will likely be affected by the increased adoption of new technologies and machine learning at the workplace. Kirsten has collaborated with governments, international development institutions and non-governmental organisations in Europe, Latin America and the Middle East. Her work has been published by multiple journals, such as *World Development*, *The Cambridge Journal of Economics*, *Development and Change*, *Regional Studies* and *Social Indicators Review*.

Almudena Sevilla is a Professor of Economic and Social Policy in the Department of Social Policy at LSE and is currently the Founding Chair of the RES UK Women in Economics Network and the LSE Women in Social and Public Policy Research Hub. She has also held positions at UCL, Queen Mary University, University of Oxford, University of Essex, and the Congressional Budget Office in Washington DC. She received her PhD from Brown University in 2004 in the fields of family and population economics and econometrics. She has a successful track record in gender economics research. Early in her career, she received the prestigious Marie

J. Langlois Prize for her doctoral research on gender economics and the status of women in the academic field. Her research is regularly published in top-tier international journals, such as the *American Economic Review*, *Demography*, and the *Journal of Labor Economics*. She also serves on the editorial boards of leading journals, including *Feminist Economics* and *Review of the Economics of the Household*. Her work has attracted substantial research funding, including the highly competitive European Research Council Consolidator Grant of over €2 million. Sevilla holds key leadership positions in major economic associations, has recently been elected President of the Society of the Economics of the Household, and is a sought-after speaker at leading academic and policy forums, where she discusses women's roles in the economy.

Ranjeeta Thomas is Associate Professor of Health Economics in the Department of Health Policy at LSE. She is an applied economist with research interests in understanding the drivers of risky health behaviours, the role of incentives in improving demand for preventative healthcare, and early childhood development and health, including the long-term benefits of childhood health and education interventions. She has been a co-investigator on grants from the National Institute of Mental Health USA and the European & Developing Countries Clinical Trials Partnership, and led consultancy projects for the Global Fund and the Bill & Melinda Gates Foundation.

Sir Paul Tucker is a Research Fellow at the Mossavar-Rahmani Center for Business and Government at the HKS, writing at the intersection of political economy and political theory. He is author of *Global Discord* (Princeton University Press, 2022) and *Unelected Power* (PUP, 2018). He is working on a book applying David Hume's political theory to today's problems. From 1980 to 2013, he was a central banker.

Miguel Urquiola is Dean of Social Science and Professor of Economics at Columbia University. He has chaired Columbia's Department of Economics and its Committee on the Economics of Education. He is also a faculty member at the SIPA, where he served as vice-dean. Outside Columbia, Urquiola is a Research Associate at the NBER and has held appointments at Cornell University, the World Bank, and the Bolivian Catholic University. He is a member of boards, such as that of the SSRC. Urquiola's research is on the Economics of Education. It focuses on understanding how schools and universities compete and how educational markets differ from other markets economists study. He has written numerous journal articles on these issues and a book on why American universities excel at research: *Markets, Minds, and Money* (Harvard University Press, 2020).

John Van Reenen is Ronald Coase School Professor at LSE and Digital Fellow at the Initiative for the Digital Economy at the MIT. Until 2020 he was Gordon Billard Professor MIT in the Economics Department and Sloan Management School. He has published over a hundred papers on many areas in economics, with a particular focus on firm performance and the causes and consequences of innovation. He was the 2009 winner of the Yrjö Jahnsson Award (the European equivalent of the Clark Medal); the Arrow Prize (2011); the European Investment Bank Prize (2014); and the HBR-McKinsey Award (2018). He is a fellow of the British Academy, the Econometric Society, the NBER, CEPR, and the Society of Labor Economists. In 2017, he was awarded an OBE for 'services to public policy and economics' by Queen Elizabeth II.

Anthony Venables is a Senior Research Fellow at the University of Oxford and part-time Research Professor at Monash University, Melbourne. He is a fellow of the Econometric Society, the Regional Science Association International, and the British Academy. Former positions include Professor of Economics at Oxford University and at LSE, and chief economist at the UK Department for International Development. He has published extensively in the areas of international trade, spatial economics, natural resources, and economic development.

Leonard Wantchekon is the James Madison Professor of Political Economy, Professor of Politics, and International Affairs at Princeton University. He is the Founder and President of the African School of Economics and the Pan African Scientific Research Council. His research centres on political economy, development economics and economic history, with regional focus on Africa and on substantive topics, such as democracy and development, education and social mobility, and the long-term social impact of slavery and colonial rule. Finally, Wantchekon is the 2023 winner of the Global Economy Prize, awarded by the Kiel Institute for the World Economy. He is a fellow of the American Academy of Arts and Sciences, the Econometric Society, the BREAD and Research Affiliate at the NBER. He served as Vice President of the APSA, and is on the Executive Committee of the IEA.

Editorial team

Mie Hoejris Dahl is a Danish independent journalist covering politics, economics, crime, environmental, and social issues in Latin America. She holds a Master in Public Administration from HKS and writes for *The Economist*, *Foreign Policy*, *Mongabay*, and other international outlets.

Thomas Graham is a freelance journalist based in Mexico who covers Latin America for *The Guardian*, the *Financial Times* and *The Economist*, among others. He holds degrees in immunology and contemporary China studies from the University of Oxford.

Ana Lankes is *The Economist*'s Brazil bureau chief, based in São Paulo. She covers politics, economics, and society in Brazil and South America. Previously, she was the paper's Latin America correspondent, based in Buenos Aires. She has also worked for the *New York Times*.

Index

Note: page numbers in italic type refer to Figures; those in bold type refer to Tables. Reference to Endnotes show both the page number and the note number (231n3).

1920s 292, 380
1930s 44, 48, 135, 238, 362, 380
1940s 380, 390
1950s 46, 71, 78, 105, 144, 328, 380, 398, 402, 523n31, 540, 555n26
1960s 78, 105, 240, 328, 340, 399, 402, 523n31
1970s 1–2, 46, 52, 85, 139, 182, 286, 303, 325, 328, 329n12, 347, 370, 386, 603
1980s 2, 9, 11, 14, 45–46, 63, 70, 97–98, 143–144, 146, 186, 219, 220, 256, 289, 314, 327, 346–348, 352, 360, 370, 379, 386–387, 394, 439 440, 539
1990s 2, 41, 45, 54, 99, 117, 127, 219, 223, 242, 256, 303, 314, 320–21, 327, 330n23, 347, 380, 426–429, 536, 539–540, 602
19th century 43, 62, 289, 468
20th century 61–62, 105, 119, 326, 469, 486, 576
21st century 2, 61, 486, 515

A

abortion 91, 617
accountability 13–16, 21, 28, 50, 108, 162, 240, 409, 551, 577, 581, 583, 588, 608–610, 615–616
  see also electoral accountability
Acemoglu, Daron 12, 44, 48, 145, 148, 321, 554, 564
adaptation 10, 29, 87, 109, 162, 217, 253, 303, 410, 476, 477, 485, 489–494, 507, 509–510, 515, 518, 520, 573, 586, 589, 604, 607
addiction 6, 24, 79, 80
  see also alcohol; drugs
Additional Credit Claims programme 44
advanced economies (AEs) 28, 61, 73, 77–79, 97–99, 105, 198, 201–202, 205–206, 219–224, *225*, 232, 248, 270, 272, 275, 315, 369, 423, 492
Advanced Research Projects Agency (ARPA) 47, 86, 88, 101
  see also Defense Advanced Research Projects Agency (DARPA)
  Energy (ARPA-E) 88
aeronautics 46–47
Affordable Care Act 465
ageing 27, 259, 275, 362–363, 389, 437, 440–441, 448–449, 464
aggregate efficiency gains (aggregate gains) 24, 117–121, 127–129, 133–134
Aghion, Philippe 8, 21, 61, 63, 71, 73–74, 82, 321, 594n56
  see also Howitt, Peter
agriculture 21, 88, 144–145, 183, 283–284, 297, 327, 360, 476, 483 485, 491, 508, 514, 517–520, 588
agroforestry 517
AIDS 303, 445
Albania 165, *316*
alcohol 52, 438, 441, 468
A levels 263, 389
Amazon 158, 257, 352
Amazon Rainforest 486, *487*
American Rescue Plan Act 213–214
Angola 516
Anna-Karenina principle 543
annual leave 259, 264–265
antitrust regulation 313, 326
anxiety 10, 52, 198
Apple 25, 186
apprenticeship 263
Argentina 11, 48, 164–165, *316*, *317*, *364*, 442
Arizona 162
Armenia 315, *316*
artificial intelligence (AI) 22, 44–45, 61–62, 64, 100, 106–107, 255–258, 260–265, 372
  see also automation; robotics
Arts 259, 586
Asian financial crisis of 1997 49, 219–220
asset 6, 16, 163, 200–206, 219–221, 231, 244, 248, 297, 367–368, 489, 513
  price 17–18, 221–222, 227, 248
Australia 120, 135, *284*, 368, 386, 438, 566, 617
Austria 154, *284*, *285*, 294, *295*, *316*, 449
autarky 192, 192n10
autocracy 11, 540, 543, 550, 557n60
automation 43, 78, 255, 260
  see also artificial intelligence (AI)

B

bad job 80, 86, 270–271
  see also good work
Balassa–Samuelson effect 145–146, 192n2, 192n9, 222
Bangladesh 120, 154, 169n32, 328, 393
banking 16–17, 221, 234n29, 239–242, 306n9, 347, 360
  see also Smart Development Banks
Bank of England 240
Bank of Korea 229
Barcelona 619
Basel III 229
Baumol, William 61, 259
Belarus 315, *316*
Belgium 99, 177, *284*, *316*, 439, 617
Belize 516, 521
Berlin Wall 2, 19, 536, 550
Biden, President Joe 85, 90, 100

Big Tech 619
see also technology
biodiversity 98, 216, 218, 488–489, 507, 515–518, 522
loss of 1, 61, 216, 218
birth rate 145, 367
Bismarckian model 380–383
Blair, Tony 5, 33n6, 89
bond market 219 221, 226, 228, 231, 247
Botswana 120, 166, 514
Bourguignon, F. 321–322
Boxing Day tsunami 491
Brazil 11, 48, 127, 228, 248, 272, *316*, 317, 326–327, 347, *364*, 439, 441, 487–488, 510, 517, 540, 594n55, 609, 616
Bretton Woods 220–221
Brexit 11, 134–136
British Leyland 46
bureaucracy 128, 403–409, 575, 577, 579, 585, 589–590, 608–609, 616
Bus rapid transport (BRT) 517

C

California 162
Calvo, Guillermo 11, 204, 226
Canada 26, 120, 135–136, *284*, *285*, 323, 366, 369, 516
see also Montreal Protocol
capitalism 41–43, 51–54, 78, 90, 101, 255, 348, 468, 536, 619
capital flow 17–18, 143–144, 219–222, 226–228, 231, 243, 245, 248
carbon border adjustment mechanism (CBAM) 140, 486
carbon emissions *see* CO2 emissions
carbon pricing 140, 484, 486, 519
carbon taxes 50, 163, 272, 348, 476, 483, 485, 519–520
career 99, 288, 294, 296, 301, 305, 367, 369, 410, 608
progression 80, 83, 99, 106, 287
caregiver 86–87, 301, 451, 583
Caribbean, the *151*, *395*, 448, *510*
Case, Anne 51–52, 438, 468
see also Deaton, Angus
cement 483, 495n15
Central Africa 509, 583
Chiang Mai Initiative 206
Chicago Board Options Exchange's Volatility Index (VIX) 221, *222*, 245, 247
Chief Risk Officer (CRO) 230
childbirth 30, 287–288, *294*, *295*, 300 301, 304, 582
see also birth rate
childcare 30, 288, 293, 296, 301, *302*, 303, 470
childhood 288, 313, 322–323, 325, 327–328, 331n45, 469, 582–583
Chile 11, 120, 144, 164–165, 204, 228, 272, 274, 285, 315, *316*, *317*, 325, 347, 369, 428, 439, 442, 480, 517, 519
China 3, 11, 21, 24, 35n30, 74, 85, 90, 99–100, 105, 120, 123, 126, 134–135, 144, 166, 186, *188*, 192n10, 256–259, 266n6, *364*, 449, 480–483, 508, 514, 536, 540, 569, 571, 575
see also US–China trade war
civil society 21, 41–42, 50–51, 53–54, 61, 64, 77, 80, 578
classroom 303, 407, *408*, 409, 584
Clean Air Act *482*, 492
clean energy 482, 493–494, 477–481, 519
see also solar energy; wind power
climate
action 509, 511, *512*, 513 514, 518, 520
change 1, 3, 10, 29, 32, 43, 51, 80, 83, 85, 88, 109, 140–141, 163–164, 216, 355, 372, 438, 475–480, 484–489, *490*, 491–494, 507–522, 554, 615
justice 475, 477, 489, 491–494, 507, 513, 521
shock 491–493
Clinton, Bill 5, 11, 89
clothing 24, 293, 297, 360, 371
CO2 emissions 43, 50, 106, 139–140, 483–484, 508, 517
see also global greenhouse (GHG) emissions
coal 6, 328, 478, 481
see also mining
coalition 13, 21, 33n6, 514, 541
coast 328, 486, 488, 521
codification 42, 146, 158
Cold War 314, 536
Colombia 48, 144, 164 166, 272, 285, 315, *317*, 325, 328, 381, 481, 517
colonialism 400, 513–514, 550–551, 583
Colorado 162
communism 134, 352, 357, 360, 404, 536, 550, 553
comorbidities 435, 438
compensation 6, 26, 86, 138, 321, 386, 493
competition policy 14, 17, 21, 42, 45, 47, 50, 52, 53, 63, 108, 161
Conditional Cash Transfer 327, 357, 365, 380–381, 437, 491–492
Congo 448, 488, 509, 514
construction 146, 481
consumerism 91
Contingent Capacities Consensus 603–606
see also Problem Driven Iterative Adaptation
Convention on Biological Diversity 518
COP28 491
copyright 64
corruption 121, 128, 175, 359, 433, 488, 516, 540, 552–554, 577, 581–582, 608, 616
anti 618
Costa Rica 163, 165–166, 177, *285*, *316*, *317*, 323, 364, 442, 449, 516
cost–benefit analysis 176
Costinot, Arnaud 133–134, 176
COVID-19 15, 29, 51, 62, 198, 204, 215–216, 239, 254, 262, 293, 303, 305,

353, 355, 357, 361 362, 372, 383, 396, 398, 428, 433, 435, 437–438, 445, 447, 464, 590, 594n57
(United Kingdom's) furlough scheme, 199
see also pandemic; vaccine
credit 16, 44–48, 79, 126, 158, 175, 197, 200–201, 207, 222–230, 240–241, 281, 289, 370, 483, 486, 517
growth 227–229
Credit Suisse 240
crime 6, 79–80, 127, 129, 175, 360, 617
see also violence
cyber-attack 22
Czech Republic 154, *285*, 316, 327

D

Dasgupta Review 216
death 52, 62, 381, 382, 432, 438, 468 *see also* suicide
rate 145
Deaton, Angus 51–52, 438, 468
see also Case, Anne
debt 14, 16, 109, 144, 165, 197–198, 200–201, 203–207, 208n9, 220, 224, 229, 245, *246*, 313, 388, 513, 521–522
burden 9, 521
crisis 9, 207n9, 220, 313–314, 346–348, 379
household 201
in emerging markets *246*
management 198, 203, 205, 215
public 197, 198, 204–206, 215, 439, 465
revenue 205–206
sustainability 211–214
Defense Advanced Research Projects Agency (DARPA) 47, 88–89, 100, 138
deforestation 476, 479, 488
democracy 1, 11, 31, 53, 91, 106, 243, 380, 535–537, 540, 550–551, 553–554, 566, 569, 616, 618–619
Democratic Republic of Congo *see* Congo
Democrats 90–91
Demographic and Health Surveys (DHS) 394, 398
demography 145, 150, 156, 351
Deneen, Patrick 90–91
Denmark 52, 154, 186, *284*, 285, 294, *295*, *316*, 327, 331n56, 362, 393, 441, 547, 579
Department of Health and Social Care (DHSC) 389
deprivation 314, 328, 468–469
developing world 1, 72, 155, 238, 319–320, 325, 346, 392, *399*, 421–422, 424, 430, *437*, 421–422, 424, 536
development clusters 535, 539, 542, 545, 547–548, 568, 570
development gap **149**
diagnostic-related group (DRG) 443–446
diagnostics 263, 405, 444, 570, 573, 587, 589
Dickens, Charles 468–469
dictatorship 11–12, 22
digital economy 64, 253, 265
disability 81, 262, 381–382
Distributional National Accounts 319
doctor 363–364, 447–449, 583
dollar 17–18, 79, 84, 145, 150, *151*, 185 186, 193, 222–224, 233n23, 247, 513
Dominican Association of Free Zones (ADOZONAS) 165
Dominican Republic 120, *316*
drugs 6, 80, 127, 352, 354, 356, 363, 370, 434, 438, 445, 450
dualism 77–80, 97, 104–105
productive 77–79, 97, 99, 105
Dutch disease 516, 523n31

E

Eastern Europe 254, 439, *510*, 550
Economic Complexity Index (ECI) 155, *156*
economic efficiency 31, 141, 219, 282–283, 304, 313, 354
Economic Job Market Rumors (EJMR) 304
Economics of Education 426
ecosystem 84, 140, 166, 476, 486–489, 516, 518
Ecuador *316*, *317*, 326, 406, 439, 442
education 5, 13, 21, 28, 30, 53, 81, 85, 105, 109, 145, 147, 259, 263–264, 281, 297, 315, 322, 325, 341–342, 347, 353, 355–357, 371, 391–397, 400–407, 421–422, 424, 428–429, 437–438, 464–465, 468–470, 541–542, 569, 584, 589 *see also* literacy; numeracy; pedagogy; schooling
distribution of 341–342
higher 46, 49, 150, 297, 388
policy 63, 401, 426–427
public 323, 421–422
systems 391, 400–410, 422
UK system 263 *see also* A levels
vocational 163–164, 389, 618
educational attainment 23, 28, 315, 317, 347, 545
Education For All conference 392
see also Jomtien Declaration
egalitarianism 5, 34n22, 292, 297, 322, 341, 343
Egypt 70, *71*, 176, 272
Eisenhower, Dwight 89
election 2, 317, 537, 538, 540, 608, 616, 618, 619
US presidential 90, 316
electoral
accountability 565, 608
systems 551, 552, 589
electric auto manufacturer 26, 514
electricity 146, 158, 164, 261, 348, 476, 478–481, 495, 515, 517, 518
electric vehicle 49–50, 64, 514
emerging economies 143, 144, 202, 223, *224*, 226, 248, 274, 478
emerging markets (EMs) 17, 105, 108, 201, 219, 223, 228, 245, *246*, 248
and developing economies (EMDEs) 105, 108–109, 206

employment 27, *73*, 78–81, *82*, 84–85, 100–101, 123, 144–145, 148, 175, 177, 184, 203, 227, 254–259, 262–263, 271–275, 283, *284*, *285*, 288–289, 301, 348, 383, 410, 468, 547, 580
aggregate 43–44
contract 14
domestic 44, 175, 177, 282–283
formal 369, 382, 545
industrial 12
per capita 145, 148
re- 123, 127–128
self- 86, 303, 328, 369, 383
state 551
status 28, 581
see also gig economy; unemployment
energy markets 19, 480–481
engineering 260, 317, 352, 479, 494, 552
entrepreneur 16, 23, 25, 42, 53, 61, 79, 91, 158, 174, 176–177, 357, 540, 550
environment 10, 29, 62, 99, 216–217, 231, 245, 348, 371, 475, 478, 483, 485, 488–489, 494, 516, 519, 522, 552, 578, 586 *see also* biodiversity; climate change
environmental, social, and governance (ESG) movement 108
Estonia *284*, *316*, 616
Ethiopia 154, 422, 488, 512, 518, 569
Euro 9, *151*, 229, 513
Euro Area debt crisis 207n9, 220
European Bank of Reconstruction and Development (EBRD) 549–550, 553
European Central Bank 44, 248 *see also* Additional Credit Claims programme
European Commission (EC) 107, 214
European Green Deal 83
European Stability Mechanism 206
European Union (EU) 48, 63, 134–136, 214, 216–217, 257, 448, 483, 486, 553, 616
Economic Policy Committee 448
Emissions Trading System (EU ETS) 216–217
Stability and Growth Pact 216
exams 404, *408*
exchange rate 9, 15, 17–18, 34n25, 143–144, 160, 176, 184–186, 202–203, 220, 224–228, 232, 233n21, 233n22, 233n23, 234n29, 379, 513
floating 34, 224–227, 232, 233n23
exclusion 64, 79–80, 437, 447
export 6, 17–18, 21–22, 25–26, 34n15, *82*, 121–124, 127–128, 134–135, 139, *153*, *154*, 168n20, 174–178, 181–186, *187*, 191, 213, 228, 257, 380, 512–513, 521, 523
see also import
export-led growth 122, 143–147, 149, 151–167, 178, 181
extinction 486

F

family 7, 12, 30, 52, 126, 200, 259, 262, 281, 287–288, 294, 296–297, 300–301, 315–316, 322–324, 326, 342, 353, 449, 565
broken 6, 80
business 281–283, 297
income 294, 315–316, 428
farming *see* agriculture
fatherhood bonus 294–296 *see also* motherhood penalty
Federal Reserve *see* US Federal Reserve
female labour force 145, 148, 156, 183, 292
feminism 293–294
fertility rate 127, 145, 148, **149**, 183, 367, 448
Finland 53, 127, *284*, *285*, *316*, 327
fiscal activism 15, 198, 203, 206–207, 215–217
fiscal policy 9, 15–16, 109, 160, 182, 197–207, 208n16, 211–214, 215–217, 233n26, 348
fisheries 297, 615
flexible work 30, 271, 288, 305
flexicurity 30, 52, 271, 362
food 10, 62, 86, 183, 293, 297, 319, 321, 327, 352, 354, 359 360, 370, 372–373, 438, 469 470, 485 486, 507, 513, 522
price 183
security 507, 509, 513, 515, 518
stamps 327
ultra-processed 438
see also National Food Service; malnutrition
foreign direct investment (FDI) 26–27, 121, 139, 175, 177–178, 379
foreign exchange 152, 158, 220, 228–230, 346
foreign investment 26, 120–121, 182, 379
fossil fuel 441, 478–479, 481, 483, 508, 512, 515–516, 519
Non-Proliferation Treaty 516
see also coal; gas, oil
foundational skills 397, 406–407
four-day week 258, 266n13
France 43, 45, 85, 99, 101, 230, 256, *284*, 285–287, *316*, 320, 403, 439, 448, 569
free trade 25, 121, 134–135, 141, 144 *see also* North American Free Trade Agreement
Friedman, Milton 18, 89, 240, 428

G

G7 countries *436*
G20 242
Gallup World Poll, *547*, *548*
Gambia, The *316*, 514
gas 478, 479, 481, 513, 516

gender 30–31, 91, 281–283, *284*, 285–289, 292, *293*, 294, 296, 300–305, 306n9, 316, 323, 329n12, 437, 547, 565
equity 282–283, 304
gap 282–283, *284*, *285*, 286–287, 292–293, 300–301
inequality 31, 281–282, 286–287, 297, 300, 316, 437
roles 287–289, 301–305, 306n9, 306n14
General Agreement on Tariffs and Trade (GATT) 134–135
general practitioners (GPs) 446
geopolitical 10, 85, 108, 109, 182, 217, 238, 243, 511, *512*
relations 182
Germany 51, 78, 101, 169n32, 199, 225, 256, 258–259, 275, 276n7, *284*, *285*, 294, *295*, *364*, 366, 441, 448–449, 480–481
Ghana 396, 399, 448, 516
gig economy 106, 258, 264, 271, 273, 276n7, 369
see also zero-hour contract
Gini coefficient 315, 319, 323–324, 327, 329n8, 382
Gladwell, Malcolm 158
Global Britain 135–136
see also Brexit
global financial cycle (GFC) 17–19, 219, 220, *221*, 222–223, 225, 227, 229, 232n6, 245–248, 323n6
global greenhouse (GHG) emissions 80, *477*, 483, 484, 486, 508, 517–519
globalisation 2, 11, 20, 23, 25, 32–33, 78, 80, 82, 89, 107–108, 117–118, 175, 178, 221, 232n1, 270, 305, 509, 513, 536, 618
anti-globalisation protests 117
globalism 91
Global North 591n1
Global South 25, 509, 511, 591n1
good job *see* good work
good work 21, 23, 79–80, 83, 85–86, 90, 98–101, 104–106, 109, 212, 253–254, 261–262, 265, 267n21, 271, 468
see also bad job
Google 257, 555n26
GPS 84, 88–89
Great Depression 2
Great Financial Crisis of 2007–09 9, 12, 15–16, 198, 200, 204, 220, 229, 239, 353
Great Gatsby Curve *324*
Greece 258, *284*, *285*, 286, *316*, 439
greedy jobs 31, 301, 306n9
green
agenda 348, 512
growth 508, 514
innovation 42–43, 49–50, 479, 483, 485
investment 484–485
technology 19, 50, 85, 140–141, 478, 484
transition 85, 90, 106, 485, 512–515
greenhouse gas emissions *see* global greenhouse (GHG) emissions
gross domestic product (GDP) 7, 28, 42–43, 48, 70, *71*, *72*, 85, 119, 146, **149**, *151*, *153*, *155*, 157, 168n15, 168n16, 185, *186*, 187–188, *190*, 199, 223–224, 259, 263, 272, 283, 289, 382–383, 403, 440, 448, 464, 516, 521, 557n60, 579, 620n7
growth acceleration 18, 139, 152
Guatemala 325
Guinea-Bissau 154
Guyana 516

H

Haiti 317
Harvard 586, 593n49
Hausmann, Ricardo 6, 18, 21–22, 54n1, 152, 155, 168n20, 168n22, 169n32, 174, 176, 178, 181–187, 191
Haut Conseil de Stabilité Financière 230
healthcare 85, 100, 271, 274, 306n9, 326, 352–353, 356, 360, 363–365, 385, 389–390, 438–451, 464–466, 467–470, 578, 583, 603
policy 464–466
reform 464–466
system 10, 29, 365–366, 369, 371–372, 385, 389, 434–435, 449, 464–466, 468, 470, 603
universal health coverage (UHC) 386, 433, *434*, 435, 437, 439, 442, 444–445, 447, 450–451, 465–466, 468, 470
see also NHS (National Health Service)
health expenditure *364*, *435*, 440, 442, 444, 446
heart disease 444, 467
Hirschman, Albert 3, 33n7
Hobbes, Thomas 437, 539
home production 20, *293*, 297n2
see also reproductive labour
Hong Kong 120
housing 6, 198, 354, 380
price 224, 226, 322, 330n28
Howitt, Peter 71, 73
see also Aghion, Philippe
human development index (HDI) 515
human resources 147, 262, 515, 587
Hungary 11, *284*, *285*, *316*
Hurricane Katrina 491

I

Iceland 186, 228, *285*, 327, 616–617
immigration 11, 27, 79–80, 159, 161
see also migration
import 1, 46, 48, 121, 123–124, 126–128, 134–136, 140–141, 144, 177, 512–513, 517, 519
see also export
income
family 294, 315–316, 428
gap 143–145, 148, 156, 174
national 6, 229, 319–320, 326, 389, 513, 518, 576
per capita 150, 152, *155*, 189, 438, 516, 545, 550

tax 14, 161, 211, 213, 318, 326, 328, 340, 342, 519, 541, 545, 579–580
see also low- and middle-income countries (LMICs); lower-income countries (LICs); wage
India 23–24, 34n22, 43, *71*, 74, 99, 119–120, 243, 289, 292–293, 297, *364*, 396–406, 409, 422, 437, 485–486, 581, 583, 593n43, 510–511, 517, 575, 578, 581, 583, 593n43, 615, 620n7
see also Rajasthan
India Education Initiatives 396
Indonesia, 70, *71*, 233n24, *316*, 398, 399, 405–406, 428, 440, 486, 488, 510
industrialisation 1–2, 78, 99–100, 118, 144, 169n32, 254, 261, 264, 270, 274–275, 284, 514, 569
export-led industrialisation (ELI) 144
industrial policy 5, 14, 20–21, 42, 45–48, 50, 64, 77, 83–86, 90, 97, 101, 106, 110, 122, 140, 142n1, 159, 211, 484–485, 510
industrial zone 146–147, 161–163
inequality 6, 12, 20, 25, 29, 31, 34n22, 35n30, 61, 78, 81–84, 89, 100, 104, 118–119, 125, 192n2, 211, 215, 264, 293, 313–328, 329n8, 330n21, 330n23, 330n28, 340–342, 347–348, 354, 357, 380, 382, 429, 437–438, 465, 615
economic 301, 321
see also gender inequality
inflation 2, 8, 17–18, 85, 90, 143–144, 204, 213, 220, 223–224, 226, 228–229, 232, 238–240, 242, 348, 355–356, 387, 480, 493
Inflation Reduction Act 85, 480
information and communications technology (ICT) 260, 582
information technology (IT) 44, 260, 265, 580
infrastructure 5, 10, 13, 19–20, 27, 65, 84, 86, 134, 139, 162, 164, 197, 215, 255, 257, 265, 356, 404, 479–481, 513–514, 517, 540–541, 545, 569, 574, 577–578, 582
insecurity 52, 80, 82, 84, 89, 449, 469, 509
Institute for Fiscal Studies 341, 581
Institute for the Future of Work 260, 262
Institutional Experiments 570–571
intellectual property (IP) 8, 25, 42, 62, 64, 82–83, 138, 141, 484, 512
interest rate 16–18, 144, 198, 202–206, 212–213, 223, 226, 228, 233n13, 240, 367, 388
Intergovernmental Panel on Climate Change (IPCC) 508–510, 512
International Centre for Taxation and Development Government Revenue Dataset 545
International Financial Institutions (IFIs) 109, 314
International Monetary Fund (IMF) 1, 9, 19, 54n1, 109, 198, 106, 216, 219, 233n26, 242–243, 245, 248, 314, 346, 357, 440, 569
internet 22, 84, 88, 158, 183, 254, 256, 264
intrinsic value 12, 548–549, 551, 564
investment 147, 162–166, 169n38, 174–178, 182, 201–205, 213, 228, 231–232, 254, 263, 286, 301, 321, 325, 327, 342, 348, 354, 367, 380, 387, 437, 439, 446, 450, 466, 481–483, 491–494, *512*, 515–522, 537, 540–547, 576, 598, 608
green 484, 491-492, 520-521
in education and training *82*, 437
in human capital 380, 391,
in innovation 8, 83, 175, 478, 513
in state capacity 15, 542, 544, 576, 589, 608
public 47, 166, 325, 327, 342, 439
R&D 44, 83, 169n38, 177, 513
Ireland 88, 165, *284*, *285*, *316*, 438, 617
irrigation 615
Israel *285*, *364*, 449, 555n20

J

Japan 1, 26, 48, 50, 86, 119–122, 165, 256, 282, *284*, *285*, 286, *364*, 367, 449, 553
Ministry of Economy, Trade and Industry 48
Jomtien Declaration 392, 410
see also Education For All conference

K

Kazakhstan 164
Kenya 405, 516, 520
Keynes, John Maynard (J. M.) 1, 44, 199, 258–259
Keynesian 1–2, 15, 77, 79–80, 89, 91, 97–98, 104 105, 198, 200, 203, 212, 234n29
neo- 97–98, 234n29
see also welfare state
Klein, Ezra 90
Krueger, Anne 1, 144
Kurzarbeit 275
Kyoto Protocol 520

L

labour force participation rate (LFPR) 183, 297
labour market 22, 28, 30, 51–52, 63, 77–85, 101, 106–107, 127–128, 146, 253–265, 270–275, 281–289, 292–297, 300–307, 314, 323, 325–326, 369, 380, 382, 384, 388, 392, 426–427, 441, 584
Latin America 1, 9, 23–24, 144, *151*, 182–183, 206, 220, 313–322, 330n21, 346–347, 349n1, 357, 379, *381*, 382–384, 394, **395**, 441–442, *510*, 609, 620n7
learning crisis, the 392–393, 398, 400–403, 410, 421–423
left behind 12, 78–79, 107, 138–139, 270, 274
legislator 239, 358–359, 565
leisure 258–259, 261, 281–283

lender of last resort (LOLR) 27, 201–204, 241–242
Leontief, Wassili 258
Lerner symmetry theorem 144
Lewis, W. Arthur 77–78, 174
liberalism 549, 553–554, 571
  see also neoliberalism
life expectancy 8, 62, 145, 147–148, **149**, 174, 183, 315, *364*, 365–368, 387, 433, 435, *436*, 437–438, 444, 545
literacy 9, 265, 347, 367, 392–400, 402
  see also numeracy
lobbying 46, 53, 64, 79, 102, 129, 135, 159, 163, 165, 211, 476
local community 6–7, 21, 27, 31, 77, 80, 86, 90, 98, 102, 406, 488–489, 493, 518, 615, 619
local currency units (LCUs) 185
low- and middle-income countries (LMICs) 174–176, 361, 369, 434, 440–448, 476, 478, 480, 483, 486, 489, 491, 507–511, *512*, 513, 515–522
low-carbon energy sources 516, 522
lower-income countries (LICs) 509, 511, 513, 516, 518, 520–522, 579–580, 584
Lucas, Jr, Robert E. 70, 160, 320
Luddite movement 44
Luxembourg *284*, *285*, 315, *316*, 439, 449
  Wealth Study 315, 319

M

Maastricht Treaty 214
macroeconomic
  crises 9, 10, 16, 197, 199, 347, 348
  policy 15–19, 89, 239, 314, 346
  risk 199
  stability 27, 54n1, 197, 213–214, 223, 226, 379–380
macroprudential regulation 16, 18
Maddison Project Database 545, 557n60
Malaria 445
Malawi 406, 588
Malaysia 120
malnutrition 347, 373
Manhattan Institute 90
Manpower Group 260
manufacturing 21, 25, 61, 78, 85, 90, 97, 99–100, 106, 123, 144–145, 159, 161, 255–257, 360, *482*, 483, 513–514
marine conservation 521
market power 62, 105, 122, 138, 326
Marmot Review 467–469
maternity leave *see* parental leave
McKinsey Global Institute 260, 401
McNamara, Robert, 46
media 54, 108, 163, 288, 292, 304, 341, 340, 617
  see also social media
medical insurance 351, 361, 363, 366–367, 371–372
  see also private health insurance (PHI)
medical savings accounts (MSAs) 439–440
medical technology 362–363, 450
  see also technology, health
Medicare 86, 443–444
medicine 29, 61, 64, 161, 443–446, 449, 451, 451n1
  cardiovascular 438, 444
Mexico 35n30, 163, 169n31, 248, *284*, *316*, *317*, 347, 364, 370, 380, 442, 510, 517, 520
Middle East 144, *151*, **395**, *510*, 540
migration 24, 27, 140, 159, 169n30, 169n31, 275, 447–448, 464, 489, 492–493
  see also immigration
Mill, J. S. 4, 33n10
Mill–Diamond–Mirrlees principle 5–6
minimum wage 7–8, 81, 86, 99, 101, 211, 272–273, 326, 340, 354, 380
mining 6, 146, 162, 328
Mitbestimmung (co-determination) 101
mobile telephony 63
monopoly 25, 62, 105, 138, 160, 166, 326, 331n55, 481, 539–540, 568, 617–618
monopsony 107, 138, 326, 619
Montreal Protocol 88
moral hazard 199, 201, 239–241, 358, 360, 362, 364–365, 372, 385
Morocco 166
mortality 51–52, 127, 438, 444, 468, 479, 486, 489, *490*
  infant 8, 315, 347, 616
  see also death rate; life expectancy
motherhood 30, 287, *295*, *296*
  penalty 30, 287, 294, *295*, *296*, 300
  see also fatherhood bonus
Mozambique 512, 516
multinational enterprise (MNE) 175, 177
multilateral development banks (MDBs) 519
Multiple Indicator Cluster Surveys (MICS) 394, 396
Mundell–Fleming 18, 226
Myrdal, Gunnar 536, 539, 542, 549, 554

N

Namibia 163, 166
National Endowment for Science, Technology, and the Arts (Nesta) 586, 593n49
National Food Service 352, 360, 372
National Labor Relations Act 565
nationally determined contributions (NDCs) 518
neo-classical growth models 157
neoliberalism 2, 7, 30, 77, 80, 87, 90–91, 97–98, 104–105, 109
  see also liberalism
Netflix 257
Netherlands, the 258, *284*, *285*, 286, *316*, 327, 369, 441, 449, 514, 523n31
  see also Dutch disease
net zero 415, 485, 508, 515, 519
Nevada 162
New Mexico 162
New Public Management 604

New York Times 90
New Zealand 135, 242, *284*, 367
NHS (National Health Service) 274, 352, 370–372, 385, 389
Nicaragua 11, 491, 512
Nigeria 154, 328, 399–400, 405–407, 509, 516, 609
Niskanen Center 90
Nixon, Richard 89
Nobel Prize 77, 175, 320, 341, 351, 355–356, 370
non-governmental organisation (NGO) 15, 396, 410, 512, 522, 551, 585–586
North Africa *151*, 281, **395**
North American Free Trade Agreement 134
Norway 186–188, *284*, *285*, 327, *364*, 516
NREGA 581–582, 593n32
numeracy 8, 392–394, 396
  see also literacy

O

Obama administration 465
  see also Affordable Care Act
obesity 62, 359, 438, 469
Occupational Health 262
'Occupy' movements 314
oil 164, 239, 314, 478, 513, 515–516, 564
Organisation for Economic Co-operation and Development (OECD) *72*, 73, 161, 282, 289, 285, 362–363, 366, 369, 382, 397, 448, 510
  Programme of International Student Assessment (PISA) 315, 316, 395, 397–398, 403, 422
organisational structures 13, 167, 541, 584, 587
original equipment manufacturer (OEM) 159
Osterman, Paul 86
out-of-pocket payments (OOPs) 433, 439, 449–450
ozone 88
  depleting substances (ODS) 88

P

Pakistan 396, 405–406, 423, 428, 582, 593n44
Panama 120, 161, 169n39
pandemic 1, 10, 14–15, 17, 23, 29, 43, 62, 199–200, 207n3, 213, 215–216, 239, 255, 293, 303, 305, 348, 353, 357, 361 362–383, 396, 433, 435, 437–438, 445, 447, 464, 542, 574, 590, 594n57
  see also COVID-19
paradigms 1–4, 8, 41–43, 73, 79–80, 85, 89, 91–92, 97–98, 104, 106, 109, 300–304, 564
  see also Schumpeterian growth paradigm
parental leave 30, 287–288, 296, 300, 305
Paris Agreement 216–217, 508, 520
patent 8, 49, 50,157, 481
pay-for-performance 443, 583, 588
payments for ecosystem services (PES) 488–489
pedagogy 326, 399, 402–403, 409–410
Peel, Robert 238, 243
Penn World Table *71*, 148, **149**
pension 8, *82*, 231, 271, 326–327, 352–354, 356, 360–361, 367–373, 374n36, 379–380, 382, 385–388, 390
  age 368, 387
  earnings-related 386–387
  Pay-As-You-Go plan 368–370, 520
  reform 272
  state 386–388, 390
Peru 120, 144, 165, 315–316, *317*, 318, 400, 403, 406, 422, 439, 442
pharmaceuticals 62, 162, 305, 351, 354, 356, 363, 370, 445, 450
Philippines, the 319, 347, 540
Pigou 160
Pillars of Prosperity database *546*, *547*, *548*, 564
Pissarides Review, the 265, 274
place-based policies 7, 32, 107, 140, 162
pluralism 288, 550
police 26, 140, 589, 617
policymaking 4, 32, 64, 89, 98, 536–537, 551, 553, 574, 590, 605, 607–608
  climate mitigation 514
  gender equality 282, 300, 304–305
  fiscal 9, 15–16, 109, 160, 182, 197–207, 208n16, 211–217, 233n26, 348
  state capacity 607–608
political stability 13, 540
politician 5, 8, 11–12, 15, 89, 91, 239–241, 341, 343, 359, 387, 466, 576, 581, 589, 602, 608–609, 617–619
Polity-IV project *538*, 540, *548*
pollution 88, 354–355, *482*, 483–484, 491, 578, 615
  agricultural 88
  air 469, 483, 492, 511, 522, 578, 615
  water 483, 492
populism/t 1, 10–12, 34n22, 62, 80–81, 87, 90, 105, 270, 554, 616
poverty 2, 24, 27, 32, 70, 79, 105, 109, 138, 174, 256, 261, 327, 343, 347, 354–356, 368–370, 381–386, 394, 437, 440, 488, 507–509, 516, 521, 543, 554
  child 469–470
  reduction 8, 24, 27, 340, 508–509, 516, 569, 583
  relief 356, 368–370, 385–386
  trap 328, 513
privacy 63–64, 447
private goods 158
  see also public goods
private health insurance (PHI) 439
privatisation 5, 7, 19, 54n1, 182, 347–348, 360–361, 372, 385, 480–481
Problem Driven Iterative Adaptation 586, 593n49, 604
production cost 25, 177

productivism 21, 77–81, *83*, 84v89, 92, 104–110
productivity 5, 22, 28, 30, 41–45, 47–48, 53, 61–64, 73–74, 78, 80, *81–83*, 86–89, 99–100, 104–108, 110, 120, 123, 145–148, 150, 156, 167, 169n29, 177, 182–183, 201, 254–259, 267n21, 272, 283, 305, 321, 326–327, 426, 429, 447, 483, 491–492, 509, 517, 542, 616
property rights 8, 42, 54, 84, 182, 379, 484, 488, 512, 541, 551, 570, 573–574
psychology 3, 13, 23, 286, 356
public debt *see* debt, public
public goods 20, 30, 90, 146, 158–159, 162–166, 355, 568, 574, 576, 580, 587
  see also private goods
public services 14, 28–29, 86, 100, 274, 322, 324, 358–359, 389–390, 440, 541, 575
purchasing power parity (PPP) 150, *151*, *153*, 185–186

Q

Qatar *153*

R

race 79, 86, 91, 316–317, 323, 329n12, 331n61, 492, 565
raising money 578–579
Rajasthan 509, 583
randomised controlled trials (RCTs) 544, 550–552, 565, 589
Rawls, John 34n13, 357, 374n18
Reagan, Ronald 2, 11, 89–90, 98, 314
recession 9, 16–17, 44, 198–202, 204, 230, 346
redistribution 4–6, 30, 77, 80–81, 84, 89, 104 105, 109, 118, 126, 128, 138, 200, 211, 283, 296, 314, 326–327, 332n64, 341–343, 353–357, 363, 380–383, 386, 388, 568
renewables 20, 479–481, 515
repression 160, 540, 543–546, 556n48
reproductive labour 293
  see also home production
Republicans 89–91
research and development (R&D) 44, 46, 48, 80, *82*, 87, 107, 147, 161–163, 169n38, 177, 255, 263, 481, 483, 618
Research on Improving Systems of Education (RISE) 400–406, 411n20
Resilience and Sustainability Trust 109
retail 85, 146, 254, 257, 480
Robinson, James 12, 148, 321, 544
robotics 255–257, 260, 266n6
  International Federation of 256, 266n6
  see also artificial intelligence (AI)
Rodríguez-Clare, Andrés 133
Rodrik, Dani 3, 18–19, 21, 23, 74n3, 97–107, 109, 144–145, 152, 266n20, 274, 321
Romer, Paul 157
Romney, Mitt 90
rotational labour mobility 27
Rubio, Senator Marco 90–91
Russia 10–11, 220, 239, *316*, 464, 540, 575, 592n9
  see also Soviet Union
Rwanda 519–520, 569, 603

S

salary 52, 123, 212, 380, 383, 389, 442, 566, 587
Saudi Arabia 164, 166, 511
Scandinavia 30, 51, 274, 294, *295*, 327
  see also Denmark; flexicurity
schooling 53, 74, 148, **149**, 281, 286, 293, 327, 391–394, 398–400, 404, 410, 421–424, 578, 393–394, 410, 584, 593n44
  basic 393–394, 410
  primary 347, 391–393, 398–400, 407, *408*
  private 28, 323, 423–424, 428, 578
  public 322 327, 423, 428
  see also education
school value-added 426–429
Schumpeter, Joseph 8, 21, 53, 61, 255, 428
  see also Schumpeterian
Schumpeterian 41–44, 48, 63–64, 72–74, 255–256
  growth paradigm 41–43, 74
Scotland 449
SCRIPTS project 569
sea-level rise 491–492, 508
self-employment 303, 369, 383
Senegal 516
September 11 163
service delivery 29, 442 443, 552, 577–578, 585, 589, 603, 609
Seychelles 521
shale gas *see* gas
shareholder 50, 80, 101–102, 108, 262, 387
Silicon Valley 166, 240
Silicon Valley Bank 240
Singapore 1, 120, 181, 186, 188–189, *190*, 233n22, 397, 439, 603
slavery 317, 566
Slovakia 166, *285*, 315, 327
Slovenia *284*, *285*, 315, 327
small and medium-sized enterprises (SMEs) 48, *83*, 105, 162
Smart Development Banks 165
social insurance 10, 81, *82*, 89, 126, 199–200, 351–352, 354, 361–362, 365–366, 371–372, 369, 379–383, 387, 434, 439–441, 449, 618
social media 22–24, 108
social sciences 32, 552, 576,
social services 27, 100, 146, 448–449, 578, 619
socioeconomic status 422, 492, 616
soil 486, 518, 590, 616
solar energy 84, 141, 327, 476, 479–480, 485, 514, 516, 519–520
  see also Solyndra
Solow, Robert 41–42, 71, 145

Solyndra 84
sortition 617
South Africa 164–166, *364*, 406, 519
Industrial Development Corporation (IDC) 165
South Korea 1, 49, 78, 85, 120, 122, 256, *285*, 449, 553
Soviet bloc 134
Soviet Union 3, 46, 127, 439
see also Russia
Spain 267n25, *284*, *285*, *316*, 323, 438, 400, 444, 449, 481, 619
see also Barcelona
special economic zones 121, 147, 161–162, 164, 169n39, 178
Spence, Michael 175, 182
Sri Lanka 347
stagflation 1, 314
stakeholder 31, 81, 101–102, 107, 262, 271, 273, 401, 404, 489, 511, 514–515, 518, 573–575, 578
Stanford Plan, The 365, 374n30
start-up 74, 162, 166, 254, 257, 480
state capabilities 13, 586, 603, 607, 609–610
state capacity 13–15, 18, 20–22, 28–29, 33, 90, 489, 510, 536, 539, 540–548, 551, 552, 555n26, 564, 568–571, 573–579, 583–587, 589–591, 591n3, 592n14, 593n28, 602–606, 607–609
state structures 542
common-interest states 539, 542, 546–548, 551, 553, 554, 556n32, 565, 568, 570
special-interest states 543, 546, 548, 568
weak states 539, 543, 546, 548, 568
steel 161, 360, 495n15
STEM (science, technology, engineering, and mathematics subjects) 23, 317
Stigler, George 163
stock market 166, 248
Stolper–Samuelson theorem 25, 35n30, 118
student finance 385, 388, 390
Sub-Saharan Africa 11, *151*, 346, **395**, 422, 423, 440, 448, 483, 569
Sudan 154, 509
Suez Canal 119–120
suicide 52, 343, 438, 468
superstar firms 45, 52–53, 62, 64, 104, 108
supply chain 10, 62, 64–65, 85, 90–91, 108, 121, 124, 177, 483, 579–580
surveillance 22, 63–64, 106, 109, 163, 447
Sweden 34n22, 154, 242, 264, 282, *284*, 285, 294, *295*, *316*, 366, 369, 448
Switzerland 181, 186, 189–190, 240, 439, 448
Sypnowich, C. 343
Syria 543

T

Taiwan 1, 85, 120, 122, 185, 553, 616
Tanzania 428
tariff 2, 23, 26, 46, 50, 90, 119–12, 125, 128–129, 134–136, 138, 140, 144, 160, 177, 480,
most-favoured nation (MFN) 135–136
taxation 5–6, 14, 19, 27–28, 81, 198, 313, 326, 328, 332n64, 341, 355–356, 359, 363, 365, 369, 386–387, 439–441, 537, 542, 545, 568–570, 579–581, 620n7
see also tax
tax
base 27–28, 161, 197, 215, 515, 573–574, 579–584
credit 48, 80, 161, 289, 326
Laffer curve 580
payer 241, 466, 580–581, 605
rate 28, 161, 197–198, 211–212, 328, 342, 519–520, 580
revenue 28, 197, 213, 440–442, 449, 541 542, 580
see also income tax
teaching 13, 313, 326–327, 356, 402–406, *408*, 409–410, 584
at the right level (TaRL) 405, 409
see also education; schooling
technocracy 12, 16, 19–20, 81, 406–407, 410, 553, 569, 571, 602
technology 6, 19–27, 32, 46, 62–64, 68, 79–80, 82, 84–85, 134, 143, 150, 152, 175–177, 192n10, 253–254, 259, 264, 271–275, 301, 317, 402, 422–446, 511, 577, 580–588, 616, 618
adoption 22, 72, 145–148, 155–158, 160, 167, 174, 576
advanced 182–185, 192, 273
clean energy 140, 478
frontier 8, 45, 48, 174
health 445–446, 450, 465
policy 21, 164
production 146, 177, 303
work 306n9
see also information and communications technology (ICT); information technology (IT); medical technology
Temin, Peter 78
Tesla 84
Thailand 120, 219, 392, 540
Thatcher, Margaret 2, 11, 33n6, 89, 98, 314
Tilly, Charles 322, 539, 541 542, 555n26
see also state capacity
time flexibility 262, 265
tobacco 438, 441
tourism 146, 271, 521
Trade Adjustment Assistance programme 126
trade
agreements *82*, 129, 134–136, 144
barriers 1, 128, 136, 144, 176, 484
flows 25, 118–119
international 117, 120–121, 123, 125–126, 133, 176, 256, 512
liberalisation 2, 23–25, 35n30, 117, 119, 126–129, 134, 136, 138, 141, 177, 346, 348

openness 26, 118–119, 133–134, 140, 181, 183–185, 188
policy 90, 121–122, 125, 129, 133, 135–136, 484–486
shocks 118, 126–128, 134, 139–141, 314
union 30, 107, 618
war 134–135
transport 128, 134, 161, 164, 256, 327, 331n61, 348, 478, 515, 517, 578
public 327, 517
see also Bus rapid transport (BRT)
tropical forest 486, *487*
Trump, President Donald 26, 90–91, 100, 135
Tuberculosis 445, 467
Turkey 11, 166, 220, 223, 245, 248n3, *284*, 511, 540

U

Ubcr 63, 264, 273
Uganda 177, *408*, 409
Ukraine 10, 19, 239, *316*, 465
war 10, 19, 239, 465
unemployment 6 7, 9, 21, 43–44, 46, 52, 81, 126, 199, 213–214, 272, 347, 351, 353, 361–362, 369, 371–372, 380, 382, 385, 491
benefits 52, 213, 352, 360, 362
union 30, 54, 107, 135, 271, 273, 289, 313, 326, 406, 428, 565–566, 618–619
United Arab Emirates (UAE) 164
United Kingdom (UK) 45, 63, 98, 133, 139, 199, 206, 225, 242, 257, *284*, *285*, *295*, 314, *316*, 341, *364*, 385, 438, 468, 581, 617
see also Global Britain
United Nations (UN) *317*, 318, 433, 437, 513
Development Programme 8
Economic Commission for Africa 514
Millennium Development Goal 393
Sustainable Development Goals 393, 395, 433, 451n1
UNICEF (United Nations Children's Fund) 347, 396
see also Multiple Indicator Cluster Surveys (MICS)
World Income Inequality Database (WIID) *317*, 318–319
United States (US) 2, 7, 11, 17–18, 26, 35n30, 45–48, 50–53, 63, 79, 85, 88–89, 98–99, 101, 105, 130n8, 133, 139, 148, 149, 163, 166, 181, *186*, 188–189, 193n12, 205–206, 240, 248, 257, *284*, *285*, 292, *295*, *314*, 316, 331n56, 331n61, 363, *364*, 365, 385, 403, 434, 465, *482*, 491, 570, 609, 619
Congress 85, 163, 565
Federal Reserve 18, 219, 220, 222–228, 239, 248, 274
Framework Convention on Climate Change 88
monetary policy 2–9, 17–18, 129, 164, 203, 212–213, 220–223, *224*, 225–229, 231–232, 232n8, 239–240, 245, 248, 603
universal basic income 275, 618
Universal Credit 271
Universal Declaration of Human Rights 410
unpaid work 281, 282, *283*, *284*, 297
upskilling 21, 254, 271
urbanisation 145, 147, 150, 156, 183, 580
US–China trade war 134
utopia 23, 89, 554, 619

V

vaccination 274, 355, 437, 542, 582–583
Value-Added Tax (VAT) 161, 212, 273, 579
Venezuela 11, 164, 347, 516, 540
venture capital 46, 166
Vietnam 120, *316*, 400, 402–403, 422, 510–511, 569
violence 12, 281, 304, 422, 539–542, 544, 546–548, 564–566, 568
domestic 281
political 539, 542, 544–548, 556n48, 556n48, 570
see also crime
VIX *see* Chicago Board Options Exchange's Volatility Index (VIX)

W

wage 7–8, 17, 22–23, 27, 30, 35n30, 44, 78, 81, 86, 99, 101, 106–107, 120, 136, 150, 181–185, 191–192, 211, 272–273, 317, 321, 325–327, 340, 354, 380, 382, 405, 441, 483, 556, 618
distribution 289, 380
gap 286, 292, 294, *295*, 296
stagnation 12
see also income; minimum wage
wage–price mechanism 181–182, 191, 192n2
war 1–2, 45, 97, 105, 134–135, 146, 239, 314, 341, 352, 371, 372, 392, 539, 545, 569
civil 539–540, 546, 555n18, 556n48
see also Cold War; Ukraine; World War II
Washington Consensus, the
10 dictums of 379–380
economic model 370
formulation of 536, 539, 544, 550, 603–604
on education 391, 429
on exchange rate 34n25, 176, 203
on exports 143–148, 178
on imports 121
policies of 2, 11, 13, 15, 16–20, 22, 30, 70, 122, 127, 133, 140–141, 163, 167, 176–177, 182, 197, 207, 215, 346–347, 385, 521, 536, 607
reforms 129, 303–304, 346
weaknesses of 175, 183, 270, 346, 370, 379–380, 385, 429, 568, 573
water 161, 293, 483, 486, 489, 492, 518, 615
see also irrigation; pollution

weapons 26
weather 10, 216, 484, 489, 493, 518
  extreme 216, 484, 489
  see also Boxing Day tsunami; Hurricane Katrina
Weber, Max 539
wellbeing 4, 6, 10, 23, 29, 80, 98, 183, 186, 198, 254–255, 261–262, 265, 270, 275, 316, 330n28, 346, 355–356, 366, 435, 475, 491, 539, 547–549, 551, 556n52, 570
welfare economics 33, 386, 390
welfare state 1, 10, 30, 77–81, *82*, 89, 97, 272, 289, 326–327, 351–360, 372, 379–382, *381*, 382–384, 385–390, 434, 566, 574, 576
  see also Keynesian
Williamson, John 2, 7–11, 23, 26, 117, 129, 134, 143, 192n4, 198, 313, 349n1, 391–392
wind power 476, 479–481, 519–520
women
  at home 283–284, 293, 303
  education of 147, 317, 321, 398, *399*, 400
  equality of 281–283, 296, 301, 304, 316
  income of 285, 287, 301
  rights of 289, 292, 296
  societies of 619
  workers 31, 86, 147, 262, 285–286, 289, 293, 321
  see also female labour force; feminism; gender gap; motherhood
worker
  domestic 175, 282
  foreign 159, 169n39, 175
  formal 381, 618
  full-time 259, 263
  healthcare 443, 447–448, 582–583
  high-educated 79
  high-skill 84, 159, 255, 273, 348
  informal 28, 273, 381–382, 618
  low-educated 78–79
  low-skill 21, 25, 78, 144, 159, 211, 255–256, 274, 347, 362, 511
  MNE 177
  transition 253–254, 263, 265, 270, 274
work–life balance 262, 271
World Bank 1–2, 7, 19, 46, 54n1, 193n12, 216–217, 314, *316*, 320, 346, 440, 513, 545, 552, 557n68, 569
  Doing Business indicators 162, 545
  International Development Association (IDA) 521
  World Development Indicators **149**, *151*, *153*, *186*, *187*, *188*, *189*, 193n11, 315, *316*, *436*, 545
  World Development Report 2006 314
  World Development Report 2018 'Learning to Realize Education's Promise' 401
world economy 1, 24, 61, 219–220, 604
World Health Organization (WHO) 437, 447, 468
  Commission on Social Determinants of Health 437, 467–468
World Trade Organization (WTO) 90, 134–135, 512
World War II 45, 97, 105, 134, 146, 329, 539
Wright, Erik Olin 617, 619
Wright's Law 160, 479

X

Xi Jinping 514

Y

Yellen, Secretary of Treasury Janet 90
Young Lives Study 402–403, 422
youth 140, 314, 361, 392–393, **395**, 396, **397**, 403

Z

Zambia 393
zero-hour contract 264, 273–274, 276n7, 369
  see also gig economy
Zimbabwe 448, 514

www.ingramcontent.com/pod-product-compliance
Ingram Content Group UK Ltd.
Pitfield, Milton Keynes, MK11 3LW, UK
UKHW020721041026
15590UKWH00002B/799

9 781911 712435